SOCIAL AND POLITICAL FOUNDATIONS OF CONSTITUTIONS

This volume explores the social and political forces behind constitution-making from a global perspective. It combines leading theoretical perspectives on the social and political foundations of constitutions with a range of in-depth case studies on constitution-making in nineteen different countries. In the first part of the volume, leading scholars develop theories that regard constitutions as coordination devices, mission statements, contracts, products of domestic power play, transnational documents, and as reflection of the will of the people, respectively. In the second part of the volume, these theories are examined through case studies of the social and political foundations of constitutions in countries like Egypt, Nigeria, Japan, Romania, Bulgaria, New Zealand, Israel, Argentina, and others. The result is an examination from various social science perspectives in social science of constitutions as social phenomena and their interaction with other social phenomena. The approach reflected in the volume combines theoretical analysis of constitutions generally with case studies of selected constitutions.

Denis J. Galligan is Professor of Socio-Legal Studies at the Centre for Socio-Legal Studies at Oxford University. He is a Professorial Fellow of Wolfson College Oxford as well as the Jean Monnet Professor of European Public Law at the Università degli Studi di Siena and a Visiting Professor at the Woodrow Wilson School of Public and International Affairs at Princeton University. He is the author of *Law in Modern Society* (2007) and *Due Process and Fair Procedures: A Study of Administrative Procedures* (1997), among many others.

Mila Versteeg is an Associate Professor at the University of Virginia School of Law. Her research and teaching interests include comparative constitutional law, public international law, and empirical legal studies. Prior to joining the University of Virginia School of Law, Versteeg was an Olin Fellow and lecturer in law at the University of Chicago Law School. Versteeg's articles have appeared in the *Journal of Legal Studies*; the *Journal of Law, Economics and Organizations*; the *California Law Review*, the *NYU Law Review*, and the *UCLA Law Review*, among others.

COMPARATIVE CONSTITUTIONAL LAW AND POLICY

Series Editors:

Tom Ginsburg, *University of Chicago*
Zachary Elkins, *University of Texas at Austin*
Ran Hirschl, *University of Toronto*

Comparative constitutional law is an intellectually vibrant field that encompasses an increasingly broad array of approaches and methodologies. This series collects analytically innovative and empirically grounded work from scholars of comparative constitutionalism across academic disciplines. Books in the series include theoretically informed studies of single constitutional jurisdictions, comparative studies of constitutional law and institutions, and edited collections of original essays that respond to challenging theoretical and empirical questions in the field.

Volumes in the Series:

Comparative Constitutional Design edited by Tom Ginsburg (2012)
Consequential Courts: Judicial Roles in Global Perspective edited by Diana Kapiszewski, Gordon Silverstein, and Robert A. Kagan (2013)
Social and Political Foundations of Constitutions edited by Denis J. Galligan and Mila Versteeg (2013)
Constitutions in Authoritarian Regimes edited by Tom Ginsburg and Alberto Simpser (2014)
Presidential Legislation in India: The Law and Practice of Ordinances by Shubhankar Dam (2014)

Social and Political Foundations of Constitutions

Edited by

DENIS J. GALLIGAN

University of Oxford Centre for Socio-Legal Studies

MILA VERSTEEG

University of Virginia School of Law

CAMBRIDGE
UNIVERSITY PRESS

CAMBRIDGE
UNIVERSITY PRESS

32 Avenue of the Americas, New York, NY 10013-2473, USA

Cambridge University Press is part of the University of Cambridge.

It furthers the University's mission by disseminating knowledge in the pursuit of
education, learning, and research at the highest international levels of excellence.

www.cambridge.org
Information on this title: www.cambridge.org/9781107032880

© Cambridge University Press 2013

First published 2013

Printed in the United States of America

A catalog record for this publication is available from the British Library.

Library of Congress Cataloging in Publication data
Social and political foundations of constitutions / edited by Denis J. Galligan, Mila Versteeg.
    pages   cm. – (Comparative constitutional law and policy)
Includes bibliographical references and index.
ISBN 978-1-107-03288-0 (hardback)
1. Constitutional law – Social aspects   2. Constitutional law – Political aspects.
3. Constitutions.   I. Galligan, D. J. (Denis James), 1947– editor of compilation.
II. Versteeg, Mila, 1983– editor of compilation.
K3165.S63   2013
342–dc23   2013009471

ISBN 978-1-107-03288-0 Hardback

Contents

Contributors

Paul Brady is a D.Phil. candidate, Faculty of Law, University of Oxford.

Kevin L. Cope is a Visiting Associate Professor of Law at Georgetown University Law Center and a Visiting Assistant Professor of Law at the Washington and Lee School of Law.

David Erdos is Katzenbach Research Fellow & Leverhulme Trust Early Career Fellow at the Centre for Socio-Legal Studies, University of Oxford.

Denis J. Galligan is Professor of Socio-Legal Studies at the Centre for Socio-Legal Studies, University of Oxford.

Tom Ginsburg is Leo Spitz Professor of International Law and Ludwig and Hilde Wolf Research Scholar.

Benedikt Goderis is Assistant Professor of Economics, Tilburg University.

Russell Hardin is Helen Gould Shepard Professor in the Social Sciences, New York University.

Binesh Hass is a D.Phil. candidate, Centre for Socio-Legal Studies, University of Oxford.

Ran Hirschl is Professor of Political Science and Law, University of Toronto School of Law.

Jeff King is a Senior Lecturer in Law, University College London.

Phoebe King is a student at the University of Chicago.

David S. Law is Professor of Political Science and Law, Washington University in St. Louis.

Clark B. Lombardi is Associate Professor of Law, University of Washington School of Law.

Pedro C. Magalhães is a Political Scientist, Social Sciences Institute of the University of Lisbon.

Anne Meuwese is Professor of Law, Tilburg University Faculty of Law.

Christina E. Parau is Department Lecturer in European Politics and Societies, University of Oxford.

Charles O. H. Parkinson is a barrister at Owen Dixon's Chambers, Melbourne.

Miguel Schor is Professor of Law, Drake Law School.

Adam Shinar is Assistant Professor of Law, Radzyner School of Law, Interdisciplinary Center, Herzliya.

Daniel Smilov is Program Director, Political and Legal Research, Centre for Liberal Strategies and Associate Professor of Political Science, Sofia University.

Brian Z. Tamanaha is William Gardiner Hammond Professor of Law and Israel Treiman Faculty Fellow, Washington University in St. Louis.

Mila Versteeg is Associate Professor of Law, University of Virginia School of Law.

Neil Walker is Regius Professor of Public Law and the Law of Nature and Nations, University of Edinburgh School of Law.

Preface

This collection of essays is the result of a program of workshops and occasional lectures that took place at Oxford University between 2009 and 2012 under the same title as the book: *Social and Political Foundations of Constitutions.* The program was sponsored jointly by the Foundation for Law Justice and Society (FLJS) and the Centre for Socio-Legal Studies (CSLS). The aim of the program was to gain a better understanding of constitutions as social phenomena and their interaction with other social phenomena. The approach we adopted, as reflected in the volume, is to combine theoretical analysis of constitutions generally with case studies of selected constitutions. The result is a set of essays on constitutions drawing on the varied perspectives of the social sciences. All but one of the chapters were presented and discussed at Oxford.

Neither the program nor the volume would have been possible without the support of the two sponsoring institutions, the FLJS and the CSLS. On this occasion, the FLJS has been the senior partner in providing support for the program. It funded the entire program, including the cost of mounting the workshops and lectures, and assumed responsibility for their organization and administration. Accordingly, we wish to acknowledge the contribution of the FLJS, and in particular its chairman, John W. Adams, and the board of trustees. The CSLS, a research institute of Oxford University dedicated to conducting research into law in society, enthusiastically supported the program and encouraged participation by many of its research staff and students.

The FLJS is an independent institution affiliated with the CSLS. It was founded in 2005 by John Adams and one of the editors, Denis J. Galligan, to provide a forum for discussion of the role of law in society, a forum in which the academic world could meet practitioners and professionals, where each would have occasion to learn from the other. We wanted to make the fruits of academic research relating to law in society more accessible to practitioners and professionals, whether lawyers, government, business, or the institutions of civil and international society, while at the same time learning from them. In publishing this collection of studies, we are confident of having achieved our purpose, for it will challenge and provoke the community of scholars, while offering much by way of guidance to those engaged in the practical tasks of creating constitutions or making them work. On behalf of all the authors, the editors wish to acknowledge with appreciation and gratitude the outstanding and unstinting support of the FLJS, its president, and the board of trustees.

We wish to thank members of the FLJS, Judy Niner and Jessica Hamilton, who organized the events, arranged travel and accommodation, and dealt with all other matters incidental to an international program of this kind. Communications, publications, and the Web site were skilfully managed by Phil Dines, communications officer at the FLJS, the quality of whose work can be seen on, and more information about the program obtained from, the excellently constructed Web site: http://www.fljs.org. Dr. Tanya Baldwin, CSLS administrator and a specialist in English language and literature, exercised fine judgment in ensuring each essay meets the exacting standards of English prose, for which we offer our warm thanks. Binesh Hass, one of the contributors, is to be thanked for providing editorial expertise at an early stage of the program. We also thank Trevor Moore, JD student at the University of Virginia School of Law, for providing editorial assistance. The Faculty of Law of Oxford University kindly provided funds to help with editing, which was vital to ensuring the quality of the essays.

We wish to thank our contributors who traveled to Oxford from far and wide to take part in the program for the time and energy spent producing studies of high quality. We also thank the editors of the series, Professors Tom Ginsburg, Zachary Elkins, and Ran Hirschl, for accepting the volume for inclusion. Finally, we express our appreciation to Cambridge University Press, New York, and to John Berger, our editor, with whom it has been a pleasure to work.

PART I

Introduction

1

Theoretical Perspectives on the Social and Political Foundations of Constitutions

Denis J. Galligan and Mila Versteeg

1.1 INTRODUCTION

The last half-century has been a period of unprecedented constitution-making. New constitutions arose from the ashes of World War II, some freely, others – such as West Germany and Japan – under the direction of the Allies. A second wave of constitutions followed the decolonization of Africa, Asia, the Pacific, and the Middle East, where in countries like Nigeria and Micronesia the colonial powers presided over the drafting process. The collapse of communism in Central and Eastern Europe in 1989 allowed more than twenty nations to rediscover their constitutional past, or, where there was little past to rediscover, to take the first steps toward entering the international community. These were the main constitutional developments in recent years, but not the only ones: South Africa led the way in the 1990s for a further round of constitutional revision in southern and central Africa, followed by various nations in South America and Asia. Most recently, new constitutions are being written in the wake of popular uprisings in North Africa and the Middle East and following foreign invasion in the cases of Iraq and Afghanistan.

These developments have been accompanied by a new generation of constitutional law scholarship dedicated to studying constitutions in their social and political context from the perspective of the social sciences. Traditional approaches have tended to follow one or other of two courses, sometimes analyzing constitutional doctrines either of particular constitutions or comparatively, at other times taking a philosophical approach to constitutional ideas and concepts. Without wishing to draw too sharp a line between the different approaches, because doctrinal and

We thank Kevin Cope, Tom Ginsburg, Carlos Guarnieri, Jeff King, Clark Lombardi, Assaf Meydani, Laurel Miller, Miquel Schor, and Adam Shinar for helpful comments on an earlier draft of this chapter.

philosophical aspects of constitutions are also relevant to a social science analysis, our purpose in this collection of essays is to contribute to the third approach: the social and political understanding of constitutions. In doing so, we have been guided by several questions: (1) what is the character of constitutions as social phenomena and what functions and purposes do they serve; (2) how are constitutions made; (3) what are the contents of constitutions and what are the main influences on content; and (4) what is meant by success and under what conditions are constitutions successful? Complete answers to each of these questions would fill a volume or more, so the analysis here is bound to be partial and contingent on the conditions of particular nations, but nevertheless of utility in advancing our understanding of constitutions.

Interest in the social and political foundations of constitutions can be traced back to the classic texts of David Hume, Adam Smith, Thomas Hobbes, and Jeremy Bentham, and even earlier to John of Salisbury, to name merely a few within the English and Scottish tradition, to which may be added names such as Montesquieu and de Tocqueville, James Madison, and Thomas Jefferson, without mentioning numerous other traditions in Europe and beyond. The present volume continues the tradition of studying constitutions as social and political phenomena, as part of the fabric of nations, and applies it to a range of issues of contemporary interest. The disciplinary approaches are those of the social sciences, including law, political science, sociology, history, and economics. The methods of research are several and diverse: comparative across constitutions, quantitative, case studies of specific issues, or historical accounts of ideas and concepts. While the contributions employ a variety of methods, reflecting their authors' backgrounds, disciplines, and interests, the common purpose is to identify different types of constitutional systems and to show, through empirical study, aspects of their social and political foundations. This volume is just a first step in such an undertaking. Considering there are more than two hundred national constitutions, not to mention the numerous state constitutions in federal systems, or the emerging regional constitutional orders such as the European Union, the scope for research has no bounds and many questions remain unanswered.

Aside from this Introduction, the volume consists of two parts. Essays in the first part offer a variety of theoretical perspectives on the social and political foundations of constitutions, which include constitutions as coordination devices, as mission statements, as social contracts, and as transnational documents, among other things. The second part consists of sixteen case studies of particular constitutions. The purpose of the case studies is to bring to life the theoretical perspectives discussed in the first part of the collection, while also opening up new ideas and providing fresh insights.

We have selected the case studies so that they represent a range of different conditions under which constitutions are written. Constitutions are often written in the wake of crisis or under an exceptional circumstance of some sort (Elster 1995, 370; Sajo 1999). Among such crises are revolutions, decolonization, regime change, war,

TABLE 1.1 *Selection of Case Studies*

Constitution	Region	Legal System	Circumstances
Japan 1947	Asia	Civil law	Postwar occupation
Portugal 1976	Western Europe	Civil law	Democratic transition
Ireland 1922	Western Europe	Common law	Independence
Bulgaria	Eastern Europe	Civil law	Postcommunist transition
Micronesia	Pacific	Common law	Postcolonial
New Zealand 1993	Oceania	Common law	No apparent transition
Nigeria 1960	Africa	Common law	Postcolonial transition
Egypt 1972	North Africa and Middle East	Civil law	Overthrow of autocratic order
Argentina	Latin America	Civil law	Democratic transition
European Union	Europe	n/a	n/a
Israel	Middle East	Common law	Democratic transition
Iceland 2011	Western Europe	Civil law	Economic crisis
South Sudan 2011	Africa	Common law	Independence
Iran 1979	North Africa and Middle East	Civil Law	Post-revolution
Romania	Eastern Europe	Civil law	Postcommunist transition
Venezuela 1999	Latin America	Civil law	Political transition
Ecuador 2008	Latin America	Civil law	Political transition
Bolivia 2009	Latin America	Civil law	Political transition

and economic downturns. Many of the constitutions studied in this volume are written in times of major transition, such as: independence, often from a colonial power, such as in Micronesia, Nigeria, and South Sudan; democratic transitions, as in Argentina and Portugal; and drastic transition from a communist system to a democracy, as in Bulgaria and Romania. Other constitutions, especially those not confined to one document, such as New Zealand, Israel, and the United Kingdom, change as ideas and circumstances change rather than in reaction to a momentous event. The conditions under which the constitution is written represent one of the variables in selecting the sixteen case studies in this collection. The case studies are also geographically diverse, exemplify different legal traditions, and apply to countries of varied size and significance, ranging from tiny Micronesia to populous Nigeria. The time scale runs from the early twentieth century in the case of Ireland (1922), through the era of colonial independence as in Nigeria (1960) and Micronesia (1986), to some of the most recent constitutional experiments, of which South Sudan (2011) and Iceland (2011) are examples. Some of the constitutions considered here, such as those of Ireland, Nigeria, and Egypt have since been replaced, although their legacy in setting the foundation for later constitutions is plain (Brady 2013). We have tried to identify constitutions that exemplify a pattern or wider set of circumstances. The constitution of Nigeria (1960) is fairly typical of the British postcolonial model (Parkinson

2013). Others, such as the constitutions of Bulgaria and Romania, display the context of constitution-making after the collapse of Soviet domination, while the constitution of Iceland (2011) reflects an unusual determination for popular involvement in constitution-making. Finally, we exclude those constitutions that have received disproportionate attention in the comparative constitutional law literature in recent years, such as the constitutions of the United States, Canada, South Africa, Germany, and India. Table 1.1 lists the different constitutions studied in this volume, as well as the circumstances under which they were made, the legal system they represent, and the geographic region to which they belong.

In the remainder of this chapter, the editors provide an overview and analysis of the theoretical issues discussed in the following chapters. We have endeavored wherever possible to integrate the findings from the case studies and to show how they confirm, illuminate, or question our understanding of these issues.

1.2 WHAT IS A CONSTITUTION?

A constitution establishes a system of government, defines the powers and functions of its institutions, provides substantive limits on its operation, and regulates relations between institutions and the people.[1] In doing so, constitutions *constrain* government: they generate a set of inviolable principles to which future lawmaking and government activity must conform. But constitutions also *enable* government, by empowering institutions and, in some cases, by mandating them to promote social welfare. Although use of the term "constitution" in this way is relatively recent, the very idea of government has always included some notion, elementary though it may be, of a constitution – that is, of rules creating, empowering, and limiting government institutions (Stourzh 1988; Sartori 1962). Constitutions are now expected to be in written form and usually contained in a single document, although even today they are not always written and not necessarily contained in one document. Nevertheless, the standard practice across the nations of the world, with just a few exceptions, is to have a single written constitutional document that sets out these basic functions.

This does not mean that the document includes all matters of constitutional concern, or that all constitutional matters can be resolved by reference only to the document. A brief encounter with any constitution will soon reveal that around the formal document arise other ideas, conventions, and practices, which influence its interpretation or even augment, modify, or render obsolete some of its provisions.[2]

---

[1] For other definitions of what is a constitution, see, for example, Dicey (1915: 22); King (2007: 3), Llewellyn (1934: 3), Palmer (2006: 592–593), Young (2007: 411); Erdos (2013); Elkins et al. (2009: 36–40).

[2] For the idea that conventions emerge around the written document, see also Llewellyn 1934: 3; Strauss 1996).

The success and endurance of Japan's constitution might be partly attributable to the ability of institutions, in this case the Supreme Court in its restrained approach to judicial review of legislation, to marginalize certain of the written provisions (Law 2013). The need to take account of informal constitutional features is the first indication that, while constitutions are distinct and separate social institutions in stating the rules of government, at the same time they interact with the social and political context around them. They present to the world two faces, one independent and autonomous, the other interdependent and interlocking with the social and political context. The interplay of the two aspects is the key to understanding constitutions as social institutions.

Independent and autonomous constitutions are characterized as a set of rules and principles on the basis of which government is conducted and its actions explained and justified or criticized and condemned. Administrative, executive, and legislative officials derive their powers from the constitution and, when challenged, have to justify their actions in accordance with it. Citizens, groups, and associations use the constitution to make claims against government bodies and officials, sometimes restraining action, at other times demanding it. Lawyers spend time advising on and arguing about what the constitution means, while the judges of constitutional courts enjoy high prestige for having the last say on constitutional questions, which for the nation are often questions of great moment. Once constitutions are viewed as interdependent and interlocking with the social and political context, they become both more complex and more interesting. On one approach constitutions are reasonably self-contained and self-referential, where the task of lawyers and judges is to interpret them according to legal doctrine and precedent. It soon becomes plain, however, that arguing over, interpreting, and ruling authoritatively on constitutions involves complex social processes that unavoidably spill over into the wider social and political context, raising questions about relations between that context and the written text. The work of lawyers and judges in interpreting the rules and principles of the constitution has long attracted the interest of social scientists, so that there is now available an extensive body of both quantitative and qualitative research.[3] From there it is a short step to wider and deeper questions about the very nature of constitutions, their purposes, their contents, how they come about, and their effectiveness. These are the questions with which many scholars and researchers are now preoccupied; they are also the questions with which several of our contributors grapple.

To summarize, it soon becomes clear from the study of constitutions in their social context that they are more than just written documents declaring the framework of government; they are also social institutions interacting with society in complex ways. In the remainder of this chapter, we examine further this interaction

---

[3]   See, for example, Martin and Quinn (2002); Ginsburg and Moustafa (2008); Garoupa (2011).

and highlight the nature and function of constitutions as social institutions, deeply rooted in, and intertwined with, particular societies. Our examination is centered on the following issues: (1) constitutions as expressions of values; (2) constitutions as manifestations of power; (3) constitutions as coordinating devices; and (4) constitutions as contracts. We show how these themes relate to each other, how they illuminate the case studies, and how the case studies in turn often provide an empirical grounding for the various theories.

1.3 CONSTITUTIONS AS EXPRESSIONS OF VALUES

A cursory reading of constitutions shows they are steeped in values. The values are many and various: some reflect a nation's "core, constitutive political commitments" and identity (J. King 2013); some reflect international or transnational norms and standards (Goderis and Versteeg 2013); and others express shared notions, such as liberty and democracy (Galligan 2013b). Values appear throughout the text, defining the content and distinguishing one nation from another. However, constitutions are not only declarations of values, and as we shall see in the following discussion, there may be tensions between aspirations and ideals, and other goals. The successful coordination of society and politics, which is or ought to be a major goal of any constitution, may require an adjustment or even compromise of aspirations and ideals. Some constitutions are the outcome of power struggles among the nation's elites, thus reflecting interests and positions that defeat or diminish idealistic goals and values (Hirschl 2013). Constitutions plainly serve diverse ends and perform various functions, yet they are invariably also a declaration of values and aspirations – an aspect we shall now consider in more detail.

1.3.1 *National Values, Identity, and Mission Statements*

National values are brought out in a constitution's dealing with the nation's past, as well as its hopes and aspirations for the future. Constitutions often look back to past events and aim to resolve past problems (Sajo 1999). They are likely to reflect shared experiences, such as Ireland's history of oppression by England (Brady 2013), Japan's subjection to a militarist government and devastation by war (Law 2013), and Hungary's liberation from the Soviet Union's domination (Arato and Miklosi 2010). How a constitution presents the ideals and aspirations of a society matters, as became evident in the depth of feeling shown and the level of controversy aroused over the wording of the preamble to the proposed 2004 constitution of the European Union (EU). At stake are not just the values of the EU but also its identity. National identity as well as national values were on the mind of the Hungarian government when, with the support of the parliament, it felt the need to rewrite the preamble to the Hungarian constitution, which was transformed into the Fundamental Law. The battle over whether the postrevolutionary Iranian Constitution should declare a "Republic," an "Islamic Republic," or a "Democratic Islamic Republic" reflects a similar search for national identity (Hass 2013).

A nation's history can feature in constitutions as a source of inspiration; it can also be something to overcome and avoid in the future. Several nations of Central and Eastern Europe, upon liberation from the Soviet yoke in 1989, were able to hark back to, and find guidance in, older constitutional traditions and the ideas and ideals informing them. Something similar is happening in the context of the Arab Spring, where constitution-makers are drawing on their own constitutional history in an attempt to design a new future (Brown 2012). But, as the study of New Zealand highlights, constitutional choices are often directed at remedying the past or escaping from its legacy. In this case, the reforms of the early 1990s "had their roots in an aversive reaction against the activities and outlook of" the prime minister, who had displayed "woeful disregard for traditional conventional understandings of how public power should be exercised" (Erdos 2013: 334). Likewise, the 1853 Argentine constitution was preoccupied with creating order and stability because of its previous experience with excessive disorder and instability (Schor 2013), while the Romanian postcommunist constitution was aimed at overcoming the communist past (Parau 2013). Other examples are the 1996 South African Constitution, which aims to overcome its apartheid past by emphasizing international rights and authorizing its constitutional court to take account of foreign and international law (Klug 2000), and the 1949 German Constitution, which, in the wake of a totalitarian regime and the dark shadow of the Holocaust, proclaims "human dignity" as one of its basic principles.[4] Whether or not a constitution cherishes the past or abhors it, there is no escape, to paraphrase Justice Oliver Wendell Holmes, from "the stories of the nation's development through many centuries" (Holmes 1881: 1–2).

In creating a system of government and dictating its powers and responsibilities, constitutions are also forward-looking, stating ideas and ideals and articulating commitments as to how government will be conducted in the future (Elster 1993, Holmes 1995, Sadurski 2009). By the very process of empowering government and defining its limits, constitutions inherently rely on ideals, principles, and values meant to guide and contain the conduct of government not just today but into the future. Features such as the sovereignty of the people, representative government, and civil, political, and socioeconomic rights are statements about the values of the nation for the future.

"Core, constitutive political commitments of the community" (J. King 2013: 73) are also commonly stated explicitly in constitutions. According to Jeff King, constitutions

---

[4] The Basic Law of the Federal Government of Germany, 1949, art. 1.

are like "mission statements," although the notion is more at home in a business context and novel to constitutions. He continues: "A constitution that exemplifies such a function will express the political ideas that animate the constitution and polity more broadly, including the type of government it represents, the rights of citizens and people, and its conception of citizenship and the values it seeks to respect in its state planning" (J. King 2013: 81). While we should urge caution against sharp distinctions between constitutions that contain mission statements and those that do not, many constitutions do explicitly set out goals and aspirations, with the preamble serving as a useful vehicle for the purpose.

The EU's *Consolidated Version of the Treaty on European Union* 2011, although not strictly a constitution, is typical of numerous constitutions: it draws inspiration from the cultural, religious, and humanist inheritance of Europe, the inviolable and inalienable rights of the human person, freedom, democracy, equality, and the rule of law; it confirms attachment to those values and to fundamental social rights; and it expresses the desire to deepen the solidarity between the peoples of Europe while respecting their history, culture, and traditions (Walker 2013). Similarly, the 2011 interim constitution of South Sudan reflects the nation's Christian heritage by paying tribute to the "[a]lmighty God for giving the people of South Sudan the wisdom and courage to determine their destiny and future through a free, transparent, and peaceful referendum in accordance with the provisions of the Comprehensive Peace Agreement" (Cope 2013: 315).

The idea that constitutions contain the "core, constitutive political commitments of the community," whether as an explicit mission statement or as implicit in the substantive provisions, fits best in the context of democratic and liberal nations, where it may be presumed that the founders intend the constitution to be taken seriously and implemented by suitable institutions of government. But mission statements are not confined to constitutions of liberal and democratic nations and often appear in those of anocratic and autocratic nations. The 1978 constitution of the People's Republic of China contains a six-page preamble that celebrates the achievements of the glorious leader Mao Zedong, the "proletarian revolution," and "socialism."[5] Although this seems an accurate reflection of Mao's mission, it is an open question whether mission statements in authoritarian constitutions are seriously intended, or whether there is a disparity between sentiment and reality (Law and Versteeg 2013).

In focusing on the expressive and aspirational aspects of constitutions, King adds a dimension to the study of constitutions that has largely escaped attention and research.[6] However, we should be careful to distinguish between the fact that mission statements are commonly included in constitutions and the claim that they

---

[5]   Constitution of the People's Republic of China 1978, Preamble.
[6]   For studies that highlight this perspective, see Jacobsohn (2010) and Breslin (2007).

perform certain social functions. Mission statements, King argues, serve several functions: to express principles, to channel and guide public bodies in decision making, to provide "an enforcement or remedial function by founding or supplementing claims in the courts or government institutions," and to legitimate the legal order (J. King 2013: 87). It is useful to separate two dimensions of analysis: one is the characterization of constitutions as statements of principles and values, the other the social consequences and effects of such statements. The first dimension is not contentious: as a matter of description, contemporary constitutions commonly express ideas, principles, and values. That constitutions are expressive in this way is simply a feature of constitutions; the expression of values is one of their functions. Claims that such expressions have additional social functions and consequences are of a different order. Rather than being common, even necessary, features of constitutions, they are claims about how constitutions work in practice, and that is contingent on the social context of each. Whether the statements of ideas, principles, and values influence officials in their actions and decisions, or are the basis for claims in courts and government institutions, will vary from one country to another and are matters to be tested by empirical research. In the absence of such empirical evidence, a note of caution should be entered as to whether aspirations typically found in constitutions are intended to, or in practice do, have any real effect on how officials and institutions behave. To promote ideals and values of the kind typically found in preambles, which tend to be open and abstract, to the status of practical standards guiding government is to obscure the difference between such aspirations and other provisions in constitutions, which are intended to be genuine guides to practical decision making and which are often justiciable in the courts.[7] Similarly, there is no empirical evidence that mission statements serve to legitimate the constitutional order, bearing in mind the notorious elusiveness of both the concept and the criteria by which it is established.

While the aspirational aspects of constitutions typically appear in the preamble, they may, in some cases, also permeate other, more substantive provisions concerning the nature and structure of government and institutions, the limits on their powers, and relations between them and the people. A constitution is by nature a statement of values, ideals, and aspirations for the future. Despite the unavoidably imprecise lines between the two – the mission statement aspects on the one hand and the provisions of a constitution of binding force and justiciable status on the other – there is utility in maintaining the distinction. Proclaiming values and identity in the preamble is relatively easy and costless, whereas justiciable standards require practical action by government bodies, which is often neither easy nor costless. An important

---

[7] Recent research suggests that even justiciable constitutional standards are often not enforced (Law and Versteeg 2013).

question for further research is whether aspirations affect substantive and justiciable constitutional choices or whether they are confined to the preamble. Some examples of national values of a justiciable character include the constitutional ban on abortion and, until recently, the prohibition of divorce in the religious context of the Irish constitution,[8] or a ban on gay rights in the equally religiously inspired Ugandan constitution.[9] The catalogue of social rights in the 1976 constitution of Portugal is, as Pedro Magalhães shows in his essay, attributable to a broad consensus among the parties with origins deep in Portuguese culture and society: "The overall conception of the role of the law and of the state in the Portuguese legal tradition, the values of social Catholicism .... and an international *Zeitgeist* favourable to social rights, all combined to form an ideological environment that was incompatible with the tenets of a 'minimal state' and 'economic liberalism'" (Magalhaes 2013: 449). Thus, as Magelheas shows, Portuguese national values and identity, albeit mixed with emerging international norms, are expressed not only in mission-statement-like preambles but are also the basis for substantive standards of social rights. Likewise, as Phoebe King demonstrates in her essay, the recent neo-Bolivarian constitutions in Venezuela, Bolivia, and Ecuador not only contain radical statements of values in their preambles but also adopt a catalogue of rights that reflect popular preferences and are directed at remedying past injustice. All three constitutions enshrine elaborate socioeconomic policies that address historic inequalities and popular grievances resulting from an era of neoliberal development, structural adjustment, and privatization, as propagated by the international community in the 1980s and the 1990s. The Venezuelan constitution, for example, grants all citizens a "right and duty to work" and "to obtain .... a dignified and decent existence," while the constitution of Bolivia grants "every person the right to water and food," which may not be "object of concession or privatization" (P. King 2013: 373).

While some of the essays here highlight the expressive function of constitutions, it is a task for future research to test how constitutions balance their past with their future and their national identity with international norms. In some systems, such as that of the United Kingdom, which have developed and evolved with relative stability over a long period, constitutional ideas are anchored in their history and almost by definition reflect national character. For most nations, however, relations between the constitution and indigenous ideas and ideals are more variable, depending on many factors, including the simple point that the very purpose of a new constitution may be to cast off the influence of old values in favor of the new ones. This has its own risks, for a set of constitutional ideas and ideals without roots in the society may soon wither and be little more than textual adornments or

---

[8]   Irish Constitution, 1937, art. 40, cl. 3; art. 41, § 3, cl. 2 (amended 1995).
[9]   Uganda Constitution, 1995, art. 31. § 2a.

a "sham constitution" (Law and Versteeg 2013). Future research might profitably explore the balance within each national constitution between the past, the present, and the future (see Ginsburg et al. 2013), while at the same time acknowledging the pressures originating from outside the nation.

1.3.2 *Transnational Values and Diffusion*

The influence of the external environment is the perspective that Benedikt Goderis and Mila Versteeg develop in their essay (Chapter 4 in this volume), where they emphasize the influence of transnational factors, international bodies, and the norms and values of foreign nations. Modern-day constitutions, Goderis and Versteeg argue, are inherently transnational documents (Goderis and Versteeg 2013), the content of which is shaped to a large extent through various processes of transnational influence. The thesis at first sight appears to be the direct opposite of the one advanced by King: constitutions do not reflect national values, ideals, and aspirations, but instead reflect more international norms and standards, promoted by other nations. However, as we shall show, on closer examination, the two perspectives supplement rather than oppose each other.

Several mechanisms of diffusion are available: (1) coercion by other nations; (2) competition among nations; (3) learning by one nation from others; and (4) acculturation. Coercion suggests that powerful nations push less powerful ones to adopt particular constitutional arrangements. This is most common in, though not confined to, situations of colonial independence and military occupation. As Charles Parkinson's study of Nigeria illustrates, the constitutions granting independence to Britain's former colonies in Africa and the Caribbean were drafted and negotiated by the British authorities, who insisted on the inclusion of a bill of rights modeled on the European Convention on Human Rights and Fundamental Freedoms (Parkinson 2007, 2013). The Colonial Office thus imposed standard constitutional provisions on states ranging from Antigua and Barbuda to Zimbabwe and Nigeria. In Micronesia, the U.S. advisors pushed for a bill of rights along the lines of the U.S. Constitution, the legacy of which not only shaped the constitutional document but the entire body of Micronesian constitutional law up to the present day (Tamanaha 2013). The 1946 Japanese Constitution offers an example of an occupation constitution, drafted by U.S. officials and naturally reflecting their notions of a suitable constitution (Law 2013). More recent versions of the same phenomenon include the constitutions of Afghanistan and Iraq, both of which were drafted "in the shadow of the gun" within parameters set by the occupying forces (Goderis and Versteeg 2013; Ginsburg et al. 2008).

The logic of the second diffusion mechanism, *competition*, is that states copy particular constitutional arrangements in order to attract foreign buyers and investors

(Law 2008). The more countries are successful in attracting investment by adopting specific constitutional rules, the more likely others are to follow and adopt the same constitutional rules (Law 2008). The case of Egypt has been suggested as an example. According to one study, the Sadat regime in Egypt realized that its "socialist and nationalist commitments obstructed inflows of capital because investors ... were always at risk of expropriation," which put the nation at a disadvantage compared with competitors (Tushnet 2009: 996*accord* Moustafa 2007). In response, the government created an independent constitutional court authorized to enforce constitutional provisions, including an anti-expropriation guarantee, and was even willing to accept unfavorable rulings for the sake of securing foreign investment (Moustafa 2007: 67–70, 77–79).[10] Egypt engaged in constitutional reform to improve its position in the global market for foreign capital.

The third mechanism, *learning*, entails a deliberate borrowing of constitutional provisions after assessing foreign constitutional models. Constitutional learning is most common among states that share certain features, because arrangements that work in one case are likely to be successful in similar cases. As the former chief justice of the Israeli Supreme Court puts it, only when "the relative social, historical, and religious circumstances create a common ideological basis" is it possible to use foreign constitutions as "a source of comparison and inspiration" (Barak 2002: 114). When states know that certain constitutional features are successful in other states, which they consider their peers, they have an incentive to follow suit. For example, the drafters of the 1866 Romanian Constitution imitated the Belgian constitution because "Belgium had thrived despite being overshadowed by great powers on all sides." By copying the Belgian constitution, the drafters hoped that Romania, similarly overshadowed by great powers, could "replicate the Belgium success story" (Parau 2013: 500). The drafters of the 1922 Irish Free State Constitution conducted a "diligent search" of numerous foreign constitutions, especially the then new constitutions in Central and Eastern Europe, which were carefully studied to get new insights on how best to "engineer" Irish society (Brady 2013: 274). This deliberate search for the best solutions suggests that the Irish constitution-makers were learning from constitutional choices elsewhere.

According to the last diffusion mechanism, *acculturation*, states copy foreign constitutional rules not because they are convinced of their intrinsic merits, but because they wish to gain international acceptance and legitimacy (Goodman and Jinks 2004). Once a critical number of states adopt certain constitutional provisions, they may become standardized norms of "world society." Conformity to such norms ensures international recognition and legitimacy. Even where states are

---

[10] For an alternative explanation of the Egyptian constitutional court, see Lombardi (2008), Brown (2009).

indifferent as to whether such provisions should be included in the constitution, the desire for international recognition can be reason enough. The government of Taiwan, having been deprived of diplomatic relations with most other nations, allegedly engaged in Western-style constitutional reform to cultivate their goodwill (Madsen 2001; Law and Versteeg 2011: 1181). Likewise, the transnational elites that drafted Romania's postcommunist constitutions consciously absorbed the constitutional standards of the West "in order to be credible with regard to [its] intentions of building a democratic policy" (Parau 2013: 514).

Transnational influences are documented in numerous essays comprising this volume. In addition to those already mentioned, where foreign influences were a crucial factor in the constitution's foundations, transnational influences are evident in South Sudan, where foreign consultants promoted international models of rights protection (Cope 2013), and the Egyptian constitution of 1923, which was modeled on the constitution of Belgium and Prussia (Lombardi 2013). Even in a highly inclusive constitution-making process, the constitutional assembly of Iceland, aware of its status as a pioneer in popular constitution-making, turned to foreign models, as "the re-writing was always going to be in part a borrowing exercise," as well as to state-of-the-art social science research, including the economic research on constitutions by Persson and Tabellini (Meuwese 2013: 485).

While it is reasonable to conclude on the basis of research to date that constitutions are rarely, if ever, written in isolation, we ought to be careful of oversimplified accounts of either the copying of foreign ideas or the role of the expert in dominating the process. As one of the editors learned from direct involvement in amending the constitution of Pakistan in 2002, while shrewd constitution-makers naturally and reasonably want to learn how other nations have solved common problems, they are not committed to blind imitation; nor does showing respect for the expert's advice preclude its being subjected to rigorous scrutiny. The degree of foreign influence and its effects on the constitution will vary from case to case, ranging from wholesale colonial imposition as in Nigeria (Parkinson 2013), to a deliberate search for Western identity as in Romania (Parau 2013), to more subtle influences in the background, such as the Icelandic constitution-makers surfing the Web for information (Meuwese 2013).

Not only does the degree of foreign influence vary from case to case; foreign influences also blend with domestic values and interests. The 1922 Irish Free State Constitution was "in many ways typical of the .... legal transplantation of the early inter-war period," but was also a reflection of national values "shaped by the intellectual presuppositions of an Irish nationalist movement that, for the most part, was a distinctive blend of Catholic, democratic, and constitutionalist influences" (Brady 2013: 290). Similarly, the study of South Sudan's 2011 Interim Constitution shows how foreign experts competed with local elites, producing what Cope (2013) calls an "Intermestic

Constitution."[11] In South Sudan's Intermestic Constitution, the foreign experts wrote the Bill of Rights, while domestic elites focused on the structural provisions. In each of these cases, transnational values blend with national values as well as the interests of local elites. The mixing of norms is not surprising, for, as discussed earlier, the writing of a new constitution gives each nation the occasion to reflect its history and the lessons of history, while looking to the future and allowing for the expression of values as to how it wishes to govern and be governed. Constitution-making is, moreover, often a politicized process in which local elites and interests groups compete for power and try to vindicate their political agenda in constitutional form (Hirschl 2013). As a result, most constitutions are bound to be a hybrid of localism and particularity on the one hand and uniformity and similarity on the other.

If the diffusion of standards and provisions is inevitable in modern constitution-making, then various questions arise as to its consequences. Perhaps the most important one is whether there is a causal connection between diffusion and the success of the constitution, judged by whether it is faithfully implemented. Intuitively, we may think that the more foreign the constitutional norms are, the harder they will be to domesticate.[12] The Nigerian Independence Constitution's disregard for ethnic tensions and persistent poverty might have contributed to its failure four years later, with the outbreak of a bloody civil war (Parkinson 2013). Though not dictated by foreign occupiers, the more experimental and transplanted elements in the 1922 Irish Free State constitution were often "found to be a dead letter" simply because some of its innovative elements were both untested and foreign to the Irish constitutional tradition (Brady 2013). Yet the Japanese case study teaches a different lesson. Here a postwar constitution dictated by the Americans was later "domesticated," – that is, interpreted and applied to match and reflect the character and values of the Japanese people. The constitution became embedded in national life and has not been amended since its promulgation in 1946 (Law 2013).[13] Bearing in mind the numerous factors contributing to a constitution's success, we have no reason to conclude that the source of the standards bears anything more than marginal relations to later success.

1.3.3 *Democratic Values and the People*

How the people are presented in modern constitutions, particularly those of democratic nations, which is the subject of Denis Galligan's essay, illustrates both

---

[11] According to Cope, an "intermestic constitution" is a constitution that combines *Inter*national and *Domestic* ideas, values, and preferences (Cope 2013).

[12] The notion that transplanted laws may not be effective in a new context as they were in the old is an old theme in comparative law. See, for example, Berkowitz et al. (2003) and Watson (1974).

[13] Similar success stories of imposed legal reforms have been documented by Acemoglu et al. (2011), who claim that Napoleon's radical externally imposed legal reforms in Germany were very successful.

diffusion and constitutions as statements of values and aspirations (Galligan 2013). After examining the way in which constitutions present the people, Galligan remarks on the "strikingly consistent way the people are presented in modern constitutions despite the diversity of the societies for which they are written." The sovereignty of the people is taken for granted and then the people hand over power to representatives, occasionally reserving the power to take initiatives, which is rarely exercised. Representative government is based on election by the people, leaving the people with no role in government; nor do the people insist on regular accountability, retaining only the ultimate power to change the representatives at the next election. Galligan concludes: "This way of presenting the people is made to appear compelling both theoretically and practically, as a universal answer to a universal problem of how a people can both govern itself and have effective government" (Galligan 2013a: 154). This could be seen as a case of diffusion, very successful diffusion, where one or a few societies over a long period have developed a way of accommodating a problem at the heart of society – how to govern or be governed, or more precisely how the people acquiesce in being governed by the few – which other nations are then willing to adopt fairly much without question. Or it could be construed, as the quotation suggests, as the common resolution through common experience and concerted reason of a problem central to all systems of government, while of special significance for democracies.

The study also illustrates the characterization of constitutions as expressions of values and aspirations. Behind the constitution lies the political ideal of democracy, which means at its most basic that the people are sovereign and self-governing.[14] How then do the constitutions of democratic nations express principles of democracy? At first sight, the principle seems to be reproduced accurately, maintaining harmony between the political ideal of democracy and its constitutional expression. A commitment to democracy sometimes appears in preambles, but the preferred language is that of sovereignty, the idea being presumably that sovereignty signifies the source and location of power, which is then used to create a system of democratic government. Many constitutions begin with the words "We the People," suggesting a clear and confident assertion that the constitution is made by and belongs to a sovereign people, while among others less bold in such assertions sovereignty is present in the text expressly or by implication. Under further scrutiny, however, a different picture emerges: in the practical and substantive provisions for government, popular sovereignty is weakened to the point of dissipation. The promise of self-government implicit in democracy gives way to government by representatives in which the people have no constitutional role, and where the representatives are

---

[14] According to the Polity Score, roughly 90 nations among 200 qualify as democracies: Marshall and Cole (2011).

required to act on behalf of the whole, with at best minimal accountability to the people other than removal at election.[15] Is this then a case of disjunction between constitutions and society? Is it a failure of constitutions to express adequately the character of democratic societies and conventions and understandings within them? On the contrary, on still further scrutiny, it becomes clear that, regardless of the language of popular sovereignty, the practice of modern democracy is as portrayed in the constitution: the people may be in some sense sovereign, but in reality hand over government to representatives just in the way described earlier. Constitutions, far from being out of step with the reality of modern democracies, in their substantive provisions for government and the place of the people, are accurate reflections of political reality. The disjunction lies instead between the aspiration of democracy as a self-governing people and political reality.

The task then is to explain how this limited sense of democracy has come to prevail in modern constitutional orders. Galligan argues that we need to dig deeply into the historical development of constitutions, especially those of the Western tradition, to understand the origin of contemporary constitutional ideas concerning the people and the practical concerns that gave rise to them. This means showing how at pivotal points in constitutional history new concepts have been developed or old concepts reinterpreted to manage the tension between the people as the source of power and the handing over of that power to government institutions and officials. The essay shows how, long before the advent of democratic commitments, the people were acknowledged as the source of constitutional authority, but the people as a corporate entity rather than as a collection of individual persons. The idea of the people as a corporate entity proves to be of considerable utility, for on the one hand it retains the notion of sovereign power in the people, while on the other hand it solves the problem of government, because a corporate entity cannot act itself but may act only through representatives. How much control the people have over their representatives varies according to the rules of the corporation, but as a matter of constitutional history it was rather low. These notions were formative of the constitutional movements of the eighteenth century, not only in the United Kingdom but also in France and the United States, and were vehicles into which ideas of popular elections could be inserted without rupturing the basic structure.

1.4 CONSTITUTIONS AS MANIFESTATIONS OF POWER

Whatever other qualities they have, constitutions are also the product of domestic power struggles. That is the perspective developed in Ran Hirschl's essay, where he argues that constitutions are "politics by other means" (Hirschl 2013: 157), reflecting

---

[15] For a fuller analysis of the place of the people, see Galligan (2013a).

bargains, interests, and the self-dealing of different elites and interest groups. Drawing on an influential literature in political science, from Robert Dahl (1991) to Martin Shapiro (1964) and others, and offering many examples, Hirschl summarizes what he calls the "strategic-realist approach" to constitutions. The premise is that "strategic behaviour by politicians, elites and courts plays a key role in explaining the tremendous variance in the scope, nature and timing of constitutional reform" (Hirschl 2013: 159). The approach is prominent in recent comparative constitutional law literature (Hirschl 2004; Ginsburg 2003; Finkel 2008; Erdos 2010). It builds on rational choice theory, which assumes that politicians are rational, self-interested, and utility-maximizing actors who, all things being equal, favor institutions that serve their interests. On the basis of this premise, the image of constitutions changes from being documents written in "constitutional moments" of higher lawmaking (Ackerman 1991: 6–7), or the products of genuine deliberation and reflection on higher values, to an image of haphazard bargains, raw power play, and the political agenda of self-interested elites.

It is no surprise that political actors take a keen interest in constitution-making. One of the primary goals of any constitution, after all, is to create, channel, and monitor power. Constitutions provide an ideal platform for "locking in certain contested worldviews, policy preferences, institutional structures, while precluding the consideration of alternative perspectives" (Hirschl 2013: 166). The writing of the constitution of the world's youngest nation, South Sudan, a process that is still unfolding, is a classic case. As Kevin Cope explains in his essay, constitution-making in South Sudan was characterized by a "my turn to eat" attitude, in which political groups tried to create institutions that would best serve their interests once the constitution were functioning. Most notably, the constitution-makers created a second legislative chamber, the "council of states," which substantially expanded the size of the national assembly, in order to create future jobs in Khartoum for the constitution-makers and their allies (Cope 2013).

Yet at face value, constitutions *do* normally constrain government by enshrining rights and mandating the judiciary to enforce them. How do we explain this apparent paradox? Why would self-interested elites constrain themselves by constitutional means? The answer, according to Hirschl and those associated with the constitutions-as-power approach, is that such arrangements in fact serve the self-interest of political elites, especially in the face of electoral uncertainty. Constitutional constraints are not adopted because of popular beliefs in rights and limited government, but because governments that are "clipping their wings" assume "they will be compensated for by the limit it might impose on rival political elements and/or the reduced probability for other non-favorable political developments down the road" (Hirschl 2013: 167).

There are different ways of explaining why constitution-makers agree to "clip their wings." One account, associated with Tom Ginsburg's work on East Asia, is that constitutional constraints, including rights and judicial review, serve as a form of "political insurance" (Ginsburg 2003; Ginsburg and Versteeg 2013). The adoption of constitutional constraints, Ginsburg argues, is a "solution to the problem of political uncertainty at the time of constitutional design." Parties who fear losing power in the future are likely to prefer constitutional review by an independent court because the court provides an alternative forum for challenging government action and mitigates the risk of electoral loss (Ginsburg 2003). On the other hand, stronger political parties will opt for fewer constraints because they anticipate being able to advance successfully their interests in the post-constitutional legislature (Stephenson 2003; Chavez 2004). Political division within the legislative branch is thus correlated with constitutional constraints. As an example of this logic, the transition to democracy in Portugal in the mid-1970s was characterized by the lack of a single political power, which made it easier for the fragmented parties to adopt constitutional review (Magalhães 2013).

In another version of constitutions-as-power, Hirschl argues that ruling elites adopt constitutional constraints when they foresee the loss of power and are thus threatened in their political status, worldviews, and policies. The timing of constitution-making is crucial, because in the final stages of their rule, elites who expect to lose power secure their future interests by entrenching suitable restraints on succeeding governments and providing for judicial enforcement. Constitutional change is a means by which outgoing elites preserve their political interests, dressed up as values, by placing them outside the scope of ordinary lawmaking (Hirschl 2004). In short, according to this "hegemonic self-preservation" theory, constitution-making is not merely "a form of Ulysses-like self-binding against one's own desires, but rather a self-interested binding of other, credibly threatening actors who advance rival worldviews and policy preferences" (Hirschl 2013: 170). Case studies of South Africa, Canada, Israel, and Mexico, among others, all appear to support the thesis (Hirschl 2004; Finkel 2008; Magaloni 2008). Other case studies, however, provide little support for the thesis. David Erdos shows in his essay in this volume how, in constitutional reform in New Zealand in the 1990s, elites interacted with civil society and the public in crucial ways, producing what Erdos describes as a process of "elite-mass" interaction, which is closer to an "Ackermanean constitutional moment" than to elite power play (Erdos 2013: 336). In a study of the constitutional situation in Hong Kong, Eric Ip contests the claim that the government's adoption of a bill of rights and judicial review "stemmed directly from its imminent evaporation of political power." On the contrary, he argues, the government faced no serious political threat, and that, as the British government was committed to peaceful withdrawal from the colony, the positions of the business and administrative elites in the new government were secure (Ip 2013). These studies suggest that the explanatory power of hegemonic self-preservation and political insurance theories is likely to be stronger in some settings than others. While elite power play and self-interest are always present in the background, in some cases they may be overcome by the power of ideas and values, or by a desire for coordination.

What sets the strategic-realist approach apart from an account of constitutions as expressions of values, according to Hirschl, is its ability to explain the *timing* of constitutional change. The theory highlights the political events that trigger constitutional change, such as elites losing power (Hirschl 2004), or major transitions that induce electoral uncertainty (Ginsburg 2003). This is an important feature of the approach and should stimulate further research into issues of timing. Its exponents suggest that the lack of attention to the timing of change is a weakness of the competing idealist approaches.[16] Idealist approaches indeed emphasize a different dimension of constitutions, namely, that they contain a declaration of values. They then go on to make claims about why those values have been chosen, why the constitution of this nation has this content, the usual answers being either because they are indigenous to the society or they have come from sources external to the society.[17] Strategic realism adds a third potential source of content: the claim is that values and institutions are in some cases included in the constitution as a direct result of the self-interest of elites. The power of elites to influence content is after all the main point of the approach. It is not the only point, given that it has the potential also to explain the timing of change. Accordingly, we see no incompatibility between the analysis of constitutions as values and strategic realism. They are, in practice, complementary: strategic realism might explain the domestic politics that lead to constitution-making in the first place; it might also show how the interests of elites at stake, in combination with indigenous values and external standards, can potentially have an influence on content.

How much does strategic realism tell us about the content of constitutions? Its exponents are right to claim a possible causal connection, but is there evidence of what that means in practice, of concrete provisions that owe their place to elite power play? Empirical research on this question is still incomplete. Ginsburg's theory holds merely that electoral uncertainty will produce constraints of some sort, while Hirschl's theory suggests that constitutions somehow reflect the interests of the losing elites, which he conceptualizes as the neoliberal right. It is possible, however, that other elite interests may be enshrined: constitutions may reflect the interests of the progressive left, for example (Bork 2003). At best, strategic-realist approaches produce broad predictions about whose interests the constitution will entrench and in which values and practices they will be clothed. Idealist

---

[16] Hirschl (2013) and others use the term "ideational approaches" (see Ginsburg 2003; Ginsburg and Versteeg 2012).

[17] They also make causal claims, as we saw earlier, about the social functions of expressions of value.

approaches, by contrast, examine the content of constitutions in more depth, and explain why countries make some constitutional choices and not others, in the light of their domestic values as well as transnational influences (for further accounts highlighting this more complete understanding of the idealist perspective, see Hilbink 2009; Magalhães 2013). In this sense, the potential of strategic realism is unrealized because of an absence of empirical research deploying that perspective and identifying causal connections between power plays by elites and the content of constitutions.

The case studies also suggest that, to the extent domestic politics impacts on substantive constitutional choices, it is more likely to affect structural provisions than preambles and bills of rights (Magalhães 2013). Structural provisions, such as the electoral system and judicial review, define the relationship between different government actors, while rights and preambles do not. As Cope points out in the South Sudan case, rights and values are potentially "cheap-talk," especially in a nation that has a long record of rights abuse, and it was therefore easy for South Sudanese elites to accept an internationally-crafted bill of rights. The structural provisions, by contrast, have a direct impact on the future role of the different elites in government, and elites fought vigorously over the structural part of the constitution. The case suggests that it is mainly bills of rights and preambles that offer a venue to articulate values, ideas, and ideals. Such values can be transnational, as in the South Sudanese case (Cope 2013), but may also be domestic, as in Portugal, where the social rights reflected genuine Catholic and left-wing sentiments (Magalhães 2013).

The strategic-realist approach draws our attention to a number of factors the importance of which may sometimes be overlooked in the study of the social and political foundations of constitutions. First, it highlights the importance of "events that did not occur" and roads not taken (Hirschl 2013), because non-decisions may also offer important insights in the politics behind the making of any given constitution. This theme is brought out in some of the case studies. Sometimes constitution-makers "decide not to decide" (Dixon and Ginsburg 2011; Lombardi 2013). The Egyptian constitution of 1972 was full of strategic ambiguities that would potentially allow the authoritarian and the liberal factions in Egyptian society to work with the same document (Lombardi 2013). The ambiguities in the text were thus a direct result of the presence of two competing political groups – both of which hoped to hold power in the future – which were unable to compromise. Israel's constitutional future was to a large extent shaped by indecision; political tensions prevented the constitutional assembly of 1949 from agreeing on a single constitutional document, which paved the way for a more gradual development of its constitutional order through the adoption of Basic Laws and their constitutional interpretation (Shinar 2013).

Secondly, the strategic realist perspective suggests that constitutional choices may often be haphazard and "accidental," the result of political deadlock and indecision, or simply chance. The case study of Israel in this volume, for example, demonstrates how political deadlock, and a failure to reach agreement over core constitutional issues, produced what Adam Shinar calls an "accidental" development of Israel's constitution, through the gradual enactment of basic laws and their interpretation. Perhaps even more accidental was New Zealand's prime minister's misreading of his notes on national television in announcing a popular referendum of electoral reform, which set off an unexpected chain of events and produced electoral reform in an "accidental" fashion (Erdos 2013: 339). Admittedly, the latter example is almost a caricature of constitutional realism, one step short of suggesting that "the constitution would depend on what the constitution-maker had for breakfast," to rephrase Llewellyn's famous claim. Even so, it draws to our attention that constitutions are not always conscious and deliberate, but riddled with sub-optimal bargains and even mistakes.

1.5 CONSTITUTIONS AS SOCIAL COORDINATION

The theory of constitutions as coordination contends that the "whole point of a constitution is to organize politics and society in particular ways." Russell Hardin adopts this approach in arguing that "[e]stablishing a constitution is itself a massive act of coordination, which, if it is stable for a while, creates a convention that depends for its maintenance on its self-generating incentives and expectations" (Hardin 2013: 61). There is in fact a double convention: "Government derives its power (not its right) to rule by some specific form of coordination that is a convention and the populace acquiesces in that rule by its own convention. Once empowered by these conventions, the government has the capacity to do many things" (Hardin 2013: 59). The two distinct episodes of coordination and two matching conventions are crucial to the thesis: establishing a system of government is one episode of coordination, which results in a convention mainly, presumably, on the part of government officials to govern accordingly; whether the constitution, and the system of government created by it, then serves to coordinate the society depends on the people adopting a second convention to acquiesce.

The distinction between the two episodes of coordination and the two conventions is vital. One reason is that both conventions are necessary for successful coordination of politics and society: the system of government must be capable of governing effectively and the people must acquiesce in it. Either one without the other destroys or reduces the system's capacity to coordinate politics and society. There is a certain logical problem in separating the two, because whether government is effective depends partly on whether the people acquiesce to it. Effective government has two parts: it means government that is both capable of coordinating politics and society *and* succeeds in practice in doing so, where success depends on popular acquiescence. In explaining the theory, however, it is useful to keep the two elements separate. The logic of effective government can be expressed in this way. It has two elements. One is a system of government capable of governing, which requires a set of institutions with powers to make and implement laws and policies. The other element is that the people acquiesce in the system of government. Only when both elements are present is the system effective, where the test of effectiveness is success in coordination. In the interests of clarity, we use the terms in the following way: coordination requires effective government; effective government requires both a capable government, as just defined, and popular acquiescence. We see why both have to be present. A system of government can be capable of governing, has the institutions and powers to govern, yet the people do not acquiesce. In the opposite case, the people acquiesce in a system of government that is incapable of governing, incapable, that is, of providing the basis for coordination, perhaps because of such factors as weak and unsuitable institutions, political strife, or corruption. There is a failure of coordination in both cases. It is only when the two elements come together that coordination is fully achieved.

Some observers will insist that what constitutes effective government is open to interpretation and should not be separated from a notion of good government, which means government's having certain qualities beyond the effective exercise of power. The quality of government is of course likely to affect whether the people acquiesce. But the reality is that people often acquiesce in systems of government even though they lack qualities that would be considered vital from, say, a liberal and democratic point of view.[18] It is enough to observe the contemporary world, let alone have recourse to history, for evidence of the kinds of government in which the people acquiesce, often apparently regardless of their lack of higher qualities. We see no obstacle to distinguishing between a notion of effective government and the particular character or quality of government, that is, the nature of the institutions – such as whether they are based on democratic ideas – and the content of the laws – such as whether they protect rights. Coordination theory requires only that government be effective, that is, capable of governing and gaining acquiescence. Above that threshold the people may insist on other qualities, but whether they do and what qualities they demand depend on the social and political context of each nation.

Whether the people acquiesce and the conditions that induce acquiescence are empirical questions awaiting further research. The existence of institutions with the capacity to make laws and policies, and to enforce and implement them, is itself a strong incentive for acquiescence. In some cases it is enough, after a period of upheaval, for instance, when the restoration of order and stability is the priority.

---

[18]   Roughly one-third of nations are ranked as democratic, yet at least some of the other two-thirds have effective systems of government in which the people acquiesce.

But, it is not always enough, and we can imagine cases of the people or a large sector of the people declining to acquiesce in a potentially capable government, after conquest or revolution, perhaps, where the new system is considered repugnant to their way of life. After having acquiesced, the people may rebel and withdraw their acquiescence, as the current situations in Egypt, Tunisia, and Syria illustrate. The work of historians on popular rebellion, a fertile source of empirical evidence on acquiescence and its withdrawal, awaits exploitation by social scientists (Wood 2002). Establishing a system of government is one thing; making it work in practice, in the sense that the people acquiesce to it, is quite another. If the two conventions are in place, the system has succeeded in organizing politics and society in particular ways. The two episodes of coordination depend not just on officials' acting in fact in accordance with the constitution and the people's acquiescing, but on a convention that in each case they do so. The point of the convention is that, once in place, the officials govern and people acquiesce in the system as a whole without having to decide whether to do so in particular cases and despite aspects of the system being contrary to their interests or occasionally working injustice.[19]

While both episodes of coordination are necessary to the effective working of a constitutional order, the emphasis in Hardin's essay is on the people's acquiescence: "Acquiescence is the compelling fact." The English and Scottish people acquiesced in the decision of their parliaments to invite William and Mary to the throne (Hardin 2013); the Israeli people appear to be acquiescing in the constitutional revolution quietly effected by the Supreme Court, despite low levels of support for some of its decisions, especially those concerning security (Shinar 2013); the people of Hungary are acquiescing in recent major changes to the constitution, although they are controversial and divisive. Acquiescence is a necessary condition of coordination because constitutions are self-enforcing, which is to say that unless the people acquiesce in their provisions and in actions taken pursuant to them, a constitution will fail.

The coordination thesis is based on the idea that once the conventions are in place and stable – that is, once the government is functioning and the people acquiescent – two consequences follow: one is that the costs of doing things differently are raised, the other that, even if the constitution does not wholly serve the interests of the people as a whole, or those of a particular group or persons, it is likely to be more in their interests to support it than to try to change it and introduce new rules or government structures. A number of the case studies indeed highlight such path dependence in constitution-making. When countries are faced with an opportunity to change their constitution, even one that was imposed by a former colony, they often maintain the old constitutional arrangements, in a process that one of the

---

[19] Russell Hardin explains more fully the notion and importance of conventions in Hardin (2007).

contributors describes as "constitutional laziness" (Meuwese 2013). Iceland prior to the 2011 amendment to the constitution largely kept the arrangements that had been imposed by Denmark in an earlier epoch. The South Sudanese interim constitution is closely related to the Comprehensive Peace Agreement for Sudan (Cope 2013). The coordination thesis suggests that constitution-makers may not just be lazy, but instead baulk at the high costs of changing the existing modalities of government.

The notion of acquiescence to some is puzzling and so a further word of explanation is warranted. To acquiesce means to accept or agree tacitly to a set of arrangements. The notion of tacit acceptance fits well. It means no more than a willingness to regard the constitution, and in turn the system of government created, as a power structure within which one finds oneself and compliance with which is practical and prudent. The people do not have to approve of the constitution in some strong sense, nor does it have to be characterized as an agreement, contract, or covenant, and whether there is a moral obligation to comply is a wholly different issue. Unlike other concepts invoked to describe the position of the people in a functioning constitutional order, acquiescence is grounded in social reality and is empirically observable. It removes the need to resort to nebulous notions such as legitimacy, the meaning of which is uncertain and existential authenticity questionable. Acquiescence means only that the people as a matter of convention regard the constitutional system as authoritative, in explanation of which they might give a variety of reasons, some ideological, others principled, while the more mundane – that is, stability and the provision of social goods such as security, protection, and a few basic rights – are likely to be the more authentic. The people, wrote Nicolò Machiavelli, "desire to be free .... in order to live securely"; they want to be able "to possess one's things freely without any suspicion .... not fearing for oneself." "Men of such a humour .... when they are governed well, neither seek nor want any other freedom" (Machiavelli, quoted in Rahe 2008: 51). The people are just as likely to have no clear reasons beyond being part of a society whose culture includes the constitutional order and its shared acceptance.

David Hume long ago pondered how "this wonder is effected" and went on to express his surprise, and that of all who "consider human affairs with a philosophical eye," at "the easiness with which the many are governed by the few; and the implicit submission, with which men resign their own sentiments and passions to those of their rulers" (Hume 2008: 24). Yet force is always on the side of the governed, for "the governors have nothing to support them but opinion." The main influence on opinion, according to Hume, is "interest," by which is meant "the sense of the general advantage which is reaped from government" (Hume 2008: 25). He added other factors shaping opinion, one that government maintains public justice (opinion of right to power), the other that government is necessary to protect property (opinion of right to property). We need not here assess the strength of such opinions, upon which Hume thought all governments are founded, although it broadly fits the idea put forward in Hardin's account of coordination theory that once a convention of acquiescence is in place, the costs of acting otherwise are high, and even if it does not suit the interests of all, it is probably as good as any alternative. As history shows, the people tend to acquiesce in the system in which they find themselves, regardless of its merits, reserving always the power to rebel and substitute one system for another, although only rarely and under extreme conditions invoking that power. Coordination is grounded in that reality, and while it would be of interest and utility to know more about the conditions under which the people acquiesce, the validity of the theory is not dependent on such empirical knowledge.

The coordination thesis addresses directly the social foundations of a constitutional order. It is "a causal thesis, not a definition of what a constitution is," for a constitution might fail to coordinate government and the people (Hardin 2013: 62). A failed constitution is still a constitution, whereas a successful constitution is necessarily one that creates and sustains an effective system of government. Let us be clear as to the nature of the thesis: the coordination thesis advances a sociological claim about the conditions that must be met in order for a nation to have an effective system of government within a constitutional framework. The claim is definitional of what a successful constitution is rather than an empirical claim to be tested by evidence. Unless a constitution creates a government able to govern, unless government is conducted according to the terms of its authority, and unless the people acquiesce in the system of government, there will be a failure of coordination. This is not to say that in designing a constitution the parties are always committed to the goal of an effective system of government, and hence effective coordination; whether they are and the extent to which they are varies according to the circumstances. Other aims and purposes may be in competition with coordination, some meritorious, such as constraints on government and protection of rights, others without merit, such as lust for power or excessive protection of sectional interests. Both can be subversive of effective government and coordination.

Notice that each of these conditions is in practice variable and a matter of degree rather than a precise standard, so that acquiescence by the people, for instance, is more or less, stronger or weaker. Notice also that the thesis is not specifically about constitutions in the narrow sense of the written document, but rather about a system of government within which the written text has a variable role, sometimes of high importance as in Germany, Australia, and the United States, and more recently Poland, where it took several years to work out the conditions for a strong and stable democracy and to settle the text accordingly (Garlicki and Garlicka 2010).[20]

---

[20] The major efforts exerted in Spain to achieve consensus at the constitution-making stage suggest a serious commitment to coordination; Bonime-Blanc (2010). A very different case is Bosnia, where

Coordination is often of low priority for constitution-makers, as shown in recent constitutional efforts in Iraq (Morrow 2010), Afghanistan (Thier 2010), and Nicaragua (Walker and Williams 2010) where constitutions were drafted quickly. In all systems there is likely to be some variation between the written text and the workings of government institutions, either by creative interpretation, or allowing some provisions to fall into disuse, or informally creating new principles and practices. A complete account of a nation's constitution would include both the text and the wider context of rules, principles, conventions, and understandings surrounding the text. Such informal means of adjusting and developing the constitution can be of utility in sustaining an effective system of government and its popular acceptance. The Japanese constitution has been a success owing in part, it is said, to the capacity for informal adjustment of the text (Law 2013). The relationship between the two – the formal and the informal – raises interesting issues for further investigation.

The coordination thesis is a forceful reminder that the practical point of a constitutional order is to provide an effective system of government. The thesis is intended as a sociological counter to normative accounts of what a constitution is and what it should contain; it is also aimed at accounts that concentrate their attention on the content of the text while taking no interest in whether it has any effect in practice. Since accounts such as these do not purport to be sociological, they are mere skirmishes along the way to confronting contract theory as the main target. Here the idea is that constitutions are best understood as contracts, albeit of a certain character (an idea considered in the next section). As for the strengths of coordination theory, it may seem obvious and even circular to contend that a successful constitutional order is one that provides for effective government, where being effective means coordinating politics and society. Yet, perhaps surprisingly, so much of the discussion of constitutions is conducted as if oblivious to this obvious fact. Constitutional orders do not always coordinate social life effectively, as the experience of the Soviet Union and neighboring nations shows; as societies they were reasonably well coordinated, but only partly as a result of the constitution and government (Kurkchiyan 2003). Societies consist of networks influencing and regulating the attitudes and actions of their members, both people and officials, so that to be effective, government has to confront and either marshal support or overcome other mechanisms of coordination (Scott 1996; Galligan 2007). Coordination according to a constitutional order is not just any coordination but coordination of a certain kind, the kind that only effective government can deliver.

---

attempts were made, presumably in order to ensure effective government, to accommodate the warring parties by allocating political positions according to ethnicity and creating a large government structure so that all parties have a role; O'Brien (2010). Whether the resulting system will in practice be effective in coordination remains to be seen.

1.5.1 *The Practical Value of Coordination Theory*

Today, all nations are expected to have written constitutions and to update them regularly. In an age where the importance of constitutions is taken for granted and constitution-making is widespread, we should be curious to know if there are causal relations between the process of making a constitution, its contents, and coordination. Does coordination have a role in guiding how a constitution is made and what it contains? Do the process and contents in turn affect coordination?

Coordination theorists contend that there is no necessary relation between how a constitution is made and coordination; the more robust among them might go further and claim the same about relations between content and coordination. Constitutional systems are capable of high coordination even though made by a select few without reference to the people, as shown in cases such as the United States, the Fifth French Republic, and contemporary Hungary. There also appears to be no necessary connection between the content of a constitution and coordination. The content of successful constitutions varies enormously, just as it does for the unsuccessful ones. The U.S. constitution is successful in coordination, as Hardin points out, in spite of its content, the suggestion being that much of the content is unsuitable for a modern nation of that size and variety.[21]

However, although there is no necessary causal connection between process, content, and coordination, the question remains whether the goal of coordination can, or has the potential to, influence the process of constitution-making and its content, and, alternatively, whether process and content can, or have the potential to, contribute to coordination. In order to understand better the causal dynamics, we propose a model of constitution-making based on relations between process, content, and coordination. The aim is to show how the text, in the sense of process and content, and the people's acquiescence can be integrated into a set of causal relationships. The logic is as follows.

1. The first step is to picture the making of a constitution as a structured process whose threshold goal is coordination through a system of effective government (using the term as earlier defined to include government with the powers to govern capably in which the people acquiesce). Whatever else the constitution aims to achieve, it ought to be effective in coordinating politics and society. The conditions of effective government are partly practical in the sense of what kinds of powers and institutions are necessary potentially to govern; they are also partly based on other qualities, such as concerns

---

[21] For an analysis of how the U.S. Constitution is out of step with modern constitutional models, see Law and Versteeg (2012).

for liberty and democracy, without which a particular people is unlikely to acquiesce. Above the threshold, there are likely to be other goals, values, and aspirations to include, some of which are unrelated to coordination, others potentially in competition with and capable of jeopardizing coordination. If coordination is the main goal, then such other factors need to be modified accordingly; if, however, they are insisted on, coordination might be in jeopardy.

2. The *content* of the constitution and coordination are potentially causally related in two ways: the goal of coordination provides guidance as to the content, while the content has the potential to influence coordination. Since capable government and popular acquiescence are the two elements of coordination, the constitution needs to be designed with those two goals in mind.

Content ↔ Coordination

There is no formula to apply in the design of an effective system of government, yet a wealth of common experience is available as to what kind of system is likely to be effective and what not, and experts and consultants have long been keen to offer such advice. If the constitution provides a well-designed system of government, then a first step has been taken toward effective government; if it also has qualities important to the society at the time, then it will encourage acquiescence. That the people expect the constitution to institute a workable system of government is normally a reasonable assumption to make. Other expectations may be held both about the qualities of government, such as whether it is democratic and representative, and the inclusion of substantive provisions dealing with such matters as the equal treatment of diverse groups, limits on the powers of government, and the protection of rights. What the people's expectations are is an empirical question that depends on the social and political conditions at the time.

Notice how coordination works reflexively: the text is guided and limited by the concern for a constitutional order that coordinates politics and society, yet substantive provisions that meet people's expectations might encourage them to accept the constitution. Where there are deep divisions in the nation, the goal of coordination could be an incentive for accommodation and compromise (Choudhry 2008). But notice also the tension: too much emphasis on democratic elements, or excessive constraints on legislative and executive institutions, have the potential to weaken government to the point of its being ineffective, while watering down the democratic elements could reduce the people's commitment. While few nowadays would vote for the stern sovereign of Hobbes's imagination, governments rendered useless by excessive constitutional constraints are not impossible to imagine.

3. The *process* of constitution-making has the potential to affect coordination along two causal lines: one is the indirect line from process to content and from content to coordination, the other the direct line between process and coordination.

Process → Content → Coordination
← ——————————————————— →

The logic of the indirect relationship is this: the process of constitution-making has the potential to influence the content – for instance, by allowing the people or their representatives to participate – which in turn, as we have just seen, can affect coordination. The second causal relationship depends on the process of constitution-making having a direct effect on acquiescence by the people. Intense participation at the process stage, for instance, might be a reason for the people acquiescing in the resulting system of government.

1.5.2 *Content and Coordination*

With this account of the logic of constitutions in mind, let us consider in more detail how coordination might affect the content of the constitution and vice versa. If constitution-makers are acting in good faith, they would want to create at least a constitutional order with capable government in which the people acquiesce. Unless they succeed in that aim, much else will be in vain. An effective system of coordination, while a major achievement, is unlikely to be their only aim. The parties will have interests to protect, past wrongs and abuses to remedy, and ideals to advance. Pressures from outside – from the international community, for instance – must be accommodated, and so on. Consider the case of past wrongs. Following the sudden end of the communist era in Central and Eastern Europe, the parties engaged in constitution-making were naturally affected by past abuses, one reason for which was the concentration of power in a small executive without adequate constraints. The inclination to distribute power among several institutions and severely to constrain each, while natural and understandable, had to be tempered by the competing aim that the new institutions be able to govern effectively, otherwise coordination would be at risk.

An example of how the content of the constitution was shaped by constitution-makers striving to achieve coordination was the 1971 Constitution of Egypt. According to Clark Lombardi, the document is best explained in terms of coordination. On the one hand, it was riddled with ambiguity and, in the absence of agreement among the parties, who represented authoritarian, liberal, and Islamist elements, left major issues unresolved. On the other hand, the constitution created a system of government that in the short term offered enough to all parties to win their acceptance and the people's acquiescence (Lombardi 2013). The making of the Constitution of Japan in 1946, where the occupying Allies managed to sideline the reactionary government and connect directly with the people, whose inclinations were more democratic, liberal, and forward-looking, also shows commitment to the creation of a viable system of government (Law 2013). Other examples could be cited, including the Commonwealth of Australia, the Republic of India, Ireland, the United States, and most recently the new constitution of Iceland (Meuwese 2013), all of which display a high regard for effective coordination.

There is no shortage of cases heading in the opposite direction. In the postcolonial context, coordination was not foremost in the minds of officials of the British Colonial Office when they insisted on a bill of rights being included in the constitution of Nigeria, despite the alien nature of such an instrument, regardless of the ethnic and tribal divisions, and apparently oblivious to the unlikelihood of its being enforced (Parkinson 2013). Other striking examples of a lack of regard for coordination are the constitutions of Iraq and Afghanistan, given that in both there is deep disparity between the text with its ideals and aspirations and a political reality of deep conflict and division that was left intact (Morrow 2010; Thier 2010). In a less clear case, the Israeli Supreme Court, in creating a new set of constitutional standards through adjudication, appears to have been motivated by the need to establish principles, without particular regard for the consequences, with the result that the coordinating capacity of such major innovation remains uncertain (Shinar 2013).

Do the case studies in this collection or elsewhere suggest any guidelines as to what contents are likely to contribute to coordination? Can we go beyond the slightly lame concession that all depends on the social and political context? The positive causal connections are always hard to prove, and this is no exception. The best that can be done is to identify potential links from case studies and then see whether they stand up to empirical scrutiny, keeping always in mind the problems inherent in making causal connections. It is possible that constitutions that align with popular and domestic values are more likely to succeed in coordination. The study of the constitution of Japan suggests that its endurance is attributable to General McArthur and his advisers making connections with the "will of the people" (Law 2013). The opposite is likely to occur where a constitution relies heavily on standard constitutional provisions or foreign imports, which are remote from popular values and imagination, as the failure of the Nigerian Independence constitution shows (Parkinson 2013). Constitutions that do not take account of social and political realities, where there is a lack of symmetry between text and reality, are at risk of failing to coordinate politics and society. The constitution of Afghanistan, while strong on provisions for moderation, democracy, an Islamic state, strong government, and the rule of law, is so far removed from the social and political realities of deep divisions and lack of consensus that failure to provide effective government is inevitable (Thier 2010). Negative lessons might also be learned from other cases, such as Iraq and several from South American constitutions, including Venezuela, Argentina, and Nicaragua.[22] The lack of symmetry between the text on the hand and the cultural and social realities on the other is a recurring negative factor. If we are to progress beyond mere impressions, further research, both quantitative and qualitative, is needed to unravel the link between substantive constitutional provisions and coordination.

1.5.3 *Process and Coordination*

The process by which a constitution is made, too, may affect coordination. Specifically, constitution-making in recent years shows a growing commitment to involving the people (Miller 2010; Elkins et al. 2009).[23] Widespread popular participation was present in the making of the 1996 South African Constitution, the 1995 Ugandan Constitution, the 1997 Constitution of Thailand, the 1997 Eritrean Constitution, and the Brazilian Constitution of 1988, just to name a few. Most recently, Iceland underwent a complicated process aimed at producing a people's constitution, a process recounted in Anne Meuwese's (2013) essay. According to some, the Icelandic case epitomizes a new gold standard in constitutional design. If true, we may expect that future episodes of constitution-making will more frequently and more intensively involve the population (Miller 2010). One reason for this new level of interest is the notion that a sovereign and democratic people ought to be engaged in the constitutional process.

Are such participatory processes conducive to coordination? The causal connection, as noted, between process and coordination takes two possible lines: one is the direct effect of process on coordination, the other the indirect effect of influencing content. The relationship is reflexive: coordination guides process, while process has the potential to influence coordination. Before examining the causal connections, we ought to be clear about the elements of process, which include such matters as: the procedures and mechanisms by which the constitution is established, the nature and powers of the entity responsible for devising the constitution, how the members are appointed, the role of advisers and experts, the position of groups and special interests, and the participation of the people. Leaving aside the possibility of a truly populist process, we find various avenues of popular participation. Perhaps the most direct are exemplified in the case of South Africa, where the people were potentially able to influence the deliberations of constitution-makers by submitting petitions and attending workshops held around the country (Klug 2000). In other cases,

---

[22] These countries are all referred to earlier in this chapter.

[23] However, the extent to which the people are so engaged in practice is highly variable even in democratic nations and much less than democratic theory dictates (Galligan 2013b).

the people elect the constitution-making authority, as in the Icelandic case, among others (Meuwese 2013). Or they may exert pressure on the constitution-makers in a more informal way, as in the Portuguese case where the constituent assembly was "not immune" to popular demands and the "streets and the fields outside . . . . brimming with activity" (Magalhães 2013). Finally, the people might participate by voting in a referendum of ratification, although fewer than half of extant national constitutions have been ratified by the people (Galligan 2013b; for an overview, see Ginsburg et al. 2009).[24]

An adequate account of how the process, both generally and with respect to specific parts of the constitution, could be influenced by the goal of coordination would require a fuller analysis than we are able to give here. It would also depend on more research than is now available. It is instructive, nevertheless, to consider in outline the possible causal links between process and coordination by studying popular participation. This is just one aspect of process but, in democratic societies, where constitutions are made in the name of the people, one of special interest. It is plain from constitutional history that popular participation is not a necessary condition of a well-designed constitution or of popular acquiescence. We know many constitutions have been effective in coordination over long periods despite the people not having been involved in their creation or adoption. Among contemporary cases are the constitutions of the Fifth French Republic, post–World War II Japan, postcommunist Hungary, and the 1971 Egyptian Constitution, all of which have been fairly successful in coordination despite participation being minimal or nonexistent. The question, however, is whether popular participation could contribute positively to both the quality of the constitution and acquiescence in the constitutional order so established. In answering, we need to keep in mind the difference between political theory and social reality, for no matter how enticing ideas of participation may be and the sense of satisfaction they induce, whether or not participation contributes to coordination is ultimately an empirical question.

In order to understand the potential causal relationship between process and coordination, we need to have a brief account of the nature of process and the ends it serves (see generally Galligan 1997).[25]

1. We often encounter the idea that procedures, especially participatory ones, are good in themselves: it just is right to hear a person before making a decision affecting his interests. This is not to be taken literally, for what it means is that

---

[24] For useful discussion of these issues, see Miller (2010).

[25] Acemoglu and Robinson argue in their recent study, *Why Nations Fail*, that the inclusiveness or exclusiveness of institutions is one of the key factors in whether nations succeed or fail; Acemoglu and Robinson (2011). Future research might find the idea of utility in assessing the causal effects of popular participation in constitution-making.

hearing a person serves some value, such as respect for persons, an acknowledgment of their autonomy and dignity. The merit of participatory procedures then lies in serving such values and is independent of whether they also contribute to some further end, such as an accurate or sound outcome.[26]

2. Procedures are potentially useful instrumentally in bringing to light issues that need to be dealt with in the constitution, but which would otherwise have been unnoticed. Procedures might ease the way for the successful resolution of issues, such as the divisions between ethnic groups or powerful interests, in advance of the text and, without which there would be no consensus later on; or, having mixed their labor in its making, the people might be more inclined to accept the product.[27]

3. Most importantly for our purposes, procedures such as participation plainly are instruments to outcomes, of which, in the constitutional context, there are two main kinds: one is the content of the constitution, the other acquiescence by the people. It is to these two possible connections that we now turn.

Whether participatory procedure encourages popular acquiescence is difficult to show in practice, and the relationship is one of subtlety and nuance. If participation influences content to the point where the people are reasonably satisfied with the text, perhaps to the point of actual agreement, the grounds for acquiescence are strengthened. The chain of causation would then be: participation influences content, content influences acquiescence. Participation also relates directly to acquiescence, the idea being that, as a result of their involvement in the process, the people are more inclined to accept or at least acquiesce in the constitution, even if the content does not fully meet their expectations. The reason often given is that if they have participated in a fair and meaningful manner in the process, the people may be – perhaps should be – willing to accept the outcome more or less regardless of its content (cf. Tyler 1988). But again the normative claim needs to be kept apart from the empirical one: whether involvement in the process creates an obligation to comply with the outcome is debatable (Pettit 1997); whether it has efficacy as a causal factor in acquiescence is contingent and variable according to the context.

It is difficult to draw general conclusions about the causal effects of popular engagement in constitution-making on content and outcome (what some have called downstream effects). There is a natural inclination in democratic societies to believe that process matters, and particularly that public involvement matters.

---

[26] For discussion, see Galligan (1997). Participation is often linked to legitimacy, that is, the constitution gains legitimacy if the people are involved in its making. Such claims suffer from two defects: one is that the concept of legitimacy is left unexplained, the other that legitimacy, whatever it means, does not necessarily result in acquiescence. On legitimacy, compare Arato and Miklosi (2010).

[27] Part of the reason for an interim constitution is to allow the parties time to negotiate difficult issues.

However, there is only limited evidence on the relationship between process and content, and even less evidence on the relationship between process and acquiescence. The former relationship, between process and content, lends itself to relatively straightforward empirical testing, and initial research demonstrates that citizens' participation in designing constitutions is positively associated with the extent of constitutional rights and the presence of certain democratic institutions in the resulting document (Elkins et al. 2009; Samuels 2006). The positive association does not prove a causal relationship, and constitutional design can be idiosyncratic, dynamic, nuanced, and contingent, a process that lends itself to careful, case-by-case process-tracing to uncover the causal mechanisms at work in individual cases (Elkins et al. 2009). There is no clear evidence that participatory processes produce constitutions that are more closely tied to the ideals and aspirations of the society, nor is there evidence that popular participation in the process counters the influence of transnational constitutional diffusion. In the Icelandic case, a notably inclusive constitution-making processes was still a "borrowing exercise," drawing heavily on foreign constitutional notions (Meuwese 2013). In the opposite case, the absence of popular participation does not necessarily prevent the constitution-makers from identifying and accurately reflecting popular values, as the case of Japan demonstrates (Law 2013).

The relationship between the popular participation and outcome – that is, attachment, acquiescence, endurance, or otherwise – is even more difficult to test empirically. The relationship is less proximate than that of process and content, and there are more intervening variables that make it difficult to uncover general patterns and prescriptions (see especially Widner 2008). While there is evidence that public involvement in constitutional adoption is associated with increased attachment to the document (Moehler 2006), increased constitutional endurance (Elkins et al. 2009), and decreased violence (Widner 2008), again, these associations do not necessarily imply causal or generalizable relationships. The case studies in this collection are no exception: the hint of a connection appears in cases like Brazil and South Africa where effective government has been achieved by constitutions that were written with widespread participation, although other factors particular to the social and political context were also instrumental. The experience of Eritrea points in the opposite direction: widespread popular participation in the process failed to produce a working system of government (Maalo 2013). The Brazilian experience adds an interesting twist: although extensive popular engagement resulted in a long, complex, and unwieldy text, effective government – and hence a high level of coordination – appears to have been achieved.

In searching for possible causal connections between process and coordination, we ought not to forget that the most common situation of all occurs where the people neither participate nor have met their expectations as to content, yet acquiesce. The most likely explanation for this fits the coordination thesis: the people acquiesce in order to secure the practical gains of a stable and effective government, despite other shortcomings. Acquiescence is of course a variable both as to degree and over time, and sometimes tips over into non-acquiescence or even rebellion, as noted earlier concerning current events in North Africa and the Middle East.

The want of evidence of a significant causal connection between process, content, and acquiescence is not a good reason for concluding that process is unimportant, or that how constitutions are made is a matter of indifference, as long as they are effective in coordination. Process has the potential to serve various ends, as we saw from the earlier discussion. In a society that respects its citizens, participation is a mark of respect and acknowledgment of their autonomy. Participation may, moreover, provide a forum in which social divisions can be discussed and perhaps resolved. These are good reasons, and there may be others, for involving the people in the making of the constitution. At the same time, procedures, even participatory ones, are not necessarily unqualified goods; they also have a darker, negative side. Brazil is often cited as an outstanding case of popular engagement, yet the resulting text, in the drafters' eagerness faithfully to reflect the varied claims and opinions put forward, is long, complex, and unwieldy. Another cautionary lesson emerging from South Africa is that intense popular involvement is prone to raise expectations of the constitution and government that cannot be met, raising the prospect of a disappointed people being more restive than a passive people.

1.5.4 *Critiques of Coordination Theory*

Coordination theory has attracted vigorous criticism, including from some of the essays in this collection (Ginsburg 2013; J. King 2013). We conclude our analysis of the theory with a brief account of the main lines of criticism and our response. The main two are: the notion that coordination is empty of content, and that it employs a measure of success that allows the constitutions of autocratic and repressive regimes to be considered successful.

The first charge is that the theory is empty of content, and that it provides no guidance as to the content a constitution should have (Ginsburg 2013). While it is true that coordination identifies "no best constitution" (Hardin 2012: 68), the complaint seems misdirected, because the joint aims of designing a workable system of government and inducing popular acquiescence plainly provide, as the preceding discussion has shown, at least some guidance as to content, both what needs to be included and what excluded. Successful coordination requires a government that is capable of adopting and implementing law and policies. Beyond that, as we have shown, particular constitutional features may contribute to coordination or militate against it. Those likely to ensure coordination are partly dependent on the local

social and political context, perhaps mainly so dependent. Yet not entirely, for as
more knowledge is gained from the combination of experience and research, guidelines of general application may possibly emerge. We already know from experience
that certain issues must be addressed in the constitution if it is to have any chance
of success. The constitution of a society divided along ethnic lines will not succeed
unless the divisions are addressed and efforts made to ameliorate the differences and
protect minorities. The same can be said of a constitution rich in ideals but bearing
no relation to the social and political realities of the society. Eliminating obvious
grounds for failure is a necessary condition of success but not its guarantor, and the
formulation of positive guidelines poses more of a challenge than the negative ones,
for social and political life is unruly and the wheel of fortune is forever turning. But
even here the painstaking study of successful constitutions – successful, that is, in
coordination – is likely to offer some guidance for the future. A good starting point –
guideline number one – would be that all those engaged in constitution-making
grasp that the first aim of their endeavors, regardless of what other goals they hope to
achieve, is to produce a constitution that coordinates politics and society.

The second complaint is that the measure of success employed by coordination theorists is compatible with a spectrum of constitutional orders, ranging from
such unappealing cases as the former Soviet Union, the Taliban government of
Afghanistan, and contemporary Belarus to those based firmly on liberal and democratic principles. The observation is accurate but does not threaten coordination
theory: unappealing systems of government are still systems of government, and
provided they meet the two conditions of effectiveness and acquiescence, they are
successful in coordinating politics and society. Why the critics object to this aspect
of coordination theory requires a word of explanation. In the minds of critics, the
theory means that the quality of government, the principles and values on which it
is based, are of no consequence. This is a misunderstanding of coordination theory,
even if some accounts of the theory lend themselves to this interpretation. The
theory provides, as we saw earlier, the threshold standards, compliance with which is
necessary for coordination. Issues of the quality of the constitutional system enter at
two stages. At the first stage, meeting the criteria of capable government and popular
acquiescence depends to a considerable degree on factors such as the character of
the nation, its history, the stage of development economically and politically, its
social and demographic features, and the expectations of the parties. Once the two
criteria are met and the threshold test is satisfied, other considerations concerning
the quality of government can be added to the constitution, provided they do not
undermine the threshold criteria of effective coordination.

To take an example, the most elementary idea of constitutionalism to which
modern societies of a broadly liberal disposition are committed requires that government be limited; unlimited government is simply incompatible with modern

expectations of a constitution. In such societies, limitations on government power might be – indeed are likely to be – a factor in both capable government and popular acceptance. The form the limitations take and their extent might also influence the quality of government above the threshold. In a different society, one not committed to limited government or to only minor limitations, the standards of capable government and popular acquiescence are likely to be satisfied by a more autocratic system of government. In short, coordination through capable government and popular acquiescence is an essential condition of a successful constitutional order, although the qualities necessary to meet the two standards depend to a substantial degree on the social and political context of each nation.

A third matter to mention is less a criticism of the theory and more in the nature of a refinement. On the account Russell Hardin advances in his essay, the constitutional text as a distinct social formation has a minor role. The emphasis instead rests on the system of government, in which of course the constitutional text has a place, but not necessarily one of importance. As the foregoing analysis demonstrated, the content of the text and the process by which it is formulated are potentially significant in achieving coordination.

1.6 CONSTITUTIONS AS SOCIAL CONTRACTS

In response to Hardin's claims for constitutions as coordination, Tom Ginsburg offers a modern defense of constitutions as contracts (Ginsburg 2013). Building on the point that coordination theory does not explain the content of constitutions, Ginsburg advances the argument that "modern developments in contract theory provide a set of very valuable tools to understand how constitutions are negotiated and maintained, and may have greater explanatory power than either classical contract theory *or* the coordination alternative in understanding actual constitutional design" (Ginsburg 2013: 182). In making the case, the author begins by refuting the standard objections to constitutions as social contracts. They are threefold: constitutions are not in fact agreed to by all the parties; while contracts are normally enforced by a third party, that is not the case with constitutions, which have to be self-enforcing; and constitutions create a system of government that is not in principle limited by time, while contracts generally anticipate a time at which the parties have fulfilled their obligations.

The essay then considers the positive advantages of drawing parallels between constitutions and contracts. One advantage occurs at the drafting stage in negotiations over design and content, which has some of the features of negotiating a contract. A second advantage of the contract approach concerns the content of the constitution. On the basis that constitutions are usually drafted by experts and lawyers, Ginsburg notes that models are used for the basic or standard provisions, which results in a high level of similarity in many modern constitutions. International treaties are another source of standard provisions, so that "the content of constitutions may, like contracts, have a form-like quality. Provisions migrate from document to document, sometimes with only minor amounts of local tailoring" (Ginsburg 2013: 197). The third advantage claimed for constitutions as contracts relates to renegotiation and endurance, where again the process of bargaining among the parties has parallels to the parties to a contract.

The challenge faced by the contract theory of constitutions is to show that it adds a layer of knowledge and understanding, and that it opens up a new perspective, which would otherwise be missed. We are concerned here with descriptive theory, not normative theories based on a notional social contract, the point of the latter being to establish the duty of the people to accept the system and obey its laws. The aim of contract theory as descriptive theory is quite different: its aim is to identify actual features of constitutions and constitution-making. The test of its worth then is whether it uncovers aspects of constitutions and constitution-making that are not included in other theories. Ginsburg rises to the challenge and sets out to show why theories of contract continue to have a central role in thinking about constitutions. Despite criticism, the notion that contract theory has something to contribute to the understanding of constitutions persists and the essay is a serious attempt to explain that persistence, citing an array of examples and drawing on a wide range of constitutional experience. Aware of the need to separate a descriptive analysis from the normative, Ginsburg suggests that there are two main ways in which contract theory contributes to the understanding of the social and political foundations of constitutions: one concerns constitution-making, while the other relates to the content of constitutions.

The making of a constitution, on this approach, resembles or is analogous to negotiating a contract. At first glance, one may express skepticism as to whether the making of a constitution is indeed like the negotiation of a contract: constitutions may be externally imposed, as in postwar and postcolonial situations, and the majority of the population is routinely excluded from the drafting process. To see the analogy requires a conceptual shift from a social contract to a private contract: even when the people are not involved in constitution-making, the constitution still represents a bargain between two or more parties. Such parties may be diverse: they might be elites, as in the roundtable talks in Venezuela, or they might be a combination of elites and outside powers, as was the case in Afghanistan, Iraq, and in the postcolonial setting of Nigeria. Only in rare cases, the people at large are actually part of the bargaining game. Thus, when we take "the people" out of the equation, constitutions become like contracts that are negotiated between a limited number of parties. To explain why the populace at large would consent to such elite bargains, Ginsburg points to coordination theory: the constitution is a contract for some, while it is merely acquiesced to by others.

Contract theory does more than shift our attention from a hypothetical social contract to an actual contract between rival groups in society. It also provides insights on the potential problems and solutions that parties – whoever they are – face in the constitutional bargaining game. Contract theory pays close attention to the specific interest of each of the bargaining parties, the information they possess, and the time pressures they are under, among other things. Applying concepts like "surplus," "hold-ups," "asymmetrical information," and "incomplete contracting," and drawing on a wide range of examples, Ginsburg shows how insights from contract theory improve our understanding also of the constitutional bargaining game. To offer just one example: in the face of imperfect information, parties may want to "write a more complete agreement, specifying contingencies," or rely on third-party enforcement. It is with these types of insights that the theory contributes most to our understanding of constitution-making.

The second reason advanced for the utility of the contract perspective is that it helps in determining the content of constitutions. Just as John Rawls used the hypothetical original position and the veil of ignorance to reveal the essential features of justice (Rawls 1972), a hypothetical contract, in the negotiation of which all parties hypothetically participate, may be of utility in designing and accounting for the content of constitutions (d'Agostino 2010). However, Ginsburg's approach is not that of the hypothetical contract. He relies rather on the observation that constitutions are normally drafted by experts and lawyers acting on behalf of the negotiating parties. And in the same way that lawyers drafting contracts rely on standard forms, so those engaged in drafting the text are prone to draw on existing models.

There are numerous historical examples of constitution-makers relying on "boilerplate constitutional provisions," as Ginsburg calls them. In the nineteenth century, a whole generation of Latin American constitutions copied verbatim from the U.S. Constitution (Billias 2009: 105; see also Goderis and Versteeg 2013: 103). Likewise, the Romanian Constitution of 1848 "faithfully copied" about 60 percent of its provisions from the French Constitution (Parau 2013), while about thirty former British colonies in Africa and the Caribbean all adopted what was essentially a carbon copy of the European Convention on Human Rights and Fundamental Freedoms as their bill of rights (Parkinson 2007). Ginsburg claims that constitution-makers rely on standardized constitutional models because "they reduce the transaction costs of negotiation." He does not, however, explore alternative explanations for why such standardized models might be relied on. As the essay by Goderis and Versteeg illustrates, there are several reasons why constitution-makers might and often do imitate foreign models: to signal conformity with the norms and values of the international community; because they carefully considered and deliberated a wide range of models as part of a learning process; because they are deliberately trying to attract economic capital; or simply because these models are coerced by outside powers (Goderis and Versteeg 2013). Considering the time and effort that is commonly put into the drafting of the constitutional document, it is at least plausible that the reliance on standardized models results from complex social relationships rather than mere cost-efficiency considerations. Moreover, there is an open question of exactly how much of the content of written constitutions is explained by the contract metaphor. It seems unlikely that all content of a constitution is determined by the use of standard forms, and so empirical evidence of constitution-making is needed to show just how much of the content and which parts are explicable on this basis. Cope's essay, for example, highlights that in South Sudan, the bill of rights appears to be based on standard forms, while the structural part of the constitution is not (Cope 2013).

Despite the advantages of the contract approach, the contract metaphor does not appear to capture all the features of constitutions. Specifically, constitutions have a strong aspirational and normative dimension not commonly found in private contracts. Even as elite bargains, constitutions include national and international values and proclamations of national identity. The mission-statement-like character of constitutions (J. King 2013) does not fit comfortably with private contracting, as private contracts tend to be rational bargains rather than symbolic documents. Constitutions, moreover, may be reinterpreted and evolve in unpredicted ways after the bargain has been concluded. This may happen because the people push for a different understanding of certain provisions or because the people develop an irrational attachment to the document, making it harder to amend even when amendment would be desirable. To illustrate the latter, it has been argued that the U.S. Constitution has been amended infrequently because the document is venerated and has evolved into a "civic religion" (Levinson 2012). Contracts, by contrast, may be subject to efficient breach: when rational actors calculate they will be better off without the contract, they simply refuse to live up to the contractual obligations. In sum, there might be something in the nature of constitutions – something sacred or irrational – that is not present in private contracting.

1.7 CONCLUSION

The essays in this collection, both the theoretical and the empirical, demonstrate the need to look beyond the idea of a constitution as simply a written document establishing a system of government. That there is much more to constitutions than that is obvious, for like any social phenomenon, constitutions interact with society in complex and varied ways. Guided by the four questions set out at the start, we have tried in this essay to provide an analysis of the interaction and the issues that arise from it. We show how different theoretical perspectives help in explaining and accounting for the social and political character of constitutions. It has also been important to point out their limitations and ways in which they need to be developed. We have considered constitutions as expressions of values, both of a national and transnational character, as products of domestic power among political elites, as coordination devices, and as contracts. Where possible we have drawn on the selection of case studies to illustrate each of the theories and to see to what extent they provide evidence, one way or another, for the different perspectives. We have also been concerned to examine the capacity of the various theories to explain aspects of constitutions. The theories and perspectives considered are not the only ones relevant to constitutions, and some readers may be disappointed to find no mention of their own favored approach. For a collection of this kind, some selection is necessary, but others may be inspired to subject other theories to similar analytical and empirical scrutiny. Explaining the social and political foundations of constitutions is the task of a lifetime. Our hope is that this essay offers a framework within which to think about and analyze constitutions in their social context, their social and political foundations, their functions and purposes, and to their practical effects.

REFERENCES

Acemoglu, Daron, Cantoni, Davide, Johnson, Simon, and Robinson, James A. 2011. 'The French Revolution: the consequences of radical reform', *American Economic Review* 101: 3286–3307.

Ackerman, Bruce 1991. *We the people: Foundations*. Cambridge, MA: Harvard University Press.

Arato, Andrew and Miklósi, Zoltán 2010. 'Constitution making and transnational politics in Hungary', in Laurel Miller (ed.), *Framing the state in times of transition: Case studies in constitution making*. Washington, DC: United States Institute of Peace Press, pp. 350–390.

Barak, Aharon 2002. 'Foreword: A judge on judging: The role of a supreme court in a democracy', *Harvard Law Review* 116: 16–162.

Berkowitz, Daniel, Pistor, Katharina, and Richard, Jean-Francois 2003. 'Economic development, legality, and the transplant effect', *European Economic Review* 47: 165–195.

Billias, George Athan 2009. *American constitutionalism heard round the world 1776–1989: A global perspective*. New York: New York University Press.

Bonime-Blanc, Andrea 2010. 'Constitution making and democratization: The Spanish paradigm', in Laurel Miller (ed.), *Framing the state in times of transition: Case studies in constitution making*. Washington, DC: United States Institute of Peace Press, pp. 417–434.

Bork, Robert H. 2003. *Coercing virtue: The worldwide rule of judges everywhere*. Washington, DC: American Enterprise Institute Press.

Brady, Paul 2013. 'Social, political and philosophical foundations of the Irish constitutional order', in Galligan, Denis J. and Versteeg, Mila (eds.), *Social and Political Foundations of Constitutions*. Cambridge: Cambridge University Press.

Breslin, Beau 2007. *From words to worlds: Exploring constitutional functionality*. Baltimore: Johns Hopkins University Press.

Brown, Nathan J. 4 April 2009. *Elections and rule of law: Democratic routes to dictatorial ends?* Paper presented for the conference 'Democracy and Development in the Middle East', held in honor of John Waterbury, Princeton.

2011. 'Americans, put away your quills', *Foreign Policy*, November 8.

2012. 'Constitutionalizing Authoritarianism and Democracy in Egypt and Tunisia' (unpublished manuscript).

Chavez, Rebecca Bill 2004. *The rule-of-law in nascent democracies*. Stanford, CA: Stanford University Press.

Choudhry, Sujit 2007. 'Migration as a new metaphor in comparative constitutional law', in Choudhry, Sujit (ed.), *The Migration of Constitutional Ideas*. Cambridge: Cambridge University Press, pp. 1–36.

2008. *Constitutional design for ethnically divided societies*. Oxford: Oxford University Press.

Cope, Kevin 2013. 'South Sudan's dualistic constitution', in Galligan, Denis J. and Versteeg, Mila (eds.), *Social and Political Foundations of Constitutions*. Cambridge: Cambridge University Press.

D'Agostino, Fred 2010. *The promise of social welfare: New foundations for the social contract*. Paper presented at the Foundation for Law Justice and Society, June 9, Oxford.

Dahl, Robert 1991. *Democracy and its critics*. New Haven, CT: Yale University Press.

Dicey, Albert Venn 1915. *Introduction to the study of the law of the constitution*. London: Macmillian.

Dixon, Rosalind and Ginsburg, Tom 2011. "Deciding Not to Decide: Deferral in Constitutional Design," *International Journal of Constitutional Law* 9: 636–672.

Elkins, Zachary, Ginsburg, Tom, and Melton, James 2009. *The endurance of national constitutions*. Cambridge: Cambridge University Press.

Elster, Jon 1993. 'Majority rule and individual rights', in Shute, Stephen and Hurley, Susan (eds.), *On Human Rights: The Oxford Amnesty Lectures*. New York: Basic Books, pp. 175–216.

1995. 'Forces and mechanisms in the constitution-making process', *Duke Law Journal* 45: 364–396.

Erdos, David 2010. *Delegating rights protection: The rise of bills of rights in the Westminster world*. New York: Oxford University Press.

2013. 'New Zealand: Abandoning Westminster?', in Galligan, Denis J. and Versteeg, Mila (eds.), *Social and Political Foundations of Constitutions*. Cambridge: Cambridge University Press.

Finkel, Jodi 2008. *Judicial reform as political insurance: Argentina, Peru and Mexico in the 1990s*. Notre Dame, IN: University of Notre Dame Press.

Galligan, Denis J. 1997. *Due process and fair procedures: A study of administrative procedures* Oxford: Oxford University Press.

2007. *Law in modern society*. Oxford: Oxford University Press

2013a. 'The sovereignty deficit of modern constitutions' (forthcoming).

2013b. 'The people, the constitution and the idea of representation', in Galligan, Denis J. and Versteeg, Mila (eds.), *Social and Political Foundations of Constitutions*. Cambridge: Cambridge University Press.

Garlicki, Lech and Garlicka, Zofia A. 2010. 'Constitution making, peace building, and national reconciliation: The experience of Poland', in Miller (ed.), *Framing the state in times of transition: Case studies in constitution making*. Washington, DC: United States Institute of Peace Press, 391–416.

Garoupa, Nuno 2011. 'Empirical legal studies and constitutional courts', *Indian Journal of Constitutional Law* 5: 25–65.

Ginsburg, Tom 2003. *Judicial review in new democracies: Constitutional courts in Asian cases.* New York: Cambridge University Press.

    2013. 'Constitutions as contract, constitutions as charters', in Galligan, Denis J. and Versteeg, Mila (eds.), *Social and Political Foundations of Constitutions.* Cambridge: Cambridge University Press.

Ginsburg Tom and Versteeg, Mila 2013. 'Why do countries adopt constitutional review?' (unpublished manuscript).

Goderis, Benedikt and Versteeg, Mila 2013. 'Transnational constitutionalism: A Conceptual Framework', in Galligan, Denis J. and Versteeg, Mila (eds.), *Social and Political Foundations of Constitutions.* Cambridge: Cambridge University Press.

Ginsburg, Tom, Elkins, Zachary, and Melton, Tom 2008. 'Baghdad, Tokyo, Kabul....: Constitution-making in occupied states', *William and Mary Law Review* **49**: 1139–1178.

Ginsburg, Tom, Elkins, Zachary, and Blount, Justin 2009. 'Does the process of constitution-making matter?' *Annual Review of Law and Social Science* **5**: 201–223.

Ginsburg, Tom, Lansberg-Rodriguez, Daniel, and Versteeg, Mila 2013. 'When to overthrow your government: The right to resist in the world's constitutions', *UCLA Law Review* **60** (forthcoming).

Ginsburg, Tom and Moustafa, Tamir 2008. *Courts in authoritarian regimes.* New York: Cambridge University Press.

Ginsburg, Tom and Versteeg, Mila 2012. *Why do countries adopt constitutional review?* Manuscript, University of Chicago, Chicago.

Goodman, Ryan and Jinks, Derek 2004. 'How to influence states: Socialization and international human rights law', *Duke Law Journal* **54**: 621–703.

Hardin, Russell 2013. 'Why a constitution?' in Galligan, Denis J. and Versteeg, Mila (eds.), *Social and Political Foundations of Constitutions.* Cambridge: Cambridge University Press.

Hass, Binesh 2013. 'The juristic republic of Iran', in Galligan, Denis J. and Versteeg, Mila (eds.), *Social and Political Foundations of Constitutions.* Cambridge: Cambridge University Press.

Hilbink, Lisa 2009. 'The constituted nature of constituents' interests: Historical and ideational factors in judicial empowerment', *Political Science Research Quarterly* **62**: 781–797.

Hirschl, Ran 2004. *Towards juristocracy: The origins and consequences of the new constitutionalism.* Cambridge, MA: Harvard University Press.

    2013. 'The strategic foundations of constitutions', in Galligan, Denis J. and Versteeg, Mila (eds.), *Social and Political Foundations of Constitutions.* Cambridge: Cambridge University Press.

Holmes, Oliver Wendell Jr. [1881] 2005. *The common law.* New Brunswick, NJ: Transaction Publishers.

Holmes, Stephen 1995. *Passions and constraint: On the theory of liberal democracy.* Chicago: University of Chicago Press.

Hume, David, Copley, Stephen, and Edgar, Andrew 2008. *Selected essays.* Oxford: Oxford University Press.

Ip, Erik 2013. *Constitutionalism under China: Strategic interpretation of the Honk Kong basic law in comparative perspective.* Doctoral Thesis, Oxford University.

Jacobsohn, Gary Jeffrey 2010. *Constitutional identity*. Cambridge, MA: Harvard University Press.

King, Anthony 2007. *The British constitution*. Oxford: Oxford University Press.

King, Jeff 2013. 'Constitutions as mission statements', in Galligan, Denis J. and Versteeg, Mila (eds.), *Social and Political Foundations of Constitutions*. Cambridge: Cambridge University Press.

King, Phoebe 2013. 'Neo-Bolivarian constitutional design: Comparing the 1999 Venezuelan, 2008 Ecuadorian, and 2009 Bolivian constitutions', in Galligan, Denis J. and Versteeg, Mila (eds.), *Social and Political Foundations of Constitutions*. Cambridge: Cambridge University Press.

Klug, Heinz 2000. *Constituting democracy: Law, globalism and South Africa's political reconstruction*. Cambridge: Cambridge University Press.

Kurkchiyan, Marina 2003. 'The illegitimacy of law in post-Soviet societies', in *Law and Informal Practices: The Post-Communist Experience*. Oxford: Oxford University Press, pp. 25–47.

Law, David S. 2008. 'Globalization and the future of constitutional rights', *Northwestern University Law Review* 102: 1277–1350.

2013. 'The myth of imposed constitution', in Galligan, Denis J. and Versteeg, Mila (eds.), *Social and Political Foundations of Constitutions*. Cambridge: Cambridge University Press.

Law, David S. and Versteeg, Mila 2011. 'The evolution and ideology of global constitutionalism', *California Law Review* 99: 1163–1257.

2013. 'Sham constitutions', *California Law Review* 101: 863–952.

Levinson, Stanford 2012. *Framed: America's 51 constitutions and the crisis of governance*. New York: Oxford University Press.

Llewellyn, Karl N. 1934. 'The constitution as an institution', *Columbia Law Review* **34**: 1–40.

Lombardi, Clark B. 2008. 'Egypt's Supreme Constitutional Court: Managing constitutional conflict in an authoritarian, aspirationally "Islamic" state', *Journal of Comparative Law* 3: 234–253.

2013. 'The constitution as agreement to agree: The social and political foundations (and effects) of the 1971 Egyptian constitution', in Galligan, Denis and Versteeg, Mila (eds.), *Social and Political Foundations of Constitutions*. Cambridge: Cambridge University Press.

Maalo, Daniel 2013. *Gathering dust: The case of Eritrea's failure to realise its constitutional dreams*. Manuscript, University of Virginia, Charlottesville.

Madsen, Robert A. 2001. 'The struggle for sovereignty between China and Taiwan', in Krasner, S. (ed.), *Problematic Sovereignty*. New York: Columbia University Press, pp. 141–193.

Magalhães, Pedro 2013. 'Explaining the constitutionalization of social rights: Portuguese hypotheses and a cross-national test', in Galligan, Denis J. and Versteeg, Mila (eds.), *Social and Political Foundations of Constitutions*. Cambridge: Cambridge University Press.

Magaloni, Beatriz 2008. 'Enforcing the autocratic political order and the role of courts: The case of Mexico', in Ginsburg, Tom and Moustafa, Tamir (eds.), *Rule by Law: The Politics of Courts in Authoritarian Regimes*. New York: Cambridge University Press, pp. 180–206.

Marshall, Monty and Cole, Benjamin 2011. *Global report 2011: Conflict, governance, and state fragility*. Vienna, VA: Centre for Systemic Peace.

Martin, Andrew and Quinn, Kevin 2002. 'Dynamic ideal point estimation via Markov Chain Monte Carlo for the U.S. Supreme Court, 1953–1999', *Political Analysis* 10: 134–153.

Meuwese, Anne 2013. 'Popular constitution-making: The case of Iceland', in Galligan, Denis J. and Versteeg, Mila (eds.), *Social and Political Foundations of Constitutions*. Cambridge: Cambridge University Press.

Miller, Laurel E. (ed.) 2010. *Framing the state in times of transition: Case studies in constitution making*. Washington, DC: United States Institute of Peace Press.

Moehler, Devra C. 2008. *Distrusting democrats: Outcomes of participatory constitution-making*. Ann Arbor: University of Michigan Press.

Morrow, Jonathan 2010. 'Deconstituting Mesopotamia: Cutting a deal on the regionalization of Iraq', in Laurel Miller (ed.), *Framing the state in times of transition: Case studies in constitution making*. Washington, DC: United States Institute of Peace Press, pp. 563–600.

Moustafa, Tamir 2007. *The struggle for constitutional power: Law, politics and economic development in Egypt*. Cambridge: Cambridge University Press.

O'Brien, James C. 2010. 'The Dayton Constitution of Bosnia and Herzegovina', in Laurel Miller (ed.), *Framing the state in times of transition: Case studies in constitution making*. Washington, DC: United States Institute of Peace Press, pp. 332–349.

Palmer, Matthew S. R. 2006. 'Using constitutional realism to identify the complete constitution: Lessons from an unwritten constitution', *American Journal of Comparative Law* 54: 587–636.

Parau, Christina 2013. 'Romania's transnational constitution: A tradition of elite learning and self-empowerment', in Galligan, Denis J. and Versteeg, Mila (eds.), *Social and Political Foundations of Constitutions*. Cambridge: Cambridge University Press.

Parkinson, Charles H. 2007. *Bills of rights and decolonization: The emergence of domestic human rights instruments in Britain's overseas territories*. Oxford: Oxford University Press.

   2013. 'The social and political foundations of the Nigerian constitution', in Galligan, Denis J. and Versteeg, Mila (eds.), *Social and Political Foundations of Constitutions*. Cambridge: Cambridge University Press.

Pettit, Pilip 1997. *Republicanism*. Oxford: Oxford University Press.

Rahe, Paul 2008. *Against throne and altar: Machiavelli and political theory under the English republic*. Cambridge: Cambridge University Press.

Rawls, John 1972. *A theory of justice*. Oxford: Oxford University Press.

Sadurski, Wojciech 2009. 'Judicial review in Central and Eastern Europe: Rationales or rationalizations?' *Israel Law Review* 42: 500–527.

Sajo, Andras 1999. *Limiting government: An introduction to constitutionalism*. Budapest: Central European University Press.

Samuels, K. 2006. *Constitution building processes and democratization: A Discussion of twelve cases studies*. Geneva: IDEA.

Sartori, Giovanni 1962. 'Constitutionalism: A preliminary discussion', *American Political Science Review* 56: 853–864.

Schor, Miguel 2013. 'The once and future democracy: Argentina at the bar of constitutionalism', in Galligan, Denis J. and Versteeg, Mila (eds.), *Social and Political Foundations of Constitutions*. Cambridge: Cambridge University Press.

Scott, W. Richard 1996 *Institutions and Organizations*. London: Sage.

Shapiro, Martin 1964. *Law and politics in the Supreme Court*. Glencoe, IL: Free Press of Glencoe.

Shinar, Adam 2013. 'Accidental constitutionalism: The political foundations and implications of constitution-making in Israel,' in Galligan, Denis J. and Versteeg, Mila (eds.), *Social and Political Foundations of Constitutions*. Cambridge: Cambridge University Press.

Stephenson, Matthew 2003. 'When the devil turns....: The political foundations of independent judicial review', *Journal of Legal Studies* 32: 59–89.

Stourzh, Gerald 1988. 'Constitution: Changing meanings of the term from the early seventeenth to the late eighteenth century', in Ball, T. and Pocock, J. G. A. (eds.), *Conceptual Change and the Constitution*. Lawrence: University of Kansas Press, pp. 35–54.

Strauss, David A. 1996. 'Common law constitutional interpretation', *University of Chicago Law Review* 63: 877–936.

Tamanaha, Brian 2013. 'Battle between law and society in Micronesia,' in Galligan, Denis J. and Versteeg, Mila (eds.), *Social and Political Foundations of Constitutions*. Cambridge: Cambridge University Press.

Thier, J. Alexander 2010. 'Big tent, small tent: The making of a constitution in Afghanistan', in Laurel Miller (ed.), *Framing the State in Times of Transition: Case Studies in Constitution Making*. Washington, DC: United States Institute of Peace Press, pp. 535–562.

Tyler, Tom R. 1988. 'What is procedural justice? Criteria used by citizens to assess the fairness of legal procedures', *Law and Society Review* 22: 103–136.

Voigt, Stefan 2003. 'The consequences of popular participation in constitutional choice – toward a comparative analysis', in Aaken, Aanne Van, List, Christian, and Luetge, Christoph (eds.), *Deliberation and Decision: Economics, Constitutional Theory and Deliberative Democracy*. Aldershot: Ashgate Publishing, pp. 199–229.

Walker, Lee Demetrius and Williams, Philip J. 2010. 'The Nicaraguan constitutional experience: Process, conflict, contradictions, and change', in Laurel Miller (ed.), *Framing the State in Times of Transition: Case Studies in Constitution Making*. Washington, DC: United States Institute of Peace Press, pp. 483–504.

Walker, Neil 2013. 'The shifting foundations of the European Union constitution', in Galligan, Denis J. and Versteeg, Mila (eds.), *Social and Political Foundations of Constitutions*. Cambridge: Cambridge University Press.

Watson, Alan 1974. *Legal transplants*. Athens: University of Georgia Press.

Widner, Jenifer 2005. *Constitution writing and conflict resolution*. Helsinki: UN University World Institute of Development Economics Research.

    2008. 'Constitution writing in post-conflict settings: An overview', *William Mary Law Review* 49: 1513–1541.

Wood, Andy 2002. *Riot, rebellion, and popular politics in early modern England*. Houndmills, Basingstoke, Hampshire: Palgrave.

Young, Ernest A. 2007. 'The constitution outside the constitution', *Yale Law Journal* 117: 408–473.

PART II

Theoretical Perspectives

2

Why a Constitution?

Russell Hardin

2.1 INTRODUCTION: TWO STRATEGIC SCHOOLS

For many centuries the world and its states were successfully governed without formal constitutions. Then why are constitutions seen as fundamentally important now? The U.S. Constitution, one of the first modern formal constitutions, was written, adopted, and put to work in 1787–1789. Why were the authors of that constitution so intent on putting it in place? The short answer is that the document set out the design for institutions of governance. There had been governing institutions in place in all of the thirteen colonies that would eventually make up the initial thirteen states of the United States, but not at the overarching national level. The Constitution made a nation of those disparate colonial entities. Contemporary constitutions do much the same thing: either they establish institutions where there were none or they replace unsatisfactory institutions, as, for example, in the case of a recently independent colony.

There are two contrary main schools of constitutional theory. The first and oldest grounds constitutions in contractual agreement, as in the long-standing contractarian tradition in political philosophy. The second grounds them in coordination. The former theories are almost all at the normative level as part of an ostensible justification of obedience to the monarch or state. The coordination theories are inherently explanatory or causal theories as well as, sometimes, normative. One might sensibly suppose that the question "Why now?" is more pertinent for the coordination than for the contractarian school. I compare the two schools briefly and then turn in later sections to in-depth analysis of the schools and to applications of them to major governmental institutions.

Much of contemporary work on constitutionalism takes up prior debates and brings them into contemporary analytical frameworks, such as game theory, bargaining theory, psychological theories of commitment, and so forth. Most of it is comparative and grounded very solidly in real-world cases. Some of it has been stimulated by recent constitutional changes in newly democratizing nations, such as those of Eastern Europe, re-democratizing nations, such as many in Latin America, and in South Africa with the enfranchisement of blacks after the end of apartheid. And some of it is now being stimulated by efforts to understand supra-state constitutions, especially that of the European Union, whose document is called a constitutional treaty. It will sharpen discussion here to address such issues.

In general, it is absurd to assess the normative qualities of a constitution from its content alone. The whole point of a constitution is to organize politics and society in particular ways. For example, modern constitutions typically organize a state apparatus, provide for representative democracy, define certain rights and civil liberties for citizens, provide a legal system, both civil and criminal, organize national defense, and sometimes provide for some degree of distributive justice, often through so-called economic and social rights, as distinct from the historical political rights of civil liberties. Hence, constitutions are inherently consequentialist devices. To judge a constitution normatively requires attention to its actual consequences. Because the consequences of a particular constitution are likely to depend to some extent on the nature of the society it is to govern, what would count as a good constitution for one society might be a poor constitution for another society. Purely abstract discussion of constitutions and constitutionalism is therefore pointless and misdirected. Constitutionalism without social science is an arid intellectual pastime.[1] For many theoretical enterprises, looking to specific examples is a necessary part of making sure the theory is polished and adequate. In the discussion of constitutionalism, looking at specific examples forces us to recognize that the theory is not unitary, but is fractured and contingent on circumstances. Who can be coordinated on what varies across time and place. This is, of course, not a theoretical but a factual claim.

I briefly compare the two main, contrary schools of constitutional theorizing before turning to in-depth accounts of the schools and applications of constitutional theory to major institutions. Then I focus on the two main problems of modern constitutional democracy: the constitutional nature and organization of representative democracy and the problem of placing enforceable limits on government.

2.2 CONTRACTARIAN THEORIES

The metaphorical claim that government is established by contract is one of the mainstays of traditional political theory. Against the metaphor, there are several objections to the claim that a constitution is analogous to an ordinary contract in any

---

[1] Rawls shares this view (see 1971/1999, section 42), as do most libertarians, as well as, of course, all political economists, including Hume and Smith.

useful sense. These objections include the following. Constitutions are enforced by social conventions as elaborated later in the chapter. Contracts are typically enforceable by a third party (usually the state); constitutions are not. Contracts typically govern a fairly limited quid pro quo between the parties; it is hard even to define who might be the parties engaged in such an exchange when a constitution is drawn up. The exchanges governed by a contract typically get completed and the contract ceases to govern further; constitutions typically govern into the distant and unforeseeable future and they have no project for "completion" in sight – they are never to be "fulfilled." Contracts require genuine agreement to make them binding: constitutions require merely acquiescence to make them work. In game theory, contracts govern exchanges, which have the strategic structure of a prisoner's dilemma; constitutions govern coordination of a population on a particular form of government and therefore have the strategic structure of coordination games. Finally, note that, if a constitution is a contract, then we must make a contract on what contract will mean. That may not be a logical impossibility, but it is an oddly circular idea. Under our coordination constitution, we can make a law of contracts to govern many of our future interactions and, indeed, to enable many of them.

Let us spell out one of these points a bit further. In a two-person prisoner's dilemma, there is an outcome that would be best for one player and worst for the other player. In a coordination game, the best outcome for each player is also the best or near best for the other player. It is implausible that the major groups involved in adopting the U.S. or any other constitution could face an outcome that was best for one very important group and worst for another, as would invariably happen in a prisoner's dilemma.

The two most important groups in the U.S. case were arguably the financial and shipping interests of the northeastern cities and the plantation interests of the southern states. Alexander Hamilton and other financiers could not have supposed they would be best off when Thomas Jefferson and other agrarians were worst off. Any regime that did not enable them to cooperate in managing the export of southern crops and the import or manufacturing of farm implements would have harmed both groups. Any regime that enabled them to cooperate more efficiently in doing these things benefited both groups. The central issue of the constitution was to eliminate trade barriers between the thirteen states and to regularize tariffs with other nations. That was the issue that brought these two groups into the design and adoption of the constitution as a mutually beneficial arrangement. They faced a relatively straightforward coordination problem (Hardin 1999: chapter 3).

Contractarian theorists typically ignore all of these issues and use the metaphor of contract to ground a claim that citizens are *morally* obligated to defer to government by their consent, as the parties to a real contract would be *legally* obligated. Traditional contractarian theorists do acknowledge one deep problem for their theories. Contractual obligation without actual personal agreement seems like nonsense, especially given that it is prior agreement that is supposed to make a contractarian order binding. Yet it is hard to ground any claim that future generations agree to an extant contractarian order. Moreover, Hume (1748/1985) compellingly dismisses even the claim that there could ever have been a genuine agreement on political order in any modern society. He also argues that actual citizens do not believe their own legal or political obligations depend on their having agreed to their social order, even though many citizens apparently do believe they and all other citizens are obligated.

Hume's arguments and facts are so devastating to the idea of the social contract that one must wonder why that idea continues to be in discussion at all. John Rawls essentially agrees with Hume's central conclusion. He says that, because citizens have not genuinely contracted for or agreed to any political obligation, they cannot have such obligations (Rawls 1971: 113–114; 1999: 97–98). Yet he still perversely classifies his theory as part of the contractarian tradition (Rawls 1971: 32–33; 1999: 28–30).[2] There seems to be a sense that contractarianism is morally superior to utilitarianism, and Rawls poses his theory this way. This is a deeply odd view. A utilitarian acts on behalf of others. Those who enter contracts typically are concerned with their own benefits and need not care about the benefits to their partners in trade. The former is other-regarding; the latter is self-seeking. It is a saving grace of contemporary claims for contractarianism that they are not about contracts. Unfortunately, they are rather about *rationalist agreement* on what are the right principles to follow as though these could merely be deduced from first principles.

A huge part of the discussion of contractarian theories addresses how we are to understand the idea of contractual obligation when there cannot be an actual contract or agreement by the relevant parties (in this case, the citizens and perhaps the governors). The nearest thing we ever have to actual contracts in politics is votes on the adoption or amendment of a constitution. But these votes typically require only some kind of majority, ranging from simple to supermajority. Unanimity is an impossible condition for a working constitution or amendment in a real society, although it is required for a legal contract to be binding. Hence, in a sense that is contrary to any plausible sense of "contractarian," contractarian constitutions must be imposed on a significant fraction of the populace, indeed on the overwhelming majority of citizens.

Traditional, straight contractarianism appears to be on the wane. Few people argue for it in principle, although many scholars continue to present contractarian arguments from John Locke (1690/1988), Hobbes (1651/1994), and others from the distant past. In part such contractarianism has simply been rejected, as by coordination theorists. In part it has been displaced by contractualist argument. Despite

---

[2]   Jean Hampton (1980) argues correctly that Rawls's theory is not contractarian.

the growing flood of work on it (the most important items include Barry 1995 and Scanlon 1982, 1998), the latter program is not yet well defined. Traditional contractarianism is relatively well defined, and therefore its deep flaws are clear. It is a peculiar but perhaps false advantage of the contractualist program that it is ill defined. Its vagueness means that debate over it will often thrive, even debate over what the program is.

Contractualism is supposed to resolve or sidestep the problem of fitting some degree of moral obligation to a regime to which one has not actually agreed. Thomas Scanlon's original definition is: "An act is wrong if its performance under the circumstances would be disallowed by any system of rules for the general regulation of behavior which no one could reasonably reject as a basis for informed, unforced general agreement" (Scanlon 1982: 110). A further statement is often taken as definitive, although it is peculiar: "On this view what is fundamental to morality is the desire for reasonable agreement, not the pursuit of mutual advantage" (*ibid.*: 115n). Why is it this desire that is fundamental rather than achieving moral action or outcomes? I will ignore the concern with this desire because it trivializes our concern. Scanlon (1998) himself has primarily been interested in applying the contractualist idea to moral theory. The most extensive and articulate defense of the idea of reasonable agreement in political theory is probably that of Brian Barry (1995: 3), who says, "I continue to believe in the possibility of putting forward a universally valid case in favor of liberal egalitarian principles."

Unfortunately, Scanlon's criterion of reasonableness is somewhat tortured and ill defined. Its use has become unmoored from his original defense of it. As first presented, the term supposedly attested to the claim that moral theory is analogous to mathematics (Scanlon 1982: 104–105). Mathematicians know mathematical truths; moral theorists can similarly know moral truths. We do not know either of these by observation but only through some inner faculty of reasoning. That the analogy is not apt is suggested by the fact that there is no terminological analog of "reasonableness" in mathematics. Every mathematician knows that the square root of two is not a rational number (that is, a number that can be expressed as a fraction in the form of whole integers in both the numerator and the denominator). No one would say further that this claim is reasonable. It just is true mathematically. If you say this is false, mathematicians will say you are a crackpot or an ignoramus, not that you are unreasonable. One wonders what the analogs of axioms and theorems are in moral theory.

The claim that morality is analogous to mathematics is a perverse variant of intuitionism in ethics.[3] Intuitionists believe they can intuit whether, say, a particular action is right or wrong. Unfortunately, they do not agree with each other. If disagreement

---

[3] Although Scanlon (1982: 109) defends it against a particular sense of intuitionism.

were similarly pervasive in mathematics, there would not be mathematics departments in great universities.

If all of us reject some principle, presumably no one would disagree with the conclusion that we should collectively reject applications of that principle in practice and, furthermore, that it is reasonable for us to do so, whatever "reasonable" might mean in this vernacular claim. Scanlon's principle must, however, be stronger than this. If you think you are reasonable to reject some principle that the rest of us support, what can we say to you? We might be quasi-Kantian and suppose that we can deduce the true principle here, and we can therefore say to you that you are simply wrong. That would surely violate the element of agreement that Scanlon and other contractualists want. They do not suppose that agreement on certain principles is incumbent on any and every one as a matter of moral or transcendental logic. They mean for agreement to be genuine, which is to say they mean that there must be a possibility of disagreement.

Rawls, on the contrary, sometimes seems to intend a quasi-Kantian principle of rationalist agreement. He assumes that any single representative person behind his veil of ignorance would reach the principles of his system of justice (Rawls 1971: 139; 1999: 120). It is hard to imagine how that could be true unless those principles are somehow definitively correct in the sense that they are rationally deducible. One who does not agree with the deduction of Rawls's rules of justice has evidently failed to understand. There is rationally no possibility of disagreement. To my knowledge there is no major, serious constitutional theorist who has such a rationalist view of the design of constitutions. Because Rawls's purpose eventually is to design the institutions of justice for a society, one might suppose that he intends for his theory to produce a constitution. Although he grants that the design of institutions would have to deal with social constraints, thus making its content contingent, he nevertheless seems to think that the content of these institutions, and hence of his constitution, must be fully determinate once his theory and the relevant social contingencies are taken fully into account.[4] If so, he holds a very strange – rationalist – position in the world of constitutional theory. No working constitutional lawyer could take that position seriously. General determinacy in constitutional theory is an implausible goal.

Note that in the coordination theories discussed later, you could well disagree with some rule we have adopted, even think it an unreasonable rule, and yet you could still think it reasonable for yourself to abide by the rule. For example (a recently painful example for many Americans), the U.S. constitution establishes an indirect device for electing presidents. That device made some sense in the era of the creation of the constitution, but it would be dismissed as a bad idea if proposed anywhere

---

4   For his views on determinacy, see Hardin (2002: chapter 7).

today. In 1789, transportation and communication were grievous obstacles, and no one had much experience with making democracy work.

The device is to count votes at the state level and then to count peculiarly weighted scores for the individual states at the level of the Electoral College, which finally chooses the president if a majority of its members agrees on a particular candidate. On three occasions (nearly 6 percent of all presidential elections), the Electoral College has elected the candidate who got the second-largest number of citizens' votes, and the candidate with the highest number of such votes lost. Most recently, this was the result in the presidential election of 2000, in which Al Gore had a clear plurality of the national vote but lost the election to George Bush in the Electoral College – with a large dollop of help from Bush's ideologically tainted friends on the Supreme Court.

Many U.S. citizens as well as many noncitizen observers think that the result of the election of 2000 was in some moral sense wrong or was a violation of democracy. But no citizen seems to have thought it right to oppose the result by taking action that would have made Gore the president. Indeed, one can imagine that a poll would show that Americans overwhelmingly agreed that the constitutional rule on election of the president should be followed, even though they might also have agreed that the system was perverse and should be changed. It would take a relatively strained effort to argue that that rule could in some sense meet the contractualist criterion. But it is easy to show why the rule arose originally and why it continues to prevail despite the possibility of a constitutional amendment to block what many people think was a travesty of democracy on the two most recent occasions when the apparent loser in the national election became president.[5]

Hence, you might morally or even merely self-interestedly reject a constitutional rule or principle. And you might readily be able to think your rejection reasonable in any sense that the contractualist would want. But still you would most likely conclude that it would be unreasonable for anyone in the system to act, in a particular election, against the application of the rule. That rule has the great force of a convention that can be altered only through the actions of large numbers in concert. The only powerful defense of it in a specific application of it, such as in 2000, is

---

[5] The first election that gave the presidency to the loser of the popular vote in a two-party split was that of Rutherford B. Hayes in 1876. But in that instance, there was a corrupt deal to distort the process. Such corruption is, of course, a travesty of democracy, but that is not an issue in the judgment of the American constitutional rules for election of presidents. The availability of the Electoral College lets the deal take the form it did, but one can imagine that the deal would have been made no matter what the system had been. The second case was the election of Benjamin Harrison in 1888. In that election, Grover Cleveland received more votes but Harrison nevertheless won in the Electoral College. The 1824 election left four candidates without a clear winner in the Electoral College, and selection passed to the House of Representatives. In 1800, an ambiguity in the system forced the final decision into the House.

that *it is the rule* and that the rule is a convention that is not readily changeable, even though presumably no one drafting a constitution today would include such a perverse institution as the Electoral College.[6] This defense does not make the rule morally *right*; it only enables the rule to *govern*. In this instance, the argument from convention trumps any argument from simple rightness or agreement unless the argument from agreement simply takes over the argument from convention. It would be unreasonable to reject a powerful convention in any specific application of it. This can, of course, be true even though it would be reasonable to change the convention before its next application.

The chief difficulty with the contractualist program for those who are not its advocates is that there is no definition of reasonableness and no clear account of how others can judge reasonableness in general even if we might suppose that the vernacular term fits some obvious cases (for which we have no need of constitutional or moral theory). The term "reasonable" has unfortunately been left as a residual notion that is not defined by the contractualists. Scanlon's definition is vacuously circular. We "desire to be able to justify [our] actions to others on grounds they could not reasonably reject." A footnote supposedly clarifies this: "Reasonably, that is, given the desire to find principles which others similarly motivated could not reasonably reject" (Scanlon 1982: 116 and 116n). This is one of the least reasonable definitions in contemporary moral and political philosophy. The historical dodges of the fact that supposedly contractarian obligations that were never literally agreed to were somehow hypothetically or tacitly agreed seem much more compelling than this murky move to ground normative claims in their "reasonableness."

Advocates of the contractualist program seem to think they can spot reasonableness when they see it. Hence, what they give us are examples of reasonableness or unreasonableness rather than elaborations of principles for assessing reasonableness. For example, Barry believes "that it would be widely acknowledged as a sign of an unjust arrangement that those who do badly under it could reasonably reject it" (Barry 1995: 7). But Rawls's difference principle might leave us with a society in which the worst-off class does badly relative to many others. This would be true if great productivity were motivated by substantial rewards to the most productive members of the society, so that they are very well-off in comparison to the worst-off groups. In that case, the worst-off might suffer far worse misery if they did not suffer such inequality. It would be hard to argue – at least to a Rawlsian – that making the worst-off citizens substantially better-off is unjust. If Rawls's theory of justice is reasonable, then even gross inequality might be seen as reasonable. We must look at

---

6   The College was designed to block pure democracy by using a forum of political elites to make the final choice of who would be president. But presumably, the architects of the College did not intend such undemocratic results as those of 1888 and 2000.

the whole picture of the society if we are to understand and to judge its justice and reasonableness.

Part of the rationale of the difference principle is causal. There is, at least possibly, a causal trade-off between efficiency of production and equality of rewards. Rawls openly supposes that the causal chain is from greater equality to lesser production, so that some inequality is required if the worst-off are not to be abjectly miserable. If this were not thought to be true, there would be no reason to have such a complicated theory as Rawls presents, because pure equality would be a credible theory. At some points, however, Barry very nearly equates reasonableness and equality.[7] Once this move is made, there is little more needed to establish a theory of distributive justice merely by definition. It might still be very difficult to design institutions that would achieve extensive equality (Hume 1751/1975: sect. 3, part 2, 193–194).

2.3 COORDINATION THEORIES

Before Hume there were three main theories of social order. These are based on theological views, contractarian agreement or consent, and draconian coercion by the state. Hume dismissively rejects all three. The theological views are simply false or at least beyond demonstration (Hume 1748/1985). Locke and others propose contractarian consent as an alternative justification for the state and an alternative ground for obligation to the state, but as noted earlier, Hume demolishes the claim for consent. Hobbes's argument from draconian force seems empirically wrong for many very orderly societies, and Hume rejects it almost entirely, although he shares many social scientific views with Hobbes. Having demolished all of the then-acceptable accounts of obedience to the state, Hume therefore has to propose a dramatically different, fourth vision.

In essence his theory is a dual-convention theory. Government derives its power (not its right) to rule by some specific form of coordination that is a convention and the populace acquiesces in that rule by its own convention. Once empowered by these two conventions, the government has the capacity to do many things, including ancillary things unrelated to the purpose of maintaining social order. This dual-convention argument is compelling for most stable governments in our time. Moreover, for democratic governments, *the dual-convention theory virtually demands constitutional limits on the power of government to interfere in democratic processes.*[8] The earlier theories could make as good a sense without constitutional provisions,

---

[7] For example, Barry (1995: 7) says, "The criterion of reasonable acceptability of principles gives some substance to the idea of fundamental equality while at the same time flowing from it."

[8] Such limits may fail to stop violations of the government's principles, as in the U.S. presidential elections of 1876 and 2000.

and the absolutist versions of the theological and draconian power visions virtually deny any role for a limiting constitution.

For both of the conventions in the dual-convention theory of government, *acquiescence is the compelling fact*. Hume argues, by example, that ten million British citizens simply acquiesced in the succession of William and Mary to the English throne, all by act of "the majority of seven hundred" in the English and Scottish parliaments (Hume 1748/1985: 472–473). Acquiescence is Hume's term (*ibid*.: 469). We acquiesce because it would be very difficult to organize what would have to be a de facto collective action to topple a going convention or to organize a new one. While we can readily just happen into a convention, such as the driving conventions of driving on the left or the right side of the road, we cannot so readily alter one once it is established. You might detest the convention we have and you might even discover that apparently most of us detest it. But you may not be able to mobilize the opposition that would be necessary to change it. The foolishness of the Electoral College has seemed perverse to many Americans ever since its first anomalous and potentially destabilizing results in 1800 and 1888. In the interim, a couple of elections came close to faltering in that system. And finally the election of 2000 was very nearly a destabilizing event that could have been very harmful if a national crisis had arisen during the period in which the result could have been in limbo. Yet there has been no substantial effort to change this bad system for electing presidents.[9]

On this account, a constitution does not commit us in the way that a contract does (Hardin 1989). It merely raises the costs of doing things some other way through its creation of a coordination convention that is itself an obstacle to re-coordination.[10] More often than not our interests are better served by acquiescing in the rules of that constitution than by attempting to change it. This is true not because we will be coerced to abide by those rules if we attempt not to, but because it will be in our interest simply to acquiesce. The forms of commitment that are important for constitutional and even for conventional social choice in many forms are those that derive from the difficulties of collective action to re-coordinate on new rules. These are not simply problems of internal psychological motivation or moral commitments and they are not problems of sanctions that will be brought to bear. They are inherent in the social structure of the conventions themselves, a structure that often exacts costs from anyone who runs against the conventions more or less automatically without anyone or any institution having to take action against the rule breaker.

---

[9] It would be hard to change because the rule seemingly gives power to small states, which together could block any amendment.

[10] The costs of changing constitutions and conventions may outweigh any benefit from the change. But a great advantage of democratic constitutions is that they reduce the costs of switching leaders.

Establishing a constitution is itself a massive act of coordination that, if it is stable for a while, creates a convention that depends for its maintenance on its self-generating incentives and expectations. Given that it is a mystery how contracting could work to motivate us to abide by a constitution to which we or our forebears have contracted, we should be glad that the problem we face is such that we have no need of a contract or its troublesome lack of enforcement devices across generations. Moreover, *the acquiescence that a successful constitution produces cannot meaningfully be called agreement.* Some citizens might prefer extant constitutional arrangements to any plausible alternative, but for those who do not, their obedience to the constitutional order has more the quality of surrender than of glad acceptance. Indeed, if our constitution is solidly ensconced, surrender or acquiescence gives us the best we can get given that almost everyone else is abiding by it – even if almost all of them are merely acquiescing or surrendering in abiding by it.

Hobbes is commonly invoked as one of the founders of the contractarian tradition in political thought. Ironically, he is even more clearly a founder of the coordination theory of government. We coordinate on obeying a single leader. The initial selection of a ruler is a matter of coordinating among all of us. Hobbes presents an argument from contract but finally dismisses it as having no likely historical precedent, a claim later seconded by Hume.[11] He then goes on to defend the powers of a ruler – or, we might prefer to say, a state or a government – on the grounds that not abiding by the rule of a state would wreak havoc in our lives. Hence, for our own good, which is to say for our mutual advantage, we should abide by the laws of our state. This is an argument that carries even for a government that usurps the powers of an extant government. Once the usurper government is well established and is able to maintain order, it should then rationally, self-interestedly be obeyed.

The difference between Hobbes the contract theorist and Hobbes the power theorist is the difference between a political philosopher and a social scientist. His arguments from contract are about an imaginary and maybe even an ideal or desirable world. That world is a cute story, not a basis for philosophical or scientific analysis. His arguments from power and coordination are somewhat abstract, but still they are about the actual worlds that he inhabited and that we inhabit. Although there are many discussions in his works on politics that have normative overtones, his most coherent and extensive discussions are arguments from political sociology. As already noted, constitutional content must be contingent on the conditions of the society that the constitution is to govern (see further, Dahl 1996). This is in the nature of coordination and convention. If a particular rule

---

[11] "There is scarce a commonwealth in the world whose beginnings can in conscience be justified" (Hobbes 1651/1994: "Review," 392/492), because they were generally established by conquest or usurpation, not by contract or agreement.

does not coordinate our actions, it cannot become one of the conventions of our constitutional regime.

2.4 CAVEATS AND CLARIFICATIONS

It should be clear that the issue here is *establishing* government. It is the strategic structure of that choice or problem that we wish to understand. This is not the same as understanding the problems that government, once established, will resolve (as in Weingast 1997: 248). The latter can be coordination, exchange (prisoner's dilemma), collective action (n-Prisoner's Dilemma), and fundamental conflict problems, all of which might be handled by a relatively strong established government, unless, for example, the conflicts are too deep for resolution. Contract theories suppose that *this problem* – establishing a constitution for a form of government – is one of exchange and bargaining between groups with varied interests. If a constitution is to work in its early years, it must, however, successfully coordinate its populace on acquiescence to the new government that it establishes.

The nature or content of debates over the design of a constitution may not fit the strategic structure of the problem of constitutional design. Much that is said at a constitutional convention is apt to be blather and the fraction of time given over to blather might far outweigh the time spent on central issues. Successful or failed coordination on a constitution and government is the core problem.

Some of the easiest resolutions for the new government under the U.S. constitution of 1787–1788 were among the hardest of the problems under the weak prior government of the Articles of Confederation. Coordinating on a central government with even modest powers implied a nearly instant resolution of such problems as certain common pool resource issues, tariff regulation, trade between the states, and military conflict between the states. Before the new constitutional order, these had been conflictual problems, with free-riding, cheating, and the threat of instability. Pennsylvania and Virginia succeeded in having a tariff-free joint trade policy, but other states went their own ways. Having a central government with sole jurisdiction over these issues turned them into, roughly, coordination problems, because on collective issues the central government must legislate for all one way or the other. No state could impose a tariff on trade with other states or with foreign countries. The possibility of free-riding on the resolution of a typical common pool resource issue was virtually eliminated because under central government the choices were reduced to the binary pair: provide the resource to all and tax all, or provide it to none and tax none.

The thesis of coordination is a causal thesis, not a definition of what a constitution is. A constitution can include anything people might want. But if it is filled with perversities, it is likely to fail to coordinate us. Even if it looks like a model constitution (suppose its text is adopted whole from another, long-successful constitution), it may fail to coordinate *us*. For example, the people of Rwanda are arguably so deeply divided that no constitution could gain wide support from both Hutu and Tutsi ethnic groups (see Hardin 1999: chapter 7). Most constitutions have failed fairly soon after their adoption (France may have set the record for failures in the decade or more after the Revolution). If a particular constitution in a particular society fails to coordinate, we would say that it is a failed constitution, not that it was not a constitution after all. It is wrong to say that a constitution is a coordination device as though by definition. But the reverse is true: a successful constitution must have been a successful coordination device.

Suppose that a particular constitution is apparently the result of a bargain. If that constitution is to work in establishing social order, it must coordinate us on acquiescence to our new government. This is likely to be a critical problem in the early years before the government has acquired the power to enforce its mandate. Hence, what makes the constitution work is that it coordinates us on social order and is virtually self-enforcing. Hobbes supposes that most regimes in the world were established by acquisition or conquest, which is to say that someone usurped the power already in place or some outside body that already had substantial power came in and established an order. He sees and states the problem of establishing power if we attempt to create a sovereign by contract. Even though we the citizens might entirely agree that we want our government to have requisite power to maintain order and to do various other things, we cannot turn our power over to a newly ensconced regime. Hobbes rightly says, "no man can transferre his power in a naturall manner" (Hobbes 1642/1983: 2.5.11, 90; see further, Hardin 1991: 168–171). Hence, the contractarian foundation crumbles before its state is empowered.

Hobbes's (1651/1994: chapter 20) account of government by acquisition or conquest suggests an important fact about a constitutionally created regime. Once it is in place and working to achieve order, it can then be seized by some group and its powers put to use in continuing an order that is far less beneficial to many who were much better served by the prior regime. This is possible simply because social order at that point is the result of general acquiescence to the regime rather than of genuine approval or support of it. Acquiescence might be readier once a government gains great power to block opposition. To get initial coordination on a constitution and its regime, however, is likely to require a fairly broad degree of support. But it does not require continuing support to maintain a regime that once has power and control of the mechanisms of office. The core issue in constitutionalism is how a government under a constitution is empowered (especially initially). Once it is, it can maintain social order and it can resolve prisoner's dilemma and other interactions, including other coordination problems. Trivially, for example, it can establish orderly traffic laws.

Constitutionalism is a two-stage problem. At the first stage, we coordinate on a constitution and its form of government. At the second stage, that government then enables us to maintain order and to resolve various ordinary problems, many of which are between individuals or small groups of individuals rather than, like the constitution, at the whole-society level.

Finally note that in the law, contracts have been pushed in two directions against the simple, classical model implicit in the discussion here. First, many issues have been taken out of the realm of binding contractual agreement no matter what we agree to. For example, your apartment lease might say you cannot have house pets but the law may say you can, and the contract for the lease is not fully binding on this issue even though you might sign it, because state policy takes precedence. Second, many issues in especially complex deals cannot be easily adjudicated by courts, so that relevant contracts are not enforceable by legal authorities but must be self-enforcing (Williamson 1985). They may, for example, be enforced by the incentives we have to maintain good relations or good reputations. In this respect, contracts have become more nearly open-ended and therefore more nearly like constitutions. One could say that the meaning of contract has changed or that we have displaced it with other devices. A defender of the social contract tradition could, falsely, say that finally we have developed a conception of contract that fits what the tradition has really been about.

2.5 WHAT CONSTITUTIONS DO

To achieve justice and social order we must design institutions or norms to bring about just resolutions. Hence, justice is inherently a two-stage concern. It will bring about mutual advantage, but the actions we take within the justice system will not each by themselves necessarily bring about mutual advantage. *It is the whole scheme of justice that is mutually advantageous, not its adjudications in specific cases.*

We might object and say that the system ought to be corrected and overridden when it does not produce the more mutually advantageous outcome in a particular case. Rawls (1955) demolishes such views in his argument that we create an institution, whose design determines the roles of individuals within it, and these roles determine behavior. In the stage of institutional design, we should do our best to make the institution achieve results that are mutually advantageous overall. Our institution of justice depends on this two-stage argument: at one stage, role holders follow the rules of their roles as defined by the institution, and at the other, "prior" stage, the institution achieves welfare.

This is, of course, the structure of constitutional government. The constitution stipulates institutions of government; those institutions make and implement policies. In a constitutional government we cannot simply decide at every turn what would be the best thing to do, even the mutually advantageously best thing to do, and then do it. We must do what can be accomplished within and by the constitutionally established institutions. It is common for citizens to miss this principle and to suppose we can do whatever they think best in this case right now. That would de facto eliminate the institutional devices that we have designed to accomplish our mutual advantage goals. Acting as many citizens want would serve us very badly and would finally make government unlimited.

Successful constitutions coordinate us at a minimum on social order without need for Hobbes's draconian enforcement. But in some contexts such coordination may be infeasible. For example, in a society that is too violently split, coordination of major groups behind a single regime may not be possible, so that any intended constitutional order breaks down. A constitution cannot motivate people who are grievously hostile to its provisions (Hardin 1999: chapter 7). A constitution is like democracy in the account of Robert Dahl (1957: 132–133), who says, "In a sense, what we ordinarily describe as democratic 'politics' is merely the chaff. It is the surface manifestation, representing superficial conflicts. [These] disputes over policy alternatives are nearly always disputes over a set of alternatives that have already been winnowed down to those within the broad area of basic agreement." Constitutional democracy can manage the chaff of political conflict but it cannot manage really deep conflict between large significant groups that are hostile adversaries.[12]

Violently opposed groups are likely to want to seize the reins of government to serve themselves, as in Rwanda. This already happens in ordinary, more or less successfully working constitutional democracies such as the United States and the United Kingdom. The 2000 election in the United States cannot possibly be seen as giving a mandate to the government of George Bush, but even his strong supporters must grant that he treated his accession to office as giving him an opportunity to undo much of the welfare and tax structures of the past and to put in their place structures to serve the wealthiest members of the society and to end environmental and other regulations that have undercut business profits. His margin of victory in the election had little or no effect on what he was able to do. What mattered was seizing control of the government.

2.6 LIMITS ON GOVERNMENT

For Hobbes, the argument for coordination on a sovereign ruler is not an argument for a constitution or a constitutional order in any sense that these terms normally connote. A typical reason for having a constitution is to place limits on government.

---

[12] This is roughly Tocqueville's (1945/1835 and 1840 1, 260) view as well: "When a community actually has a mixed government – that is to say, when it is equally divided between adverse principles – it must either experience a revolution or fall into anarchy." We should qualify Dahl's claim with the note that "the broad area of basic agreement" need only be an area in which the politically effective groups are in agreement (Hardin 1999: chapter 7).

Indeed, "constitutional government" is commonly taken to mean limited government. Hobbes wants no limits on government sovereignty, in part because he cannot imagine how those limits could be imposed without opening up the possibility of overriding the government more generally. That would mean that the government is not sovereign.

Hume (1739–1740/1978: Book 3) resolves such issues in social order with the introduction of the idea of conventions that are de facto self-regulating or endogenously self-enforcing (see further, Hardin 1982: chapters 10–14; Hardin 1999: chapters 1 and 3).[13] Understanding this possibility resolves some of Hobbes's problems. With the power of conventions to block actions of many kinds, government can be limited in many respects even while it can be powerful in those arenas in which its power would be beneficial to the populace.

Among the early advocates of limited government are Locke (1690/1988), Sidney (1698/1990), Hume, Adam Smith (1776/1976), Wilhelm von Humboldt (1854/1969), and Mill (1859/1977). Locke and Sidney argue against the theocratic theory of Robert Filmer (1680/1949), who advocates, with Hobbes, absolute power for the sovereign, although Filmer wants only monarchs as sovereigns and not bodies of aristocrats as Hobbes would allow. Hume and Smith especially argue against mercantilist economic policies that protect native industries against imports. In an argument against using government to achieve "perfect" equality, Hume (1751/1975: s. 3, part 2, 193) also contends that this would empower government far too grievously. This is, of course, partially a straw man argument because no one other than perhaps Gerrard Winstanley (1652/1973) and the Levellers of the seventeenth century in England seriously advocates perfect equality. Most theorists who argue for egalitarianism generally mean only to bring about substantially greater equality of distribution than typical wealthy societies achieve, as in the noteworthy cases of Rawls (1971/1999) with his difference principle and Barry (1995) with his concern for fairness. The workings of Rawls's difference principle turn on social possibilities, so that it is conceivable that it would allow very substantial inequalities.

Hume's task therefore is largely to show that government officials can be constrained to act for the general good. Why? In part because they act on general principles that do not directly affect their own interests. The consequences of today's breach of equity are remote and cannot counterbalance any immediate advantage of better behavior (Hume 1739–1740/1978: 3.2.7, 535). When we consider actions in the distant future, all their minute distinctions vanish, and we give preference to the greater good (*ibid.*: 536). The trick is to change our circumstances to make us observe the laws of justice as our nearest interest. We appoint magistrates who have

---

[13]   See further Przeworski's discussion of self-enforcing democracy.

no interest in any act of injustice but an immediate interest in every execution of justice (*ibid.*: 537).

This last claim is too optimistic. Insofar as our magistrates have no interest in the injustices committed by others, we can generally expect them not to have a bias in favor of injustice. Indeed, through sympathy we can expect them to have at least a slight bias in favor of justice in any matter that does not concern themselves. All we need to do to constrain them from acting unjustly, therefore, is to block any actions that they might take on their own behalf or on behalf of their relatives and friends. We can do this to some degree by having different offices overseeing each other. This is not merely the separation of powers, which is typically intended to block institutions from acting on some institutional agenda rather than to block individual office holders from acting in their own personal interest against the public interest. It is rather more nearly Madison's (1788/2001b: 268) device of having ambition counter ambition, person to person. Montesquieu argues for separation of powers. Hume and Madison propose the monitoring of all by all, which is Hume's device for a small society regulated by norms (or conventions), so that such a society might not need constitutionally devised institutions of government.[14]

It is not clear that the Hume-Madison device works. It has more in common with competitors in a market than with Montesquieu's hiving off some duties to one agency and other duties to other agencies. I block your action because I think it is wrong, but I do so because I have a slight leaning toward the public interest through the influence of my concern for mutual advantage, which includes my own advantage as a likely minor part. My action against you is apt to be costless to me and it might even be rewarded by other officeholders or even by the citizens who, if they have no direct interest in the matter at issue, also have a slight leaning for the mutual advantage. I therefore have a motive from interest to block your illegitimate self-interested action.

2.7 CONCLUDING REMARKS

To argue that a particular constitutional system is "necessary" or "right" is very hard, because there is commonly evidence that other possibilities are attractive, plausibly

---

[14] Hume supposes that, although our present interest may blind us with respect to our own actions, it does not with respect to the actions of others, so we can judge the latter from sympathy with the general effect of those actions (Hume, 1739–1740/1978, 3.2.8, 545) or, as we might prefer to say, out of concern for the mutual advantage. Most members of our small community can therefore be expected to sanction misbehavior that affects the interests of others. Government itself has more of the character of a small society than does the whole society that it governs. (This would have been far more nearly true in Hume and Madison's day than it is today, with our enormous government agencies whose total populations exceed the national populations of their day.)

even superior in principle. The pseudonymous Caesar (1787), writing during the debates over the adoption of the U.S. Constitution, put the case clearly: "Ingenious men will give every plausible, and, it may be, pretty substantial reasons, for the adoption of two plans of Government, which shall be fundamentally different in their construction, and not less so in their operation; yet both, if honestly administered, might operate with safety and advantage." Caesar's conclusion is a defining principle in the coordination theory of constitutionalism. There may be no best constitution, although there may be many that are comparably good and far more others that would be bad.[15]

Still it may be clear that to change from a system we already have in place to some in-principle more attractive alternative would be very difficult and plausibly too costly to justify the change. The more pervasive, articulated, and important the system is, the more likely this will be true. Swedes could change their convention of driving on the left to driving on the right at modest cost, as they did in 1967 (Hardin 1988: 51–53); they could not change their system of jurisprudence or the remnants of their Judeo-Christian moral system at low enough cost to justify serious thought to select superior systems. To this day, the people of the state of Louisiana, formerly part of colonial France, live under a legal system that is based on the Napoleonic Code, while the U.S. federal system and the systems of the other forty-nine states are based on the British common law.

The only thing that might make an extant system right is that it is extant. We could not expect to design an ideal or even a much better system because we could not be sure how it would work in the longer run. As Madison (1787/2001a: 183) writes in *Federalist* 37, "All new laws, though penned with the greatest technical skill, and passed on the fullest and most mature deliberation, are considered as more or less obscure and equivocal, until their meaning be liquidated and ascertained by a series of particular discussions and adjudications." Hence, rationalist theories of morality and government are inherently irrelevant to our lives. At the margins, however, we might be able to revise our constitutional system by drawing on the experience of others.

Conventions do not have a normative valence per se. Some are beneficial and some are harmful. Both beneficial and harmful conventions can be self-reinforcing even when their only backing is sensibly motivated individual actions. If we could easily redesign government, law, norms, practices, and so forth, we might immediately choose to do so in many cases. The very strong Chinese convention of footbinding was horrendously harmful, and it was deliberately changed (Mackie 1996).

---

[15] John Locke's 1669 "constitutions" for Carolina included, as its last substantive clause, the silly, naïve proviso that it "shall be and remain the sacred and unalterable form and rule of government of Carolina forever" (Locke 1669/1993: 232).

The still surviving convention of female genital mutilation is similarly horrendously brutal and it is being eradicated in some parts of the world. In the light of such harmful norms, we must grant in general that it is possible to contest whether some pervasive convention costs us more than it harms us; but successful major constitutional change is rare in any given society.

We face the fundamental problem that we need government to enable us to accomplish many things and to protect us from each other, but that giving government the power to do all this means giving it the power to do many other, often harmful things as well. We depend on constitutional cleverness to design institutions that accomplish the former and block the latter. The cleverest person in this task historically was probably Madison. But Americans have long since lived past the institutions he helped design, and the present government under his constitution would be unrecognizable to him. These changes have happened while a few hundred million Americans essentially acquiesced.

2.8 METHODOLOGICAL NOTE

Crossing or underlying all of these discussions is a background methodological and intentional theory: political economy (see Brennan and Hamlin 1995). The political economy approach to politics and institutions is based on economic motivations, somehow defined, indeed very often crudely defined. Thomas Hobbes says that if mere consent to living in justice were sufficient, we would need no government "at all, because there would be peace without subjection" (1651/1994: chapter 17, 86/107). This claim is wrong for the reason that undercuts others of Hobbes's arguments; we would still need coordination on many purposes and we would need collective actions in many contexts in which spontaneous provision, even by those who consent to live in justice, would be unlikely. But Hobbes's dismissal of the likelihood that people can be universally motivated by commitment to justice is compelling. That dismissal, his individualist focus, and his arguments for the quasi-economic kinds of motivations people actually have make him an early political economist. This is not to say that our only or even chief motivation is economic, but merely that this is a centrally important motivation, especially in the context of how we might want our constitution to be designed.

Against the assumptions of political economy, some moves in contemporary political philosophy depend on attributing very strong motivations of fairness or public spiritedness to citizens. For example, Brian Barry supposes that if people have the right motivations, contractualism will work. But there is no good reason to suppose that a population can be reeducated into having powerful motivations of – in Barry's hope – fairness rather than self-seeking. Constitutional political economy seems bound to deal with cases in which interests often enough trump, so that what we need are safeguards against each other. Rawls supposes that once we establish a just regime, that regime will educate future generations to be just. Institutions "must be not only just but framed so as to encourage the virtue of justice" (1971: 261; 1999: 231). He also says that once we have just institutions, the initial condition of self interest no longer applies and citizens and legislators have a duty to support such institutions (1971: 334; 1999: 293–294). To design a constitutional order on the assumption that such motivations will generally trump self interest, family interest, and narrow group interests of various kinds runs against experience and against James Madison (1788/2001b: 268–269) and David Hume's (1742/1985) view that we should design the institutions themselves to be proof against abuse by officeholders. Madison and Hume see liberalism as inherently grounded in distrust of political officeholders, not in supposing that these leaders will generally work for the public interest. Madison's constitution is the preeminent constitutional response to liberal distrust (see further, Hardin 2002).

The central claim that grounds constitutionalism in political economy is that, in general, it is to our *mutual advantage* to preserve social order because it is the interest of *each of us* that it be preserved. There may, of course, be collective action problems in preserving it, so that its serving mutual advantage does not guarantee its survival. Indeed, mutual advantage can have more than one implication in cases of unequal coordination and very commonly in cases of multiple possible coordinations that are all more or less equally attractive, at least when viewed ex ante.

REFERENCES

Barry, B. 1995. *Justice as Impartiality*. Oxford: Oxford University Press.
Beer, S. H. 1993. *To Make a Nation: The Rediscovery of American Federalism*. Cambridge, MA: Harvard University Press.
Berle, A. A., and G. C. Means. 1932. *The Modern Corporation and Private Property*. New York: Macmillan.
Brennan, G., and A. Hamlin. 1995. Constitutional Political Economy: The Political Philosophy of Homo Economicus? *Journal of Political Philosophy* 3(3).
Burke, E. 1774/1969. Speech to the Electors of Bristol (in 1774). In *Speeches and Letters on American Affairs*, E. Burke. London: Everyman.
Caesar, no. 2. 1787/1987. In *The Founders' Constitution*, edited by P. B. Kurland and R. Lerner. Chicago: University of Chicago Press. Available at http://press-pubs.uchicago.edu/founders/documents/v1ch2s13.html.
Calhoun, J. C. 1853/1992. *A Disquisition on Government*. In *Union and Liberty: The Political Philosophy of John C. Calhoun*, edited by R. M. Lence. Indianapolis: Liberty Fund.
Dahl, R. A. 1957. *A Preface to Democratic Theory*. Chicago: University of Chicago Press.
    1996. Thinking about Democratic Constitutions: Conclusions from Democratic Experience. In *Political Order: Nomos XXXVIII*, edited by I. Shapiro and R. Hardin. New York: New York University Press.
Downs, A. 1957. *An Economic Theory of Democracy*. New York: Harper.

Filmer, R. 1680/1949. *Patriarcha: A Defence of the Natural Power of Kings against the Unnatural Liberty of the People*. In *Patriarcha and Other Political Works of Sir Robert Filmer*, edited by P. Laslett. Oxford: Oxford University Press.

Hampton, J. 1980. Contracts and Choices: Does Rawls Have a Social Contract Theory? *Journal of Philosophy* 77(6).

Hardin, R. 1982. *Collective Action*. Baltimore, MD: Johns Hopkins University Press for Resources for the Future.

　　1988. *Morality within the Limits of Reason*. Chicago: University of Chicago Press.

　　1989. Why a Constitution? In *The Federalist Papers and the New Institutionalism*, edited by B. Grofman and D. Wittman. New York: Agathon Press.

　　1991. Hobbesian Political Order. *Political Theory* 19(2).

　　1999. *Liberalism, Constitutionalism, and Democracy*. Oxford: Oxford University Press.

　　2002. Liberal Distrust. *European Review* 10(1).

　　2003. *Indeterminacy and Society*. Princeton, NJ: Princeton University Press.

　　2004. Transition to Corporate Democracy? In *Building a Trustworthy State in Post-Socialist Transition*, edited by J. Kornai and S. Rose-Ackerman. New York: Palgrave Macmillan.

Hibbing, J. R., and E. Theiss-Morse. 2002. *Stealth Democracy: American's Beliefs about How Government Should Work*. Cambridge: Cambridge University Press.

Hobbes, T. 1642/1983. *De Cive*, edited by H. Warrender. Oxford: Oxford University Press.

　　1651/1994. *Leviathan*, edited by E. Curley. Indianapolis: Hackett.

Humboldt, W. 1854/1969. *The Limits of State Action*, edited by J. W. Burrow. Cambridge: Cambridge University Press. Reprinted by Liberty Press, 1993.

Hume, D. 1739–1740/1978. *A Treatise of Human Nature*, edited by L. A. Selby-Bigge and N. H. Nidditch, 2nd edition. Oxford: Oxford University Press.

　　1742/1985. Of the Independency of Parliament. In *David Hume: Essays Moral, Political, and Literary*, edited by E. F. Miller. Indianapolis: Liberty Classics.

　　1748/1985. Of the Original Contract. In *David Hume: Essays Moral, Political, and Literary*, edited by E. F. Miller. Indianapolis: Liberty Classics.

　　1751/1975. *An Enquiry Concerning the Principles of Morals*, edited by L. A. Selby-Bigge and N. H. Nidditch, 3rd edition. Oxford: Oxford University Press.

Locke, J. 1669/1993. The Fundamental Constitutions of Carolina. In *Political Writings of John Locke*, edited by D. Wootton. New York: Mentor.

　　1690/1988. *Two Treatises of Government*. Cambridge: Cambridge University Press.

Lupia, A., M. D. McCubbins, and S. L. Popkin. 2000. *Elements of Reason: Cognition, Choice, and the Bounds of Rationality*. Cambridge: Cambridge University Press.

Mackie, G. 1996. Ending Foot-Binding and Infibulation: A Convention Account. *American Sociological Review* 61(6).

Madison, James. 1787/2001a. *The Federalist* #37. In *The Federalist*, A. Hamilton, J. Jay, and J. Madison, edited by G. W. Carey and J. McClellan. Indianapolis, IN: Liberty Fund.

　　1787/2001b. *The Federalist* #51. In *The Federalist*, A. Hamilton, J. Jay, and J. Madison, edited by G. W. Carey and J. McClellan. Indianapolis, IN: Liberty Fund.

Manin, B. 1997. *The Principles of Representative Government*. Cambridge: Cambridge University Press.

Mill, J. S. 1859/1977. *On Liberty*. In *Collected Works of John Stuart Mill*, edited by J. M. Robson. Toronto: University of Toronto Press.

Miller, A. 2001. *On Politics and the Art of Acting*. New York: Viking.

Rawls, J. 1955. Two Concepts of Rules. *Philosophical Review* 64(1).

1971/1999. *A Theory of Justice*. Cambridge, MA: Harvard University Press.

Reid, J. P. 1989. *The Concept of Representation in the Age of the American Revolution*. Chicago: University of Chicago Press.

Richie, R. 2002. *Fair Elections Update: Election 2002 and the Case for Reform*. Washington, DC: Center for Voting and Democracy.

Scanlon, T. M. 1982. Contractualism and Utilitarianism. In *Utilitarianism and Beyond*, edited by A. Sen and B. Williams. Cambridge: Cambridge University Press.

1998. *What We Owe to Each Other*. Cambridge, MA: Harvard University Press.

Schumpeter, J.A. 1942/1950. *Capitalism, Socialism and Democracy*. 3rd edition. New York: Harper.

Sidney, A. 1698/1990. *Discourses Concerning Government*, edited by T. G. West. Indianapolis, IN: Liberty Classics.

Smith, A. 1776/1976. *An Inquiry into the Nature and Causes of the Wealth of Nations*, edited by R. H. Campbell, A. S. Skinner, and W. B. Todd. Oxford: Oxford University Press; reprinted by Liberty Press, 1979.

Tocqueville, A. 1945/1835 and 1840. *Democracy in America*, 2 vols. New York: Knopf.

Weingast, B. R. 1997. The Political Foundations of Democracy and the Rule of Law. *American Political Science Review* 91(2).

Williamson, O. E. 1985. *The Economic Institutions of Capitalism: Firms, Markets, Relational Contracting*. New York: Free Press.

Winstanley, Gerrard. 1652/1973. *The Law of Freedom in a Platform or, True Magistracy Restored*, edited by R. W. Kenny. New York: Schocken Books.

Wittman, D.A. 1995. *The Myth of Democratic Failure: Why Political Institutions Are Efficient*. Chicago: University of Chicago Press.

Wood, G. S. 1969. *The Creation of the American Republic, 1776–1787*. Chapel Hill: North Carolina University Press; reprinted by Norton, 1972

3

Constitutions as Mission Statements

Jeff King

3.1 INTRODUCTION

The purpose of this essay is to outline and defend a function for constitutions which, though immediately recognisable, has been too little discussed in the English-language literature on constitutions. I argue in Section 3.3 that constitutions in liberal democracies can and sometimes do function as mission statements. The expression 'mission statement', borrowed from the world of business, means in this chapter a statement of core values and commitments that constitute or form part of the purpose of the state, and are meant to guide its decision making. Constitutions have multiple functions, and being mission statements is merely one, contingent feature of them. They do so by means of various provisions, which for ease of reference I call mission statement provisions. These provisions will often set out the core and constitutive political commitments of the community, not only as a record of pre-existing sociopolitical conditions and conventions, but often also as a proactive programme of development. These commitments take various forms, which I enumerate in Section 3.3. I argue that the constitutional enshrinement of these types of provisions can produce positive consequences in four particular ways: expressiveness, guiding, enforcement and legitimation. I argue that, in particular, to carry out the legitimation function well, mission statement provisions ought to be egalitarian and non-minimalist. This view of what constitutions can and ought to do may conflict with some accounts of the function of constitutions, and in particular, one that considers constitutions to be

Senior Lecturer, Faculty of Laws, University College London. The author would like to thank Nick Barber, Denis Galligan, Samuel Hawke, Alon Harel, Mila Versteeg and Grégoire Webber for helpful feedback on earlier drafts. He would also like to thank Russell Hardin and especially Maurice Adams, as well as other participants, for feedback delivered at workshops held by the Foundation for Law, Justice and Society in Oxford on 2 October 2010 and 17 June 2011.

vehicles for coordination for mutual advantage. I thus commence in Section 3.2 with a discussion of some common accounts of the purposes of constitutions, and their attendant flaws, before introducing the alternative account.

There are a number of objections to the idea that constitutions can serve as mission statements, and especially to the idea that such statements should be non-minimalist. I examine five of these in Section 3.4. I reject the claims that mission statements are (1) destabilizing, (2) pious wishes having no real impact or (3) mere instruments for entrenching elite bargains. Two remaining arguments are, however, stronger and require careful accommodation. There is a real danger that non-minimalist mission statements could lead to (4) constitutional conservativism by entrenching values that are not easily amended, or to (5) judicial supremacy if the operating presumption is that all mission statement provisions are judicially enforceable. These dangers require vigilant attention to these problems at the stage of constitutional design, as well as in the interpretive doctrines adopted by judges thereafter. Yet that attention is both possible and often likely, so these objections qualify but do not rebut the claim that constitutions can and ought to function as mission statements. The analysis in this chapter is ultimately intended to be both descriptive and normatively prescriptive. The descriptive component is the claim that many contemporary constitutions contain provisions that are best understood as mission statements, and that an account of constitutions that neglects them is incomplete. The normative argument is that constitutions can legitimate a political order in the sense of making it more justifiable normatively and more acceptable to citizens. In my contention, if constitutions are to play this role appropriately, they ought to include mission statement provisions setting out proactive state goals that are egalitarian and non-minimalist.

3.2 SOME EXISTING ACCOUNTS OF THE PURPOSE OF DEMOCRATIC CONSTITUTIONS

One could be forgiven for finding the question about what a constitution is 'for' a bit odd – somewhat like asking what Jupiter is for. On that (pedantic) view, a constitution merely is. And what it is, to take one definition from many, is 'the set of the most important rules and common understandings in any given country that regulate the relations among that country's governing institutions and also the relations between that country's governing institutions and the people of that country' (King 2007: 3). This 'thin' sense of defining a constitution is not merely a parochial definition to accommodate the unwritten elements of the British constitution (on 'thin' conceptions, see Raz 2001: 153–154), and on this view, one can certainly conclude that constitutions just 'are' and need not be 'for' anything. However, nearly all constitutions in the world include codified, written charters, and henceforth this is the aspect of constitutions that I am referring to unless otherwise stated. The design of such codified constitutions is an affirmative political act, guided by a set of individual or collective purposes. Designers of constitutions ordinarily intend for the written document to help serve particular ends, *to do something*. So constitutions have functions, and are instruments enlisted in grand projects of statecraft. This is all the more true given that such codified constitutions are not a political necessity, even in complex states like the United Kingdom, New Zealand, or Israel.

Three influential accounts of the purpose of modern constitutions comprise claims that (1) they serve as forms of a social contract, (2) are instruments for limiting government or (3) are vehicles through which we coordinate the actions of key constituencies for mutual advantage. I argue here that none of these views is complete, and take the third of such views, the idea of coordination, as the departure point for why it is necessary to affirm and defend a role for constitutions as mission statements.

3.2.1 *The Social Contract*

There are two forms of social contract theory that are at times offered as an account of what a constitution is or represents. The older one, affirmed by writers such as Locke, Rousseau and Hobbes, suggests that a constitution is an actual agreement between citizens on the principles of government. This agreement is sometimes explicit, but more often it is tacit. As Jean Jacques Rousseau put it in *The Social Contract*, 'When the state is instituted, residence constitutes consent; to dwell within its territory is to submit to the Sovereign' (Rousseau 1762: 277).

These theories have been dismissed as implausible by a number of philosophers. For one thing, there never was an actual agreement with current or past residents. For another, the idea that one consents to law merely because one refuses 'to build a new life under a foreign flag' is simply untrue (Dworkin 1986: 192–193; Raz 1995). Further, Russell Hardin in his contribution to this volume has shown that there are several other ways in which constitutions are not analogous in form or in substance to real contracts (Hardin 2013).

So a second type of social contract theory, originating with Immanuel Kant and finding contemporary expression in the work of John Rawls, is the idea of a hypothetical social contract. This tradition departs from the idea of actual consent, and rather uses a hypothetical contract scenario as a device to explain what the requirements of a particular theory of justice would require. In Rawls's case, the theory was justice as fairness (Rawls 1971, 1993). But this approach, as an account of the requirements of justice, is vulnerable to two further objections. The first is that '[a] hypothetical contract is not simply a pale form of an actual contract; it is no contract at all' (Dworkin 1978: 17–18). If the social contract theorist replies by emphasising that the theory is merely a device for expounding a particular substantive conception of justice, then she risks impaling herself on the horn of the other objection, namely that the device of a contract does nothing more than obscure a substantive philosophical theory of what reasonable people ought to accept. In such a case, as Hardin implies, the device of a social contract can become irritating (Hardin 2013). Ultimately, we can sidestep this issue by concluding that whatever its value, the social contract tradition furnishes no good account of the *purpose* of constitutions. If actual or tacit agreement among the subjects of political authority is not attainable, then to say that the purpose of the constitution is to embody consent is untenable. And if one resorts to the hypothetical social contract as a justificatory device, then one offers an account of the outcome of a hypothetical procedure that would yield a just set of constitutional principles, not an account of the function of constitutions themselves (see Rawls 1971: 197, n2, 198ff).

Tom Ginsburg's essay in this volume defends the idea of constitutions as a social contract against some of Hardin's objections. He argues that social contract theory may suffer as a normative theory for legitimizing constitutions, but it remains the best account of the actual formation of constitutions. Yet this defence rescues the idea of a social contract by dispensing with its traditional role in argumentation. The social contract tradition has always been an account of why and under what conditions people ought to accept political authority as legitimate. It is true that Hardin is concerned to say that contract theory is neither descriptively accurate nor normatively ideal, but he aims both points at the general argument that the tradition aims to provide – that is, an account of the legitimacy of political authority. Ginsburg responds to Hardin's complaint about the lack of actual agreement in any real constitutional scenario by stating that on the one hand, many constitutions are elite-bargains (and so are like contracts), and on the other, many in fact tacitly consent – a 'form of explicit, if coerced, consent' (Ginsburg 2013). That latter phrase at least appears oxymoronic (a bit like 'accepting' an offer one cannot refuse), although some have argued that the mere acceptance of the benefits of citizenship implies consent to the order (Locke 1991: 347–349; cf Rawls 1971: 118; Nozick 1974: 90–95). And the idea of an elite-bargain will hardly serve to legitimate political authority. So Ginsburg's 'social contract' would be of the sort having nothing to do with the tradition Hardin is primarily interested in criticising.

Although I doubt the relevance of social contract theory as an account of the *function* of constitutions, I do not claim that such theories are irrelevant to constitution-making. It is still useful to the project because, if correct, it tells us something about the content of a just constitution and potentially something about the conditions under which it should be determined. It is therefore not superfluous or obfuscating. The Rawlsian contract device (to take the most prominent example) maintains that the basic structure of society be framed such that it would be chosen by free, equal and rational persons under conditions of fairness. This shows respect for persons. If such a theory is used to defend the content of a particular constitution, that constitution is always vulnerable, in a good way, to the quite democratic objection that it would be *unacceptable* to some real persons in the given situation (Rawls 1971: 17). It may also suggest that constitutional design procedures and the content of the constitution itself ought to be adopted under egalitarian conditions (rather than be constituted by elite-bargains), which would indicate a role for consultation, referenda, basic rights provisions or constitutional renewal when the constitution is too remote in time or content from what free, equal and reasonable people would presently accept. The benchmark of acceptability is a potent normative standard.

3.2.2 *Limited Government*

Another common view of constitutions is that they are meant to limit government. The origins of constitutional government in the United Kingdom, for instance, concerned limitations on the powers of the monarch with the Magna Carta 1215 and the Bill of Rights 1689. When the expression 'constitutional monarchy' is used, it signifies a monarchy limited by constitutional rules and principles. As Elkins, Ginsburg and Melton put it, 'arguably the most important role of constitutions is to limit the behavior of government. Constitutions generate a set of inviolable principles and more specific provisions to which future law and government activity more generally must conform' (Elkins et al. 2009: 38). Unlike the idea of contract, the concept of limited government does not require any consent.

This idea is often (though not always) backed up by a view that strong governments can be a threat to liberty, and the function of constitutions is to constrain them, harness their power, and control their arbitrary temperament. The idea of constitutions as limitations on government is a key theme in the libertarian writings of Friedrich von Hayek:

> The formula that all power derives from the people referred not so much to the recurrent election of representatives as to the fact that the people, organized as a constitution-making body, had the exclusive right to determine the powers of the representative legislature. The constitution was thus conceived as a protection of the people against all arbitrary action, on the part of the legislative as well as other branches of government. (von Hayek 1960: 155–156)

But this view of constitutions is itself very limited. For one it is substantively irreconcilable with the provisions of contemporary constitutions that recognise a role for the social state and for the protection of social welfare rights. More importantly, the idea overlooks the extremely important *enabling* function of constitutions. Constitutions are meant to enable groups to achieve goals together as well as provide for accountable government. No better illustration of this is to be found than in the

Federalist cause and its case for a Union between the thirteen states in America after the American Revolution. The central project of the Federalists was the creation of a federal state, and the principal antagonists were individuals representing state interests, who opposed its creation on grounds that it would amount to a new form of despotism (Madison et al. 1788; Ketcham 1986). So, to read the table of contents of the Federalist Papers is to read a catalogue of the ways in which a federal state will enable the states collectively to do things they could not otherwise do effectively, culminating in the Federalist 23 ('The Necessity of a Government at Least Equally Energetic with the One Proposed'). Similarly, Jürgen Habermas's call for a constitution for Europe, which finds itself at the similar crossroads, was based chiefly on the way in which the creation of a stronger European polity could increase the power of European states to protect their distinctive brand of welfare state and social solidarity (Habermas 2001: 8–11). That is not a view of limited government at all. It is rather a vision of constitutions facilitating the creation of a new system of politics to achieve things that could not otherwise be achieved.

3.2.3 *Coordination and Stability*

Hardin's view is that constitutions are devices for both enabling and constraining (Hardin 1999: 133). According to him, the basis of organised government is best understood as a social convention, and not as a contract between constituents or elite groups. Conventions do not require agreement, but they may provide the seed for understanding why an arrangement not formally agreed to is legitimate. It is legitimate because it works to our mutual advantage (Hardin 1999: chapter 3; Gauthier 1986). Conventions are underpinned by acquiescence, not by commitment. This is what Hardin calls the compelling fact of constitutions (Hardin 2013). Constitutions gain acquiescence by raising the costs of change. For Hardin, constitutions are a form of a complex dual-convention: one convention is the convention concerning how government derives its power to rule; another is the convention of popular acquiescence.

Thus far, there is nothing objectionable in Hardin's argument, and much to be admired, for it overcomes the key problems found with both previous accounts. But we are presented with one problem with the coordination thesis, which I will call the under-determination problem. That is, like the concept of human dignity, the idea of coordination may explain too much, because it appears that most constitutional arrangements might be sold on the hypothesis that they will coordinate behaviour well. Not so, thinks Hardin, because the coordination thesis carries with it an important implication. 'Establishing a constitution is a massive act of coordination that, if it is stable for a while, creates a convention that depends for its maintenance on its self-generating incentives and expectations' (Hardin 2013: 61). For him, 'constitutionalism works when and only when it serves to coordinate a population' (Hardin 1999: 1). It is crucially the self-enforcing nature of conventions that must be appreciated. Hardin tells us that '[t]o judge a constitution normatively requires attention to its actual consequences' (Hardin 2013: 52). Constitutions, unlike contracts, do not have external enforcement agencies. Therefore they must be self-enforcing if they are to work. To maintain that set of incentives, the constitution must reflect 'our own good, our mutual advantage.' So now we move closer to the upshot: '[a] constitution can include anything people might want. But if it is filled with perversities, it is likely to fail to coordinate us' (Hardin 2013: 62). So it emerges that the constitution must work for the mutual advantage of politically effective groups, that is, those in a position to destabilise the constitution (Hardin 1999: 105). He adds that this is an account of the necessary conditions for a successful constitution, but not the sufficient conditions for a just one.

Hardin's account has affinities with a quite significant and commonly asserted function of constitutions – that they should provide stability and continuity in political societies (Raz 2001: 153). No doubt this is one of the important aims of constitutions. It may be a good explanation of the success and longevity of the British constitution, which has not experienced an unconstitutional change of government since the Glorious Revolution of 1688. Moreover, the idea of coordination is the key overriding purpose ascribed to law more generally by John Finnis, and regarded also as among law's central purposes by Raz as well (Finnis 1979: chapters IX and X; Raz 1979).

My key concern with Hardin's thesis, and potentially with the idea of treating stability as the supreme virtue, is that it undersells the potential of constitutionalism as an instrument for liberal statecraft. A weaker reading of his thesis would suggest that a constitution must work if it is to be useful, so it should not attempt the impossible. That lesson is one no one will deny. Stability is a precursor for whatever else a state may wish to do. A stronger reading of his thesis is more insidious. It is that the interests of politically effective groups must predominate if the constitution is to last. On this view, one does not get a seat at the bargaining table without a sword behind one's smile. Such a view would not only be consistent with the literature suggesting that constitutions are often a form of elite-bargain, but it would lend support to the practice, possibly suggest it is a precondition for an effective constitution. This is by no means a necessary consequence of a coordination theory of constitutions, but it is one plausible reading of Hardin's work. It is exactly the type of reading taken from his earlier work by some commentators (Ordeshook 1993: 202, 206–207), and it is the one I take issue with.

In my opinion, such a view would encourage constitutions to be conservative rather than proactive. One can think of all manner of constitutional innovations that were strongly opposed by powerful groups. These would include the expansion of the franchise in Britain and the United States first to propertyless men and then to women. It would also have lent cold comfort to those advocating the development of agency government in the New Deal United States, which prompted a constitutional crisis there, as well as the introduction of the People's Budget in the United Kingdom by the then-Chancellor of the Exchequer David Lloyd George in 1909, which led to the House of Lords refusing to pass the budget and the eventual crisis resulting in the Parliament Act 1911. Another innovation that might have fallen foul of the coordination thesis is the ambitious Charter of the United Nations, adopted in 1945, which outlawed international aggression but also enshrined a commitment to international human rights. Those goals were highly idealistic at the time – but the march towards international peace and respect for basic rights since then has been astonishing, if viewed in historical perspective. The entire concept of 'transformative constitutionalism' is the idea that the constitution should be an ally in reshaping the social power structures that exist, by redistributing rights and privileges in a more egalitarian fashion, and by empowering the state to take action against inequalities where they are prevalent (Klare 1998). These ideas and occurrences are not marginal counter-examples to the coordination thesis. They were epoch-defining in important areas of the world. And their lesson is clear. Sometimes a measure of idealism that challenges the status quo is a part of successful constitutionalism. Of course, mortal instability would be foolish, but I will shortly consider and reject the supposition that ambitious mission statement provisions lead to constitutional mortality.

Hardin does argue that the coordination thesis is not a complete theory of a just constitution. Yet if the implications to which I have drawn attention earlier are true, then it is not only incomplete, but may counsel against the kinds of constitutions that I consider in the next section. I argue there that a good constitution ought to *legitimate* the legal and political order. A constitution that seeks coordination alone, one favouring the interests of powerful groups, is one that favours the status quo, and might even give a veneer of legitimacy to it. Whether that is required for constitutional survival is quite doubtful; that it is manifestly unfair is beyond doubt.

3.3 CONSTITUTIONS AS MISSION STATEMENTS

The accounts examined in Section 3.2 fail to emphasise the role of the constitution as a mission statement. Any account of constitutional purposes ought ideally to fit, to an important extent, the current practice, at least in those political communities at which the argument is aimed (in my case, liberal democracies). A survey of a range of the world's codified constitutions (including some non-democratic ones) shows that there are at least three key functions that continuously recur: (1) the legal establishment or recognition of the basic institutions and departments of the state,

including federal or other sub-national units within it; (2) the division and allocation of responsibilities between the institutions or departments of state; and (3) the
articulation of a set of foundational political principles to which the institutions of
the state are meant to give effect, and which typically include a list of human or
citizens' rights or related state duties. My claims about constitutions as mission statements naturally pick up on the third of these functions, whose form and broader
purpose I now turn to examining.

3.3.1 *The Nature of Mission Statements*

The basic idea expounded here is that constitutions may outline the core, constitutive political commitments of the community, and are meant to guide the institutions of the state in dealings *inter se*, as well as in their dealings with citizens and
foreign persons and organisations (including foreign states). It is necessary to address
some of the features of mission statements before proceeding to examine their form
and putative functions.

First, it is necessary to distinguish between 'constitutions as mission statements'
and 'mission statement provisions'. The first is a claim about how a constitution may
serve holistically to provide normative guidance for proactive state planning and policy. I envisage no threshold for how much guidance is required for a constitution to
be called a mission statement; it is a matter of degree. And I merely draw attention to
one particular feature of constitutions, one that is contingent rather than necessary.
The mission statement provisions, by contrast, are those provisions in the constitution that provide individual commitments or statements of principle. The constitution's holistic mission statement (should there be a coherent one) is determined by
construing these provisions as a whole, in light of the rest of the written constitution
and any other constitutional values and principles instantiated in the community's
constitutional practice. It is a matter of constructive interpretation (Dworkin 1986:
chapter 2). The greater the range of mission statement provisions in the constitution,
the more guidance the constitutional authors will have provided to the interpreter.

Second, the distinguishing feature of mission statements is the feature of proactive guidance and purpose. Constitutional rules and conventions may guide action
without being clear as to any holistic purpose. And they may also serve as constraints rather than normative goals in themselves. Constitutions can be minimalist,
expressly renouncing any aim to articulate a state philosophy. A constitution that
serves as a mission statement, by contrast, will rather express the political ideas that
animate the constitution and polity more broadly, including the type of government
it represents, the rights of citizens and the people, and the values it seeks to respect
in its state planning. Mission statements are about state ends, not only state means,
still less about constraints or "no-go areas."

Third, it is important also to distinguish between mission statement provisions as observable features, characteristics of constitutions, or normative statements, on the one hand and the social functions that such constitutional statements *actually* perform on the other. Many constitutions are loaded with what could analytically be described as mission statement provisions, but which are routinely ignored in practice. If so, then the mission statements are present, but the functions outlined later in this chapter are not served. Further, the functions I outline later are some of the positive functions that mission statements may play. I acknowledge and address the potentially negative ways they may function in Section 3.4. Whether particular mission statement provisions serve positive or negative functions, or no function at all, is a contingent empirical matter.

Lastly, it is necessary to clarify that mission statement provisions, as I explain further in the following section, may be either general statements of principle not intended to found legal actions or be provisions largely intended for judicial enforcement. The line between these is not strict; general statements of principle can guide judges, just as respect for binding constitutional rights will hopefully guide legislators. This relates to recent discussion of aspirational constitutionalism (Dorf 2009; Scheppele 2003). While there are important links between mission statements and aspirational constitutionalism, there is an unfortunate connotation of 'hope' to the word 'aspiration', one which invites contrast with the idea of 'binding commitments'. In my view, mission statements provisions can be either judicially enforceable or largely declaratory. Preambles can serve as mission statements, and so can the bill of rights. What is functionally important is normative guidance and the institutional declaration of key values, not judicial enforceability. From the point of view of guidance, the role of judicial enforceability is neither a determinative factor nor, in many constitutions, even a crucial one in estimating the extent to which the constitution serves to guide states.

3.3.2 *The Forms of Mission Statement Provisions*

Mission statement provisions come in various forms:

- *Basic Organising Principles of the State*: More contemporary constitutions typically begin with a section on basic principles. So for example, in recent cases, we have the Kyrgyz Republic (2010) section 1 ('General Provisions'), Djibouti (2010) ('On the State and Sovereignty') and Kenya (2010) chapter 1 ('Sovereignty of the People and Supremacy of This Constitution').[1] The same is true of slightly older constitutions like Brazil (1998) Title 1 ('Fundamental

[1] References to all constitutions in this essay are to those found in Wolfrum and Groter (1971) (with updates). A reference to a constitution in the form, for example, Germany (1949), means it is the constitution for the Federal Republic of Germany, adopted in 1949, and which is presently in force.

Principles'), China (1982) chapter 1 ('General Principles') and Greece (1975), part one ('Basic Provisions'). And ones appearing after World War II also had more attenuated versions of these sections: France (1958) Title 1 ('On Sovereignty'), Italy (1948) Articles 1–15 ('Fundamental Principles') and even as far back as Norway (1814) A. ('Form of Government and Religion'). In all these cases, the constitutions contain a variety of provisions of some vagueness but which set out the founding and core principles of the nation. Notably, in every case, these basic principles are set out in sections other than those dealing with fundamental rights. There is a noticeable increase in the usage of these sections of constitutions. For instance, Belgium amended its 1994 constitution in 2007 by adding the following article under the heading of 'General Political Objectives': 'In the exercise of their respective powers, the Federal State, the Communities and the Regions follow the objectives of lasting development in its social, economic and environmental aspects, taking into account the solidarity between the generations'.

- *Bills of Rights*: Such bills or chapters of constitutions represent the most obvious set of normative political principles meant to guide the state. In more recent times, bills of rights have been quite expansive, embracing socio-economic rights and increasingly rights to a healthy environment. One might argue that rights are not like mission statements: they rather represent side-constraints on whatever else the state may wish to do (Nozick 1974: chapter 3). But that is an unconvincing account of rights, especially those of more recent generations, because such rights are meant to empower and even command the state to take action as much as they are meant to limit it. Any view to the contrary is radically out of step with both international law and comparative constitutional law.

- *Directive Principles of State Policy*: Directive principles of state policy were an Irish and subsequently Indian contribution to constitutionalism. So, in Ireland (1937), for example, art.45(4)(1) reads, 'The State pledges itself to safeguard with especial care the economic interests of the weaker sections of the community, and, where necessary, to contribute to the support of the infirm, the widow, the orphan, and the aged'. And in India (1950), art.39 states, 'The State shall, in particular, direct its policy towards securing – (a) that the citizen, men and women equally, have the right to an adequate means of livelihood;(b) that the ownership and control of the material resources of the community are so distributed as best to subserve the common good; (c) that the operation of the economic

In most cases, the constitutions indicated have been amended subsequently. Any provision I cite that was subject to an amendment after the adoption of the main text is indicated in the text of this essay. Any details provided about any constitution that are not apparent in the text of the constitution were derived from the introductory essays published in Wolfrum and Groter (1971).

system does not result in the concentration of wealth and means of production to the common detriment; (d) that there is equal pay for equal work for both men and women'. These types of directives are typically made expressly non-justiciable, and their character is vague. The extent of their impact is debatable, but their role is established quite firmly. They are presently found also in the constitutions of Eritrea, Gambia, Ghana, Nepal, Nigeria, Papua New Guinea, Sri Lanka, Sudan, Swaziland, Thailand, Uganda and Zambia. Another form of a similar idea is to outline the duties of the state, either as examined previously or in a stand-alone chapter such as the example of directive principles.

- *Ad Hoc Statements of Principle*: Sometimes a country will wish to break clearly with a past event and make such a break part of its constitutive identity, something Kim Lane Scheppele calls 'aversive constitutionalism' (Scheppele 2003). South Africa renounced apartheid in this way, Germany renounced Nazism, Poland (1997) both fascism and communism (art.13), and Rwanda (2003) the horrors of genocide (art.9(1)). On the other hand, countries may wish to fully embrace principles to underline their core role in the new polity. Some may wish to make adherence to a religious doctrine part of its constitutive identity (e.g. Israel, Iran) or institute a strong policy of secularism (France (1958), art.1, United States Bill of Rights (1791), First Amendment). Others still may wish to make clear a commitment to items like the social state principle (Germany (1949), art.20(1)), or commitments to address regional disparities (Canada (1982), s.36), or to acknowledge the status of aboriginal peoples (Canada (1982), s.35; Ecuador (1998), art.84, Venezuela (1999), ch.VIII).
- *Preambles*: Although preambles are not directly enforceable, they may, like directive principles, influence the decisions of courts and of political actors (Orgad 2010; Levinson 2011). The U.S. constitution (1789) opens with commitments to 'establish Justice, insure domestic Tranquility, provide for the common defence, promote the general Welfare, and secure the Blessings of Liberty to ourselves and our Posterity'. The preamble of the constitution of Ireland (1937), notably, finds the people accepting the constitution while '[h]umbly acknowledging all our obligations to our Divine Lord, Jesus Christ, Who sustained our fathers through centuries of trial' (Levinson 2011: 170–171; Hirschl 2010). Other preambles tend to highlight historical circumstances, as in South Africa (1996), with its accent on healing (e.g. 'We, the people of South Africa ... Believe that South Africa belongs to all who live in it, united in our diversity ... We ... adopt this Constitution so as to ... [h]eal the divisions of the past and establish a society based on democratic values, social justice and fundamental human rights').

These are the forms in which core commitments may be set out in constitutions. They may be quite specific or more abstract in character. And the role for judicial enforcement can vary widely: only one of these five forms is ordinarily expected to be directly enforceable in legal proceedings, and this point too requires some qualification depending on the rights concerned.

3.3.3 *Four Positive Potential Functions of Mission Statement Provisions*

The first is the *expressive function* of constitutive political principles either agreed at the time of formation or which were instantiated in practice or even conventions when constitutional reform was undertaken (Sunstein 1995–1996; Raz 2001: 153–154; Brennan and Hamlin 2006: 333–338; Jacobson 2010: 7, 13, 31). Put simply, these principles help to manifest what the state and the political community stands for. Although expressive, such statements can have important consequences. They can become reference points in public debate. They can give recognition to important groups and constituencies. They can inform judicial interpretation of not only the constitution, but of statutes and the civil law. It is difficult or impossible to say what the causes are of public political commitments to ideas that are also reflected in the constitution – that is, whether the constitution only mirrors political practice or vice versa. But we do not need to subscribe to either of these polarities, and can rather adopt a more moderate claim that mission statement provisions may reinforce political rhetoric in a subtle and sometimes not so subtle way. For example, the French constitutional commitment to republicanism and secularity (*Laïcité*) in all probability reinforces the extreme strength of these values in French political debate, just as the Second Amendment right to bear arms does in American discussions of gun control. Likewise, the German preoccupation with suppressing hate speech and excluding extremist groups from the federal and *Land* parliaments is borne of its experience under fascism, but is also supported by art.18 of its constitution, which is concerned with those who would 'abuse' their basic rights 'in order to combat the free basic democratic order'.

More than simply expressing values symbolically, it must have been intended that constitutions would *channel* or *guide* the state's public institutions and provide an agreed normative standard for public criticism. Such principles can serve as political beacons that both direct the institutions of state and demarcate certain topics as fundamental and important, signalling that adverse tampering requires the utmost care and public scrutiny. It would be naïve to think this is the everyday role for such principles, but foolish to deny that role altogether. The guiding potential of the constitution will largely be a function of its specificity. The German constitution contains a few examples:

- Art. 20a: 'Mindful also of its responsibility toward future generations, the State shall protect within the framework of the constitutional order the natural bases of life and the animals by legislation and, in accordance with law and justice, by executive and judicial power'.

- Art. 21: 'Political parties shall participate in the formation of the political will of the people. They may be freely established. Their internal organization must conform to democratic principles. They must publicly account for their assets and for the sources and the use of their funds'.
- Art.23(1): 'With a view to establishing a United Europe, the Federal Republic of Germany shall participate in the development of the European Union that is committed to democratic, social and federal principles, to the rule of law, and to the principle of subsidiarity, and that guarantees a level of protection of basic rights essentially comparable to that afforded by this Basic Law'.

These provisions contain enough substance to guide officials towards definitive outcomes, and can found political and possibly legal claims that lethargic institutions are failing in their positive constitutional commitments. Of a similar nature one finds the following statement in the Draft Treaty Establishing a Constitution for Europe (2003):

- Article 3(3): 'The Union's Objectives' 'The Union shall work for the sustainable development of Europe based on balanced economic growth, a social market economy, highly competitive and aiming at full employment and social progress, and with a high level of protection and improvement of the quality of the environment. It shall promote scientific and technological advance.

  It shall combat social exclusion and discrimination, and shall promote social justice and protection, equality between women and men, solidarity between generations and protection of children's rights.

  It shall promote economic, social and territorial cohesion, and solidarity among Member States.

  The Union shall respect its rich cultural and linguistic diversity, and shall ensure that Europe's cultural heritage is safeguarded and enhanced'.

Whatever scorn the cynic might heap upon such a lofty declaration, one can immediately tell, beyond any doubt, that the Union is not the United States, and neither is it China. The idea of a social market economy giving high priority to equality and a focus on social exclusion was at the heart of Jürgen Habermas's influential appeal for a constitution of Europe – so that it could provide a progressive bulwark against the power of global market forces (Habermas 2001: 8–11). Clearly, the effectiveness of the guiding function of the mission statement provisions will depend on the strength of the rule of law in the relevant society. Just as one might say that there are many examples of constitutions not guiding (i.e. being ignored) in many countries, much the same could be said about statute law. Yet we will not infer from that fact that statutes are not meant to guide behaviour.

A third function of such core political principles is their *enforcement* or *remedial* function, which can be realised by their grounding or supplementing claims in the courts or other institutions such as constitutional councils or parliamentary committees. While this remedial function might seem obvious, in fact many constitutions contain standards that aim to guide but are rarely expected to found legal actions. Constitutional conventions are an obvious and quite important example of such norms in the UK constitution, but written constitutions also abound with such clauses, such as Canada's clause on regional disparity ((1982), s.36), and the French provisions on republican government ((1958), Title 1). The ordinary route for the enforcement of the provisions of the constitution is of course via the courts. They can enforce the constitution both directly and indirectly. While the first is familiar in constitutional rights litigation, the second refers to when constitutional principles serve as interpretive guides for interpreting other constitutional provisions, legislation or common or civil law principles (including *droit commun*). The doctrine of statutory interpretation known as purposive or teleological interpretation can be invigorated by even quite vague constitutional statements of principle. So many examples of this abound in the laws of the liberal democracies that elaboration is hardly necessary.

The last function is the *legitimation* of the legal order. The concept of legitimacy has both normative and descriptive senses (Barker 1991: 59; c.f. Fallon Jr. 2005). The normative sense is concerned with the conditions under which political authority can be justified to those required to obey it (Rawls 1993; Raz 1986: chapter 4; Raz 1979: chapter 1; Habermas 1996; Habermas 1975). This sense of legitimacy is concerned, at heart, with the fairness and justifiability of political authority. A legitimate constitution in this sense, I would argue, is one that can be regarded as reasonably acceptable to all citizens by treating them fairly and as equals, which would include recognising important differences or needs in key constituencies (on which, see the discussion later in this chapter). The descriptive sense of legitimacy, on the other hand, refers to the conditions under which the subjects of authority will *in fact* accept the authority as issuing valid and binding directives, even when the subjects of such directives disagree with their content. This line of study about legitimacy is to some extent attitudinal – it examines the psychological states of particular persons, to determine their propensity both to obey rules *and* accept them as legitimate (Weber 1964; Hart 1961; Tyler 1990; Rasinski et al. 1985). Some writers have emphasised that the concept of legitimacy can only be correctly understood by considering both the normative and descriptive senses of legitimacy (Barker 1991: 11, 59; Habermas 1979: 205ff). This is because descriptive claims alone would disregard the important role played by moral principles in shaping notions of acceptability, and normative claims alone would be blind to the actual conditions under which general acceptance (rather than mere obedience) is gained.

In my view, mission statement provisions can legitimate constitutions in both of these senses, in many cases they do, and at any rate they ought to be used for that purpose. They can make the constitutions more normatively justifiable, and, one hopes, thereby lead to wider public acceptance. The normative claim made here follows from the view that a constitution is more defensible if it reflects the views and interests of all the main constituents and interest groups of society. It should treat all as equally important when establishing the key departments and core principles of the state. Mission statement provisions are one way to accomplish this. Of course, to achieve this type of legitimacy, it is not only the content of the constitution that matters. The process of constitutional design matters as well. Yet, unsurprisingly, there is a direct correlation between the inclusivity of the drafting process (measured somewhat imperfectly by prevalence of a referendum procedure for approving the constitution) and more rights provisions and other mission statement provisions in constitutions (Samuels 2006; Ginsburg, Elkins and Blunt 2009: 217–218; see also Elkins et al. 2009: 139). So both the design process and content of constitutions tend to move together so far as normative legitimacy is concerned. One might take the view that it is morally irrelevant whether or not a constitution textually 'speaks' to a particular constituency. What matters is whether the constitution and its operation are just. However, my view is that constitutional recognition of interests itself can be important to particular constituencies, and thus normatively required (in the absence of compelling counterarguments) (Kymlicka 1995; Fraser and Honneth 2003). A further, more empirically contingent claim is that mission statement provisions offer enough guiding *potential* that there is a strong normative case for their inclusion. And even where they fail to guide, they can serve as reference point for critique or even adjudication. Each of these normative claims, however, is of course entirely contingent on the content of the mission statement provisions themselves not being immoral or elitist. I consider this problem further in Section 3.4.

The other branch of legitimation is concerned with acceptability, and this is a straightforwardly empirical question. Do more (or a critical mass of) mission statement provisions lead to greater public acceptance? This is difficult causal claim to make out, and I am not aware of any empirical study on that precise matter. However there are studies of inclusive design procedures and public acceptability. In law more generally, there is an established record showing that citizens who believe that the fairness of the procedure under which a decision or law was made are more likely to accept the outcome as legitimate, even if they disagree with it substantively (Tyler 1990; Lind et al. 1993; Stryker 1994). The studies of inclusivity of constitution-making and public acceptability are, however, both more limited and more divided (see Ginsburg et al. 2009: 214–215). Some suggest a positive correlation between inclusivity and wider public approval and acceptance (Samuels 2006; Ginsburg et al. 2009: 215; cf Voight 2003). South Africa's constitution, designed with highly publicised popular participation, is often given as a model example in this regard. Other studies suggest that greater inclusiveness has had no decisive impact on popular acceptance of the resulting constitution. In a rigorous qualitative and quantitative study, Devra Moehler, for example, found that the Ugandan constitution (1995) was not more supported by those citizens active in the design process than by those who were not (Moehler 2008).

In spite of this incomplete record, I would advance the following argument:

1. Constitutions that are subject to approval by popular referendum will, all else being equal, tend to have greater popular acceptance than those that do not.
2. Constitutions subject to referendum generally include more mission statement provisions.
3. The inclusion of more mission statement provisions is probably caused by either or both of (a) a strategic desire among drafters or elites to gain greater popular support at the referendum stage and (b) a good-faith desire among drafters to create an inclusive constitution that will be approved.
    Therefore,
4. A greater scope of mission statement provisions in a constitution is either indicative of, or a potential cause of, greater levels of public approval for that constitution.

The first of these premises is not, to my knowledge, established empirically, but it would be highly surprising if it turned out to be false. The burden of proof lies on the person denying a link between referenda and public acceptability. The second premise is established in the study by Ginsburg, Elkins and Blount (as noted earlier in the chapter). The third premise is a claim regarding causation that is not established empirically; however, in my view it offers two plausible explanations for the prevalence of mission statement provisions in constitutions approved by referenda. The conclusion follows from these three premises. It would be well to remember here that, of course, public approval is not an unalloyed good. A popular constitution can be highly oppressive to minorities. Approval in a referendum is compatible with a constitution that does not recognise or protect marginalised constituencies. So popular acceptance has an uncertain relation to egalitarian forms of normative legitimacy.

Previously I said that mission statements can and often do legitimate constitutions, but I also argued that they *ought to be* used to legitimate them. A constitution that is successful in this sense, or just, or morally attractive, would in my view tend to reflect at least three characteristics: (1) it should be egalitarian in showing equal concern for all (and especially the main constituencies); (2) it should not be minimalist; and (3) it should be adopted using inclusive constitutional design procedures. These three items are all related, for in practice a constitution adopted under inclusive procedures will tend to contain more detail, and that detail will tend to recognise the interests of more groups, and therefore make the constitution (at least superficially) more egalitarian (Elkins et al. 2009: chapters 2, 5, 6). To be reasonably egalitarian, a constitution would give recognition to key constituencies and recognise the role of the state in promoting the interests of all. Recognition of and attention to the interests of such groups will be an important factor in making the political authority justifiable to them (Fraser and Honneth 2003). Recognition of marginalised groups such as indigenous peoples and certain regional minorities or groups is one technique (as is the case in Canada (1982) (s. 23, minority language rights, s.35, rights of Aboriginal Peoples), Sweden (1974) Art. 20, and the same may be true of giving recognition in more diverse pluri-national communities (South Africa (1996)), as well as recognition to groups such as women (Irving 2008). Similarly, in my view, a contemporary constitution ought also to reflect the state's commitments not only to civil liberties and immunities, but also to positive state duties (whether judicially enforceable or not) to recognise and give effect to basic social rights (on the profusion of which see Law and Versteeg 2011: 138; Elkins et al. 2009: 27–28; Langford 2009; King 2012). Now, clearly, a constitution can reflect all these things and not be supported by political action. That it reflects these items would merely be a necessary but by no means sufficient condition for achieving a just constitutional state.

Any constitution that reflects these indicia of egalitarianism will, of course, be non-minimalist. So non-minimalism and moderate egalitarianism are the flip sides of the same coin. Likewise with inclusive design procedures, it will be the rare constitution that is imposed fairly on a foreign country or imposed fairly by a domestic elite on a disenfranchised population. Both, of course, happen regularly enough (Ginsburg et al. 2009: 206). But the constitutions adopted in such cases cannot ordinarily be regarded as legitimate or as treating the citizens of the country as worthy of equal treatment when the basic rules and principles governing their lives are designed without their input or approval. Where just, they are borne of extraordinary circumstance or pure necessity.

An important caveat must be added. When I suggest that constitutions should not be minimalist, neither am I endorsing the maximalism to be found in some constitutions that seek to virtually micromanage the day-to-day workings of politics (see e.g. Venezuela (1999)). Obviously some balance should be had between the need for some specificity and the need for some flexibility in working arrangements, to accommodate different political views within a framework of democratic self-government that gives high priority to the principle of equality through majority decision making.

3.4 OBJECTIONS

The preceding argument has been that mission statements can perform a positive function in the constitution, and that they ought to be egalitarian and non-minimalist. However, this is liable to a number of objections, the more important of which I address below.

3.4.1 *Mission Statements Are Destabilising*

A challenging objection arising from the line of reasoning presented in Hardin's work is that non-minimalist and egalitarian mission statements will lead to powerful groups not getting their way. This will destabilise the constitution by making it more likely for such groups to abandon the constitutional compromise, potentially with violence. This is an unlikely scenario in most wealthy liberal democracies, but is a potential threat in many emerging ones.

Such claims about constitutional mortality have been based largely on deductions from postulates about bargaining behaviour and incentives to obey (especially game theoretic ones), rather than empirical study. Elkins, Ginsburg and Melton's *The Endurance of National Constitutions* offers insights from both fields, and its conclusions tend to support the claims made here rather than those of Hardin and others. On the subject of what I call non-minimalism they conclude that constitutions having greater scope and detail (i.e. are longer) tend to have greater endurance (Elkins et al. 2009: 103–104, 141). Scholars studying conflict resolution have found positive correlations between representative constitutional design (determined by reference to the character of the deliberative body that is tasked with writing the constitution) and decreases of post-constitutional violence. Those constitutions that were adopted using more inclusive and participatory procedures also tend to have more extensive progressive rights provisions (Ginsburg et al. 2009: 217–218; Samuels 2006). Elkins, Ginsburg and Melton also find that 'constitutions written under inclusive conditions, and that also then incorporate inclusive provisions, are more likely to survive than those that do not. The effect is fairly dramatic' (Elkins et al. 2009: 139–140). On the whole, then, the evidence suggests that mission statement provisions and inclusive design procedures not only do not destabilise but may even contribute to constitutional endurance.

3.4.2 *Mission Statements Are Pious Wishes*

This objection argues that mission statement provisions will often be empty, may be misleading, could raise false hopes, or, worse, might debase the currency of the constitution by inserting non-justiciable provisions into what should be a legally enforceable charter. A related objection is that my argument in this chapter depends on an empirical claim that mission statements actually make a difference to political practice, a claim that can be doubted or rejected.

I should begin by distinguishing an important argument that constitutions are somehow expressive of the unique social and political identity of a particular nation. Mila Versteeg has presented considerable evidence to show this is a myth (Versteeg 2013). My argument about mission statements is not that they are distinctive of national identity, but rather that they can and do serve to articulate state goals. These goals can be widely shared, and mission statements can be transplanted between similar cultures without any concern for originality of form, much like other regulatory models or statutory frameworks.

The claim about debasing the legal currency of the constitution seems particularly off. There is no strong evidence of it, but there is plenty to the contrary. Germany's constitution, as noted earlier in the chapter, gives recognition to some core principles (such as the social state, and now to its role vis-à-vis the European Union) and its Constitutional Court is among the world's most activist. It has, on one estimate, invalidated nearly 5 per cent of federal laws between 1951 and 1990 (Landfried 1995: 308). The same is true of India and its activist Supreme Court, notwithstanding the expressly non-justiciable directive principles of state policy, which the courts there have nonetheless used to interpret and, indeed one might say, enrich other provisions of the constitution (Elkins et al. 2009: 151–157; Sathe 2001). Indeed, if anything, the evidence suggests that the more minimal substantive character of the U.S. constitution has led to the libertarian interpretation of its bill of rights and obstructionist attitude of the *Lochner*-era courts to the creation of the administrative state. The failure of the constitution to enable administration to develop in this way was at least a potential source of the problem. Judicial obstructionism was far more attenuated in Britain, but the lack of any constitutional commitment to the social state also permitted that problem there too (Laski 1925–1926). It is at least as likely that a more minimalist constitution has likely withheld the benefits of a more positive socio-economic rights jurisprudence in the courts.

This leaves us with the claim that mission statements are likely to be ineffective. This objection follows from the sceptical literature that argues that courts and rights have little impact (Rosenberg 1991; Klarman 2004; Horowitz 1977: 34–51), and the common observation that there is a difference between law on the books and law in action. One might deflect this objection with the following argument: if mission statements are harmless on one view but potentially helpful on another, we ought to include them as a safe bet. However, I want to go further and suggest that mission statement provisions do offer real potential in the area of channelling and guiding state behaviour. On the one hand, it is absurd to suggest that constitutional commitments to the separation of powers, to the separation of church and state, to republicanism in the U.S. and French constitutions were hollow. They have had an enormous impact on political behaviour in both countries, and the other examples of core political principles adduced in Section 3.3 are similar, if less dramatic. Of course, we can gather examples from countries that neglect the rule of law, but these are not the acid test for the claims set out in this chapter. That would be like saying anti-corruption legislation is pointless because it does not work in Bangladesh.

The hollow-hope objection to the efficacy of courts raised by Rosenberg cuts much closer to the bone, however, because he is arguing that even legally enforceable rights provisions in wealthy countries with strong traditions of judicial review like the United States do not lead to significant social reform. The question of whether rights adjudication really amounts to a hollow hope is a complex one, and this is not the place for a close examination of it. It can be said with confidence, however, that while Rosenberg's arguments about courts being engines for *significant* social reform are important and well heeded, there are a plethora of studies that show how courtroom litigation has had an important impact on administration and substantive law, and in particular, how legal mobilization by activists commonly uses litigation and campaigning in iterative symbiosis to achieve notable victories (Scheingold 1974; McCann 1994; Epp 1998, 2010; Canon and Johnson 1999; Vanhala 2011; King 2012: 63–70). As with any social phenomenon, the changes created by litigation are complex, varied and inconsistent over time. But the weight of opinion supports the view that rights litigation is more than a hollow hope, and therefore that rights provisions are more than a pious wish for those with modest expectations.

3.4.3 *Mission Statements Give Effect to Elite Bargains*

Indeed, a more challenging view is that core principles do count in practice – perhaps too much. They may count in a bad way by expressing the wrong principles, guiding the state in the wrong ways, and offering false legitimation to what is actually an elitist hijacking of the drafting process. There is no doubt that many constitutions are heavily influenced by elite groups (Burton and Higley 1987). What important public process isn't? If the point of this objection is that constitutions are nothing but bargains between elites that exclude the people, then it is ludicrous in a state where a pre-adoption referendum is held. The point might be more subtle, however, and suggest that elites have disproportionate influence and that it can be nuanced and insidious, possibly slipping past a transparent referendum procedure (Hirschl 2004: chapter 3). The risk of promoting mission statement provisions is that it will give such elites an option to promote their interests further, thereafter backing it up with legal enforcement and firm entrenchment.

This argument tends to assume two things, neither of which is necessarily true. The first is that the core political principles I refer to serve the interests of a dominant, typically neo-liberal agenda. It is of course true that the shape of some constitutions will reflect the power of dominant groups. So a communist or theo-cratic constitution will contain overt commitments to those ideals. But constitutions adopted recently under democratic conditions, and ratified by a referendum, tend to show the opposite tendency. These constitutions tend to be more rather than less inclusive, more rather than less egalitarian. The second untrue assumption is that elites would be better served by engaging in constitutional standard-setting than by leaving the constitution silent and advocating their interests through the legislative process. There is also little evidence for this view (at least outside highly unstable non-democratic countries negotiating the transition to a more inclusive constitu-tional state). While whether elite groups exert powerful and illegitimate control over modern constitution-making remains a debateable hypothesis, that they have perva-sive influence over legislative decision making is an old and trite observation (Dahl 1989: 19). Contemporary democratic constitutions are for the most part subject to the requirements of considerable publicity and of national ratification through a referendum. Publicity is achieved because constitution-drafting is a 'constitutional moment' when the People and press pay attention, more so (quite often) than dur-ing the course of day-to-day politics (Ackerman 1991: chapter 10). And as Justice Louis Brandeis pointed out so long ago, 'sunlight is said to be the best of disinfec-tants' (Brandeis, 1913).

Furthermore, there is evidence that constitutional silence serves elites rather well. A minimal constitution can deprive marginalised groups of a textual root for their advocacy claims, and it can forego the possibility of nudging institu-tions in the directions provided in the constitution. We do know that the United Kingdom, with its famously non-committal 'political constitution' (Griffith 1979), is nearly the most unequal of the original EU-15 states and has nearly the worst record of child poverty among them (Hills 2004: 57, 66–71). We also know that the U.S. constitution's silence on social questions outside the bill of rights fits well with its manifest non-commitment to regulation and economic equality, and also with the agenda of libertarian groups who fetishise the constitution and call for a retrenchment of the state to fit with a narrow reading of the constitution (*The Economist* 2010).

Clearly, constitutions will, to some extent, reflect the interests of elite groups. And it is also true that when elite and popular opinions clash in the constitution-making process, it can cause friction and instability, particularly in countries prone to violence. Nonetheless – and for the moment leaving aside the question of judi-cial enforcement and of imposed constitutions – the truth is that there is at least as much evidence of constitutional silence being a threat to equality as is the pros-pect of elites hijacking the statements of principle embodied by mission statement provisions.

3.4.4 *Mission Statements Are Inescapably Conservative*

One potential issue with setting out core principles is that, as with the U.S. constitution, they may be hard to amend. They could thus freeze the evolution of political thinking. This is a serious problem, because the clear virtue of legislative decision making over constitutional reform is that it can be carried out by simple majority. There are well-known problems with the view of constitutions as pre-commitment devices used by a people to bind itself; the reality is that the authors of constitutions also bind other people as well (Holmes 1995; Elster 2000: chapter 2; Waldron 1999: chapter 12). Majority decision making, for all its flaws, lays a good prima facie claim to treating everyone as equals (Beitz 1990; Waldron 1999: chapters 5, 11).

This type of problem is serious and cannot be dismissed without constructive engagement. But it is a problem that afflicts all forms of constitutionalism, so the problem is not unique to mission statements. If the problem is taken seriously and a solution offered, then the solution will apply equally to mission statements. One could argue, however, that enthusiasm about mission statements could exacerbate this problem because its non-minimalism could extend the influence of conservative groups and obstruct the channels of progressive change even further. But this would mean that most mission statement provisions have a conservative bent. It seems to me that the evidence is precisely the opposite in most constitutions, apart from theocratic constitutions (which Hirschl (2010) argues, in fact, serve to limit the extent of religion on the state rather than extend its dominion). I have already addressed the idea that constitutions allow for more elite influence than day-to-day democratic politics.

Admittedly, this issue can be a significant problem if the constitution is particularly inflexible. Constitutional flexibility is a matter that has been examined empirically. Arend Lijphart has shown how various democracies can be plotted on a spectrum of constitutional flexibility, with only six of thirty-six countries being capable of constitutional amendment by simple majority at the time of writing (Lijphart 1999: 220). Elkins, Ginsburg and Melton find that constitutional flexibility is one reliable indicator of the longevity of written constitutions, with the more rigid ones living less long (Elkins et al. 2009).

In my view, the appropriate approach to this issue is to reconsider the tradition of strong entrenchment of constitutions. Consensus decision making can be particularly crucial for highly divided societies. But stern supermajority requirements can lock constituencies into unjust arrangements, in some cases perpetuating extreme forms of inequality of influence, such as in the U.S. Senate, where Alaska and California have the same number of senators notwithstanding the fact that the latter is over fifty times more populous (see generally Dahl 2002: 43–54). Some of the main benefits of constitutionalism arise, or could arise, from the process that surrounds constitutional reform. It is the act of convening the citizenry and its luminaries for a national dialogue on fundamental principles that, in my view, lends special legitimacy to the constitutional arrangements. It may be possible to achieve those benefits, therefore, through procedural requirements for anything from the holding of referenda to the calling of a national convention under specified conditions – or even by means of a simple legislative majority or special parliamentary procedure.

I am not calling for the universal abandonment of supermajority entrenchment. Whether to observe a supermajority requirement for constitutional amendment is a complex question that is dependent on political circumstances. It is unlikely that the United Kingdom, for example, given its constitutional stability, has any need for a supermajority amendment procedure. But it may be perfectly fitting for ethnically divided communities such as Northern Ireland, Belgium or Switzerland. Further, it may be possible to give less flexibility to particular portions of the constitution where particular needs or sensitivities exist. It may be equally possible to provide that the constitution may be amended by *adding* new provisions of a particular type by means of a simple majority or special procedure. The possibilities are so manifold that further exploration is beyond the scope of this chapter. The point remains that mission statements do not necessarily lead to conservatism, and a well-planned constitution can respond to the concern in an adequate manner.

3.4.5 *Mission Statements Invite Judicial Supremacy*

The final objection I address is that having non-minimalist mission statements will invite judges to extend the domain of judicialisation (Hirschl 2004: chapters 4–6; Shapiro and Stone Sweet 2002). The fear is that by making constitutions more normatively ambitious, we invite judges to interfere ever more profoundly in policy making.

This fear is by no means unfounded, but it risks eliding two separate factors: the expanding judicial role in protecting and enforcing rights, and the increasing use of statements of core principles in constitutions. These may have occurred around roughly the same time. But it would be wrong to link them causally. For one thing, it has been historically common for some nations, such as Sweden, Finland, and (still) the Netherlands (1983) (art.120), to have had extensive incorporation of principles into their constitutions while historically denying the courts the capacity to engage in aggressive constitutional judicial review of laws. European constitutions as well as many constitutions from around the world are replete with constitutional principles that may be considered by courts in their exercise of legal interpretation, but which are not meant ordinarily to found legal claims in the courts. And there is notably little litigation over the basic founding principles of constitutions, which, as I have shown in Section 3.3, are widespread. The courtroom activity is rather concentrated on provisions of bills of rights, which were very much intended to be the subject of litigation.

Another approach taken in the courts of countries in Europe is to assert interpretive jurisdiction over the legal terms in question, and thus to recognise that it imposes legal constraints, but to accord a significant interpretive latitude, or a margin of appreciation, or margin of discretion, or to exercise of judicial restraint, when reviewing other institutions' conduct in respect of such a principle (King 2008). This is sometimes called the 'underenforcement of constitutional norms' (Sager 1978). This type of approach is common under the European Convention, in EU law and in the law of the United Kingdom.

This too is a complex problem, and only the sketch of an answer can be furnished. It is a matter on which courts and constitutional framers must proceed cautiously. The role of the judiciary may also depend on the nature of the judicial appointments process, which varies quite radically. The question in each case, of course, will be whether to constitutionally indicate a role for judicial enforcement or restraint. The question is radically contextual. The answer will depend on institutional roles and interrelationships, constitutional text, the extent to which the practice is already embodied in custom, and the nature of the task comprised by the particular mission statement provision at hand. But where the combination of such factors weighs against giving judges a role in interpreting the requirements of the core principles (or presents serious risks of harm), the solution need not be to abandon the idea of mission statement provisions. The role for judges can be calibrated as desired, by adding constitutional indications of intensity of review, interpretive sections or provisions, demarcating certain provisions as non-justiciable (e.g. Ireland, India), by designating some provisions as principles rather than more categorically enforceable rights (as in Part II of the Charter of Fundamental Rights in the European Union) or by giving the judiciary a weak-form review power that can be overridden by a simple legislative majority. Dispensing with the broader political objectives of a non-minimalist constitution is not an obvious solution to concerns over judicial supremacy. Here, critics of judicial supremacy risk overshooting by depriving the constitution of its straightforwardly *political* benefits the fear of overreaching judges.

3.5 CONCLUSION

In brief, I have argued that existing accounts of the purpose and character of written constitutions in a liberal democracy are problematic and incomplete. While the problems with the social contract theory and the concept of a constitution as a limitation on government are reasonably well recognised, Hardin's more developed thesis about coordination for mutual advantage presents new challenges. The coordination thesis can support constitutional conservatism of an unjustifiable kind, and it does not give the legitimating function of constitutions the role they ought to have. It also does not fit a rather large spread of constitutional practice in countries other than the United States.

I examined a companion idea, which is that constitutions can function as mission statements, setting out core political principles that the community accepts as expressions of its constitutive values, and as a guide for decision making and programme for action. It is a companion because it is not meant to articulate the central function of constitutions, but merely one of their important functions. Mission statements appear in statements of general principles, in bills of rights and directive principles of state policy, as well as in ad hoc formulations in various parts of constitutions aiming at particular issues in given polities. The positive social functions these can play include the expressive, guiding, enforcement and legitimation functions. This chapter takes no idealistic perspective on these functions. I do not assert that they make a revolutionary difference in political practice. Yet I do think they make a worthwhile difference in some cases and can do so in others. The upshot of the legitimation role, in particular, is that constitutions should show equal respect for all constituencies, and a corollary of this idea is that the constitution should not be minimalist. It should recognise key disadvantaged constituencies – along ethnic, gender and socio-economic lines – and seek to reflect their interests in the constitution.

The objections that including such mission statements would be destabilising, be pious wishes or entrench elite bargains fall flat for want of convincing evidence. However, the potential for conservative inertia or judicial supremacy is a real danger. These two objections contain enough truth to warrant some responsive constitutional engineering that will need to adjust the terms of the constitution to the requirements of the particular society. But in neither case is the solution to exclude mission statements altogether. Constitutional silence can speak quite loudly.

REFERENCES

Ackerman, B. 1991. *We the People: Foundations*. Cambridge, MA: Belknap Press.
Alexy, R. 2002. *A Theory of Constitutional Rights*. Oxford: Oxford University Press.
Barker, R. 1991. *Political Legitimacy and the State*. Oxford: Clarendon Press.
Beitz, C. R. 1990. *On Political Equality: An Essay in Democratic Theory*. Princeton, NJ: Princeton University Press.
Brennan, Geoffrey and Hamlin, Alan 2006. 'Constitutions as Expressive Documents', in Weingast, B. and Wittman, D. A. (eds.), *The Oxford Handbook of Political Economy*. Oxford: Oxford University Press.
Burton, M. G. and Higley, J. 1987. 'Elite Settlements', *American Sociological Review* **52**: 295.
Canon, B. C. and Johnson, C. A. 1999. *Judicial Policies: Implementation and Impact*. Washington, DC: Congressional Quarterly.

Case C-438/05 *International Transport Workers' Federation* v. *Viking Line ABP* [2007] ECR I-000.

Case C–341/05 *Laval un Partneri Ltd* v. *Svenska Byggnads-arbetareförbundet and others* [2007] ECR I-000 ("Viking and Laval").

Charter of Fundamental Rights of the European Union, 7 December 2000, OJ [2007] C303/1.

Dahl, R. A. 1989. *Democracy and Its Critics*. New Haven, CT: Yale University Press.

　2002. *How Democratic Is the American Constitution?* New Haven, CT: Yale University Press.

Dorf, M. C. 2009. 'The Aspirational Constitution', *George Washington Law Review* 77: 1632.

Dworkin, R. 1978. *Taking Rights Seriously*. Cambridge, MA: Harvard University Press.

　1986. *Law's Empire*. Cambridge, MA: Harvard University Press.

Elkins, Zachary, Ginsburg, Tom and Melton, James 2009. *The Endurance of National Constitutions*. Cambridge: Cambridge University Press.

Elster, J. 2000. *Ulysses Unbound*. Cambridge: Cambridge University Press.

Epp, C. 1998. *After the Rights Revolution: Lawyers, Activists and Supreme Court in Comparative Perspective*. Chicago: University of Chicago Press.

　2010. *Making Rights Real*. Chicago: University of Chicago Press.

Fallon Jr., R. 2005. 'Legitimacy and the Constitution', *Harvard Law Review* 118:1787.

Feeley, M. and Rubin, E. 2000. *Judicial Policy Making in the Modern State: How the Courts Reformed America's Prisons*. Cambridge: Cambridge University Press.

Finnis, J. 1979. *Natural Law and Natural Rights*. Oxford: Clarendon Press.

Fraser, N. and Honneth, A. 2003. *Redistribution or Recognition?: A Political-Philosophical Exchange*. London: Verso.

Gauthier, D. 1986. *Morals by Agreement*. Oxford: Oxford University Press.

Ginsburg, Tom 2013. 'Constitutions as Contract, Constitutions as Charter', in Galligan, Denis and Versteeg, Mila (eds.), *Social and Political Foundations of Constitutions*. Cambridge: Cambridge University Press.

Ginsburg, Tom, Elkins, Zachary and Blount, J. 2009. 'Does the Process of Constitution-Making Matter?' *Annual Review of Law and Social Science* 5: 201.

Griffith, J. A. G. 1979. 'The Political Constitution', *MLR* 42: 1.

Habermas, J. 1975. *Legitimation Crisis*. Boston: Beacon Press.

　1979. *Communication and the Evolution of Society*, Boston: Beacon Press.

　1996. *Between Facts and Norms*. Cambridge: Polity Press.

　2001. 'Why Europe Needs a Constitution', *New Left Review* 11: 5.

Hardin, R. 2013. 'Why a Constitution?', in Galligan, Denis and Versteeg, Mila (eds.), *Social and Political Foundations of Constitutions*. Cambridge: Cambridge University Press.

Hardin, Russell 1999. *Liberalism, Constitutionalism and Democracy*. Oxford: Oxford University Press.

Hart, H. L. A. 1961. *The Concept of Law*. Oxford: Clarendon Press.

Hills, J. 2004. *Inequality and the State*. Oxford: Oxford University Press.

Hirschl, R. 2004. *Towards Juristocracy*. Cambridge, MA: Harvard University Press.

　2010. *Constitutional Theocracy*. Cambridge, MA: Harvard University Press.

Holmes, S. 1995. *Passions and Constraint*. Chicago: University of Chicago Press.

Horowitz, D. 1977. *The Courts and Social Policy*. Washington, DC: Brookings Institution.

Irving, H. 2008. *Gender and the Constitution: Equity and Agency in Comparative Constitutional Design*. Cambridge: Cambridge University Press.

Jacobson, G. 2010. *Constitutional Identity*. Cambridge, MA: Harvard University Press.

Ketcham, R. (ed) 1986. *The Anti-Federalist Papers and the Constitutional Convention Debates*. New York: Signet.

King, A. 2007. *The British Constitution*. Oxford: Oxford University Press.

King, J. 2012. *Judging Social Rights*. Cambridge: Cambridge University Press.

King, J. A. 2008. 'Institutional Approaches to Judicial Restraint', *Oxford Journal of Legal Studies* 28: 409.

Klare, K. 1998. 'Legal Culture & Transformative Constitutionalism', *South African Journal on Human Rights* 14: 146.

Klarman, M. 2004. *From Jim Crow to Civil Rights*. New York: Oxford University Press.

Kymlicka, W. 1995. *Multicultural Citizenship: A Liberal Theory of Minority Rights*. Oxford: Oxford University Press.

Landfried, C. 1995. 'Germany', in Tate, C. N. and Vallinder, T. (eds.), *The Global Expansion of Judicial Power*. Oxford: Oxford University Press.

Langford, M. (ed.) 2009. *Social Rights Jurisprudence: Emerging Trends in International and Comparative Law*. Cambridge: Cambridge University Press.

Laski, H. J. 1925–1926. 'Judicial Review of Social Policy in England', *Harvard Law Review* 39: 836.

Law, David and Versteeg, Mila 2011. 'The Evolution and Ideology of Global Constitutionalism', *California Law Review* 99: 101.

Levinson, S. 2011. 'Do Constitutions Have a Point? Reflections on "Parchment Barriers" and Preambles', in Paul, E. Frankel, Miller, F.D. Jr., and Paul, J. (eds.), *What Should Constitutions Do?* Cambridge: Cambridge University Press.

Lijphart, A. 1999. *Patterns of Democracy: Government Forms and Performance in Thirty-Six Countries*. New Haven, CT: Yale University Press.

Lind, E. A., Kulik, C. T. and Ambrose, M. 1993. 'Individual and Corporate Dispute Resolution: Using Procedural Fairness as a Decision Heuristic', *Administrative Science Quarterly* 38: 224.

Locke, J. 1991 (1690). *Two Treatises of Government* (Laslett, P., ed.) Cambridge: Cambridge University Press.

Madison, J., Hamilton, A. and Jay, J. 1788. (I. Kramnick, ed.) 'The Federalist Papers', in Kramnick, I. (ed.) 1987. *The Federalist Papers*. London: Penguin.

McCann, M. 1994. *Rights at Work: Pay Equity Reform and the Politics of Legal Mobilization*. Chicago: University of Chicago Press.

Moehler, D. C. 2008. *Distrusting Democrats: Outcomes of Participatory Constitution-Making*. Ann Arbor: University of Michigan Press.

Nozick, R. 1974. *Anarchy, State and Utopia*. Oxford: Basil Blackwell.

Ordeshook, P. C. 1993. 'Some Rules of Constitutional Design', *Social Philosophy and Policy* 10(2): 198.

Orgad, L. 2010. 'The Preamble in Constitutional Interpretation', *International Journal of Constitutional Law* 8: 714.

Rasinski, K., Tyler, T. R. and Fridkin, K. 1985. 'Exploring the Function of Legitimacy: Mediating Effects of Personal and Institutional Legitimacy on Leadership Endorsement and System Support', *Journal of Personality and Social Psychology* 49: 386.

Rawls, John 1971. *A Theory of Justice*. Cambridge, MA: Harvard University Press.

1993. *Political Liberalism*. New York: Columbia University Press.

Raz, J. 1979. 'The Functions of Law', in Raz, J. (ed.), *Authority of Law*. Oxford: Oxford University Press.

1986. *The Morality of Freedom*. Oxford: Clarendon Press.

1995. 'Government by Consent', in Raz, J. (ed.). *Ethics in the Public Domain*. Oxford: Clarendon Press.

2001. 'On the Authority and Interpretation of Constitutions: Some Preliminaries', in Alexander, L. (ed.). *Constitutionalism: Philosophical Foundations*. Cambridge: Cambridge University Press.

Reference re Secession of Quebec, [1998] 2 S.C.R. 217 (SCC).

Reich, N. 2008. 'Free Movement v. Social Rights in an Enlarged Union – the Laval and Viking Cases before the ECJ', *German Law Journal* 9: 128.

Rosenberg, G. 1991. *The Hollow Hope: Can Courts Bring About Social Change?* Chicago: University of Chicago Press.

Rousseau, J. J. 1762. *The Social Contract* (trans. Cole, GDH 1993). London: Everyman.

Sager, L. 1978. 'Fair Measure: The Legal Status of Underenforced Constitutional Norms', *Harvard Law Review* 91: 1212.

Samuels, K. 2006. *Constitution Building Processes and Democratization: A Discussion of Twelve Cases Studies*. Geneva: IDEA.

Sarat, A. and Scheingold, A. (eds.) 2010. *Cause Lawyers and Social Movements*. Stanford, CA: Stanford University Press.

Sathe, S. P. 2001. 'Judicial Activism: The Indian Experience', *Washington University Journal of Law & Policy* 6: 29.

Scheingold, S. 1974. *The Politics of Rights: Lawyers, Public Policy and Political Change*. New Haven, CT: Yale University Press.

Scheppele, K. Lane 2003. 'Aspirational and Aversive Constitutionalism: The Case for Studying Cross-Constitutional Influence through Negative Models', *International Journal of Constitutional Law* 1: 296.

Shapiro, M. and Stone Sweet, A. 2002. *On Law, Politics and Judicialization*. Oxford: Oxford University Press.

Stryker, R. 1994. 'Rules, Resources and Legitimacy Processes: Some Implications for Social Conflict, Order and Change', *American Journal of Sociology* 99: 847

Sunstein, C. R. 1995–1996. 'On the Expressive Function of Law', *University of Pennsylvania Law Review* 144: 2021.

'The Perils of Constitution Worship', *The Economist*, 23 September 2010.

Thompson, E. P. 1975. *Whigs and Hunters: Origin of the Black Act*. New York: Pantheon Books.

Tyler, T. 1990. *Why People Obey the Law*. New Haven, CT: Yale University Press.

Tyler, T. R. 1994. 'Governing Amid Diversity: The Effect of Fair Decisionmaking Procedures on the Legitimacy of Government', *Law & Sociology Review* 28: 809.

Vanhala, L. 2011. *Making Rights a Reality? Disability Rights Activists and Legal Mobilization*. Cambridge: Cambridge University Press.

Versteeg, Mila. 2014. 'Unpopular Constitutionalism,' 89 *Indiana Law Journal*.

Voight, S. 2003. 'The Consequences of Popular Participation in Constitutional Choice – toward a Comparative Analysis', in Van Aaken, A., List, C. and Luetget, C. (eds.). *Deliberation and Decision*. Aldershot: Ashgate.

Von Hayek, Friedrich 1960. *The Constitution of Liberty*. London: Routledge.

Waldron, J. 1999. *Law and Disagreement*. Oxford: Oxford University Press.

Weber, M. 1964. *The Theory of Social and Economic Organization* (T. Parsons, ed.). New York: Free Press.

Wolfrum, R. and Groter, R. 1971. *Constitutions of the Countries of the World*. New York: Oxford University Press.

Young, I. M. 1990. *Justice and the Politics of Difference*. Princeton, NJ: Princeton University Press.

4

Transnational Constitutionalism

A Conceptual Framework

Benedikt Goderis and Mila Versteeg

4.1 INTRODUCTION

Constitutions are commonly transported across national borders. In the nineteenth century, a whole generation of Latin American constitutions was copied largely verbatim from the U.S. Constitution, in what Simon Bolivar dubbed a "craze for imitation" (Horowitz 2009: 505; Billias 2009: 105). Around that same time, the founding fathers of the Australian constitution, who reportedly demonstrated a "hypnotic fascination" with the U.S. Constitution, also borrowed from it extensively (Horowitz 2009: 509). Across the globe, the Romanian Constitution of 1848 "faithfully copied" roughly 60 percent of its provisions from the French Constitution (Parau 2013). More than a century later, about thirty former British colonies in African and the Caribbean adopted as their bill of rights what was essentially a carbon copy of the European Convention on Human Rights and Fundamental Freedoms (Parkinson 2007).

Other constitutions reflect a more diverse range of foreign influences. In Ireland, the drafters of the 1922 Constitution extensively studied a range of foreign documents and imported various experimental elements they discovered (Brady 2013). In Eastern Europe, postcommunist constitution-makers drew up lists of foreign constitutions "worthy of emulation" (Howard 1996: 383, 402; Horowitz 2002: 15) and used them as a source of inspiration. Constitution-making in this region, it has been said, was characterized by a "conscious emulation" of the "democratic constitutions of the Western world" (Scheppele 2003: 303; Parau 2013). At this very moment, the

We thank Kevin L. Cope, Tom Ginsburg, Denis Galligan, David Erdos, Binesh Hass, Jeff King, Anne Meuwese, Laurel Miller, Christina Parau, Neil Walker, and participants in the Oxford Workshop on the Social and Political Foundations of Constitutions for helpful comments and suggestions.

democratically elected drafters of the Icelandic constitution are likely surfing the Internet, studying constitutional choices made elsewhere to aid the writing of their new constitution (Meuwese 2013).

In some cases, foreign influences may be subtler and are easily misunderstood by the casual observer. French jurists acquainted Romanian judges with U.S. constitutional law, who, in turn, invented judicial review in a *Marbury v. Madison*-like decision (Parau 2013). In another twist on U.S. constitutional influence, the often celebrated limitations clause from the 1983 Canadian Charter was strongly inspired by U.S. constitutional case law, even though the U.S. Constitution itself is largely devoid of limitations clauses (Jackson 2012). Conversely, the Japanese Constitution – which at first glance appears to be an exclusively U.S. product secretly drafted by General McArthur after the Second World War – actually turned out to reflect Japanese popular opinion fairly accurately (Law 2013).

Regardless of the source of influence, the systematic empirical study of the substance of written constitutions reveals remarkable similarities across countries. In earlier work (2011), we analyzed the written constitutions of 188 countries for the 1946–2006 period and found that an important predictor of whether a country has adopted a particular right is whether certain other countries previously did the same thing. Specifically, we found evidence that constitutional rights diffuse between countries that share the same legal origins, the same religion, a common colonizer, and a common aid donor. Law and Versteeg (2011) show that as a result of these diffusion processes, constitutions are fairly standardized documents that vary along a limited number of underlying dimensions. The existing empirical evidence thus suggests that constitutions, at least in part, are *transnational documents*, shaped by a range of foreign influences.

What explains this standardization of written constitutions? Why do constitution-makers turn abroad for foreign guidance? Who borrows from whom and why? This chapter is an attempt to conceptualize the transnational influences in constitutional design. In particular, it expands the framework introduced in our earlier work to analyze in more detail four different pathways of foreign influence, that is, mechanisms of diffusion, in constitutional design. It does so by discussing both a range of real-world examples and the empirical findings from the quantitative literature on this topic (in particular, Goderis and Versteeg (2011), but also Law and Versteeg (2011), and Elkins, Ginsburg and Simmons (2013)).

The first diffusion mechanism we identify is *coercion*, which suggests that powerful states, like former colonizers and aid donors, push for the adoption of specific constitutional arrangements in less powerful states. The second diffusion mechanism is *competition*, the logic of which suggests that states strategically imitate foreign constitutions in order to attract foreign buyers and investors. The third diffusion mechanism is *learning*, which entails a functional borrowing of constitutional provisions among states that share important preexisting similarities, such as a similar legal system. The last-diffusion mechanism is *acculturation*, the logic of which suggests that states emulate foreign constitutional rules not because they are convinced by the intrinsic merits of these rules, but because they aim to gain international acceptance and legitimacy. These four diffusion mechanisms provide insights into both why constitution-makers might adopt foreign constitutional models and whose models they are most likely to adopt. The claim we make in this chapter, and which we have explored empirically elsewhere, is that these mechanisms produce transnational constitutions, or national constitutions that reflect a range of foreign influences.

This chapter unfolds as follows. It first discusses the two diffusion mechanisms that operate by altering material costs and benefits, that is, coercion and competition. It next discusses diffusion through altered beliefs, or learning. Finally, it discusses diffusion through social benefits and cognitive pressures, that is, acculturation. The chapter concludes by examining the impact of each of these mechanisms on global constitutionalism, and to what extent they are responsible for a global constitutional convergence.

4.2 MECHANISMS OF CONSTITUTIONAL DIFFUSION

To conceptualize the mechanisms of transnational influence in constitution-making, we draw on a rich literature on diffusion, developed in economics, geography, political science, and sociology alike. Diffusion is "the process by which the prior adoption of a trait or practice in a population alters the probability of adoption for the remaining non-adopters" (Strang 1991: 324–325). Put simply, the more actors adopt a particular practice, the more likely that others are to follow. The literature has documented numerous examples of such diffusion, including democracy (Gleditsch and Ward 2006: 911), economic liberalization (Simmons and Elkins 2004: 171), central bank independence (Polillo and Guillén 2005: 1764), and bilateral investment treaties (Elkins et al. 2006: 811). Laws and legal institutions, likewise, have been shown to diffuse, although transnational influences in lawmaking are more commonly studied as "transplantation" in the (small-N) comparative law literature (Twining 2005: 210–213). We ourselves have shown that constitutional rights diffuse across countries (Goderis and Versteeg 2011).

The four diffusion mechanisms that we conceptualize in this chapter – coercion, competition, learning, and acculturation – describe the behavior of "states" in the aggregate. Admittedly, "state" is an abstract entity that in reality consists of a range of different actors, often with diverging interests. It is therefore hard to establish whether the state is learning, competing, acculturating, or being coerced. The same is true for constitution-makers. Constitution-makers comprise numerous actors, such as the constitutional assembly, a technical drafting committee, foreign experts, the legislature, the executive, and, in some cases, the constitutional court. All of these actors may have their own agenda, which may include the objects to expand their institutional mandate (Ginsburg et al. 2009; Cope 2013). At times, moreover, charismatic individuals are involved – like Nelson Mandela in South Africa or Atatürk in Turkey – who are influential beyond their designated institutional role.

In our analysis, we abstract from the particular actors involved in the drafting process, instead focusing on "states" or "constitution-makers." We do so because our goal is to understand how and why norms diffuse from one constitution to the other, rather than to get a full picture of all the different actors and their motivations. The latter would require a range of in-depth case studies of the kind presented in this volume. And even with such studies, it is hard to draw conclusions on whether the involvement of particular actors – ranging from foreign experts to the people as a whole – is associated with particular outcomes (Galligan and Versteeg 2013). When abstracting from the exact players on the constitutional playing field, however, there exist certain overarching motivations for incorporating foreign norms and standards into a constitution, regardless of who is promoting these norms or who is writing the constitution. It is these motivations that this chapter seeks to examine.

4.3 ALTERED MATERIAL PAYOFFS: COERCION AND COMPETITION

The first two diffusion mechanisms discussed in this chapter – coercion and competition – are a function of rational states calculating material costs and benefits. They built on the assumption that states are "rational and self-interested actors that calculate the costs and benefits of alternative courses of actions," and act accordingly (see, e.g., Goldsmith and Posner 2005: 3; Hathaway 2002: 1944). Constitutions, under this logic, are strategic instruments, used to achieve strategic goals (Cooter 2000; Hirschl 2013). When countries borrow from each other's constitution, they do so for strategic reasons.

4.3.1 *Coercion*

If coercion is at work, the content of written constitutions is shaped at least in part by the carrots and sticks of powerful foreign states. Some states, of course, are stronger than others, and when stronger nations exploit power asymmetries to impose their constitutional preferences on weaker nations, constitutional diffusion takes place (Simmons et al. 2006: 790; Goodman and Jinks 2004: 633). Constitutional coercion includes the imposition of constitutional rules by force, but also more subtle incentives and sanctions.

The hardest form of constitutional coercion is the use of military force, or the constitutional version of "gunboat diplomacy." Somewhat less hard is the use of carrots and sticks, or the manipulation of material costs and benefits. An even softer version is what Joseph Nye calls "soft power," whereby states are influential because of the attractiveness of their culture, ideals, and policies, even without the use of force or material pressures (Nye 2004; Simmons et al. 2006: 791). The focus of this subsection is on the harder forms of coercion, "bombs and guns" and "carrots and sticks," but not on (far less tangible) forms of "soft power." The softer forms of coercion are considered as part of the discussion on acculturation (see Dixon and Posner 2011).

There are some well-known examples of the hardest form of constitutional coercion, where constitutions have been imposed upon a nation. Probably most paradigmatic for this scenario are the postcolonial constitutions, or the constitutions drafted as part of the decolonization process. For example, the independence constitutions of Britain's former colonies in Africa and the Caribbean required British consent as a quid pro quo for colonial independence. As part of the negotiations for independence, Britain insisted on the inclusion of a bill of rights modeled after the European Convention of Human Rights (Parkinson 2007: 1–19). To this day, many former British colonies are governed by these "boilerplate" bills of rights (Ginsburg 2013), which were once drafted by the Colonial Office in London. Likewise, the United States staged the 1935 constitution-making process in the Philippines. In 1934, the United States adopted the McGuffie Act, which paved the Philippines' way to colonial independence, but also stated that the new constitution was to include a bill of rights and a republican form of government. Indeed, the resulting 1935 constitution bore a close resemblance to the U.S. Constitution (Billias 2009: 229–233). A similar phenomenon occurred with the Micronesian independence constitution, which was adopted under close supervision of the United States, as recounted in Brian Tamanaha's (2013) contribution to this volume. Similarly, the constitutions of the former colonies of France were deeply influenced by the constitution of the French Fifth Republic (Go 2003: 71, 74). In general, it has been observed that postcolonial states commonly adopted the constitutional model of their former imperial master, thus producing, as one commentator puts it, a "constitutional world of empires" (*ibid.*: 73, 74).

Other examples of constitutional imposition through force – or "hard coercion" – can be found in the context of occupation, in the constitutions drafted after war under the influence of the war victors. According to Fred Schauer, the best example of a "truly imposed" constitution is the Japanese Constitution of 1947. That document, drafted under heavy influence from U.S. occupiers, was "more the contribution of Douglas MacArthur than of internal Japanese decision" (Schauer 2005: 907–908; *but see* Law 2013). Another well-known imposed constitution, the German Basic Law of 1949, was drafted after Germany's defeat in the Second World War in a process created and managed by the occupying powers. Though allowing local input, the occupying powers insisted on a veto power over the final constitution (Elster 1993: 459–460; Schauer 2005: 908). Even the U.S. Constitution, which is often heralded for its democratic nature (see, e.g., Rubenfeld 2004: 1994), contains traces of this type of coercion. In particular, after the American Civil War, the Southern states were denied representation in Congress until they ratified the Thirteenth, Fourteenth, and Fifteenth amendments (Schauer 2005: 908; Harrison 2001: 375). Such coercive pressures in constitution-making under occupation persist to this day. While the 2005 Constitution of Iraq was drafted with local participation, it was drafted "in the shadow of the gun," after the dictatorial regime had been overthrown by an outside power, and in a process staged and dominated by this outside power (Feldman 2005: 858; Katz 2006: 185). Similar coercive pressures were present in the writing of the new constitution of Afghanistan, the constitutions of the republics of the former Yugoslavia, and the constitution of East Timor, which were all drafted in conditions "of de facto or de jure occupation" (Feldman 2005: 858).

But in an age of widespread commitment to democracy, transnational pressures, in most cases, are likely to be subtler than wholesale imposition (Feldman 2005: 858; Schauer 2005: 909). While constitutions like those in Afghanistan and Iraq may be drafted in the shadow of the gun, there is also a widespread commitment to democracy and local participation, producing what Noah Feldman calls the "latest, most sophisticated form of imposed constitutionalism" (Feldman 2005: 858). More often than not, it is carrots and sticks (or material benefits and sanctions) rather than bombs and guns that produce constitutional coercion.

One example of constitutional coercion through material incentives, or carrots and sticks, involves conditioning membership in international organizations on adoption of certain constitutional norms. To become a member of the Council of Europe, for example, prospective members must "accept the principles of rule of law and the enjoyment by all persons within its jurisdiction of human rights and fundamental freedoms" (Statute of the Council of Europe, Article 3). Thus, the benefits of membership are conditional upon averred respect for human rights. Turkey's Bill of Rights has been described as a product of this logic. According to Paul Magnarella (1994: 516), rights commitments in the Turkish Constitution did not result from the traditional values of the Turkish people, but from the ruling elite's calculation that "Turkey's best prospects for economic development and security from Soviet aggression lay in alliances with the West." To secure such alliances, Turkish elites had to commit to constitutional democracy, human rights, and the rule of law (*ibid.*). Likewise, constitution-making in postcommunist Romania was characterized by a widespread borrowing from Western nations because Romanians felt "they had no chance of entering the Council of Europe without a new constitution that was fundamentally different from ... [its predecessor]" (Parau 2013).

Like conditional membership in international organizations, international trade agreements are commonly tied to human rights. The European Union, for instance, does not conclude trade agreements without a human rights clause (Leino 2005: 329). Through such trade agreements, nations may be "forced to be good" (Hafner-Burton 2009). Empirical evidence suggests that human rights clauses in trade agreements do in fact improve the human rights records of the treaty partners (Hafner-Burton 2005: 593). Such trade agreements, moreover, may result in the constitutional incorporation of free market guarantees (Schneiderman 2000). For example, when Mexico acceded to the North Atlantic Free Trade Agreement (NAFTA), it promulgated thirty constitutional amendments to its 1917 Constitution in order to conform to the investment rules of the treaty. Despite widespread popular protest, this move resulted in radical amendment of the economic chapter of the Constitution, including the repeal of a constitutional provision for the redistribution of communal lands (*ibid.*: 764–767).

Perhaps the most important carrots and sticks for constitutional design involve foreign aid and foreign assistance. The past two decades have seen a growing consensus among economists that "good institutions" are crucial to economic growth (North 1990). Without certain institutions, such as secure property rights and an independent judiciary, most economic reform might be in vain. As a result, substantial financial resources have been committed to rule-of-law reforms and "getting the institutions right" (Rodrik 2007: 184). By one estimate, the World Bank has spent $2.9 billion on rule-of-law reforms since the early 1990s (Trubek 2006: 74). This type of rule-of-law assistance often directly affects the constitution (Hirschl 2004: 47). The constitution is instrumental to the protection of property and civil liberties, as well as to the establishment of an independent judiciary, all of which tend to be crucial ingredients for the rule-of-law agenda. It is no surprise, therefore, that foreign aid donors and international organizations are often at the forefront of constitutional reform (Hirschl 2004: 46–47). In the case of the 2005 Iraqi Constitution, for example, it was the representatives of these international organizations, combined with the mixture of neoliberal advocates of the free market, human rights advocates, and conservative religious lobbyists, that promoted Westernized constitutional rights (Feldman 2005; *see also* Jackson 2009: 265).

Foreign aid has also been used as a strategic tool to promote certain laws and policies that the international community deems beneficial. Aid conditionality occurs when aid donors set requirements for foreign aid or loans (Jacoby 2000: 29). Some of these conditions are couched in terms of policy content, such as lowering tariffs and subsidies or devaluating the exchange rate (the "Washington consensus"). But other types of conditionality involve the imitation of institutions that exist elsewhere, such as the adoption of an independent constitutional court (*ibid.*). Human rights have also been part of aid conditionality. In the United States, federal law prohibits the allocation of foreign aid to nations that engage in "gross violations of internationally recognized human rights" (Foreign Assistance

Act, 22 U.S.C. par. 2151(a) (2000)). Empirical research suggests that human rights practices do affect the direction of aid flows (Alesina and Dollar 2000; Svensson 1999; Neumayer 2003).[1]

If aid donors reward good human rights practices – and the empirical evidence suggests they do – then aid recipients face incentives to constitutionally commit to human rights. Foreign aid can also induce a process of constitutional competition: if one aid recipient successfully attracts aid through constitutional reforms, others may follow, in what will be a "race to the top" (Law 2008: 1281, 1292–1293). Bilateral aid donors may even resort to "aid tournaments," explicitly inducing competition among potential aid recipients by offering aid to the contestants that are most successful in implementing certain laws or policies (Gibson et al. 2005). In our earlier work, we find evidence that constitutional rights diffuse among countries with the same aid donors, which suggest that aid donors do in fact shape constitutional design in recipient countries (Goderis and Versteeg 2011).

It makes sense that constitution-drafting states would respond to economic incentives. But conversely, why would powerful states want to affect constitutional arrangements elsewhere? An idealist might suggest that altruism drives their involvement, that constitutional reform, as one commentator put it, is "the gift of freedom from one country and culture to another" (Katz 2006: 184). The realist assumption, however, is that powerful nations are involved in constitutional design elsewhere because it is in their best interest to do so. At the height of the Cold War, for example, the United States and the Soviet Union sought to promote their respective liberal or socialist constitutional arrangements among their allies to secure political loyalty.

Today, powerful states may be involved in constitutional reform abroad in order to promote liberal democracy. Liberal democracy, apart from potential benefits for the democratizing nation, can have global spillover effects in the form of increased global security and trade (Gowa 1999). The link between liberal democracy and global security has its basis in Immanuel Kant's famous "democratic peace" thesis, which holds that democracies do not fight each other. There is now a wealth of international relations scholarship finding empirical support for this thesis (see, e.g., Maoz and Russett 1993: 624). Its straightforward policy implication is that global security can be enhanced by enlarging the number of democracies. The link between liberal democracy and trade has its basis in a related body of international

---

[1] Svensson (1999) and Alesina and Dollar (2000) find that government respect for political and civil rights has a positive impact on allocated aid for some recipient countries but not for others. Neumayer (2003) documents that a higher level of respect for political and civil rights increases allocated *bilateral* aid but that within-country improvements in this respect do not. For personal integrity rights he finds the exact opposite: while improvements in respect for these rights increase *bilateral* aid, a higher level does not. Neumayer (2003) also finds that only improvements in respect for political and civil rights are rewarded with more *multilateral* aid.

relations literature, which finds that democracies enjoy stronger trade relationships, and simply trade more (Oneal and Russett 1997: 270–271; Mansfield et al. 2000: 318). These insights, in fact, constituted a central premise of the Clinton administration's foreign policy, which stressed that "[a]ll of America's strategic interests – from promoting prosperity at home to checking global threats abroad before they threaten our territory – are served by enlarging the community of democratic and free market nations" (the White House 1995, 22, cited in Gowa 1999, 3).

When powerful states promote certain constitutional features such as liberal democracy, they do not necessarily promote their own constitutional arrangements. Take the example of the twentieth-century colonial powers: in some cases, they modeled the postcolonial constitutional landscape after their own, as the United States did in the Philippines and Micronesia (Billias 2009: 229–233). But in other cases, they used some other template, like the United Kingdom, which imposed a bill of rights on its colonies even though it notoriously lacked such a bill of rights itself. The same may be true for aid donors. As an example, the United States may seek to promote rule of law and democratization without propagating the U.S. Constitution as a model. The U.S. Constitution, after all, contains relatively few enumerated rights and includes some esoteric rights like the right to bear arms (Law and Versteeg 2012). Moreover, there is a growing consensus that a strong presidential system, as embodied by the U.S. Constitution, may carry hazards for young democracies, as a strong executive can easily morph into a dictatorship (Skach 2005). For these reasons, U.S. officials may not view their own constitution as an ideal template for young democracies today.

In sum, coercion has two possible outcomes. Constitutions may come to resemble the constitutions of a powerful state. But perhaps more plausibly, the constitutions of coerced nations, all being the products of the same coercive pressures, may come to resemble one another. Indeed, Goderis and Versteeg (2011) find empirical evidence of diffusion among countries with the same aid donor and the same colonizer, but not from aid donor to aid recipient or from colonizer to former colony directly. This finding suggests that foreign aid indeed impacts constitutional design, but that donors do not necessarily impose their own constitutional models.

But while foreign aid has been an important determinant of constitutional design, in recent years, the prudence of a one-size-fits-all approach to institutional reform has increasingly been challenged in development circles (Trubek 2006: 81–94). There is a growing recognition that, as the World Bank has put it, "attempts to transplant formalist rule of law to developing and/or democratizing countries could actually be counter-productive for economic, institutional and political development" and that the "economic impact of a particular set of institutions often depends on context" (*ibid.*). As a result, the notion that constitutions ought to be tailor-made to local circumstances and supported by the people has recently been gaining adherents

(Miller 2010; Ginsburg et al. 2009). It is possible, therefore, that the appetite for promoting constitutional solutions abroad may decrease in the future.

4.3.2 *Competition*

A second diffusion mechanism is constitutional competition (Law 2008). Competition refers to the rivalry between two or more states for material benefits. It is well established that policy choices in one jurisdiction can produce economic externalities in others. Competition is induced when those policy choices affect the flow of economic resources between jurisdictions (Brueckner 2003).

The idea that nations compete for foreign capital is not new: as early as 1776, Adam Smith wrote that "the proprietor of stock is properly a citizen of the world, and is not necessarily attached to any particular country. He would be apt to abandon the country in which he was ... assessed to a burdensome tax, and would remove his stock to some other country where he could either carry on his business or enjoy his fortune more at his ease." Likewise, Karl Marx observed that

> the intellectual creations of individual nations become common property.... The bourgeoisie, by the rapid improvement of all instruments of production, by the immensely facilitated means of communication, draws all, even the most barbarian, nations into civilization.... It compels all nations, on pain of extinction, to adopt the bourgeois mode of production; it compels them to introduce what it calls civilization into their midst, i.e. to become bourgeois themselves. In one word, it creates a world after its own image. (Jacoby 2000: 4, citing Marx)

Let us consider the logic of constitutional competition for economic resources. Where economic resources move freely across borders, countries will act strategically to attract these resources to their jurisdiction. Thus, countries may compete for foreign capital or exports through the adoption of policies or institutions that are attractive to investors and buyers in international markets (Bartolini and Drazen 1997: 139). Such economic competition has been shown to take place through trade liberalization (Simmons and Elkins 2004: 171), the adoption of welfare policies (Figlio et al. 1999: 437–454), the adoption of tax policies (Tiebout 1956), the signing of bilateral investment treaties (Elkins et al. 2006), and even the introduction of democracy (Jensen 2003). In all these cases, the empirical evidence suggests that if a given country adopts a particular policy or institution, its competitors are likely to follow, so as to safeguard their position in export and international capital markets.

David Law has argued that nations may also use their constitution to attract foreign capital, because foreign investors value property and basic human rights. Investors would not dedicate long-time investments to countries where their property may be expropriated. For example, in a recent (and somewhat controversial) trend, multinational corporations increasingly buy farmland in developing countries, particularly in Sub-Saharan Africa, to produce biofuels and increase food supplies.[2] But such land buying, it seems, occurs only in countries where property rights are secure. As one investor puts it, "[w]e only operate in counties where we can have clear land title. If ... we don't have a 99-year lease from the government then we won't operate in that country" (Hunt 2009). In general, secure property rights increase long-term investment because they reduce uncertainty and stabilize expectations (North 1990: 52). In the absence of secure property rights, investors will invest only in projects with a short time horizon or refrain from investment altogether (Furubotn and Pejovich 1972: 1139). It is for these reasons that development assistance is often conditioned on the adoption of property rights, as in the Washington consensus (Stiglitz 2002: 73–74).

Foreign buyers and investors may also be interested in the protection of human rights more broadly. This possibility is less obvious, as it contradicts the more cynical, "classical" view of the cost-conscious capitalist, who favors repressive states with low wages and poor working conditions. Child labor, long working days, and low wages all lower the cost of production, or so the argument goes (Law 2008: 1313). But this classical view is increasingly challenged by new empirical evidence which suggests that foreign buyers and investors actually prefer a high level of respect for basic human rights (Busse and Hefeker 2007: 397–415; Blanton and Blanton 2006; Law 2008: 1314–1315). *Ceteris paribus*, they invest in the countries that respect human rights, for a number of strategic reasons. First, regimes with strong human rights records are typically stable ones. Stable regimes tend to enjoy relatively high levels of popular support, and are not plagued by social clashes and uprising. Instability makes it hard for investors to anticipate relevant future developments that will affect their activities and to calculate the potential returns to their investments. Thus, because of their attachment to stability, investors may favor countries with a strong human rights record (Law 2008: 1317–1318). Second, foreign investors may favor protection of basic civil liberties so that they will be able to attract skilled workers, who typically would not want to work in countries where their basic rights are not secure (*ibid.*: 1321–1342). Third, there are negative reputational effects for foreign buyers and investors who invest in countries with a bad human rights record. Consumers prefer fair trade and reject products manufactured at the expense of human rights. They do not want blood diamonds or clothes manufactured through child labor. For example, when Apple was

---

[2]   The Economist, *Buying Farmland Abroad: Outsourcing's Third Wave* (May 21, 2009).

confronted with a wave of suicides by iPad laborers, it was quick to increase sala-ries.[3] Bad human rights are bad publicity, and bad publicity is costly. Therefore, all things being equal, foreign buyers and investors may favor those countries with a strong human rights record.

If economic capital indeed favors human rights, the constitution may be used to offer attractive bundles of human rights to foreign buyers and investors (Law 2008: 1282, 1307–1342).[4] The fact that a constitution is typically a highly visible legal docu-ment, judicially enforceable and hard to amend, renders it particularly suitable to do so. Constitutional commitments are potentially credible ones and send a strong signal to potential buyers and investors (Farber 2002: 85–94, 98).

Thus, by offering attractive bundles of constitutional rights, governments may attract economic benefits. For example, in Egypt, the autocratic regime realized that its "socialist and nationalist commitments obstructed inflows of capital because investors ... were at risk of expropriation." (Tushnet 2009: 996*accord* Moustafa 2007). As a result, the government created an independent constitutional court authorized to enforce the constitution that included an anti-expropriation guaran-tee. Even when the court exercised its independence to weaken the government's authoritarian control over elections, the government accepted this limit, again because of economic benefits (Moustafa 2007: 67–70, 77–79). The New Zealand bill of rights has also been described as a product of a transition to a neoliberal economic order, and was reportedly adopted with the goal of facilitating large-scale foreign borrowing (Hirschl 2004: 84–88). Likewise, the South African consti-tution embraced judicially enforceable constitutional property rights to "prevent capital flight and to attract foreign investment" (*ibid.*: 95–96).

If constitutional protection of rights attracts foreign investors and buyers, this phe-nomenon may induce constitutional competition among states. If one state reaps economic benefits by strategically offering attractive bundles of constitutional rights, others may follow its example, producing a race to the top. Thus, where governments in the absence of economic competition might have preferred a low rights-equilibrium, competitive pressures push them in a different direction. As a result, constitutional rights may diffuse among economic competitors. Our earlier work explored competi-tion among trade competitors that export to the same export markets, but we did not find evidence that constitutional rights diffuse through such competition. Whether countries use their constitution to compete for foreign direct investment, however, has thus far gone untested for lack of data on foreign direct investment that is specific to certain sectors of the economy (Goderis and Versteeg 2011).

---

[3] The Independent, *Concerns Over Human Costs Overshadows IPad Launch* (May 27, 2010).
[4] The notion that constitutions may be used in economic competition is also developed by Tushnet (2009: 991); Sunstein (1994: 383–384); Howard (1996: 405).

Supreme Court Justice Breyer puts it, foreign law "casts an empirical light on the consequences of different legal solutions to a common problem."[6]

Constitution-drafting has, at times, been described in such terms. For example, Mario Eindauni describes the writing of the 1948 Italian Constitution as an eighteen-month genuine and deliberative learning process. The drafters of the Italian Constitution, he says, intellectually engaged with the constitutional classics: "continuous reference was made in the many thousands of pages of debate to the classical political philosophers from Aristotle to Montesquieu and Rousseau.... The communists called in the authority of George Washington and Benjamin Franklin to weaken the argument for an upper chamber, while the Christian Democrats quoted at length the authority of Stalin to support the thesis that the chambers had to be of equal power" (Eindauni 1948: 662). And the drafters deliberated thoughtfully on foreign practice: "[t]he Bonapartist regimes, the Weimar experiment, and the faith of the French constitutional project of 1946 – all were considered" (*ibid.*). The resulting document reflected "the influence of many lands" (*ibid.*). Likewise, the drafters of the 1922 Irish Free State Constitution conducted a "diligent search" of numerous foreign constitutions, especially the then-new constitutions in Central and Eastern Europe, which were carefully studied to get new insights on how to best "engineer" Irish society (Brady 2013).

However, in most cases, real-world constitutional learning is likely to be limited by imperfect information and cognitive biases that favor the constitutional practices of some countries more than others. Like other policy makers, constitution-makers lack both the information and cognitive capacity to make the best possible choices and necessarily rely on a variety of imperfect heuristics (Elkins and Simmons 2005: 43–44). According to Mark Tushnet, real-world constitution-making is often akin to "bricolage," wherein the constitution "assembled from provisions that a constitution's drafters selected almost at random from whatever happened to be at hand when the time came to deal with a particular problem" (Tushnet 1999: 1285–1301). Because of such limitations, constitution-makers are likely to rely on those systems they are actually familiar with. They will learn from states to which they are somehow "close," or from a "reference-group" of likeminded countries (Rogers 2003:18). As Israeli Supreme Court Justice Barak puts it, only when "the relative social, historical, and religious circumstances create a common ideological basis, it is possible to refer to a foreign legal system for a source of comparison and inspiration" (Barak 2002: 114).

In the comparative law literature, the presence of the common or civil law system has often been singled out as an important determinant for the diffusion of legal

---

[6] Printz v. United States, 521 U.S. 898, 977 (1997) (Breyer, J., dissenting); *but see* Lawrence v. Texas, 539 U.S. 558 (2003) (Scalia, J., dissenting) (arguing that the United States has nothing to learn from "foreign fads and fashions").

rules (Spamann 2010). The common and civil law traditions are themselves a product of foreign influence: the English colonizers have spread the common law system
throughout their empire, while the civil law system has its root in Roman law, which
diffused throughout continental Europe, and was subsequently transplanted to other
parts of the world through the French and Spanish colonial empires. While it is
frequently argued that today constitutional law transcends the traditional boundaries
between common law and civil law systems (Weinrib 2007: 89–90; Tushnet 2009:
985–986), there are reasons to believe that constitution-makers are more likely to
consult the constitutional practices of nations with similar legal systems. From a practical perspective, constitutional designs borrowed from similar legal systems are likely
to "fit" better with existing local legal practice (Berkowitz et al. 2003). In addition, it
has long been argued that countries with similar legal systems hold similar beliefs on
how to protect freedom by constitutional means. Specifically, common law systems
have a long tradition of limiting government through a strong judiciary, while civil
law systems have a more subordinate judiciary and traditionally empower the government to fulfill positive rights and equality rather than to constrain its actions (Hayek
1960; Mahoney 2001; Law and Versteeg 2011). Countries with the same legal origins
also interact more and exchange more information. Common law countries interact
in the Commonwealth, which has a number of formal settings for legal exchange,
most notably the Privy Council (Spamann 2010; Jackson 2009: 40). Commonwealth
countries also receive legal development assistance from the British Institute of
International and Comparative Law (BIICL) and its "commonwealth legal advisory
service" (Spamann 2010). Moreover, students from Commonwealth countries are
often trained in the United Kingdom, where they may qualify for special recognition
such as the Rhodes and other scholarships. Civil law countries also have a number
of forums for legal exchanges. For example, the French National Magistrates School
trains about 3,000 civil law judges per year and the "Organisation Internationale
de la Francophonie" disseminates legal information from civil law systems (*ibid.*).
And whereas students from common law systems traditionally studied in the United
Kingdom, civil lawyers received their legal education in France (*ibid.*). Countries
with the same legal origin thus have a long tradition of exchanging legal materials,
which may also facilitate constitutional exchanges (*ibid.*).

Indeed, in our previous work, we have found evidence that constitutional rights
diffuse among countries that share the same legal origins (Goderis and Versteeg
2011). We found such an effect even when controlling for colonial and linguistic
ties. Law and Versteeg (2011) also find that because of such diffusion, common law
systems and civil law systems have bills of rights that have distinct ideological orientations. Bills of rights in common law systems are "libertarian" in character – that
is, they portray the state as a threat to individual liberty and emphasize judicial
protection of traditional civil and political rights from state interference – while bills

of rights in civil law systems are more "statist" in character and emphasize positive rights and envision an active role for the state in pursuing social welfare (Law and Versteeg 2011).

Of course, the presence of a civil or common law system is not the only source of similarity that may facilitate the spread of constitutional norms across different systems. In our previous work, we not only found evidence that constitution-makers learn from those with whom they share the same legal origins, but also that they follow countries with the same majority religion (Goderis and Versteeg 2011). Future research may uncover additional channels through which learning takes place.

4.5 SOCIAL BENEFITS AND COGNITIVE PRESSURES: ACCULTURATION

A fourth diffusion mechanism is acculturation. Acculturation is "the general process by which actors adopt the behavioral patterns of the surrounding culture" (Goodman and Jinks 2004: 626). The same mechanism has also been described as "emulation," "mimicry" (Meyer and Rowan 1977), "status maximization," "social influence" (Young 2009), and "reputational cascades" (Sunstein and Posner 2006: 161). In a nutshell, the basic idea is that constitution-makers emulate foreign models to obtain social rewards, even when there are no apparent material benefits and they are not persuaded by the content of these models.

Acculturation has its roots in the new institutionalist tradition of organizational sociology. Scholars working in this tradition have demonstrated that organizations routinely follow taken-for-granted models regardless of their functional utility (Meyer and Rowan 1977; DiMaggio and Powell 1983). Models are adopted not because of their functional utility but because of their legitimacy and the social relationships they represent. These insights have been translated to state behavior by the "world polity school" in sociology (see Meyer et al. 1997). The core premise of this school of thought is that "many features of the contemporary nation-state derive from worldwide models constructed and propagated through global cultural and associational models" (*ibid.*: 144–145). States conform to global cultural models not because of their functional utility but because they represent the social norms of the international community, or "legitimate scripts of modern statehood" (Frank et al. 2000: 102–103). This insight is not new: as the philosopher Hegel noted centuries ago, "if a civilized nation lacks in its eyes and the eyes of others a universal and universally valid embodiment in laws, it fails to secure recognition from others" (Hegel et al. 1991: para 39).

Acculturation is different from coercion and competition in that states copy the constitutional provisions of others, not because of *material* cost and benefits but because of *social* rewards and sanctions. To some extent, these social rewards and sanctions are external, as foreign states may try to influence behavior through naming and shaming or back-patting. It is for this reason that acculturation is sometimes seen as a form of "soft-coercion" (Dixon and Posner 2011). But unlike for coercion, the logic of acculturation suggests that states also feel an internal desire to belong to self-identified groups of peers. States conform to the social norms of other states simply to enhance status and legitimacy on the global plane, even when they cannot ascertain that doing so will advantage them materially (Meyer et al. 1997: 145).

States thus conform to global templates, regardless of their content. The content of the adopted template is less important than the social relationship it represents. In this respect, acculturation is also different from learning. Where learning takes place, a message is actively assessed, internalized, and accepted, as a result of which beliefs are altered. With acculturation, laws or policies are adopted, but their underlying logic or underlying norms are not internalized. As a result, outward conformance may be detached from internal acceptance (Goodman and Jinks 2004: 638–656). Thus, acculturation may result in outward conformity (adoption) without private acceptance or corresponding changes in behavior (implementation and compliance) (Goodman and Jinks 2008: 726). The result is a "structural decoupling" between the adopted scripts and actual practices (Goodman and Jinks 2005: 1760). Sociologists have documented numerous examples of such structural decoupling: states adopt environmental policies in the absence of environmental problems (Frank et al. 2000: 96); they adopt social welfare policies without a budget for implementation (Strang and Chang: 1993); they establish state ministries that serve no functional purpose (Kim et al. 2002); and they sign international human rights agreements without intending to comply (Goodman and Jinks 2004: 638–656).

The nature of written constitutions makes constitution-making prone to processes of acculturation. Constitutions are widely acknowledged to have both an instrumental and a more symbolic function. On the one hand, constitutions are functional instruments to design desirable traits like democracy, rule of law, or wealth (see, e.g., Cooter 2000). On the other hand, they are also expressive documents that reflect the nation's highest ideals and values (Versteeg 2013). Commentators commonly surmise that the expressive function steers nations toward constitutional diversity, as different nations have different identities (Tushnet 1999; Breslin 2007; Kreimer 1999: 648–650; Schauer 2005: 912; Jacobsohn 2010). Yet Meyer and Boli-Bennett (1980: 526) argue exactly the opposite: because constitutions are expressive, they can be used to signal conformance to international norms and standards or global constitutional blueprints. Constitutions may express identity, but identity is shaped through a global world polity of nation-states. Thus, under the logic of acculturation, constitutions and bills of rights are "scripts of modernity" and a symbol of modern statehood (Meyer et al. 1997: 148). They are adopted for reasons of external legitimacy, to express international values and to signal conformity to the norms of the international community, not to reflect internal practices.

There are a number of potential examples of constitutional acculturation, that is, where countries have amended their constitutions to secure recognition from the international community. In Japan, for example, the Meiji Restoration of the late nineteenth century led to the adoption of a Western-style cabinet and parliamentary government (Reischauer 1988: 87), in order to secure for Japan "the respect of the Western powers" (*ibid.*) and to convince the rest of the world that Japan was "a modern nation that was the equal of the Western powers, one that would be respected internationally as a modern, 'civilized' society" (Westney 1987: 18–19; see also Law and Versteeg 2011: 1181). A similar logic motivated postcommunist constitutional reform in Romania, where constitution-makers "approached the new constitution instrumentally, with a view to being accepted by their betters" and to convince the world that Romania was "building a democratic polity" (Parau 2013). Likewise, when Iran was writing its new constitution after the revolution of 1979, Khomeini's statements that Iran's republic would be "the same as any other republic in the world" reflected at least a rhetorical commitment to the norms of the international community (Hass 2013). As another example, post-apartheid South Africa illustrates how a former "pariah nation" may elevate its standing in the eyes of the international community by absorbing foreign constitutional ideas (Schauer 2000: 259). According to Heinz Klug, it was the "the emergence of a thin, yet significant international political culture" that explains why a nation in which the majority of citizens had suffered years of oppression under a European legal system adopted a Western liberal constitutional model with a powerful judiciary (Klug 2000: 7). Even though the South African constitution-making process has been praised for its broad and inclusive drafting process, the content of the South African constitution was shaped by international norms, not by local identities.

Processes of acculturation are usually considered to be global in nature. States conform to "global scripts of modernity" that have been institutionalized by a global "world polity" and that result in "global isomorphism" (Goodman and Jinks 2005: 1755, 1758). Various commentators have indeed conceptualized a global constitutional order (de Wet 2006: 51). Philip Bobbitt (2002: 636–637) characterizes world society as currently possessing a "constitution" in the form of the "Peace of Paris" that marked the close of the Cold War. At the heart of this "constitution" is the 1990 Charter of Paris, which "places dramatic emphasis upon democratization and human rights" (*ibid.*; see also Law and Versteeg 2011: 1180). Like the Peace of Paris, international human rights treaties may serve as global models for constitutional design. Especially the International Covenant of Civil and Political Rights and the International Covenant on Economic, Social and Cultural Rights, jointly referred to as "the International Bill of Rights," carry strong normative value. Since these documents reflect norms that are agreed

on and consented to by the international community at large, states that want
to signal conformity to the norms of the international community may enshrine
the rights set forth in these documents into their constitutions (Elkins, Ginsburg,
and Simmons 2013). Anecdotal evidence suggests that constitution-makers have
at times consulted international human rights treaties (Heyns and Viljoen 2001).
At the same time, there exists little evidence that there has been a global constitutional convergence on a single model, or that countries commonly enshrine
treaty models into their constitutions (Law and Versteeg 2012).

Transnational influence through acculturation need not be global. Acculturation
suggests that states influence each other through cultural channels. Scholars associated with the world polity school usually assume that culture is global. But to the
extent acculturation entails conformity to the "behavioral pattern of surrounding
culture," constitutional borrowing may also follow more specific cultural channels.
Culture may differ across countries, and some countries may share more cultural
commonalities than others. As a result, transnational influence may also follow
more specific cultural traits, such as common language or common religion, or
some other measures of culture. Indeed, in our earlier work, we have found that
rights diffuse among countries that share the same religion (Goderis and Versteeg
2011), which might result from acculturation.

4.6 THE END OF CONSTITUTIONAL HISTORY?

If constitutions are shaped by foreign influences, does that mean that the world's
constitutions have converged on a common model? Comparativists have at
times proclaimed that the world has witnessed "the rise of world constitutionalism" (Ackerman 1997: 771–797), which is characterized by "striking similarities"
(Goodin 1996: 223), "a new constitutional paradigm" (Tushnet 2009: 985), "generic
constitutional law" (Law 2005: 662–728), "strange multiplicity" and an "enterprise
of uniformity" (Tully 1995: 58), the breaking down of "traditional boundaries"
(Weinrib 2007: 89–90), "the global convergence of national constitutions" (Yeh
and Chang 2008: 1), and a "world constitution" (Bobbitt 2002: 481–485), just to
name a few.

These alleged growing similarities are often linked to "globalization," or the "cluster
of technological, economic, and political innovations that have drastically reduced the
barriers to economic, political, and cultural exchange" (Law 2008: 1307–1342). In the
face of globalization, constitutional convergence is, in Mark Tushnet's words, simply
"inevitable" (Tushnet 2009). Globalization increases economic interdependence and
fosters constitutional competition (Law 2008). According to some, it has drastically
transformed international politics into a "new world order" where political actors

operate in transnational networks (Slaughter 2005b). Judges fly around the world, meet at international conferences, and are developing a common practice and conception of constitutionalism, as reflected by the growing judicial citations of foreign and international law (Tushnet 2009: 998). Constitution drafters are only a mouse click away from foreign constitutions, which are stored in several online databases. Such observations are further reinforced by Fukuyama's startling prediction that the world has witnessed "the end of history." According to Fukuyama, after the end of the Cold War, a liberal model of constitutional democracy has triumphed over all competing models. This model constitutes, in Fukuyama's words "the end point of mankind's ideological evolution, and the final form of human government, and as such the end of history" (Fukuyama 1992: xi).

The case studies documented in this volume suggest, however, that foreign influences were present also in the eighteenth and nineteenth centuries – before globalization and before the alleged end of history – at the very dawn of modern constitution-making (see, e.g., Parau 2013) yet the nature of foreign influence might have changed. Through globalization, foreign influences have become more complex, and constitutions written today reflect a range of different sources. While early constitutions copied foreign documents (and in particular the French and U.S. Constitutions) wholesale, constitutionmakers today surf the Web, fly in foreign consultants from different continents, and consider numerous foreign documents. It is these kinds of documents that are genuinely transnational.

But the rise of transnational constitutionalism does not necessarily imply that all constitutions have converged on a common model, or that we have witnessed the end of constitutional history. The mechanisms discussed in this chapter suggest that transnational influences are likely to be more complicated, and subtler than is oftentimes suggested in literature. While each of the diffusion mechanisms implicates substantial interdependence among states, they do not necessarily imply that all constitutions are alike.

Under the logic of *coercion*, weaker states will converge upon the models provided by stronger states. In theory, there may be one constitutional hegemon that coerces all others. But more likely, different powerful states may promote different constitutional models. During the Cold War, the U.S. and Soviet Union both tried to attract countries to their respective constitutional ideologies. Or as another example, the influence of the colonial powers was limited to their own colonies, and did not extend to the colonies of other states. Britain's former colonies followed the prescriptions made by Britain, while France's former colonies followed France. Thus, to the extent there exists multiple powers, there will exist multiple models upon which constitutions could converge.

Under the logic of *competition*, constitutional convergence is confined to economic competitors, or states that share the same export markets or compete for the same foreign direct investment. Again, in theory, all states could compete with one another. But in the real world, different countries compete for different types of FDI and for different types of exports. In particular, poor countries with predominantly low-skilled labor will attract different types of FDI than rich countries with mostly high-skilled workers. It seems plausible, for example, that India and South Africa would compete for a clothing factory, while the U.S. and France compete for the Microsoft head office. Similarly, countries that export high-tech luxury goods may face different sorts of competitive pressures than countries that export raw materials, such as crude oil. While some basic rights such as property and basic civil liberties may be attractive to all types of economic capital, there likely exist relevant differences as well, with certain bundles of rights being more attractive to high-skilled workers (Law and Versteeg 2011).

Under the logic of constitutional *learning*, constitutional convergence is likely to be confined to certain "reference groups" of countries that are functionally similar and exchange information (Elkins and Simmons 2005: 42–45). In a world with full and perfect information, learning might have been global, and constitution-makers may have considered the successes and failures of all foreign constitutions equally. However, all available evidence suggests that this type of learning is limited by information constraints, and that states consider the constitutional arrangements they are actually familiar with, or that appear to be particularly relevant, such as the arrangements of countries with a similar legal system.

It is only under the logic of *acculturation* that one would expect constitutional convergence to be global. Even without a genuine learning, states may be acculturated into the constitutional norms of world culture.

The existing empirical evidence does not lend support for the claim that the world has witnessed a global constitutional convergence. In our study of the diffusion of 108 rights across 188 countries and a 61-year time period, we found no evidence of global diffusion (Goderis and Versteeg 2011). Instead, we found that diffusion is confined to particular groups of countries only. Specifically, we found evidence of diffusion among countries that share a common aid donor or a common colonizer, which suggests that constitutions are affected by coercive pressures from aid donors and former colonizers. We also found that countries borrow from countries that share the same religion and the same legal origin, which suggests that constitution-makers learn through legal and religious ties. In sum, our study suggests that while transnational influences are widespread, they are confined to certain groups of countries. In some cases, diffusion is even confined to particular types of rights only. For example, we found that negative liberty rights are borrowed from aid donors, whereas socioeconomic rights diffuse through trade relationships, and fair trial rights diffuse through export competition only (Goderis and Versteeg 2011). These findings further reveal that diffusion is a retail process, whereby bits and pieces are borrowed from different countries. Convergence, by contrast, is a whole-sale process, whereby entire constitutional orders become more alike. Along similar lines, Law and Versteeg (2011) find that while constitutions are fairly standardized, they vary (1) in the number of rights they enshrine and (2) in their ideological character, with some constitutions being more libertarian than others. In sum, while there is substantial evidence that modern constitutions are transnational constitutions – shaped by foreign influences and varying along a limited number of underlying dimensions – there is no evidence of a global constitutional convergence.

4.7 CONCLUSION

This chapter has conceptualized in some detail four different mechanisms through which constitutional provisions diffuse: coercion, competition, learning, and acculturation. Its central claim is that through such diffusion mechanisms, modern-day constitutions have become transnational constitutions. This claim is supported by in-depth case studies of the kind presented in this volume (Parau 2013; Tamanaha 2013; Brady 2013; Cope 2013). It is also supported by a number of quantitative studies that have documented transnational influences in constitutional design (Goderis and Versteeg 2011; Law and Versteeg 2011). However, at the time of this writing, some questions still remain unanswered and await further research.

First, there is only limited research on how foreign norms interact with indigenous values. Constitutions are unlikely to be entirely transnational; imported norms blend with national values, as proclaimed in preambles, for example (King 2013). Moreover, it is possible that some constitutional features are immune from diffusion altogether. While there is evidence that constitutional rights diffuse, it is not a priori clear whether the same is true for the power structures defined in the constitution. To illustrate, the 2011 South Sudanese bill of rights was a transnational document, drafted with strong involvement of foreign experts, but the structural part of the constitution was more an indigenous national product, producing what Kevin Cope calls an "intermestic constitution" that blends international and domestic elements (Cope 2013). Future research may uncover how foreign norms relate to domestic values, and if and how they interact.

Second, while there is evidence to suggest that modern constitutions are transnational documents, it is not currently clear whether their subsequent interpretation is also affected by foreign norms and standards. In the case of Micronesia, not only was the Micronesian Constitution modeled on the U.S. Constitution, but its subsequent interpretation also turned out to be a borrowing exercise from U.S. constitutional law (Tamanaha 2013). In other cases, constitutional courts may domesticate foreign elements by interpreting them in light of national values and traditions, as was arguably the case in Japan (Law 2013). Anecdotal evidence suggests that constitutional courts commonly rely on foreign case law in interpreting the constitution (Slaughter 2005a). Where courts are citing foreign law, they may be engaged in the same processes as constitution-makers: they may learn, compete, or acculturate. While courts are rarely forced to take account of foreign law when interpreting their constitution, they may be "persuaded" by foreign decisions and decide to incorporate them into their own decisions as part of a learning process (Slaughter 2005a). Alternatively, judicial borrowing might be part of a process of acculturation, whereby courts are simply nose counting and following the common denominator in order to seek international approval (Young 2009). Judges may even be engaged in competition and cite foreign law to ease cross-border transactions (Sunstein and Posner 2006). The framework provided in this chapter might guide future research into judicial citations of foreign law.

Finally, we have little knowledge on if and how transnational elements in the constitution affect its operation in practice. Intuitively, we may think that the more foreign the constitutional norms are, the harder they will be to domesticate. The comparative law literature long found that transplanted laws are less effective in their new environment than in their old one (Berkowitz et al. 2003). To illustrate, the bill of rights in the Nigerian independence constitution modeled after the European Convention on Human Rights and Fundamental Freedoms was plainly less effective in Nigeria than it was in Europe. Specifically, its disregard for the ethnic tensions and persistent poverty in Nigerian society likely contributed to its failure four years later, with the outbreak of a bloody civil war (Parkinson 2013). The framework provided in this chapter provides some tentative insights into the question whether transnational influences negatively impact the subsequent operation of rules. Specifically, whether or not transnational influences undermine the effectiveness of the constitutional document is likely to depend on which diffusion mechanism was at work. If constitutional borrowing reflects a genuine learning, constitution-makers carefully assess foreign norm and decide whether these might offer a solution to domestic problems. Foreign constitutional provisions adopted through such a learning process may do fairly well in their new context. But transnational elements in constitutions could also signal an unthinking emulation of seemingly modern and legitimate norms, or a constitutional imposition on unwilling recipients. Constitutions that are written for an international audience or that are simply dictated by powerful external actors may be less likely to be effective in practice. In this latter scenario, it remains to be seen whether "the enlightenment hope of written constitutions" (Ackerman 1997: 772) is not in fact a false dawn.

REFERENCES

Ackerman, Bruce 1997. 'The rise of world constitutionalism', *Virginia Law Review* **83**: 771–797.

Alesina, Alberto and Dollar, David 2000. 'Who gives foreign aid to whom and why?' *Journal of Economic Growth* **5**: 33–63.

Barak, Aharon 2002. 'Foreword: A judge on judging: The role of a supreme court in a democracy', *Harvard Law Review* **116**: 16–162.

Bartolini, Leonardo and Drazen, Allan 1997. 'Capital account liberalization as signal', *American Economic Review* **87**: 138–154.

BBC News 2010. 'Turkish reform vote gets Western backing', *BBC News*, September 13. Available at http://www.bbc.co.uk/news/world-europe-11279881.

Berkowitz, Daniel, Pistor, Katharina, and Richard, Jean-Francois 2003. 'Economic development, legality, and the transplant effect', *European Economic Review* **47**: 165–195.

1995. 'Incumbent behavior: vote-seeking, tax-setting, and yardstick competition', *American Economic Review* **85**: 25–45.

Billias, George Allen 2009. *American constitutionalism heard around the world, 1776–1989: A global perspective.* New York: New York University Press.

Blanton, Shannon L. and Blanton, Robert G. 2006. 'Human rights and foreign direct investment', *Business and Society* **45**: 464–485.

Bobbitt, Philip 2002. *The shield of Achilles: War, peace, and the course of history.* London: Penguin.

Boli-Bennett, John and Meyer, John W. 1980. 'Constitutions as ideology', *American Sociological Review* **45**: 525–527.

Brady, Paul 2013. 'Social, political and philosophical foundations of the Irish constitutional order', in Denis Galligan and Mila Versteeg (eds.), *Social and political foundations of constitutions.* Cambridge: Cambridge University Press.

Breslin, Beau 2007. *From words to worlds: Exploring constitutional functionality.* Baltimore: Johns Hopkins University Press.

Brooks, Sarah M. 2005. 'Interdependent and domestic foundations of policy change: The diffusion of pension privatization around the world', *International Studies Quarterly* **49**: 273–294.

Brueckner, Jan K. 2003. "Strategic Interaction Among Governments: An Overview of Empirical Studies." *International Regional Science Review* **26**:175–88.

Busse, Matthias and Hefeker, Carsten 2007. 'Political risk, institutions and foreign direct investment', *European Journal of Political Economy* **23**: 397–415.

Cooter, Robert D. 2000. *The strategic constitution.* Princeton, NJ: Princeton University Press.

Cope, Kevin L. 2013. 'South Sudan's dualistic constitution', in Denis Galligan and Mila Versteeg (eds.), *Social and political foundations of constitutions.* Cambridge: Cambridge University Press

DiMaggio, Paul J. and Powell, Walter W. 1983. 'The Iron Cage revisited: Institutional isomorphism and collective rationality in organizational fields', *American Sociological Review* **48**: 147–160.

Dixon, Rosalind and Posner, Eric A. 2011 'The limits of constitutional convergence', *Chicago Journal of International Law* **11**: 399–423.

Eindauni, Mario 1948. 'The constitution of the Italian republic', *American Political Science Review* **42**: 661–676.

Elkins, Zachary, Guzman, Andrew T. and Simmons Beth A. 2006. 'Competing for capital: The diffusion of bilateral investment treaties: 1960–2000', *International Organization* 60: 811–846.

Elkins, Zachary and Simmons, Beth A. 2005. 'On waves, clusters and diffusion: A conceptual framework', *Annals of the American Academy of Political and Social Science* 598: 33–51.

Elkins, Zachary, Ginsburg, Tom and Simmons, Beth A. 2013. *'Getting to Rights: Treaty Ratification, Constitutional Convergence, and Human Rights Practice'*, *Harvard Journal of International Law* 54: 61–94.

Elster, Jon 1993. 'Constitutional bootstrapping in Philadelphia and Paris', *Cardozo Law Review* 14: 549–575.

Etzioni, Amitai 2000. 'Social norms: Internalization, persuasion and history', *Law and Society Review* 34: 157–178.

Farber, Daniel A. 2002. 'Rights as signals', *Journal of Legal Studies* 31: 83–98.

Feldman, Noah 2005. 'Imposed constitutionalism', *Connecticut Law Review* 37: 857–889.

Figlio, David N., Kolpin, Van W., and Reid, William E. 1999. 'Do states play welfare games?' *Journal of Urban Economics* 46: 437–454.

Frank, David J., Hironaka, Ann, and Schofer, Evan 2000. 'The nation-state and the natural environment over the twentieth century', *American Sociological Review* 65: 96–116.

Fukuyama, Francis 1992. *The end of history and the last man.* London: Penguin.

Furubotn, Eirik and Pejovich, Svetozar 1972. 'Property rights and economic theory: A survey of recent literature', *Journal of Economic Literature* 10: 1137–1162.

Galligan, Denis and Versteeg, Mila (eds.) 2013. *The social and political foundations of constitutions.* Cambridge: Cambridge University Press.

Gibson, Clark C., Andersson, Krister, Ostrom, Elinor, and Shivakumar, Sujai 2005. *The Samaritan's dilemma: The political economy of aid allocation.* New York: Oxford University Press.

Ginsburg, Tom 2013. 'Constitutions as contract, constitutions as charter', in Denis Galligan and Mila Versteeg (eds.), *Social and political foundations of constitutions.* Cambridge: Cambridge University Press.

Ginsburg, Tom, Elkins, Zachary, and Blount, Justin 2009. 'Does the process of constitution-making matter?' *Annual Review of Law and Social Science* 5: 201–223.

Gleditsch, Kristian Skrede and Ward, Michael D. 2006. 'Diffusion and the international context of democratization', *International Organization* 60: 911–933.

Go, Julian 2003. 'A globalizing constitutionalism? Views from the postcolony, 1945–2000', *International Sociology* 18: 71–95.

Goderis, Benedikt and Versteeg, Mila 2011. *Transnational Constitutions.* Paper presented at the 6th Annual Conference on Empirical Legal Studies, Chicago. Available at http://papers.ssrn.com/sol3/papers.cfm?abstract_id=1865724.

Goldsmith, Jack L. and Posner, Eric A. 2005. *The limits of international law.* New York: Oxford University Press.

Goodin, Robert E. 1996. 'Designing constitutions: The political constitution of a mixed commonwealth', in Bellamy, Richard and Castiglione, Dario (eds.), *Constitutionalism and transformation: European and theoretical perspectives.* Oxford: Blackwell, pp. 223–234.

Goodman, Ryan and Jinks, Derek 2004. 'How to influence states: Socialization and international human rights law', *Duke Law Journal* 54: 621–703.

2005. 'Towards an institutional theory of sovereignty', *Stanford Law Review* 55: 1749–1788.

2008. 'Incomplete internalization and compliance with human rights law', *European Journal of International Law* 19: 725–748.

Gowa, Joanne S. 1999. *Ballots and bullets: The elusive democratic peace.* Princeton, NJ: Princeton University Press.

Gray, Virginia 1973. 'Innovation in the states: A diffusion study', *American Political Science Review* 67: 1174–1185.

Haas, Peter M. 1992. 'Introduction: Epistemic communities and international policy coordination', *International Organization* 46: 1–35.

Hafner-Burton, Emilie M. 2005. 'Trading human rights: How preferential trade agreements influence government repression', *International Organization* 59: 593–629.

2009. *Forced to be good: Why trade agreements boost human rights.* Ithaca, NY: Cornell University Press.

Harrison, John 2001. 'The lawfulness of the reconstruction amendments', *University of Chicago Law Review* 68: 375–462.

Hass, Binesh 2013. 'The juristic republic of Iran', in Galligan, Denis J. and Versteeg, Mila (eds.), *Social and Political Foundations of Constitutions.* Cambridge: Cambridge University Press

Hathaway, Oona A. 2002. 'Do human rights treaties make a difference?' *Yale Law Journal* 111: 1935–2041.

Hayek, Friedrich A. 1960. *The constitution of liberty.* Chicago: University of Chicago Press.

Hegel, Georg Wilhelm Friedrich, Wood, Allen W. and Nisbet, Hugh Barr 1991 (1820). *Elements of the philosophy of right.* Cambridge: Cambridge University Press.

Heyns, Christoph & Viljoen, Frans 2001. 'The impact of the United Nations human rights treaties on the domestic level', *Human Rights Quarterly* 23: 483–535.

Hirschl, Ran 2004. *Towards juristocracy: The origins and consequences of the new constitutionalism.* Cambridge, MA: Harvard University Press.

2013. 'The strategic foundations of constitutions', in Galligan, Denis and Versteeg, Mila (eds.), *Social and political foundations of constitutions.* Cambridge: Cambridge University Press.

Horowitz, Donald L. 2002. 'Constitutional design: Proposals versus processes', in Reynolds, Andrew (ed.), *The architecture of democracy.* New York: Oxford University Press, pp. 15–36.

2009. 'The Federalist abroad in the world', in Shapiro, Ian (ed.), *The Federalist Papers.* New Haven, CT: Yale University Press, pp. 502–532.

Howard, A. E. Dick 1996. 'The indeterminacy of constitutions', *Wake Forest Law Review* 31: 383–402.

Hunt, Katie 2009. 'Africa investment sparks land-grab fear', *BBC News*, August 5. Available at http://news.bbc.co.uk/2/hi/business/8150241.stm.

Jackson, Vicki C. 2009. *Constitutional engagement in a transnational era.* New York: Oxford University Press.

2012. 'Comment on Law and Versteeg', *New York University Law Review* 87: 2102–2117.

Jackson, Vicki C. and Tushnet, Mark 1999. *Comparative constitutional law.* New York: Foundation Press.

Jacobsohn, Gary Jeffrey 2010. *Constitutional identity.* Cambridge, MA: Harvard University Press.

Jacoby, Wade 2000. *Imitation and politics*. Ithaca, NY: Cornell University Press.

Jensen, Nathan M. 2003. 'Democratic governance and multinational corporations: Political regimes and inflows of foreign direct investment', *International Organization* 57: 587–616.

Kahneman, Daniel 2002. *Maps of bounded rationality: A perspective on intuitive judgment and choice*. Nobel Prize Lecture. Available at http://neuroeconomics-summerschool. stanford.edu/pdf/kahneman1.pdf.

Katz, Stanley N. 2006. 'Democratic constitutionalism after military occupation; Reflections on the United States' experience in Japan, Germany, Afghanistan and Iraq', *Common Knowledge* 12: 181–196.

Kim, Young S., Jang, Yong Suk, and Hwang, Hokyu 2002. 'Structural expansion and the costs of global isomorphism: A cross-national study of ministerial structure, 1950–1990', *International Sociological Review* 17: 481–503.

King, Jeff 2013. 'Constitutions as mission statements', in Galligan, Denis and Versteeg, Mila (eds.), *Social and political foundations of constitutions*. Cambridge: Cambridge University Press.

Klug, Heinz 2000. *Constituting democracy: Law, globalism and South Africa's political reconstruction*. Cambridge: Cambridge University Press

Kreimer, Seth F. 1999. 'Invidious comparisons: Some cautionary remarks on the process of judicial borrowing', *University of Pennsylvania Journal of Constitutional Law* 1: 640–650.

Ladha, Krishna K. 1992. 'The Condorcet jury theorem, free speech and correlated votes', *American Journal of Political Science* 36: 617–634.

Law, David S. 2005. 'Generic constitutional law', *Minnesota Law Review* 89: 652–742.

   2008. 'Globalization and the future of constitutional rights', *Northwestern Law Review* 102: 1277–1350.

   2013. 'The myth of imposed constitution', in Galligan, Denis and Versteeg, Mila (eds.), *Social and political foundations of constitutions*. Cambridge: Cambridge University Press.

Law, David S. and Versteeg, Mila 2011. 'The evolution and ideology of global constitutionalism', *California Law Review* 99: 1163–1257.

   2012. 'The declining influence of the U.S. constitution', *New York University Law Review* 87: 763.

   2013. 'Sham constitutions', *California Law Review* 101: 863–952.

Leino, Päivi 2005. 'European universalism? The EU and human rights conditionality', *Yearbook of European Law* 24: 329–383.

Mahoney, Paul G. 2001. 'The common law and economic growth: Hayek might be right', *Journal of Legal Studies* 30: 503–525.

Magnarella, Paul J. 1994. 'The comparative constitutional law enterprise', *Willamette Law Review* 30: 509–532.

Mansfield, Edward D., Milner, Helen V., and Rosendorff, B. Peter 2000. 'Free to trade: Autocracies, democracies, and international trade', *American Political Science Review* 94: 305–321.

Maoz, Zeev and Russett, Bruce 1993. 'Normative and structural causes of peace, 1946–1986', *American Political Science Review* 87: 624–638.

Meuwese, Anne 2013. 'Popular constitution-making: The case of Iceland', in Galligan, Denis and Versteeg, Mila (eds.), *Social and political foundations of constitutions*. Cambridge: Cambridge University Press.

Meyer, John W., Boli, John, Thomas, George, and Ramirez, Francisco 1997. 'World society and the nation-state', *American Journal of Sociology* **103**: 144–181.

Meyer, John W. and Rowan, Brian 1977. 'Institutionalized organizations: Formal structure as myth and ceremony', *American Journal of Sociology* **83**: 340–363.

Michelman, Frank I. 2004. 'Reflection', *Texas Law Review* **82**: 1737–1761.

Miller, Laurel E. (ed.) 2010. *Framing the state in times of transition: Case studies in constitution making*. Washington, DC: United States Institute of Peace Press.

Moustafa, Tamir 2007. *The struggle for constitutional power: Law, politics and economic development in Egypt*. Cambridge: Cambridge University Press.

Neumayer, Eric 2003. 'Is respect for human rights rewarded? An analysis of total bilateral and multilateral aid flows', *Human Rights Quarterly* **25**: 510–527.

North, Douglass C. 1990. *Institutions, institutional change, and economic performance*. Cambridge: Cambridge University Press.

Nye, Joseph S. Jr. 2004. *Soft power: The means to success in world politics*. New York: Public Affairs.

Oneal, John R. and Russett, Bruce M. 1997. 'The classic liberals were right: Democracy, interdependence and conflict, 1950–1985', *International Studies Quarterly* **41**: 267–294.

Parau, Christina 2013. 'The transnational constitution: Eastern elites in search of a Western ideal', in Galligan, Denis and Versteeg, Mila (eds.), *Social and political foundations of constitutions*. Cambridge: Cambridge University Press.

Parkinson, Charles 2007. *Bills of rights and decolonization: The emergence of domestic human rights instruments in Britain's overseas territories*. Oxford: Oxford University Press.

Parkinson, Charles H. 2013. 'The social and political foundations of the Nigerian constitution', in Galligan, Denis and Versteeg, Mila (eds.), *Social and political foundations of constitutions*. Cambridge: Cambridge University Press.

Polillo, Simone and Guillén, Mauro F. 2005. 'Globalization pressures and the state: The worldwide spread of central bank independence', *American Journal of Sociology* **110**: 1764–1802.

Posner, Eric A. and Sunstein, Cass R. 2006. 'The law of other states', *Stanford Law Review* **59**: 131–180.

Reischauer, Edwin O. 1988. *The Japanese today: Change and continuity*. Cambridge, MA: The Belknap Press of Harvard University Press.

Ritchie, David T. 2004. 'Critiquing modern constitutionalism', *Appalachian Journal of Law* **3**: 37–49.

Rodrik, Dani 2007. *One economics, many recipes*. Princeton, NJ: Princeton University Press.

Rogers, Everett M. 2003. *Diffusion of innovations*, 5th edition. New York: Free Press.

Rubenfeld, Jed 2004. 'Commentary: Unilateralism and constitutionalism', *New York University Law Review* **79**: 1971–2028.

Schauer, Frederick 2000. 'The politics and incentives of legal transplantation', in Nye, Joseph S. Jr. and Donahue, John D. (eds.), *Governance in a globalizing world*. Washington, DC: Brookings Institute Press, pp. 253–270.

2005. 'On the migration of constitutional ideas', *Connecticut Law Review* **37**: 907–919.

Scheppele, Kim Lane 2003. 'Aspirational and aversive constitutionalism: The case for studying cross-constitutional influence through negative models', *International Journal of Constitutional Law* **1**: 296–324.

Schneiderman, David 2000. 'Investment rules and the new constitutionalism', *Law and Social Inquiry* **25**: 757–787.

Schor, Miguel 2008. 'Mapping comparative judicial review', *Washington University Global Studies Law Review* 7: 257–287.

Simmons, Beth A., Dobbin, Frank, and Garrett, Geoff 2006. 'Introduction: The international diffusion of liberalism', *International Organization* 60: 781–810.

Simmons, Beth A. and Elkins, Zachary 2004. 'The globalization of liberalization: Policy diffusion in the international political economy', *American Political Science Review* 98: 171–189.

Skach, Cindy 2005. *Borrowing constitutional designs: Constitutional law in Weimar Germany and the French Fifth Republic*. Princeton, NJ: Princeton University Press.

Slaughter, Anne-Marie 2003. 'A global community of courts', *Harvard International Law Journal* 44: 191–219.

2005a. 'A brave new judicial world', in Ignatieff, Michael (ed.), *American exceptionalism and human rights*. Princeton, NJ: Princeton University Press, pp. 277–303.

2005b. *New world order*. Princeton, NJ: Princeton University Press.

Somek, Alexander 1998. 'The deadweight of formulae: What might have been the second Germanization of American Equal Protection review', *University of Pennsylvania Journal of Constitutional Law* 1: 284–324.

Spamann, Holger 2010. 'Contemporary legal transplants: Legal families and the diffusion of (corporate) law', *Brigham Young University Law Review* 2009: 1813–1877.

Stiglitz, Joseph E. 2002. *Globalization and its discontents*. London: Penguin.

Strang, David 1991. 'Adding social structure to diffusion models: An event history framework', *Sociological Methods and Research* 19: 324–353.

Strang, David and Chang, Patricia Mei Yin 1993. 'The International Labor Organization and the welfare state: Institutional effects on national welfare spending, 1960–80', *International Organization* 47: 235–262.

Sustein, Cass R. 1994. 'On property and constitutionalism', in Rosefeld, Michel (ed.), *Constitutionalism, identity, difference and legitimacy: Theoretical perspectives*. Durham, NC: Duke University Press, pp. 383–412.

2003. 'Why conditional aid does not work and what can be done about it?' *Journal of Development Economics* 70: 381–402.

Svensson, Jakob. 1999. "Aid, Growth and Democracy." *Economics and Politics* 11(3):275–297.

Tamanaha, Brian Z. 2013. 'A battle between law and society in Micronesia,' in Galligan, Denis and Versteeg, Mila (eds.), *Social and political foundations of constitutions*. Cambridge: Cambridge University Press.

Tiebout, Charles M. 1956. 'A pure theory of local public expenditures', *Journal of Political Economy* 64: 416–424.

Trubek, David M. 2006. 'The rule of law in development assistance: Past, present and future', in Trubek, David M. and Santos, Alvaro (eds.), *The new law and economic development*. New York: Cambridge University Press, pp. 74–94.

Tully, James 1995. *Strange multiplicity: Constitutionalism in an age of diversity*. Cambridge: Cambridge University Press.

Tushnet, Mark 1999. 'The possibilities of comparative constitutional law', *Yale Law Journal* 108: 1225–1309.

2009. 'The inevitable globalization of constitutional law', *Virginia Journal of International Law* 49: 985–1006.

Twining, William 2005. 'Social science and diffusion of law', *Journal of Law and Society* 32: 203–240.

Versteeg, Mila. 2014. 'Unpopular Constitutionalism.' *Indiana Law Journal* (forthcoming)

Weinrib, Lorraine 2007. 'The postwar paradigm and American exceptionalism', in Choudhry, Sujit (ed.), *The migration of constitutional ideas*. Cambridge: Cambridge University Press, pp. 84–112.

Westney, D. Eleanor 1987. *Imitation and innovation: The transfer of western organizational patterns to Meiji Japan*. Cambridge, MA: Harvard University Press.

Wet, Erika de 2006. 'The international constitutional order', *International and Comparative Law Quarterly* **55**: 51–76.

The White House 1995. *A national security strategy of engagement and enlargement.* Washington, DC: The White House.

Yeh, Jiunn-Rong and Chang, Wen-Chen 2008. 'The emergence of transnational constitutionalism: Its features, challenges and solutions', *Penn State International Law Review* **27**: 89–124.

Young, H. Peyton 2009. 'Innovation diffusion in heterogeneous populations: Contagion, social influence, and social learning', *American Economic Review* **99**: 1899–1924.

5

The People, the Constitution, and the Idea of Representation

Denis J. Galligan

5.1 INTRODUCTION

Modern constitutions are presented as a declaration by the people as to how they are to be governed. By "the people" I mean the members of a society as a collective entity. In accordance with classic republican ideas, society consists of free men and women, where being free entails being self-governing. The concept of the people needs further elaboration and may not be as straightforward as I make it sound, but the definition is enough for the purpose of this essay, which is concerned with how the people, as distinct from the notion of individual persons, are presented in constitutions. Although constitutions vary from one nation to another, a study of a wide selection shows a recurring pattern in their general structure and in the way the people are depicted. Constitutions create the institutions of government, prescribe the process for appointing officials, specify their powers, and define their limits. Constitutions normally go on to dictate the relationship between the organs of government and individual persons and groups, sometimes expressing the relationship in terms of rights, at other times simply as limits on government. The people typically make three appearances in the constitution: (1) to declare that the constitution has been made by the people; (2) to provide for the election of representatives; and (3) in some cases to vote on amendments to the constitution.[1] Having created government and defined its powers, the people leave the conduct of government to their representatives and to officials appointed by the representatives, although some constitutions allow for direct action by the people.

The people generally retain for themselves no constitutional role in the conduct of government or in supervising government to ensure it acts in their best interests.

The author wishes to thank David Robertson of St. Hugh's College Oxford for comments on an earlier draft.

[1] For a detailed analysis of sixty constitutions, being the constitutions of nations toward the democratic end of a scale from democratic to autocratic, see Galligan (2013b).

It is not as if this is the only imaginable form, as if the imperatives of liberty, democracy, and rights, as well as effective government or any other factors, necessarily result in the people being presented in this way. Why, we might ask, do the people's constitutions not confer on the people more power, more engagement in government, more control over government? If all political power derives from the people, why do they hand it over to legislators, executives, and administrators, even judges, who, once in power, are beyond their control? Why have we come to accept that delegating power to others, whether elected representatives or appointed officials, is the only way to gain effective government? Robert Dahl contends that I it was perfectly obvious to the Framers of the U.S. constitution, as well as to us, that a republican government would have to be a *representative* government (Dahl 2001). But surely it is not so obvious. Representative government is not simply a practical means for dealing with a technical problem, a compromise of stronger forms of democracy in order to ensure effective government. On the contrary, representative government derives from, and is central to, a definite and distinct form of constitutionalism, which is the product of ideas and events in certain societies, England, France, and the United States especially. Social factors, ways of understanding the world, and ideals and visions for the future combine to produce a very particular understanding of the nature of government, and of how a nation can best govern itself, from which follows a view of constitutions, their purposes, and their contents.

The aim of this essay is to explain this paradigm of modern constitutions and the place of the people within them. My assumption is that, in understanding the social world and the role of law within it, the constitution matters, matters in the sense that it influences actions. It follows that how the people are presented in the constitution, the place assigned to them, also matters. It is enough for my purposes that they matter, even if how much they matter is uncertain. This essay is part of a program of research and discussion whose purpose is to examine the connections between constitutions and their social and political foundations. Since the place of the people sketched earlier is common to modern constitutions – in fact, is among their distinguishing features – then its investigation should reveal something of interest about constitutions and their social foundations. A social account of the people in constitutions has three parts: (1) what constitutions say about the people; (2) the ideas that support and make sense of those provisions; and (3) the social context from which the ideas emerge. The emphasis in this essay is on the second part, the ideas, whereas the first and third parts are considered at length in a forthcoming study.[2] By ideas I mean the way the main actors at various times think about constitutions, how they understand their nature and content, the ideals and visions

---

[2] The fuller study is in the process of completion and proceeds under the working title: *The Hidden Constitution of the People* (completion, 2014).

of what constitutions should be – in short, their *mentalité*. In analyzing the ideas behind modern constitutions, I draw on historical events, but by way of illustration rather than systematic historical explanation. I am not putting forward a normative claim about the place the people should have in the constitution, despite the tendency to assume that anyone writing about the subject must have an ideal in mind, a view about what that place should be. That may or may not be the case, and it is not the case here, my purpose being to identify, understand, and explain the place of the people, not to prescribe what it should be. The comparisons I make between representative government and more direct forms of democracy are to illuminate different positions rather than to argue for one or the other.

5.2 THE PEOPLE IN THE CONSTITUTION

The people appear in the constitution in four main ways. They declare the constitution to be theirs, created by them in the exercise of their authority. The constitutions of the United States, Japan, India, and many others begin with the words "We the People," while the Act to constitute the Commonwealth of Australia refers to the agreement of the people of the states to unite in a Federal Commonwealth.[3] The Fundamental Law of the Republic of Hungary is made in the name of "the members of the Hungarian nation" who declare that all power belongs to the people, who exercise sovereignty through elected representatives or "in exceptional circumstances directly."[4] That the constitution is the act of the people, in some sense belongs to them, is a common theme of these and many other constitutions.[5] The people often, but not invariably, make a second appearance in affirming the representative character of government and stating how representatives are to be elected. The Australian Constitution, in line with many others, states that the two Houses of Parliament shall be "directly chosen by the people," while in many other constitutions no express reference is made to the election of representatives, although the assumption is that they will be, leaving such matters to be provided for elsewhere.[6] Once elected, representatives are rarely subject to processes of accountability to the people other than the final power to vote them out of office. The third reference to the people occurs in provisions for amending the constitution. The people in a few cases are able to initiate constitutional change,[7] but

---

[3] Commonwealth of Australia Constitution Act 1900, Preamble.

[4] Constitution of the Republic of Hungary 2011, Article 2.2.

[5] Some constitutions vest sovereignty in representatives rather than the people: the constitutions of Argentina and Brazil are examples; other constitutions are based on parliament rather than the people: United Kingdom, Australia, and Canada are examples.

[6] Thirty-five percent of the cohort of sixty provide expressly for election of representatives; the other 65% make no reference.

[7] Seven constitutions in the cohort allow the people to initiate a referendum for constitutional change, but only under very restrictive conditions.

more often they are asked to consider changes proposed by government; even then only half the constitutions in the cohort provide for a confirmatory referendum, often at the discretion of parliament, the other half allowing change by special parliamentary majorities without reference to the people. The fourth and final appearance of the people relates to direct action that takes several forms, the most common being voting on a referendum to amend the constitution or initiating a referendum to propose a new law or abrogating an existing one.[8]

Beyond these points of reference, and occasional exhortations that government be conducted for the good of the people, constitutions say little about the people. The result is a constitutional structure in which the people have a significant but limited role. Although constitutions often declare the people's sovereignty or supremacy, the extent to which they are involved in making the constitution or even ratifying it is highly variable and often more a case of acquiescence than positive consent. And as we have just seen, their presence in the constitution is limited and narrowly defined. The high-sounding declarations of the sovereignty and supremacy of the people are important symbolically but do not translate into a vigorous engagement in government. The authority to amend the constitution, where it exists, is by no means insignificant, yet amendments, being exceptional, do not engage the people in constitutional affairs on a regular or frequent basis. That leaves the authority to elect representatives, mainly legislative, sometimes executive. The election of representatives is fundamental to even the leanest notion of democracy, and there is a world of difference between having the right to elect and not. Nevertheless, to confine the constitutional role of the people to the election of representatives is to opt for a very particular constitutional scheme. It is a scheme in which the people have no constitutional authority to involve themselves in government, by which I mean in the formulation of policy and the making of law; nor in the executive, administrative, and even judicial aspects of government; nor do the people have, as a matter of constitutional right, direct power of supervision or control over government.

An immediate objection might be made that the people have ample opportunities to influence and guide the conduct of government through political action. Quite apart from how true that is in practice, which varies from place to place and group to group, the focus here is on the constitution, not on the political process. The question is about the place the people have in the constitution, which is quite different from questions about the way the people conduct themselves in politics. Another objection, the one voiced by Dahl noted earlier, is that constitutions reflect the realities of modern societies, where the idea of a more positive role for the people in the

---

[8] It was noted earlier that half the constitutions in the cohort provide for confirmatory referenda on constitutional amendments, while in seven cases the people may take the initiative. Seventeen constitutions in the cohort of sixty provide for initiatives of the people, which in practice, in general, are not easy to mount and are not often used.

constitutional scheme, however attractive in principle, is ruled out as impracticable. The appeal is to common sense: government is large and complex, and must be conducted by a select few, who act on the advice of experts and professionals. Whatever the merits of the argument, it does not end the enquiry, for implicit in it are empirical claims about the nature of modern societies and government, which, to be plausible, would need to be broken down into a multitude of different issues and closely examined. Only then would it be possible to determine whether a modern government requires such wholesale delegation of authority to officials and necessarily excludes the people from being involved in a range of ways. In the absence of any such analysis, the general claim based on the necessities of modern government is rather weak and should not deter further investigation into the role of the people in the constitution.[9]

The Constitution of the United States occupies a special place in constitutional development. It is the outcome of extensive debate by intelligent men dedicated to creating a new constitutional order, some of whom, like James Madison, were well-versed in the history, the rise and fall, of countless constitutional orders. The U.S. Constitution is backward-looking in embracing the fundamental constitutional understandings of the English of the time, while forward-looking as a point of reference for the future – the paradigm, some think, of what a constitution should be. How it fits within the scheme outlined earlier is well put by J. G. A. Pocock, who writes that, for the Federalists, the "crucial revision [of competing democratic theories] was that of the concept of the people" (Pocock 1975: 517). He continues: "There was a distinction between the exercise of power in government, and the power of designating representatives to exercise it; and it could be argued both that all government was the people's and that the people had withdrawn from government altogether" (*ibid.*). If this is the culmination of a course of history, the summit of constitutional endeavor, as I think it must be regarded, then we may ask: how did it come about? What social factors made it not just possible but seemingly inevitable, the natural and necessary accommodation of two competing notions: the people as masters of their own destiny and the practical needs of government? Claims to either naturalness or necessity as to the form of social institutions are usually suspect, and this case is no exception. From the premise that the people are free and self-governing, and yet have to find a way of living together, a way of governing and being governed, from that premise different conclusions may be drawn, different forms of government and constitution devised.

An obvious alternative, one that casts its spell over centuries of constitutional thought, is contained in a tradition with its origins in Greek and Roman history, finds its expression in the Roman Republic and Roman Law, and was the foundation

---

[9] An assessment of the arguments from practicality is made in the larger study referred to earlier.

of the Italian republics. This republican approach, despite the term "republican" now having been emptied of much of its original meaning, has at its core the question of how free men – where being free entails being self-governing – could enter into association with others, could consent to government, and yet remain free. The answer, despite many variations and complications, in turn has at its core the notion of direct participation and involvement in government. Government is seen not only as a necessity but also as a good, and engagement by its citizens a source of virtue. How that should be expressed in practice is also open to interpretation and local variation, but the idea in its simplest form remains constant. Polybius, the Greek historian of the third century, whose text stands out from an abundance of texts for its clarity, simplicity, and influence, expresses the perfect constitution as one that combines the three elements of monarchy, aristocracy, and democracy, each checking and balancing the other (Polybius, 1979). That is not so extraordinary in itself, for even Charles I of England, in *His Majesties Answer to the Nineteen Propositions of Both Houses of Parliament* put to him in June 1642, could propound a similar constitutional scheme (Kenyon, 1986: 21–23).

Everything turns on the third element: democracy. For Polybius and the tradition he represents, democracy means active engagement of the people in the affairs of government. This is not what Charles I had in mind. He did use, surprisingly, the word "democracy," which, to a seventeenth-century Englishman, normally meant anarchy. He was referring, however, to the House of Commons as the democratic part of Parliament, which represented the people, although its members were elected by only a small percentage of them. The House of Commons might be "an excellent conservor of liberty," Charles concedes, but it is a representative house where the elected members are actually present, the people only notionally so. The institutional structure, the balancing of the three estates, fits the form of the republican tradition, but the substance is crucially different, for the idea of the people as active participants in government is absent. The people, as real persons with needs, interests, and aspirations, are replaced by a corporate notion of "the people" capable of expressing itself only through representatives, who, as representatives of the corporate whole, should not and need not be too closely tied to interests or localities.

Somewhere down the historical line, a major transformation has taken place: the old issue of how to reconcile the people as free and self-governing with the demands of effective government has been resolved by redefining the people in such a way that they speak only through representatives, and so are rendered distant from government. Government is a matter for king, aristocracy, and commons, who collectively constitute the sovereign authority, who act for and in the name of the people, and who are the only ones capable of so acting. The transformation took place for reasons internal to the constitutional affairs of the medieval and early modern English nation, but its significance is universal. That government should be, can only effectively be, conducted by representatives is the premise on which James Madison designed the Constitution of the United States, from where it found its way into practically every constitution of the modern world. At almost the same time and on the same basic premise, Abbé Emmanuel Sieyés, in the ferment of the French Revolution, was attempting to put the study of constitutions on a more scientific footing and to provide practical guidance in their design. I shall return to Sieyés's ideas shortly.

5.3 ON THE NATURE OF CONSTITUTIONS

Chief Justice Marshall of the U.S. Supreme Court, writing in 1803, states concisely one view of modern constitutions: "Certainly all those who have framed written constitutions contemplate them as forming the fundamental and paramount law of the nation."[10] Marshall here gives expression to an idea gradually emerging but until then imperfectly formed: that the fundamental law of a nation is found in the written constitution, and that there is no sense of fundamental law outside the written document. Fundamental law, the rules of government, and the constitution merge into one written document. That in turn gives birth to other ideas: that the constitution defines the relationship between government and the people in terms of the rights of individual persons, and that the authoritative interpretation of the constitution is the domain of the courts. These are two of the distinctive features of modern constitutions.

"Constitution" came only recently to be viewed in this way. In the seventeenth century it meant something different, an account of which, and how it changed, will help in unravelling the place of the people (Stourzh 1988). In the seventeenth century, especially the period around the English Civil War, men of affairs spoke in language now strange. They spoke of the "body politic" by analogy to the body natural and of "constitution" as the state of health and well-being of the body politic. The health and well-being of the body politic consists of those features essential to its nature and well-functioning. The Parliamentary complaint was that, during twelve years of Personal Rule of King Charles I, the body politic was of poor constitution and needed to be restored to health. The purpose of Parliament's criticism of the king and its proposals for reform was restoration of the body politic to good constitution. In a speech in the House of Commons in 1642, Stephen Marshall spoke of Parliament's purpose in its contest with the king being "to restore the nation" to "the fundamental and vital liberties, the propriety of our goods, and freedom of our persons" (Judson 1949: 353). To violate those qualities, as the king was accused of doing, was to ruin the health of the nation and hence its constitution; restoration

---

[10] *Marbury v. Madison*, 5 U.S. (1 Cranch) 137 (1803).

meant bringing government into line with those qualities and so restoring the nation's constitution. Parliament becomes the "Physician" whose task is to care for the "Patient" and restore it to health. If the "body be distempered," Parliament is best suited to restore it to health. When the Levellers enter the scene in the mid-1640s, they accuse Parliament, now ruling, of failing in its duty, of perpetuating the ills rather than curing them. They then set out to find another route to good health (Galligan 2013b).

Law, more than anything else, was essential to the health of the nation. Men of the seventeenth century, writes Margaret Judson, a historian of the constitutional crisis of the 1640s, "held a profound belief in the importance of law" (Judson 1949: 44). Edward Sexby, a Leveller branded a dangerous radical, was one of those men. He explains the law as being essential to social life and that we achieve social life only by subjection to the law. "Laws," he writes, drawing on the image of a body and its health, "are the nerves or sinews of every society or commonwealth, without which they must necessarily dissolve and fall asunder" (Sexby 1986: 371).[11] Why is law so basic to the health of the nation, why are laws "things of constitution," as an unnamed author wrote, which constitution is "written in the very heart of the Republique" (unnamed author 1643: 3–4)? The answer is that laws are not just instruments to ends; they constitute the society in the sense that they define the rights and duties of the people and relations between the people and the Crown. If the first duty of the king is to govern for the welfare and safety of the people, the *salus populi* – an ancient idea invoked in Parliament's attack on the king, and later in the Levellers' attack on Parliament – then laws express the *salus populi* and define the welfare and safety of the people. Being a law-based constitution, the English constitution is a constitution of rights, a feature often neglected; and we might add in passing how salient a feature that is in comparison with the classic republican constitution, which was one of active civic engagement rather than law and rights. The English constitution was not based on civic engagement of the people, indeed the opposite: the constitution allowed no room for general civic engagement.[12] It relied instead on the wisdom of king, lords, and commons governing for the good of the people, governing that is in accordance with law and respecting the rights created

---

[11] In their search for fundamental law, the Levellers went back to a pre-Norman England to an idealized vision of Anglo-Saxon England; that proving not to be entirely satisfactory, they finally concluded that fundamental law is right reason: see further, Galligan (2013b). Very similar bodily imagery had been used two centuries earlier by John Fortescue, a seasoned judge who survived the Wars of the Roses; he wrote: "The law ... resembles the sinews of the physical body, for, just as the body is held together by the sinews, so this body mystical is bound together and preserved as one by the law"; Fortescue (1997).

[12] Although the people were excluded from civic engagement, they held the ultimate extra-constitutional power to withdraw their acquiescence, the threat of which is a constant theme in early modern English history. Civic engagement did occur at the local and shire levels; see, for instance, Hindle (2000).

under law, from which all the people benefited. Within this perfect constitutional order, as it was often proclaimed to be and not only by Englishmen, there was neither constitutional need nor constitutional space for an active citizenry. This was the inheritance of early Americans, who, although rebelling against tainted implementation of the English constitution, based their own on similar foundations: good and wise government guided by law and rights. They had to concede a wider franchise, but that, as we shall see, did not ruin the foundations.

The connection between law and constitution and the health of the nation is now established. Law is pivotal, yet it has a special and rather elusive sense. It is more than statutes and common law, although both are part of it. When men of the seventeenth century spoke of law, invoked law in their cause, they meant more than what we would now call positive law. What they had in mind is not always clear, but includes a notion of fundamental principles, which are to be found not only in such public declarations as Magna Carta,[13] but appear also in the conventions, understandings, and practices that constitute the body politic, at whose heart lay the rights and duties of freeborn Englishmen. Conventions, understandings, and practices they may be, but, as that anonymous author writes, they are things of constitution, the things "written in the very heart of the Republique, far firmlier than can be by pen and paper" (unnamed author, *ibid.*).

The rules and institutions of government have a place but are only part, and not the most important part, of a constitution. They are, in a way, instruments for sustaining fundamental law, and so the welfare and safety of the people, and in turn the health of the nation. They are also more than instruments, for the understanding was that a certain pattern of rules and institutions of government is closely tied to the nation's welfare. In his last significant statement on the constitution, through his advisers Culpeper and Hyde, in *His Majesties Answer to the Nineteen Propositions of Both Houses of Parliament*, King Charles I affirms that laws are made by king, lords, and commons, and that government is trusted to the king. He then states that authority in the king "is necessary to preserve the laws in their force, and the subjects in their liberties and properties." The House of Commons, he goes on to explain, "is an excellent conserver of liberty, but never intended for any share in government, or the choosing of them that should govern. – The power presently placed in both houses is more than sufficient to prevent and restrain the power of tyranny" (Wootton 1986: 171). The good of the nation is, in the king's view, inseparable from the institutions of government, a view from which few seventeenth-century men, at least before 1642, could dissent. By 1642 it was too late: Parliamentarians were now ambitious for a greater share in government, which in turn required changes to the balance between Parliament and the king. And while this meant changing an

---

[13]   For an analysis of Magna Carta, see Holt (1992).

element of the constitution, it concerned changes at the institutional level, leaving the fundamentals intact.

We might think of the organic constitution as consisting of several layers around a core. The core is the welfare and safety of the people, part of which, indeed a crucial part, consists of certain rights and liberties, which are wrapped in fundamental law, around which an institutional structure is built. The layers are interconnected to make an organic whole. Adjustments and modifications can be accommodated, although drastic change to one layer may threaten the whole. Changes to the institutional structure are the easiest to cope with, but even the core idea of the safety and welfare of the people and the standards of fundamental law can be reformulated. This idea of a constitution as an organic whole, as an expression of the well-being of the nation, is strikingly different from the notion expressed by Chief Justice Marshall. An obvious difference is the absence of a single document stating the fundamental law. Even more salient, fundamental law is less concerned with the institutions of government than with the understandings on which the society is based and which are expressed and reexpressed in practical actions. Another difference follows, for now the very idea of law suggests not so much rules or even definite standards, but something less tangible, something more amorphous, something more in the nature of understandings, assumptions, and expectations. These were the basis for Parliament's indictment of the king in 1642 and a few years later the Levellers' indictment of Parliament, the claim being that both were violating the fundamental law.

5.4 THE PEOPLE AND THEIR REPRESENTATION

Most important of all, the organic constitution is inseparable from – indeed, is another way of describing – the social structure. The nation is in good health when its many parts and its different layers come together in a harmonious whole. To know what constitutes a harmonious whole, one looks to the social order. The image of well-being of the body politic, with the king at its head and lords and commons combining to constitute the sovereign body, directly reflects and reproduces at the constitutional level the structure of society. That structure is clear and settled, and, just as property and status determine the social order, they also identify those, the few, who should govern, who are fit to govern. The people, the many, know their place in the social order and, however much they resent it, only rarely raise a voice in protest. One case occurred during the New Model Army debates in Putney Church in October 1647, when Colonel Rainsborough argued with haunting simplicity the case for soldiers, the ordinary men who had fought for Parliament in the Civil War, having a say in electing the government. But just as the possession of property and social status secure the place of the higher orders in political affairs, its lack serves equally well to exclude the lower orders. Without property or commercial endeavor, the people lack that "permanent interest" in the nation, which Henry Ireton invoked in order to reject their pleas (Galligan 2013b). Only those with property and status have sufficient interest to sustain a social order that turns on property and status; to allow the vote to those without would put the social order at risk. In Ireton's own words: "the most fundamental civil constitution of this kingdom . . . is, above all, the constitution by which I have my property."[14] Oliver Cromwell adds another reason: widening the franchise "tends to anarchy, must end in anarchy; for where is there any bound or limit set if you take away this limit, that men that have no interest but the interest of breathing shall have no voice in elections" (*ibid.*).

Yet the constitution of the seventeenth century, in common with the constitution of earlier centuries, was celebrated for requiring government with the consent of all and for the safety and welfare of all. King, lords, and commons all accepted that the authority of government derives from the people, that the people must in some sense consent to government, and that the powers of government should be used for their safety and welfare. The Coronation Oath expresses the bond between the people and the king, for as Margaret Kelly writes: "[T]he basis of the oath is the willingness of the people or peoples to accept the person about to take the oath as king" (Kelly 1998: 165). The sovereign body, the King-in-Parliament, also depends on the people, as Charles I states in his *His Majesties Answer*: "In this kingdom the laws are made jointly by a king, by a house of peers, and by a house of commons chosen directly by the people, all having free votes and particular privileges" (Wootton 1986: 171). Since neither king nor peers were elected by the people, and the House of Commons by a small portion of the people, in what sense was government based on the consent of the people?[15]

The answer lies in *representation*. Representation is a complex notion, open to a range of meanings.[16] The proclamation accompanying the succession of James I to the English throne explains one sense of representation, a sense at the center of early constitutional thought, with brevity and clarity: "[I]n this High Court of Parliament, where the whole body of the realm, and every particular member thereof, either in person or by representation . . . are by the laws of this realm deemed to be personally present" (Kelly 1998: 126). The idea is both powerful and remarkable: the whole realm comes together in Parliament, the people are *deemed to be personally present*. When Parliament, in the sense of the King-in-Parliament, decides, the nation decides. Since the people are present in Parliament, there can be no gap between them and Parliament. It is not a matter of Parliament deciding and then seeking the

---

[14] *Putney Debates*, p. 37.
[15] Roughly one-fifth of the adult male population had the vote; see Kishlanksy (1986).
[16] See further, Pitkin (1967) and Manin (1997).

consent of the people: the decisions of Parliament are the decisions of the people. "Every Englishman is entitled to there be present," wrote Thomas Smith in 1628, and "the consent of Parliament is taken to be everie man's consent" (Judson 1949).

In order to understand this notion of the people being present through their representatives, we must put aside two pillars of modern constitutional thought. One is the modern idea that election by the people is the normal and legitimate way of appointing government, from which it follows that consent of the people means consent positively displayed through elections.[17] Things were seen differently in the seventeenth century. We noticed earlier why popular election had no place in a nation based on property and status. Even the Commons had its origins in members being selected by the King and only later came to be the elected chamber (Maddicott 2010). Vital to this way of thought is the notion that good government depends on the quality of those who govern, not on how they are selected. The other feature of seventeenth-century thought at odds with modern ideas is that "the people" constitute a corporation, a *universitas*, which has a legal identity separate and distinct from its members, in the same way that a modern corporation has legal identity separate and distinct from its shareholders. The idea is inherent in the very word "people," which can be singular or plural depending on that to which it refers: the welfare of the people, singular, is then the welfare of the corporation, the people as a whole, and what constitutes the welfare of the corporation of the people is determined by those who represent it. The modern tendency is to repudiate or at least much diminish the sense of the people as a corporation (although vestiges remain) in favor of the people, plural, as a collection of individual persons with different ideas and interests.

The sense of the people as a corporation is at the heart of the seventeenth-century constitution. It was taken for granted; it was the way men of affairs thought, the notion they had in mind when they spoke of the people, made claims on the people's behalf, or wielded power in their name. The people as *universitas* has its origins in Roman Law, was imported into medieval Canon Law in order to solve problems of government within the Church, and from there made its way into secular constitutional thought (Tierney 1982; Monahan 1987). Once the "people" is understood in the corporate sense, some of the puzzles of seventeenth-century constitutional thought dissolve. The corporation of the people, being an entity distinct from its members, acts only through its representatives, who are appointed according to the rules of the corporation. Acts of the representatives are therefore acts of the people. The king's claim that his authority derives from the people and that he in turn

---

[17] On the nature of popular consent and its origins, see Monahan, A. P. *Consent, Coercion and Limit: The Medieval Origins of Parliamentary Democracy* (Kingston: McGill-Queens University Press, 1987) and Clarke, M. V. *Medieval Representation and Consent* (New York: Russell & Russell, 1964).

represents them now makes sense; the king acts for and on behalf of the people as a distinct entity. The fact that he was not elected by the people is not relevant.[18] The narrow electoral base of the commons is unimportant, because the commons represents the people as a corporate entity rather than as individuals or groups, and for that the object is to have able representatives rather than elected ones. Perhaps most importantly, the notion of the people as a corporate entity enables us to understand parliamentary sovereignty. When king, lords, and commons come together as King-in-Parliament, they represent the corporation of the people, and are the only ones with authority to represent it, and their actions are the actions of the corporation. And if we add the strange idea that the people are also there assembled, Parliament's claim to sovereignty is complete.

Although the notion of the people as a corporation explains much about early modern constitutional thought, it is unstable. Why should the real people accept a fiction, which, no matter how rich in history and pregnant in symbol, precludes their presence in the constitution and the political process authorized by the constitution? If the ordinary people tended to accept their constitutional exclusion as mere "breathers," to borrow Cromwell's term, it is because that was their place in the social order, of which the constitution was the mirror image. Despite the exclusion of the people, various rebellions and disturbances over the centuries had influenced the constitutional order,[19] but it was not until the upheavals of the 1640s that one stream of social rebellion in the form of the Leveller movement paved the way for a constitutional revolution that would have pierced the corporate veil to reveal the real people. But the moment passed and the Leveller movement came to nothing. After eleven years of a turbulent commonwealth, the monarchy was restored on terms favorable to lords and commons, while keeping intact the corporate identity of the people. It took the very different social order that grew up in the American colonies to enable the real people to emerge, to proclaim the constitution as theirs, and to secure the right to elect their representatives. Sovereignty moved from the Queen-in-Parliament in England to the people in the American colonies, and a wedge was driven between the two, so that government is of the people with only such powers as the people confer, from which it follows both that the people may change the terms of the conferral and that government must be chosen by the people.

[18]   There was a body of opinion that the king was elected by the people: that was John Fortescue's view, a view recently endorsed by Margaret Kelly (Fortescue 1997; Kelly 1998). This must be regarded as election in a special sense; for an analysis of consent and its relation to election, see Monahan (1987).

[19]   For an account of the impact the people had in shaping events and constitutional ideas, see Rollison, D. *A Commonwealth of the People: Popular Politics and England's Long Social Revolution, 1066–1649* (Cambridge: Cambridge University Press, 2010) and Watts J. *Henry VI and the Politics of Kingship* (Cambridge: Cambridge University Press, 1996).

That the people are able to take control of the constitution and elect their representatives are major advances on the seventeenth-century English constitution. Yet features of the old order remain. In the first place, the veil was pierced but not destroyed, so that the corporate notion of "We the People" lives on side by side with the people as real people with local and particular needs and interests.[20] Modern constitutions retain elements of both, with representatives sometimes acting for the corporate sense of the people and at other times for local and particular interests. Secondly, although the constitution is the people's constitution, the old notion survives according to which the people act only through their representatives. The constitutional role of the people is confined to the choice from time to time of who should represent them, with the result that the main focus of political action is influencing representatives.[21] The republican spirit of self-governing citizens, where self-government not only protects liberty but has positive virtue for those engaging in it, is not dead but much weakened. That weakening has led to a strengthening of another feature of the old constitutional order, the peculiarly English notion that liberty depends on law, not virtue, a notion that assumes a prominent place in the new order through the constitutional enunciation of rights and leads over time to the transfer of final authority to the courts.

5.5 REPRESENTATION AS THE FOUNDATION OF MODERN CONSTITUTIONS

That early modern ideas of constitution and government, themselves a direct expression of the social order of the time, should have persisted to become the foundation of modern constitutions suggests they contain something universal. Universal, that is, in relations between the people and the government, something transcending time and place, something to be confronted in any constitutional order. The voice that tried to move beyond the particular to the universal, to identify a sociological truth common to all systems of government, which should be credited with providing a foundation for modern constitutions, is that of the Abbé Emmanuel Sieyés (1748–1836). Described as "a theoretical architect of the French Revolution" of 1789, Sieyés, while writing of those events, intended also to advance a general account of constitutions (Sieyés 2003: vii).

In a pamphlet published in 1791, entitled *Qu'est-ce que le tiers état?*, Sieyés argues that to understand constitutions we must first consider the formation of political society, which has three stages. At the first stage, individual persons unite to form a nation, which consists of the combination of individual wills, or in Sieyés's words, "a

---

[20] For further discussion of the corporate aspects of modern constitutions, see Galligan (2013b).
[21] Max Weber's analysis of modern democracy proceeds along this line; see Weber (1978: 983 *ff*).

body of associates living under a *common* law, represented by the same legislature" (Sieyés 2003: 97). They then coordinate their activities and agree on common needs and how to achieve them, which marks the change from a coming together of individual wills to the formation of a common will, a progression essential to a nation's existence. The third stage is the crucial one: it marks the creation of a constitutional order and system of government, consisting of the delegation by the community to its representatives. Only at this stage can the common will of the community be identified and developed, and only then is a mature political society realized. But at this stage, says Sieyés, "it is no longer a *real* common will that acts, but a *representative* common will" (Sieyés 2003: 135). So, in a mature political society, relations between the people, the government as their representatives, and the constitution, are made plain: the people as a nation are the *constituent* power, the government is the *constituted* power, and the terms on which it functions are the *constitution*.

Sieyés's approach is that of the social scientist describing a constitution as a necessary element of a modern nation, an element whose properties and functions can be analyzed and generalized. The central ideas are simply stated. Firstly, the people as a nation needs government in order to achieve its common goals, for government can organize and coordinate the nation more effectively than the people acting as a collection of individuals. Secondly, the people *are* the nation, but the people *is* the constituent or sovereign authority, which expresses its wishes only through representatives. Thirdly, the people adopt a constitution that delegates powers to a group of officials as representatives, the constituted authority, which has only those powers so conferred. From this it follows that the affairs of government are left to the representatives as the constituted authority without involvement or interference from the people, first, because, as a practical matter, involvement or interference would threaten the point of delegating authority to government, and second, because government officials as representatives of the people act for and on behalf of the people and in its name. The authority of government is never more than a delegated authority that is held subject to the terms of the constitution and that government may not alter. The people retain the constituent power, from which they cannot be divested and with which they may alter the constitution. Sieyés goes on to explain that the drafting of a constitution and its later amendment should be entrusted to a second type of representative, *extraordinary* representatives, who are appointed by the nation for that purpose and who act on its behalf (Sieyés 2003: 142).

Sieyés's account of constitutions, proposed in the late eighteenth century, in the heat of revolution, purports to be a sociological account of general application and fits well with modern constitutions. Gone is nostalgia for the past, for restoring what was lost, and in its place is optimism for a new constitutional order based on reason and utility. Constitutions are no longer tied to notions of bringing the body politic back to good health, but are instead practical means to serve the ends of a political society. The task is to understand the structure of political society and then to devise a suitable constitution to serve its ends. The people, the Third Estate, now constitutes the nation, is the constituent power, the bearer of sovereignty (a term Sieyés does not use but which would be apt).[22] Unless the people as an undifferentiated collective is acknowledged as the nation, as the source of government authority, a genuine political society cannot form. In such a society there is no place for privileged orders, so that failure of the English to grasp this basic idea renders its constitution a "monument to gothic superstition" (Sieyés 2003:131). But the nation can act only through its representatives. This is the most salient feature of Sieyés's account and the most contentious. The medieval notion of the people as a corporation also has long since gone, yet its work in shaping constitutional history has been done, for here in modern dress, at the very center of the constitution, is the same old idea: the nation has a distinct identity that is separate from its individual members and that can be expressed only through representatives. The people do not govern themselves but are governed by their representatives. There are major differences between the premodern and the modern: one is that in the modern constitution the people choose the representatives; the other that the powers of the representatives are limited by the constitution. As important as these two factors are to the nature of modern constitutions and in recognizing the ultimate authority of the people, they do not touch the more basic notion that the nation acts through and only through its representatives.

5.6 REPRESENTATION, DEMOCRACY, AND RIGHTS

The English constitution of the seventeenth century and the theoretical account of Abbé Sieyés of the late eighteenth century both have at their center the people, and yet neither is dependent on or in any necessary way linked to democracy. Whereas today we could not imagine discussing the place of the people in political society in terms other than democracy, in seventeenth-century England and eighteenth-century France, democracy was not part of the discourse. Ideas of the people and their representation had different origins and a different logic. The English notion of the people as a corporate entity kept at a distance the real people, who were a threat to the social order, while Sieyés's account of political society, constitution, and government depends on the people but not on democracy. The people are governed through their representatives, but who should be representatives and how they should be selected are open to different approaches. Popular election is not ruled

---

[22] Sieyés's criticism of the English constitution, although meriting admiration for its continuity, is severe: "this much-vaunted masterpiece," he writes, "cannot withstand an impartial examination based on the principles of a genuine political order" (Sieyés 2003: 131).

out, but Sieyés, in debate with Thomas Paine, argued strenuously for a monarch as the supreme representative, even in some circumstances justifying a hereditary one (Sieyés 2003).

By the time of the American Revolution, and the working out of the federal constitution, the people had gained a foothold in political affairs that could not be denied in the constitution. James Madison, the dominating presence in constitutional affairs, after adverting to the need to control the "violence of factions" that inevitably results from popular government, asks in *Federalist* 1 whether the form of government has to be republican. His answer is plain: "no other form would be reconcilable with the genius of the people of America" (Madison 1971). By that Madison meant the right of the people, albeit only adult males, to engage in the political process to the extent of voting for representatives. That, for Madison, is the key difference between republicanism and monarchy. What the Levellers in England had advocated in vain more than a century before was now achieved in the American states, so successfully that it became a basic premise of American constitutionalism and its repudiation unthinkable: the people were now entitled to choose their representatives. Beyond that, the new constitution inherited and naturalized the English notion that government be conducted through representatives and that the people have no part in government other than choosing who its members should be.

In *Federalist* 10, Madison's fear of the people, of the "interested and overbearing majority," leads him to draw even more deeply on the foundations implicit in the English constitution. The "great object" of the new constitution, he states, is to secure two competing ends: on the one hand, the protection of the public interest and in particular private property, and, on the other hand, "the spirit and form of popular government." The solution is a representative republic, where views held in society are passed "through the medium of a chosen body of citizens, whose wisdom may best discern the true interest of their country, and whose patriotism and love of justice will be least likely to sacrifice it to temporary or partial considerations" (Madison 1971). It may be that the voice of the people, "pronounced by the representatives" of the people, will be "more consonant to the public good than if pronounced by the people themselves" (*ibid.*).[23] The tide of support for republican government is unstoppable, but, by confining it to representative republicanism, the risks to the social order are reduced and made manageable. Just as king, lords, and commons represent the people and could be relied on to protect the English social order, well-chosen representatives are likely to be the kind of persons who do likewise for American society.

---

[23] For a catalog of restrictions on the majority under the original federal constitution, see Dahl (2001: 15 *ff*).

Fifty years later, some of that mistrust had dissipated and the mature Madison was less sure that majorities would unite to threaten the common good (Dahl 2001: 33 *ff.*). By 1821, the right to vote "is a fundamental Article of the Republican Constitution" and should not be tied to ownership of freehold property. To restrict the right to vote in this way "violates the vital principle of free government that those who are bound by laws, ought to have a voice in making them" (Dahl 2001: 35). Rainsborough's plea in Putney Church nearly two centuries before is at last vindicated in a foreign land. Majority rule of course has its dangers, but of all forms of government, adds Madison: "The recommendation of a Republican form is that the danger of abuse is less than any other" (Madison 1953: 46). Despite Madison's changing opinion as to the place of the people in a Republic, it was too late; the federal constitution was already based on the more cautious version of republicanism, some of whose features were later altered, but whose basic structure remains.[24]

The point of present interest is that both the Constitution and the ideas behind it are situated within a model of representative government in which the representatives know how best to govern and should be left to govern without intervention by the people. Madison devoted much time to explaining republicanism and showing how it differed from other forms of government. But the form of republicanism he settled on is not that of the classical tradition; it is rather a form of government with its roots firmly in the English constitution, into which Madison inserts wider voting rights. Republicanism in the classic sense embraces a quite different role for the people: it is based on the citizen actively participating in government, not merely in choosing government and delegating authority to it. How active citizenship is to be realized, and what form participation takes, are variables dependent on the circumstances. But the premise is plain: republican government is government by the active engagement of the people and does not countenance a handing-over of authority to representatives. Republican government in the classic sense had a place in the discourse of the eighteenth century, and was even experimented with in some states, vestiges of which are still visible.[25] But the idea was short-lived and deemed a failure. One reason was its impracticability: the choice of representative government was the response of practical men to the impossibility of the citizens of thirteen states assembling to enact laws.[26]

A more important reason, I suggest, is that those practical men thought and worked within a frame of reference in which the nature of constitutions, government, and the place of the people was settled. The English constitution contained truths about the nature of society and social relations, which the Americans had no

---

[24] For an account of the changes, see Dahl (2001: *ibid*).
[25] For a historical account, see Wood (1968) and Manin (1997).
[26] Dahl considers this the decisive reason; see Dahl (2001: 160).

reason to question. Madison's views at the time of the federal constitution on the purposes of government, on who is fit to govern, and on the need to keep the people out of government occurred within that frame of reference, which had matured over centuries in English constitutional thought. Representative government is the form of government that best fits the frame of reference, which offers the best resolution of the dilemma that government is the government of the people, and yet government must be conducted by those who know how to govern for the common good. That such ideas had their origins in English constitutional thought would not have been enough to secure their passage into a new and in some respects revolutionary order; indeed, the opposite, for some central aspects of the English constitution, the monarchy and the lords, for instance, could be discarded as unsuitable. But while the monarchy and the lords are mere institutions of government rather than organs of good constitution, the same cannot be said of the place of the people, for that is a matter of the very essence of good constitution and the social order sustaining it, which is fixed and permanent and oblivious to time and place. Madison was not alone in coming to the realization that one had to distinguish between those parts of the constitution that were fixed and permanent because they reflected and protected the social order and those parts that were impermanent and mutable. We must remember that at the time Madison was designing a constitution for the new United States, Abbé Sieyés was formulating a general social science of constitutions and reaching substantially the same conclusions.

The tension between the two competing ends of government and the constitution – the public interest and private property on the one hand and the spirit and form of popular government on the other – shows itself more plainly in the debate on whether to include a bill of rights in the federal constitution. The initial opposition of Madison, Hamilton, and others could have been taken from the English debates of the 1640s, namely that liberty is at the heart of good government and liberty depends on the government acting for the good of the people, for liberty and the good of the people go together – in essence, they are different ways of saying the same thing. Public opinion and "the general spirit of the people," urges Hamilton, "would afford a better recognition of popular rights than volumes of those aphorisms" that fill bills of rights (Madison 1971: no. 84). Charles Stuart would have agreed for, in his view, king, lords, and commons embodied the spirit of the people and were the protectors of liberty and the laws on which liberties depend. Hamilton's argument would also have appealed to that anonymous writer of the seventeenth century referred to earlier, for whom the rights and liberties of freeborn Englishmen depend on "a Law held forth with more evidence, and written in the very heart of the Republique, far firmlier than can be pen and paper." Since in the American context the general spirit of the people favored liberty, a bill of rights was held unnecessary, "even denigrating to the people" (Ketchem 1993: 91). The reasons against did not prevail and, for other reasons, a bill of rights finally was included in the constitution.

To the Americans, the English constitution ran into trouble partly because king, lords, and commons collectively had lost sight of its fundamental principles, and partly because the people were excluded. The American case would be different because sovereignty lay in the people, who would be active and vigilant in ensuring that government pursued the common good. But notice how two different modes of discourse, two different models of a constitution, are now in play: one is that of an active and engaged citizenry, the discourse of classic republicanism; the other is that of representative government, the inheritance of the English constitution, in which the role of the people is confined. That nature and scope of that role is defined by the logic and structure of each model: one assumes the active citizen of classic republicanism, whose image Madison and others invoke; the other assumes the represented citizen, kept at the margins. Madison the architect of the constitution valued both but had already opted for security over active citizenship. The later Madison might have chosen otherwise, but by then the more cautious approach was entrenched in the constitution. Whether active citizenship has emerged and prevailed despite the constitutional odds against it, whether the foundation of the American nation and its government is the general spirit of the people, whether history has proved Madison and Hamilton right about the spirit of the people are questions beyond my present purposes. Writing of early America, de Tocqueville praised the engagement of the people at many levels of government (Wolin 2003). Whether that was an accurate account at the time is arguable; whether it has been maintained in the manner or to the extent envisaged by the architects of the constitution is questionable.

One final attempt to keep at the heart of the constitution that older republican tradition comes perhaps unexpectedly from a 1943 judgment of Justice Felix Frankfurter, in which he refused to rule invalid a law of the state of Virginia, which he considered foolish and unjust, requiring the children of Jehovah Witnesses to salute the flag, despite their strong religious objections and the imposition of severe sanctions.[27] For the court to invalidate the law, he argued, would be to undermine the fundamental premise of a self-governing society, for such a society depends on the vitality of the people and their active engagement in preserving liberal values. Look, he urged, not to the consequences of the law, unfortunate though they be; look instead to its origins in the elected government.[28] Elected government is accountable to the people and it is up to the people to ensure their representatives do not pass laws infringing rights and liberties. To rely on the courts to intervene,

[27] *West Virginia State Board of Education v. Barnette* (1943) 319 US 624.
[28] The ideas are well expressed in Ketchem (1993: 113 *ff*).

to correct the mistakes of representatives, would diminish the responsibility of the people for their own government. The tendency to regard the law "as all right if it is constitutional" is described as "a great enemy of liberty." Frankfurter continues: "Reliance for the most precious interests of civilization, therefore, must be found outside of their vindication in courts of law. Only a persistent positive translation of the faith of a free society into the convictions and habits and actions of a community is the ultimate reliance against unabated temptations to fetter the human spirit."[29]

In defending this vision of the role of the people, a vision with which the mature Madison and Hamilton would have been at ease, Frankfurter was a minority of one against declaring the Virginia law unconstitutional. His words have about them the air of elegy, a last call for the virtues of the classic republic and the image of the free man as a self-governing citizen. Alas, it was too late: for just as the republic of active citizenship had long before been displaced by a constitution of representation, law, and rights, so its language became ill-suited to the new order. The rest is history. What Frankfurter feared has come to pass, and the courts are now central to political life. Few would charge the courts with being a "great enemy of liberty," but what is plain is that, as the courts ascend the peaks of public life, the role of political action and hence of the people declines. The mantle of the enemy of liberty has passed to the executive and administration, which have moved to the center of power, a position conceded without resistance from the people or their representatives. That, however, is another story; how to account for the people not meeting the expectations of the mature Madison and the reflective Frankfurter, how to explain the reliance on the courts to decide the great issues of the nation, are complex matters. Part of the explanation is likely to be the rift between what is expected of an active people and the constitutional structure imposed on them.

In conclusion, this essay is prompted by the strikingly consistent way that the people are presented in modern constitutions despite the diversity of the societies for which they are written. This way of presenting the people is made to appear compelling, both theoretically and practically, as a universal answer to a universal problem of how a people can both govern itself and have effective government. While allowing that both parts of the answer, the theoretical and the practical, have merit, they must be seen in the social and historical setting at different formative periods of constitutional history. There we see the relations between society and the constitution, filtered through the prevailing pattern of social and legal relations; through the way leaders thought about and understood the social world, and in turn the nature of government and constitutions; and through the aspirations and ideals the leaders of the new world had of the future, of a better constitutional order than that they left behind, yet at the same time being, if not in thrall to, strongly influenced by, the old order.

---

[29] Justice Felix Frankfurter in: *West Virginia State Board of Education v. Barnette* 319 U.S. 624 (1943).

REFERENCES

Clarke, M. V. 1964 *Medieval Representation and Consent* New York: Russell and Russell

Dahl, R. A. 2001 *How Democratic Is the American Constitution*. New Haven: Yale University Press

Fortescue, J. 1997 *In Praise of the Laws of England* (1643) (ed) Lockwood, S. *Sir John Fortescue: On the Laws and Governance of England* Cambridge: Cambridge University Press

Galligan, D. J. 2013a "The Sovereignty Deficit of Modern Constitutions" (2013) **33** *Oxford Journal of Legal Studies* (forthcoming)

2013b "The Levellers, the People, and the Constitution" in *Constitutions and the Classics* (ed) D. J. Galligan (forthcoming)

Hindle, S. 2000 *The State and Social Change in Early Modern Britain, 1550–1640* Basingstoke: Palgrave

Holt, J. C. 1992 *Magna Carta* Cambridge: Cambridge University Press

Judson, M. A. 1949 *The Crisis of the Constitution* New Brunswick: Rutgers University Press

Kelly, M. R. L. L. 1998 *King and Crown* (Doctoral Thesis) Sydney: Macquarie University

Kenyon, P. 1986. *The Stuart Constitution: Documents and Commentary*. Cambridge: Cambridge University Press.

Ketchem, R. 1993 *Framed for Posterity: The Enduring Philosophy of the Constitution* Lawrence: University Press of Kansas

Kishlansky, M. A. 1986 *Parliamentary Selection: Social and Political Choice in Early Modern England* Cambridge: Cambridge University Press

Maddicott, J. R. 2010 *The Origins of the English Parliament 924–1327* Oxford: Oxford University Press

Madison, J. 1971 *The Federalist or the New Constitution* London: Glazier & Co.

Records, in R. A. Dahl 2001 *How Democratic Is the American Constitution* New Haven: Yale University Press

1953 Letter to Thomas Ritchie, in *The Forging of American Federalism: Selected Writings of James Madison*, edited by S. K. Padover. Harper Torchbooks.

Manin, B. 1997 *The Principles of Representative Government* Cambridge: Cambridge University Press.

Monahan, A. P. 1987 *Coercion and Limit: The Medieval origins of Parliamentary Democracy* Kingston: McGill-Queens University Press

Pitkin, H. F. 1967 *The Concept of Representation* Berkeley: University of California Press

Pocock, J. G. A. 1975 *The Machiavellian Moment: Florentine Political Thought and the Atlantic Republican Tradition* Princeton: Princeton University Press

Polybius 1979 *The Rise and Fall of the Roman Empire*, translated by I. Scott-Kilvert, with an introduction by F. W. Walbank London: Penguin

Rollison, D. 2010 *A Commonwealth of the People: Popular Politics and England's Long Social Revolution* Cambridge: Cambridge University Press

Sexby, E. 1986 *Killing Not Murder* (1657) in *Divine Right and Democracy*, edited by D. Wootton London: Penguin.

Sieyés, A. 2003 *An Explanatory Note of M. Sieyés, in Answer to the Letter of Mr. Paine* in *Sieyés: Political Writings*, edited by M. Sonenscher. Cambridge and Indianapolis: Hackett Publishing.

Sonenscher, M. (ed.) 2003 *Sieyés: Political Writings*. Cambridge and Indianapolis: Hackett Publishing

Stourzh, G. 1988 Constitution: Changing Meanings of the Term, in *Conceptual Change and the Constitution* (eds) Ball, T. and Pocock, J. G. A. Lawrence: University Press of Kansas

Tierney, B. 1982 *Religion, Law and the Growth of Constitutional Thought, 1150–1650* Cambridge: Cambridge University Press

Watts, J. 1996 *Henry VI and the Politics of Kingship* Cambridge: Cambridge University Press

Weber, M. 1978 *Economy and Society* (ed) Roth G. and Wittich C. Berkeley: University of California Press

Wolin, S. 2003 *Tocqueville between Two Worlds* Princeton: Princeton University Press

Wood, G. 1968 *The Creation of the American Republic, 1776–1787* Chapel Hill: University of North Carolina Press.

Wootton, D. 2001 Introduction, in *Divine Right and Democracy: An Anthology of Political Writing in Stuart England* London: Penguin

6

The Strategic Foundations of Constitutions

Ran Hirschl

6.1 INTRODUCTION

The past few decades have seen sweeping global convergence toward democracy, real or professed, alongside a convergence on constitutional supremacy and a corresponding increase in the political salience of constitutional courts and judicial review worldwide. In that period, more than 150 countries and supranational entities, ranging from Russia to South Africa to the European Union and covering approximately three-quarters of the world's population, have gone through major constitutionalization processes. Even countries such as Canada, Israel, Britain, and New Zealand – described merely three decades ago as the last bastions of Westminster-style parliamentary sovereignty – have embarked on a comprehensive constitutional overhaul aimed at introducing principles of constitutional supremacy into their respective political systems. The widespread adoption of this all-encompassing form of managing public affairs has been reinforced by an almost unequivocal endorsement of the notion of constitutionalism and judicial review by scholars, jurists, and activists alike. According to the generic version of this canonical view, judicial review by constitutional courts is a necessary supplement to, and a core element of, a viable democracy.

Although this trend is arguably one of the most important phenomena in late-twentieth- and early-twenty-first-century government, the diffusion of constitutions remains largely under-explored and under-theorized. Until the early 2000s, the literature on the subject was dominated by two main threads: *ideational* and *functionalist*. In the past decade, an alternative strand of scholarship has emerged in response to these canonical understandings of constitutionalization and judicial review. This *strategic-realist* approach is premised on the notion of constitutional law as a form of politics by other means. It attempts to provide a richer explanatory account of the proliferation and role of constitutions and constitutional courts as reflecting a worldly, even strategic set of considerations, interests, and choices. A core finding here is that strategic behavior by politicians, elites, and courts plays a key role in explaining the tremendous variance in the scope, nature, and timing of constitutional reform. In the following pages, I elucidate the strategic-realist approach's main arguments and insights, and then illustrate these with examples drawn from the real world of new constitutionalism. But before turning to the strategic-realist account, a brief critical outline of the ideational and functionalist approaches to constitutionalization is in order.

6.2 THE IDEATIONAL STORY

Ideational theories suggest that the meaning and quality of ideas are key factors in explaining their prevalence or demise; the more normatively appealing ideas are, the greater the likelihood that they prevail (and vice versa). According to such theories, ideas matter a great deal in explaining political change. Political actors and institutions advance certain ideas primarily because they genuinely deem those ideas to be right, just, and suitable. Such an idealist vision of politics has played a key role in explaining the rise of constitutionalism, primarily of the liberal variety.

The large-scale convergence toward constitutional supremacy worldwide is typically portrayed as stemming from modern democracies' post–World War II acceptance of and commitment to the notion that democracy means more than mere adherence to the principle of majority rule. Not least, we are often reminded, it reflects every "mature democracy's" (in Ronald Dworkin's terms) subscription to the view that democracy must protect itself against the tyranny of majority rule through constitutionalization and judicial review, most notably by way of checks on government action and an entrenched, self-binding protection of the rights of vulnerable groups and individuals (Dworkin 1990; Weinrib 2007). According to this common account, liberal constitutionalism is both normatively superior to other alternatives and is the most effective way to prevent despotism, advance democratic politics, and protect basic rights and freedoms. The morally elevated status of these values – the fact that they reflect a just ideological platform, and that many political leaders, institutions, and voters believe this to be the case – is the main factor that explains the spread of constitutionalism in the past half-century.

Even according to this prevalent narrative – resplendent as it is with myths about the liberalizing power of rights, the Herculean capacities of judges, and a supposedly authentic, "we the people" quest for constitutional protection – fear is a main driving force of constitutionalization. The ineffectiveness of the Weimar Republic constitution and horrors of the Third Reich and the Nazi era are commonly invoked as a stark illustration of why strong constitutions are necessary. In its pre-commitment guise constitutions are viewed (and justified) as self-binding precautions that responsible right-holders who are well aware of their weaknesses (e.g., at times of national panic or mass hysteria) have taken against their own imperfections. Fearful of succumbing to their own future desires, constitutional pre-commitments may reduce the probability that such harmful measures will be adopted and carried out.

To the extent that concrete societal factors matter in this prevalent story, it is often in the context of supposedly authentic, bottom-up calls for a liberalizing constitutional change. During such "constitutional moments," massive popular mobilization – often accompanied by international cheering by rights advocates, Western media, and democracy supporters – leads to mounting pressure on a despotic regime to relinquish power, democratize politics, and protect individual rights through constitutional reform. Accordingly, a given polity's constitution is often taken to be the most genuine reflection of a polity's popular will, worldviews, and aspirations. Constitutional courts that are said to be removed from the pressures of partisan politics, and whose judges are neutral, apolitical adjudicators, are responsible for translating the constitutional provisions into practical guidelines for public life in a way that, to paraphrase Ronald Dworkin, takes rights "seriously" and reflects the polity's "enduring values."

While appealing from a normative standpoint, the prevalent ideational account of what constitutions are, what they do, and how they come about encounters several nontrivial challenges. Rights-based explanations often tell a broad, at times vague, so-called demand-side causal story that is difficult to operationalize. The analytical distinction between the force of ideas per se and the instrumental interests of actors and agents that adhere to and advance those ideas is quite fuzzy. There is no doubt that ideas do shape (or delimit) behavior to some extent. Rights ideology is indeed a key component of the post–World War II constitutional discourse and one of the reasons why constitutions are adopted. However, these insights are incapable of independently explaining the tremendous variance in the institutional design, forms of constitutional review, scope of judicial activism, and above all the precise timing of constitutionalization. And whereas commitment to certain ideas or values may well explain the substantive content of constitutional documents, that aspect too may reflect transnational diffusion and imitation trends (Goderis and Versteeg 2011; Elkins 2010). As ideologically appealing or normatively superior as liberal constitutionalism may be, the variance within the global constitutional domain is simply too large for the ideational story to be the sole explanatory factor.

Canada adopted a constitutionally entrenched bill of rights in 1982, Hong Kong did the same in 1991, Jamaica joined the constitutionalization-of-rights trend in 2011, and Australia and the United Kingdom remain without a constitutional bill of rights to date. What accounts for these considerable variations in the nature, scope, and timing of constitutional reforms? Surely, there are more concrete factors at play in each of these settings than those accounted for by the generic rights-based ideational storyline. The variable status of constitutional courts is another example of this limitation. In some settings, powerful constitutional courts have emerged whereas in other, substantively similar settings, such courts have been repeatedly criticized, tinkered with, or simply dissolved and replaced with a more compliant body. The ideational narrative alone cannot account for these differences.

Supporters of historically disenfranchised groups, advocates of women's or minority rights, lawyers concerned with the rights of the accused, and a host of other ideational agents have supported the constitutionalization of rights for much of the past half-century, and in any case long before it has been formalized in many countries. Yet the establishment of constitutional review in Israel happened between 1992 and 1995 and not a decade earlier or later. The adoption of the Canadian Charter took place in 1982, not in 1972 or in 1992. At best, then, ideational factors may provide a broad, fuzzy pro-constitutionalization ambience, within which key political actors operate. An explanation of why the Charter was adopted in 1982 or why Israel embarked on its constitutional revolution precisely when it did must be far more concrete.

What is more, rights-based explanations tend to posit a somewhat romantic notion of constitutionalization as reflecting massive political mobilization and genuine popular will. The reality, however, is that the vast majority of constitutional revolutions of the last few decades are culminations of elite bargains, or otherwise do not fit the "bottom-up" story. Indeed, as Denis Galligan demonstrates in Chapter 5 of this collection, the notion of substantive popular participation in constitutionalization processes is largely fictitious (Galligan 2013). Instead, constitutional revolutions were either negotiated among rival parties during times of political transition (e.g. South Africa), promoted by external actors (as was the case in Afghanistan in 2004 and Iraq in 2005), are often seized by influential stakeholders (consider the constitutional transformation in Egypt following the toppling of President Mubarak in 2011), or were initiated in the first place by political elites whose interests do not necessarily reflect popular will at the time (consider the continuous attempt by "Eurocentric" politicians, bureaucrats, and jurists to create an "ever closer union" in Europe by the adoption of an EU constitution). In other words, popular will or other forms of bottom-up pressures may be a pro-constitutionalization factor, but they are certainly not a necessary, let alone sufficient condition for such reform to actually take place.

In fact, many constitutions simply do not reflect the prevalent worldviews in their respective polities (see Jacobsohn 2010). India and Turkey are consistently cited as two of the most religious polities in the world in the sense that members of these polities are among the most likely to define themselves by their religious affiliation, attend religious services, or resort to religion for guidance in their everyday life. Yet the constitutions of both advance distinctly secular visions of politics that do not reflect the wills of their people. Furthermore, if genuine long-term ideational processes are indeed that significant in promoting constitutionalization, how are we to explain the fact that so many constitutional orders get changed or abolished so frequently? In their empirical study of the lifespan of constitutions worldwide, Elkins et al. (2009) report that only half of all constitutions last more than nine years, with an overall average of nineteen years.[1] Such frequent change of constitutional orders must reflect either a rapidly changing ideological platform or, more likely, changes in the concrete conditions and constellations of power within which constitutions emerge, function, and ultimately die.

6.3 THE FUNCTIONALIST STORY

A second canonical thread sees constitutions as offering efficient responses to systemic information and coordination problems. Institutional economists, for example, have depicted constitutions as credible commitment instruments that foster predictability and enhance economic performance by establishing limits on erratic government action. Rationality and efficiency, so the argument goes, warrant the adoption of legal mechanisms that enhance investors' trust, most often exemplified by the constitutional protection of property rights, legal mechanisms that have led to economic growth in various historical contexts (North and Thomas 1973). Douglass North and Barry Weingast, for example, have illustrated how legal limitations on rulers' arbitrary power in early capitalist Europe increased legal security and predictability for external lenders who were protected by law from the seizure of their capital (North and Weingast 1989; Weingast 1993). By reducing the risks associated with lending, capital became more readily accessible, economic growth increased, and the relative positions of countries where sovereigns had limited themselves improved markedly. Federalism has likewise been linked to enhanced economic development by coordinating competition among subunits for people, resources, and investment (Weingast 1995). More recent empirical studies have established a statistical link between the existence of certain constitutional rules and economic growth (see, for example, Mahoney 2001; Persson and Tabellini 2005).

Related to this is the idea that the constitution of a given polity may provide the outer world with a reliable proxy or a signal of the set of values and practices to which that polity is committed. The two main problems with such institutional economics-driven arguments remain their tendency to draw on retrospective analyses of events that fit the theory (see, for example, Shapiro and Green 1994) and,

---

[1] An average of seventeen years in nondemocratic settings; an average of twenty-three years in stable democracies, notably less if a few outlier cases are not taken into account, such as the U.S. constitution; Norway's constitution, which was adopted in 1814 and is the second-oldest constitution currently in existence; Sweden's 1809 constitution, which was replaced in 1974, at the age of 165; and the 1874 constitution of Switzerland, which was replaced by a new one in 1999, at the age of 125.

more importantly, their inability to account for the considerable variance across polities in the precise timing of constitutionalization.

Another set of functionalist or systemic need-based arguments see constitutions as establishing effective governance arrangements in multilevel polities. By its very nature, the establishment of a democratic regime entails the establishment of some form of separation of powers among the major branches of government, as well as between the central and provincial/regional legislatures. It also entails the presence of a set of procedural governing rules and decision-making processes to which all political actors are required to adhere. The persistence and stability of such a system, in turn, requires at least a semiautonomous, supposedly apolitical judiciary to serve as an impartial umpire in disputes concerning the scope and nature of the fundamental rules of the political game. Constitutional separation of powers and active judicial review are both a prerequisite and a by-product of viable democratic governance in multilayered federalist countries (Shapiro 1999). Along the same lines, the functionalist approach attributes the upsurge of constitutionalization in recent decades to the proliferation in levels of government and the corresponding emergence of a wide variety of semiautonomous administrative and regulatory state agencies (Shapiro and Stone-Sweet 2002). Independent and active judiciaries armed with judicial-review practices are seen as necessary for the efficient monitoring of the ever-expanding administrative state. Some accounts of the rapid growth of judicialization at the supranational level also portray it as an inevitable institutional response to complex coordination problems deriving from the systemic need to adopt standardized legal norms and administrative regulations across member-states in an era of converging economic markets (Stone-Sweet 2000).

As with the ideational approach, accounting for the timing of constitutional change is a major analytical challenge to this variant of the functionalist argument. Ultimately, it remains unclear whether the complexity of multilevel governance or set of administrative institutions in a given polity has indeed reached a point that necessitates the adoption of a constitution or the establishment of judicial review at precisely the time a constitution was adopted in that polity. Even if we ignore the fact that many of the countries in the world of "new constitutionalism" are unitary – in itself a challenge to the federalism aspect of the multilevel governance point – it would be difficult to argue convincingly that the nexus of government institutions and administrative agencies in Ireland reached a level of complexity that required a major constitutional overhaul precisely in 1937, whereas that level of institutional complexity in France was reached in 1958 and in New Zealand in the early 1990s.

Although this approach provides a plausible explanation for the rise of administrative review as facilitating coordination among state agencies at various levels, it cannot account for the spread of American-style high-voltage constitutionalism and judicial review. Additionally, both the economic pre-commitment and systemic needs-based theories of constitutions tend to ignore human agency, particularly the fact that constitutional innovations require constitutional innovators, and take lightly or altogether overlook the crucial self-interested intervention of those political power-holders who are committed to judicial expansion in an attempt to shape their institutional settings to serve their own agendas.

It is therefore hardly surprising that against the prevalent ideational and functionalist canons, a "realist" approach to constitutionalization has emerged. It is premised on the notion that the constitutional domain is rife with struggles for power, the pursuit of interests, and political conflicts more generally. Instances of constitutionalization, or the absence thereof, are not driven solely – or even primarily – by bottom-up pressures for rights entrenchment or the pursuit of efficient responses to systemic coordination problems. Ideational and structural factors may delimit or frame the range of options available to pertinent stakeholders, but the actual form of constitutional revolutions (and certainly their timing) is explained by concrete political factors.

6.4 CONSTITUTIONS AS STRATEGIC INSTRUMENTS OF POWER

As the seminal works of Robert McCloskey, Robert Dahl, Martin Shapiro, Walter Murphy, and others have established, constitutional courts and their jurisprudence are integral elements of a larger political setting and cannot be understood independent of it. Meanwhile, scholars critical of the prevalent status of rights in constitutional and political discourse suggested that the dominant notion of rights as negative freedoms is based on an atomistic view of society as composed of unencumbered individuals operating within an autonomous and self-sufficient private sphere. This in turn is considered reflective of social and economic neoliberalism, expanded private sphere, and a "small state" ideology (see, for example, Tushnet 1984; Waldron 1987; Bakan 1997). Constitutional discourse more generally helps promote a perceived contrast between the relative openness and integrity of the judicial process and the corruptibility of political bargaining (Scheingold 2004).

Unlike the idealist notion of constitution-making that is shaped by popular will and reflects a principled vision of politics, a pragmatic vision of constitution-making sees it as helping constitute the demos and providing a framework for its establishment and evolution. (It is little wonder that this latter view of constitutionalism has been popular among advocates of a European Union constitution – much like an EU currency, a supposedly pan-European demos-building instrument.) A voluminous body of literature on constitutional design and engineering suggests that when constitution-drafting is seen as a pragmatic – rather than principled – matter, it can be employed to mitigate tensions in ethnically divided polities through the adoption of federalism, secured representation, and other trust-building and power-sharing mechanisms (for a prominent exponent of this view, see Lijphart 1977). The literature on constitutional design of this kind, often referred to as "consociational-ism" (or "accommodation-centered" constitutionalism) emphasizes the significance of joint-governance institutions, mutual veto points, power-sharing mechanisms, and the like (Lijphart 2004). In its more strategic, "centripetal" (or "integrationist") guise, this brand of scholarship advocates the adoption of institutions that would make the political process more attractive to recalcitrant stakeholders, encourage moderation, and defuse the causes of strife by providing incentives to vote across group lines (Horowitz 1985). The entire exercise is driven by pragmatic political bargaining thinly disguised as principled constitutionalism.

From Fiji to Lebanon and Nepal, dozens of constitutions worldwide reflect such a "second-order" problem-solving form of constitutionalism that is not driven by sophisticated ideational platforms but by political necessities. A prime illustration is the Constitution of Bosnia and Herzegovina (BiH), brokered by international mediators in 1995 as part of the Dayton Accords. It creates a complex system of checks and balances among BiH's three constituent peoples (Bosnian, Croats, and Serbs). According to the 1995 Constitution, the BiH constitutional court, to pick one example, consists of two judges of Croat descent, two of Serb descent, two of Bosnian origin, and three international jurists appointed by the European Court of Human Rights, who cannot be citizens of BiH or of any of its neighboring states.

Recent studies appear to confirm the relative significance of strategic constitu-tional design. Elkins et al. (2009), for example, report that enduring constitutions emerge by virtue of a relatively open drafting stage that engenders "buy-in" by diverse constituencies, tend to be specific, and more often than not are adaptable by way of practicable amending formulae and provisions for incorporating modern practices. These three design choices "result from the constitution-making process itself, but are also features of ongoing practice. All three mutually reinforce each other to pro-duce a vigorous constitutional politics in which groups have a stake in the survival of the constitution" (Elkins et al. 2009: 89). Likewise, astute constitutional design may faciliate transition to and consolidation of democracy by lowering the costs of upholding the democratic bargain, inter alia by allowing outgoing authoritarians a role in the new democratic order, as happened, for example, in post-Pinochet Chile (Alberts et al. 2012). Strategic constitution-making is also evident in the area of executive term limits and their evasion (Ginsburg et al. 2012). Attempts to tinker with constitutionally imposed term limits have taken place in dozens of countries, ranging from Algeria to Venezuela and Colombia, and from Russia to Honduras and Uganda, although on the whole, term limits have worked in a vast majority of cases (*ibid.*: 374). Having said that, the independent contribution of strategic constitu-tional designs to the stabilization of troubled polities is very much an open question. As Ginsburg and colleagues readily admit in another piece, "constitutional design processes are loaded with expectations about endurance, efficacy, the resolution of conflicts, and political reconstruction.... In the real world, however, most constitutions fail" (Ginsburg et al. 2009: 223).

Taking the notion of constitutions as political institutions even further, recent political science scholarship, quantitative and qualitative, suggests that constitutionalization and the expansion of judicial power more generally are an important manifestation of the concrete social, political, and economic struggles that shape a given political system. This body of scholarship attempts to move beyond the traditional focus on constitutionalization as emanating from broad demand-side or organic pressures, and identify the concrete political conditions that are conducive to constitutional reform. It focuses on specific "supply-side" factors such as the arrival of a new constellation of power and the changing interests and incentives of pertinent political stakeholders as a key determinant of constitutionalization and judicial empowerment.

This strategic-realist approach to constitutionalization rests on a number of preliminary assumptions and insights some, though not all, of which embrace what may reflect a "rational choice" approach to constitutional politics.[2] First, constitutional transformation does not develop in a vacuum and cannot be analyzed separately from the concrete social, political, and economic struggles that shape a given political system. Indeed, it is an integral part and an important manifestation of those struggles and cannot be understood in isolation from them. Any attempt to portray the constitutional domain as a predominantly legal or philosophical, rather than political, arena is thus destined to yield incomplete accounts of the origins and consequences of constitutionalization. Moreover, constitutions are human-made institutions; their establishment, amendment, or abolition is carried out by identifiable actors – not abstract ideas or amorphic organic pressures, but real people who make concrete decisions and choices.

Second, when studying the political origins of constitutionalization (as well as the political origins of other large-scale institutional reforms), it is important to take into account events that did not occur, choices not taken, and the motivation of political power-holders for inaction or for not behaving in certain ways. As Bachrach and Baratz (1962) suggest, much like active decisions, nondecisions and inaction reflect concrete choices, implicit or invisible as they may be. In other words, the political origins of constitutional reform cannot be studied in isolation from the political origins of constitutional stalemate and stagnation.

---

[2] As with any other theory, if one questions the basic assumptions on which a theory rests, in this case that politicians tend to favor, *ceteris paribus*, institutional settings that work to their advantage, advance their agenda, or otherwise serve their interests, then the entire argument or theory may seem questionable.

A third assumption on which the strategic-realist approach rests is that legal institutions – be they property rights, labor law, or electoral rules – produce differential distributive effects: they privilege some groups, interests, and policy preferences over others (see, for example, Moe 1990). This effect is further accentuated when it comes to constitutions, the raison d'être of which is to create, channel, and monitor power. Given their entrenched status and relative difficulty to change or replace, constitutions provide an ideal platform for "locking in" certain contested worldviews, policy preferences, and institutional structures, while precluding the consideration of alternative perspectives. Given the high stakes, prominent political, economic, and judicial actors are therefore likely to favor the establishment of institutional structures most beneficial to them. There is no reason to believe that when it comes to constitutional law and courts, pertinent stakeholders behave in an altogether different, purely principled way. In fact, if we take the constitution to be an instrument of utmost political significance, the likelihood of pertinent stakeholders voluntarily behaving in a self-defeating fashion when it comes to constitutionalization is quite low.

It is no doubt true that prevalent ideational platforms are among the factors that determine the range of options for institutional change, including constitutional change. This is certainly true in certain post-authoritarian settings, where the familiar "democratization via constitutionalism" post–World War II story has some bite. However, to drive the ideational message home, proponents of such an approach ought to have shown a series of instances where ideational factors *run against the interests* of pertinent stakeholders, and successfully tilts their behavior in a self-defeating direction. Such a set of examples would have provided a possible *alternative* explanation, not a complementary one, to the strategic approach. This, alas, very few canonical constitutional theorists do, as the ideational story they tell is always aligned with the interests of those who, according to a given strategic take, push toward constitutional review.

A fourth basic notion here is that of constitutions as risk- or threat-reducing instruments. A threat of civil war or of a given polity's dissolution often brings to mind a pragmatist vision of constitutions as conflict-mitigating or assurance-providing instruments. But a more concrete, self-interested sense of threat and risk aversion is also at play when it comes to constitutionalization. Think of the simple logic of insurance. Those who are absolutely confident do not buy it. Residents of California buy insurance against earthquake damage. Residents of the Netherlands or the Maldives buy insurance against flooding. By contrast, flood insurance is not common, it is safe to assume, in the Gobi Desert (one of the driest areas in the world) or in La Paz, Bolivia (the world's highest capital). Likewise, if, having bought insurance policy against flooding, one happens to move from the Netherlands to the Gobi Desert, one would want to stop paying for the flooding insurance pronto, as the risk level would be deemed negligible. In short, it is the balance between the level of risk, real or perceived, and the insurance policy costs that is a main determinant of choices regarding insurance. A similar logic may be applied to conceptualize pertinent stakeholders' willingness to engage in constitutionalization as a type of insurance policy in an insecure political environment (see, e.g., Ginsburg 2003; Hirschl 2004).

The basic premise that people tend to be risk-averse under conditions of systemic uncertainty has been advanced by a wide array of thinkers in other scholarly domains, from John Rawls's "principles of justice" agreed on behind a veil of ignorance, to Marshall Sahlins's paradigm-shifting explanation for the lack of food accumulation or storage among hunter-gatherer societies (a perception of unlimited resources and a pervasive belief in a "giving environment"), to Tversky and Kahneman's seminal work on the psychology of choice under conditions of uncertainty (Rawls 1971; Sahlins 1972; Tversky and Kahneman 1981). It is an equally prevalent notion in the context of constitutional design (see, e.g. Vermeule 2013). Either way, it is the "risk-aversion as a key pro-constitutionalization factor" point where the strategic approach to constitutions comes close to the generic "constitutions as pre-commitments" metaphor, although the focus here is on strategic pre-commitment by concrete, self-interested actors, not on pre-commitment in its abstract, public-choice sense.

A fifth presupposition of the strategic-realist approach is that because constitutions and judicial review hold no purse strings, have no independent enforcement power, but nonetheless limit the institutional flexibility of political decision makers, self-limitation through constitutionalization seems, prima facie, to run against the interests of power-holders in legislatures and executives. Unless proven otherwise, a plausible explanation for self-limitation through constitutionalization is therefore that political stakeholders who either initiate or refrain from blocking such reforms estimate that it serves their interests to abide by the limits imposed by such constitutional constraints and the consequent judicial monitoring of the political sphere. Political actors who voluntarily establish institutions that appear to limit their institutional flexibility (such as constitutions and judicial review) must assume that the clipping of their wings under the new institutional structure will be compensated for by the limits it might impose on rival political elements and/or by the reduced probability for other non-favorable political developments down the road. In other words, those who are eager to pay the price of constitutional constraints of one kind or another are likely to assume that their position (absolute or relative) vis-à-vis other pertinent trends, forces, scenarios, or actors within the body politic would be improved under a new constitutional setting.

Political scientists and economists who study the constitutional domain have built upon these five core assumptions to identify concrete scenarios and motivations that are likely to lead pertinent political stakeholders to favor constitutionalization, and the expansion of judicial power more generally.

That an expansion of the constitutional domain, indeed of the judicial sphere more generally, is often in line with the interests of constitutional courts, judges, lawyers, and the legal academia – all are vying for symbolic stature and other profes- sional and reputational perks – is a quite intuitive insight. But what about the politi- cians? The idea of delegation as an effective risk-reduction measure first appeared in the mid-1980s in the literature on the political motivations behind the creation of independent administrative agencies (see, for example, Fiorina 1982; McCubbins and Schwartz 1984; McCubbins, Noll, and Weingast 1987, 1989). From the politi- cians' point of view, delegating policy-making authority to the courts may be an effective means of reducing decision-making costs as well as shifting responsibility, thereby reducing the risks to themselves and to the institutional apparatus within which they operate. If delegation of powers can increase credit and/or reduce blame attributed to the politician as a result of the policy decision of the delegated body, then such delegation can be beneficial to the politician (Voigt and Salzberger 2002). At the very least, the transfer to the courts of contested political "hot potatoes" offers a convenient, "blame deflection-like" retreat for politicians who are unwilling or unable to settle public disputes in the political sphere. Delegation also helps poli- ticians avoid difficult or "no win" decisions and/or the collapse of deadlocked or fragile governing coalitions (Graber 1993). Courts and judges, on their part, may take hold of an issue as a means of expanding their ambit of influence or reshaping their public image in the face of hesitation, disagreement, or inaction in the legisla- tive or executive realm. Politicians may seek to gain public support for contentious views by relying on national high courts' public image as professional and apolitical decision-making bodies. Alternatively, when politicians are obstructed from fully implementing their own policy agenda, they may favor the active exercise of consti- tutional review by a sympathetic judiciary in order to overcome those obstructions (Whittington 2005).

Judicial empowerment may likewise reflect the competitiveness of a polity's elec- toral market or governing politicians' time horizons. So, for example, when a ruling party expects to win elections repeatedly, the likelihood of an independent and pow- erful judiciary is low (Landes and Posner 1975; Ramseyer 1994). When a ruling party has a low expectation of remaining in power, it is more likely to support a powerful judiciary and attempt to staff courts with sympathetic judges to ensure that the next ruling party cannot use the judiciary to achieve its policy goals. In more general terms, under conditions of electoral uncertainty, the more independent courts (or other semiautonomous regulatory agencies) are, the harder it will be for the succes- sive government to reverse the policies of the incumbent government.

When it comes to constitutions, several complementary strategic motivations come to mind. First, constitutionalization may allow governments to impose a cen- tralizing, "one-rule-fits-all" policy on enormous and diverse polities (Morton 1995).

(Consider the standardizing or centralizing effect of an overarching constitution and an apex court jurisprudence in exceptionally diverse polities such as the United States, India, or the EU.) Second, constitutions may be adopted so as to ease off pressure for a comprehensive political change, or in order to signal a regime's prima facie acceptance of a set of international standards or expectations with respect to the openness of the political process and the rights of the polity's members. Third, as Tom Ginsburg and others have argued, the "electoral market competitiveness" logic may be expanded to suggest that contractually insecure environments create a political setting that is highly conducive to the creation of constitutional review and independent courts as an "insurance" mechanism (Ginsburg 2003; Finkel 2008). During periods of political transition when no obvious winner is projected to emerge, the establishment of constitutional review may provide a safety net for all involved parties, thereby facilitating a transition to democracy. Put differently, under conditions of electoral uncertainty, constitutional review may emerge as a "form of insurance to prospective electoral losers during the constitutional bargain" (Ginsburg 2002: 54; but see Popova 2010). This compelling "rational-strategic" account of constitutional review identifies the actual negotiating parties as the main agents, and their expectations or time horizons as the main factors in the constitutionalization game. The substantive positions or worldviews advocated by the parties do not play a role here.

A fourth, related argument combines "rational-strategic" impulses with elite-driven struggles over worldviews and policy preferences as the main driving forces behind constitutionalization. As I have argued elsewhere, the threat of losing control over pertinent policy-making processes and outcomes may be a significant driving force behind attempts to constitutionalize matters (Hirschl 2004). Embattled elites and their political representatives are more likely to opt for constitutional reform when present or prospective transformations in the political system threaten their own political status, worldviews, and policy preferences. Such threatened occupiers of a polity's symbolic "center" – these could be either old-timers on their way down or emerging hegemons who fear a comeback of their sociopolitical rivals – may favor constitutionalization as a hegemony-preserving maneuver when their grip over politics, cultural dominance, or the allocation of core perks and benefits are, or are likely to be, challenged in majoritarian decision-making arenas. In this fashion, threatened elites can get through the constitutional domain what they cannot get through the electoral market.

The time horizons and perceived threats to power-holders are key factors here. It is the arrival of credible political competition, or a new constellation of power, that makes those who operate in an insecure political environment, either politicians, parties, or social groups, see the utility of constitutional protection and powerful courts. Those that have better control over and affinity with the constitutional arena are more likely to resort to it as a power-preserving measure when present or prospective transformations in the political system threaten their own political status, worldviews, and policy preferences. In short, constitutionalization is often not merely, or even mainly, a form of Ulysses-like self-binding against one's own desires, but rather a self-interested binding of other, credibly threatening actors who advance rival worldviews and policy preferences.

6.5 FROM THEORY TO PRACTICE

The electoral market thesis – a key thread of the strategic-realist approach – is quite insightful when analyzing the politics of constitution-making processes during periods of regime change and political transition. Its main assertions – most notably, that the degree of political uncertainty facing politicians, either those on the decline or those insecure in their newly acquired power, is an important predictor of whether or not a constitutional court will be established – have been supported in a variety of studies ranging from formal modeling or large-N statistical analyses to detailed comparative studies of constitutionalization (see, for example, Stephenson 2003; Ramos 2006). Scholars within the latter camp have drawn on the logic of insurance to explain the variance in the choice of constitutional institutions between different periods in the late-nineteenth-century United States, between two Argentine provinces, among several polities in Eastern Europe, and, most famously, among post-authoritarian Asian countries (South Korea, Mongolia, and Taiwan). Here is a less frequently cited illustration: as Pedro Magalhães points out in this volume (Chapter 16) and elsewhere, the transition to democracy in Spain and Portugal in the mid-1970s was characterized by the lack of a single core of post-authoritarian political power, thereby leading to the rapid adoption of strong constitutional review mechanisms. In Greece, by contrast, the post-authoritarian constituent process was dominated by a single party (Constantine Karamanlis's New Democracy), which enjoyed more than 70 percent of the seats in the assembly and did not have to worry about elections following the approval of the new constitution. "The result was that Greece, with similar authoritarian and civil law legacies as Spain and Portugal, and involved in an almost simultaneous democratic transition, remained the only Southern European democracy without constitutional review of legislation" (Magalhães 2003: 127; Magalhães, 2013).

The hegemonic preservation guise finds support in other notable examples of constitutionalization. Having opposed judicial review for most of the twentieth century, white elites in South Africa miraculously discovered the virtues of judicial review when it became clear that the days of apartheid were numbered. Pierre Elliott Trudeau's drive to adopt the Canadian Charter of Rights and Freedoms came on the heels of his electoral defeat in 1979, the rise of the separatist Parti Québécois in 1976, and above all the credible threat of Quebec's secession as signaled by the 1980 secession referendum. In Mexico, the ruling Institutional Revolutionary Party (PRI) was indifferent to judicial review for more than seventy years but discovered its charms in the mid-1990s when credible political opposition emerged. Israel's Labor Movement and its predominantly secular Ashkenazi constituencies were agnostic toward constitutional reform for decades, but embraced constitutional supremacy and judicial review once their cultural and electoral dominance began to erode, their historic grip over Israel's governing bodies faded, and "new elites" and their policy preferences had gained considerable influence. The constitutional revolution of the mid-1990s then followed. In the years leading to the 1992–1995 constitutional revolution, electoral support for the Labor Party and the old Ashkenazi establishment plummeted, while several other hitherto "peripheral" groups and interests – very few of which have been represented, let alone proportionally, on the Supreme Court bench – gained momentum. And there are more examples of such defensive moves too. Having been in opposition for forty-four years, and fearful of the return of the socialist establishment, the first thing the right-wing coalition in Sweden did when it finally ousted the Social Democrats in 1976 was to recognize the courts' authority to exercise judicial review. Conversely, little or no judicial empowerment has taken place in countries such as Japan or Singapore where a single political force has controlled the political system for most of the last half-century. The same logic may explain why the ANC, now the undisputed ruling party in South Africa, has become considerably less keen on judicial activism compared to its initial support for the practice during the tumultuous transition of the early 1990s.

In Thailand, the historically hegemonic yet electorally challenged coalition of monarchists, army generals, and state bureaucracy resorted to a hitherto passive judiciary, to support a military coup, and later to carry out a massive constitutional overhaul to depose the anti-establishment Prime Minister Thaksin Shinawatra and his Thai Rak Thai Party, and later to topple Prime Minister Samak Sundaravej. The judiciary was also called upon to disband much of the People's Power Party (an offshoot of the formerly banned Thai Rak Thai), which had won the 2007 parliamentary election (see generally Dressel 2012). The Kemalist elite in Turkey discerned the benefits of a strong constitutional court in the last few decades, when religious parties seriously challenged its historical grip over Turkish politics. Having dissolved two pro-Islamist parties in 1998 and 2001, the Constitutional Court has become a bastion of Kemalist interests in their fight to curb the influence of the popular Justice and Development Party (AKP). In 2008, the Court came very close to banning the AKP; six of the eleven judges – one vote shy of the necessary seven votes – found the AKP platform unconstitutional. In so doing, the judges signaled that no further Islamization would be tolerated by the Court and its secularist and military establishment backers. A few weeks later, the Court declared unconstitutional a constitutional amendment that had been passed legally by the AKP-controlled parliament that would have directly challenged the official state policy of militant secularism. Little wonder why the AKP-led government reacted in 2010 by proposing a set of constitutional amendments that would, among other things, alter the composition of the Constitutional Court so as to better suit the interests of the ruling party. In early 2012, the Philippine's President Benigno Aquino III impeached through a senate hearing the Chief Justice of the Supreme Court, Renato Corona. The impeached chief justice was a last-minute appointment of the previous president, Gloria Macapagal Arroyo, named just two days before her electoral loss to Aquino. This apparent violation of a constitutional prohibition on last-minute appointments required a timely and helpful decision from the Supreme Court, a ruling that the pro-Arroyo court happily delivered, and so Corona was allowed to take office. And in Egypt, the Supreme Constitutional Court has become the main ally of the military apparatus in its attempt to preserve the army's privileged position in Egypt's political system. In 2012, to pick one example, the Court ordered the dissolution of the Muslim Brotherhood-dominated parliament, having found that one-third of its members were elected illegally. This has led to a clash between the Court and newly elected President Mohammed Morsi of the Freedom and Justice Party backed by the Muslim Brotherhood movement.

And there are other variations on this uncertainty or perceived threat element. Having defeated President Musharraf in the February 2008 elections and in anticipation of a Phoenix-like rise from the ashes of a military regime, the newly elected government of Pakistan led by the Pakistan People's Party (PPP) was quick to ratify the International Covenant on Economic, Social, and Cultural Rights and sign the International Covenant on Civil and Political Rights in April 2008. A similar logic may explain the 1994 incorporation of ten international covenants into Argentine constitutional law. Scholars have identified many earlier examples of such strategic incorporation of international standards into domestic law (see, for example, Moravcsik 2000). While for many years Britain was unwilling to incorporate the provisions of the European Convention on Human Rights into its own legal system (let alone to enact a constitutional bill of rights of its own), it enthusiastically promoted the entrenchment of Convention rights in the "independence constitutions" of newly self-governing African states as devices for protecting established interests from the "whims" of independent majoritarian politics. The 1991 constitutionalization of rights in British-ruled Hong Kong took place shortly after the British Parliament had ratified the Joint Declaration on the Question of Hong Kong, whereby Britain was to restore Hong Kong to China in July 1997. In fact, some scholars of British constitutional history even argue that the events known as the Glorious Revolution (1688–1689), most notably the establishment of a constitutional monarchy and the adoption of the English Bill of Rights, were aimed at protecting the interests of the propertied classes against Dutch invasion and the ensuing political instability.

A similar logic may be applied to explain the proliferation of quasi-constitutional economic arrangements at the supranational level (think WTO, NAFTA, and other regional trade and monetary agreements) as an attempt to solidify the foundations for a business-friendly global economic order that is largely beyond national political control and the vicissitudes of democratic politics more generally. As Stephen Gill observes, the new constitutionalism "is a macro-political dimension of the process whereby the nature and purpose of the public sphere has been redefined in a more privatized and commodified way ... it can be defined as the political project of attempting to make trans-national liberalism, and if possible liberal democratic capitalism, the sole model for future development. It is therefore intimately related to the rise of market civilization" (Gill 1995: 412). It is intended to "lock in commitments to liberal forms of development, frameworks of accumulation and of dispossession so that global governance is premised on the primacy of the world market" (Gill 2003: 132). David Schneiderman (2008) has likewise talked about the emergence of a global investment rules regime that places the interests of international corporations beyond the reach of domestic politics. Whether by coincidence or not, the global spread of democracy and the rise of corporations-friendly supranational constitutionalism have been, as a matter of fact, simultaneous.

More nuanced manifestations of strategic constitution-making are also evident. For fifteen years (1996 to 2011), the constitution of Morocco remained unchanged. As the so-called Arab Spring of 2011 began to gain momentum, the royal family and its political allies introduced a new constitution aimed at preempting and staving off democratic demands while maintaining King Mohammed VI's grip on power. The amended constitution gives more power to the parliament and the prime minister and guarantees the independence of the judiciary, while still leaving control in the hands of the king. Having been through a vicious civil war, Algeria adopted a new constitution in 1996. Article 2 states that "Islam is the religion of the State." Article 42 allows for the formation of political parties. However, it also states that the right to form political parties "cannot be used to violate the fundamental values and components of the national identity ... as well as the democratic and Republican nature of the State. Political parties cannot be founded on religious, linguistic, racial, sex, corporatist or regional basis." Article 1 of the Tunisian Constitution likewise establishes Islam as the state religion. Article 38 further states that the President of the Republic must be a Muslim. Article 8 of the constitution guarantees the right to form political parties but states that "political parties must respect the sovereignty of the people, the values of the republic, human rights, and the principles pertaining to personal status. Political parties pledge to prohibit all forms of violence, fanaticism, racism and discrimination. No political party may take religion, language, race, sex or region as the foundation for its principles, objectives, activity or programs." So although Islam is the official state religion and must be the religion of its leader, no political party may take Islam as the sole basis of its principles.

Even in Iran, where politics are supposedly modeled on a principled, religious platform, strategic maneuvering has come to dominate the constitutional arena. In 1989, Ayatollah Khomeini introduced the Expediency Council in order to block popular pressures from the generally more progressive Consultative Assembly (*majlis*) and the distinctly more conservative Guardian Council. What is more, in 1993, the Iranian Majlis approved the Free Zones Act, which established Kish Island, Qeshm Island, and the Port of Chabahar as the Free Zones of Iran: free-trade zones in Iran, each of which offers various perks to the international investor, such as full exemption from "Islamic banking" hurdles, tourist attractions, guaranteed repatriation of capital and accumulated profit in case of nationalization, and other benefits that are, by any stretch of the imagination, not fully compatible with a straightforward reading of Shari'a. In other words, worldly interests may trump ideological platforms even in the most principled of constitutional settings.

So-called Islamic constitutionalism illustrates another important aspect of strategic constitutionalism. How North American or European constitutional law is coping with the resurgence of religiosity has been the subject of numerous journalistic and academic accounts. Less well known is the fact that in the past four decades, at least thirty of the world's predominantly Muslim polities declared Shari'a (Islamic law) "a" or "the" source of legislation. Although virtually none of these polities' constitutions were adopted in an authentic bottom-up, "we-the-people" fashion – in fact, quite the opposite is true in most cases – Islamization does reflect a set of values that a large portion of the population in these countries seems to support. It is thus hard not to assign at least some genuine ideational, principled, or aspirational motives to these constitutional regimes.

In practice, however, these countries' actual adherence to and implementation of these principles is often selective, instrumentalist, and self-serving. Every effort is made by moderate, pragmatic regimes, even those who claim to be zealous guardians of tradition, to circumvent certain aspects of religion that are deemed non-beneficial while preserving aspects of religion that are mainly symbolic or that are too costly to transform. A comparison between the light, "form over substance" approach to many religious economic and redistributive directives, as opposed to the notably more solemn approach to family and personal status aspects of religious law, provides a simple yet effective illustration of the non-idealist, earthly tone of constitutional theocracy.

As I argue elsewhere, all things considered, the constitutional establishment of religion is not only an ideational or a regime legitimacy-enhancing move, but also a rational, prudent strategy that allows opponents of theocratic governance in religion

-laden polities to talk the religious talk without walking most of what they regard as theocracy's unappealing, costly walk (Hirschl 2010; 2012). Constitutional law and courts, as symbols of state sovereignty and authority, owe their existence to the body politic, not to a divine authority. They share an inherent antipathy toward rival interpretive hierarchies. Many of the jurisdictional, enforcement, co-optation, and access-to-power advantages that gave religious legal regimes an edge in the premodern era are now aiding the modern state and its laws in its effort to contain religion. The "constitutional" in a constitutional theocracy thus fulfills the same restricting function it carries out in a constitutional democracy: it brings theocratic governance under check and assigns to state-controlled constitutional law and courts the task of a bulwark against the threat of radical religion.

The formal constitutional establishment of religion and the granting of certain jurisdictional autonomy to its tribunals may be portrayed as capitulating to religion, but in reality it may, paradoxically, help limit the potentially radical impact of religion in non-secular settings by bringing religion and its interlocutors under state control. Although establishment of religion does not come without some compromise on universal outlooks, the jurisdiction of constitutional courts in such settings, even if formally religious in some sense, will inevitably reflect a less militant view of religious identity (Hirschl 2010). In short, turning to constitutional law and courts to bring religiosity under check or defuse its potentially radical edge is a rational choice of action by secularists and moderates. Despite occasional and inevitable setbacks, it is a prudent, judicious gamble. Even in presumably aspirational constitutional settings, strategic considerations, writ small or large, matters a great deal.

The realist-strategic approach further suggests that once established, constitutional courts and judges themselves may speak the language of legal doctrine but their actual decision-making patterns reflect ideological preferences and attitudinal tilts, as well as strategic considerations vis-à-vis their political surroundings (the initial foundation for such accounts was laid down in Murphy 1964). This can be explained by reference to the costs that judges as individuals or courts as institutions may incur as a result of adverse reactions to their unwelcome decisions, or through the various benefits that they may acquire through the rendering of strategically tailored decisions (see, for example, Epstein and Knight 2000: 625; Spiller and Gely 2008; Segal 2008; Epstein and Jacobi 2010).

Examples of strategic behavior by constitutional courts are plenty. Here is a less frequently cited illustration. In 2000, the Supreme Court of Pakistan, including then-Justice Iftikhar Chaudhry, unanimously rubber-stamped (based on the doctrine of "state necessity" and the principle of *salus populi suprema lex*) then-President Musharraf's 1999 coup d'état and ousting of Prime Minister Nawaz Sharif. In 2009 (Musharraf was already in exile at the time), the same court, now led by Chief Justice Chaudhry, declared unconstitutional (this time based on principles of judicial independence and *ultra vires*) Musharraf's 2007 ousting of Chaudhry. In other words, a military coup d'état against an elected government is constitutional; ousting a judge is not. Translation: constitutional ideas and doctrines are many. Their selective deployment in politically charged cases is often strategic.

The strategic interplay does not end there. Once a system of constitutional review is put in place, powerful political stakeholders continue their quest to control the composition of courts and to ensure jurisprudential support for their agendas. Occasionally, courts may side with non-canonical worldviews or actors. This is done either on the merits of the arguments, as a court legitimacy-building measure, or simply because courts assess that the political tide has shifted or is likely to shift (Helmke 2002). However, when courts issue rulings that threaten to seriously alter the political power relations in which they are embedded, the political sphere generally responds to quell unfavorable judgments or to hinder their implementation. As the recent history of comparative constitutional politics tells us, recurrent manifestations of unsolicited judicial intervention in the political sphere in general – and unwelcome judgments concerning contentious political issues in particular – have triggered significant political backlashes aimed at clipping the wings of overactive courts. These include legislative overrides of controversial rulings, political tinkering with judicial appointment and tenure procedures to ensure the appointment of compliant judges and/or to block the appointment of undesirable judges, "court-packing" attempts by political power-holders, disciplinary sanctions, impeachment or removal of judges deemed by powerful political stakeholders as objectionable or overactive, the introduction of jurisdictional constraints, or limiting jurisdictional boundaries and curtailment of judicial review powers. The recent government-versus-court wars in Hungary, Romania, or Pakistan provide a textbook illustration of many of these sanctions in action. In some instances (e.g., Russia in 1993, Kazakhstan in 1995, Zimbabwe in 2001, Thailand in 2006, on three occasions in Ecuador from 2004 to 2007, or in Niger 2009), such a backlash has ended in constitutional crisis, leading to the reconstruction or dissolution of constitutional high courts. A struggle for political power and influence, not constitutional principles, an ideological outlook, or systemic functionalism, was a main driving force behind any and all of these events.

Overactive courts do learn the lesson. A wide array of empirically grounded studies suggest that harsh political responses to unwelcome activism or interventions on the part of the courts, or even the credible threat of such a response, can have a chilling effect on judicial decision-making patterns. Variations on the same logic explain prudent and/or strategic judicial behavior in countries as different as Argentina, Brazil, Germany, Pakistan, Canada, Russia, South Korea, Taiwan, Georgia, Ukraine, and Kyrgyzstan (Helmke 2005; Kapiszewski 2011; Vanberg 2005; Newberg 1995; Radmilovic 2010; Epstein, Knight, and Shvetsova 2001; Chang 2010; Trochev 2008, 2013).

6.6 CONCLUSION

Akin to any other major socio-legal phenomenon, the spread of constitutions and judicial review across a wide spectrum of settings results from a confluence of factors rather than any single cause. Until the early 2000s, the pertinent literature on the origins and consequences of constitutionalization was preoccupied with broad ideational and functionalist factors. The realist-strategic approach, by contrast, identifies a set of concrete political vectors, interests, and incentives that affect the introduction of new constitutional orders and, consequently, the interplay between political and constitutional actors and institutions. A quest for lowering risks and costs – most notably attempts to enhance regime legitimacy or lock in a certain set of contested worldviews and policy preferences – is a major determinant of constitutionalization and the corresponding behavior of constitutional institutions, courts, and judges. This, in a nutshell, is the take-home message of the strategic turn in comparative constitutional studies. While this approach does not provide a complete explanation for all instances of constitutionalization, it marks an important theoretical and empirical departure from both formalist legal analyses and overly idealistic normative accounts, as well as from political scientists' and economists' traditional emphasis on functionalist, systemic needs-based explanations of how constitutions emerge and what they do. More than any other extant theory, the strategic-realist approach rests on genuinely comparative, empirically grounded findings, and provides a plausible explanation for the considerable variance worldwide in the scope, nature, and timing of constitutionalization.

REFERENCES

Alberts, Susan, Chris Warshaw and Barry Weingast. 2012. "Democratization and Countermajoritarian Institutions: Power and Constitutional Design in Self-Enforcing Democracy," in Tom Ginsburg, ed., *Comparative Constitutional Design* (Cambridge: Cambridge University Press), 69–100.

Bachrach, Peter and Morton S. Baratz. 1962. "Two Faces of Power," *American Political Science Review* **56**: 947–952.

Bakan, Joel. 1997. *Just Words: Constitutional Rights and Social Wrongs* (Toronto: University of Toronto Press).

Chang, Wen-Chen. 2010. "Strategic Judicial Responses in Politically Charged Cases: East Asian Experiences," ICON *International Journal of Constitutional Law* 8: 885–910.

Dressel, Björn. 2012. "Thailand: Judicialization of Politics or Politicization of the Judiciary?" in Björn Dressel, ed., *The Judicialization of Politics in Asia* (New York: Routledge), 79–97.

Dworkin, Ronald. 1990. A *Bill of Rights for Britain* (Ann Arbor: University of Michigan Press).

Elkins, Zachary. 2010. "Diffusion and the Constitutionalization of Europe," *Comparative Political Studies* **43**: 969–999.

Elkins, Zachary, Tom Ginsburg and James Melton 2009. *The Endurance of National Constitutions* (Cambridge: Cambridge University Press).

Epstein, Lee, Jack Knight and Olga Shvetsova. 2001. "The Role of Constitutional Courts in the Establishment and Maintenance of Democratic Systems of Government," *Law & Society Review* 35: 117–164.

Epstein, Lee and Tonja Jacobi. 2010. "The Strategic Analysis of Judicial Decisions," *Annual Review of Law and Social Science* 6: 341–358.

Epstein, Lee and Jack Knight. 2000. "Toward a Strategic Revolution in Judicial Politics: A Look Back, a Look Ahead," *Political Research Quarterly* 53: 625–661.

Finkel, Jodi. 2008. *Judicial Reform as Political Insurance: Argentina, Peru, and Mexico in the 1990s* (South Bend, IN: University of Notre Dame Press).

Fiorina, Morris P. 1982. "Legislative Choice of Regulatory Forms: Legal Process or Administrative Process?" *Public Choice* 39: 33–66.

Galligan, Denis J. 2013. "The People, the Constitution, and the Idea of Representation," in Denis J. Galligan and Mila Versteeg, eds., *Social and Political Foundations of Constitutions* (Cambridge: Cambridge University Press), forthcoming.

Gill, Stephen. 1995. "Globalization, Market Civilization, and Disciplinary Neoliberalism," *Millennium* 24: 399–423.

    2003. *Power and Resistance in the New World Order* (New York: Palgrave Macmillan).

Ginsburg, Tom. 2002. "Economic Analysis and the Design of Constitutional Courts," *Theoretical Inquiries in Law* 3: 49–85.

    2003. *Judicial Review in New Democracies: Constitutional Courts in Asian Cases* (New York: Cambridge University Press).

Ginsburg, Tom, Zachary Elkins and Justin Blount. 2009. "Does the Process of Constitution-Making Matter?" *Annual Review of Law and Social Science* 5: 201–223.

Ginsburg, Tom, Zachary Elkins and James Melton. 2012. "Do Executive Term-Limits Cause Constitutional Crises?" in Tom Ginsburg, ed., *Comparative Constitutional Design* (Cambridge: Cambridge University Press), 350–379.

Goderis, Benedikt and Mila Versteeg. 2011. *The Transnational Origins of Constitutions: An Empirical Investigation*, available at: http://papers.ssrn.com/sol3/papers. cfm?abstract_id=2216582

Graber, Mark A. 1993. "The Nonmajoritarian Difficulty: Legislative Deference to the Judiciary," *Studies in American Political Development* 7: 35–73.

Helmke. Gretchen. 2002. "The Logic of Strategic Defection: Court-Executive Relations in Argentina under Dictatorship and Democracy," *American Political Science Review* 96: 291–303.

    2005. *Courts under Constraints: Judges, Generals, and Presidents in Argentina* (Cambridge: Cambridge University Press).

Hirschl, Ran. 2004. *Towards Juristocracy: The Origins and Consequences of the New Constitutionalism* (Cambridge, MA: Harvard University Press).

    2010. *Constitutional Theocracy* (Cambridge, MA: Harvard University Press).

    2012. "The Political Economy of Constitutionalism in a Non-Secularist World," in Tom Ginsburg, ed., *Comparative Constitutional Design* (Cambridge: Cambridge University Press), 164–192.

Horowitz, Donald. 1985. *Ethnic Groups in Conflict* (Berkeley: University of California Press).

Jacobsohn, Gary. 2010 "The Disharmonic Constitution," in Stephen Macedo and Jeffrey Tulis, eds., *The Limits of Constitutional Democracy* (Princeton, NJ: Princeton University Press), 47–65.

Kapiszewski, Diana. 2011. "Tactical Balancing: High Court Decision Making on Politically Crucial Cases," *Law and Society Review* 45: 471–506.

Landes, William and Richard Posner. 1975. "The Independent Judiciary in an Interest Group Perspective." *Journal of Law & Economics* 18: 875–901.

Lijphart, Arend. 1977. *Democracy in Plural Societies: A Comparative Exploration* (New Haven, CT: Yale University Press).

2004. "Constitutional Design for Divided Societies," *Journal of Democracy* 15: 96–109.

Magalhães, Pedro. 2003. *The Limits to Judicialization: Legislative Politics and Constitutional Review in the Iberian Democracies* (PhD dissertation, Ohio State University).

2013. "Explaining the Constitutionalization of Social Rights: Portuguese Hypotheses and a Cross-National Test," in Denis J. Galligan and Mila Versteeg, eds., *Social and Political Foundations of Constitutions* (Cambridge: Cambridge University Press), forthcoming.

Mahoney, Paul G. 2001. "The Common Law and Economic Growth: Hayek Might Be Right," *Journal of Legal Studies* 30: 503–525.

McCubbins, Matthew and Thomas Schwartz. 1984. "Congressional Oversight Overlooked: Police Patrols versus Fire Alarms," *American Journal of Political Science* 28: 165–179.

McCubbins, Matthew, Roger Noll and Barry Weingast. 1987. "Administrative Procedures as Instruments of Political Control," *Journal of Law, Economics, and Organization* 3: 243–277.

1989. "Structure and Process, Politics and Policy: Administrative Arrangements and the Political Control of Agencies," *Virginia Law Review* 75: 431–482.

Moe, Terry. 1990. "Political Institutions: The Neglected Side of the Story," *Journal of Law, Economics, and Organization* 6: 213–253.

Moravcsik, Andrew. 2000. "The Origins of Human Rights Regimes," *International Organization* 54: 217–252.

Morton, F. L. 1995. "The Effect of the Charter of Rights on Canadian Federalism," *Publius: The Journal of Federalism* 25: 173–188.

Murphy, Walter F. 1964. *Elements of Judicial Strategy* (Chicago: University of Chicago Press).

Newberg, Paula R. 1995. *Judging the State: Courts and Constitutional Politics in Pakistan* (Cambridge: Cambridge University Press).

North, Douglass and Robert Thomas. 1973. *The Rise of the Western World: A New Economic History* (Cambridge: Cambridge University Press).

North, Douglass and Barry Weingast. 1989. "Constitutions and Commitment: The Evolution of Institutions Governing Public Choice in Seventeenth Century England," *Journal of Economic History* 29: 803–832.

Persson, Torsten and Guido Tabellini. 2004. "Constitutional Rules and Fiscal Policy Outcomes," *American Economic Review* 94: 25–45.

2005. *The Economic Effects of Constitutions* (Cambridge, MA: MIT Press).

Popova, Maria. 2010. "Political Competition as an Obstacle to Judicial Independence: Evidence from Russia and Ukraine," *Comparative Political Studies* 43: 1020–1229.

Radmilovic, Vuk. 2010. "Strategic Legitimacy Cultivation at the Supreme Court of Canada: Quebec Secession Reference and Beyond," *Canadian Journal of Political Science* 43: 843–869.

Ramos, Francisco. 2006. "The Establishment of Constitutional Courts: A Study of 128 Democratic Constitutions," *Review of Law & Economics* 2: 103–135.

Ramseyer, J. Mark. 1994. "The Puzzling (In)dependence of Courts: A Comparative Approach," *Journal of Legal Studies* 23: 721–747.

Rawls, John. 1971. *A Theory of Justice* (Cambridge, MA: Harvard University Press).

Sahlins, Marshall D. 1972. "The Original Affluent Society," in *Stone Age Economics* (London: Routledge), 1–39.

Scheingold, Stuart. 2004. *The Politics of Rights: Lawyers, Public Policy, and Political Change* (Ann Arbor: University of Michigan Press).

Schneiderman, David. 2008. *Constitutionalizing Economic Globalization: Investment Rules and Democracy's Promise* (Cambridge: Cambridge University Press).

Segal, Jeffrey. 2008. "Judicial Behaviour," in Keith Whittington, Daniel Kelemen, and Gregory Caldeira, eds., *Oxford Handbook of Law and Politics* (New York: Oxford University Press), 19–33.

Shapiro, Ian Shapiro and Donald Green. 1994. *Pathologies of Rational Choice Theory: A Critique of Applications in Political Science* (New Haven, CT: Yale University Press).

Shapiro, Martin. 1999. "The Success of Judicial Review," in Sally J. Kenney, William Reisinger and John Reitz, eds., *Constitutional Dialogues in Comparative Perspective* (New York: MacMillan), 193– 219.

Shapiro, Martin and Alec Stone-Sweet. 2002. *On Law, Politics, and Judicialization* (New York: Oxford University Press).

Spiller, Pablo and Raphael Gely. 2008. "Strategic Judicial Decision Making," in Keith Whittington, Daniel Kelemen, and Gregory Caldeira, eds., *Oxford Handbook of Law and Politics* (New York: Oxford University Press), 34–45.

Stephenson, Matthew. 2003. "'When the Devil Turns…': The Political Foundations of Independent Judicial Review," *Journal of Legal Studies* 32: 59–89.

Stone-Sweet, Alec. 2000. *Governing with Judges: Constitutional Politics in Europe* (New York: Oxford University Press).

Trochev, Alexei. 2008. *Judging Russia: The Role of the Constitutional Court in Russian Politics 1990–2006* (Cambridge: Cambridge University Press).

2013. "Fragmentation, Defection, and Disputed Elections: Why Judges Joined the Post-Communist Color Revolutions," in Diana Kapiszewski, Gordon Silverstein, and Robert Kagan, eds., *Consequential Courts: New Judicial Roles in Global Perspective* (Cambridge: Cambridge University Press), 67–92.

Tushnet, Mark. 1984. "An Essay on Rights," *Texas Law Review* 62: 1363–1403.

Tversky, Amos and Daniel Kahneman. 1981. "The Framing of Decisions and the Psychology of Choice," *Science* 211: 453–458.

Vanberg, Georg. 2005. *The Politics of Constitutional Review in Germany* (Cambridge: Cambridge University Press).

Vermeule, Adrian. 2014. *The Constitution of Risk* (Cambridge: Cambridge University Press), forthcoming.

Versteeg, Mila. 2014. "Unpopular Constitutionalism," *Indiana Law Review* 89, forthcoming.

Voigt, Stefan and Eli M. Salzberger. 2002. "Choosing Not to Choose: When Politicians Choose to Delegate Powers," *Kyklos* 55: 289–310.

Waldron, Jeremy. 1987. *"Nonsense Upon Stilts": Bentham, Burke, and Marx on the Rights of Man* (London: Routledge).

Weingast, Barry. 1993. "Constitutions as Government Structures: The Political Foundations of Secure Markets," *Journal of Institutional and Theoretical Economics* **149**: 286–311.

1995. "The Economic Role of Political Institutions: Market-Preserving Federalism and Economic Development," *Journal of Law, Economics & Organization* **11**: 1–31.

Weinrib, Lorraine. 2007. "The Postwar Paradigm and American Exceptionalism," in Sujit Choudhry, ed., *The Migration of Constitutional Ideas* (Cambridge: Cambridge University Press), 83–113.

Whittington, Keith. 2005. "'Interpose Your Friendly Hand': Political Supports for the Exercise of Judicial Review by the United States Supreme Court," *American Political Science Review* **99**: 583–596.

7

Constitutions as Contract, Constitutions as Charters

Tom Ginsburg

7.1 INTRODUCTION

Contractual theories have long played a central role in thinking about the social and political foundations of constitutions, and have been controversial (Barnett 2009; Fallone 2010). In the last two decades, an important line of critique of contractual thinking has come from coordination theorists, beginning with Hardin (1989) and followed by Ordeshook (1992), Weingast (1997), and others. These thinkers, informed by modern game theory, have revived Hume's views, which emphasized coordination, over those of Locke, who emphasized contract. In Chapter 2 of this volume, Hardin lays out the critique with some force.

The social contract metaphor criticized by Hardin and others is primarily a normative one. For early thinkers in the liberal tradition, contract was a natural metaphor for helping explain why a constitution ought to be legitimate in a society composed of fictively autonomous individuals. Hardin's critique is that the contract metaphor is both descriptively and normatively inaccurate. In its place, he argues that coordination provides a better descriptive account of why people comply with constitutional provisions they have not and potentially would not agree to.

I am largely in agreement with this position. However, in this chapter, I argue that, in emphasizing the coordinating role of constitutions, we should not be too quick to reject contractual thinking in its entirety (see also Stone Sweet 2012). Indeed, modern developments in the theory of *private* contracts provide a set of very valuable tools to understand how at least some constitutions are negotiated and maintained, and may have greater explanatory power than either classical social

Thanks to Rosalind Dixon and Mila Versteeg for helpful discussions. Part of this chapter draws on joint work with Zachary Elkins and James Melton .

contract theory *or* the coordination alternative in terms of understanding actual constitutional design in many countries. Coordination theory is a valuable heuristic for explaining positive and normative acquiescence to constitutional provisions, but not particularly useful for generating predictions about the circumstances under which actual constitutions will be formed and endure. A successful coordinating device is simply recognizable by the presence of a constitution in force that is generally accepted; however, we do not have anything within game theory that provides insight into what the equilibrium will be. In contrast, modern contract theory helps us make sense of constitutional bargaining in many real-world cases because it allows us to specify interests and trace negotiations and to understand the possible pareto-superior outcomes. Whatever their deficiencies as a normative theory of constitutionalism, contractarian theories are very helpful for understanding how constitutions are formed and operate as a positive matter – in other words, they help us understand the actual social and political foundations of constitutions, as opposed to the theoretical foundations.

I also wish to be clear that I am not attacking coordination as a concept. Indeed, coordination plays a central role in upholding and maintaining the constitutional contracts that I identify (see Elkins et al. 2009). But coordination is not sufficient as a complete account of constitutional formation and endurance, and itself tells us little about the processes and outcomes of constitutional design processes. Contract, on the other hand, does provide a helpful metaphor for these issues because contracts, like constitutions, are negotiated. The concept of contract, then, should not be discarded too easily and can supplement a coordination perspective.

7.2 THE COORDINATION CRITIQUE: THREE OBJECTIONS

I will not rehearse the long debate over social contract theories, but focus instead on the critique levied by Hardin and others who favor a coordination account. I focus on three objections to contract theory in particular: the lack of actual subjective agreement to constitutional terms, the lack of third-party enforcement, and differences in prospective temporal scope.

First, a central challenge for social contract theorists is the casual observation that constitutions are not in fact agreed to by all their subjects, a point made by Hume himself.[1] There is no moment of universal mutual acceptance, and many subjects will not in fact agree to the terms of the constitution under which they must live. This may be because the constitution was adopted long ago, or perhaps because the subjects have opposed the adoption of the constitution but lost in the founding

---

[1]   Hume, David. 1978. *Of the Original Contract*. Edited and Translated into HTML by Jon Roland. Available at: http://www.constitution.org/dh/origcont.htm.

debates. Surely agreement cannot explain acquiescence, and coordination theory does a superior job on this point. As a descriptive matter, under coordination theory, citizens will have a reasonable basis for complying with constitutional provisions notwithstanding the absence of actual or even implicit agreement to so abide. They will do so because they expect that noncompliance will lead to penalties, or perhaps because of network benefits of remaining in the constitutional order. In this sense, coordination theory is a superior account of acquiescence.

The second objection to contract theory is the fact that contracts are typically enforceable by a third party (e.g., judges). Constitutions cannot rely on such a claim: even judicial enforcement of the constitution depends on higher-order coordination or agreement that the court is to be obeyed as an authoritative interpreter. So constitutions, to be effective, must ultimately be self-enforcing (Ordeshook 1992; Weingast 1997).

Third, constitutions set up an elaborate governance structure, not, in principle, one that is temporally limited, whereas most contracts do anticipate a stage of fulfillment of mutual promises. In this sense, contract is asserted to be an imperfect analogy because contracts can generally be fulfilled whereas constitutions cannot, or at least optimally are not, but endure forever (but see Elkins et al 2009).

Let us take each of these points in turn to see whether they constitute fatal objections for contractual analogies.

7.2.1 *Agreement*

As for the problem of agreement, it is true that coordination theory provides a superior basis for understanding the phenomenon of acquiescence by nonparties. But coordination theory does not explain the *content* of constitutional agreement or how it is produced. Here, the notion of a bargain *is* helpful, particularly for the category of constitutions known as *pacts*. Political scientists have used the notion of a pact to represent negotiated transitions to democracy in which elite bargains are sufficient for transition to occur (Burton and Higley 1987; O'Donnell and Schmitter 1986; Przeworski 1991).[2] Prominent examples include the roundtable talks following the fall of communism in Europe, and the Venezuelan elite bargain from 1958 to 1991.[3] Typically, though not always, such pacts are captured in a formal written constitu-

---

[2] Consider also the supranational constitution of the European Union, which originates in contract-like treaty negotiations by independent states but set in motion a process that led to constitutionalization. See Stone Sweet and Brunnel (1998).

[3] In Venezuela in 1958, a military-civilian coalition overturned a military leader. The three leading political parties concluded what became known as the Punto Fijo pact to form a government of national unity after new elections and to draft a new constitution for the country. The multiparty commission produced a document that survived for thirty-eight years after promulgation in 1961 – the longest-enduring constitution in Venezuela's history.

tion. For these constitutions, bargaining *is* an accurate description of the elite-level negotiations that produce the text (about which we will say more later).

This bargaining is *not* the hypothetical bargain between ruler and subjects offered in classical social contract theory. Rather it is more akin to private bargaining among parties exchanging mutual promises and dividing assets. If the various elite groups are backed by broader social forces, it may not go too far to say that pacted constitutions have the implicit agreement of many of the citizens. But social agreement is not the main mechanism that is of concern. The bargains are simply among powerful parties, who may have the will or ability to coerce others to join them.

What of those who do *not* agree to the constitutional bargain? There will always be some fraction of the populace that is unrepresented in the elite negotiations. These citizens and groups may face the choice of remaining outside the constitutional order, perhaps by secession, or of joining a constitutional scheme that they consider unjust. Some of these citizens and groups *may* decide to join because of the network benefits of being in the system.[4] For these actors, coordination takes the form of explicit, if coerced, consent.

Of course many citizens and groups may have no such choice at all. For example, a geographically dispersed ethnic or political minority may have no effective opportunity to secede and so may be effectively coerced to join the constitutional order without either explicit or implicit consent. For such citizens, the contract metaphor runs out, and coordination again provides a superior account of acquiescence. But for the other categories of citizens, the social contract metaphor does a decent job. The point is that a given constitutional order can have both elements of contract and coordination: acquiescence is explained by contract for some groups and coordination by others.

To illustrate, consider the bargaining that produced the constitution of the United States. It is true that many of the principles that were instantiated in that document – popular sovereignty, republicanism, rights – had developed as conventions over a long period of experiments with colonial and American government. But to assert that these simply sprung into being as a result of coordination would be quite wrong. The decisions produced by the constitutional convention were bargained over, among states with diverse interests. The controversies – over slavery, tariffs, voting rules, and amendment – were resolved through contract-like negotiations among the players. Once adopted, of course, the players and the publics they represented had to coordinate. Even reluctant states like Rhode Island, which had not ratified or agreed to the initial deal, found it in their interests to acquiesce. But the formation of the deal was in some sense contractual, involving promises of performance among several discrete sovereigns.

---

[4] We know that the purportedly more contractual environment of international treaties features some similar dynamics. In 1993, for example, developing countries were effectively given a choice by the EU and the United States of remaining outside the new GATT/WTO regime or remaining in the old system without access to rich country markets.

7.2.2 *Third-Party Enforcement*

Next let us consider the objection about third-party enforcement. Russell Hardin has emphasized this point in his sustained critique of the contractual analogy. Contracts derive their authority from the consent of the parties, as well as a set of outside principles that are enforced by the state that bound and limited the contractual space. In the case of constitutions, this second source of authority is lacking. There is no outside authority that can guarantee enforcement of the constitutional contract, in most cases.

As the highest law of the land, it seems unreasonable to assume that there is an external enforcer of the constitution (Finn 1991: 26). Treating judicial review as a third-party enforcement mechanism simply raises the higher-order question of why it is that parties obey the court's pronouncements. Coordination does provide some insight here: even a court without any coercive authority can help parties select focal points in situations of multiple equilibria (Ginsburg and McAdams 2004; Law 2007). One might think of constitutional courts as providing third-party coordination to facilitate self-enforcing contracts rather than third-party enforcement of ordinary contracts drafted in the shadow of a state legal system.

All this said, Hardin may overstate the case. First, in contemporary constitution-making, international actors may provide a degree of external enforcement of the constitutional bargain. True self-enforcement may not in fact be necessary. This is most easily illustrated with regard to constitution-making exercises imposed by external occupation, or when the United Nations or international community as a whole act as constitutional midwife, as in East Timor in 1999 (Ginsburg et al. 2008). But, you might say, this is exceptional. However, a closer look suggests that international involvement is becoming more the norm than the exception. The Afghan constitution of 2004 was produced by a process that began with the Bonn Agreement of late 2001, in which the United Nations was a party along with the various non-Taliban Afghan representatives. The Kenyan constitution of 2010 came into being as a result of a process initiated by Kofi Annan among warring factions in 2008, and was subject to continual outside monitoring (and indeed lobbying). The list of constitutions produced under some sort of international auspices is long and growing, and in such cases an external actor may in fact play an enforcement role.

Nor is international constraint on constitution-making a new phenomenon. Consider the problem of constitution-making in the early part of the twentieth century for several eastern European nations emerging out of the ashes of the Austro-Hungarian Empire. These states were concluding fragile constitutional bargains in an era of nationalistic self-determination. They included within their constitutions rights for minority groups to preserve and develop their own cultural and linguistic practices.[5] The governments of these states *also* concluded treaties with the great powers of the day, promising to uphold minority rights. This was an instance of duplicate mechanisms of constitutional enforcement, but it is not a stretch to say that the external powers provided a means of external enforcement of the constitutions.

Another example of external enforcement comes from the long tradition of ex-British colonies retaining the jurisdiction of the Privy Council in London as a court of final appeal. This not only helped keep these countries tied to the overall development of the common law, but also helped enhance their credibility with investors and others (Voigt et al. 2007).

The power relationships involved in external enforcement are quite clear in the case of constitutions adopted under occupation (Ginsburg et al. 2008). Some occupying military powers, especially France, the United States, and the Soviet Union, had constitutions written at their behest. For example, Afghanistan had seven constitutional documents written between 1979 and 2004, some of which showed profound influence from the Soviet and U.S. occupiers. One might doubt that constitutions drafted by foreigners are likely to develop into self-enforcing bargains, but there may be certain provisions that the external actors would step in to enforce. This might, under some circumstances, undermine local self-enforcement. If citizens believe a foreign power will punish transgressions, they will have little incentive to pay the costs necessary to organize and challenge the ruling elite and may become unaccustomed to challenging transgressions. Constitutions written under occupation are likely to create a culture of acquiescence in which citizens are explicitly absolved of any responsibility for enforcement. Under such circumstances, the coordination function of constitutions is anemic at best. Leaders anticipate citizen apathy and are more likely to transgress constitutional terms.

Consider as an example the Platt Amendment and the U.S. intervention in Cuba (Carrington 2008). After the Spanish-American War, the United States occupied Cuba and proceeded to prepare the island for self-governance. In a misguided maneuver, the U.S. Senate adopted the Platt Amendment to a military appropriations bill, explicitly stating that U.S. intervention would be forthcoming when and if democratic institutions failed in an independent Cuba. This provision was ultimately included in the 1902 Cuban constitution. As Carrington (2008: 1087) so well describes, it "begot the disorders it was designed to prevent." Domestic factions refused to compromise and each sought to induce the United States to intervene on their own side, preventing stable self-enforcing democracy from taking hold.

More broadly, even those constitutions that do not formally allow for external monitoring are in some sense externally enforced in an era of global attention to human rights issues and a nascent doctrine of humanitarian intervention. The

---

[5]　E.g., constitution of Poland 1921, Articles 109–110.

record of the international community intervening in cases of massive human rights violations is surely inconsistent, but the number of instances has grown. One can think of intervention as an enforcement action to ensure that certain core constitutional obligations are in fact enforced.

7.2.3 *Ongoing Governance*

Finally let us consider the objection that constitutions are designed for *governance*, not simply performance of a discrete set of specific obligations. This objection centers on a model of contract as an agreement of limited duration and purpose in which parties can in principle fulfill their obligations and be done with the contract.

To be sure, constitutions do not generally specify a termination date, although there are some exceptions.[6] But the disanalogies are less than what meets the eye. Contracts are intended to endure, and some contractual provisions, such as restrictive covenants, are perpetual (Finn 1991: 23). Like contracts, constitutions specify a structure of future action for their subjects, providing for some actions that are required, others that are prohibited, and some that are unspecified. Sometimes designers will explicitly specify periods of performance, typically in transitional provisions. "Sunset" clauses might be used for particularly controversial constitutional articles: examples include the U.S. constitution disempowering Congress from regulating slave importation for twenty years, and the Australian constitution limiting several national powers in relation to federalism.[7]

Constitutions, while intended to endure, do not typically do so. In a recent book, Elkins, Ginsburg, and Melton (2009) have shown that constitutions can be expected to last nineteen years on average. In this sense, parties to the constitutional bargain seem quite willing to renege, breach, and start anew. One can describe this as a failure of coordination, which then may lead to a new round of attempts to coordinate. But the process of coordination involves genuine negotiation, akin to other legal documents, including contracts. And so analogizing to contracts may be helpful.

Consider a particular kind of legal document, namely the corporate charter. Modern charters are, of course, a particular type of contract; indeed in one influential view they are nothing more than a "nexus of contracts" (Alchian and Demsetz

---

[6] The Fiji constitution of 1990 required a review within seven years, and then regular reviews every decade thereafter. The latter mechanism is a feature of many U.S. state constitutions.

[7] U.S. Constitution, Art. I, s. 9, cl 1. The Australian constitution capped the percentage of customs duties that the Commonwealth could apply to its own purposes for a ten-year period; limited the automatic power of the Commonwealth to grant state aid to a similar period; and allowed one state (Western Australia) to impose special import duties after the imposition of otherwise uniform customs duties, but only for a five-year period: see Const. of Australia 1901 ss. 87, 95. Thanks to Rosalind Dixon for this point.

1972; Meckling and Jensen 1976). They are contracts that set out governance institutions for a process of ongoing decision making; like constitutions, they have a fundamental purpose and aim. They are also principal-agent documents in which structures of delegation are defined and regulated. Citizens face an agency problem very much like corporate shareholders who need to strike a balance between giving managers enough power to govern but not so much power that managers can extract resources. Another aspect in which corporations are like constitutional orders is that they have internal organizational cultures that persist over time. And like constitutions that, in one view, *create* identity, charters establish new institutional structures that are distinct from the wills of their creators.

To be sure, a polity is a more complex entity than even a large corporation, in the sense that shareholders are assumed to have a relatively discrete set of objectives, or even a single overarching goal of maximizing firm value. In reality, however, some shareholders may care about others, including employees, creditors, or the public. Some shareholders will be only nominal shareholders, who seek to own shares in order to exercise voice about company policies. Shareholders are not coextensive with stakeholders.

As a historical matter, it is worth remembering that the early written constitutions evolved out of contractual arrangements called charters. The Magna Carta was nominally a charter, which in medieval terms was of the same character as royal promises granting land or incorporating cities or companies. Although nominally between the King and the landholding nobles, some of its provisions benefited those who were not directly parties to it. Like contracts, a *carta* required formalities, and had to contain the ruler's signature along with the signatures of witnesses such as important clergy or nobility. Furthermore, like a contract, the *carta* was directed at future action: it is essentially a promise by the ruler to continue to recognize rights and privileges (in land or otherwise) in the future (Robertson 1939: xv–xvi). It was used by the Anglo-Saxon kings to grant land or rights to subjects and would be signed by lay and ecclesiastical members of the king's court (Martin 1979: 140). An example of a charter granting both land and rights would be royal charters of cities, declaring their boundaries and also their rights of local government. A similar usage of charters also existed in Normandy and continued to be used in Norman England (see, for example, Stenton 1955). So it came to be that William the Conqueror's son Henry Beauclerk, or Henry I, combined the *carta* with the Anglo-Saxon tradition of the written coronation oath in issuing the "Charter of Liberties" on his coronation in 1100 (Pollock 1898/1999: 99).

The early charters of the American colonies provided substantive limitations on the powers of the colonial authorities (Amar 1987). They also established organs for ongoing governance. For example, the Massachusetts Bay Company Charter empowered the offices of the governor, deputy governor, assistants, and regular "general court[s]" of freemen of the company. The latter group was comprised of the shareholders in the body, and understood itself to have a role in governance (Bailyn 1967: 190). In some states (Connecticut and Rhode Island), these charters served as actual constitutions for several decades after the founding of the United States (Wood 1969: 276–278).

Charters were historically broad in purpose and akin to a kind of legislative license. Any corporate entity came into being only by a sovereign act – they had to be granted by the monarch, regardless of whether their purpose was private or public, or whether the entity was governmental in character. Corporation traditionally referred to human associations, of which government was only one type. This view was echoed in late-nineteenth-century Prussian thought, particularly the ideas of Georg Jellinek and Otto van Gierke. These thinkers explored the distinctive law of communal associations (Mogi 1932; Emerson 1928: 129–142).[8]

The founding fathers of the United States frequently used the notion of a charter (as well as the contractual notion of compact) to describe the powers of the government created under the constitution.[9] They contrasted the American experience from the European one: American governments were, in Madison's view, *"great charters,* derived not from the usurped power of kings, but from the legitimate authority of the people."[10] The charter idea was that the government had been granted its authority by the people, and the terms of that grant were limited by the text (Fallone 2010: 1080–82).

The corporate analogy meant that there were limitations on the power of the agents and that these were set out in written form (Amar 1987: 1434). The logical

---

[8]   As part of the historical school associated with Friedrich von Savigny, von Gierke sought to develop normative theory out of historical inquiry into the development of German legal institutions. According to von Gierke, it was in the possibility of forming collective organizations that human society flourished, and the state emerged only out of a very long process of evolution of such associations. Although rooted in a logic of voluntary associations, the state had distinctive qualities as it encompassed all other collectivities. As he put it, "the state alone cannot be subordinate as sovereign collective person to any organized will power external to and above it, and consequently it cannot be limited in its will and action by a higher community participating in its decisions" (von Gierke, *Die Genossenschaftstheorie,* 641–642, quoted in Mogi 1932).

[9]   See, e.g., Letter from James Madison to Spencer Roane (June 29, 1821), *in The American Enlightenment,* 461, 461–462 (Adrienne Koch ed., 1965) ("Our Governmental System is established by a compact, not between the Government of the [United] States, and the State Governments; but between the States, as sovereign communities, stipulating each with the others, a surrender of certain portions, of their respective authorities, to be exercised by a Common Govt. and a reservation, for their own exercise, of all their other Authorities."); Madison wrote: "[T]he Government holds its powers by a charter granted to it by the people …. Hitherto charters have been written grants of privileges by Governments to the people. Here they are written grants of power by the people to their Governments." Letter from James Madison to A. Stevenson (November 27, 1830), *in The American Enlightenment, supra* note 66, at 478, 479.

[10] James Madison, 'Charters: Powers and Liberty,' *National Gazette,* January 19, 1792, reprinted in *The American Enlightenment,* at 508, 508.

extension was that these limits could be enforced by those traditionally responsible for doing so: judges. This idea, in which violations of constitutional provisions are analogized to violations of contractual provisions, is part of the building block of judicial review. In *Federalist* No. 78, Hamilton evokes the argument that:

> There is no position which depends on clearer principles than that every act of a delegated authority, contrary to the tenor of the commission under which it is exercised, is void. No legislative act, therefore, contrary to the Constitution, can be valid. To deny this would be to affirm that the deputy is greater than his principal; that the servant is above his master; that the representatives of the people are superior to the people themselves; that men acting by virtue of powers may do not only what their powers do not authorize, but what they forbid.... [T]he Constitution ought to be preferred to the statute, the intention of the people to the intention of their agents.

There are, of course, differences between modern corporate charters and constitutions. The chief distinction is the possibility of exit. Shareholders can sell out their interests, whereas citizens who find a particular set of arrangements unsatisfactory cannot opt out (Amar 1988: n. 152; Chander 2003: 160; Hirschman 1970). This has led some to argue that constitutions should care more about minority protections than including corporate law rules, notwithstanding the fact that minority shareholders are frequently a target of protective corporate regulation in battles for corporate control and similar actions (Chander 2003: 160).[11]

The lack of exit poses a problem to charter theorists of constitutions. Citizens are not able to bargain freely for entry with various alternative polities, unless they happen to be possessors of very high levels of human or financial capital (Law 2007). Without any bargaining leverage, the idea that one is in a contractual relationship with the jurisdiction in which one happened to have been born stretches the ordinary meaning of the term. Even here, however, there may be a sense in which competition does operate at the level of constitutional provisions. In a world of mobile citizens, states that compete for capital and labor have some competitive incentives to offer attractive packages of civil rights, at least packages that are attractive to high-end mobile workers who are in demand in many jurisdictions (Law 2007).

In short, the charter analogy suggests that contractual thinking may have some relevance in thinking about problems of constitutional design. The familiar agency problem in both contexts and the need to handle unspecified problems of ongoing governance are similarities, even if the exit condition is not met in the case of (most) constitutions.

---

[11] See also Paramount Commc'ns Inc. v. QVC Network Inc. 637 A.2d 34, 46, 48 (Del. 1993) (expressing concern that shift to control by large shareholder necessitated judicial intervention.)

7.3 CONSTITUTIONS AS CONTRACTS

Having made the case that some of the critiques of contract thinking about constitutions are overstated, I now wish to argue that there are significant payoffs to the application of modern contract theory to constitutional design. Again, this theory has been developed in the context of private contracts, not political or social contracts, but it provides useful resources for understanding constitutions. I focus on three issues: constitutional formation and negotiation, the content of constitutions, and constitutional renegotiation and endurance. I draw on the economics literature on incomplete contracts, which has advanced our theoretical understanding of why some things are written and others left unwritten.

7.3.1 *Constitutional Negotiation*

7.3.1.1 Constitutional Incompleteness and Bargaining

A good place to start is to think about how constitutions are actually produced in the real world. One set of parameters that will influence the bargain is the nature of the drafting process. Drafting processes, of course, differ in the degree to which they facilitate bargaining. Three different variables are the degree to which the process is open or closed, time-constrained or leisurely, participatory or exclusive.

In terms of being open or closed, Elster (1995) claims that more transparent processes can lead to more arguing than bargaining, in which parties spend time and energy on posturing before their respective principles. We do not know whether this conjecture is correct but it seems plausible. Another major factor is time. Time constraints might pressure parties to leave more things unspecified if they run out of time to write them down; at the same time, they can reduce the possibility of strategic behavior in the negotiation process. If time for drafting were unlimited, parties might never sit down to sort out the hard issues.

A third factor is the range and diversity of parties to the constitutional negotiation process. It is a fact of constitution-making that it typically takes place among groups or factions who represent, to one degree or another, the individual subjects of the constitution. These might be ethnic or religious groups, as in the recent cases of Bosnia or Iraq, or they may simply have divergent interests, as did Southern planters and Northern financiers during the negotiation of the American founding. The groups may differ with respect to resources, geography, ideology, or other dimensions – the content of their disagreement is not particularly material for present purposes.

Let us first assume a discrete number of groups, and also that there is some "surplus" to be gained from concluding a constitutional deal.[12] Note that the notion

---

[12] See generally Elkins et al. (2009).

of a negotiating surplus is directly drawn from contract theory, and in the present context, the surplus might include goods like international legitimacy, economic stability, and security. The constitutional bargaining process is costly, requiring the expenditure of time and political capital during both the negotiation and approval phases. Furthermore, each bargainer must be concerned with ensuring that his supporters can be delivered, which provides some constraints. The parties at the table will conclude a bargain or not, based on an expected stream of benefits to particular groups less the transaction costs of negotiation. Parties will also consider alternative arrangements depending on their feasibility. The concept of a *reservation price* from contract theory is relevant here. A reservation price refers to the least favorable point at which a party will accept a negotiated agreement, and depends in part on the value of alternative arrangements.

To provide an example, suppose there are two ethnic groups, A and B, located in different areas of the country, with 70 percent and 30 percent of the population, respectively, as well as a military faction M. Any two of these three players can conclude a constitutional bargain, excluding the other. Ethnic group A would like to conclude a bargain with the military, shutting out group B from political goods. But B has the capacity to impose costs on A; if it does not receive at least 20 percent of the political goods, it would prefer to secede or organize violent demonstrations. If these threats are credible, the 20 percent is the reservation price for Group B. The parties come together and negotiate, and let us assume that they negotiate an arrangement wherein A gets 70 percent of the anticipated stream of political payoffs, B 20 gets percent, and M gets 10 percent.

Note that other stable arrangements are possible, and choosing among them involves coordination – but only among those that lie on the "pareto frontier." Contract theory helps illuminate the range of possible deals because it pushes us to specify, ex ante, the perceived interests of the negotiators.

Contract theory has identified the problem of bilateral monopoly, which occurs in markets where there is only one buyer and one seller. When there is asymmetric information, these markets are subject to "holdout problems" in which each party signals that its reservation price is more extreme than the real price, and parties cannot conclude a deal. Suppose, in our earlier example, there are only two parties to the constitutional bargain, groups A and B. Each one has private information on its actual reservation price. A says that it will only conclude a constitution with a system of parliamentary sovereignty, while B, the smaller and weaker party, says that it will only conclude a bargain in which courts have a powerful role in protecting minority rights. If neither is willing to compromise, a bargain may not be concluded, and in many cases civil strife may result. Something like this seemed to happen in the constitutional negotiations in Iraq, in which Sunni representatives refused to participate in negotiations without prior guarantees of their position. The other parties – various representatives of Shiite and Kurdish groups – did conclude an agreement, under severe pressure from an externally imposed timetable.

Contract theory also provides useful language for understanding downstream renegotiation. The initial bargain will of necessity be "incomplete," in that the parties will be unable to specify every future contingency (Persson, Roland, and Tabellini 1997: 1165; Gillette 1997: 1355). Because of transaction costs to negotiation, parties that seek to specify every contingency will never conclude a deal. This means that the bargain will be subject to unanticipated "shocks" that occur downstream. Just as parties to a contract may find, for example, that prices of supplies increase, forcing a renegotiation of the deal, constitutional bargainers may need to adjust their bargain down the road if anticipated benefits do not materialize. This might involve a constitutional amendment or even a replacement of the constitution with a new one.

Another source of pressure on constitutional bargains is that each party may be unaware of other parties' true capabilities and intentions. In contract theory this is called the problem of hidden information, and is ubiquitous. A party to negotiation may misrepresent its own endowments and intentions for strategic reasons.

Constitutional bargaining sometimes involves attempts to induce counterparties to reveal private information. The Spanish transition to democracy, marked by the Constitution of 1978, was negotiated through an elite pact among political parties brokered by President Suarez (Linz and Stepan 1996). The context was one in which memories of the bloody civil war of the 1930s were quite raw, and both left and right had to reassure each other. The left was seen as divisive and republican, while the right was seen as favoring military intervention in politics. The negotiation process of the so-called Moncloa pact facilitated the left's acceptance of the monarchy, with the right's agreement to dismantle the institutions of Franco's dictatorship. This set of mutual promises set in motion a series of events in which the parties learned to trust each other, culminating in the 1982 election of the socialist party that retained the monarchy. The bargain held, both during constitutional transition and during the long period of socialist rule from 1982 to 1996.

In the U.S. context, hidden information about intentions was a key factor in constitutional negotiations. The intense negotiation over the majority required to pass navigation acts reflected not just different views on morality but hidden information. The South believed that the North was likely to tax the South on exports, which would both subsidize Northern shipping interests and harm the South (Goldstone 2005: 161–163). It thus demanded that navigation acts require a two-thirds legislative supermajority. The North, however, was able to resist this demand, in part because it had conceded so much to the South on other points. The point is that the constitutional negotiation was one in which the South distrusted the true intentions of its negotiating partner and sought to specify further detail and veto power as a way of preventing harm to its interests.

As we note in our account of constitutional endurance (Elkins et al. 2009), the problem of hidden information is particularly severe in the first period of constitutional performance. As parties interact in performing the terms of the constitutional bargain, they are likely to reveal information to each other more fully than can be done in the bargaining phase. They may even develop the constitutional equivalent of a "course of dealing," a set of informal norms that supplement their formal arrangements. As time goes on, information on the "type" of partner they have is likely to increase. For example, Spain's left and right wings grew to trust each other in the course of dealing with each other over time. This is just one example of a type of problem illuminated using modern contract theory.

It is worth considering solutions to each of the information problems laid out earlier: the problem of incomplete information because of external shocks, and hidden information that results from strategic incentives in bargaining. One standard answer to the problem of incomplete information is to write loosely defined contracts that allow flexible adjustment over time as new information is revealed. The parties will be able to specify performance within general parameters in light of changing circumstances. The economic theory of contract, however, has identified a risk of moral hazard from loosely specified contracts. Vague language might allow a party to claim that circumstances have changed in order to take a greater share of the constitutional "surplus." Indeed, knowing that this is a possibility down the road, a party might seek to conceal its intentions and endowments from its constitutional partners.

In contrast, a standard response to the problem of hidden information is to write a more complete agreement, specifying contingencies. By forcing the other party to reveal information, one can minimize strategically generated surprises down the road. But this solution to the problem of hidden information, of course, exacerbates the risk of being too rigid in the face of exogenous change. The more one tries to solve one problem, the more one exacerbates the other.

Another standard solution to problems of hidden and incomplete information is to rely on third parties. Analogizing to contract law, one might imagine a theory of constitutional review in which the courts seek to correct problems that arise during the bargaining process. Contract theorists have identified an important role for courts in providing "default rules" that reflect their understanding of what the bargain would have been in the presence of complete information (Ayres and Gertner 1989). In contract theory, courts that play this role can provide a disincentive for parties to hide information from each other. However, there are significant problems with expecting courts to be able to play this function in the constitutional context because no matter what decision the court makes, the relevant parties *still* face the decision as to whether or not to comply with the court decision. Furthermore, independent and competent courts are themselves a product of constitutional bargaining, and cannot be assumed to exist ex ante. Hardin is correct that self-enforcing provisions are key.

These two sources of uncertainty, caused by exogenous shocks and strategic incentives to hide information, mean that parties are unable to produce a complete contract. For each of them, information revealed later in time, either by a party or by new states of the world, may affect the parties' perceptions of the arrangement. This may lead to moments of potential adjustment – or breakdown – of the constitutional arrangement down the road.

This discussion does not exhaust all potential sources of information constraint in constitutional design. Parties have bounded rationality and may be unable to anticipate the costs and benefits accurately. Doing so requires a certain level of social scientific reasoning in institutional design (Tarrow 2010), which may be suspect in the real world. In short, we should expect a certain amount of unanticipated pressure on constitutional bargains.

7.3.2 *The Content of Constitutions*

Contracts are typically drafted by law firms acting on behalf of the parties. Constitutions are drafted by experts, government officials and lawyers acting on behalf of the negotiating groups. In either case, the drafters are likely to take the same initial approach. Rather than draft the document from scratch, they will look for a model, or several models, to see how the document is organized and what subjects it covers (Choudhry 2007).[13] I call these boilerplate provisions of constitutions (see also Law 2005 describing "generic" constitutional law).

As example of boilerplate provisions in constitutions, consider the rights provisions of Commonwealth constitutions (Versteeg, 2013). Many of the constitutions adopted by former British colonies at the moment of independence were drafted in very similar circumstances, involving the so-called Lancaster House negotiations under the auspices of the Foreign Office. These involved local elites who were encouraged to produce constitutions as a condition of independence. The drafting of many of these documents is remarkably similar, particularly those sections related to rights, as they were modeled on the European Convention of Human Rights (Simpson 2001).[14] More generally, Law and Versteeg (2011) have identified the contents of global templates of rights provisions in constitutions.

International treaties can sometimes provide templates for constitutional drafters. With my coauthors I have found that constitutions drafted after the adoption of

---

[13] See also Symposium on Constitutional Borrowing, 1 *International Journal of Constitutional Law* 177–324 (2003); Symposium: Comparative Avenues in Constitutional Law Borrowing, 82 *Texas Law Review* 1737 (2004).

[14] See also, for example, the constitutions of Antigua and Barbuda, The Bahamas, Barbados, and Belize.

the International Covenants on Civil and Political/Economic and Social Rights are more likely to include the rights listed in those documents than other rights (Elkins, Ginsburg, and Simmons 2012; but see Versteeg 2013). In short, the content of constitutions may, like contracts, have a form-like quality. Provisions migrate from document to document, sometimes with only minor amounts of local tailoring. These can reduce the transaction costs of negotiation.

This approach has the virtue of not reinventing the wheel, and need not be viewed pejoratively. If one believes that constitutional provisions have been adopted by other countries based on an independent assessment of their benefits, borrowing can represent a form of social learning, by which states learn from others' experience. Further, some provisions of a constitution may be directed externally, such as rights provisions that are designed to act as signals to international audiences (Farber 2002). It might make sense for drafters to use conventional forms of rights language to achieve this signaling purpose. On the other hand, boilerplates can lead to adoption of provisions without much local meaning. Perhaps it is not surprising that the paradigmatic phrase "we the people" appears in thirty-eight national constitutions in history; but it may be somewhat surprising to learn that the idiosyncratic phrase "cruel and unusual" punishment appears in ten constitutions, and "due process" appears in sixty-seven, ranging from Afghanistan to Yugoslavia.[15] This latter phrase has a specific historical meaning in common law countries, and yet has been widely adopted in countries with different legal tradition. If there is less local understanding of what the provisions entail, there is less likelihood of effective enforcement in practice (Weingast 1997).

Boilerplate provisions have the advantage of saving on transaction costs of negotiation. Furthermore, in the constitutional context, the usual objections to "boilerplate" in contracts between buyers and sellers – namely that they involve a power imbalance in favor of drafters – are less salient (Ben-Shahar 2007). On the other hand, in the constitutional context, there are few of the mechanisms of market discipline that some believe restrain the use of "inefficient" boilerplates in the contractual setting (Ben-Shahar and White 2007). We cannot be confident that the phrases being borrowed are in fact the best provisions.

Both contracts and constitutions rely to a certain extent on background principles and understandings not specified in the text (Finn 1991: 24). These can include the parties' expectations of proper behavior, unwritten norms and understandings, or other legal documents that are seen as having normative force and are relevant to the terms of the deal. Contract theorists emphasize the importance of such unwritten terms in "relational contracts" in which parties engage in a long-term relationship. This concept has obvious application to constitutional bargains.

---

[15] Data on file with author. Data drawn from Comparative Constitutions Project, available at http://www.comparativeconstitutionsproject.org

Beyond form and unwritten supplements, certain constitutional provisions are nicely understood using contractual language. I have argued previously that those who are prospective losers in the post-constitutional political process have a greater incentive to empower a constitutional court than those who are prospective winners (Ginsburg 2003). The inclusion of judicial review and other minoritarian institutions operates as an *insurance term* in the constitutional bargain, providing an alternative forum to reconsider policies in the event that the bargainer finds him/herself out of power. Other constitutional provisions might benefit from this kind of analysis.

In contracts and corporate law, but not constitutions, the terms of the bargain are supplemented with mandatory law and default rules, which form, in some sense, implicit additional terms to the contract. Default rules consist of provisions that will apply as long as parties do not bargain around them. Mandatory rules of law limit the ability of parties to choose their terms of cooperation freely. There are few analogies here in the constitutional realm, save perhaps the international law of *jus cogens*, norms of such universal acceptance that no deviation from them is allowed. Hypothetically, for example, a constitution that purported to legalize torture would provoke international outrage and potentially lead to enforcement efforts to prevent implementation.

7.3.3 *Changed Circumstances and Constitutional Renegotiation*

A central problem for constitutional endurance is that, although the constitutional bargain may be an optimal arrangement for the parties at the time it is drafted, conditions may change over time. A constitution that fails to anticipate the various risk factors to which it will be subjected can be considered genetically defective and unlikely to survive. One that does anticipate such factors may better withstand the waves of exogenous change, surviving through adjustment down the road.

The contract theory notion of efficient breach suggests that parties in some circumstances can and should violate their prior agreements when it is efficient to do so. For every period after the initial negotiation, the parties to a contract or a constitution have to make a decision about whether to remain in the current bargain or renegotiate. Sometimes pressure for renegotiation may result from the revelation of information that was strategically hidden during initial negotiations. Sometimes pressure can result from an external shock that changes costs and benefits over time, leading parties to renegotiate the deal. And sometimes the costs and benefits may simply shift because of internal changes, reflecting the rise of a minority group or newly emerging social force seeking to enhance its position.

Consider the 1926 constitution of Lebanon, supplemented by the so-called National Pact of 1943 that divided power among confessional groups. A 1943 amendment provided that the sects would be represented in an equitable manner "as a temporary arrangement."[16] Under the National Pact, the president of the country would be a Maronite Christian, the prime minister a Sunni Muslim, and the speaker of the parliament a Shiite; parliament would have a 6:5 ratio of Christians to Muslims. This arrangement was stable for some decades, but ultimately demographic change meant that the constitution no longer fitted the society, and it died in a bloody fourteen-year civil war. Surely a firmer sunset provision might have prevented the "temporary arrangement" from breaking down in such a horrific manner.

The proponents of renegotiation can be the relative winners or losers in the initial constitutional bargain. The relative winners are often seeking a larger share of the constitutional surplus. On the other hand, it may be a relative loser who seeks to renegotiate the bargain for a larger share of the constitutional surplus. Even if losers do not have the power to win in ordinary politics, they may be able to impose sufficient costs on the winners so as to force renegotiation.

Renegotiation can take several forms. The formal amendment process is one mechanism; however, if that is unavailable or difficult, parties may use informal mechanisms such as judicial interpretations or unwritten understandings. If, on the other hand, formal constitutional amendment is relatively simple, there may be less need for judicial or other institutional reinterpretation of the constitution.

If renegotiation through amendment does not work, one party or another may seek to start the bargain over. This is typically costly. The bundled character of institutional change, with many different issues to be decided, means that parties will find it more difficult to predict ex ante what the trade-offs across issues will be. Furthermore, there is some risk that major shifts will inure to the detriment of the group(s) that called for a renegotiation. We have some real-world examples of such dynamics. In the aftermath of the South African Constitutional Court's 1995 decision in *State v. Makwanyane*, in which it found the death penalty unconstitutional, some elements of the National Party sought a constitutional amendment to overrule the case. The African National Congress (ANC), however, responded by calling for amendment of the property rights provisions that had been central to the country's negotiated transition and were of great interest to the National Party. These had been subject to grave criticism within the ANC's constituencies because they slowed down popular land reform (Atuahene 2011). Rather than risk losing property rights protection, the National Party quickly quieted calls for amendment of the death penalty provision. Ten years later, the Constitutional Review Committee recommended that neither provision be amended.[17]

Termination of constitutions, as a legal matter, would seem to require unanimous agreement, even if this is not true as a political matter. Lincoln, in his First

---

[16] Constitution of Lebanon, Article 95 (1946).
[17] Parliamentary Monitoring Group 2005.

Inaugural Address, wrestled with the issue, arguing that termination required unanimity, or else would be considered a breach. "If the United States be not a government proper, but an association of States in the nature of contract merely, can it, as a contract, be peaceably unmade by less than all the parties who made it? One party to a contract may violate it – break it, so to speak – but does it not require all to lawfully rescind it?"[18] Yet we do observe breach and rescission quite frequently in the comparative context.

Some constitutions will be fragile, and others not. This has to do with factors related to the environment as well as certain design features that may be within the control of the drafters. Elkins et al. (2009) report that constitutional flexibility (in terms of ease of amendment), inclusive processes, and constitutional detail help constitutions endure over time.

Not all the effects of time are harmful for constitutional endurance, nor are they for contracts. In either context, time can erode the initial bargain as new circumstances arise, but it can also reinforce it. Scholars who emphasize the importance of path dependency focus on how certain choices, once made, will provide increasing returns from continued investment. Although originally developed in the context of the economy, path dependency is what scholars in political science and law are now turning to as an explanation of why some phenomena endure and others do not (e.g., Pierson 2005; Hathaway 2001). One can imagine that constitutions may generate increasing and continuing support for their institutions, making it less likely that parties would like to exit from current arrangements, "locking in" the current configuration and insulating it from exogenous shocks (Arthur 1994). This is what we might call the self-reinforcing constitution.

In the constitutional context, self-reinforcement first requires that constitutions give actors a stake in participating in the political institutions that are established. As actors invest resources in utilizing these political institutions, they may find that the investments pay off and return political goods to the investor. Over time, actors may develop an increasing stake in constitutional viability.[19] The public, too, can gain an increasing familiarity with and attachment to the founding document over time, making it more likely that they will enforce the bargain, as discussed later.[20] The self-enforcing constitution is sustained by self-reinforcing dynamics.

---

[18] First Inaugural Address.

[19] Note that this analysis deviates from one point emphasized in the current literature on self-enforcement. Weingast (1997) emphasizes that self-enforcement requires reducing the stakes of politics so as not to trigger actors' rational fears, which might cause a constitutional breakdown. We agree with this point, but also note that self-*reinforcement* requires raising the stakes of politics, so as to give actors an incentive to participate and to produce increasing levels of collective goods.

[20] Widner (2008: 6 n. 6) provides the example of new multiparty constitutions in Africa. When leaders sought to amend these constitutions to extend their terms beyond the original bargain, popular resistance has been effective in countries where drafting was consultative, but not so when drafting was highly elite driven.

7.4 CONCLUSION

Social contract is the central metaphor in modern Western constitutional thought, and informs the imaginations of constitutional designers as well as scholars. For example, in a recent comment on the transitional constitution of the Sudan, a government official relied heavily on the claim that "constitutions are contracts between people and the government" in arguing for greater public participation in the constitution-making process.[21] Such thinking forms the normative basis for constitutionalism.

This contractual analogy has a long history but has been subjected to recent attack on normative and positive grounds. I agree with the normative critique but in this essay claim that positive contractual analysis can provide helpful perspectives to help us understand how constitutions are formed and what their content is. In this sense I am trying to revive the contract analogy, not as a normative matter for understanding constitutional acquiescence by those who oppose its terms, but as a positive matter for understanding constitutional formation and endurance. My argument is not a defense of social contract theory, as much as an argument that we should move to different elements of the contractual analogy to understand fully the lived social and political bases of constitutions.

REFERENCES

Alchian, Armen and Demsetz, Harold 1972. 'Production, Information Costs, and Economic Organization', *American Economic Review* **62**: 777–779.

Amar, Akhil 1987. 'Of Sovereignty and Federalism', *Yale Law Journal* **96**: 1425–1520.
    1988. 'Philadelphia Revisited: Amending the Constitution Outside Article V', *University of Chicago Law Review* **55** (4): 1043–1104.

Arthur, W. Brian 1994. *Increasing Returns and Path Dependence in the Economy*. Ann Arbor: University of Michigan Press.

Atuahene, Bernadette 2011. 'South Africa's Land Reform Crisis: Eliminating the Legacy of Apartheid', *Foreign Affairs* **90**(4): 121–129.

Ayres, Ian and Gertner, Robert 1989. 'Filling Gaps in Incomplete Contracts: An Economic Theory of Default Rules', *Yale Law Journal* **99**: 87–130.

Bailyn, Bernard 1967. *The Ideological Origins of the American Revolution*. Cambridge, MA: Harvard University Press.

Barnett, Randy E. 2009. 'The Misconceived Assumption About Constitutional Assumptions', *Northwestern University Law Review* **103**(2): 615–662.

Ben-Shahar, Omri (ed.) 2007. *Boilerplate: The Foundation of Market Contracts*. Cambridge: Cambridge University Press.

Ben-Shahar, O. and White, J. 2007. 'Boilerplate and Economic Power in Auto-Manufacturing Contracts', in Ben-Shahar (ed.), *Boilerplate: The Foundation of Market Contracts*. Cambridge: Cambridge University Press, pp. 29–45.

---

[21] Sudan Radio Service, June 7, 2011.

Burton, Michael and Higley, John 1987. 'Elite Settlements', *American Sociological Review* 52: 295–307.

Brown, Nathan 2008. 'Reason, Interest, Rationality, and Passion in Constitution Drafting', *PS: Political Science and Politics* 6(4): 675–689.

Carrington, Paul 2008. 'Could and Should America Have Made an Ottoman Republic in 1919?', *William and Mary Law Review* 49: 1071–1108.

Chander, Anupam 2003. 'Minorities, Shareholder and Otherwise', *Yale Law Journal* 113: 119–178.

Choudhry, Sujit (ed.) 2007. *Migration of Constitutional Ideas.* Cambridge: Cambridge University Press.

Diamond, Larry, Hartlyn, Jonathan, and Linz, Juan 1989. 'Introduction', in Larry Diamond, Juan J. Linz, and Seymour Martin Lipset (eds.), *Democracy in Developing Countries: Latin America.* Boulder, CO: Lynne Rienner.

Eisenberg, Melvin 1976. *The Structure of the Corporation: A Legal Analysis.* New York: Beard Books.

Elkins, Zachary, Ginsburg, Tom, and Melton, James 2008. 'Baghdad, Tokyo, Kabul: Constitution-Making in Occupied States', *William and Mary Law Review* 49: 1139–1178.

Elkins, Zachary, Ginsburg, Tom and Melton, James 2009. *The Endurance of National Constitutions.* Cambridge: Cambridge University Press.

Elkins, Zachary, Ginsburg, Tom and Simmons, Beth 2013. 'Getting to Rights: Treaty Ratification, Constitutional Convergence, and Human Rights Practice in the Late Twentieth Century', *Harvard International Law Review* 54: 61–95.

Elster, Jon 1995. 'Forces and Mechanisms in the Constitution-Making Process', *Duke Law Review* 45: 364–396.

Emerson, Rupert 1928. *State and Sovereignty in Modern Germany.* New Haven, CT: Yale University Press.

Fallone, Edward A. 2010. 'Charters, Compacts, and Tea Parties: The Decline and Resurrection of a Delegation View of the Constitution', *Wake Forest Law Review* 45: 1067–1124.

Farber, Daniel 2002. 'Rights as Signals', *Journal of Legal Studies* 31: 83–98.

Finn, John 1991. *Constitutions in Crisis: Political Violence and the Rule of Law.* Oxford: Oxford University Press.

Ginsburg, Tom 2003. *Judicial Review in New Democracies.* New York: Cambridge University Press.

Ginsburg, Tom and McAdams, Richard 2004. 'Adjudicating in Anarchy: An Expressive Theory of International Dispute Resolution', *William and Mary Law Review* 45(4): 1229–1339.

Ginsburg, Tom, Zachary Elkins, and James Melton 2008. 'Baghdad, Tokyo, Kabul: Constitution-making in Occupied States', *William and Mary Law Review* 49: 1139–1178.

Gillette, Clayton 1997. 'The Exercise of Trumps by Decentralized Governments', *Virginia Law Review* 83(7): 1347–1418.

Goldstone, Lawrence 2005. *Dark Bargain: Slavery, Profits, and the Struggle for the Constitution.* New York: Walker Publishing Company.

Hardin, Russell 1989. 'Why a Constitution?' in Grofman, Bernard and Wittman, Donald (eds.), *The Federalist Papers and the New Institutionalism.* New York: Agathon Press, pp. 100–120.

1999. *Liberalism, Constitutionalism, and Democracy.* Oxford: Oxford University Press.

Hathaway, Oona 2001. 'Path Dependence in the Law: The Course and Pattern of Change in a Common Law Legal System', *Iowa Law Review* 86: 601–661.

Hirschman, Albert O. 1970. *Exit, Voice, and Loyalty: Responses to Decline in Firms, Organizations, and States.* Cambridge, MA: Harvard University Press.

Issacharoff, Samuel 2009. 'Pragmatic Originalism?', *New York University Journal of Law and Liberty* 4: 517–534.

Jackson, Vicki and Greene, Jamal 2011. 'Constitutional Interpretation in Comparative Perspective: Comparing Judges or Courts?' in Ginsburg, Tom and Dixon, Rosalind (eds.), *Comparative Constitutional Law.* Chelthenham: Edward Elgar Publishing, pp. 599–623.

Jensen, Michael C. and Meckling, William H. 1976. 'Theory of the Firm: Managerial Behavior, Agency Costs and Ownership Structure', *Journal of Financial Economics* 3(4): 305–360.

Kronman, Anthony T. 1985. 'Contract Law and the State of Nature', *Journal of Law, Economics, and Organization* 1 (1): 5–32.

Law, David S. 2005. 'Generic Constitutional Law', *Minnesota Law Review* 89: 652–742.

2007. 'Globalization and the Future of Constitutional Rights', *Northwestern Law Review* 102(3): 1277–1349.

2009. 'A Theory of Judicial Power and Judicial Review', *Georgetown Law Review* 97(3): 723–801.

Law, David and Versteeg, Mila. 2011. 'The Evolution and Ideology of Global Constitutionalism', *California Law Review* 99: 1163–1258.

Linz, Juan and Stepan, Alfred 1996. *Problems of Democratic Transition and Consolidation.* Baltimore: Johns Hopkins University Press.

Manning, John 2010. 'Clear Statement Rules and the Constitution', *Columbia Law Review* 100(2): 101–153.

Martin, Charles B. 1979. 'Anglo-Saxon Diplomatics: An Introduction to Sources', *South Central Bulletin* 39(4): 140–142.

Mogi, Sobei 1932. *Otto von Gierke: His Political Teachings and Life.* London: P.S. King and Son.

O'Donnell, Guillermo and Schmitter, Philippe C. 1986. *Transitions from Authoritarian Rule.* Baltimore: Johns Hopkins University Press

Ordeshook, Peter C. 1992. 'Constitutional Stability', *Constitutional Political Economy* 3(2): 137–175.

Persson, Torsten, Roland, Gerard, and Tabellini, Guido 1997. 'Separation of Powers and Political Accountability', *The Quarterly Journal of Economics* 112(4): 1163–1202.

Pierson, Charles W. 2005. *Our Changing Constitution.* Boston: IndyPublish.

Pollock, Sir Frederick and Maitland, Frederic William 1898. *The History of English Law before the Time of Edward I, Vol. 1.* Cambridge: University Press. (2nd printing 1999).

Przeworski, Adam 1991. *Democracy and the Market; Political and Economic Reforms in Eastern Europe and Latin America.* New York: Cambridge University Press

Robertson, A. J. 1939. *Anglo-Saxon Charters.* Cambridge: Cambridge University Press.

Simpson, A. W. Brian 2001. *Human Rights and the End of Empire: Britain and the Genesis of the European Convention.* Oxford: Oxford University Press.

Stenton, Frank 1955. *The Latin Charters of the Anglo-Saxon Period.* Oxford: Oxford University Press.

Stenton, Frank Merry 1908 [1967]. *William the Conqueror: and the Rule of the Normans.* London: G. P. Putnam's Sons.

Sweet, Alec Stone 2012. 'Constitutional Courts', in Rosenfeld, M. and Sajo, A. (eds.), *Oxford Handbook of Comparative Constitutional Law.* Oxford: Oxford University Press, pp. 816–30.

Sweet, Alec Stone and Brunell, Thomas L. 1998. 'Constructing a Supranational Constitution: Dispute Resolution and Governance in the European Community', *American Political Science Review* 92: 63–81.

Tarrow, Sidney 2010. *Power in Movement.* New York: Cambridge University Press.

Versteeg, Mila 2013. *Unpopular Constitutionalism.* Manuscript.

Voigt, Stefan, Ebeling, Michael, and Blume, Lorenz 2007. 'Improving Credibility by Delegating Judicial Competence – the Case of the Judicial Committee of the Privy Council' *Journal of Development Economics* 82(2): 348–373.

Walton, Nina 2010. 'On the Optimal Allocation of Power Between Shareholders and Managers', *University of Southern California Center in Law, Economics and Organization Research Paper Series.* Research Paper No. C10–12, USC Legal Studies Research Paper No. 10–13.

Weingast, Barry R. 1997. 'The Political Foundations of Democracy and the Rule of Law' *American Political Science Review* 91(June): 245–263.

Widner, Jennifer 2008. 'Constitution Writing in Post-Conflict Settings: An Overview', *William and Mary Law Review* 49(4): 1513–1541.

Williamson, Oliver E. 1985. *The Economic Institutions of Capitalism: Firms, Markets, Relational Contracting.* New York: Free Press.

Wood, Gordon 1969. *The Creation of the American Republic, 1776–1787.* Chapel Hill: The University of North Carolina Press.

PART III

Case Studies

8

Accidental Constitutionalism

The Political Foundations and Implications of Constitution-Making in Israel

Adam Shinar

8.1 INTRODUCTION

This chapter describes and evaluates Israel's constitution-making process. Unlike most democratic constitutional regimes, the events that gave rise to Israel's constitutional structure did not come about as a result of a constitutional convention, referendum, civic mobilization, or any other deliberate process that characterizes traditional constitution-making. Instead, the process has been gradual, incremental, contingent, and piecemeal, often lacking a clear trajectory, intention, or defined purpose, and involving the rarely coordinated contribution of multiple institutions, particularly the legislature and the Supreme Court. Indeed, as will be detailed later in the chapter, several framers of the modern Israeli constitutional regime did not perceive themselves to be constitutional framers at all. The making of Israel's constitution, I argue, should be understood as accidental, a process best described as accidental constitutionalism.

Accidental constitutionalism can raise problems of legitimacy. A constitution is grounded in the idea that it is the people, either directly or through their representatives, who are involved in constitution-making and amending, whereas courts should confine themselves to application and interpretation. A constitution must mediate between conflicting conceptions of the good, creating a broad base of consensus that most people in a polity will find agreeable. This is especially important in deeply divided societies (Gavison 2006: 346–357; but see Ginsburg et al. 2009: 215 [finding that the impact of participatory design on the constitution's legitimacy is mixed but ultimately largely untested]). These principles were not observed in Israel. Instead, Israel's constitutional framework is a result of legislative-judicial interactions over

For helpful comments and suggestions, I thank Ori Aronson, Denis Galligan, Claire Houston, Shay Lavie, Liav Orgad, Jennifer Shkabatur, Anna Su, Mila Versteeg, and Ruvi Ziegler.

several decades. Crucially, constitutional milestones, such as declaring the suprem-acy of some laws over others and the establishment of judicial review, were initiated by the Supreme Court. Indeed, the determination that Israel even has a constitution was made by the Court.

Although this aspect of Israeli constitutionalism has been the focus of most scholarly writing, it obscures how the Israeli constitutional structure has produced arrangements that are both stable and similar to those of countries whose constitu-tion originated in more conventional processes. My intention, then, is to reply to the argument that Israel's controversial constitutional regime results in instability (Gavison 2006: 394). My claim is that no such instability exists.

This chapter argues that the ad hoc making of Israel's constitution has had rela-tively little impact on the day-to-day manageability and workability of that structure. The more general argument this chapter pursues is that there is no necessary rela-tionship between a polity's constitution-making process and the particular features that process generates. Although Israel's constitutional structure came about in an unconventional way, I argue that when examining the consequences of such a pro-cess, the similarities to traditional constitutions outweigh the differences. In other words, the features that could be thought to be unique to accidental constitution-alism can be found in other constitutional orders. It may be that over time, after Israel's constitutional structure has been consolidated, concerns over its origins will take a back seat to concerns over its interpretation and manageability, concerns that are shared by all constitutional orders. The third argument, which I raise here only to bracket for future research, is that accidental constitutionalism may gener-ate differences of degree rather than kind when compared to other constitutions. It could be, for example, that accidental constitutions are more susceptible to future accidents than constitutions that were deliberately produced, but such an assertion requires a much more detailed examination than can be taken here.

Section 8.2 describes the Israeli constitution-making process from its founding to the present day, highlighting the process of accidental constitutionalism. Section 8.3 delves deeper into Israeli accidental constitutionalism, suggesting three theories to explain its origins. The first theory offers a constructivist account, grounding con-stitutionalism in an ideological fermentation that reflected a consensus view among the Israeli public. The other two theories ground their explanations in Israel's polit-ical structure. While one theory invokes fragmentation in Israeli politics, the other argues that Israeli constitutionalism can best be explained as a move by embattled elites concerned with losing political power. Each theory raises problems; instead of looking for one explanation, I argue that it was the combination of political and ideological forces that made Israeli constitutionalism possible. Section 8.4 exam-ines five potential consequences of accidental constitutionalism: increased judicial power, a decrease in legislative development of constitutional norms, decline in public support for the Supreme Court, noncompliance with judicial decisions, and diminished constitutional discourse. I argue that while conventional wisdom suggests that these consequences are assumed to be associated primarily with accidental constitutionalism, it turns out that there is little difference between Israeli constitutionalism and that of countries that had an orderly, comprehensive, deliberate, and deliberative constitution-making process. This calls into question the common assumption that constitutional origins have a particular effect on subsequent constitutional developments.

8.2 A BRIEF HISTORY OF ISRAELI CONSTITUTION-MAKING AND THE RISE OF ACCIDENTAL CONSTITUTIONALISM

In his writing on constitution-making, Jon Elster has argued that "new constitutions almost always are written in the wake of a crisis or exceptional circumstance of some sort" (Elster 1995: 370). Among such crises are revolutions, decolonization, regime change, war, or economic downturns (Elster 1995: 370–371). These transformative moments aptly describe the creation of the U.S. constitution, the postcolonial Indian constitution, the post–World War II Japanese constitutions, the post-Soviet Eastern European constitutions, and the post-apartheid South African constitution. At its founding, Israel too had all the makings of an Elsterian "constitutional moment" that could give rise to a written constitution. A new state was established, a major war had just been won against the surrounding Arab countries, and the new Israeli regime stood in marked contrast to the British mandatory rule that preceded it. Indeed, Israel's declaration of independence provided that a constitution shall be drafted by a constituent assembly no later than October 1, 1948, only four and a half months after the Declaration (Declaration 1948).

This, however, was not to be. Fraught with internal tensions between secular and religious Jews, disagreements over the desired political arrangements, and facing an existential threat not alleviated by winning its War of Independence, as well as a substantial resident Arab minority that was not part of the originally planned demos, Israel failed to adopt a constitution in those decisive days. Unlike other constitutions, the making of the Israeli constitution, insofar as it has one (see Gavison 1997: 31 [Israel is perhaps the only country where scholars still argue whether it has a constitution]),[1] was "accidental." It was not the culmination of intense public mobilization and spirited discussion. Nor was there a formal decision-making mechanism like voting, which would lead to a written constitution. Instead, the constitution-making process in Israel has been piecemeal, extended over time, and chaotic, the product resembling more a patchwork than a complete document. The

---

[1] The controversy, not expounded in this chapter, is whether Israel's set of basic laws amount to a written constitution like those of other democracies. No one argues that Israel does not have a set of constitutional arrangements similar to Britain's material constitution.

Israeli constitutional moment of 1948 did not generate a constitution, but rather brought about, incrementally, a set of basic laws enacted through normal legislative processes and majorities by the Knesset (Israel's parliament). At the time of their passing, these basic laws were considered minor, did not engage the entire Knesset, and reflected ambiguity about what exactly were the rights that were included, as well as about the normative level of these basic laws vis-à-vis other Knesset legislation. It was only later, as a result of judicial intervention, that the basic laws were elevated to a constitutional status. This section provides an account of these events, beginning first with legislative developments and then describing how the constitutional enterprise was received by the Israeli Supreme Court sitting as a High Court of Justice (hereinafter the Court).[2]

8.2.1 *Legislative Constitution-Making*

According to Israel's Declaration of Independence, promulgated by the People's Council, a semi-democratic representative body of the Jewish population in pre-1948 Palestine, an independent constituent assembly would be elected.[3] Its task would be to draft a constitution, after which a legislature would be elected in line with the processes stipulated in the new constitution (Rubinstein and Medina 2005: 35). A constituent assembly was elected by popular vote in January 1949, but instead of drafting a constitution, the assembly enacted the Transition Law 1949, according to which the legislature shall be called the Knesset, and the constituent assembly be the first Knesset. Thus, the assembly changed its designation from a body in charge of creating a constitution to a regular legislature.

One of the main reasons for the switch was the inability of the constituent assembly to agree not only on the provisions of a constitution, but whether a constitution should be enacted at all. Several reasons are usually offered to explain why the disagreement was intractable. First, some were concerned that Israel, being a young country, had not established any set character and identity. Expecting massive immigration waves, they argued it would be hasty and unwise for a small group of people to determine the institutional and political structure for generations to come. Secondly, the grave security situation around the time of establishment gave rise to concerns that a constitution would unduly restrict the government's power to safeguard the nation. While a constitution could, in theory, grant broad deference

---

[2] The Israeli Supreme Court sits as both a court of criminal and civil appeal and as a high court of justice. The latter is an institution preserved from the time of British mandatory rule. In this capacity, the court sits as a court of first instance over the majority of constitutional and administrative affairs. For the development of this function, see Sagy (2008).

[3] This echoed the UN Partition resolution of 1947, which specified that the new Jewish and Arab states shall have a constitution.

to military and security exigencies, some MKs (Member of Knesset) argued that such deference would upset the protection of human rights (Barak-Erez 1995: 314). Paradoxically, the desire to protect human rights required that the constitutional project be postponed.

The bigger obstacles, however, were objections from religious parties, on the one hand, and the ruling Mapai Party, headed by Israel's first prime minister, David Ben Gurion, on the other. Religious parties opposed a constitution in principle, arguing that the Bible should be Israel's constitution, and that any future constitution conflicting with requirements in the Torah would be invalid. More importantly, religious parties were concerned that constitutional guarantees would upset arrangements that buttressed the Jewish nature of the state, in particular marriage and divorce laws and policies that respected the Sabbath (Barak-Erez 1995: 314).

The most significant hurdle, however, came from the Mapai Party. In the state's first three decades (1948–1977), Mapai dominated Israeli politics. While it never controlled the Knesset, it was consistently the largest party and needed few (and relatively weak) partners to form a coalition. Mapai was concerned that a constitution would constrict its power, benefiting the judiciary and minorities (Hirschl 2001: 326). Given the nation-building project it was pursuing at the time, this was especially problematic (Segev 2007: 420). Thus, Mapai opted for the British constitutional model of parliamentary sovereignty without a written constitution.

Consequently, the constituent assembly was deadlocked. The core disagreements between various parties about what a constitution should look like and the contested identities the constitution should embody resulted in a decision to not decide.[4] As a way out, in 1950, the Knesset passed what came to be known as the Harari Resolution, named after the MK who proposed it (5 Knesset Records 1743 [1950]). The Resolution provided that "[t]he First Knesset charges the Constitution, Law, and Justice Committee to prepare a draft constitution. The constitution will be comprised of chapters, in a way that each will be a fundamental law unto itself. The chapters will be brought before the Knesset, if the committee finishes its work, and all the chapters together will become the constitution of the state."

The Harari Resolution, vague and incomplete as it was, became Israel's constitution-making method. The Resolution gave no timeline for the completion of a constitution and did not provide any guidelines as to its content, form, or mode of creation. And yet, it was precisely this ambiguity that could command a majority. The Resolution had two main consequences. First, it put to rest the attempt to

---

[4] On the contestation regarding Israel's identity that prevented a creation of the constitution, see Tushnet (2000: 1337) ("Israel is distinctive here … precisely because the identity of Israel's people is still open in a way that French or U.S. identity is not. In France and the United States, contests over what the nation is occur within an agreed-upon framework, while in Israel what is at stake is precisely what that framework ought to be.").

enact a comprehensive constitution (Salzberger 2007: 232). Secondly, it regularized the constitution-making process, relegating it to the ordinary processes of politics (Tushnet 2000: 1337). The creation of basic laws, then, would be erratic, and subject to the prevailing (and contingent) political vicissitudes (Gavison 1997: 31; Jacobsohn 1993: 106 [equating the Harari Resolution to *Brown's* all-deliberate-speed formula]).

From 1958 to 1991, the Knesset passed nine basic laws, most of them dealing with structural aspects, including the composition and powers of the various governmental bodies.[5] Progress on the basic laws was possible because of broad legislative consensus at the time. In 1992, the Knesset overcame its traditional reluctance to pass basic laws that addressed individual rights by passing two: Basic Law: Freedom of occupation, guaranteeing the right to pursue an occupation of one's choice; and Basic Law: Human Dignity and Liberty, securing various liberal rights such as rights to life, human dignity, liberty, freedom to leave and enter the country, privacy, and property.

Because these two basic laws served to launch what became known as Israel's Constitutional Revolution,[6] their story merits brief discussion. In 1992, the Minister of Justice submitted for the government's approval a comprehensive Basic Law essentially providing for a constitutional bill of rights. Although coalition considerations prevented this proposed basic law from moving forward, it was picked up by several MKs who split its contents into four basic laws, the aim being to secure majority support for the least controversial rights guarantees. However, only the provisions regarding freedom of occupation (a right that has been judicially recognized since 1949, although it could not trump primary legislation [H.C. 1/49 Bejerano v. Minister of Police]) and those entailed in human dignity and liberty were passed. These basic laws were different in two ways. Basic Law: Freedom of Occupation was fully entrenched, requiring sixty-one MKs to amend it.[7] Basic Law: Human Dignity and Liberty, though not entrenched, included a limitation clause, providing that infringement could only be done by a law befitting the values of the state of Israel, for a worthy purpose, and where the harm caused by the infringement was proportionate with the value brought about by the rights-infringing legislation.[8]

Despite being the first basic laws addressing anything resembling a bill of rights, they received little public attention. They passed without any kind of special majority,

---

5   See Basic Law: The Knesset, Basic Law: Israel Lands, Basic Law: The President, Basic Law: The Government, Basic Law: The State Economy, Basic Law: The Military, Basic Law: Jerusalem Capital of Israel, Basic Law: The Judiciary, Basic Law: The State Comptroller.

6   The term "constitutional revolution" was coined by Professor Claude Klein in an op-ed, but was made famous by then-President Aharaon Barak. See Barak (2004: 5); Barak (1992: 9).

7   However, the Basic Law does include an override provision, which states that, if explicitly stated, a regular law can override its protections, but only for a limited time.

8   A similar limitation clause was attached to Basic Law: Freedom of Occupation in a new version passed in 1994.

as part of the Knesset's normal legislation process (Karp 1993: 325 [indeed, the constitutional revolution they supposedly heralded was not made explicit by the Knesset, but by the Supreme Court three years later]). The atmosphere surrounding the basic laws during their drafting was not one of elation, but of compromises and struggles.[9] Those who opposed the bill were concerned that by entrenching the basic law and including a limitation clause the Knesset was inviting judicial review, but they were assured by one of the framers of the bill that no judicial review would be forthcoming (Sapir 2008: 582). Others called the initiative partial and not sufficiently protective of rights (Karp 1993: 326–327). Importantly, the bills reflected three notable compromises. First, a right to equality was tossed out, reflecting religious parties' concerns over who would be defined as a Jew, the possible invalidation of the exemption of ultraorthodox men from the military, a state recognition of nonorthodox streams of Judaism, and a possible conflict with the Law of Return, which guarantees preferential treatment to Jews in matters of immigration. Similarly, the Knesset dispensed with protections for free speech, religious freedom, and association, mostly because of concerns that such protections could undermine the secular-religious status quo. Secondly, the Knesset specified that the values of Israel are those of a Jewish and democratic state, without defining what constitutes either or determining which vision should trump in case of conflict. Third, the Knesset immunized all arrangements existing prior to the enactment of the Basic Law: Human Dignity and Liberty, primarily in order to protect religious arrangements and emergency legislation in case of conflict with the new basic law.

It is possible that the success in passing basic laws resulted from the prevailing understanding that they did not enjoy supreme status. At the time of their promulgation, the Knesset, the legal community, and the Supreme Court all held that basic laws, unless specifically entrenched, were not supreme to regular legislation and could be changed through ordinary laws (H.C. 148/73 *Kaniel v. Minister of Justice*). The prevailing conception was that at some point in the future there might be a constitution, and that the basic laws would eventually comprise that constitution. Moreover, enacting basic laws was done against a background of no judicial review of primary legislation. Up until 1995, with one minor exception,[10] the Supreme Court refused to recognize the power of judicial review over legislation (H.C. 142/89

---

[9] According to one of the drafters, MK Amnon Rubinstein, the majority that passed these basic laws took advantage of the "anarchy" that was then present in the Knesset, before going into general elections, and with a lack of governmental leadership. See Avnun (1995: 423). See also Bendor (1995: 443).

[10] See H.C. 98/69 Bergman v. Minister of Finance, 23(1) P.D. 693 (1969) (establishing judicial review only when the Knesset violates an entrenched provision of a basic law. In effect, this only applied to election laws that impacted the equality of elections and which were passed without the stipulated requisite majority of 61 MKs). See also H.C. 246/81 Derekh Eretz Ass'n v. Broadcasting Authority, 35(4) P.D. 1 (1981); H.C. 141/82 Rubinstein v. Speaker of the Knesset, 37(3) P.D. 141 (1983); H.C. 149/89 Laor v. Speaker of the Knesset 44(3) P.D. 529 (1990) (applying the Bergman precedent to other cases).

Laor v. Speaker of the Knesset). Basic laws could thus be passed without the threat of future invalidation. This was precisely why the introduction of judicial review in 1995 in the landmark case of *United Mizrahi Bank* (C.A. 6821/93) effectively ended the passing of additional basic laws, especially those that sought to protect individual rights.[11] As discussed later in the chapter, the judicial constitutional project put an end, if not in theory then in practice, to the legislative development of rights-protecting constitutional norms.

The process of Israeli constitution-making has been haphazard. Faced with a reluctant legislature, basic laws were enacted incrementally, without regard to substantive or procedural criteria, and mostly codified existing political arrangements.[12] Importantly, two issues that any constitution addresses – rigidity and supremacy – were conspicuously avoided in order to secure majority support. Thus, it could be said that whatever constitutional strides the Knesset made since 1950, they were relatively minor. Despite the occasional calls to enact a comprehensive constitution, the political reality and the fundamental disagreements about the nature of the state prevented such a constitution from passing. The Israeli public could not agree on the core values that such a constitution should embody. Having a constitution early in Israel's life would have embroiled the country in rifts and divisions its leaders sought to forestall. But postponing the constitution-making process had the effect of making only piecemeal progress realistic. Indeed, virtually all attempts to enact basic laws that established judicial review and sought to protect a more expansive set of rights have failed (Segev 2007: 465–466). The reason for their failure was similar to the failure in 1949: persistent disagreements between various parties over the core rights that should be respected and unwillingness to cede power to the judiciary.[13]

8.2.2 *Judicial Constitution-Making*

The legislative impasse that prevented a written constitution from coming into being helped confirm the Israeli judiciary's status as the guardian of the rule of law. Prior to establishment of judicial review of legislation in 1995, the rule of law was considered the most important limiting device of partisan politics (Edelman 1994: 33). Faced with a need to secure individual rights, but without the tools of a written

---

[11] The one exception being a temporary basic law that allowed for passing a budget every two years. See Basic-Law: State Budget for 2009 to 2012 (Special Provisions) (Temporary Provision). There were also *amendments* to *existing* basic laws, but those did not involve rights protection.

[12] For an argument that this is a desirable approach in deeply divided societies, see Lerner (2010: 68).

[13] It should be noted that both of the 1992 basic laws were amended and re-ratified by a large majority in 1994, at a time when the argument that judicial review is possible was already made by some judges (though yet to be recognized by the Court). Therefore, one can argue that even in 1992 the Knesset was hostile to judicial review; it was more receptive in 1994.

constitution to do so, the Court developed a judicial bill of rights based on Israel's professed status as a democracy committed to the rule of law. In this way, the court recognized various rights such as the right to pursue an occupation, freedom of conscience and religion, procedural due process, free speech, and equality (see, e.g., H.C. 73/53 *Kol Ha'am v. Minister of Interior* [recognizing the right to free speech]). However, the protection of individual rights was limited to infringements by the executive, not the legislature (Dorner 1999: 1327). Because these rights derived from case law, they could not be used to strike down legislation. Administrative action that infringed on these rights, without clear statutory authorization, was deemed *ultra vires* and violating the rule of law.

The dramatic change in administrative adjudication in the 1980s also portended constitutional consequences. Rocked by political scandals and political fragmentation as a result of Mapai's loss of electoral dominance, Israeli society became more polarized. Trust in elected representatives and democratic institutions declined, and calls were made for the drafting of a constitution by a burgeoning social movement. The Supreme Court responded by asserting a more meaningful and powerful role in Israeli politics and governance, a step mostly welcomed by the public, which viewed the Court as an impartial and apolitical institution representing a consensus view of Israeli society (Mautner 2011; Meydani 2011).

The Court embarked on a significant relaxation of standing and justiciability requirements. It moved from a standing doctrine that intervened only when the plaintiff asserted a concrete and personal interest to one that granted broad standing to public petitioners, including NGOs, requiring only that the petitioner assert a violation of the rule of law or a violation of human rights (H.C. 910/86 *Resler v. Minister of Defence*). The Court's argument in support of this change was rooted in its perception that if it were to abstain from ruling, the rule of law would be undermined (H.C. 270/80 *Segal v. Minister of Interior*). In this vein, the Court has argued that supervisory mechanisms such as parliamentary or public control cannot substitute judicial review (Rubinstein and Medina 2005: 180). Similarly, the Court eliminated its justiciability doctrine (H.C. 910/86), assuming the doctrine would silence public examination of policy choices (Rubinstein and Medina 2005: 200).[14]

Easy access to the Court, the fact that the Supreme Court is a court of first instance in constitutional matters, that it hears no witnesses, and that filing fees are very low, all contributed to the Court's increased opportunities for exercising its activism (Salzberger 2007: 234). On the administrative front, the Court began reviewing administrative actions for their "reasonableness" (H.C. 389/80 *Dapei Zahav v. Broadcasting Authority*; Rubinstein and Medina 2005: 260) and proportionality. This allowed the Court to intervene in areas it had previously avoided or

---

14   For an elaboration of the Court's standing and justiciability doctrines, see Barak (2003: 97–110).

supervised in a limited fashion. This included scrutinizing the Attorney General's prosecutorial discretion (H.C. 935/89 *Ganor v. Attorney General*); intervention in security matters, especially in the discretion of military authorities in the Occupied Palestinian Territories, such as house demolitions, administrative detentions, deportations, and the legality of torture, targeted killings, and the separation barrier (H.C. 2056/04 *Beit Sourik Village Council v. Government of Israel*; H.C. 7957/04 *Mar'abe v. Prime Minister of Israel*);[15] intervening in internal Knesset procedures and the legislative process(H.C. 652/81 *Sarid v. Speaker of the Knesset*; H.C. 4885/03 *Chicken Farmers Org. v. Government of Israel*); intervening in political appointments (H.C. 6163/81 *Eisenberg v. Minister of Housing*; H.C. 4885/03 *The Movement for Quality Government in Israel v. Government of Israel*); and even examining the legality of negotiations held between an interim government and the Palestinian Authority (H.C. 5167/00 *Weiss v. Prime Minister of Israel*). In one case, the Court went so far as to require the state to create protected spaces in towns subject to missile attacks from Gaza, deeming the state's protection plan unreasonable (H.C. 8397/06 *Wasser v. Minister of Defence*).

While administrative adjudication expanded, constitutional review was left mostly untouched. This changed in 1995. In a landmark decision, *United Mizrahi Bank v. Migdal Cooperative Village*, the Court seized the two basic laws of 1992 to declare that a constitutional revolution has taken place; that by enacting these basic laws the Knesset had been acting as a constituent assembly. Employing the logic of *Marbury v. Madison*,[16] the Court reached the conclusion that the hierarchy of norms has to be enforced by some institution, and absent a contrary constitutional provision, the courts are the most suitable institution to the task.[17] The Court held that the two basic laws are, in fact, part of a written constitution that is normatively superior to ordinary legislation. In subsequent decisions, the Court declared that all the basic laws are now supreme to regular legislation (E.A. 92/03 *Mofaz v. Election Commissioner*; L.C.A. 3007/02 *Yitzhak v. Mozes*; H.C. 1384/98 *Avni v. Prime Minister*; H.C. 212/03 *Herut National Movement v. Election Commissioner*), and that all legislation must be interpreted in light of the basic laws (F.H. 2316/95). Finally, the Court, through constitutional interpretation, expanded the scope of the basic laws to include rights the Knesset sought to exclude. In particular, the Court, as part of its interpretation of human dignity, announced constitutional rights of equality,

---

[15] This is not to say that the substance of the intervention was by any means appropriate or adequate. My point is only that the Court saw itself as entitled to adjudicate such issues.

[16] Marbury v. Madison, 5 U.S. (1 Cranch) 137 (1803).

[17] It could be argued that establishing judicial review in Israel was similar to *Marbury v. Madison* in the United States. But the differences between the two jurisdictions complicate matters considerably. The United States did have a written constitution; judicial review was considered by some of the Framers, and many believed that it was inevitable because of the constitution's Supremacy Clause.

free exercise, association, free speech, and a minimal set of social and economic rights (Sommer 1997: 257).

While the Court has struck down very few statutes since 1995, the most notable being a statute that authorized prison privatization (H.C. 2605/05 *Ganimat v. Israel*), it is impossible to overstate the shift in Israeli constitutional law and culture as a result of these moves: from a state with no written constitution or judicial review to a state that, at least from the Court's perspective, transitioned almost overnight to a full-blown constitutional regime complete with judicial review, with very little public engagement, deliberation, or intention.[18] This transformation consolidated the Court as a major policy-making institution. From an arbiter of individual disputes the Court became a "political institution that participates in determining the values that prevail in the country and the distribution of its material resources" (Mautner 2011: 73).

What made this transformation possible? How was it that a state that could not agree on its basic constitutional essentials ended up with what the Court and the legal community now consider to be a written constitution? It is to these questions that I now turn.

8.3 THREE THEORIES OF ACCIDENTAL CONSTITUTIONALISM

What might explain the development of accidental constitutionalism? What accounts for the particular timing of significant constitutional developments, specifically the transfer of power from the legislature to the judiciary? Several theories have been offered by scholars and by those who pushed for constitutionalism in Israel. Here I consider the three I believe most powerful: a constructivist thesis, a political fragmentation thesis, and a political hegemony thesis. Each theory bears some explanatory power, although I will argue that a combination of the three best explains these constitutional developments.

8.3.1 *The Constructivist Thesis*

The constructivist thesis holds that passage of the 1992 basic laws and the concomitant assertion of, and increase in, judicial power is a result of an ideological shift viewing protection of individual rights as favorable.[19] Like other democracies and

---

[18] Indeed, Haim Ramon, a prominent MK, called the scope of the constitutional revolution an "accidental constitutional revolution" because "it was not intended by the legislator." 191 Knesset records, 5799 (1998), cited in Sapir 2008:592 n. 74.

[19] See, e.g., Ginsburg (2003: 11) (describing, though not completely accepting, the thesis as it applies to the rise of global constitutionalism); Dworkin (1990) (arguing that a mature democracy protects minorities and vulnerable groups against majority rule, and tying the protection of individual rights

formerly communist countries that ratified formal constitutions that provided for
bills of rights and judicial review, the framers of Israel's new basic laws were driven
by similar commitments. Spearheading Israel's constitutional efforts was the liberal
MK Amnon Rubinstein, Israel's foremost constitutional authority and the author of
the leading treatise on constitutional law. Similar ideological commitments were
shared by other MKs who advanced constitutional reform efforts. The Constitution,
Law, and Justice Committee, responsible for working on basic laws, was similarly
comprised of individuals who were either committed to the idea of individual rights
or could be persuaded to vote in favor of such bills (Lin and Loya 2012). Judges
on the Supreme Court were influenced by the ideas of their foreign colleagues,
from whom they borrowed extensively, especially when it came to the protection
of individual rights. For example, the free speech doctrine expressly invoked the
U.S. commitment to free expression, and the Court's proportionality formula relied
on German and Canadian sources (see, e.g., H.C. 73/53; H.C. 1715/97 *Investors
Management Bureau v. Minister of Finance*). The judicial elite thus seized the new
basic laws to affirm their own preexisting liberal commitments.[20] On the civil society
front, the declining faith in electoral politics (fallout from the 1973 war, the 1982
Lebanon war, political corruption, and a severe economic crisis), coupled with the
high public trust in the Supreme Court, signaled the public's willingness and desire
to impose substantive limits on the political process.

The constructivist thesis explains particular ideological commitments among
segments of Israeli society and how those commitments coalesced and were made
feasible. However, the constructivist thesis puts a moralistic gloss on a much more
complicated process. For example, many MKs who voted for the 1992 basic laws
were taken aback by the introduction of judicial review in 1995, suggesting that they
did not anticipate this development (Sapir 2008: 585). Thus, if the pro-rights, pro-
judicial review camp was so strong, what are we to make of the legislative backlash
generated by the judicial assertion of power? Indeed, if the Knesset was heading
down a consensual, public-backed path, why were the basic laws split into separate
bills? Examining the legislative process that made the 1992 basic laws possible reveals
that relatively few MKs actually turned out to vote, suggesting that the constitutional
moment was not considered transformative.[21] Finally, an ideological coalescence

---

to judicial review). In his contribution to this volume (Chapter 6), Hirschl discusses constructivist
accounts under the label of "ideational theories."

[20] This is not to say that all judges had liberal commitments in the partisan sense, but the influential
judges who turned the basic laws into a constitution, most notably President Aharon Barak, explicitly
endorsed traditional liberal values such as the rule of law and individual rights, and the centrality of
the Court in enforcing limits on government.

[21] However, eighty-two MKs did turn out to ratify amendments to the basic law in 1994. Amnon
Rubinstein and Uriel Lin explain that the dearth in attendance should be attributed to primary campaigns that required MKs to lobby for their reelection. See Lin (2012); Rubinstein (2012).

does not explain the Knesset's numerous (albeit mostly unsuccessful) court-curbing attempts that followed the Court's declaration of a constitutional revolution, on the one hand, and the legislative disengagement from constitutional law, on the other, manifesting in an almost complete cessation of basic law legislation (Gavison 1997:137 [arguing that the constitutional project has come to a halt in the legislature because legislators feel cheated and do not trust the court]).

8.3.2 *The Political Fragmentation Thesis*

The political fragmentation thesis, advanced mostly by Menachem Mautner (2011), holds that the fragmentation of Israeli politics facilitated the consolidation of the Supreme Court as the constitutional leader and as an alternative site of political power. The Israeli political system has undergone four phases. First, between 1948 and 1977, Israel was dominated by the Mapai party, which lost its hegemony in 1977, bringing about an era of two large parties that could never quite control parliament and often had to enter into national unity governments (1977–1992). The national unity governments, instead of allowing one party to rule effectively, enabled mutual vetoes. Each large party could block the initiatives of the other. Religious parties, which were always coalition members, had a similar veto power when it came to the religious status quo (Hofnung 1996: 593).

Over time, the combined power of the two largest parties declined, and sectorial parties (parties designed to help particular sectors such as religious persons, immigrants, settlers, and Arabs) became more prominent. The political fragmentation generated a proliferation in government ministries and spending to appease and secure cooperation of smaller parties that were needed to maintain fragile coalitions. This coalition building often prevented important policy objectives from being raised or addressed, which allowed the status quo to prevail. The constant need to manage a volatile security situation vis-à-vis neighboring countries and the Palestinians also prevented important issues from being fully addressed in the political process (Meydani 2011: 74–75).

The second phase in Israeli politics – the 1980s and 1990s – saw a series of political crises that could not be resolved because of the deadlock between the two large parties and the disproportionate power exerted by small parties who could provide the swing votes. To alleviate political blockages, the elections for the Knesset and prime minister were separated. The hope was that the executive could be strengthened and its dependence on the Knesset reduced. This, however, brought about increased polarization in the Knesset, because voters were now able to split the ticket between their preferred candidate for office and their desired political party.[22] Consequently,

---

[22] For example, in 1996, 20 parties ran for a seat in the 120-member Knesset, and in 1999, 33 parties ran for a seat.

the old system was reinstated, but without any solution to the problem of political fragmentation (Arian et al. 2002: 87–94).

The decline in political stability and the parallel loss of trust in the political branches, mentioned earlier, explains the rise in the Court's power. The public turned to the Court because it was perceived as a stable and objective entity that could step into a vacuum left open by the Knesset.[23] Similarly, non-governability encouraged politicians to shift responsibility to the Court with the expectation that it would decide contentious issues, while also serving as a battleground for politicians who petitioned the court when they lost in the political process.[24] Judicialization, then, was not simply a result of judicial aggrandizement, but rather a societal choice. Given the inability and unwillingness of the political system to address the deep social cleavages in Israeli society, the Court gradually became more interventionist. In other words, citizens and NGOs exited the political system and exercised their voice through the Court, guaranteeing the supply of the governmental services that the political process could not secure (Meydani 2011: 58).

These trends were reflected in the development of judicial doctrine. Up until and around 1977, the Court limited its intervention and insisted more forcefully on standing and justiciability requirements. The increased intervention, mostly in the adoption of liberal access requirements, came at the height of the political deadlock of the 1980s, and was aptly done in a case that sought to resolve the long-standing issue of recruitment of ultraorthodox men to the Israeli military, an issue that the elected majorities in the government and Knesset could not address given minority religious parties' insistence on maintaining their constituents' exemption from service. Shortly thereafter, the Court expanded judicial review, a move that was supported by the majority of the Israeli public, though not necessarily the Knesset (Barzilai et al. 1994).

The political fragmentation thesis goes beyond the constructivist thesis by presenting a more complicated and nuanced picture of a highly polarized society that encountered difficulties in the deadlocked political sphere and thus turned to the Court for help. Yet the fragmentation thesis leaves at least three questions unanswered.[25] First, it fails to account for the precise timing of the transfer of power from the political sphere to the judicial one. While it is true that political polarization correlates with an increase in judicial power, the thesis does not explain why a particular development happened at a particular time. Secondly, the thesis treats political fragmentation as a binary situation: either it exists or it does not. However, if the political system was indeed fragmented, it is unclear how it managed to pass the 1992

---

[23] During those times, the Court enjoyed exceedingly high levels of trust and legitimacy compared with the Knesset and government. See Barzilai et al. (1994).

[24] On the latter point, see Dotan and Hofnung (2005: 75).

[25] These questions are raised in (Hirschl 2001: 317).

Basic Laws when all previous attempts failed. One would imagine that political fragmentation would hinder constitutional progress. Finally, the fragmentation thesis overlooks the role particular individuals played in making constitutional reform possible. Legal innovators have their own unique interests to further, and those do not necessarily depend on the existence of fragmentation. We therefore need a theory that is able to answer these questions.

8.3.3 *The Political Hegemony Thesis*

The political hegemony thesis aims to answer the questions left open by the political fragmentation thesis. The theory, developed most forcefully by Ran Hirschl, argues that constitutionalization can best be explained as a process fueled by politically threatened hegemonic elites attempting to secure their gains for the day they lose power. They seek judicial independence to prevent future governments from harnessing the judiciary for its policy goals. The choice to transfer power to the judiciary is not accidental; elites hold more power in the legal arena, thus guaranteeing that their preferences will be less contested there. Establishing judicial review and a bill of rights, then, are not the result of ideological fermentation or political polarization, but rather the strategic interplay between political elites and the legal profession interested in preserving their power (Hirschl 2001: 318–319; Hirschl 2004; Hirschl 2013). Similarly, Menachem Mautner argues that the groups that wanted to make Israel a more liberal Western society controlled important positions in Israeli civil society (press, business, academia, arts) but could not secure control over the political process and state administration, explaining their choice to advance their interests through the Court, which shared similar liberal preferences (Mautner 2002: 201).

According to Hirschl, the constitutional revolution was initiated by a political cross-section of the secular Ashkenazi bourgeoisie (whose hegemony had increasingly become threatened by periphery towns, immigrants, blue-collar workers, religious parties, and Mizrahi Jews), economic leaders, the managerial class, and industrialists, who pursued a neoliberal economic agenda that favored the constitutionalization of property rights, among others. This effort was supported by Israel's legal elite, which was urging a constitution, partly to increase its relative power in Israeli governance (Hirschl 2001: 320–321). What was at stake was not partisan control of the Knesset, but the declining power of particular groups in the policy-making process. Indeed, from 1981 to 1999, the secular bourgeoisie and the neoliberal wing of the Likud party lost a third of their seats to the new parties that resulted from the aforementioned demographic shifts. In 1996, the old guard enjoyed a bare majority – 62 seats in the 120-member Knesset (Hirschl 2001: 322–323). Consequently, these groups banded together to secure political power by decreasing the overall power of the Knesset, where they believed they were about to lose power.

While the political hegemony thesis explains the precise timing of the constitutional revolution and the role political elites played in furthering constitutional
reform, it fails to explain all aspects of Israeli constitutionalism. Hirschl focuses on
the 1992 basic laws and the introduction of judicial review in 1995. However, the
preceding analysis has demonstrated that the transfer of power to the court has been
gradual and incremental.[26] Further, the Court often asserted its power either through
petitions filed by marginalized groups or issues that, for parliamentary coalition
considerations, could not be addressed via the political channels (see Dotan 1999:
1059 [arguing that the Court functions as a representative of the common citizen
and that the haves enjoy only a limited advantage compared with the have-nots]).
While some of these decisions were compatible with elite preferences, not all were
the result of a conscious transfer of power. Moreover, to argue that Israel's constitutional revolution is a consequence of embattled hegemons seeking their preservation discounts the fact that many who voted in favor of the 1992 basic laws did not
belong to the hegemonic elite. In addition, many who opposed the basic laws and
later judicial review did belong to the elite. Consequently, it would seem that either
the hegemonic elite was not exclusively interested in maintaining its own power,
or that it was divided in its strategy to maintain its power. Finally, many who voted
for the basic laws claimed that they did not anticipate the establishment of judicial
review. Indeed, one of the central framers of the Basic Law: Human Dignity and
Liberty assured the Knesset that it retained all its powers and that no power would
be transferred to the Court (Lin and Loya 2012). Therefore, one must conclude that
either the passage of the basic laws was done by way of deception – an extremely
unlikely claim given the amount of time and meetings held to discuss the bills in
the Knesset[27] – or that the future application was unclear, thus undermining the
claim of a decisive plan to transfer power to the Court and to preserve the power of
political elites.

The available theories, on their own, do not explain the dynamics of gradual,
piecemeal, incremental, and contextual developments. Instead, it is the combination of ideological, institutional, political, and other contingent factors that explain
this trajectory. The ideological impulse favoring a bill of rights and judicial review
has been present since Israel's founding, at least among some sectors of society. It
materialized, however, through a series of political events and societal conditions
that reflected the deep divisions in Israeli society: tensions between secular and
religious Jews, between Jews and Arabs, between Ashkenazi and Mizrahi Jews, and
conflicts that stemmed from Israel's precarious security situation, including, but not

---

[26] Ruth Gavison argues that the 1992 basic laws were not a revolution but an evolution. It was made a
     revolution because judges started to refer to it as such, persuading the public and the political sphere
     that this was a revolution; Gavison (1997: 129).
[27] This option is considered and largely dismissed in (Sapir 2008: 582–592).

limited to, the occupation of Palestinian territories since 1967 and the construction of settlements. These tensions and conflicts, in turn, were reflected in the political sphere. The loss of Mapai dominance, the subsequent fragmentation of politics, and the resulting increase in the Court's power gave rise to a perhaps unintended, partial, and crippled constitutional regime, but a constitutional regime nonetheless.

In the next section, I consider the consequences of accidental constitutionalism. Some consequences are more pronounced in the Israeli context. However, insofar as the Israeli case study reveals important conclusions, I argue that the differences, if any, between accidental and ordered constitutionalism are of degree, not kind. Although accidental constitutionalism may be normatively problematic because it lacks the proper democratic foundations, it can be just as durable and stable as constitutions that have been ratified in a collective, organized, deliberate, and deliberative process. In other words, shaky and questionable origins do not necessarily portend problems of application and endurance.

8.4 THE CONSEQUENCES OF ACCIDENTAL CONSTITUTIONALISM

What happened as a result of accidental constitutionalism? How were the constitutional developments received by the political branches and the people? In this section I examine what I consider to be the five most important developments that Israeli constitutionalism has generated. I focus on these developments because the move to constitutionalism triggers both institutional and cultural changes having to do with each branch's relative power, the political repercussions of such changes, and the discursive shifts that may or may not have occurred as a result of those power transfers. To that end, I examine the increase in the Court's power and the resulting decrease in the Knesset's constitutional activity, the legitimacy of the Court as manifested in public support and compliance with judicial decisions, and the constitutional discourse after the Court asserted judicial review powers over primary legislation. My examination leads to the conclusion that despite a different constitutional structure (e.g., a set of basic laws and few enumerated rights), in many respects there is a convergence between Israel's accidental constitution and constitutions that benefited from a more ordered constitution-making process. Put differently, the subsequent analysis demonstrates that there is no necessary relationship between a constitution's origins and the dynamics to which it later gives rise.

8.4.1 *Delegation of Power to the Judiciary*

The first consequence I examine is the steady increase in power held by the Supreme Court at the expense of the political branches. While the Court's unique institutional location facilitated this increase, its erosion of justiciability doctrines, the expansion of administrative review, and the subsequent establishment of constitutional review were additional contributing factors. As the various explanations demonstrate, the power shift was accompanied and made possible by growing political fragmentation, political instability, and ideological ferment favoring entrenched individual rights. The Court took on the role of a consensus institution, representing "the people" in lieu of a fragmented legislature and an often hamstrung executive. Similarly, the Court encouraged public petitions, strengthened the role of NGOs, and sought to arbitrate political disputes. Indeed, politicians themselves turned to the Court when dissatisfied with results generated by the political system or when they believed they could garner positive exposure from litigation (Dotan and Hofnung 2005). In other words, most of what the Court did was to expand its jurisdiction. This judicial activism, then, was largely an activism of access rather than of outcome.

The constitutional revolution embodied in the establishment of judicial review bolstered these trends by subjecting all governmental and legislative actions to the basic laws. The constitutional revolution was seen by the Court both as a vindication of its constitutional path and an authorization going forward. Thus, the Court took it upon itself to continually develop the scope of the basic laws through constitutional interpretation. In particular, the Court has interpreted the right to dignity as including rights to equality, free speech, and free exercise – precisely the rights the Knesset was careful to leave out. For the most part, it seems, the public has accepted these actions (Barzilai et al. 1994: 75 [showing 65 percent support for judicial review and 73 percent support for relaxing justiciability requirements]). To be sure, in particular areas, especially security matters and the adjudication of Palestinians' claims, support for the Court has been relatively low. However, the Court enjoyed diffuse institutional support, which endured irrespective of substantive disagreements in particular cases, precisely because there was a consensus view of its overarching purpose and function – limiting the excesses of the political system (Barzilai et al. 1994: 129–130).

Unsurprisingly, these developments have triggered charges of judicial activism (Posner 2007: 53; *but see* Medina 2007). As is usually the case, activism is rarely defined with precision and is hard to disentangle from the commentator's political preferences. Most writers refer to a judicial body's willingness to strike down democratically enacted legislation, departures from established precedent, or "result-oriented" judging (Kmiec 2007). On this account, Israel's Supreme Court has in fact struck down very few laws. Its "activism" is characterized more by its willingness to entertain petitions, even if they are ultimately rejected.

Yet even if Israel is a relative outlier in terms of the activism level of its Supreme Court, it is surely part of a larger trend in the democratic world. Allegations of judicial activism are repeatedly made in virtually all common law jurisdictions;[28] the judicialization of politics as a worldwide phenomenon is now a common phrase (Hirschl 2004 ; Sweet 2000; Gibson et al. 1998 [noting that the "judicialization of politics seems to be a truly global phenomenon and may be or may become one of the most significant trends in late-twentieth and early-twentieth -first-century government" (internal quotations omitted); Tate and Vallinder 1995]). While Israel may be firmly within the category of countries with activist judiciaries, that category includes countries with entrenched constitutions developed through an orderly, deliberate, and deliberative process. Although one can claim that in these countries the constitution designates a specific role for the judiciary, suggesting that activism could be justified, or at least understandable and "legal," this is not always the case. Famously, charges of judicial activism are common in the United States, even though the constitution does not explicitly provide for judicial review.

8.4.2 *Cessation of Legislative Constitutional Development and Increase in Court-Curbing Efforts*

A second consequence of Israel's accidental constitutionalism, and a corollary of judicial accretion of power, has been the almost complete cessation of constitutional development by the Knesset. The 1992 basic laws were the last time the Knesset passed major basic law legislation.[29] Subsequent attempts to pass a comprehensive constitution have failed.[30] Instead, the Knesset has been consumed by efforts to constrain the power of the Court. For example, the Knesset has tried to institute a notwithstanding provision, allowing it to override a judicial decision of invalidation.[31] It has also tried to limit the Court's jurisdiction by narrowing standing and constraining the matters it can hear.[32] Proposals have been made to prohibit or limit the Court from issuing orders on security matters,[33] immigration,[34] foreign affairs, war powers,

---

[28] See the essays in Dickson (2007) (discussing activism in Australia, New Zealand, Britain, India, South Africa, and the United States). See also Bork (2003).

[29] Two other constitutional developments passed since then were the direct election for the prime minister and the passing of a temporary provision that allowed the passing of a budget every two years. These reforms are relatively unimportant. The first has since been cancelled. The second is limited in time and will expire in 2014.

[30] Two notable attempts to pass a constitution are the Constitution, Law, and Justice Committee's draft constitution, available at http://www.knesset.gov.il/huka, and the Israeli Democracy Institute, available at http://www.idi.org.il/hebrew/article.asp?id=2351. Both attempts have not been put to a vote.

[31] Proposed Basic Law: Adjudication (Amendment – Judicial Review of a Statute's Validity), Private Bill 2056/18.

[32] Proposed Basic Law: Adjudication (Amendment – Public Petitioner). Private Bill 3134/18.

[33] Proposed Basic Law: Adjudication (Amendment – Authority of the High Court of Justice), Private Bill 2018/18.

[34] Memorandum on Proposed Basic Law: Human Dignity and Liberty (Amendment – Citizenship, Residency, and Entrance to Israel).

establishment of commissions of inquiry, and the allocation of budgetary funds.[35] Attempts were also made to change the appointment process for Supreme Court judges and to institute public confirmation hearings.[36] Finally, a bold plan was put forward in 2000 to establish a special constitutional court that would decide challenges to legislation and whose bench would more closely reflect the social/political makeup of the population (Meydani 2011: 109).

While these attempts should be viewed against a background of displeasure with the Court's increased power, a closer analysis reveals the durability of Israel's constitutional revolution. First, virtually all the proposed reforms failed, suggesting that a majority in the Knesset has accepted, even if grudgingly, the transformation to a constitutional regime.[37] Secondly, attempts to alter some of the details of the constitutional arrangements reflect the Knesset's acknowledgment and acceptance that the major features of the constitutional revolution – that is, the supremacy of the basic laws and the establishment of judicial review – are now an integral feature of Israeli constitutionalism. At most, the proposed bills (with the important exception of the plan for a constitutional court) sought to limit the scope of the constitutional change, not its underlying premises. Notably, very few bills sought to overturn particular decisions. Thirdly, it seems that legislative obsession with the Court's power is confined to distinct periods of political concern.[38] Most of the bills were proposed in a period of heightened scrutiny of the judicial system, largely because the then-minister of justice was ideologically opposed to the increase in the Court's power. When this chapter was initially written, Israel was in the midst of another such period, with bills trying to change the composition of the judicial appointments committee in order to reflect current political preferences, and another bill attempting to limit the court's broad rules of access for public petitioners. These bills did not pass. This too serves to confirm the durability of the constitutional developments.

Although the legislative backlash to the judicial assertion of power may seem intense, it is hardly unique. In the United States, for example,[39] Congress regularly

---

[35] Memorandum on Basic Law: Adjudication (Amendment – Justiciability) – 2008.

[36] Eventually only one change was made. The nine-member committee that decides on judicial appointment now has to have a majority of seven members in order to appoint a Supreme Court judge.

[37] Another possibility is that the Knesset is too fragmented to institute constitutional changes, even if there is a provisional majority willing to do so. It is possible that legislative attempts in themselves likely have a chilling impact on adjudication, even if they do not reach fruition. In countries with a solidly entrenched constitution, the court knows that it is nearly impossible to amend the constitution, or at least that amendment cannot be achieved by mere legislative will.

[38] An alternative explanation is that the bills achieved their purpose by "threatening" the Court, making it more reluctant to issue bold decisions. This hypothesis has yet to be empirically tested.

[39] Court-curbing tendencies are less pronounced in other jurisdictions. In Canada, they are mostly espoused in Quebec and among conservative provincial politicians. See Morton and Knopff (2000).

attempts to constrain the Supreme Court by introducing bills that reduce the Court's power of judicial review, strip the Court's jurisdiction in a specific area, or alter the Justices' terms of service. However, out of about 360 court-curbing attempts between 1937 and 2008, very few were successful. For example, term limits, mandatory retirement, and reconfirmation bills were proposed more than sixty times during the Warren and early Burger Courts. Between 1962 and 1987, fifteen measures were introduced to require a supermajority or unanimity in cases that implicated overturning state or federal law. None of these measures passed (Farganis unpublished). Similar to Israel, many court-curbing measures came after controversial court decisions, but the Court's institutional legitimacy prevented their success. Thus, while court curbing may be popular among legislators, it generally does not pose a major threat to courts, and should be seen as a mostly symbolic attempt to signal displeasure with the Court's activity (Devins 2006).

A similar experience, albeit with different outcomes, has been the political reaction to activist constitutional courts in Russia and Hungary. Both courts became very powerful and popular after transitioning from communist rule. However, in both countries, the courts were effectively neutralized after a period of heightened constitutional scrutiny. In Hungary, the government, displeased with high levels of activism, simply did not reappoint the "problematic" judges to new terms, thus replacing the court with judges favorable to the government's agenda. In Russia, the court was literally shut down from 1993 to 1995 because of President Yeltsin's displeasure with the court's pro-parliament rulings. It was then reconstituted and six new judges were added. As a result, the court became much less interventionist (Scheppele 2003).

Court curbing occurs irrespective of the way the constitutional arrangement came about. It likely has more to do with particular decisions the legislature is railing against than dissatisfaction with the overall constitutional framework.[40] Its chances for success derive from the constellation of political forces rather than the constitutional source of the court's power.

8.4.3 *Legitimacy of the Supreme Court*

A possible consequence of accidental constitutionalism might be a low level of public trust in the Court. If the Court is perceived as usurping the legislature, instituting judicial review, and intervening in political affairs, all without clear authorization,

---

Worth mentioning is the use of the Notwithstanding Clause to override particular judicial decisions. See (Kahana 2002). For India, see Memorandum on Proposed Basic Law: Human Dignity and Liberty (Amendment – Citizenship, Residency, and Entrance to Israel).

[40] For a confirmation of this argument with respect to India, see Iyer (2007).

then this might jeopardize its support among the citizenry. Although it is too soon to tell, it seems that this concern is partially warranted in Israel.

The Israeli Supreme Court has traditionally enjoyed high levels of public trust explained by a public suspicion of the political branches. A comprehensive study in 1991, prior to the constitutional revolution, found that among those who were surveyed (a representative sample of the Jewish population), the Court was perceived as apolitical (85 percent of respondents) and therefore attracted high levels of public trust. Moreover, support for the Court was diffuse and did not stem from a particular decision. Seventy-one percent thought the Court was the highest moral authority in the country (Barzilai et al. 1994: 60, 72). Sixty-five percent favored judicial review of primary legislation, even before the Court declared it had the power to do so (Barzilai et al. 1994: 75). The authors have concluded the Court has leeway to forge ahead in its protection of rights and intervention in the political process and become an institutional leader without undermining its public legitimacy; the public would accept the Court's authority even in decisions that conflicted with public opinion (Barzilai et al. 1994: 178, 180).

This conclusion may have been premature. Indeed, the Court forged ahead, but the public has not followed. A major study conducted over a ten-year period (2000–2010) (five years after establishing judicial review) of a representative sample of Israelis documented a steady decline in the Court's legitimacy. From an 80 percent approval rate in 2000, the Court declined to 56 percent in 2010 (Zarhin 2010). This figure does not include ultraorthodox Jews and settlers, the two groups that traditionally distrust the Court (9 percent of ultraorthodox Jews and 25 percent of settlers trusted the Court in 2010). The steep decline in trust, according to the study, may be traced to increased intervention in controversial matters, especially religion and security.

There are indications, however, that the decline in trust is not directly related to features of accidental constitutionalism. There has been a steady decline in trust in all governmental institutions (Hattis-Rolef 2006). For example, another study documents a decline in trust in the Knesset from 41 percent in 1995 to 14 percent in 2000 (Meydani 2011: 113). Another explanation for the decline in trust cites criticism of the Court's de facto control over the judicial appointment process (Mautner 2011: 164–167) and the personalities and statements of particular judges (Posner 2007).

From a comparative perspective, the level of public support for the Israeli Supreme Court is not unique. In the United States, there is agreement that public support for the Court is high and not dependent on partisan or ideological divisions that influence support for other institutions. Americans view the Court as legitimate not because they necessarily agree with its decisions, but because they support its underlying authority to adjudicate disputes (Caldeira and Gibson 1992; Gibson and

Caldeira 2009).[41] Some groups, such as African Americans, exhibit less support for the Court, but overall support is high, and similar to that of the Israeli Supreme Court (Gibson 2007). Shifts in support occur not when the Court takes a particular ideological position, but when that position diverges from the ideological preferences of the citizenry (Durr et al. 2000). While the shifts in support are less marked than in Israel, this may be attributed to the long history of the Court and its role in U.S. politics. Unlike the Israeli Supreme Court, which is relatively young, the U.S. Supreme Court's authority has already been established and withstood several crises. Indeed, younger courts may face more difficulties in their quest to establish public support. For example, a study from 2002 found that the South African Constitutional Court enjoyed relatively low legitimacy compared with other high courts.[42] And, similar to the United States and Israel, legitimacy varies across racial and social groups (Gibson and Caldeira 2003; Roux 2009). Finally, comprehensive cross-sectional data of national high court legitimacy shows that Israel sits comfortably among other democracies such as Canada, France, Italy, and the Netherlands (Gibson 2011; Bühlmann and Kunz 2011: 322 [presenting similar findings regarding judicial systems as a whole]).

In conclusion, despite a sharp drop in trust in the Israeli Supreme Court, current levels of trust are generally in line with other constitutional regimes. Moreover, it is possible that the decline in trust may be quite healthy and reflective of a maturation of civil society. From an unrealistic perception of the court as a mythical institution, the public has come to hold more complex views that accord with those held in other mature democracies. Crucially, there does not seem to be a correlation between constitutional origins – accidental or orderly – and the level of public support and confidence in the judicial system and in the high court. Of course, increased activism has contributed to declining trust, but this has to do with the particular way in which judicial review is exercised rather than its existence.

8.4.4 *Compliance with Judicial Decisions*

Compliance is a complex phenomenon. Here I focus only on the political branches' acceptance of judicial rulings as binding and their good-faith attempts to implement them. On this view, compliance is an aspect of legitimacy. The less support the Court has among the citizenry and government institutions, the more we can expect its decisions to be flouted. Given the questionable origins and developments of Israeli

---

[41] It may very well be that the Court's legitimacy stems not just from the high regard the public holds the Court, but also from what Russell Hardin terms mere "acquiescence" to the conventional rules of a regime. See Hardin (1989).

[42] South Africa's case, however, is not dispositive. Several Eastern European constitutional courts have been successful in garnering public support early on. See Schwartz (2000).

constitutionalism, we might expect only partial compliance with judicial decisions. If the Court's constitutional authority is contested by the political branches and the people and rests on the Court's assertions about its own power, it may be difficult for the Court to enforce its decisions should it decide to rule against government preferences. While there is evidence of some noncompliance, the overall picture is one of compliance. Moreover, even though no reliable metric is available, it seems that noncompliance in Israel is not all that different from countries that had an orderly constitution-making process.

During Israel's early decades, direct noncompliance with court decisions was rare. The few times it did occur, pressure from the press, Knesset, and the public was applied to ensure government compliance with the Court's ruling (Shetreet 1994: 68–69). Although there is no study documenting current levels of noncompliance, there is anecdotal evidence of an increase in noncompliance over the last decade. For example, the state has failed to comply with decisions ordering the removal of segments of the separation barrier in the Palestinian Territories; ordering the building of classrooms for Palestinian students in East Jerusalem; allowing migrant workers freedom to leave one employer for another; and appointing representatives of Reform and Conservative Judaism to state religious councils. Bordering on noncompliance is the practice of the state following an unfavorable district court decision to implement the decision as applied to the parties, but choosing not to appeal or change its policy, leading to re-litigation of the same issues (Kashti and Zarhin 2010).

It is perhaps no coincidence that noncompliance occurs when the decisions implicate minority rights, Palestinian rights, and groups with little political clout such as immigrants and migrant workers. It is also no coincidence that the increase in noncompliance is correlated with the decline in public support for the Court. However, it is not clear that the instances of noncompliance can be traced to the processes of accidental constitutionalism that have been discussed here. None of the cases involve invalidation of primary legislation; all concern the striking down of military decrees or administrative regulations, powers the Court has exercised for decades. Therefore, a more plausible explanation for noncompliance is that the political branches disapprove of the ruling on the merits and try to postpone its implementation. Because the beneficiaries of the judicial decision lack political power, and because the decision is unpopular among the citizenry, this postponement can take place.[43]

As troubling as noncompliance may be, it does not appear that Israel is unique in that regard. There is a dearth of research on compliance with court decisions. Almost

---

[43] I do not mean that the accidental origins do not matter at all. It is possible that the atmosphere counts. If the Court is already under attack for its constitutional moves, it may be easier to disregard its decisions in other spheres.

all research has examined the United States, and it is either theoretical or focused on particular case studies, so it is difficult to draw conclusions regarding overall compliance. Still, noncompliance clearly occurs. Like Israel, noncompliance with judicial rulings is usually a consequence of particularly controversial decisions such as school desegregation or abolishing school prayer (Anderson 2010; Klarman 2004: 290–442; Bartley 1969; Dolbeare 1971). The strategy of complying with lower court decisions without changing the underlying policy also occurs in other jurisdictions (Hume 2009; Coenen 1991; Estreicher and Revesz 1989). The same is true of poor enforcement. In India, for example, the Supreme Court has encountered significant difficulties in achieving governmental compliance with its decisions. Some of this can be traced to substantive disagreements with judicial decisions, but another cause is the under-resourcing of administrative agencies and political interference that often amounts to corruption (Iyer 2007: 164).

In conclusion, noncompliance is a feature of public law litigation. There seems to be little correlation, if any, between the constitution-making processes and adherence to judicial decisions. Although noncompliance may be traced to public support of judicial institutions, that support, as I argued earlier, is not necessarily linked to the constitution's origins.

8.4.5 *Constitutional Discourse and Constitutional Ignorance*

An active citizenry engaged in critical assessment of government increases the quality of democracy. When the constitution is a part of everyday life, citizens may safeguard their rights and hold officials accountable to their constitutional obligations. For this to occur, debate over the meaning and adequacy of the constitution is essential. But to argue intelligently about the constitution, one must first be knowledgeable about its substantive content. It stands to reason, then, that constitutional consciousness will be achieved more easily in countries that had a transformative, collective, orderly, deliberate, and deliberative constitution-making process that engaged large swaths of the population. In countries where all governmental institutions reference the constitution, where the constitution authoritatively determines the structure of government and the rights citizens have, we may expect that citizens will be relatively familiar with these arrangements. In countries where there is still disagreement over the respective powers of each branch, the limitations on legislation, and the possibility of judicial review, let alone whether a constitution exists, we may expect less constitutional knowledge among the citizenry.

Although there is no study documenting constitutional consciousness in Israel, it is safe to say that the constitutional revolution only partially trickled down to the citizenry. Ordinary political discourse in Israel only occasionally refers to the 1992 basic laws or the supremacy of the basic laws over primary legislation. Knowledge of the Court's work is relatively limited and reserved to particular controversial cases. The constitutional developments have resonated mostly within legal academia, the lawyer class, elected representatives, and governmental institutions, most prominently the Ministry of Justice and the Knesset. Legislative sessions on proposed bills now regularly include input from the Knesset's legal advisor regarding considerations of constitutionality (Lis 2011). Constitutional discourse, then, has mostly remained in the legal professional domain, only partially informing ordinary political discourse.[44]

Whether limited constitutional consciousness demonstrates the weakness of Israeli democracy is an important question. However, Israel's limited constitutional consciousness is not that different from countries with a constitution enacted by an orderly process. Again, the comparison to the United States is telling.[45] Study after study has revealed that Americans are ignorant of constitutional essentials (Hatch 2009: 1035). According to one study, only 16 percent of Americans claim a "detailed knowledge" of the constitution (Nichol 2003: 622).[46] Another study showed that although very few people actually possess knowledge of the constitution, 91 percent say it is important to them (Jipping 2000: 368 [citing National Constitution Center, 1997 NCC Constitution Poll]). Thus, while the majority of Americans venerate the constitution, and while references to "the Constitution" are replete in the media and politics, very few Americans are actually informed about specific constitutional provisions (Mazzone 2005: 692).

Knowledge about the constitution may have little to do with the way that constitution came to be. Indeed, the oldest and shortest constitution in the world results in large amounts of constitutional ignorance, suggesting that it is not the constitution, but rather the political culture, including educational priorities,[47] that is responsible for this phenomenon. Constitutional discourse in Israel has similarly not trickled down to the citizenry (as opposed to legal-professional elites); less clear, however, is the role that the constitution-making process plays in this.

---

[44] However, the relative pliability of Israel's constitutional structure, the fact that basic laws can be easily amended, and that basic arrangements are still up for grabs do explain the admittedly huge strides in constitutional consciousness, which would probably not exist otherwise.

[45] There is limited research in English regarding non-U.S. constitutional awareness. See, e.g., Dakolias (2006: 1126) (stating that there is not enough data about citizens' knowledge of the UK constitution); Perez-Perdomo (2006: 189) (stating that citizens have relatively little knowledge of the constitutions in Latin America).

[46] Another study found that 45% of those surveyed believed that the U.S. constitution embodies the principle of "From each according to his ability, to each according to his need"; 49% believed that the president can suspend the constitution whenever he declares a national emergency; and 51% believed that the constitution does not permit citizens to speak in favor of a revolution. See Tribe (1987: 5).

[47] For example, the No Child Left Behind Act, in an attempt to boost science and math performance, has cut funding for civics classes. Today, half the states do not require learning civics to graduate from high school. See (Levinson 2009: 1243).

Of course, constitutional discourse does not operate independently of the particular constitution. The U.S. constitution is a powerful symbol in American life, as are, for example, the South African and Indian constitutions. This symbolic aspect is absent in the Israeli context, even though the Court and the basic laws consistently draw the attention of professional elites. The Israeli constitutional framework's muted and haphazard history is likely responsible for this symbolic or expressive loss. However, it is not clear that the origins and processes of Israel's constitution have led to a constitutional ignorance significantly different than that in other democracies with an established constitutional order.

Despite its distinctive origins, I have argued that the Israeli constitutional state of affairs may not be all that different from constitutions that have been created and ratified via a non-accidental process. Similar to other countries, Israel has a more or less complete set of basic laws that are superior to ordinary legislation, along with a rich body of case law interpreting them. Judicial review has been affirmed, and, as long as the Knesset does not enact new basic laws, the Court will continue the constitution-making process through constitutional interpretation. The legislative-judicial dynamics, though often fraught with tension, are not exceptional. The Court still enjoys a relatively high level of public trust, especially compared with the political branches. There is governmental noncompliance with Court decisions, but this also is not significantly different than in other countries. On the symbolic and discursive level, constitutional discourse has only been partially successful in penetrating ordinary politics, but this could be the result of Israel's brief experience with constitutionalism. Over time this will likely change and resemble other countries with established constitutional orders.

8.5 CONCLUSION

The argument I have put forward in this chapter is that Israel's constitution-making process, which I defined as accidental, has generated remarkable stability in a relatively short time. This calls into question the deep-rooted assumption, often implicit, regarding the relationship between the process of constitution-making and its attendant consequences.[48] The Israeli case study reveals that despite shaky origins and contested developments, Israel's constitutional patterns are more or less consistent with democratic constitutional regimes that had an orderly constitution-making process. With the passage of time, they are likely to become even more so.

---

[48] For example, Ruth Gavison has argued that because the status of the constitutional regime is controversial, this weakens the legitimacy of constitutional arrangements and results in instability. My argument is that this instability did not happen; Gavison (2006: 394).

Of course, the fact that an accidental constitution can end up operating like an ordered constitution is not an endorsement of the former. Israeli accidental constitutionalism has resulted in several pathologies that, although shared by ordered constitutional regimes, may be more pronounced. In particular, the preceding analysis has demonstrated how the Court became the almost exclusive agent of constitutional change, with the Knesset almost completely abdicating this role. This judicial dominance, in turn, resulted in a decline of public support for the Court, which may ultimately make it harder for the Court to make good on its countermajoritarian promise. To be sure, Israel is not exceptional in these respects, although it is possible that its constitution-making method has exacerbated these pathologies.

In the end, however, Israel's accidental constitutionalism is proving to be just as durable as other constitutions, while also sharing many of their dynamics. Warnings of constitutional instability have turned out to be unwarranted. Although there are periods of tension, noncompliance, and obsession with judicial authority, those seem to be localized and, however disconcerting, should not give rise to overarching concerns for those who believe in a judicially enforced version of constitutionalism. Indeed, the fact that the system is weathering these storms attests to its entrenchment and to the public's acceptance of Israel's constitutional structure.

REFERENCES

5 Knesset Records 1743 (1950).

Anderson, Karen 2010. *Little Rock: Race and Resistance at Central High School.* Princeton, NJ: Princeton University Press.

Arian, Asher, Nachmias, David, and Amir, Ruth 2002. *Executive Governance in Israel.* New York: Palgrave.

Avnun, Dan 1995. "'The Enlightened Public': Jewish and Democratic or Liberal and Democratic," *Law and Government,* 3: 417–452.

Barak, Aharon 1992. "The Constitutional Revolution: Protected Human Rights," *Law and Government,* 1: 9–10.

   2003. "A Judge on Judging: The Role of a Supreme Court in a Democracy," *Harvard Law Review,* 116: 19–162.

   2004. "The Constitutional Revolution at Twelve," *Law and Business,* 1: 3–58.

Barak-Erez, Daphne 1995. "From an Unwritten Constitution: The Israeli Challenge in American Perspective," *Columbia Human Rights Law Review,* 26: 309–355.

Bartley, Numan 1969. *The Rise of Massive Resistance: Race and Politics in the South during the 1950s.* Baton Rouge: Louisiana State University Press.

Barzilai, Gad, Yuchtman-Yaar, Ephraim, and Segal, Zeev 1994. *The Israeli Supreme Court and the Israeli Public.* Tel Aviv: Papyrus, Tel Aviv University Press.

Bendor, Ariel 1995. "Flaws in the Enactments of the Basic Laws," *Law and Government,* 2: 443–454.

Bork, Robert 2003. *Coercing Virtue: The Worldwide Rule of Judges*. Washington, DC: American Enterprise Institute.

Bühlmann, Marc and Kunz, Ruth 2011. "Confidence in the Judiciary: Comparing the Independence and Legitimacy of Judicial Systems," *Western European Politics*, **34**: 317–345.

CA 6821/93 United Mizrachi Bank v. Migdal Cooperative Village, 49(4) P.D. 221 (1995).

Caldeira, Gregory and Gibson, James 1992. "The Etiology of Public Support for the Supreme Court," *American Journal of Political Science*, **36**: 635–664.

Coenen, Dan 1991. "The Constitutional Case against Intracircuit Nonacquiescence," *Minnesota Law Review*, **75**: 1339–1444.

Dakolias, Maria 2006. "Are We There Yet?: Measuring Success of Constitutional Reform," *Vanderbilt Journal of Transnational Law*, **39**: 1117–1232.

Declaration of Independence 1948, Official Gazette, May 14, 1948, 1. 1 L.S.I. 3.

Devins, Neal 2006. "Should the Supreme Court Fear Congress?" *Minnesota Law Review*, **90**: 1337–1362.

Dickson, Brian (ed.) 2007. *Judicial Activism in Common Law Supreme Courts*. Oxford: Oxford University Press.

Dolbeare, Kenneth and Hammond, Philip 1971. *The School Prayer Decisions: From Court Policy to Local Practice*. Chicago: University of Chicago Press.

Dorner, Dalia 1999. "Does Israel Have a Constitution?" *St. Louis University Law Journal*, **43**: 1325–1336.

Dotan, Yoav 1999. "Do the 'Haves' Still Come out Ahead: Resource Inequalities in Ideological Courts: The Case of the Israeli High Court of Justice," *Law and Society Review*, **33**: 1059–1080.

Dotan, Yoav and Hofnung, Menachem 2005. "Legal Defeats – Political Wins: Why Do Elected Representatives Go to Court," *Comparative Political Studies*, **38**: 75–103.

Durr, Robert, Martin, Andrew, and Wolbrecht, Christina 2000. "Ideological Divergence and Public Support for the Supreme Court," *American Journal of Political Science*, **44**: 768–776.

Dworkin, Ronald 1990. *A Bill of Rights for Britain*. London: Chatto & Windus.

EA 92/03 Mofaz v. Election Commissioner, 57(3) P.D. 793 (2003).

Edelman, Martin 1994. *Courts, Politics, and Culture in Israel*. Charlottesville: University of Virginia Press.

Elster, Jon 1995. "Forces and Mechanisms in the Constitution-Making Process," *Duke Law Journal*, **45**: 364–396.

Estreicher, Samuel and Revesz, Richard 1989. "Nonacquiescence by Federal Administrative Agencies," *Yale Law Journal*, **98**: 679–772.

FH 2316/95 Ganimat v. Israel, 49(4) P.D. 589 (1995).

Farganis, Dion unpublished. "Court Curbing in the Modern Era: Should Supreme Court Justices Really Worry about Attacks from Congress?" Available at http://papers.ssrn.com/sol3/papers.cfm?abstract_id=1430723.

Gavison, Ruth 1997. "The Constitutional Revolution: A Reality or a Self-Fulfilling Prophecy?" *Mishpatim* **28**: 21–44.

2006. "Legislatures and the Quest for a Constitution: The Case of Israel," *Review of Constitutional Studies*, **11**: 345–400.

Gibson, James 2007. "The Legitimacy of the U.S. Supreme Court in a Polarized Society," *Journal of Empirical Law Studies*, **4**: 507–538.

2011. "Public Reverence for the United States Supreme Court: Is the Court Invincible?" Available at http://papers.ssrn.com/sol3/papers.cfm?abstract_id=1898485.

Gibson, James and Caldeira, Gregory 2003. "Defenders of Democracy? Legitimacy, Popular Acceptance, and the South African Constitutional Court," *Journal of Politics*, **65**: 1–30.

2009. *Citizens, Courts, and Confirmations: Positivity Theory and the Judgments of the American People*. Princeton, NJ: Princeton University Press.

Gibson, James, Caldeira, Gregory, and Baird, Vanessa 1998. "On the Legitimacy of National High Courts," *American Political Science Review*, **92**: 343–358.

Ginsburg, Tom 2003. *Judicial Review in New Democracies: Constitutional Courts in Asian Cases*. Cambridge: Cambridge University Press.

Ginsburg, Tom, Elkins, Zachary, and Blount, Justin 2009. "Does the Process of Constitution-Making Matter?" *Annual Review of Law and Social Science*, **5**: 201–223.

Hardin, Russell 1989. "Why a Constitution?" in Grofman, Bernard and Wittman, Donald (eds.), *The Federalist Papers and the New Institutionalism*. New York: Agathon Press.

Hatch, Orrin G. 2009. "The Constitution as the Playbook for Judicial Selection," *Harvard Journal of Law and Public Policy*, **32**: 1035–1044.

Hattis-Rolef, Sheila 2006. *Public Trust in Parliament – A Comparative Survey*. Knesset Information and Research Center. Available at http://www.knesset.gov.il/mmm/data/pdf/m01417.pdf.

H.C. 1/49 Bejerano v. Minister of the Police, 2 P.D. 80 (1949).

H.C. 1384/98 Avni v. Prime Minister, 52(5) P.D. 206 (1998).

H.C. 141/82 Rubinstein v. Speaker of the Knesset, 37(3) P.D. 141 (1983).

H.C. 148/73 Kaniel v. Minister of Justice, 27(1) P.D. 795 (1973).

H.C. 149/89 Laor v. Speaker of the Knesset 44(3) P.D. 529 (1990).

H.C. 1715/97 Investors Management Bureau v. Minister of Finance, 51(4) P.D. 367 (1997).

H.C. 2056/04 Beit Sourik Village Council v. Government of Israel, 58(5) P.D. 807 (2004).

H.C. 212/03 Herut National Movement v. Election Commissioner, 57(1) P.D. 750 (2003).

H.C. 246/81 Derekh Eretz Ass'n v. Broadcasting Authority, 35(4) P.D. 1 (1981).

H.C. 2605/05 Academic Center for Law and Business v. Minister of Finance (unpublished).

H.C. 270/80 Segal v. Minister of Interior, 34(4) P.D. 429 (1980).

H.C. 389/80 Dapei Zahav v. Broadcasting Authority, 35(1) P.D. 421 (1980).

H.C. 4885/03 Chicken Farmers Org. v. Government of Israel, 49(2) P.D. 14 (2004).

H.C. 5167/00 Weiss v. Prime Minister of Israel, 55(2) P.D. 455 (2001).

H.C. 5657/09 The Movement for Quality Government in Israel v. Government of Israel, (unpublished).

H.C. 6163/92 Eisenberg v. Minister of Housing, 47(2) P.D. 229 (1993).

H.C. 652/81 Sarid v. Speaker of the Knesset, 36(2) P.D. 197 (1982).

H.C. 73/53 Kol Ha'am v. Minister of Interior, 7 P.D. 871 (1953).

H.C. 7957/04 Mar'abe v. Prime Minister of Israel, (unpublished).

H.C. 8397/06 Wasser v. Minister of Defense, (unpublished).

H.C. 910/86 Resler v. Minister of Defense, 42(2) P.D. 441 (1988).

H.C. 935/89 Ganor v. Attorney General, 44(2) P.D. 485 (1990).

H.C. 98/69 Bergman v. Minister of Finance, 23(1) P.D. 693 (1969).

Hirschl, Ran (2013). "The Strategic Foundations of Constitutions," in Galligan, Denis and Versteeg, Mila (eds.). *Social and Political Foundations of Constitutions*. Cambridge: Cambridge University Press.

2001. "The Political Origins of Judicial Empowerment Through Constitutionalization: Lessons from Israel's Constitutional Revolution," *Comparative Politics*, **33**: 315–335.

2004. *Towards Juristocracy: The Origins and Consequences of the New Constitutionalism*. Cambridge, MA: Harvard University Press.

Hofnung, Menachem 1996. "The Unintended Consequences of Unplanned Constitutional Reform: Constitutional Politics in Israel," *American Journal of Comparative Law*, **44**: 585–604.

Hume, Robert 2009. *How Courts Impact Federal Administrative Behavior*. London: Routledge.

Iyer, Venkat 2007. "The Supreme Court of India," in Dickson, Brian (ed.), *Judicial Activism in Common Law Supreme Courts*. Oxford: Oxford University Press.

Jacobsohn, Gary 1993. *Apple of Gold: Constitutionalism in Israel and the United States*. Princeton, NJ: Princeton University Press.

Jipping, Thomas 2000. "From Least Dangerous Branch to Most Profound Legacy: The High Stakes in Judicial Selection," *Texas Review of Law and Politics*, **4**: 365–460.

Kahana, Tsvi 2002. "Understanding the Notwithstanding Mechanism," *University of Toronto Law Journal*, **52**: 221–274.

Karp, Yehudit 1993. "Basic Law: Human Dignity and Liberty: A Biography of Power Struggles," *Law and Government*, **1**: 323–384.

Kashti, Or and Zarhin, Tomer 2010. "This Is How the State Ignores Supreme Court Decisions," *Haaretz*, March 5, 2010.

Klarman, Michael 2004. *From Jim Crow to Civil Rights: The Supreme Court and the Struggle for Racial Equality*. Oxford: Oxford University Press.

Kmiec, Keenan 2007. "The Origins and Current Meanings of 'Judicial Activism'," *California Law Review*, **92**: 1441–1478.

LCA 3007/02 Yitzhak v. Mozes, 56(6) P.D. 592 (2002).

Lerner, Hannah 2010. "Constitution-Writing in Deeply Divided Societies: The Incrementalist Approach," *Nations and Nationalism*, **16**: 68–88.

Levinson, Sanford 2009. "What Should Citizens (as Participants in a Republican Form of Government) Know about the Constitution?" *William and Mary Law Review*, **50**: 1239–1260.

Lin, Uriel and Loya, Shlmoi 2012. "The Contribution of the Constitution, Law and Justice Committee of the Twelfth Knesset to Israel's Constitutional Law," *Law and Business*, **14**: 261–290.

Lis, Yehonatan 2011. "How the Legal Advisor to the Knesset, Attorney Eyal Yinnon, Became a Key Figure in Shaping Israeli Democracy," *Haaretz*, May 21.

Marbury v. Madison, 5 U.S. (1 Cranch) 137 (1803).

Mautner, Menachem 2002. "Law and Culture in Israel: The 1950s and the 1980s," in Harris, Ron, Kedar, Alexandre, Lahav, Pnina, and Likhovski, Assaf (eds.). *The History of Law in a Multi-Cultural Society: Israel 1917–1967*. Aldershot: Ashgate.

2011. *Law and the Culture of Israel*. Oxford: Oxford University Press.

Mazzone, Jason 2005. "The Scholarship of Lawrence M. Friedman: The Creation of a Constitutional Culture," *Tulsa Law Review*, **40**: 671–698.

Medina, Barak 2007. "Four Myths of Judicial Review: A Response to Richard Posner's Critique of Aharon Barak's Judicial Activism," *Harvard International Law Journal Online*, **49**: 1–9.

Meydani, Assaf 2011. *The Israeli Supreme Court and the Human Rights Revolution: Courts as Agenda Setters*. Cambridge: Cambridge University Press.

Morton, Frederick and Knopff, Rainer 2000. *The Charter Revolution & the Court Party*. Toronto: University of Toronto Press.

Nichol, Gene 2003. "Toward a People's Constitution: How Democratic Is the American Constitution?" *California Law Review*, 91: 621–639.

Perez-Perdomo, Rogelio 2006. "Rule of Law and Lawyers in Latin America," *Annals*, 603: 179–191.

Posner, Richard 2007. "Enlightened Despot," *The New Republic*, April 23.

Roux, Theunis 2009. "Principle and Pragmatism on the Constitutional Court of South Africa," *International Journal of Constitutional Law*, 7: 106–138.

Rubinstein, Amnon 2012. "The Story of the Basic Laws," *Law and Business*, 14: 79–109.

Rubinstein, Amnon and Medina, Barak 2005. *The Constitutional Law of the State of Israel, 6th Edition*. Tel Aviv: Shoken.

Sagy, Yair 2004. "For the Administration of Justice: On the Establishment of the High Court of Justice of Israel," *Tel Aviv University Law Review*, 28: 225–298.

Salzberger, Eli 2007. "Judicial Activism in Israel," in Dickson, Brian (ed.), *Judicial Activism in Common Law Supreme Courts*. Oxford: Oxford University Press.

Sapir, Gidon 2008. "The Israeli Constitutional Revolution – How Did It Happen?" *Law and Government*, 11: 571–597.

Scheppele, Kim Lane 2003. "Constitutional Negotiations: Political Contexts of Judicial Activism in Post-Soviet Europe," *International Sociology*, 18: 219–238.

Schwartz, Herman 2000. *The Struggle for Constitutional Justice in Post-Communist Europe*. Chicago: University of Chicago Press.

Segev, Joshua 2007. "Who Needs a Constitution? In Defense of the Non-Decision Constitution-Making Tactic in Israel," *Albany Law Review*, 70: 409–490.

Shetreet, Shimon 1994. *Justice in Israel: A Study of the Israeli Judiciary*. Boston, MA: Springer.

Sommer, Hillel 1997. "The Non-Enumerated Rights: On the Scope of the Constitutional Revolution," *Mishpatim*, 28: 257–340.

Sweet, Alec S. 2000. *Governing with Judges: Constitutional Politics in Europe*. Oxford: Oxford University Press.

Tate, Neal and Vallinder, Torbjorn (eds.) 1995. *The Global Expansion of Judicial Power*. New York, London: New York University Press.

Tribe, Laurence 1987. "Bicentennial Blues: To Praise the Constitution or to Bury It?" *American University Law Review*, 37: 1–8.

Tushnet, Mark 2000. "The Universal and the Particular in Constitutional Law: An Israeli Case Study," *Columbia Law Review*, 100: 1327–1346.

Zarhin, Tomer 2010. "A Report Reveals: A Sharp Decline in the Public's Trust in the Courts," *Haaretz*, June 22.

9

The Myth of the Imposed Constitution

David S. Law

> "Is there any point to which you would wish to draw my attention?"
> "To the curious incident of the dog in the night-time."
> "The dog did nothing in the night-time."
> "That was the curious incident," remarked Sherlock Holmes.
>
> – Sir Arthur Conan Doyle, *Silver Blaze*

9.1 INTRODUCTION: THE MYSTERIOUS CASE OF THE IMPOSED YET ENDURING CONSTITUTION

Postwar constitutionalism in Japan can be likened to the story of the dog that did not bark: the absence of the most routine forms of constitutional change is a source of mystery. Since its promulgation in 1947, the Nihonkoku Kenpō has yet to be amended even once, a record unmatched by any other constitution currently in force (Elkins et al. 2009: 180). (By way of comparison, the average national constitution lasts only nineteen years before it is replaced [*ibid.*, 129], to say nothing of how frequently it is amended. Germany alone has amended its postwar constitution more than fifty times.) Nor would it seem that judicial lawmaking has supplanted formal amendment. The Supreme Court of Japan almost never strikes down laws on constitutional grounds: since its establishment in 1947, it has done so just eight times. (Germany's constitutional court, created at roughly the same time, has struck down more than 600 laws; the U.S. Supreme Court's tally over the same period is roughly 900.)[1]

The author wishes to thank Wen-Chen Chang, Denis Galligan, Tom Ginsburg, John Haley, Jau-Yuan Hwang, Hiroshi Itoh, Colin Jones, Li-Ju Lee, Craig Martin, Tokujin Matsudaira, Mitsuo Matsumoto, Hiroshi Miyashita, Mila Versteeg, Ming-Li Wang, the University of Wisconsin Discussion Group on Constitutionalism, and the participants at faculty seminars at Hitotsubashi University Law School in Tokyo and National Taiwan University College of Law in Taipei for their highly constructive comments and suggestions. Elizabeth Drake Mohan provided diligent research assistance. I am especially indebted to Azusa Tanaka, specialist librarian at Washington University, for her invaluable expertise and help in unearthing Japanese public opinion surveys from decades past.

[1] See, e.g., Law 2011: 1426 (reviewing competing explanations for the Japanese Supreme Court's extreme reluctance to strike down laws on constitutional grounds); Law 2009: 1547 (stressing the

By any standard, the longevity of the Kenpō has been remarkable. That longevity becomes even harder to fathom, however, if one accepts the conventional narrative that the Kenpō was imposed on an unwilling nation by force. It is commonly held that Japan offers the "classic," and most successful, example of imposed constitutionalism that the world has seen in the last century (Schauer 2005: 907).[2] "Some pre-war Japanese legal and political traditions were explicitly or implicitly incorporated in the document," writes Frederick Schauer, "but these were comparatively minor, and the Japanese Constitution may remain as the best example we have of a truly imposed constitution" (*ibid.*, 908). Some wax nostalgic for a bygone era when the United States could successfully impose a constitution by force. Laments Noah Feldman: "Gone are the days when American legal officers could write the constitution of Japan, translate it into Japanese, and extract the acquiescence of such a Japanese government as existed under the auspices of U.S. occupation and the reign of Supreme Allied Commander General Douglas MacArthur" (Feldman 2005: 857). Japanese conservatives, meanwhile, have self-serving reasons to perpetuate the view that the Kenpō was imposed: characterization of the document as a foreign imposition is a strategy for depriving the document of legitimacy and undermining public support for the provisions that formally limit the country's military capabilities (Beer and Maki 2002: 83; Shōichi 1997: 251; Chinen 2005: 93).

Scholars have struggled to explain how an ostensibly imposed constitution could survive completely intact for so long. To the extent that an explanation can be discerned, the success of the Kenpō has been attributed to some uniquely Japanese capacity for acquiescence and internalization. For Feldman, Japan's long-running failure to replace or even amend its postwar constitution, even after its "imposed foreign origins" came to light, is "acquiescence" of a sort "one cannot imagine … being reproduced" today (Feldman 2005, 859). "No modern nation ever has rested on a more alien constitution," writes John Dower in his celebrated account of postwar Japan, "and few, if any, alien documents have ever been as thoroughly internalized and vigorously defended as this national charter

combined impact of political and institutional factors in shaping the Japanese Supreme Court's behavior).

[2]   This view has drawn its share of scholarly criticism. See, e.g., Beer and Maki 2002: 83, 92 (deeming it a "myth that the document was simply imposed on a helpless Japan," and arguing that this myth fails to "do justice" to the efforts of the many "intelligent, well-informed, and democratically committed" Japanese who sought constitutional reform); Elkins et al. 2009: 199 (observing that, although "the Japanese constitution would seem to be a paradigmatic case of imposition," "the facts are more complex"); Scheppele 2003: 306–06 & n.18 (2003) (questioning the view that the constitution was simply "imposed" on the Japanese government, and arguing that "there was far more Japanese input and less American input" than some believe).

would come to be" (Dower 1999: 347). But the notion of internalization raises more questions than it answers. What is internalization? Why was this particular constitution internalized? Under what conditions, if any, could a similar feat be repeated elsewhere?

Failure to explain the success of the Kenpō translates directly into failure to explain how that success might be replicated by constitution-writers today. And that is no small failure. At a time when U.S.-supported efforts at constitution-writing in Iraq and Afghanistan appear highly vulnerable to long-term failure, learning from the past ought to be a matter of some urgency. The Kenpō in particular ranks among the greatest constitutional success stories of the twentieth century: perhaps no constitution ever prepared by an occupying power, and certainly no constitution-writing project undertaken by the United States, has enjoyed greater longevity or popular appeal. The story of the Kenpō therefore offers a rare and valuable opportunity to understand the conditions for successful adoption of a transformative new constitution in a distant, post-conflict setting. But one cannot replicate a success that one cannot explain. And as long as scholars accept the simplistic view perpetuated by Japanese conservatives that the Kenpō was imposed, the endurance of the Kenpō will continue to defy explanation.

This conventional narrative of imposition and internalization glosses over two crucial facts that, taken together, go far toward explaining the constitution's unusual longevity. First, the Japanese have made their constitution their own and molded it to fit their needs. A lack of formal amendment or judicial elaboration of the Kenpō should not be mistaken for a lack of constitutional evolution. It is essential to distinguish between the de jure or "large-C" constitution, or the formal document that bills itself as the constitution, and the de facto or "small-c" constitution, which consists of the continually evolving set of rules, practices, and understandings that actually govern the operation of the state (Law 2010: 377–378). In Japan as in many other countries, reconciliation of the large-C and small-c constitutions has been achieved partly by stretching the meaning of the constitutional document to accommodate actual constitutional practice. It can be argued that Japan possesses cultural, historical, and institutional attributes that have rendered the document particularly malleable, to the point that formal amendment has proven unnecessary. Ultimately, however, neither the need for syncretic constitutionalism nor the mechanisms employed to achieve it are unique to Japan.

Second, it is a gross oversimplification, if not an outright mistake, to say that the Kenpō was imposed. Postwar Japan was not monolithic. To say that the new constitution was imposed begs the question of *upon whom* it was imposed. The conservative politicians who populated the Cabinet grudgingly supported the proposed constitution insofar as it guaranteed the survival of Emperor Hirohito in the face of Allied demands that he face trial as a war criminal.[3] In contrast to their reactionary leaders, however, the general public largely welcomed the sweeping changes introduced by their new constitution. It is this popular support, above all, that has thwarted decades of effort by the center-right Liberal Democratic Party (LDP) to curtail the Kenpō's conspicuously pacifist and liberal aspects.

Thus explained, the remarkable longevity of the Kenpō holds valuable lessons for constitution-writers today. Contrary to what some scholars have argued,[4] popular support plays a larger role in a democratic society than elite support in determining the long-term prospects for constitutional success. Indeed, the case of Japan demonstrates that the support of the public can be sufficient to overcome not only resistance from a country's political elites, but also any stigma that might be associated with foreign authorship. Conversely, a constitutional bargain engineered by local political leaders cannot be expected to endure over the long run in the face of popular opposition.[5] Such niceties as fully indigenous authorship, a genuinely transparent and inclusive drafting process, and the complicity of local elites may improve a constitution's prospects, but the Japanese experience suggests that they are not indispensable.

9.2 THE U.S. ROLE IN THE DRAFTING OF THE 1947 CONSTITUTION

It is not difficult to see why adoption of the Kenpō is typically considered a paradigmatic case of imposed constitutionalism. To summarize a series of events that remained secret for years but by now forms the conventional account (Shōichi 1997: 1), General MacArthur initially sought to encourage the Japanese leadership to take the initiative in drafting a new constitution that would be consistent with certain broad and nonnegotiable principles – namely, demilitarization, civilian control of the military, popular sovereignty as opposed to imperial rule, and broad suffrage. To that end, the Supreme Commander for the Allied Powers (or SCAP, as MacArthur's group was collectively known) gave encouragement and guidance to the constitutional revision

---

[3]   Moore and Robinson (2004: 4) characterize the adoption of the Kenpō as a "conspiracy" between conservative Japanese leaders, who sought to protect Emperor Hirohito from the prospect of dethronement and trial, and General MacArthur, who sought to protect Hirohito without appearing to usurp the prerogatives of either the other Allied powers or U.S. domestic political actors to ultimately decide Hirohito's fate.

[4]   For example, Feldman argues that an "occupying power" that seeks to impose a constitution "badly needs validation from local political elites," whereas "the opinion of the general public, real or imagined, functions as only one – often relatively weak – constraint on the negotiations" (Feldman 2005: 879). Feldman's argument is discussed in Section 9.6 of this chapter.

[5]   Malaysia's independence constitution is perhaps illustrative: although it represented a "'bargain' struck among communal leaders," opposition by a younger generation of Malays led to riots in 1969 and ultimately forced a constitutional overhaul that entrenched the privileges of ethnic Malays (Hassall & Saunders 2002: 155, quoting Haji Ahmad Zakaria).

efforts of Prince Konoe, who promptly proceeded to embarrass SCAP by announcing publicly that he had been charged with the responsibility of writing a new constitution within American guidelines. Konoe, himself a former prime minister but no longer a member of the Cabinet, labored in good faith to generate a genuinely Japanese document that would also satisfy SCAP's demands, but was at this point notified that he faced trial for war crimes and chose instead to take his own life (Moore and Robinson 2004: 64–72). Stung by this fiasco, SCAP left the new Shidehara Cabinet to its own devices to produce a new draft. Operating without guidance from SCAP, the Shidehara Cabinet, in turn, failed to grasp the magnitude of the changes that would be required; an early draft, which was condemned by the Japanese media as wholly inadequate, demonstrated that the government intended to propose little more than cosmetic changes to the existing Meiji Constitution (*ibid.*: 93).[6]

At this point, SCAP took aggressive but covert action. Realizing that the Shidehara Cabinet's bungling had created both the need and the opportunity for a vigorous alternative, but also mindful of the fact that proposal of a new constitution was arguably not within his remit and could anger the other Allies, MacArthur tendered a concise, indeed almost cryptic, memorandum of basic principles to his staff at General Headquarters (GHQ) who, working in total secrecy and without the knowledge of the other Allied powers or even the State Department, forged a complete draft in less than two weeks (*ibid.*: 91–106, Gordon 1997: 103–120). The American drafters relied in part on the constitutional proposals offered by various Japanese academics, legal reform groups, and political parties, but MacArthur's principles defined the basic parameters of their task (Beer and Maki 2002: 78; Sims 2001: 244).

The result of their labors, also delivered in secret, came as a complete shock to the Shidehara Cabinet. SCAP emphasized, however, that if Japan's conservative political leaders wished to save their cherished emperor from dethronement or trial as a war criminal, they had little choice but to preempt such action by proposing the draft constitution as their own (Moore and Robinson 2004: 109).[7] Following SCAP's resounding rejection of a Japanese rewrite that purported merely to incorporate the "fundamental principles and basic forms" of what the Americans had devised (*ibid.*: 126), the Shidehara Cabinet ultimately capitulated and offered up the SCAP draft as its own with only minor modifications (Martin 2008a: 297). Subsequent deliberations

---

[6] The manner in which the so-called Matsumoto draft was leaked to the press and the subsequent reaction to the draft are discussed in Section 9.6, immediately following note 28.

[7] MacArthur's support for Hirohito, in turn, appears to have rested in substantial part on a pragmatic calculation that removal of the emperor would have created a power vacuum and greatly complicated the tasks of occupation and reconstruction. In the words of Brigadier-General Elliott Thorpe: "otherwise we would have had nothing but chaos. The religion was gone, the government was gone, and he was the only symbol of control. Now, I know he had his hand in the cookie jar, and he wasn't any innocent little child. But he was of great use to us, and that was the basis on which I recommended to the Old Man [MacArthur] that we keep him" (Dower 1999: 327).

in the Diet resulted in a significant number of meaningful amendments, not all of which were to SCAP's liking.[8] Nonetheless, the Diet's work was itself monitored and stage-managed by SCAP in a variety of ways (Dower 1999: 385–386).

9.3 LOST IN TRANSLATION?

So much for the imposition part of the conventional narrative. No sooner had SCAP delivered its draft constitution, however, than the process of translating (in more ways than one) a formal constitutional document into actual constitutional practice began in earnest. This process of Japanization sometimes took the form of a cat-and-mouse game, in which each side jockeyed for advantage unbeknownst to the other. On occasion, it was the Americans who played games. Notwithstanding its much-vaunted power to impose its will, SCAP approached the process of proposing a new constitution as an exercise in bargaining. The SCAP draft's provision for a unicameral legislature, for example, mystified and appalled the Japanese, who were quick to point out that even the United States itself employed a bicameral legisla-ture (Okudaira 1990: 23). GHQ countered that the simultaneous lack of a federal structure and the abolition of the hereditary peerage rendered a second legislative chamber superfluous, but its defense of the proposal was half-hearted, and it has been reported that SCAP had little genuine interest in adoption of a unicameral legislature and had included that provision with the expectation that it might be deleted later as a concession (Shōichi 1997: 91; Dower 1999: 376).

Meanwhile, the inevitable vagaries of translation worked to the advantage of the Japanese government. The American side suspected that its lack of familiarity with linguistic nuance had been targeted for exploitation.[9] In the view of Colonel Kades, a principal author of the SCAP draft and key player throughout the constitution-making process, Japanese ideographs were "susceptible to equivocation," and it was a deliberate strategy on the part of the Japanese government to use "colloquial ideographs" with "connotations inconsistent with the concepts accepted" in earlier discussions where SCAP's view had prevailed (Kades 1989: 234). For its part, the Japanese side attempted to secure a number of substantive changes under the guise of translation. For example, the SCAP draft provided that the emperor would act only with the "advice and consent" of the Cabinet, but the initial Japanese version

---

[8]   Among the more interesting of the "thirty-odd amendments" made by the Diet (Beer and Maki 2002: 85, quoting Kades) were the addition of a guarantee of "minimum standards of wholesome and cul-tured living," the rejection of a legislative override of Supreme Court decisions, and the elimination of a balanced budget requirement (*ibid.*: 85–87).

[9]   Beer and Maki take a skeptical view of the actual significance of language barriers: they argue that "cul-tural differences within languages" generated no "substantive misunderstandings" between the Japanese and American drafters, and that differences between the English and Japanese wording have never produced "a noteworthy problem in subsequent Japanese constitutional law" (Beer and Maki 2002, 92).

of this provision contained only the equivalent of the word "advice" (*hohitsu*) and not the word for "consent" (*kyōsan*). When the Americans challenged this omission, Jōji Matsumoto, the minister responsible for constitutional revision and a former law professor at the University of Tokyo, countered that the concept of *kyōsan* made sense only in relation to the Diet. Discussions deteriorated to the point that Matsumoto walked out for fear that he would come to blows with Kades and left his assistant, a mid-level functionary in the Cabinet Legislation Bureau, to fend single-handedly for himself and his government.[10]

SCAP was less successful, by contrast, at guaranteeing the equal treatment of aliens. In a provision guaranteeing equality of all natural persons before the law, the Japanese side had translated "persons" not as *min* but instead as *kokumin*, a word connoting a member of the polity. SCAP rejected that translation but at the same time abandoned its insistence on a separate provision explicitly guaranteeing equal treatment of foreigners, in response to Japanese objections that the latter provision had been rendered redundant (Moore and Robinson 2004: 130).[11] Subsequent reintroduction of the term *kokumin* ultimately deprived foreigners in Japan of the protection that SCAP had sought to guarantee them.[12]

In other cases, the Americans were either unsure or unaware of the potential implications of drafting choices made by the Japanese. Of particular importance was the so-called Ashida amendment to Article 9, the pacifist provision of the Kenpō included at MacArthur's insistence and the most controversial provision in recent years by far. As with a number of other provisions of the Kenpō, such as those guaranteeing welfare rights and the right to unionize and engage in collective bargaining, Article 9 can be understood in part as a product of its time – a time when New Deal progressivism could still hold some sway over U.S. foreign policy, and before the harsh geopolitical realities of the Cold War had fully taken hold.[13] The prefatory language added by the Ashida amendment is italicized:

(1) *Aspiring sincerely to an international peace based on justice and order*, the Japanese people forever renounce war as a sovereign right of the nation and the threat or use of force as means of settling international disputes.

[10] By his own account, an exasperated Matsumoto eventually demanded of Kades: "Have you come to Japan to correct our Japanese?" Matsumoto's assistant had little choice but to remain, as Kades locked the doors and would not allow anyone to leave the building until the remainder of the translation had been reviewed (Moore and Robinson 2004: 125–126; see also Dower 1999: 380).

[11] Beer and Maki (2002: 86) suggest that the American side acquiesced in the deletion of this provision in light of the fact that the United States itself had not extended equal treatment to aliens as of the 1940s.

[12] In 1964, the Japanese Supreme Court interpreted the term *kokumin* as encompassing foreigners (Martin 2010: 174). Having acknowledged that aliens are in principle entitled to equal treatment, however, the Court has done little to enforce their equality in practice (Matsui 2011b: 158–162).

[13] See Moore and Robinson 2004: 98 (observing that everyone at SCAP "had lived through the New Deal," and that the progressivism of that era therefore "seemed natural" to them, "even to conservative Republicans such as MacArthur").

(2) *In order to accomplish the aim of the preceding paragraph,* land, sea, and air forces, as well as other war potential, will never be maintained. The right of aggression of the state will not be recognized.

Read literally, Article 9 would seem clearly to prohibit the maintenance of any "war potential" for any reason. There is strong evidence, moreover, that this is precisely how the provision was understood at the time of its adoption. During the ratification debates in the Diet, the Shidehara government represented repeatedly that Article 9 would preclude Japan from keeping military forces even for the purpose of self-defense, and it was on the basis of these representations that the proposed constitution mustered broad support from nearly every party (Dower 1999: 395–397, 399–400).

With the advent of the Korean War, however, the United States performed an abrupt about-face and began to push Japan to expand its military capabilities and activities, a trend that continues to this day. In this context, the Ashida amendment was invoked to justify the Japanese government's adoption in 1954 of the position that Article 9 does not preclude the acquisition of military self-defense capabilities or the contribution of force to United Nations operations. The government ultimately took the view that the only force prohibited by Article 9, read in the context of the Ashida amendment, is force threatened or exercised for reasons inconsistent with "an international peace based on justice and order."[14] The interpretive possibilities created by the Ashida amendment thus eventually proved highly congenial to U.S. interests, years after the fact. It is unclear, however, whether SCAP foresaw the potential significance of the amendment at the time it was adopted.[15] Whatever the intended implications of the Ashida amendment, SCAP either failed to perceive them or chose to remain uncharacteristically silent on a matter of utmost importance.

9.4 THREE MECHANISMS OF INFORMAL CONSTITUTIONAL ADAPTATION: NONENFORCEMENT, INTERPRETATION, AND FUNCTIONAL OBSOLESCENCE

If a written constitution is to succeed – where success is defined as some combination of longevity, acceptance, and relevance to actual practice – it must be at least

---

[14] Ashida, who was Home Minister at the time, himself propounded this view of the amendment in later years, but contemporaneous evidence suggests that Ashida had no such idea in mind at the time the amendment was actually adopted (see, e.g., Samuels 2004; Chinen 2005: 96–97; Martin 2008: 302–303).

[15] Decades later, Kades would report that he understood the "rather vague" Ashida amendment at the time as permitting Japan to possess "a home guard and a coast guard, sufficient to repel any invasion as well as contribute to an armed contingent to a United Nations international force," and that the Chinese had regarded the amendment as potentially reauthorizing Japanese remilitarization (Kades 1989: 237–238; see also Martin 2008: 302–303 n. 97).

somewhat adapted to its environment. In Japan, the need for such adaptation was only heightened by the unusual manner in which the Kenpō was adopted and the geopolitical upheaval that followed: its American drafters lacked intimate, firsthand knowledge of Japanese society, and the Cold War soon made the pacifist core of the new constitution look decidedly anachronistic to many. The most conspicuous way in which constitutional adaptation can occur is via the formal amendment process. Yet formal amendment procedures tend, by design, to be at least somewhat unwieldy. Even under the best of circumstances, constitutional revision occurs in fits and spurts; in Japan's case, it has not occurred at all. The Japanese experience offers, instead, a stark demonstration of how even relatively dramatic constitutional evolution can bypass not only the formal amendment process, but also the courts.

The history of Article 9 illustrates two of the three most obvious ways in which any written constitution – imposed or otherwise – can over time be adapted to actual practice and the wishes and demands of the present day without the need for formal amendment. The first is via a lack of enforcement; the second is via interpretation. For constitutional scholars who are accustomed to studying judicial decisions, the notion that the meaning of a constitution can change radically via processes of interpretation is hardly new. What is both distinctive and illuminating about the Japanese experience, however, is the degree of judicial disengagement from constitutional interpretation and enforcement. As noted previously, the Supreme Court of Japan has invalidated a law on constitutional grounds on only eight occasions in its entire history (Law 2009: 1547; Matsui 2011a: 1388), and Japanese judicial review is consequently considered "the most conservative and cautious in the world" (Beatty 1995: 121).

From the outset, the Court has effectively relinquished responsibility for interpreting or enforcing Article 9 by erecting insurmountable jurisdictional barriers. In the 1959 Sunagawa case,[16] the Court took the position that only obvious and flagrant violations of Article 9 were justiciable, and in the 1982 Naganuma case,[17] it took a narrow view of standing to bring Article 9 claims. The effect was, of course, not simply to reject the Article 9 claims in those particular cases, but also to prevent potentially liberal-minded lower courts from acting on such claims. The acquiescence of the lower courts has on occasion been grudging, but the prospect of reversal by the Supreme Court, as well as outright defiance on the part of the government, has sufficed to preclude judicial enforcement of Article 9. By way of a recent example, the Nagoya High Court concluded in 2008 that the Self-Defense Forces' (SDF) air support operations in Iraq had violated Article 9, but it simultaneously denied relief

---

[16] 13 Keishū 3225 (Sup. Ct. G.B., Dec. 16, 1959).
[17] Uno et al v. Minister of Agriculture, Forestry, & Fisheries, 36 Minshū 1679 (Sup. Ct. P.B., Sept. 9, 1982).

on the ground that the plaintiffs lacked standing. The fact that the denial of relief obviated reversal by the Supreme Court did not prevent the government from taking the further step of vowing publicly to ignore the reasoning of the decision.[18]

The interpretive vacuum left by the courts has instead been filled by the bureaucracy. The leading role in the interpretation of Article 9 has been assumed by the Cabinet Legislation Bureau (CLB), an organization of elite bureaucrats modeled on the French Conseil d'État that is responsible for, inter alia, advising the government on the constitutionality of proposed legislation (Boyd and Samuels 2005: 6–11). Although the meaning of Article 9 remains a subject of fierce controversy, the CLB has – with occasional prodding from the government – cultivated and institutionalized a permissive reading of Article 9 that has authorized a growing range of activities by Japan's artfully named Self-Defense Forces, which are backed by one of the ten largest military budgets in the world (Matsui 2011b: 240; Stockholm International Peace Research Institute 2012: 152) and have in recent years conducted naval refueling operations in the Persian Gulf and air support operations in Iraq (Samuels 2004). This combination of judicial nonenforcement and bureaucratic interpretation has been justly characterized as amounting to de facto amendment of Article 9 (*ibid.*). The result is that Article 9 has never meant in practice what it says on paper or, indeed, what it was said to mean at the time of its adoption. Although amendment of Article 9 has long been a central plank of the LDP platform and is now ostensibly championed by the Democratic Party of Japan (DPJ) as well (Hughes 2012: 31–33; Moore and Robinson 2004: 320), it might be said that formal amendment has been rendered increasingly unnecessary as a practical matter.

Nonenforcement and creative interpretation are not, however, the only ways to reconcile a written constitution with actual constitutional practice or bypass formal amendment. It is not at all unusual for a written constitution to stipulate arrangements that persist in form and theory but not in substance or practice. Such arrangements remain capable of performing their originally intended functions but no longer do so – or perhaps never did so – because changes elsewhere in the political system have rendered them functionally obsolete, irrelevant, or moot. This category encompasses a variety of formal constitutional rules that are technically respected but are more akin to formalities than to rules that govern and define how things are actually done: adherence is forthcoming, but it is adherence to the letter, as opposed to the spirit, of the text. Constitutional provisions of this type endure in a formal sense but are, for all practical intents and purposes, dead. They are, in other words, zombie provisions.

---

[18] See Martin 2008b (quoting Cabinet Secretary Machimura's public statement that the government "could not accept such a court ruling").

Neither truly alive nor officially dead, zombie provisions persist in form and not in function. In Canada, for example, Section 33 of the 1982 Charter of Rights and Freedoms, also known as the notwithstanding clause, theoretically enables a legislative supermajority to explicitly override certain rights, but this provision is not a part of actual constitutional practice; it has fallen into desuetude on account of its unpopularity with the public (Hogg and Bushell 1997: 83–84; Fletcher and Howe 2000: 21, 25; Kahana 2001: 268–272). Likewise, the governor general nominally enjoys the power to withhold royal assent to legislation, and all legislation is duly presented to the governor general for approval, without which it is not law. Nevertheless, it would be unthinkable for the governor general to refuse that approval. In the United States, the Electoral College persists in form as the means by which presidents are chosen, but it does not in substance make the decision, as the framers of the Constitution had intended; rather, its members are expected to cast their votes in accordance with the wishes of those who elected them (Levinson 2006: 81–97; Dahl 2002: 79–89; Hardin 2013).

Japan, too, has its share of zombie provisions. A little-noticed but interesting example involves the practice of *hanken koryu*, or the routinized exchange of personnel on a temporary basis between the judiciary and the Ministry of Justice. The Kenpō provides strong formal guarantees of judicial independence roughly comparable to those found in the U.S. constitution, but the reality is not nearly the same. The Japanese judiciary is, in the words of a former member of the Supreme Court, "just another bureaucratic organization" (Law 2009: 1547). The judges themselves are in a myriad ways at the mercy of the administrative arm of the Supreme Court, the General Secretariat, which is said to punish ideological heterodoxy by dispatching deviant judges to undesirable assignments in remote locations for years at a time (Ramseyer and Rasmusen 2003: 10, 22–24). The bureaucratic practices and conventions of the judiciary do not formally violate the constitution's guarantees of judicial independence, but they do limit the practical significance of those guarantees.

Under the Meiji Constitution, the judiciary fell under the Ministry of Justice and was thus under the formal control of the nation's prosecutors. With the support of the judges themselves, the judiciary achieved independence in the postwar constitution, but close ties remained, including the practice of *hanken koryu*: judges are assigned to the Ministry of Justice to serve as government attorneys for a period of time, with the result that approximately one-fifth of Japanese judges have prosecutorial experience. A substantial number of prosecutors are likewise appointed to serve as judges on a temporary basis (Miyazawa 1991: 50–51).

The problem, however, is that the Kenpō does not provide for temporary judicial appointments. Article 80 provides instead that judges shall be appointed by the Cabinet and "shall hold office for a term of ten years with privilege of reappointment," subject to a mandatory retirement age. In other words, once appointed a

judge, a prosecutor who decides that he prefers being a judge cannot constitutionally be compelled to return to his or her previous job. When I asked a Japanese
district court judge how the temporary assignment of prosecutors to judgeships can
be reconciled with Article 80, he replied that the prosecutors are expected to resign
their judicial posts upon demand and invariably comply. When I inquired further as
to why prosecutors comply with this demand, notwithstanding the fact that Article
80 would appear to entitle them to refuse, he invoked the oft-expressed idea that
Japanese culture emphasizes *wa*, or harmony, and stated without further elaboration
that "judges and prosecutors know it causes trouble if they refuse to resign in such
a situation."

The phenomenon of zombie provisions illustrates that it is unnecessary to amend
or even reinterpret – much less openly violate – a constitutional provision in order to
alter its meaning or defeat its purpose. There is ultimately little to prevent political
actors from developing expectations and coordinating behavior in such a way that
formal constitutional rules become practically irrelevant.

9.5 FORMAL VERSUS INFORMAL CONSTITUTIONAL ADAPTATION: WHICH WAY AND WHY?

There are a number of reasons why constitutional evolution in any given country
might favor an informal path over a formal one. Any explanation must account,
however, for the relative ease and attractiveness of informal as opposed to formal
amendment. Several factors render informal change the path of least resistance in
Japan. On the one hand, the hurdles to formal amendment of the Kenpō – a two-
thirds majority of all members of each house of the Diet, followed by popular ratification by simple majority vote[19] – are even more daunting in practice than on paper.
For most of Japan's postwar history, the Socialists held a sufficient number of seats
in the Diet to thwart any amendment effort by the center-right LDP, which in turn
held the reins of power (Elkins et al. 2008: 1165–1168; Elkins et al. 2009: 200–201).

On the other hand, the adaptation or Japanization of the large-C Constitution
(or, in this case, the large-K Kenpō) by informal means has arguably been facilitated
by certain characteristics of Japanese language and culture. As a threshold matter,
there is good reason to be wary of quick resort to cultural explanations. The temptation is to exoticize foreign practices as the product of some alien belief system
rather than to explain them. To say that culture is responsible for a certain pattern
of behavior begs the question of whether culture actually explains the behavior or
is instead simply the accretion of how things tend to be done, which in turn merely
returns us to the initial question of why they are done that way.

---

[19] Kenpō, Article 96.

Nevertheless, constitutional amendment has been so rare throughout Japanese history that explanations specific to Japan may deserve consideration. Although it is striking that the Kenpō has endured for so long without formal amendment, it is also the case that its predecessor, the Meiji Constitution, was also never amended prior to its forced replacement in 1947. Indeed, the predecessor to the Meiji Constitution, the Tang Dynasty code, remained formally intact for centuries until its replacement in 1889, although its reach had by that point been pruned to a tiny pocket of Kyoto (Haley 1991: 29–30).

It could be argued that the Kenpō owes its durability in part to characteristics of Japanese language and culture that leave considerable room for interpretive disagreement. Concepts such as "democracy," "justice," and "rule of law" are widely popular in part because they are so open to interpretation (Gallie 1956; Collier et al. 2006). Likewise, a constitution that is capable of meaning many different things to many different people is unlikely to generate intense opposition. Although the Japanese language may not be inherently imprecise from a linguistic perspective, deliberate vagueness and circumlocution are common in actual usage (Reischauer and Jansen 1995: 381), and the American drafters experienced frustration at the extent to which their Japanese counterparts employed ambiguous ideographs (Kades 1989: 234). It has also been suggested that Japanese legal and linguistic culture are characterized by an aversion to literalism. Speaking off the record, a retired member of the Japanese Supreme Court explained to the author that the judiciary's exceedingly loose reading of Article 9 exemplifies a "characteristically Japanese way of dealing with principles and their application": "They do believe in the power of words, but not in the literal meaning of words expressed."[20]

The idea that Japanese legal culture might treat constitutional principles and language as malleable seems at least superficially at odds with the civil law conception of adjudication as a largely technical task. It is consistent, however, with the notion that Japan is a "non-axial society," meaning that the idea of absolute or transcendental truth is largely absent from Japanese society and thinking (Law 2011: 1433–1434).[21] The absence of a sense of higher truth and, more specifically, the substitution of status and consensus for truth as normative and evaluative criteria presumably have legal and political implications, one of which may be a constitutional culture that neither confers the status of scripture upon the formal constitution nor treats the principles enshrined in the document as categorical commands.

Judicial reluctance to enforce the Kenpō's explicit guarantees of equality, for example, might be said to reflect both an overall lack of constitutional absolutism and a weak conception of equality in particular. Confucian societies such as Japan

---

[20] The retired justice in question was interviewed by the author on July 22, 2008, in Tokyo.

[21] For the social and historical basis of this evaluation of Japanese normativity, see Haley 1991: 195.

are not renowned for their social egalitarianism; instead, it is understood that people are born unequal, occupy unequal positions, and have distinctive roles to play (Reischauer and Jansen 1995: 203–204, 175–176). Hierarchy and status distinctions are further hardwired into the language itself: the need to select among gradations of courtesy that reflect the social relationship between the speaker and the listener serves as a constant reminder and reinforcement of one's position relative to others. In an interview with the author, a member of the Japanese Supreme Court identified cultural norms as a reason for which Japanese courts have approached the concept of "equality" very differently from U.S, courts. This jurist characterized Christians and Buddhists as having a more "absolute" concept of equality than the Japanese, who, in his view, subscribe to a more "relative" conception of "equality" that has spared Japanese judges from having to strike down laws on the ground that they violate constitutional guarantees of equality (Law 2011: 1434).

9.6 PUBLIC SUPPORT FOR THE "IMPOSED" AND "ALIEN" CONSTITUTION

The question of whether or to what extent the Kenpō should be characterized as an alien imposition is of much more than academic or theoretical interest. At stake are the long-standing ambitions of conservatives to amend Article 9 and the equally long-standing opposition of the left to any dilution of Article 9 that might facilitate Japanese militarization (Berger 2012: 15; Martin 2008a: 67; Matsui 2011b: 262–265). On the one hand, to characterize the Kenpō as "imposed" is to undermine the legitimacy of the document in its present form and thus to pave the way for amendment; on the other hand, to defend the Kenpō as an expression of deeply held values and aspirations is to blunt the case for amendment (Beer and Maki 2002: 83; Shōichi 1997: 251; Chinen 2005: 93). Consequently, one's position on whether the Kenpō should be amended is liable to reflect one's stance on whether the Kenpō was imposed, and vice versa.[22]

It is both imprecise and misleading to say, without qualification, that the Kenpō was "imposed" upon "Japan." Such claims reflect a combination of two errors. The first error is to conflate the preferences of the Japanese government with those of the Japanese people. "Japan" was not, in 1945 or indeed at any time in its history, a monolithic entity. If the question is whether the Kenpō was imposed upon the conservative elites who controlled the government at the time of its adoption, the

---

[22] The extent to which characterization of the Kenpō as "imposed" serves as a proxy for the desirability of constitutional amendment is evident from the clashing views and rationales on display in the Final Report of the Diet's Research Commission on the Constitution. See Taro Nakayama et al., Research Commission on the Constitution, The House of Representatives: Final Report, April 2005, at xi–xxi, 285–290.

answer is a qualified yes (wherein the "yes" must be qualified by the fact that those elites successfully negotiated and maneuvered their way to a number of meaningful victories along the way). But if the question is whether the Kenpō was imposed upon the Japanese *public*, the answer is most likely no.[23]

The second error is to minimize the impact of the public on the constitution-making process, and to consider only the sentiment of political elites. For example, Feldman argues that, in post-occupation constitution-making processes, "[t]he occupying power badly needs validation from local political elites; better, it cannot afford repudiation by those elites," whereas "the opinion of the general public, real or imagined, functions as only one – often relatively weak – constraint on the negotiations" (Feldman 2005: 879). Arguments about the overriding importance of elites tend to sound plausible for several reasons. Political leaders are the most *visible* participants in any constitution-making process, and it is tempting to infer from this fact that they are also the most *important* participants, or even the *only* important participants. The notion that only elites matter is also enticing because it smacks of hard-nosed realism about what is necessary for a constitution to succeed. In particular, the distinction between political elites and the general public evokes a false dichotomy between what is politically necessary and what is normatively desirable: the fact that public support for a new constitution is desirable on democratic grounds might seem to imply that such support is *merely* desirable *as opposed to* necessary.

In reality, however, the Japanese public was not simply a lumpenproletariat mass that could be either ignored or relied on to embrace whatever constitutional bargains might be struck by politicians behind closed doors. Instead, public support shielded the Kenpō from the hostility of conservative politicians and has continued to do so long after the end of the occupation. What emerged in 1947 was a two-on-one dynamic in favor of the new constitution: conservative ruling elites were caught between a population supportive of political liberalization and democratization, on the one hand, and an external force capable of bypassing reactionary leaders and proposing a constitution that would tap these latent but frustrated popular sentiments, on the other.

Public opinion data, the beliefs held by various participants in the constitution-making process, and a range of anecdotal evidence all suggest that there was considerable popular enthusiasm for sweeping constitutional reform along the lines pursued by SCAP. There is every indication that the Americans sought to devise a constitution that would enjoy popular support, and that they succeeded in doing

[23] See, e.g., Hasebe 2003: 225–226 (arguing that, "although the new Constitution was indeed imposed upon the government, it is not true that it was imposed against the will of the Japanese people"); Sakaguchi 2009: 235, 239 (contrasting the imposition of the 1946 constitution "on an extremely reluctant conservative Japanese government" with the "overwhelmingly favourable … reaction of the Japanese people to the new constitution").

so. SCAP did not even submit its draft to the Japanese Cabinet until it had first
consulted "key opinion leaders" in order to "gauge the likely public reaction."[24]
Alfred Oppler, an influential member of GHQ's legal reform team who witnessed
the constitutional reform effort firsthand, reported that the sentiment of the "man
on the street" did in fact favor SCAP's constitution, and that MacArthur had "some
reason to believe that the majority was in accord with the principles of the new
Constitution" (Oppler 1976: 46–47).[25] To the extent that SCAP erred, it appears
to have erred on the side of caution: its draft did not go as far as the constitutional
proposals advocated by various Japanese organizations – proposals that the Japanese
government had studiously ignored, but the Americans at SCAP gladly read.[26]

Polls conducted both before and after the adoption of the Kenpō in 1947 tend
to confirm that there existed widespread support not merely for the overall cause
of constitutional reform, but also for the specific reforms championed by SCAP. A
survey commissioned by the Japanese government and conducted in late 1945 by
the Kyodo News Service suggests that the Japanese people, having been led into
devastation and defeat, were keen to revise the constitutional arrangements that
had so badly disappointed them.[27] Fully three-quarters of the respondents deemed
constitutional reform "necessary." The specific reform that received the greatest support was some combination of limits on the powers of the emperor and expansion
of the powers of the Diet, which was favored by nearly one-quarter of respondents;
the next most popular reform was abolition or reform of the House of Peers, the
Diet's upper house consisting largely of hereditary peers and imperial appointees.
Next on the list were greater government responsiveness to the will of the people
(favored by 14 percent), followed by greater protection for individual rights and freedoms (11 percent). The constitutional draft eventually produced by SCAP adopted,
in one form or another, all of these reforms. A later poll conducted by the *Mainichi
Shimbun* shortly after the proposed constitution became public in 1946 revealed
strong and immediate support for its most important features. A whopping 85 percent supported retention of the emperor "in a reduced symbolic role," for instance,
while 72 percent deemed Article 9 "necessary" (Beer and Maki 2002: 81–82).

The ostensibly imposed constitution continued to enjoy broad acceptance in the
years that followed. A 1954 survey performed by the Cabinet Office found that only

---

[24] See Nakayama et al., supra note 22, at 292 (citing the testimony of Shōichi Koseki).

[25] See also Sims 2001: 244 (characterizing the new constitution as "not out of keeping with the popular
mood in Japan in 1946").

[26] See, for example, Moore and Robinson 2004: 64–78 (discussing how at first Konoe, and then the
Matsumoto Committee, had ignored the progressive drafts circulated by private legal reform groups
and academics); Scheppele 2003: n. 18 (noting that some Japanese wanted "more radical reform of the
constitutional structure than the Americans had wanted").

[27] *Kenpo Kaisei ni Kansuru Yoron Chosa Hokoku*, December 19, 1945, summarized in English at http://
www.ndl.go.jp/constitution/e/shiryo/02/048shoshi.html.

25 percent of the public favored any kind of amendment of the Kenpō, while a plurality of 29 percent opposed any change at all. Another 8 percent responded that constitutional amendment "does not matter," while 26 percent indicated that they were unsure.[28] Other surveys arrived at similar results. A 1955 survey by the *Asahi Shimbun*, for example, revealed only 30 percent support overall for amendment of the Kenpō.[29] A higher fraction, 37 percent, favored amendment of Article 9, yet it is striking that this number still fell far short of a majority, notwithstanding the fact that the Korean War had only recently occurred on Japan's doorstep and the Cold War was by then in full swing.

The overwhelmingly negative public reaction to a leaked version of the Shidehara Cabinet's own draft constitution is further evidence that the Japanese public strongly supported sweeping constitutional liberalization, and that the government's grudging approach to reform placed it significantly to the right of public opinion. In the aftermath of Prince Konoe's tragically failed efforts, and in the void left by SCAP's passivity at the time, Shidehara had initially charged a committee under Jōji Matsumoto's leadership, the so-called Matsumoto Committee, to draft a constitution. Much to the dismay of the Cabinet, the *Mainichi Shimbun* published a leaked copy of a "provisional draft" of the Matsumoto Committee's efforts (Dower 1999: 359). The government quickly disavowed the draft as inauthentic and unrelated to the committee's actual efforts, but it was in fact a hybrid version of two drafts under contemplation by the committee. This "provisional draft" failed to propose more than cosmetic changes to the Meiji Constitution yet was nevertheless more liberal than what the committee would eventually produce (*ibid.*; see also Shōichi 1997: 61). Reaction to the draft was, as more than one scholar has put it, "extremely unfavorable" (Shōichi 1997: 61, Sakaguchi 2009: 238). The *Mainichi Shimbun's* own comments on the draft summed up the prevailing sentiment: "We think that most people will feel disappointed that it is so conservative and does nothing more than preserve the status quo" (Shōichi 1997: 61). Polls conducted in the immediate aftermath of the publication of the Matsumoto draft indicated that a "great majority of Japanese" not only supported revision, but preferred to "elect their own commission to study the problem" (Dower 1999: 361).

The Diet's overall response to the Kenpō likewise suggested the existence of a broad, preexisting, and indigenous wellspring of political support for the most liberal provisions of the Kenpō, including quite specifically those provisions most opposed by the conservative Shidehara Cabinet that demoted the emperor and enshrined popular sovereignty. Of the various parties in the Diet, only the Communist Party

---

[28] *Kokumin no seidjiteki taido (jijimondai) ni kansuru seronchōsa* [Cabinet Office, Public Relations Office, Public Opinion Survey (Current Affairs), Popular Political Attitudes], http://www8.cao.go.jp/survey/s29/S29–10–29–02.html (last visited September 10, 2012).

[29] The results were published on p. 3 of the December 13, 1955 issue of the *Asahi Shimbun*.

opposed the draft constitution, on the grounds that any continuation whatsoever of the *tennō* (emperor) system was antidemocratic, and that it was also "unrealistic and discriminatory to deny any nation the right to self-defense" (*ibid.*: 387). The Socialists, by contrast, not only supported Article 9 but claimed that the government's new position (which in reality meant SCAP's position) was what they had always wanted. Tetsu Katayama, a Socialist who would later become prime minister, explained that his fellow Socialists supported the new constitution precisely because it placed "sovereign power … in the hands of the people" and renounced the use of force entirely. Katayama rooted support for Article 9, in particular, in preexisting public sentiment: this provision had "by no means been given or dictated from outside but is an expression of a strong current of thought which has been running in the hearts of the Japanese people" (Kades 1989: 242).[30]

Perhaps as important as the actual level of public support for sweeping constitutional reform was the fact that both SCAP and the Shidehara Cabinet strongly believed that such support existed. On the Japanese side, the Shidehara Cabinet appears to have realized that it was in the position of fighting a rearguard action against not only the Americans, but also its own people. Anticipation of the likely popular opposition to the draft devised by the Matsumoto Committee was an explicit factor in the Shidehara Cabinet's decision to capitulate to SCAP's demands and present the SCAP draft as its own. Prime Minister Shidehara's initial reaction to the SCAP draft had been, quite simply, that "we cannot accept this" (Moore and Robinson 2004: 112).[31] In response, Home Minister Hitoshi Ashida (author of the Ashida amendment) and other ministers – including Matsumoto himself – pointed out that if SCAP carried out its threat to publish the draft on its own without the government's endorsement, the draft would likely be embraced by the media and rival political parties, and the Cabinet itself might be forced to resign as a result (Moore and Robinson 2004: 112; Hasebe 2003: 225–226).

Meanwhile, on the American side, SCAP personnel "strongly believed they were helping to create the less oppressive society that most Japanese desired but could not obtain from their own leaders" (Dower 1999: 366). The Potsdam Declaration stipulated that the occupation was to end after "a peacefully inclined and responsible

---

[30] See also Nakayama et al., supra note 22, at viii (offering a slightly different translation of Katayama's remarks) ("[T]he renunciation of war is not a clause that was imposed on us, but a great idea that was present as an undercurrent in the hearts of the Japanese people."). Indeed, it is possible that the government itself may have lent support to the idea of Article 9: both MacArthur and Shidehara would subsequently claim that Shidehara had suggested the idea of a pacifism clause to MacArthur a few days before MacArthur included what would eventually become Article 9 in his brief charge to the SCAP constitutional group (Elkins et al. 2008: 1164).

[31] The Cabinet's decision at that juncture was to seek more time to prepare a draft of its own that would merely incorporate the basic principles and ideas of the SCAP draft; only when this too was soundly rejected did the Shidehara Cabinet arrive at the conclusion that it had exhausted its options.

government" had been established "in accordance with the freely expressed will of the Japanese people," but SCAP also had reason to doubt whether the Shidehara Cabinet necessarily expressed that will. In the language of constitutional theory, one might say that the members of SCAP's impromptu constitutional drafting committee saw their role in part as one of "representation-reinforcement" (Ely 1980): their willingness to impose upon the Japanese government reflected their view that, in doing so, they were compensating for the democratic deficits of that government and vindicating the popular will. So confident, in fact, were the Americans that they, and not the Japanese government, were acting to effectuate the popular will that, in response to Japanese arguments that the SCAP draft was an awkward transplant ill suited to local conditions, MacArthur threatened explicitly to "take the constitution to the people directly and make it a live issue in the forthcoming [election] campaign in order that the people will have the opportunity to enact the constitution" (Kades 1989: 231; Hasebe 2003: 225–226). Although no formal referendum on the constitution was ultimately held – perhaps because the Meiji Constitution itself called for constitutional amendments to be proposed by the emperor and approved by the Diet, without direct popular participation[32] – MacArthur's goal, according to Kades (1989: 233), was to have the draft constitution published long in advance of the next election so that the election would serve as a de facto plebiscite on his constitutional reforms.

Consistent with this emphasis on electoral legitimacy, SCAP appears to have treated the deliberations of the subsequently elected Diet as endowed with a stronger democratic pedigree, and thus entitled to greater deference and respect, than the Cabinet. Tatsuo Sato, the bureaucrat who was forced to defend the government's draft after Matsumoto himself had left in anger, observed that the firmness of SCAP's approach appeared to vary with the degree of popular legitimacy that SCAP perceived behind the government's actions, with a lighter touch being reserved for the actions of the Diet than for those of the Cabinet:

> They [GHQ staff] were very strict about the [preamble] and the chapter on the Emperor. They would make no concessions. Only a few minor wording changes were allowed. But they granted a great many of our points and objections about other parts of the draft.... [U]nlike their attitude at the stage when we were preparing the government draft [based upon the GHQ draft] the GHQ applied hardly any direct pressure on the Diet's deliberations on the constitution. Indeed they seemed to have great respect for the Diet as the supreme representative of the people. With the revisions as well they needed SCAP's approval, but 80 or 90 percent of our changes were allowed to stand.[33]

---

[32] Meiji Constitution, Article 73.
[33] Kades 1989: 242; see also, for example, Dower 1999: 388, also quoting Sato's memoirs and his impression of American receptiveness to the views of the Diet, and Shōichi 1997: 251, quoting Prime Minister

The Diet that considered the proposed constitution was the first in Japanese history to be elected on the basis of universal male and female suffrage and in an atmosphere of political freedom (Matsui 2011b: 21; Beer and Maki 2002: 81, 83). The approval and even praise that the new constitution garnered from various quarters of the Diet were thus at least somewhat indicative of broad acceptance outside the confines of the "geriatric" Shidehara Cabinet (Dower 1999: 386).

Deafening indifference to the prospect of either a second round of review by the Diet or a popular referendum on the Kenpō itself offered further evidence of the document's broad appeal. At the behest of the Far Eastern Commission, MacArthur instructed the newly installed Yoshida government that the new constitution ought to receive a second round of formal review by the Diet "between the first and second years of its effectivity," and he further raised the prospect that the Allies might "require a referendum or some other appropriate procedure for ascertaining directly Japanese opinion" (Shōichi 1997: 243, quoting MacArthur). Yoshida's two-line demurral reflected his certainty that Japanese public opinion was "diametrically opposed" to revision of the new constitution (*ibid.*: 250). As he expected, reactions across the Japanese media and the major political parties were decidedly unenthusiastic, and both constitutional revision and the idea of a popular referendum were ultimately abandoned (*ibid.*: 247, 253–254).

To the extent that SCAP's approach can be faulted for departing from public sentiment, its most notable failure may be that it cooperated too closely with the Shidehara Cabinet on the status of the emperor. SCAP's instrumental strategy of preserving the emperor, albeit only as a figurehead, placed it in cahoots with Japan's conservative leadership on the one issue that most concerned the leadership.[34] The deep attachment of Japanese governing elites to the *tennō* system reflected a powerful combination of ideology and self-interest: for centuries, the notion of the emperor as the embodiment of all sovereign power was a potent legal fiction that elites with de facto power invoked to justify and legitimate their own rule (Itoh 2010: 7–9). This system of government had profoundly discredited itself in the eyes of the Japanese people, however, by steering the country into disaster in the name of the emperor (Dower 1999: 65–84; Beer and Maki 2002: 84). MacArthur himself sensed that public support for the emperor was unstable: the two threats he perceived to the *tennō* system were the United States' wartime allies and the Japanese people themselves, whose "republican" ideas would, in his estimation, "only grow stronger with the passage of time" (Dower 1999: 362). The language in the Kenpō reducing the

Shigeru Yoshida's observation that, during the post-drafting negotiations, "there was nothing that could properly be termed coercive or overbearing in the attitude of the Occupation authorities toward us. They listened carefully to the Japanese experts and officials charged with the work, and in many cases accepted our proposals."

[34] MacArthur's motives for protecting the Emperor are discussed in note 7 to this chapter.

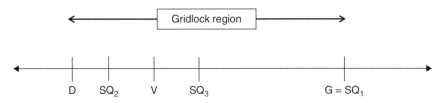

FIGURE 9.1 Unidimensional spatial model of the constitution-making process.

emperor to a mere "symbol of the state and of the unity of the people"[35] might thus be characterized not as an act of American imposition upon the people of Japan, but rather as an act of collaboration with a discredited government that sacrificed budding republicanism for the sake of expediency.

9.7 A MODEL OF THE CONSTITUTIONAL POLICY-MAKING GAME

The logic behind the interaction between the public, the government, and the occupation authorities can be illustrated by modeling the constitution-making process as a game. The relevant players in this game are those who possess the power to propose or reject constitutional changes. The two possible types of power that a player can enjoy are: (1) agenda control, or the ability to propose constitutional policies in the first place; and (2) veto power, or the ability to block changes in constitutional policy. Agenda control is potentially outcome-determinative: the ability to keep particular proposals from being considered at all can prevent even the most popular of constitutional policies from being adopted. Once a policy has tentatively been put in place, however, mere veto power is sufficient to keep the policy from being altered.

The diagram in Figure 9.1, a deliberately simplified unidimensional spatial model of the constitution-making process, depicts this policy-making game in visual form.[36] The point of the model is not to depict the actual process or the relative positions of the relevant actors in a fully accurate way, but rather to illustrate, using the logic of formal models borrowed from the study of legislation, the nature of SCAP's intervention and the reason for which its constitutional legacy has endured. The line itself represents an ideological spectrum of policy alternatives, from left to right. G represents the preferred policy, or ideal point, of the Japanese government, in the form of the Shidehara Cabinet. SQ_1 represents the initial status quo, namely the Meiji Constitution or Dai Nippon Teikoku Kenpō of 1889. SQ_2 represents the new

---

[35] Kenpō, Article 1.
[36] Models of this type have been a prominent innovation of the political science literature on the legislative process. See, e.g., Krehbiel 1998: 20–48; Cameron 2000: 83–122.

status quo selected by SCAP, namely the Nihonkoku Kenpō of 1947. D represents a relatively left-leaning member of the Diet who is more conservative than exactly one-third of the Diet and therefore determines whether conservatives can muster a two-thirds supermajority in favor of constitutional amendment.[37] Finally, V represents the ideal point of the median member of the voting public.

Prior to SCAP's intervention, the only actor with the power of agenda control was the Japanese government. Even after a crushing military defeat and a purge of the most right-wing elements, the conservative Shidehara Cabinet had little desire to put into place a constitution that would, inter alia, reduce the emperor to figurehead status, place individual rights beyond the reach of the legislature, foreclose remilitarization, and end discrimination against foreigners and women.[38] The changes that it initially proposed were largely cosmetic, and even those minimal changes might not have been proposed had it not been inescapably clear that SCAP expected something to be done. Accordingly, the model treats the Cabinet's ideal point on the policy spectrum as the existing Meiji Constitution, which is depicted by setting G equal to SQ_1. This is merely a formal way of saying that, left to its own devices, the Cabinet was unlikely to propose significant changes to the constitution.

At the same time, the median voter, V, lacked the power to propose, ratify, or veto changes to the status quo, SQ_1. The Meiji Constitution placed the formal power to initiate amendments in the emperor and required approval by a two-thirds vote of each house of the Diet but contained no requirement of popular ratification.[39] The will of the Diet, in turn, was not much of a proxy for the will of the people as of 1945. At the time of its acceptance of the Potsdam Declaration as the instrument of its surrender, Japan was not a thriving democracy but instead a military-dominated authoritarian state that had retained some of the institutional trappings of a democracy. SCAP was thus justifiably skeptical that the Japanese leadership truly acted or spoke on behalf of the Japanese people in opposing the most progressive elements of SCAP's constitutional program. The democratic pedigree of the government, after years of de facto right-wing military rule had undermined and oppressed liberal and leftist elements, was suspect at best.

---

[37] Because approval of a constitutional amendment requires two-thirds approval of both houses of the Diet, there are in fact two legislators – one in each house – whose votes are pivotal to the formation of a two-thirds supermajority in favor of a conservative constitutional amendment. For the sake of simplicity, the Diet is modeled here as a unicameral rather than bicameral legislature.

[38] Indeed, it has been argued that even now, "the political forces in power in post-war Japan fail to accept the legitimacy of the constitution and fully embrace the concept of constitutionalism" (Sakaguchi 2009: 235).

[39] Meiji Constitution, Article 73.

Accordingly, the model depicts the government's ideal point, G, as falling significantly to the right of the median voter's ideal point, V.

SCAP's actions structured this constitutional policy-making game in ways that would make the Kenpō difficult to change for decades to come. First, SCAP ensured that all constitutional policy making would occur within a procedural framework of its own creation by systematically neutralizing threats to the survival of the new constitutional order. As Russell Hardin has observed, a constitutional order cannot survive if those with the raw power to overthrow the order lack an interest in its survival and prefer instead to subvert or destroy it (Hardin 1999: 139–140, 276–277). MacArthur's purges of the rightists and militarists eliminated most of those with the ability and the inclination to threaten the new order, but the most significant remaining threat – the one person with the greatest ability to rally mass resistance – was unquestionably Hirohito. SCAP faced two basic options for dealing with this threat: it could incapacitate him (by allowing him, for example, to be tried as a war criminal, as many of the United States' allies, citizens, and leaders demanded), or it could give him a stake in the survival of the new regime by ensuring his personal safety and that of his family. It chose the latter. In hindsight, this may not have been the only viable option, but it did not prove an obvious mistake either.

Second, SCAP determined both what the default policy would be and who would have the power to block changes to that policy. Its forceful intervention in the constitution-making process temporarily stripped the government of agenda control and moved the status quo significantly to the left, from SQ_1 to SQ_2. Meanwhile, amendment rules requiring a two-thirds majority in both houses of the Diet ensured for decades that left-leaning opposition parties would possess the ability to ward off the constitutional changes most coveted by the right-wing LDP (Berger 2012: 14–16; Boyd and Samuels 2005: 25–26; Elkins et al. 2008: 1165–1168; Elkins et al. 2009: 200–201). The pivotal left-leaning Diet member whose vote would be needed to meet the two-thirds threshold for approval of a constitutional amendment is represented in the model by D. It has been suggested by some scholars that the recent demise of the Socialist Party as a political force and the concomitant rise of the DPJ, which has taken a lukewarm position on constitutional revision (Hughes 2012: 42–43), bode the end of this long stalemate (Elkins et al. 2008: 1168). The possibility that a two-thirds legislative supermajority in favor of constitutional amendment now exists can be modeled by relocating D to the right of SQ_2.

Opposition parties were not, however, the only actors empowered by the occupation to block subsequent constitutional changes. SCAP's intervention wrought a number of profound changes that empowered the general public in both theory and practice. These changes included extension of the franchise to women, democratization of the upper house of the Diet via elimination of the peerage, enhanced freedom of political expression (except when it came to criticism of SCAP's own activities) and, not least of all, an explicit constitutional requirement that subsequent changes to the constitution be ratified by a popular majority.[40] This empowerment of the public can be modeled by depicting the median member of the electorate, V, as a player in the constitutional policy-making game who lacks agenda control but possesses veto power.

The central premise of the resulting model is that the public not only prefers the new status quo to the old status quo, but also now wields the power to defend the status quo against unwanted change. From this premise, several important consequences follow. This introduction of a new veto player, the median voter, dramatically restricts both the likelihood and range of future amendments. The end of the occupation restored both the government's ability to control the policy agenda (by deciding what amendments will be submitted to the voters for ratification) and, by corollary, its de facto veto power over unwanted changes (by refusing to propose such changes in the first place). However, the government cannot secure a return to its preferred position, SQ_1, because the median voter is now empowered to block any change that would move the policy further away from its ideal point, V. Instead, the entire space between V and G is characterized by complete policy gridlock. The existence and scope of a *gridlock region*, as labeled on the diagram, is conditional upon the location of the status quo policy relative to all players with veto power. If the status quo happens to fall between any two players with veto power – in this case, between V and G – no change is possible: no matter what is proposed, any change in policy will benefit one player at the expense of the other, and so the latter player will veto the change.

Only if the policy selected by SCAP falls outside the gridlock region – perhaps because it was too liberal even for the median Japanese voter, or because the median voter has shifted to the right over time, or some combination of the two – is any amendment possible. In this scenario, the government's power of agenda control will shift the ultimate outcome in its favor, but only within limits. To see why, assume that the status quo established by SCAP, SQ_2, falls to the left of V (as depicted in the diagram). The government's best option is to propose a new policy, SQ_3 – that is, as close to its own ideal point (G) as possible – while still being at least marginally closer to V than the existing status quo, SQ_2. As long as SQ_3 is closer to V than SQ_2 – even if only by the smallest of margins – the median voter should, in theory, accept the change. (In contrast, if the median voter were given the power to initiate

[40] Kenpō, Article 96.

constitutional amendments, he or she would propose a policy at precisely his or her ideal point, V, and the government would in turn accept V as the new policy because it is closer to the government's ideal point, G, than the alternative, SQ_2.)

Whether the Kenpō is, or has become, too liberal for the tastes of the average voter – and, thus, whether constitutional amendment is a plausible possibility within the terms of the preceding analysis – is open to debate. Various public opinion polls tend to demonstrate mainly that the popular appetite for constitutional amendment fluctuates from year to year, and from poll to poll. On the whole, however, it is questionable whether there exists a decisive and durable majority in favor of amending the Kenpō at all, much less in favor of amending any specific provision (Berger 2012: 16–19). Surveys conducted by the *Asahi Shimbun* over the last decade, for example, indicate that support for some kind of amendment has varied from a low of 47 percent (in 2001 and 2010) to a high of 58 percent (in 2007). In the same year that the *Asahi Shimbun* reported that peak figure of 58 percent, however, a similar survey by Japan's national broadcaster, NHK, found less than 41 percent support for any kind of amendment whatsoever.[41]

Moreover, even assuming majority support for some kind of constitutional amendment, there is no guarantee that conservatives would take comfort in the kinds of amendments that the public might favor. The public's desire for additional rights and institutional reforms appears to exceed its appetite for revision of Article 9 (Berger 2012: 18). A relatively detailed survey commissioned by the United States Information Agency in 2000 found that nearly 80 percent of respondents either "strongly" or "somewhat" favored constitutional amendment of some kind.[42] The strongest support, however, was for a constitutional provision that would "require information disclosure by authorities," which was favored by nearly half of those surveyed (*ibid.*). By contrast, less than one-fifth singled out Article 9 for revision.[43] Likewise, the *Asahi Shimbun's* polls suggest that popular support for amendment of Article 9 has hovered between roughly one-quarter to one-third of respondents, and even that limited degree of support conceals substantial disagreement over how exactly Article 9 ought to be amended.[44]

---

[41] NHK Broadcasting Culture Research Institute, *The People's Awareness of the Debate on Constitutional Reform* (December 2007), http://www.nhk.or.jp/bunken/english/reports/summary/200712/05.html.

[42] Shin Joho Center, USIA Poll # 2000-I20012: Foreign Companies/Relations with US/Military Issues, May 18, 2000, *available at* http://webapps.ropercenter.uconn.edu/CFIDE/cf/action/catalog/index.cfm (registration required; select "Japan" from country pulldown menu and 2000 as date range).

[43] *Ibid.*; see Boyd and Samuels 2005: 53 (noting that "[p]ublic opinion is far more enthusiastic about constitutional revision in general than it is about changing Article Nine").

[44] There is conflicting evidence as to whether popular support for amendment of Article 9 is growing (Boyd and Samuels 2005: 53; Chinen 2005: 82–83) or declining (Berger 2012: 19).

9.8 CONCLUSION: THE MYTH OF THE UNIMPOSED CONSTITUTION

The notion that constitutionalism in postwar Japan has been the story of the imposition and internalization of an alien document is both inadequate and misleading. Roles and arguments were inverted in ways that complicate any effort to characterize the Kenpō as imposed. Arrayed on the one side were the occupation authorities, who sought to vindicate the popular will by imposing their own will. On the other side stood the Japanese government, which pursued reactionary, anti-egalitarian, and anti-democratic goals by depicting the demands of Japanese culture and the needs of Japanese society as incompatible with the ham-fisted imposition of a foreign constitutional blueprint.

Compounding these ironies and contradictions was the fact that the constitution that the Japanese government sought to defend against foreign imposition was itself of largely foreign origins. The Meiji Restoration of the late nineteenth century precipitated the widespread adoption of Western technology, law, and institutions, including a Western-style constitution (Reischauer and Jansen 1995: 87). This foreign innovation, meanwhile, had itself been imposed on the Japanese people by Emperor Mutsuhito and his government (Hasebe 2003: 226). Thus, in their own minds, the Americans were not to be blamed for sullying an indigenous, deeply rooted, democratically legitimate constitutional order with heretical and alien Western ideas, but were attempting instead to redeem an already "hermaphroditic creature," the Meiji Constitution, that had "Prussian tyranny as its father, and British representative government as its mother."[45]

But the notion that the Kenpō exemplifies a phenomenon called "imposed constitutionalism" is vulnerable to conceptual as well as historical attack. To say that one constitution was "imposed" while another was not implies a false dichotomy between "imposed" and "unimposed" constitutions. Constitution-making routinely implicates multiple authors, constituencies, and narratives in a process that is part negotiation, part dialectic, and part coercion. This multiplicity of participants and processes makes it difficult to say with confidence what is an "imposed" constitution and what is not. On the one hand, even an ostensibly imposed constitution can reflect a considerable measure of local input and influence. The history of the Kenpō demonstrates as much.

On the other hand, elements of imposition and alienation are arguably endemic to all constitutions, regardless of how or where they are authored.[46] The politics of constitution-making are like any other kind of politics: there are invariably both

---

[45] The quoted language is from a "Guide to Japan" prepared for U.S. troops during World War II (Dower 1999: 346).

[46] See, e.g., Hahm and Kim 2010: 848 (observing that "controversy over 'imposed constitutions'" falsely presupposes "an ideal type of autonomous constituent agent utterly free from external influences"); Hassall and Saunders 2002: 68, 241 ("There are few instances [in the Asia Pacific region] in which

winners and losers, and the losers may resent the outcome. The mere fact that a constitution has been drafted by local actors is no guarantee that it expresses the wishes of the people that it purports to bind. Indeed, as the Japanese experience demonstrates, a constitution authored and championed by domestic politicians can do a worse job of speaking for the people than an ostensibly imposed constitution of foreign provenance. Indigenous constitutions routinely reflect bargaining among political actors of unequal strength. Some of the most intensely affected parties may be underrepresented in the constitution-making process or even excluded entirely. Moreover, even if genuine participation in the process is available on generous terms, there is still no guarantee that all sides will view the results of the process as entitled to their acceptance and obedience. Are such constitutions not in some sense imposed?

Consider, for example, a scenario in which the white male inhabitants of a heavily agrarian society foist upon the members of a highly diverse, postindustrial society a constitution that contains irrelevant, unrealistic, and even immoral provisions. Adopted initially without the participation of more than half the adult population (namely, blacks and women), this constitution has at various points enshrined immoral behavior (in the form of systematic and widespread human slavery), dictated controversial moral rules (as in the prohibition of alcohol), and created institutional arrangements that people have little interest in using (such as an electoral college) or are profoundly anti-democratic (such as grossly unequal representation in the Senate). With respect to a sizeable portion of the population (in the form of a confederacy of breakaway states), this constitution was imposed by brute military force. At the same time, this constitution fails even to acknowledge, much less to regulate, fundamental aspects of the actual machinery of government, such as the existence of political parties and a large-scale bureaucracy. Finally, as if to ensure that it will not be adjusted to reflect the needs and wishes of the polity, this constitution entrenches itself by raising a variety of formidable obstacles to amendment. Is the Constitution of the United States not, in some ways, as alien to the United States as the constitution that the United States devised for Japan? What constitution does not become – in some sense, to some people, at some point in time – a stranger in its own land?

REFERENCES

Beatty, David M. (1995), *Constitutional Law in Theory and Practice*, (Toronto: University of Toronto Press).
Beer, Lawrence W. and John M. Maki (2002), *From Imperial Myth to Democracy: Japan's Two Constitutions, 1889–2002*, (Boulder: University Press of Colorado), 216.

'the people' participated in any genuine sense in creating the independence constitution.... [W]hile most independence constitutions claim to be 'autochthonous', they were invariably influenced by the constitutions and the legal systems of their colonial masters.").

Berger, Thomas U. (2012), 'Ripe for Revision? The Strange Case of Japan's Unchanging Constitution', in Wakefield, Bryce (ed.), *A Time for Change?: Japan's "Peace" Constitution at 65* (Washington, DC: Woodrow Wilson International Center for Scholars), 12–22.

Boyd, J. Patrick and Richard J. Samuels (2005), *Nine Lives?: The Politics of Constitutional Reform in Japan*, (East-West Center Washington).

Cameron, Charles M. (2000), *Veto Bargaining: Presidents and the Politics of Negative Power*, eds. Calvert, Randall and Thráinn Eggertson, (Cambridge: Cambridge University Press).

Chinen, Mark (2005), 'Article 9 of the Constitution of Japan and the Use of Procedural and Substantive Heuristics for Consensus', *Michigan Journal of International Law*, **27**, 55–114.

Collier, David, Fernando Daniel Hidalgo, and Andra Olivia Maciuceanu (2006), 'Essentially Contested Concepts: Debates and Applications', *Journal of Political Ideologies*, **11** (3), 211–246.

Dahl, Robert A. (2002), *How Democratic Is the American Constitution?*, (New Haven, CT: Yale University Press).

Dower, John W. (1999), *Embracing Defeat: Japan in the Wake of World War II*, (New York: W. W. Norton & Company).

Elkins, Zachary, Tom Ginsburg, and James Melton (2008), 'Baghdad, Tokyo, Kabul.: Constitution Making in Occupied States', *William & Mary Law Review*, **49**, 1139.

(2009), *The Endurance of National Constitutions*, (Cambridge: Cambridge University Press).

Ely, John Hart (1980), *Democracy and Distrust: A Theory of Judicial Review*, (Cambridge, MA: Harvard University Press).

Feldman, Noah (2005), 'Imposed Constitutionalism', *Connecticut Law Review*, **37**, 857–889.

Fletcher, Joseph F. and Paul Howe (2000), 'Canadian Attitudes toward the Charter and the Courts in Comparative Perspective', *Choices*, **6** (3), 4–29.

Gallie, W. B. (1956), 'Essentially Contested Concepts', *Proceedings of the Aristotelian Society*, **56**, 167.

Gordon, Beate Sirota (1997), *The Only Woman in the Room: A Memoir*, (Kodansha International).

Hahm, Chaihark and Sung Ho Kim (2010), 'To Make "We the People": Constitutional Founding in Postwar Japan and South Korea', *International Journal of Constitutional Law*, **8** (4), 800–848.

Haley, John Owen (1991), *Authority without Power: Law and the Japanese Paradox*, (New York: Oxford University Press).

Hardin, Russell (1999), *Liberalism, Constitutionalism, and Democracy*, (New York: Oxford University Press).

(2013), 'Why a Constitution?', in Galligan, Denis and Mila Versteeg (eds.), *Social and Political Foundations of Constitutions*, (Cambridge: Cambridge University Press).

Hasebe, Yasuo (2003), 'Constitutional Borrowing and Political Theory', *International Journal of Constitutional Law*, **1** (2), 224–243.

Hassall, Graham and Cheryl Saunders (2002), *Asia-Pacific Constitutional Systems*, (Cambridge: Cambridge University Press).

Hogg, Peter W. and Allison A. Bushell (1997), 'The Charter Dialogue between Courts and Legislatures', *Osgoode Hall Law Journal*, **35**, 75–105.

Hughes, Christopher W. (2012), 'Japan, Constitutional Reform, and Remilitarization', in Wakefield, Bryce (ed.), *A Time for Change? : Japan's "Peace" Constitution at 65* (Washington, DC: Woodrow Wilson International Center for Scholars), 23–49.

Itoh, Hiroshi (2010), *The Supreme Court and Benign Elite Democracy in Japan*, (Farnham, Surrey: Ashgate).

Kades, Charles L. (1989), 'The American Role in Revising Japan's Imperial Constitution', *Political Science Quarterly*, **104** (2), 215–247.

Kahana, Tsvi (2001), 'The Notwithstanding Mechanism and Public Discussion: Lessons from the Ignored Practice of Section 33 of the Charter', *Canadian Public Administration*, **44** (3), 255–291.

Krehbiel, Keith (1998), *Pivotal Politics: A Theory of U.S. Lawmaking*, (Chicago: University of Chicago Press).

Law, David S. (2009), 'The Anatomy of a Conservative Court: Judicial Review in Japan', *Texas Law Review*, **87**, 1545–1593.

 (2010), 'Constitutions', in Cane, Peter and Herbert Kritzer (eds.), *The Oxford Handbook of Empirical Legal Research* (New York: Oxford University Press), 376–398.

 (2011), 'Why Has Judicial Review Failed in Japan?', *Washington University Law Review*, **88**, 1425–1466.

Levinson, Sanford (2006), *Our Undemocratic Constitution: Where the Constitution Goes Wrong (And How We the People Can Correct It)*, (New York: Oxford University Press).

Martin, Craig (2008a), 'Binding the Dogs of War: Japan and the Constitutionalizing of Jus Ad Bellum', *University of Pennsylvania Journal of International Law*, **30** (1), 267–357.

 (2008b), 'Rule of Law Comes Under Fire: Government Response to High Court Ruling on SDF Operations in Iraq', *Japan Times*, May 3, http://search.japantimes.co.jp/print/eo20080503a1.html.

 (2010), 'Glimmers of Hope: The Evolution of Equality Rights Doctrine in Japanese Courts from a Comparative Perspective', *Duke Journal of Comparative and International Law*, **20** (2), 167–246.

Matsui, Shigenori (2011a), 'Constitutional Adjudication in Japan: Context, Structures, and Values', *Washington University Law Review*, **88** (6), 1375–1423.

 (2011b), *The Constitution of Japan: A Contextual Analysis*, (Oxford: Hart Publishing).

Miyazawa, Setsuo (1991), 'Administrative Control of Japanese Judges', *Kobe University Law Review*, **25**, 45–61.

Moore, Ray A. and Donald L. Robinson (2004), *Partners for Democracy: Crafting the New Japanese State under MacArthur*, (New York: Oxford University Press).

Okudaira, Yasuhiro (1990), 'Forty Years of the Constitution and Its Various Influences: Japanese, American, and European', *Law & Contemporary Problems*, **53** (1), 17–49.

Oppler, Alfred C. (1976), *Legal Reform in Occupied Japan: A Participant Looks Back*, (Princeton, NJ: Princeton University Press).

Ramseyer, J. Mark and Eric B. Rasmusen (2003), *Measuring Judicial Independence: The Political Economy of Judging in Japan*, (Chicago: The University of Chicago Press).

Reischauer, Edwin O. and Marius B. Jansen (1995), *The Japanese Today: Change and Continuity*, (enlarged edn., Cambridge, MA: Belknap Press).

Sakaguchi, Shojiro (2009), 'Japan', in Thiel, Markus (ed.), *The 'Militant Democracy' Principle in Modern Democracies* (Farnham, Surrey: Ashgate), 219–242.

Samuels, Richard J. (2004), 'Politics, Security Policy, and Japan's Cabinet Legislation Bureau: Who Elected These Guys, Anyway?', *Japan Policy Research Institute*, Working Paper No. 99.

Schauer, Frederick (2005), 'On the Migration of Constitutional Ideas', *Connecticut Law Review*, 37, 907–919.

Scheppele, Kim Lane (2003), 'Aspirational and Aversive Constitutionalism: The Case for Studying Cross-Constitutional Influence through Negative Models', *International Journal of Constitutional Law*, 1 (2), 296–324.

Shōichi, Koseki (1997), *The Birth of Japan's Postwar Constitution*, (Ray A. Moore ed. & trans., Boulder, CO: Westview Press).

Sims, Richard (2001), *Japanese Political History since the Meiji Renovation 1868–2000*, (London: Palgrave Macmillan).

Stockholm International Peace Research Institute (2012), *SIPRI Yearbook 2012: Armaments, Disarmament and International Security*, (Revised edn., New York: Oxford University Press).

Social, Political and Philosophical Foundations of the Irish Constitutional Order

Paul Brady

10.1 INTRODUCTION

Although replaced in 1937 by the constitution which remains in force to this day, the Irish Free State Constitution of 1922 established the modern Irish state and was a major influence on the drafting of its successor (Hogan 1997; Keogh and McCarthy 2007; also see Appendix at the end of this chapter). It thus played a formative role in both the foundation and evolution of Ireland's current legal and political order. This work considers some of the social, political and philosophical influences that shaped the transplantation of British, American and European constitutional forms and ideas into the 1922 Constitution. I focus on transplantation because, although the drafters were more or less confined to working within the basic parameters laid down by the 1921 Anglo-Irish Treaty, the Constitution is particularly notable for its novel arrangement of constitutional features drawn from a variety of legal jurisdictions and traditions.

This chapter has two main parts. The first part (Section 10.2) offers a brief overview of the immediate historical and political background to the drafting and enactment of the 1922 Constitution. The second part (Section 10.3) comprises the substance of the paper. It seeks to examine several of the more innovative and important features of the 1922 Constitution from a comparative perspective. My discussion seeks to highlight the Constitution's experimental character by noting some of the discrepancies that emerged between how the drafters imagined their provisions would operate and the political realities (or what some call the 'small c constitution') that actually resulted.

The author acknowledges the support of the AHRC and the NUI Travelling Studentship scheme for the research presented in this paper.

10.2 IMMEDIATE HISTORICAL BACKGROUND TO THE 1922 IRISH FREE STATE CONSTITUTION

10.2.1 *The Rise of Sinn Féin and the First Dáil*

The Sinn Féin party (literally: Ourselves Alone) was founded in Dublin in 1905 by the journalist Arthur Griffith. By contrast to the "home rule" strategy of constitutional nationalists, who sought to achieve a national parliament for Ireland through engagement with and participation in the Westminster political process, Sinn Féin sought to achieve Irish self-rule through political abstentionism, economic self-reliance and the (non-violent) creation of a parallel administrative system (civil and judicial) entirely separate from the existing British authorities. Although in 1914 Sinn Féin still had only a small number of branches outside of Dublin, this was all to change within a few years. By 1918 it was a wholly revitalized organization as a consequence of the radicalization of mainstream Irish nationalism in the wake of the heavy-handed response of the British military authorities to the 1916 Easter Rising in Dublin and, later, the controversial attempt by British Prime Minister Lloyd George to introduce conscription into Ireland and his proposal to postpone self-government under the Government of Ireland ("Home Rule") Act 1914. At a party convention in October 1917, Sinn Féin dropped its earlier preference for a dual-monarchy model of Irish-British relations and endorsed a formula devised by Éamon de Valera, which read: "Sinn Féin aims at securing the international recognition of Ireland as an independent Irish Republic. Having achieved that status the Irish people may by referendum freely choose their own form of government." De Valera was elected party president and Sinn Féin went on to become the umbrella organisation under which every section of Irish nationalism could unite to contest the general election in December 1918 on a common separatist platform.

The transformation of Irish popular opinion (together with the extension of the electorate from 701,475 to 1,936,673 voters brought about by the Representation of the People Act, 1918) changed the party political landscape in Ireland in the run-up to the election. Sinn Féin emerged victorious, winning 73 of the 105 seats and signalling the death knell of the once dominant Irish Parliamentary (or Home Rule) Party.

True to the party's founding project of absenting its MPs from Westminster and instead peacefully establishing parallel institutions of self-government, the parliamentary assembly known as Dáil Éireann met for the first time on 21 January 1919 in Dublin's Mansion House. According to Brian Farrell, the meeting of the First Dáil in 1919 "at the outset of what was to be become a war of independence is now accepted as the constitutional foundation stone of the new Irish state" (Farrell

1969: 127).[1] The order of business included, inter alia, the adoption of (1) Bunreacht Dála Éireann (Constitution for Dáil Éireann), (2) a Declaration of Independence, (3) a Message to the Free Nations of the World, and (4) a Democratic Programme.

The 1919 Constitution remained, with only minor amendments, the basic law of the emerging state up to 1922. It was a short and business-like document of only five articles that set out a very elementary framework for a parliamentary system of democratic government.[2] Farrell notes that the constitution appears "bare and arid" when "set beside the rhetoric" of the other documents, but argues that it "was a major link in the chain of Irish political and institutional development as the country passed from colonial dependency to national independence" (Farrell 1994: 68–69). And as he concludes elsewhere: "All examination of the 1919 Constitution, in its drafting, development and usage serves to confirm the more general impressions of the period: that the founders of the new state were constitutionalists within a strongly developed parliamentary tradition" (Farrell 1969: 135; see also Ward 1994: vii). This is an important finding that helps set the political and legal scene for the drafting of the 1922 and 1937 Constitutions for it shows that "Irish political culture was already developed into an established and sturdy parliamentary mould prior to political independence" (Farrell 1971: 83).

10.2.2 *From the First Dáil to the 1922 Irish Free State Constitution*

The policy of unilateral self-rule soon met with a robust response from the British government, which ultimately spilled over into violence and what became known as the War of Independence. The conflict ran from the summer of 1919 until a truce came into effect on 10 July 1921, and subsequent negotiations resulted in the "Articles of Agreement for a Treaty between Great Britain and Ireland" (known in Ireland simply as "the Treaty"). It was signed on 6 December 1921 and paved the way for the creation in the new year of a British-recognized Provisional Government.

The terms of the Treaty, however, split the Sinn Féin movement and it was only ratified by the Dáil by a slim majority of 64 to 57 on 7 January 1922.[3] De Valera voted

---

[1] This was later given express legislative recognition by the Irish Free State in s. 2(7) of the Interpretation Act 1923.

[2] For text, see Farrell 1969.

[3] The split was an example of the common phenomenon whereby a campaigning movement or organisation is divided when faced with a settlement offer that with regard to some aspects of the movement's core concerns makes things better but with regard to others either makes things worse or leaves them unchanged. The Treaty granted a substantial measure of independence to Ireland but with a number of downsides that struck at the heart of Irish republicanism, most significantly: (1) the acceptance of the partition of the island of Ireland into a Protestant/Unionist majority northern part and a Catholic/nationalist majority south created by Westminster's Government of Ireland Act 1920; and (2) the specification of an oath of fidelity to the king to be taken by all members of the legislature in the South.

against the Treaty and subsequently resigned as President of the Dáil, his place being taken by Arthur Griffiths. The passion and depth of conviction behind this division of opinion ultimately led to the outbreak of civil war in June of that year, shortly after the general election for a new Dáil, intended to be a constituent assembly for the proposed Irish Free State Constitution, returned only 35 out of 128 seats for the anti-Treaty side.

10.2.3 *The Drafting of the 1922 Constitution*

In early 1922, the chairman of the new Provisional Government, Michael Collins, set up a special committee to draft a constitution for what was to become known as the Irish Free State (Saorstát Éireann). The members of the committee were Hugh Kennedy,[4] James Douglas,[5] Darrell Figgis[6] (who as secretary was the only paid member of the committee), James MacNeill,[7] Clement J. France,[8] Kevin O'Shiel,[9] James Murnaghan,[10] John O'Byrne[11] and Alfred O'Rahilly.[12] The Constitution Committee ultimately produced three drafts for the consideration of the Provisional Government. Draft A and B were essentially two versions of a common working pool of provisions and were identical in most respects, the most significant disagreement being over the design of the executive and the election of the Seanad (second chamber of the legislature). Draft A was signed by Figgis, MacNeill and O'Byrne. Draft B was signed by Kennedy, Douglas and France. Draft C was written by Professor Alfred O'Rahilly

---

[4] A successful Dublin barrister, Kennedy had been chief legal advisor to the Irish negotiators in London for the Treaty talks and was later appointed Attorney General to the Provisional Government. In 1924, he became the first Chief Justice of the Irish Free State.

[5] A Dublin Quaker businessman who co-founded the Irish White Cross to assist the distribution of U.S. relief aid to civilians affected by the war of independence. He was well-versed in constitutional questions and was a trusted friend of Michael Collins.

[6] Poet, writer and author of *The Gaelic State in the Past & Future* (Maunsel & Co. Dublin 1917), which advocated a future Irish state governed in part by vocational councils.

[7] A former official in Indian civil service who had been Douglas's principal co-worker in the White Cross. He was the brother of Minister for Education Eoin MacNeill.

[8] A lawyer from Seattle who was sent to Ireland in January 1921 as part of a delegation from the American Committee for Relief to Ireland, which funded the White Cross.

[9] A barrister, legal advisor to the provisional government on the boundary clauses of the Treaty and former Sinn Féin judge during the war who was a long-time friend and associate of Collins. An infrequent attendee because of the pressures of his other assignments, he did not sign any of the resulting drafts.

[10] Professor of Jurisprudence, Roman Law and International Law at University College, Dublin.

[11] A successful young Dublin barrister who was subsequently Kennedy's successor as Attorney General. He was appointed to the High Court in 1926 and the Supreme Court in 1940.

[12] O'Rahilly was professor of mathematical physics and Registrar at University College Cork. A personal friend of Michael Collins and a former Jesuit novice. A prolific polymath, he was the founder of Cork University Press and later president of the university, establishing the chair in sociology.

independently of the Committee's working draft(s) when it became apparent to him that the differences of opinion between himself and his colleagues were too great to be ironed out in the time available to the Committee to complete its task. Professor James Murnaghan subsequently signed his name to Draft C.

In the end it was Draft B that formed the basis for the deliberations of the Provisional Government and thus for the Government Draft which they produced. As the Constitution would ultimately have to be confirmed by the British Parliament, this draft was then shown to the British government, which insisted on a number of changes in order to bring it into line with what they saw as the requirements of the Treaty and the essentials of the constitution of the British Commonwealth. Kennedy was the chief legal advisor of the Irish government during this period of negotiations with the British. The Agreed Text was published in London and Dublin on 16 June 1922 and was later debated by the Third Dáil, sitting as a Constituent Assembly, from 18 September until its approval on 25 October as a schedule to the Constitution of The Irish Free State (Saorstát Eireann) Act, 1922. In sum, it is clear that the drafting of the 1922 Constitution unfolded in four key stages as follows:

1. Appointment of Constitution Committee by Provisional Government and production of three alternative drafts by them: January – March 1922;
2. Confidential circulation of drafts by government to interested parties, feedback and criticism and finalization by government of a single draft: March – May 1922;
3. Negotiations with British government and production of a jointly agreed text: June 1922;
4. Consideration and revision by Dáil Éireann (Irish parliament elected to sit as a constituent assembly for ratification of the new constitution): September – December 1922.

From the above it is possible to identify six key documents relating to the drafting of the 1922 Constitution, namely:

(1) – (3) The three drafts produced by the Constitution Committee, known then (and referred to herein) as Drafts A, B and C;[13]

(4) The draft produced by the Provisional Government, referred to herein as the Government Draft;[14]

(5) The draft agreed by the Irish and British Governments, referred to herein as the Agreed Text;[15]

---

[13] For text of Drafts A and B, see Akenson and Fallin 1970b. For text of Draft C, see Farrell 1971.
[14] For text, see Akenson and Fallin 1970a.
[15] 1922 [Cmd. 1688] Draft Constitution of the Irish Free State (Constitution).

(6) The Agreed Text as amended and finally approved by the Irish constituent assembly[16] (and later confirmed by the British Parliament[17]), referred to herein simply as the Constitution.

10.3 SOME POINTS OF PARTICULAR RELEVANCE FOR COMPARATIVE LEGAL STUDY

In many ways the 1922 Constitution is a textbook example of the phenomenon of legal transplantation. In particular, it was at the first and third stages of the drafting process as outlined earlier that international influences were brought to bear most heavily on the framing of the constitution.

At the first stage, the Constitution Committee was formally constrained in its work only by the express terms of the Treaty and the agreement with the Southern Unionists that there would be a proportional representation system of election and a second parliamentary chamber providing minority (Protestant) representation. Farrell summarizes the common features of the Committee's three drafts as follows:

> Despite the differences in detail and tone the three drafts produced shared a common desire to break with the rigid disciplined parties of the existing British model of cabinet government.... All were in this sense radically democratic, experimental and open to an independent economic policy.... The drafts offered were, in short, typical of the optimism about constitutional engineering which was briefly and deceptively recaptured after the first World War. (Farrell 1970b: 355)

Farrell is right to locate the Committee's work within the broader international pattern of constitutionalisation at that time. Considerable efforts were made by the Committee to acquire English translations of as many foreign constitutional texts as possible. As the distinguished German scholar Leo Kohn put it in his landmark study of the Constitution: "A diligent search of foreign Constitutions was instituted, particular attention being devoted to the Constitutions of the new States of Central and Eastern Europe. Theoretical inclination and republican outlook alike led the framers of the Irish Constitution to seek inspiration from Continental models, however experimental, rather than from the empirical framework of the British Constitution" (Kohn 1932: 78).

Kennedy himself, when later addressing the American Bar Association in 1928 in his capacity as Chief Justice of the Irish Free State, stated that the key influences on the original drafting process had been "the written constitution of the USA, of

---

[16] Constitution of the Irish Free State (Saorstát Eireann) Act, 1922. Available at http://www.irishstatutebook.ie/1922/en/act/pub/0001/index.html

[17] Irish Free State Constitution Act 1922.

Germany and of Switzerland, as well as that body of principles which make up the unwritten constitution of Great Britain" (Kennedy 1928b: 443). It was at the third stage of the drafting process, during negotiations with the British government, that this latter body of constitutional "principles" made its biggest impact on the formalities – if not always the practical substance – of the constitution. It is to a consideration of some of the results of the melding of these various influences that I now turn.

10.3.1 *Transplantation and Transformation of British and Dominion Constitutional Form and Substance*

Arguably the most significant feature of the British model to be adopted, albeit in various amended forms, by all three of the drafts prepared by the Constitution Committee was the system of parliamentary or representative government. In Britain this model of government is regulated by what Dicey famously called "laws of the constitution" and "conventions of the constitution." As Ward notes:

> What is true of the British constitution is also true of the constitution of the British colonies that achieved self-government between 1852 and 1910: Australia, Canada, New Zealand, and South Africa. Their constitutions from the outset were mixtures of law and convention, with convention determining the character of the executive.... In 1922 the Irish Free State broke from this pattern by adopting a constitution that described, for the first time in constitutional law, the British model of the executive as it actually functions. (Ward 1994: 2–3)

In a sense, the Free State constitution "broke the pattern" in two distinct ways. First, it featured a radical twist on the usual model of representative government in its provisions for the appointment of "external ministers," that is, members of the executive who were not elected members of the legislature. Second, as emphasized by Ward and Kohn, it was unique in the manner in which it described the functioning of the executive. I shall consider each in turn.

10.3.1.1 The Modification of British Practice in the Constitution

Although Irish nationalists were steeped in the British parliamentary mode of democratic government, nevertheless, common to all of the drafts produced by the Constitution Committee was a concern to move away from what its members saw as the defects of the British system of responsible government. In particular they sought to reduce the control of the executive over the legislature and to rescue domestic policy issues from party politics. They identified the fusion of membership of the executive and legislature as being at the root of these problems, and all of the drafts sought to remedy this by allowing, in one way or another, for the appointment of ministers from outside of the legislature.

But there were other motivations too. Because Clause Four of the Treaty only required "Members of the Parliament of the Irish Free State" to swear the oath of fidelity to the king, the creation of external ministers would allow for the possibility of including members of the anti-Treaty side of Sinn Féin (whose rejection of the oath would bar them from the legislature) in the government of the Free State – and thus, it was hoped, help foster a new unity and forestall a slide into civil war.

Ultimately, the Government Draft adopted, with some minor changes, the recommendations of Draft B. When these provisions were ultimately considered by the British, however, the loophole in respect of the oath to the king was immediately spotted and, on their insistence, removed. All ministers would be required to take the oath. With this amendment secured, the British delegation was content to make known their disapproval of the novel scheme without demanding that it be changed. In the end, it was during the Dáil debates that the proposals for external ministers faced their toughest opposition, and the version finally adopted drew a clear line between the ministers who were members of the Dáil and together formed the Executive Council and those external ministers who would be nominated, appointed and removed largely as set out in the original Government Draft but would not be members of the Executive Council.[18] In reality the supposedly supra-party-political ministers became simply nominees of the President of the Executive Council, and the scheme was subsequently abolished for all practical purposes in 1927 by the Constitution (Amendment No. 5) Act 1927 which increased the maximum size of the Executive Council from seven to twelve, thus making it unnecessary to appoint any external ministers to head the existing departments.

10.3.1.2 Innovations in the Description of British and Dominion Practice

As already noted, a pioneering feature of the 1922 Constitution with respect to British and Dominion law generally was the manner in which it formally expressed in writing the constitutional conventions governing the functions and power of the executive. Thus, for example, the principle of the responsibility of the cabinet to the legislature is expressed twice (Articles 51 and 54), and the convention that the cabinet must resign if it loses the support of the majority is stated in positive law (Article 53).

The Constitution was no less pioneering, however, in its treatment of the relationship between the institutions of the new state and the British Crown. Clause 2 of the Treaty had stated that: "Subject to the provisions hereinafter set out ... the law, practice and constitutional usage governing the relationship of the Crown or the representative of the Crown and of the Imperial Parliament to the Dominion of Canada shall govern their relationship to the Irish Free State."

[18]   Constitution, Articles 51–56.

The Irish delegation in the Treaty negotiators had deliberately pegged the Irish Free State to Canadian "practice," for as Kennedy later put it, "[Canada] had outgrown her colonial status as well as her constitution, and in the gradual evolution of law, practice and constitutional usage had reached national stature and exhibited marks of national sovereignty" (Kennedy 1928a: 750).

The significance of this may be hard to grasp for those unfamiliar with the workings of a partly unwritten constitutional order like that of the United Kingdom. In such an order the actual practice or the custom as it evolves and is accepted assumes an equal and often greater importance than that of formally expressed rules. Thus, Canada, by 1922, was in many respects effectively an independent nation-state, although formally still a dominion of the British Crown. Nevertheless, there was a rowing back on this commitment to Canadian forms during the first stage of the drafting process. Draft C made no mention whatsoever of the Crown. Drafts A and B contained only a minimal and formalistic reference toward the end of their respective texts, in relation to the promulgation of enacted legislation, which appeared, with only minor alterations, in Article 75 of the Government Draft.

This draft was given to the assistant secretary of the British Cabinet on Saturday 27 May 1922. The British were furious with what they considered a deliberate effort to renounce the express terms of the Treaty. On 29 May, the British government replied with a memo setting out the reasons for their refusal to accept the draft as it stood. There is not enough space to consider the ensuing negotiations in detail nor the full list of changes that were made to bring the Government Draft into closer conformity to both the Treaty and Commonwealth constitutional forms (see Towey 1977; Mohr 2008), but it suffices to mention the Irish strategy that shaped the results of their eventual capitulation to the British demands, which was recorded in the minutes of meeting of the Provisional Government on 6 June, as follows: "[I]t was decided that in the event of the British representatives insisting on insertion of the letter of Canadian Law in the Constitution, the Irish representatives should insist that the practice obtaining in Canada be also explicitly embodied in the Constitution."[19]

The result was memorably described by Towey as a "curious juxtaposition of constitutional fiction and fact" throughout the Constitution – what Townshend has dubbed "Kennedy's principal contribution to the evolution of state forms of the [Irish Free State]" (Townshend 1998: 61). As Towey explained:

> The British were concerned to get the letter of dominion law into the Constitution; Kennedy was determined to have the practice stated whenever possible.... In order to meet the needs of both sides contradictory intentions were juxtaposed within

---

[19] Irish National Archives (hereafter NA) Taois/S 8 955A.

the same articles. For example, the President of the Executive Council would be appointed by "the Representative of the Crown," but only after he had been nominated by the Dáil.... The Oireachtas [trans.: Parliament] would be summoned and dissolved by the representative of the Crown, but only on the advice of the Executive Council." (Towey 1977: 358–359)

With respect to three of the royal prerogatives insisted upon by the British – the exercise of the executive authority of the king through his representative, the power to reserve Bills, and the right to appoint the Crown representative – Kennedy sought to restrict any potential for their abuse by inserting as a qualification to the recognition of each one the express requirement that they only be exercised in accordance with the "practice" and "constitutional usage" relating to the Dominion of Canada (Towey 1977: 361).[20] The result was masterfully and succinctly summarized by Kohn:

> The Constitution of the Irish Free State bears the paradoxical impress of a dual inspiration. Moulded in the frame of the Dominion Constitutions and subject to their formal limitations, it yet derives its origin from the enactment – "in the exercise of undoubted right" – of an Irish Assembly which acknowledges "that all lawful authority comes from God to the people" and implicitly denies any other. Its structural design is that of a limited monarchy, but its tenor is essentially republican.... The internal structure of the Constitution exhibits the characteristic features of the British system, but a multiplicity of novel devices indicates the influence of foreign models, while a consistent effort to modify the fundamental conventions of the former reveals an anti-authoritarian tendency alien to its basic inspiration. (Kohn 1932: 13)

It is with a consideration of some of these "novel devices" that the next three sections of this part of the chapter are concerned.

10.3.2 *Vocational Councils*

A vocational organisation exists, according to the definition proposed by the 1944 report of the Irish Government's Commission on Vocational Organisation, "when members of a vocation [i.e. profession, trade, industry] associate for some purpose concerned with their vocation and form an organic body with power to speak and act for the vocation" (O'Leary 2000: x). A vocational council can be understood as a political institution designed to give certain rights of representation and decision making within the national system of government to a vocational organisation or group of such organisations. Commonly, advocates of such councils have drawn parallels with the guilds of medieval European society and have seen them as

---

[20] See Constitution, Articles 51, 41 and 60, respectively.

representing an important alternative model of social organisation that respects the principle of subsidiary and thus avoids the extremes of market-dominated capitalism and state-dominated socialism (O'Leary 2000: xi–xiii).

All three of the Committee's drafts had endorsed the idea of vocational councils which was much in vogue, particularly in Catholic thought, at the time (O'Leary 2000: 29–32). These were ultimately provided for in Article 45 of the Constitution. Article 56 allowed for the possibility that these councils might nominate the external ministers in place of the Dáil committee provided for this function in Article 55. O'Leary observes that Article 45 "catered for an unusual convergence of interests between Southern Unionism and social Catholicism – the limitation of the powers of central government was of fundamental importance to both" (O'Leary 2000: 31).

Provisions for vocational councils also appeared in Article 68 of the Constitution of the Polish Republic (1921) and in Article 165 of the Constitution of the German Realm (1919). As it turned out, the option to create vocational councils was never taken up by any Irish Free State government, and vocationalism, despite its increasing prominence in Irish Catholic intellectual circles throughout the 1930s (Mullarkey 1999), was given only token recognition in Articles 18 and 19 of the 1937 Constitution, which provided for the election of certain members of the Seanad (the second house of the Oireachtas) from panels representing different sectors of society. As with the 1922 regime, the seemingly radical potential of these provisions on paper was never acted upon by any subsequent administration.

10.3.3 *Citizen Initiatives and Referendums*

Another "novel device" which distinguished the Irish Free State Constitution from the British system was the role given to citizen initiatives and referendums. According to Kohn:

> The introduction of the machinery of direct legislation into the structure of the Irish Constitution reflects the democratic radicalism of its framers.... Its model is to be found less in the older American, Australian and Swiss precedents than in the post-War Constitutions of the new Continental Republics. In the latter democratic zeal, political doctrinarism and distrust of the mechanism of parties and Parliaments combined to produce a highly involved design of direct legislation interwoven with the fabric of representative institutions. On that elaborate pattern the Irish system was framed. (Kohn 1932: 238)

All three of the drafts produced by the Constitution Committee provided in some manner for initiatives and referendums. Draft A and B contained four identical articles dealing with (1) referral of legislation to a popular vote, (2) initiation of legislation by citizen petition, (3) popular authorization for the declaration of war, and (4) approval of constitutional amendments by referendum. For reasons of space, I shall limit discussion to a brief consideration of (1), (3), and (4).

10.3.3.1 Referral of Legislation

The provisions for the referral of Bills to a popular vote contained in Article 47 largely mirrored those of Germany, although they omitted a number of the safeguards contained in that model. No legislation was ever referred to the people under the Article and it was deleted in 1928. A similar scheme, but closer to the German model in its safeguards, reappeared in Article 27 of the 1937 Constitution. To date the procedure has never been used.

10.3.3.2 Popular Authorization for the Declaration of War

Another radical expression of direct democracy proposed by both Drafts A and B of the Constitution Committee was the requirement that "save in the case of actual invasion, Saorstát Éireann shall not declare war upon any other State or Nation or be committed to participation in any war without the assent of the majority of the voters on the register obtained in a Referendum." This did not survive the review by the Provisional Government. Having endorsed the referendum and initiative provisions, they drew the line at supporting such a radical curtailment of representative political authority. Nevertheless, in a reflection of the depth of the commitment, at least at that time, among Irish nationalist elites to a strengthening of the role of the parliamentary assembly, they amended the article so that the approval of a majority of the Oireachtas was required.

10.3.3.3 Approval of Constitutional Amendments by Referendum

As Kohn pithily observed, "In a written Constitution the provisions governing its amendment constitute the acid test of its legal status" (Kohn 1932: 251). It is significant, therefore, that every one of the preliminary drafts, from those of the Constitutional Committee up to the text agreed with the British government, provided that amendments to the constitution proposed by the Oireachtas required approval by the people in a referendum. In Dominion terms, Ireland was here following the Australian model. It was only during the Dáil debate of the Agreed Text that a government-sponsored amendment allowed for the amendment of the constitution by ordinary legislation for a period of eight years after its enactment. Sixteen Amendment Acts were passed within that eight-year period, the last of which, enacted in 1929, extended the period for amendment by ordinary legislation for a further eight years (see further discussion in Subsection 10.3.4.2 below).

10.3.4 *Rights Declarations and Judicial Review of the Constitutional Validity of Primary Legislation*

10.3.4.1 Rights Declarations

The decision to include European- and U.S.-style declarations[21] of popular sovereignty and of basic political and civil liberties does not seem to have been the subject of any discussion by the Constitution Committee and was taken almost at the outset when the Committee decided to adopt the scheme of work set out in a memo by Darrell Figgis, the vice-chair of the Committee.[22]

Among the Kennedy papers there is what appears to be a draft briefing document for the Cabinet, introducing and explaining a draft which is very close to the official Draft B. It gives some insight into the thinking of the drafters and the unselfconscious nature of their decision to include a declaration of rights: "Article 5 to 9 inclusive deal with the personal rights of the citizens, and include all of the personal rights and liberties usually guaranteed in Constitutions of democratic States."[23]

The justification by reference to the usual practice of other "democratic States" is telling in two ways. First, it underscores the important influence of the study of other constitutions undertaken by the Committee in preparing their drafts. Second, it reveals the Committee's primarily pragmatic, rather than philosophical, approach to the choice of which rights to include. The selection was determined by the desire to establish a "free democratic constitution" – as Michael Collins had instructed the Committee at its first meeting. Thus, it is from the perspective of Irish nationalism's long-established espousal of democracy and religious non-discrimination in the face of parliament-endorsed discrimination and oppressive departures from the rule of law that one must approach the decision of the drafting Committee and the Dáil to include declarations concerning the fundamental rights of individuals. In this regard, comparison can be made with at least one of the nineteenth-century trends that led to the general emergence of a politicised Catholicism in Europe after the First World War (Buchanan and Conway 1996: 19).

In respect of the opening declarations of the Government Draft, there were some significant exchanges with the British representatives during the June negotiations.

---

[21]   Constitution, Articles 1–11. See also Appendix (Section 10.5).
[22]   "Document 2" University College Dublin Archives (hereafter UCD) P4/320. Farrell 1970a: 126.
[23]   UCD P4/308.

The British were "shocked by what Austen Chamberlain, then Lord Privy Seal, called the 'Soviet character'" (Mohr 2008: 172) of Articles 1 and 2 – the text of which came from the writings of Padraic Pearse and the 1919 Democratic Programme. They read:

> Article 1. The Nation's sovereignty extends not only to all the men and women of the Nation, but to all the material possessions of the Nation, the Nation's soil and all its resources and all the wealth and wealth-producing processes within the Nation; and all right to private property is subordinated to the public right and welfare of the Nation.
>
> Article 2. It is the duty of every man and woman to give allegiance and service to the commonwealth, and it is the duty of the Nation to insure that every citizen shall have opportunity to spend his or her strength and faculties in the service of the people.

On the first day of redrafting, Kennedy conceded to the removal of these articles in exchange for an important new Article 1 which implicitly recognised the notion of an Irish nation by stating: "The Irish Free State … is a co-equal member of the Community of Nations forming the British Commonwealth of Nations." By contrast, the Irish delegation persistently and obstinately refused to alter the wording of Article 3 of the Government Draft (later Article 2, in light of the aforementioned amendment). It stated: "All powers of government and all authority, legislative, executive, and judicial, in Ireland are derived from the people of Ireland." It was arguably the most revolutionary statement in the entire document and was a sine qua non for the Irish side. Remarkably, and with great symbolic significance for the pro-Treaty side, it survived the negotiations intact. Of course, it remained somewhat incongruous when juxtaposed with the reintroduction of the king into the articles defining the legislature, parliamentary oath, executive, and right to petition for special leave to appeal to the Privy Council.[24] Nevertheless, it was a foundation stone of the new constitutional order that was subsequently built upon and amplified by the text and jurisprudence of the 1937 Constitution.

10.3.4.2 Judicial Review

Although all of the drafts produced by the Constitution Committee departed from British and Dominion tradition in their inclusion of rights declarations, the three drafts differed considerably in their assessment of the U.S. practice of rights-based judicial review. Draft C provided for judicial review of executive acts but not of legislation. Drafts A and B provided for review by the High Court and Supreme Court of

---

[24] Constitution, Articles 12, 17, 51 and 66.

the "validity" of primary legislation with respect to the terms of the Constitution. But Draft B further required that any law declared unconstitutional be submitted to a referendum of the people, "unless the Oireachtas be able to meet the constitutional objection by an amendment of the law." Unusually, the Provisional Government chose to follow Draft A in this instance and in the end it was its system of strong judicial review that appeared in the Constitution (Article 65) and was later carried over into the 1937 Constitution (Article 34.3.2).

It should be noted, however, that unlike its successor, the 1922 Constitution ultimately failed to secure in practice the judicial review of legislation. Its failure in this regard was strikingly displayed in *State (Ryan) v. Lennon.*[25] The case was a habeas corpus challenge to the detention and trial of the applicants by a special military tribunal established under the terms of the Constitution (Amendment No 17) Act 1931 which inserted a new Article 2A into the Constitution creating an extraordinarily draconian state security apparatus under the sole control of the executive and expressly exempted from all constitutional checks and balances and judicial oversight. The applicants challenged the validity of the Act on two main grounds. The first was that the provisions of Article 50 (specifying the procedure for a constitutional amendment), which its enactment had relied upon, were themselves the result of an invalid amendment. The second was that the Act's provisions were repugnant to the fundamental principles of the Constitution and could not be deemed to have amended them. The first argument reveals the flaw in the 1922 Constitution that facilitated the debasing of its rights declarations. Under the terms of Article 50 as adopted by the Constituent Assembly, any amendment to the Constitution required a referendum unless it was passed by the Oireachtas within eight years of the Constitution coming into force. The Constitution (Amendment No. 16) Act 1929 extended the eight-year grace period to sixteen years. It was thanks to this extension that the severe measures of Article 2A were introduced. The applicants argued that the legislature had acted *ultra vires* in purporting to amend by legislation the powers of amendment granted to them by the Constituent Assembly.

Fitzgibbon J, who had occupied the Trinity College seat in the Constituent Assembly as an independent Unionist, rejected both sets of arguments. Murnaghan J, who had been a member of the Constitution Committee and a signatory of Draft C, also decided against the applicants but was sharply critical of the "extreme rigour" of Article 2A, stating that "the judicial mind is staggered at the very complete departure from legal methods in use in these Courts."[26]

Hugh Kennedy, who at this point was Chief Justice, dissented from the majority in a judgement that is famous in Irish legal history for its ringing endorsement of a

---

[25] [1935] 1 IR 170 (SC).
[26] *State (Ryan) v Lennon* [1935] 1 IR 170 at 237.

natural law account of political and legal authority which he argued underpinned the Constitution. His dissent can be seen as an attack on the unravelling of the constitution scheme of rights-based judicial review by the doctrine of "implied amendment." This doctrine, most fully articulated only shortly before by O'Connor MR in *R (Cooney) v. Clinton*,[27] and expressly approved by Murnaghan J in *Ryan*, essentially held that no enactment of the Oireachtas could be deemed unconstitutional so long as it occurred within the period allowed for constitutional amendment by ordinary legislation, because any such enactment could be taken as having implicitly amended the constitution. Such an approach was a creature of that judicial deference to legislative enactments which Free State judges, schooled in the canons of British constitutional theory, proved reluctant to shake off, and it had the effect of nullifying the superior courts' role as a constitutional watchdog.

Nevertheless the failure of the 1922 Constitution's scheme for constitutional review, inadvertently caused by desire to facilitate easy amendment in the early years of its enactment, was to some extent a *felix culpa* insofar as it proved highly instructive to the framers of the 1937 Constitution. They avoided making the same mistake by means of a special provision included among the transitory articles of the 1937 document. The article allowed for the amendment of the constitution by ordinary legislation during a period of three years after its enactment but included the express qualification that neither it nor Article 45, which provided that any amendment to the Constitution required the approval of the majority of those voting in a referendum, could be amended by ordinary legislation during that three-year period.

10.3.5 *The Philosophical Underpinnings of the 1922 Constitution*

With the exception of Alfred O'Rahilly, none of the protagonists in the drafting process appear to have viewed their work as concerned with articulating a distinctively liberal or natural law theory of political authority or law (to adopt the two labels most often used by some commentators to describe what they see as the competing intellectual traditions present in the 1937 Constitution). Rather, leaving aside the many sensitive and complicated political issues surrounding the precise nature of the newly created relationship between Ireland and Britain, which dominated national debate generally at the time (and continues to dominate historical discussion of the period), it seems clear that the overriding design principle was provided by the idea of a "free democratic constitution," an idea which was deeply woven into the historical practice and rhetoric of Irish (and Irish Catholic) nationalist politics, albeit often without any sustained philosophical reflection on its foundational principles or intellectual origins.

[27] [1935] 1 IR 245.

10.3.5.1 The "Structure of Normality" of pre-Independence Irish Nationalism

Enda McDonagh identifies three "historical and local circumstances" which had a "decisive influence" (McDonagh 1961: 132) on the 1937 Constitution, but I believe his analysis applies equally well to the genesis of the 1922 document.

"The first and perhaps most important of these was the democratic and non-denominational character of Irish political nationalism as it developed in the XIXth century and was inherited by Mr de Valera's generation and by our own" (*ibid.*). McDonagh's analysis is largely confirmed by the scholarly attention later given to the causes and history of the acceptance of democratic thought and practice in Irish nationalism and in nineteenth-century Irish society more generally (Prager 1986; Ward 1994; Garvin 1996; Townshend 1998: 45; Kissane 2002). McDonagh notes that the "democracy creed is a marked characteristic" (McDonagh 1961: 132) of Irish revolutionary nationalism from Tone, through Davis and Young Ireland, the Fenians and up to Sinn Féin and the organisers of the 1916 Easter rising. Likewise, Irish constitutional nationalism was committed to democratic values as exemplified in the campaigns of O'Connell, Butt, Parnell and Redmond. Importantly, however, both of these strands of Irish nationalism included, in their understanding of the essentials of democratic political order, "express guarantees of religious freedom for all and the exclusion of any discrimination on religious grounds" (McDonagh 1961: 132–133). This is not to deny the phenomenon of sectarian strands of cultural nationalism. It is nevertheless my argument that such views were not determinative of the constitutional projects of the elites who drafted the 1922 and 1937 Constitutions (Keogh 1995a).

The second important influence which McDonagh stresses is "the religious spirit of the Irish people" and of the leaders of both the revolutionary and constitutional movements within Irish nationalism throughout the nineteenth and twentieth centuries. It is because of this distinctive sociological phenomenon that "it would be a mistake to compare the strict non-sectarianism of Irish political theory and practice with the hostile or indifferent attitude to religion which was frequently the case in other countries" (McDonagh 1961: 133). Commenting on the notions of national and popular sovereignty found in the 1922 and 1937 Constitutions, Basil Chubb considered that "Irish Republican thought, though deriving in general from American and French ideas, was never in the main stream of European liberal theory. It had on the whole never been doctrinaire or dogmatic and was now, with national independence achieved, becoming ever more qualified and modified by the influence of Catholic teaching" (Chubb 1978: 24–25).

McDonagh further observes that "this religious spirit was combined with a remarkable sensitivity to the distinction between politics and religion, between State authority and ecclesiastical authority" (McDonagh 1961: 133). Commenting on the same phenomenon, Keogh states: "According to the shibboleth, O'Connell took his religion from Rome and his politics from home. That was a distinction which the post-independence generation of political leaders, William T. Cosgrave, Éamon de Valera and John A. Costello, sought to uphold" (Keogh 1995b: 2). However, he goes on to note: "But it was sometimes difficult to distinguish between these two spheres." And indeed it was a distinguishing feature of Irish political culture that the successful engagement of devout Catholic laymen with liberal popular causes was not just tolerated by the Irish hierarchy but actively encouraged and supported by them (MacMillan 1993: 98; O'Ferrall 1985: 42). Nevertheless, the third influence mentioned by McDonagh is "the consistent attitude by the Irish hierarchy over 200 years to relations with civil authorities" whereby the Church maintained a respectful, cooperative but clear distance, retaining the right to criticise specific government measures on moral grounds and refusing any formal association or financial endowment (McDonagh 1961: 133).

This combination of policies of the Irish bishops in the second half of the nineteenth century, falling somewhere between the Radicalism of Gladstone and the reactionary concerns of the Syllabus, has been termed "orthodox Irish Catholic Liberalism" (Norman 1965: 453). By the 1920s and 1930s, with the renewal of political and social studies within Catholic academic circles in response to the encyclicals of Leo XIII and Pius XI (Whyte 1980: 62–95; O'Leary 2000), the exceptionalism of "orthodox Irish Catholic Liberalism" was already on its way to becoming, as it did, the post–World War II Catholic norm. The complementary relationship between natural law philosophy (as communicated to them at the time in the form of Catholic social and political theory) and democratic values and systems assumed by Irish Catholic nationalism was later to become a prominent theme of twentieth-century natural law theory and Catholic reflection on democracy and human rights (Simon 1951; Maritain 1951, Vatican Council II 1965b: paras 73–76; Vatican Council II 1965a: paras. 1–8). But in the 1860s, the Irish hierarchy's involvement with politics (such as its membership of the National Association, a movement including Irish MPs and the Radicals and Dissenters of the English Liberation Society which, inter alia, opposed state funding for any church) represented an advanced position that was in tension with Roman thinking at the time (Norman: 1965).

Discussing the contribution of Daniel O'Connell to the Irish and British political scene of the nineteenth century in a way that draws together the three factors offered by McDonagh, Garvin observes that: "O'Connell was the man who tried to give Ireland a combination of liberalism, democracy, and popular Catholicism ... The new state [in 1922] was ... to be a pioneering experiment in Catholic democracy and was, for a long time, to be the only stable Catholic democracy in the world"

(Garvin 1996: 181; see also MacMillan 1993: 87). O'Ferrall also recognizes the exceptionalism of Irish Catholic liberalism from its birth in the nineteenth century: "In the European context, where Catholicism after 1815 supported absolutism ... Irish liberal Catholicism was indeed exceptional. In this era of Papal conservatism and Metternichian reaction only in Ireland did the Catholic Church become committed to a great popular political struggle ... liberalism and Catholicism were linked together in a Catholic country" (O'Ferrall 1985: 284; see also Keogh and O'Driscoll 1996: 275; Buchanan and Conway 1996: 6).

So it is no surprise that one of the most prominent Catholic apologists and nationalist public intellectuals of the 1920s and after, Alfred O'Rahilly, published a series of articles in the prominent Irish Jesuit periodical *Studies* in the years just prior to his appointment to the Constitution Committee, which argued not only that Catholicism and democracy were compatible but that modern democracy itself was historically a product of Catholic thought and practice (O'Rahilly 1918, 1919a, 1919b, 1920, 1921).

10.3.5.2 Evidence from the Absence of Debate: The Source of Political Authority

Alasdair MacIntyre has insightfully argued that "[t]he structure of normality provides the most basic framework for understanding action. Acting in accordance with those structures does not require the giving or the having of reasons for so acting, except in certain exceptional types of circumstance in which those structures have been put in question" (MacIntyre 1988: 24). This is an important point to remember when attempting to reconstruct the motives or intentions of those acting in the past. The philosophical presumptions of the drafters and ratifiers of the 1922 Constitution were rarely explicitly stated but they are often readily identifiable from what went unstated. In this regard it is surely significant that the inclusion of a reference to God in the preamble of the Act creating the Constitution does not appear to have been the subject of any debate in the constituent assembly. It began as follows: "Dáil Éireann sitting as a Constituent Assembly in this Provisional Parliament, acknowledging that all lawful authority comes from God to the people ... hereby proclaims the establishment of the Irish Free State."

It is clear from an examination of the minutes of the Cabinet meetings and the various opinions provided to the government concerning the preamble that the choice of words was significant and carefully considered. It clearly rejects the populist and tokenistic approaches to the inclusion of a reference to God's blessing, which had been mooted in memos to the Cabinet by Figgis[28] and

---

[28] 21 April 1922, NA S 8952.

O'Shiel,[29] in favor of a formula almost identical to that which O'Rahilly had described to the government in an explanatory memo as the "fundamental tenet of Christian democracy."[30] That this specification of the origin of "all lawful authority" aroused no comment among the Irish political elites who subsequently steered the process of constitutional design through its final stages suggests a shared "structure of normality" that was, at the very least, willing to accept the natural law tradition of political philosophy as a silent foundation for Irish nationalist rhetoric on democracy and popular sovereignty. This is perhaps best confirmed by the judgement of Kennedy CJ, arguably the chief architect of the Free State legal order (Townshend 1998: 60; Towey 1977, 355), in *Ryan*, which expressly cites the preamble as the basis for a natural law argument against the constitutionality of the draconian state security apparatus erected by the 1931 Act.

10.3.5.3 Evidence from the Presence of Debate: The Purpose of a Written Constitution and the Appropriate Content of Rights Declarations

If one turns to consider the sort of issues that were the subject of debate and detailed consideration by the Constitution Committee, it becomes clear that they were primarily questions of political science rather than political philosophy. Indeed, the first major debate concerned the design of the Seanad and the second that of the executive. By contrast, the disagreements which led Alfred O'Rahilly to draw up an entirely separate document, Draft C, were of a more extensive and fundamental nature. According to Farrell: "O'Rahilly's attachment to a more specifically Christian concept of the state was obviously out of tune with the strongly secularist tone of the Committee" (Farrell 1970a: 130). The term "secularist," however, is unfortunately ambiguous. It can represent a form of either non-religious or anti-religious sentiment but it can be equally grounded in a traditional Christian understanding of the proper distinction between Church and State. It is surely to some version of the latter that the majority of the committee subscribed.[31]

Primarily, O'Rahilly was concerned that a section entitled "Family, Education, Religion" needed to be added to the Constitution to supplement the proposed fundamental declarations. In his memo to the Provisional Government of 12 April, mentioned earlier, he stated that this section of his draft was "the most distinctive Chapter in the Constitution. Not a word of it occurs in either of the other two

---

[29] Circa 15 March 1922, NA S 8953.
[30] 12 April 1922, NA S 8953.
[31] See, for example, the letter from Kennedy (and endorsed by the signatories of Drafts A and B) to the Provisional Government, 6 March 1922, NA S 8955A.

drafts.... It embodies the Christian ideal of marriage, parental authority, protection of women and children, education, religion in a mixed State.... In drafting Chapter 8 I am confident I express the views of the vast majority of the people of Ireland."[32] His draft also contained seven articles in a section headed "Economic Life." He also sought to flesh out in more detail the civil and political rights covered by Drafts A and B. Unsurprisingly, O'Rahilly's draft was approximately a third longer than Draft B.

When one compares Draft C with the other two produced by the committee, however, it is by no means clear that the difference between them is best summed up in Farrell's terms of a Catholic/secularist divide. Rather, it appears that the committee diverged from O'Rahilly in their conception of what sort of provisions it was appropriate to include in the organic law of a state. O'Rahilly's draft contained a large amount of material which one may properly classify as substantive "ideals"[33] and directions for future legislation rather than procedural rights. Moreover, these policy statements, some quite radical, tended to be either very detailed or very vague.[34]

By contrast, in a letter to the Provisional Government, the acting chair of the drafting committee, Darrell Figgis, clearly set out the drafting philosophy of the majority of the committee: "From the beginning it was our desire to make our Constitution as brief as possible."[35] Later, in a published collection of newspaper articles written after the official draft text was made public, Figgis reiterated his position as follows: "Plainly there should be nothing written into a Constitution that is of a temporary, experimental, or questionable nature, or which should fall to the lot of ordinary law-making and the changing convenience of practice" (Figgis 1922: 15).

This seems to have been the dominant view among the members and advisors of the Provisional Government as well,[36] and it tallied with the views expressed in a number of documents by the chairman of the Provisional Government, Michael Collins.[37] The issue of what type of rights it was appropriate to include

---

[32] NA S 8 953.

[33] "Memorandum on Draft 'C' by Messrs. Murnaghan and O'Rahilly" NA S 8953.

[34] See, for example, Articles 53(1) (on marriage), 55(3) (placing certain restrictions on employment of children and women), 61(1) (on duties of citizens), 61(4) (on nullity of "usurious contracts" and "transactions opposed to morality") and 67 (on social legislation for diffusion of property, cooperative ownership and formation of professional guilds).

[35] Letter from Figgis to Collins, 8 April 1922 (responding to memo and criticisms of T M Healy) NA S 8952.

[36] See memos by Minister for Education Eoin MacNeill (March 1922, UCD P4/339), Minister for Local Government William T Cosgrave (who later succeeded Collins and was President of the Provisional Government during the constitutional debate in the constituent assembly) (1 May 1922, NA S 8953) and Minister for Foreign Affairs George Gavan Duffy (11 April 1922, NA 1922 Committee, Box V-W).

[37] See letter to Douglas, 30 January 1922, NA S 8952, instructing that the constitution "should be as simple as possible"; see also Draft of Memo from Collins to TM Healy, NA S 6541, referred to by Townshend 1998: 58.

in the constitution also arose at several points during the Dáil debates. Rejecting a proposal by the Labour Party to include a lengthy article on children's rights, Minister for Home Affairs Kevin O'Higgins, who had been charged with seeing the Constitutional Bill through the Dáil, argued that, "In a Constitution of this kind, I submit the "fundamental rights" should be simply and boldly set out, and that that is all that is necessary to set out in the Constitution. It is not necessary to set out in full detail all the most modern and up-to-date amplifications of those rights."[38]

The 1922 Constitution is often contrasted with the 1937 version on the grounds that it represents a more secular alternative to the latter's distinctly Christian and, many would contend, Catholic tone. It is certainly true that they display very different drafting styles. But as I have argued here, it is nevertheless a mistake to view their differences in terms of a Christian/secular (or natural law/liberal) divide. The real difference between them concerned the question of what was appropriate to include in the text of a constitution. De Valera's position in 1937 was essentially that of O'Rahilly in 1922 (O'Rahilly 1936: 2). But O'Rahilly's approach was rejected at that time by those who preferred, mostly for pragmatic and political reasons, an organic law to be as short and simple as possible. That this approach to drafting was no longer the dominant view in 1937 is attributable to several factors, including, for example, (1) the genuinely devout Catholicism of de Valera himself, (2) the political challenges facing his Fianna Fáil party, particularly in terms of rehabilitating their standing in the eyes of the Irish Church (which during the Civil War had excommunicated the anti-government forces), and (3) the increased interest in Catholic social thought in Ireland generally (Mullarkey 1999; Whyte 1980: 62–95). All were factors favoring a drafting philosophy that would be expressly supportive of, rather than merely implicitly compatible with, Catholic social teaching of the time.

10.4 CONCLUSION

The 1922 Free State Constitution is best viewed as an ambitiously innovative and historically significant political experiment which, though in many ways typical of the constitutional creativity and legal transplantation of the early interwar period, was nevertheless shaped by the intellectual presuppositions of an Irish nationalist movement that, for the most part, was a distinctive blend of Catholic, democratic, and constitutionalist influences. Its various "novel devices" were the result of an open-minded approach by the original drafting committee to the transplanting of political structures and legal forms from many different jurisdictions and legal traditions. Its

---

[38] Dáil Debates, 1, cols. 697–698, 25 September 1922. See also the remarks of the Minister for Local Government Ernest Blythe (Dáil Debates, 1, cols. 700–701, 25 September 1922) and the later comments of O'Higgins (Dáil Debates, 1, cols. 754–755, 26 September 1922).

fusion of these influences in the search for a "free democratic constitution" and on the basis of idealistic (though often empirically untested) arguments meant that many of its more distinctive elements (particularly those attempting to significantly alter the relationships between the general electorate, the political parties, the legislature and the executive apparent in the Westminster system) were subsequently either deliberately removed by an inconvenienced governing elite or simply found to be dead letters in practice. But many other features stood the test of time and were carried over, and sometimes improved upon, by the 1937 Constitution, such as the acknowledgement of the divine source of political authority, the robust assertion of popular sovereignty, the specification of the basic civil and political rights of the individual and the commitment to judicial review of the constitutional validity of legislation and to constitutional amendment by referendum.

The relative silence of the drafters at the time of the 1922 Constitution's adoption on the philosophical issues which divide liberalism and natural law theory must be interpreted within the context of the turbulent political circumstances of the day and the dominant structure of normality of the period. This structure can be glimpsed indirectly in such telling events as (1) the inclusion of a reference to God in the preamble, (2) the selection and wording of the rights declarations, (3) the social morality evident in the legislative agenda of the Free State governments (Nolan 1975; Whyte 1980: 60–61; Murray 2000: 108–116), and (4) the invocation of natural law rhetoric by Kennedy in his dissenting opinion in *Ryan*. Cumulatively, these strongly suggest that the "scale of values"[39] which underlay the commitment to liberal democracy embodied in the 1922 Constitution was not that of a doctrinaire liberalism. Rather, given what we know of the intellectual and cultural climate of the time and, in particular, the prevalent belief in the compatibility of Catholic political theory and democratic government, it was much more likely to have been informed by a broadly natural law understanding of the legal and political order which was subsequently more explicitly and elaborately expressed in the text of the 1937 Constitution and, indeed, was articulated broadly across Europe in the Christian democratic movements later in the century.

10.5 APPENDIX: INFLUENCE OF THE 1922 CONSTITUTION ON THE 1937 CONSTITUTION

Prior to his decision to replace the 1922 Constitution, the then-president of the Executive Council of the Irish Free State, Éamon de Valera, established a committee

---

[39] The phrase is used by Maritain to account for the differences in interpretation and emphasis which can arise when advocates of different philosophical schools come to concretely apply a commonly agreed set of abstract rights declarations; Maritain 1949: 16.

"to examine the Constitution with a view to ascertaining what Articles should be regarded as fundamental, on the ground that they safeguard democratic rights, and to make recommendations as to steps which should be taken to ensure that such Articles should not be capable of being altered by the ordinary processes of legislation."[40] The committee produced its report on 3 July 1934.[41] Three of its four members were subsequently involved in the drafting of the new constitution, and many of the articles from the 1922 Constitution which it cited as fundamental were incorporated into the 1937 text. The following table sets out the principal rights of individuals expressly protected by the 1922 Constitution and subsequently included in the 1937 Constitution, although it should be noted that many other procedural and institutional provisions relating to the operation of a liberal democracy were also carried over from the 1922 Constitution.

Right	1922 Constitution	1937 Constitution
Equality of citizenship/before the law	Article 3	Articles 40.1 & 9.1
Liberty of the person/habeas corpus	Article 6	Article 40.4.1
Inviolability of the dwelling	Article 7	Article 40.5
Freedom of conscience and free profession and practice of religion	Article 8	Article 44.2.1
Right of free expression, peaceable assembly and formation of associations	Article 9	Article 40.6
Right to free elementary/primary education	Article 10	Article 42.4
Right to trial in accordance with law (with jury)	Article 70 (72)	Article 38.1 (38.5)
Freedom from ex post facto legislation	Article 43	Article 15.5
Bar on state endowment of religion	Article 8	Article 44.2.2

REFERENCES

Akenson, D. H. and J. F. Fallin. 1970a. The Irish Civil War and the Drafting of the Free State Constitution: Collins, De Valera, and the Pact: A New Interpretation. *Eire-Ireland* 5(28).

1970b. The Irish Civil War and the Drafting of the Free State Constitution: The Drafting Process. *Eire-Ireland* 5(42).

Buchanan, T. and M. Conway. 1996. *Political Catholicism in Europe 1918–1945*. Oxford: Oxford University Press.

Chubb, B. 1978. *The Constitution and Constitutional Change in Ireland*. Dublin: Institute of Public Administration.

Courtney Murray, J. 1946. How Liberal Is Liberalism? *America* 75(6).

Farrell, B. 1969. A Note on the Dáil Constitution, 1919. *Irish Jurist* 4(27).

[40] Initialled memorandum, 24 May 1934, NA Taois/ S 2679, cited in Keogh and McCarthy 2007: 70. See generally Hogan 1997.

[41] For a table detailing the articles of the 1937 Constitution which correspond with the articles selected in the report see, Keogh and McCarthy 2007: 72.

1970a. The Drafting of the Irish Free State Constitution I. *Irish Jurist* 5(115).

1970b. The Drafting of the Irish Free State Constitution II. *Irish Jurist* 5(342).

1970c. The Drafting of the Irish Free State Constitution III. *Irish Jurist* 6(113).

1971b. *The Founding of Dáil Éireann: Parliament and Nation Building*. Dublin: Gill and Macmillan.

1994. The First Dáil and its Constitutional Documents. In *The Creation of the Dáil*, edited by B. Farrell. Dublin: Blackwater Press.

Figgis, D. 1922. *The Irish Constitution Explained*. Dublin: Mellifront Press Ltd.

Garvin, T. 1996. *The Birth of Irish Democracy*. Dublin: Gill and Macmillan.

Hogan, G. The Constitutional Review Committee of 1934. 1997. In *Ireland in the Coming Times: Essays to Celebrate T.K. Whitaker's 80 Years*, edited by F. ó Muircheartaigh. Dublin: Institute of Public Administration.

Kennedy, H. 1928a. The Association of Canada with the Constitution of the Irish Free State. *The Canadian Bar Review* 6.

1928b. Character and Sources of the Constitution of the Irish Free State. *American Bar Association Journal* 14(443).

Keogh, D. 1995a. Church, State and Pressure Groups. *Doctrine and Life* 45(42).

1995b. *Ireland and the Vatican: The Politics and Diplomacy of Church-State Relations 1922–1960*. Dublin: Cork University Press.

Keogh, D. and F. O'Driscoll. 1996. Ireland. In *Political Catholicism in Europe 1918–1965*, edited by T. Buchanan and M. Conway. Oxford: Clarendon Press.

Keogh, D. and A. McCarthy. 2007. *The Making of the Irish Constitution, 1937* Cork: Mercier Press.

Kissane, B. 2002. *Explaining Irish Democracy*. Dublin: University College Dublin Press.

Kohn, L. 1932. *The Constitution of the Irish Free State*. London: George Allen & Unwin.

MacIntyre, A. 1988. *Whose Justice? Which Rationality?* London: Duckworth.

MacMillan, G. M. 1993. *State, Society and Authority in Ireland: The Foundations of the Modern State*. Dublin: Gill and Macmillan.

Maritain, J. 1949. Introduction. In *Human Rights: Comments and Interpretations*, edited by UNESCO. London: Allan Wingate.

1951. *Man and the State*. Chicago: Chicago University Press.

McDonagh, E. 1961. Church and State in the Constitution of Ireland. *Irish Theological Quarterly* 28(131).

Mohr, T. 2008. British Involvement in the Creation of the First Irish Constitution. *Dublin University Law Journal* 15(166).

Mullarkey, K. 1999. Ireland, the Pope and Vocationalism: The Impact of the Encyclical *Quadragesimo Anno*. In *Ireland in the 1930s: New Perspectives*, edited by J. Augusteijn Dublin: Four Courts Press.

Murray, P. 2000. *Oracles of God: The Roman Catholic Church and Irish Politics, 1922–37*. Dublin: University College Dublin Press.

Nolan, M. 1975. Influence of Catholic Nationalism on the Irish Free State Legislature. *Irish Jurist* 10(128).

Norman, E. R. 1965. *The Catholic Church and Ireland in the Age of Rebellion 1859–1873*. London: Longmans.

O'Ferrall, F. 1985. *Catholic Emancipation: Daniel O'Connell and the Birth of Irish Democracy 1820–30*. Dublin: Gill and Macmillan.

O'Leary, D. 2000. *Vocationalism and Social Catholicism in Twentieth-Century Ireland: The Search for a Christian Social Order*. Dublin: Irish Academic Press.

O'Rahilly, A. 1918. Suarez and Democracy. *Studies* 7(1).
    1919a. The Catholic Origin of Democracy. *Studies* 8(1).
    1919b. The Sources of English and American Democracy. *Studies* 8(189).
    1920. The Democracy of St Thomas. *Studies* 9(1).
    1921. The Sovereignty of the People (Part I & II). *Studies* 10(39).
    1936. The Constitution and the Senate. *Studies* 26(1).
Prager, J. 1986. *Building Democracy in Ireland: Political Order and Cultural Integration in a Newly Independent Nation*. Cambridge: Cambridge University Press.
Simon, Y. R. 1951. *Philosophy of Democratic Government*. Chicago: University of Chicago Press.
Towey, T. 1977. Hugh Kennedy and the Constitutional Development of the Irish Free State. *Irish Jurist* 12(355).
Townshend, C. 1998. The Meaning of Irish Freedom: Constitutionalism in the Free State. *Transactions of the Royal Historical Society* 45.
Vatican Council II. 1965a. *Dignitatis Humanae ('On the Right of the Person and Communities to Social and Civil Liberty in Religious Matters')*.
    1965b. *Gaudium et Spes ('Pastoral Constitution on the Church in the Modern World')*.
Ward, A. J. 1994. *The Irish Constitutional Tradition: Responsible Government and Modern Ireland, 1782–1992*. Dublin: Irish Academic Press.
Whyte, J. B. 1980. *Church and State in Modern Ireland 1923–1979*. 2nd ed. Dublin: Gill and Macmillan.

11

South Sudan's Dualistic Constitution

Kevin L. Cope

11.1 INTRODUCTION

In a seven-day referendum held in January 2011, 98.8 percent of Southern Sudanese voters elected to sever Southern Sudan's ties with the Republic of Sudan and form an independent nation (BBC 2011). The vote culminated six years of southern autonomy, twenty-two years of civil war, and centuries of tension between the ethnically Arab, largely Islamized North and the primarily ethnically African, Animist, and Christian South. A composite of social and economic forces fueled the wars and the independence movement, principal among them economic marginalization of the South, the South's perceived exclusion from national politics, and the government's foisting Shari'a on the South (Nouwen 2007: 119; Eltahir 2010: 62). In simplistic terms, the schism was a backlash to the imposition of political and economic power and foreign social values on the people of Southern Sudan. But with the referendum, the Southern Sudanese people gave themselves the right to decide for themselves the core principles that would underlie their new sovereignty.

One of the prerogatives of this sovereignty was adopting a new constitution. In contrast to the populist exercise that enabled South Sudan's independence, the country's first constitution was developed and shaped largely by two very different

This chapter is a modified version of an article that appeared in the *Virginia Journal of International Law* in the spring of 2013. I thank the editors for granting permission to adopt portions of the article for this volume.; I thank Denis Galligan, Tom Ginsburg, Jason Gluck, Mark Fathi Massoud, David Stewart, Susan Stigant, Mila Versteeg, and Don Wallace for their helpful comments. I also received valuable feedback from participants at the University of Oxford Foundation for Law, Justice and Society December 2011 workshop, the June 2012 Law and Society Association Annual Conference in Honolulu, and the Willamette University College of Law Symposium in February 2012. Finally, I thank the activists, scholars, government officials, and past and present public officials cited later – anonymously and by name – whom I interviewed while researching for this chapter.

influences: international constitutional models and the political priorities of leaders within the dominant domestic party. It is unsurprising that an important political process would lack meaningful, broad public participation in a country whose parent is notorious for its autocratic rule and abysmal human rights (Galligan 2013). But what makes South Sudan's constitution noteworthy is its dualistic structure. That is, the two influences – international models and domestic politics – primarily operated on one of the constitution's two discrete components, namely, the bill of rights and the structural provisions, respectively. With a few key exceptions, the bill of rights replicates an international template reflecting an emerging global consensus on human rights. In many ways, it resembles recently enacted constitutions of countries such as South Africa, Brazil, Turkey, and Finland. In contrast, the document's structural provisions, although certainly not untouched by external influence, have largely been crafted to advance the priorities of the drafters. Some of these provisions flout both democratic and liberal values, making them quite incongruous with the structural provisions of model democratic countries, such as South Africa, Canada, and Germany (Law and Versteeg 2012). Because of this arrangement, domestic officials and participating foreign consultants can point to their successes in helping codify important human rights, while party and government officials enjoy the fruits of their structural power play.

This chapter proceeds in three parts. It first gives a brief overview of two sets of theories on influences of constitution-making. It then details the origins of the new nation of South Sudan and its interim and transitional constitutions. Finally, it sets forth the dualistic nature of the South Sudan constitution, focusing on the transnational bill of rights and the reasons for indigenousness and self-dealing in the constitution's structural provisions.

11.2 CONSTITUTIONAL DIFFUSION, TRANSNATIONALISM, AND INSTITUTIONAL SELF-DEALING

That international and domestic influences coexist in one constitution is hardly self-evident. In fact, much of the constitution-making scholarship to date attempts to characterize constitutions as either the mass products of external, international forces (Law and Versteeg 2011) or, alternatively, as reflecting either the nation's citizens' unique values and interests or indigenous national politics (Jacobson 2011). Two sets of phenomena commonly underlie these two viewpoints: constitutional diffusion and transnationalism on one hand, and institutional self-dealing on the other.

First, it is commonly and traditionally believed that constitutions should, and often do, reflect the unique values of the societies they govern (Elkins et al. 2009: 38; ButleRitchie 2004: 38–39), although more recent research (as described in Chapter 4 of this volume) suggests that constitutions are increasingly homogenous, transnational documents that instead reflect international norms (Goderis and Versteeg 2013).[1] The social sciences have long embraced the concept of *policy diffusion*, or the process by which substantive norms move across national borders. That principle has recently been applied to constitutional norms; substantive explanations for why constitutions are transnational are often characterized by a phenomenon called *constitutional diffusion*. Another perspective of constitutional transnationalism examines the role of transnational actors in constitutional processes (Goderis and Versteeg's contribution to this volume). This view takes account of the various pathways for transnationalism, including fraternization among lawyers and government officials at universities and international conferences, activist foreign consultants, and drafters spontaneously choosing to mimic existing constitutional approaches.

In contrast to constitutional diffusion and transnational actor perspectives, another view, *institutional self-dealing*, focuses on how constitutions are shaped by the institutional interests of domestic drafters (Ginsburg et al. 2009). The institutional self-dealing view thus presents a perspective on constitutional influence quite different from that of transnational constitutionalism or the transnational actor approach. Each set of theories offers important insights, but at least initially, they would appear to be incompatible.

The South Sudan experience shows otherwise. Under South Sudan's dualistic constitution, transnational constitutionalism and self-dealing theories exist side by side. How and why this phenomenon materialized in South Sudan is explored in the rest of this chapter. To understand better how the concepts of diffusion and self-dealing simultaneously give rise to a transnational rights and a local power structure in South Sudan, we first turn to the history of Sudan and South Sudan, including the events giving rise to the current South Sudanese constitution.

11.3 SOUTHERN SUDAN: KUSH TO INDEPENDENCE

11.3.1 *Colonization and Civil War*

Modern-day Sudan and South Sudan find their origins to the Kingdom of Kush, an ancient Nubian state centered on the Blue Nile, the White Nile, and the River Atbara. Around 540 AD, a Byzantine Christian missionary traveled to Nubia,

---

[1] While empirical studies show that bills of rights are shaped by transnational influences, only limited evidence exists suggesting that this phenomenon occurs for institutional or structural provisions. Compare Benedikt Goderis and Mila Versteeg, *The Transnational Origins of Constitutions: An Empirical Analysis* (2011) (finding empirical evidence of rights diffusion), with Tom Ginsburg and Mila Versteeg, *Why Do Countries Adopt Constitutional Review?* (2013).

in present-day northern Sudan, to spread the gospel. The widespread practice of Christianity quickly followed. A century later, Islam began to diffuse south through the region from Egypt. Explorers from Belgium had colonized much of the region in 1896, and pursuant to a Belgian-British bilateral agreement, Belgium turned the region over to Great Britain in 1909. From 1899 until 1956, Sudan was a condominium of the United Kingdom and Egypt (which was itself a British protectorate until 1922).

Soldier mutinies in 1955 helped convince the British that they could no longer control the region, and in 1956, Sudan attained independence from Egypt and the United Kingdom, becoming the first British territory to do so after World War II. The process was not entirely amicable; it has been argued that rather than being achieved "by a national consensus expressed through constitutional means," Sudan's independence was "thrust upon" the Sudanese before they had agreed on a constitution, structure of government, or were otherwise prepared for it. One commentator has argued that Sudan's independence process set a "precedent" that has "haunted Sudanese politics ever since," that is, "taking the popular will for granted, and therefore circumventing agreed legal procedures in all major constitutional issues." Through this process, it has been suggested, the Sudanese "learned from Britain at the very inception of the Sudan's independence the rewards for ignoring democratic and constitutional procedures" (Johnson 2003: 30).

At independence, the two major parties had initially been unable to agree on the nature of the new state, and Sudan's first constitution was a transitional document drafted by a British constitutional expert in a process comparable to that of the Nigerian independence constitution (Parkinson 2013). Less than a year before its independence, political and cultural tensions between the tribes of the northern and southern regions had erupted into what is now known as the First Sudanese Civil War (or Anyanya rebellion), a conflict that lasted eighteen years (O'Ballance 1977). In 1972, the Southern Sudan Liberation Movement – then the dominant Southern Sudan political party – and the Khartoum government signed the Addis Ababa peace agreement, ending the civil war and recognizing the "historical, cultural, and economic differences" between northern and southern Sudan (Murray and Maywald 2006: 1206). An uneasy peace followed. That peace was shattered in 1983 when the government imposed Shari'a law throughout the country, triggering the Second Sudanese Civil War. In fact, the period of peace was so tenuous that some regard the first and second civil wars as a single, continuous fifty-one-year conflict. Over the subsequent twenty-two years, the war was responsible for the death of an estimated two million people, the most of any civil war in world history (U.S. Committee for Refugees 2001).

11.3.2 *The Modern Schism*

Africa's longest civil war was rooted in a host of cultural and economic disputes, but arguably, two were paramount: (1) economic marginalization of the Sudanese periphery, including Southern Sudan; and (2) imposition of Northern, norm-based values and policy on the South (Johnson 2003). These power plays were facilitated in part by Sudan's long history of authoritarian, one-party-dominated government. Throughout the war, Southern leaders charged that the National Congress Party (NCP)-controlled Sudanese government was exploiting the South's national resources – meaning, essentially, its oil, which accounted for three-quarters of the country's GDP (Ahmed 2009: 140) – and otherwise denying economic opportunity to the South (Antwi-Boateng and O'Mahoney 2008: 149–150). For instance, to lock down oil resources, the Sudanese government used tribal militias to secure oil fields that were marked for exploration by transnational companies. With implicit government approval, these militias displaced local communities in favor of new settlers. Southern leaders also complained that the Sudanese government had focused its development plans on the capital Khartoum and central Sudan, ignoring the rest of the country (Wassara 2010: 259–260).

Arguably, political and cultural issues were comparably divisive. The nationalist Sudanese movements that replaced Sudan's colonial powers developed nationwide policies based largely on both race and religion (Wassara 2010: 259). Since (and perhaps prior to) Sudan's independence, Northern leaders marginalized the South politically and rejected Southern leaders' demands for greater autonomy (Dagne 2011: 15). In a 1989 coup, Colonel-turned-President Omar al-Bashir rose to the Sudanese presidency, and in the early 1990s, his military government imposed nationwide Shari'a. This move sparked the emergence of the (Southern) Sudanese People's Liberation Movement (SPLM), a Southern Sudan-based opposition party (Sidahmed and Soderlund 2008: 80). Through the 1990s, the South's sense of alienation increased, strengthening the SPLM's political hand (U.S. Department of State 2011). Sudan's one-party government further exacerbated the schism by, according to some critics, "excluding voices of mediation and opposition" (Antwi-Boateng and O'Mahoney 2008: 137).

Consistent with this approach, the NCP, influenced by the growing Islamist political organization, the National Islamic Front (NIF), began to view either total Islamization or total military victory as the only palatable options for resolving the north-south conflict (Ahmed 2009: 140, n. 13). President Bashir escalated the Islamization policy that his predecessor had begun (Lango and Patterson 2010: 121). That policy included, among other things, removing nearly all non-Muslims from political, military, and judicial office, and subjecting both Muslims and non-Muslims to severe, Islam-based punishments for violations of Shari'a

(Pimental 2010:11). Such hard-line, religion-charged policies were chief among the reasons why Sudan ultimately failed either to achieve cultural accord or to maintain political unity. These human rights abuses, along with the Darfur genocide in the early 2000s, helped draw negative international attention to the country, its government, and its domestic policies (Ahmed 2009: 140, n. 13).

Although national actors had been working toward a negotiated end to the second civil war since the late 1980s, those efforts did not bear fruit until 2002, when, with the aid of various external groups, the two sides began the productive negotiations that would lead to Sudan's Comprehensive Peace Agreement (CPA) (Dann 2006: 443). Given the extent of the north-south rift, the SPLM would agree to a cessation of hostilities only with the promise of an opportunity for independence. The CPA provided that promise.

11.3.3 *The Comprehensive Peace Agreement*

The CPA came about only after the SPLM and government of Sudan had reached a military impasse in the war, and the cost of continuing the conflict was beginning to outweigh the likely benefits to the North of consolidating power, even were it to eventually achieve victory (Dann 2006: 443). In that sense, the NCP and SPLM's goals partially aligned, allowing for productive negotiations between the two. The NCP hoped to maintain its grip on the North, and the SPLM hoped to secure an autonomous, secular state in the South. As the parties came to terms with the fact that military victory was not soon viable, they also came to embrace the possibility of a negotiated peace (Ahmed 2009: 136, 144).

Military calculations were not the only forces bringing the parties to the negotiating table. For example, the NCP faced significant international pressure to negotiate, in particular from the United States. When the NIF-driven Bashir government began reaching out to terrorist organizations like Egyptian Islamic Jihad in the 1990s, Sudan's international image deteriorated. In the early 2000s, the handling of the Darfur crisis further embarrassed the Sudanese government. In 2008, the International Criminal Court indicted Bashir for genocide, crimes against humanity, and war crimes in Darfur. In essence, ending the Second Civil War presented an opportunity to begin restoring the image of both the regime and the country. In addition, the NCP's religious authority was called into doubt internally after party leaders removed influential Islamist leader Hassan al-Turabi from power. The NCP's willingness to negotiate may have also reflected its desire for internal legitimacy and credibility (Ahmed 2009: 136).

The SPLM also faced external and internal pressure to negotiate. In the early 2000s, the group's military wing, the Sudanese People's Liberation Army (SPLA), lost several bases in Ethiopia to rebels backed by the Sudanese government. As neighboring countries increasingly pressured the sides for peace, the SPLM realized that its campaign would eventually become impracticable (Ahmed 2009: 134, 136; Antwi-Boateng and O'Mahoney 2008: 134). In addition, an internal schism in the SPLM between advocates of secession and those favoring a unified Sudan (Ahmed 2009: 136) turned violent, producing more casualties in the 1990s than the Second Civil War during the same period (Antwi-Boateng and O'Mahoney 2008: 134).

Once the parties began the peace talks leading to the CPA, the international presence only intensified. Negotiated from 2002 to 2004 and signed in January 2005, the CPA is a series of bilateral protocols between the SPLM and the NCP, prepared with the assistance of numerous nongovernmental organizations (NGOs), intergovernmental organizations (IGOs), and individual government-sponsored consultant groups (Nouwen 2007: 144). For the drafting of the CPA, three types of foreign entities were involved: (1) an IGO; (2) representatives of foreign states; and (3) foreign and international NGOs. The Intergovernmental Authority on Development, a consortium of states including Djibouti, Ethiopia, Kenya, Somalia, Sudan, Uganda, and Eritrea, organized the negotiations. The negotiations were funded by Italy, Norway, the United Kingdom, and the United States. A variety of other foreign and international actors, such as a UN representative and the Max Planck Institute for Comparative Public Law and International Law, participated directly in drafting the accord. Domestically, the NCP and SPLM dominated the talks; there was essentially no participation from either Northern Sudanese or Southern Sudanese indigenous opposition parties (Murray and Maywald 2006: 1205; Nouwen 2007: 114, 120; Dann 2006: 445, 446).

Although international actors participated in the CPA's drafting, it appears that midway through the negotiations, the SPLM and NCP began to rebuff their influence. Some in the international community – particularly the Western countries – appear to have overplayed their diplomatic hand, diminishing their opportunity to influence some terms of the agreement. Initially, these international parties dominated the discussion, pushing their respective agendas onto the talks with a pro-South slant (Dann 2006: 446). Once this influence was revealed more widely, however, some party officials criticized the international mediators, and the two negotiating parties "took ownership of their agreement, pushing back influence of external resource persons and observers" (Nouwen 2007: 120). However, the Intergovernmental Authority on Development and observer countries continued to play two important roles: "firstly to keep the parties at the negotiating table" and secondly to "exert enough pressure to prevent a breakdown of the talks" (Dann 2006: 446).

The key purpose of the agreement was to provide greater autonomy to the South and an option for full independence. The CPA's provisions giving Southern Sudan meaningful autonomy – in other words, a government that was decentralized and federalistic – and a chance for total sovereignty after six years were central to the agreement and were crucial to achieving peace (Antwi-Boateng and O'Mahoney 2008: 141). In that sense, the CPA does much more than set forth the military and political terms of a negotiated peace; it redefines key aspects of government. In fact, some commentators have characterized the CPA as a compromise intended primarily to secure political power for the two groups – the SPLM and NCP – who negotiated it (Antwi-Boateng and O'Mahoney 2008: 134).

Recognizing the political, cultural, social, and economic disputes that fueled the conflict, the CPA attempts to resolve the primary disagreements over each of those issues (Nouwen 2007: 2). As such, the CPA comprises eight protocols, including, among other things, provisions for conflict resolution, wealth sharing, and power sharing between the government of Sudan and a semiautonomous Southern Sudan. Disputes over oil allocation were central to the schism, and an entire CPA protocol (Chapter III) is devoted to distribution of natural resources and their resulting revenue. The protocol's oil-revenue-sharing agreement was crucial to the agreement, as it marked the Sudanese government's first recognition that the Southern Sudanese people had a legal right to the oil within Southern Sudan (Antwi-Boateng and O'Mahoney 2008: 146).

The last protocol, the Protocol on Power Sharing (Chapter II of the CPA), sets forth the parameters for both a new nationwide Interim Constitution of Sudan and a Southern Sudan regional constitution. The Protocol on Power Sharing recognizes both "the sovereignty of the nation as vested in its people" and the "need for autonomy for the Government of Southern Sudan and States throughout the Sudan." The protocol provides for the adoption of a separate constitution for Southern Sudan, which was required to comply with the terms of Sudan's yet-to-be-written Interim National Constitution. It emphasizes nationwide decentralization, specifying that "[t]here shall be a decentralized system of government with significant devolution of powers, having regard to the National, Southern Sudan, State, and Local levels of government."

The CPA may not have been intended as a constitution itself, but the founders envisioned that it would form the template for the new Sudanese constitution (Antwi-Boateng and O'Mahoney 2008: 134). Like a constitution, the Protocol on Power Sharing contains a bill of rights, entitled "Human Rights and Fundamental Freedoms." According to a former high-ranking diplomat who was privy to the process, that section was drafted primarily by the Intergovernmental Authority on Development Secretariat for Peace in Sudan, sponsored by the U.S. State Department, with an American legal advisor, Susan Page, leading the effort. Moreover, the provisions were not developed specially for the CPA; they were "cut and pasted from international conventions." In fact, these provisions were largely taken directly from treaties to which Sudan was already a signatory, and as such, there was little or no debate among the Sudanese over their inclusion. Reportedly, it was generally expected by those involved in the process that these same provisions would be transferred directly into Sudan's new 2005 Interim National Constitution.

The protocol lists "[t]he rights and freedoms to be enjoyed under Sudanese law," and explicitly incorporates rights from various international treaties. For example, the document guarantees that "[a]ll persons are equal before the law and are entitled without any discrimination to the equal protection of the law." It also states that "[n]o one shall be subjected to torture or to cruel, inhuman or degrading treatment or punishment." The protocol references international human rights treaties throughout, stating that "[t]he equal right of men and women to the enjoyment of all civil and political rights set forth in the International Covenant on Civil and Political Rights ... shall be ensured." According to an official at the National Democratic Institute (a U.S. organization acting in cooperation with the United States Agency for International Development (USAID)), the SPLM representatives were eager to see these rights enshrined in the CPA, as they saw them as some measure of protection from continued imposition of Northern cultural norms. As a result, even before work on the Interim Constitution of Southern Sudan began in August 2005, the CPA and the Republic of Sudan's Interim National Constitution (which together provided the framework for Southern Sudan's Interim Constitution) had already resolved the most important political issues (Murray and Maywald 2006: 1213, n. 44). According to USAID, "[i]n many ways, the constitutional process used by Southern Sudan is a model for transitional democracies" (USAID 2011).

After the CPA's signing but before work on an interim constitution began, Southern Sudan President John Garang was killed in a helicopter crash returning from a meeting in Uganda with Yoweri Museveni. Vice President of Southern Sudan Salva Kiir Mayadit (Vice President Kiir) assumed the presidency. A veteran of the Second Civil War, Kiir enjoyed overwhelming support among Southern Sudanese (*Sudan Tribune* 2010).

11.3.4 *The 2005 Interim Constitution of Southern Sudan*

Work on the Interim Constitution began when a technical committee met in Rumbek, Southern Sudan, to begin the drafting process soon after the Republic of Sudan's National Legislative Assembly adopted the Interim National Constitution. Over the course of approximately three weeks, the technical committee worked to produce a draft, which was given to a forty-member drafting committee appointed by President Kiir. The drafting committee comprised twenty-eight members of the SPLM, six members of the NCP, and six representatives from other parties. It spent three weeks reviewing the technical committee's draft, though it made few substantive changes (USAID 2011). The resulting draft consisted of 16 parts, comprising 116 pages. The document establishes a federalist system with significant decentralization: it provides for meaningful state-government autonomy, including powerful independent state governors and state courts. Equally important, it enumerates twenty-five individual human and civil rights.

Like the process leading to the CPA, the 2005 Interim Constitution was created under international scrutiny: as with the CPA, a cadre of international observers and interveners descended on the process. The National Democratic Institute provided technical assistance in the drafting process. The European Union funded the German Max Planck Institute for Comparative Public Law and International Law to act on its behalf (Steinitz 2009: 219–220). The Southern Sudan Constitutional Technical Drafting Committee also received assistance from Sudanese Civil Society (Murray and Maywald 2006: 1213, n. 44). The U.S. law firm Latham & Watkins represented the SPLM throughout the process on a pro bono basis (Steinitz 2009: 219–220).

Although the 2005 process was subject to input from interested parties around the world (Ajawin 2005: 6), reports on the degree of the specific groups' substantive impact are mixed (Nouwen 2007: 120; Dann 2006: 446). On one hand, it is reported that certain of these groups provided drafts for consideration by the committee, but that those drafts were ultimately rejected as models, with the committee choosing to adhere more closely to the language of Sudan's Interim National Constitution for many provisions (Murray and Maywald 2006: 1213, n. 44). (The bill of rights of that document was itself modeled on the CPA's power-sharing protocol.) On the other hand, the Max Planck Institute reports that it drafted the initial version of the 2005 constitution, and that it later conducted a series of workshops that attempted to refine that draft (MPIL 2012).[2] Three of these workshops were reportedly held with SPLM lawyers, with the rest conducted with South Sudanese lawyers from other groups (USAID 2011). Each workshop prepared proposals, which were then negotiated among all parties. Max Planck reportedly "reviewed the output of the Southern Sudanese constitutional drafting committee for compatibility with the [Interim National Constitution] before its final reading in September 2005," and that the assembly "adopted most of the suggestions the [Institute] gave" (MPIL 2012).

One of the foreign entities, the National Democratic Institute (NDI), also notes that its representatives may have influenced the bill of rights by encouraging the addition of certain key provisions. According to an NDI official, that group's mission is to assist the *process* of constitution-making, not to push for specific substantive

---

[2] The English-language version of the report characterizes its contribution as the "elaboration" of a draft version, but the German-language version of the report states that its contribution was the "Erarbeitung" of a draft version, and that it "erarbeitete" the 2005 draft. The better English translations of these German terms appears to be "drafting" and "drafted," respectively.

constitutional provisions. According to USAID, however, NDI "made procedural and substantive contributions throughout the entire process" (USAID 2011). USAID further reports that NDI may have substantively influenced the Interim Constitution in several ways, among them the inclusion of a provision for separation of church and state, a gender-based affirmative action provision, and a provision for a right of access to information. Acknowledging that "it is always difficult to demonstrate 'cause and effect,'" USAID lists several provisions and areas of the Constitution "where NDI's comments and suggestions directly influenced the draft constitution, both in concept and in language" (USAID 2011). Of the eight contributions to the 2005 document that USAID highlights, seven of them concern individual rights (with the eighth addressing the 2011 independence referendum) (USAID 2011). Notably, USAID's announcement says nothing about NDI's helping to shape any of the constitution's structural provisions.

Indeed, the 2005 bill of rights does add various rights to the CPA's list, including sections on the right to found a family, the rights of women, the "right to litigation," the right to own property, the right to education, and the rights of access to information, among others. But a comparison of the two documents reveals that the bulk of the 2005 bill of rights comes essentially verbatim from the CPA's list of Human Rights and Fundamental Freedoms. After all, the 2005 Interim Constitution borrowed its rights provisions heavily from the 2005 CPA, which, as discussed, "reads more like a constitution than like a peace treaty." In essence, "the 'real' constitution-making" in 2005 took place "in the guise of peace talks" leading to the CPA (Dann 2006: 447–448).

In addition to enumerating rights, the Interim Constitution also anticipates and provides the road map for possible Southern Sudanese secession from (or continued unity with) the Republic of Sudan. Article 208(7) states that "[i]f the outcome of the referendum on self-determination favours secession, this Constitution shall remain in force as the Constitution of a sovereign and independent Southern Sudan, and the parts, chapters, articles, sub-articles and schedules of this Constitution that provide for [Republic of Sudan] national institutions, representation, rights and obligations shall be deemed to have been duly repealed." Had Southern Sudan remained part of Sudan, the region would have continued to enjoy a large measure of autonomy, including the right to its own subnational constitution.

Pursuant to that provision, in October 2010, an All-Southern Sudanese Political Parties Conference was held in Juba. Titled "Southern Sudanese united for a free, fair, transparent and peaceful referendum," its purpose was to "build consensus" on the upcoming independence referendum. According to a conference final *communiqué*, twenty political parties participated. The conference produced a series of resolutions, including several provisions that would take effect should the referendum result in independence (All-Southern Sudanese Political Parties Conference 2010).

11.3.5 *The 2011 Transitional Constitution of South Sudan*

On January 21, 2011, following the overwhelming vote for independence, President Kiir (who had been reelected in an April 2010 landslide) appointed a "Technical Committee" to review the 2005 Interim Constitution. The president chiefly charged the committee with converting the Interim Constitution into one appropriate for an independent state.[3] The 2011 Transitional Constitution of South Sudan was adopted in July 2011 and, as of June 2013, remained in force while discussions continued on how to approach the drafting of the next version.

According to the United Nations Mission in Sudan, the mandate of the 2011 transitional revision process was to remove references to a united Sudan and "re-cast existing government structures in the south at a regional level as the institutions of a sovereign nation-state" (Miday 2011: 7). Developing these structural changes proved less straightforward than the mandate suggested. This process was complicated by, among other things, the fact that members of the Republic of Sudan's National Legislature who hailed from the South were now without jobs, and many aspired to continued lawmaking roles in the new South Sudan government (Miday 2011: 7; International Crisis Group 2011).

The 2011 Technical Committee was initially chaired by Legal Affairs and Constitutional Development Minister (and SPLM member) John Luk Jok. The committee contained twenty members and four observers and comprised various experts, including attorneys and other technocrats. Despite the October 2010 conference resolution's calling for an "all party constitutional conference" (All-Southern Sudanese Political Parties Conference 2010), initially, nineteen of the twenty committee members, including the chair, were SPLM members. Protesting this composition, the single non-SPLM member initially boycotted the committee. Responding to complaints about its political homogeneity, in February 2011, President Kiir signed a second order adding eleven additional seats for opposition parties, as well as two for the Council of Churches and one for Muslim contingents, for a total of fourteen new members. This move substantially tilted the committee's balance of power, as more than 40 percent were now non-SPLM members. In response to protests from his own party, the president later added seventeen more SPLM members. In turn, many non-SPLM members walked out of the process. The committee eventually began work, but its appointment process and composition engendered a backlash against Kiir and the SPLM (International Crisis Group 2011: 10–11).

---

[3] Presidential Decree no. 002/2011, Office of the President, Government of Southern Sudan, January 21, 2011 (creating a technical committee to review the Interim Constitution and mandating, among other things, that the committee present a final draft of a transitional constitution to the president no later than April 25, 2011).

Some domestic opposition groups protested the committee's political homogeneity and began plotting to circumvent the committee and contribute independently to the constitutional review process (International Crisis Group 2011: 10, n. 59). The SPLM responded that the committee's task was essentially technical, not political: it was, after all, charged only with transforming the 2005 constitution of a semiautonomous region into that of a sovereign nation, and therefore only technical changes were needed. According to USAID, "[a] sweeping overhaul of the existing constitution was never contemplated" at that stage (Miday 2011: 7). The SPLM also emphasized the importance of having a new constitution in place immediately after independence and insisted that the process to form the permanent constitution would include wider participation (International Crisis Group 2011: 10). But minority groups believed that inclusiveness should begin on the first day of independence, not a year or more later.

Some of these domestic groups who tried to participate in the revision process faced criticism that they were threatening national security and unity. During the transitional process, members of Southern Sudan's civil society, including women and disabled groups, advocated for provisions such as stronger affirmative action programs and protection of disabled rights. President Kiir condemned these groups, insisting that by proposing "alternative" constitutions to that being developed by the official Technical Committee, they were undermining national unity. Kiir characterized the groups' contributions as undermining what Southerners had fought for, and he implicitly likened these groups' advocacy to the actions of rebel militias then threatening violent overthrow of state governments.

As with the processes for the previous documents, foreign and international groups were conspicuously present. During the 2011 revision process, the Public International Law and Policy Group (PILPG), a "global pro bono law firm" based in Washington, DC, reportedly had the greatest access to that process, as it provided legal counsel directly to the SPLM (PILPG 2012). But other groups were also deeply involved. The Max Planck Institute brought several South Sudanese to Heidelberg in the spring of 2011 to begin developing a draft. Max Planck states that its Africa Team "invited South Sudanese stakeholders to a High Level Meeting of Legal Experts on the South Sudanese Constitutional Order ... in Heidelberg, Germany" in which various Southern Sudanese leaders "reviewed the Interim Constitution ... and discussed technical changes," after which "[t]he resulting document ... was personally presented to the Minister of Legal Affairs and Constitutional Development" before "[t]he proposal was internally discussed in the Technical Committee, and members of the Africa Team introduced it to" the Southern Sudan Legislative Assembly (MPIL 2012). NDI, the United States Institute of Peace, and the International Development Law Organization (IDLO) also supported the process. Indeed, the report of the 2011 committee thanks several international organizations.[4]

Whatever influence various stakeholder exerted on the prior documents' rights provisions appears to have carried over into the 2011 version now in force: only two provisions affecting individual rights changed between the 2005 and 2011 constitutions. First, because the 2005 document was subservient to the Sudanese Interim National Constitution, it named both Arabic and English as "official working languages," but Arabic was removed in the 2011 document. Second, unlike the 2005 document, the 2011 version does not explicitly proscribe implementation of a state religion, although it maintains that religion and state "shall be separate." The 2011 constitution adds procedural protections under the right to a fair trial, as well as a right to housing. Notably, these are both initiatives for which many international organizations, in some form or another, often advocate.

Thus, while it is impossible to determine with certainty the influence each of these groups respectively exerted on the final document, it is clear that every stage of the drafting process, from the CPA to the 2011 Interim Constitution, was performed under intense international scrutiny and with vigorous foreign involvement. And when those groups speak publicly about their influence, their claims deal primarily with individual rights. Empirically, the rights provisions show no meaningful change from 2005 to 2011 (although some Arabic speakers took exception to making English the sole official language). Comparing the four pertinent documents – the Human Rights and Fundamental Freedoms of the CPA, Interim Nation Constitution of Sudan, Interim Constitution of Southern Sudan, and Transitional Constitution of South Sudan – shows that the rights provisions transcended the four documents with very few changes, thereby preserving the CPA's internationally influenced bill of rights.

The structural provisions tell a different story. The SPLM-dominated committee made several key changes that, by design or accident, appear directly to benefit their members. First, the 2011 Transitional Constitution adds a second legislative chamber, creating a "council of states," thereby substantially expanding the national assembly. Even though some members of minority parties also benefitted from this change, one motivation for this move may have been to provide job opportunities for the (now-unemployed) former Southern members of Sudan's National Legislature. More important, the document rolls back decentralization. It has been suggested that decentralization was a futile goal from the start, given the states' lack of means for generating tax or other revenue. But decentralization also benefited members of

⁴ *Report of the Technical Committee to Review the Interim Constitution of Southern Sudan, 2005* (April 2011) (thanking USAID, IDLO, NDI, Max Planck Institute, PILPG, USIP, United Nations Development Programme [UNDP], and United Nations Mission in Sudan [UNMIS]).

the central party leadership, where SPLM hegemony is greatest. The Transitional Constitution places all public attorneys under national control and eliminates state-level courts, thereby nationalizing the entire national judiciary. It also gives the president the power to dissolve both state councils and the National Legislature and to dismiss state governors during any (presidentially determined and initiated) "state of emergency." During a state of emergency, the president may suspend most parts of the bill of rights and may take any measure "deemed necessary," which "shall have the force of law." The president may, "by law or orders, take any measures … as provided herein: … to dissolve or suspend any of the state organs or suspend such powers conferred upon the states under this Constitution." The basis for a state of emergency can include, for example, a natural disaster, an epidemic, or "imminent danger" to the "economy" of any part of the country. (South Sudan lives under near-perpetual threat from both invasion and epidemic.) The revisions also remove the role of the legislature in dismissing federal justices, arguably giving the president unilateral authority to remove justices (i.e., members of the Supreme Court) for bases that include not just gross misconduct and incapacity, but also "incompetence."

In total, the 2011 revision process's lack of inclusiveness and under-the-radar structural power shifts proved a political debacle that provoked widespread public anger at the Kiir administration; after the initial committee-composition controversy, "the [political] damage was done and opposition suspicions reinforced." It raised public doubts about whether the new nation's government would be transparent, inclusive, or truly democratic (International Crisis Group 2011: 10). It also demonstrated the SPLM's willingness to concede to additional human rights while altering government structures in ways that would yield future political gains: in other words, to self-deal institutional power to its most prominent members, including its president.

11.4 GLOBAL CONSTITUTIONALISM MEETS LOCAL STRUCTURALISM

The ten-year constitution-making process in Sudan and South/ern Sudan was an international affair, as a confluence of external actors and national elites played a role. All three governing documents – the CPA, 2005 Interim Constitution, and 2011 Transitional Constitution – were created under an international magnifying glass, with representatives from interested foreign-aid organizations, government-funded agencies, and intergovernmental alliances all involved in supervising, providing consultation to NCP and SPLM officials, and drafting some of the provisions themselves.

But foreign influence (whatever its form) touched the two different parts of the constitution – the bill of rights and structural provisions – in two different ways. With just a few exceptions, the 2011 constitution's bill of rights is very much of an international template. It closely resembles the corresponding rights provisions of many Sub-Saharan African documents, recently adopted bills of rights, and international treaties, especially the African Charter on Human and Peoples' Rights. The structural provisions, on the other hand, bear several marks of South Sudanese power politics and self-dealing. They (like the bill of rights) originated from the early 2000s negotiations between the two dominant factions: the SPLM and Khartoum-based NCP. Although the 2011 revision process had relatively little effect on the human rights provisions, it noticeably altered the character of the structural provisions: not only did it recast what had been subnational structures within Southern Sudan into national ones within a new South Sudanese state, it altered power within the country, shifting authority both to the new South Sudanese state executive and to the entire central government, expanding opportunities in the central government while removing positions in the state governments. Thus, while the 2011 bill of rights remains comparatively internationalist and transnational, the institutional provisions bear the stamp of local power politics. The result has produced a two-part constitution that embodies sets of values from two distinct sources.

11.4.1 *The Transnational Bill of Rights*

Transnational diffusion can take several procedural pathways, and active advice from foreign consultants is just one of them. As Paul Brady notes in his contribution to this volume (Chapter 10), constitutional drafters often look to foreign models, with or without the help of outsiders (see also Howard 1996: 402). Thanks in part to modern communication systems, including the Internet, and to the relative ease of international travel and information sharing, South Sudan's constitution-drafters were likely keenly aware of the contents of constitutions throughout the world. They were also undoubtedly aware of the ramifications for those countries and their governments of choosing the various models available to them. For the reasons explained in this section, the availability of these information channels surely eased the process of constitutional diffusion.

This international effect can be seen in more than just the tales from those who participated. When using other documents as models, strikingly similar constitutional products can result. To some degree, this phenomenon can be measured empirically, and in South Sudan, a quantitative comparison of the Transitional Constitution's rights provisions with those of the world's constitutions and various international rights treaties shows an internationally modeled document.

In earlier related work, I compared systematically the rights-related content of the South Sudanese constitution with that of the constitutions of the rest of the world (Cope 2013). This analysis yields several important insights that lend support to the notion that the bill of rights was shaped by transnational influences. Three

TABLE 11.1. *The 2006 Constitutions' Rights Provisions Most Similar to South Sudan's 2011 Provisions*

Country	Similarity Rank
Sudan	1
Niger	2
Dem. Rep./Congo	3
Togo	4
Benin	5
Sao Tome & Principe	6
Spain	7
South Africa	8
Burundi	9
Cameroon	10
Serbia and Montenegro	11
Eritrea	12
Gambia	13

observations stand out: (1) the bill of rights is highly typical among global constitutions and similar to the African Charter on Human and People's Rights; (2) the bill of rights is more similar to bill of rights of Sub-Saharan Africa than to those of the rest of the world; (3) the bill of rights is more similar to constitutions of younger nations than of older ones.

Demonstrating the second observation, Table 11.1 shows the similarity indexes of the South Sudanese bill of rights to other bills of rights. The bill of rights that is most similar to that of South Sudan is the constitution of its mother country, the Republic of Sudan. This fact merits reflection: from one perspective, it is surprising that the centuries-old value schisms that partially fueled the Sudanese civil wars, and eventually separation, did not manifest themselves in meaningfully different rights provisions in the two nations' governing documents. That they did not is one example of the power of human rights' transnationalism. The international template (i.e., the CPA's international treaty-derived rights provisions, the parent of both the Transitional Constitution and Sudan's Interim National Constitution) appears to have trumped any cultural or ideological differences that might have given rise to a different set of rights.

The next five closest cousins of the South Sudan constitution include Niger, the Republic of the Congo, Togo, Benin, and Sao Tome and Principe, all of which are located in Sub-Saharan Africa. In fact, of the thirteen most similar constitutions, eleven are those of Sub-Saharan African nations.

These relationships do not establish the cause for the South Sudan constitution's rights provisions' international character, but they do bolster the respective notions that (1) South Sudan's human rights constitution follows patterns that were gleaned from a recently emerging international template; and (2) those provisions are most likely to emerge in developing countries (which are, perhaps, in relatively weak positions to refuse international pressure, and thus more susceptible to that international template). In aggregate, the correlations suggest strongly that the South Sudan constitutional human rights provisions are, at least in part, an international product.

The finding that South Sudan's bill of rights bears an international character begs the questions: what processes facilitated this diffusion, and, perhaps more interesting, *why* did it occur? Indeed, the processes responsible for diffusion are difficult to pinpoint. As discussed, there is mixed evidence of the extent to which foreign entities helped shape the various documents' rights provisions: some groups self-report their influence on these provisions, while other accounts suggest that the South Sudanese largely rebuffed outsiders' proposals.

This uncertainty highlights the importance of the distinction between process and substantive motivation. While the pathway for the international diffusion is unclear, the fact that diffusion occurred is indisputable, and the question of *why* it occurred – that is, what motivated the drafters to accept an international template bill of rights – is more susceptible of analysis. In short, the diffusion of internationally ubiquitous rights provisions into the CPA, through the Interim Constitution, and then into South Sudan's current constitution may have been a product of the drafters' making a series of simple, though perhaps unconscious, cost-benefit analyses. In light of the significant benefits and low costs involved for the Southern Sudanese drafters and political leaders, accepting a robust, rights-laden bill of rights entailed appreciable benefits without many costs. As such, those actors were strongly incentivized to adopt a rights model that was both consistent with an emerging regional trend and acceptable to the international community.

For several reasons, Sudan and South Sudan together are strategically important to much of the international community. There are numerous other tangible trade, security, and other diplomatic advantages to entering the good graces of the world's military and economic powers.[5] Conversely, adopting an international bill of rights also pays dividends for various stakeholders outside of South Sudan. It has been argued that the international human rights community – and most international human rights initiatives, including treaties – tend to focus more on individual humanitarian rights than on the intricacies of government structure. One key role of human rights groups is public "naming and shaming." Adherence to substantive rights protections, such as prohibition of torture or protection of free speech, captures the public's imagination more effectively than do issues like federalism and separation of powers. Enlisting public support for their causes is a key tool for

---

[5]   In South Sudan's case, China is likely the most relevant economic power outside the West: China is the Republic of Sudan's biggest trading partner, possessing a 40% share in Sudanese oil projects.

human rights organizations to both mobilize assistance and secure public/private funding. Assuming human rights groups disproportionately focused their attention on South Sudan's rights provisions as they had elsewhere, it is unsurprising to find their achieving greater progress in this area. In South Sudan's case, the focus of some key foreign consultants to the CPA drafting process appears to have been cultural and rights protection issues, such as curtailing the influence of Shari'a in both Southern Sudan and in the predominantly Islamic north (Dann 2006: 446).

The international rule-of-law community values incorporating human rights provisions, but adopting such provisions can also benefit domestic leaders. For the reasons discussed earlier, doing so can potentially placate international supporters. And by appeasing constituent interests through the provision of certain rights (such as gender equality and affirmative action), it can also buy leaders domestic political capital, as well as helping to legitimize the new government in the eyes of citizens.

Moreover, as Noah Feldman has observed in the case of Iraq and Afghanistan regarding international human rights treaties (Feldman 2005: 871–872), the constitutions of Sudan have been "ignored in the past"; the failure of leaders to respect written rights has been well documented over a number of years. A recent study shows that as of 2006, the then-unified Republic of Sudan exhibited the world's greatest disparity between the human rights its constitution promised and those its government delivered (Law and Versteeg 2013). In other words, written constitutional guarantees in Sudan have been comparatively meaningless. And although they struggled for decades against marginalization by the government of Sudan, the SPLM-affiliated constitutional founders are well acquainted with this Sudanese de jure/de facto rights schism: as historical accounts and recent empirical studies suggest, their primary experience with individual constitutional guarantees is that they do not meaningfully constrain government. Given the Sudanese government and its leaders' history of failing to uphold constitutional promises, the drafters could reasonably have assumed that the pattern would continue, such that incorporating international norms into the various documents would entail few real costs. If these Southern Sudanese leaders did view written rights largely as "cheap-talk," they may have been more willing to accept significant (nominal) constraints on their fledgling government.

As South Sudan was preparing for independence, a common refrain heard from Southern Sudanese citizens was, "I hope Juba doesn't become the next Khartoum." There was good reason for concern. The impressively comprehensive bill of rights has thus far proved little use to citizens, and perhaps even less of a burden on the government. For instance, the constitution guarantees that "[n]o person shall be subjected to torture or to cruel, inhuman or degrading treatment or punishment." Yet, in the year since its independence, the South Sudanese government and the SPLM have repeatedly engaged in politically motivated kidnappings, detentions, torture, and other rights abuses (U.S. Department of State 2011: 2). The constitution also provides that "[e]very citizen shall have the right to the freedom of expression," and that "[a]ll levels of government shall guarantee the freedom of the press and other media." But over the past year, activists who organized antigovernment protests or who criticized high-ranking officials were arrested and held for long periods – in some cases indefinitely – without trial or charges (U.S. Department of State 2011: 8). The constitution also provides for an independent judiciary. But according to the U.S. State Department, "civil courts were neither independent nor impartial" (U.S. Department of State 2011: 4). Finally, the Constitution guarantees every citizen the right to education, stating, "Education is a right for every citizen and all levels of government shall provide access to education without discrimination," and that "[a]ll levels of government shall promote education at all levels and shall ensure free and compulsory education at the primary level." Yet as Human Rights Watch reports, "[l]ess than half of primary school age children are in schools and only 16 percent of women are literate" (Human Rights Watch 2012). Similar gaps between constitutional guarantees and constitutional realties existed in prison conditions, health care, and other areas.

It appears, then, that government abuse of authority and citizens' lack of access to basic needs, which together made the Republic of Sudan one of the worst human rights offenders (and gave it the distinction of having the world's *most* "sham" constitution) (Law and Versteeg 2013) have continued in South Sudan. The Constitution's robust array of rights protecting free speech, bodily integrity, due process, and fair trial have not prevented officials from violently intimidating critics and political opponents, nor have they required government allocation of (perhaps virtually non-existent) resources to a basic judicial infrastructure, humane prison conditions, or the establishment of basic primary and secondary education. Thus far, these rights have created few consequential duties for the government of South Sudan.

11.4.2 *Self-Dealing in Constitutional Structure*

While the South Sudan bill of rights largely mirrors numerous other recent constitutions, the provisions that establish the structure of government found their own, more provincial way. Indeed, outside the human rights provisions, South Sudan's Transitional Constitution is in many ways uniquely South Sudanese. That identity starts trivially, with its preamble thanking "Almighty God for giving the people of South Sudan the wisdom and courage to determine their destiny and future through a free, transparent, and peaceful referendum in accordance with the provisions of the Comprehensive Peace Agreement." But a colorful preamble says little about the document's substance, and many of the structural provisions appear only to *undermine* the "the people['s]" aspirations to "determine their destiny" and much of which the bill of rights aspires to facilitate. Rather, many of the actual drafters, themselves mostly SPLM elites, appear to have taken advantage of their nation's new autonomy and of their role in that process in bending South Sudan's constitution to favor their political objectives.

Many who have lived in Sudan and studied its politics characterize the governance philosophy of Sudan's political leaders as a "my turn to eat" philosophy. Under this view, for the Sudandese political leadership, it is ousting incumbent leaders and securing positions of power for themselves (not, say, running the country more effectively) that primarily drives governing policies. In other words, the precedent of "taking the popular will for granted," of "circumventing agreed legal procedures in all major constitutional issues" (Johnson 2003: 30), established at its 1956 independence, has not yet been exorcized. This unfortunate philosophy is obviously not limited to Sudan, but it has markedly impacted law and policy in that country for several decades. And based on the recent observations of public corruption and human rights abuses, it appears that this philosophy may have continued in South Sudan.

Granted, much of the Transitional Constitution's structural sections do resemble the structural provisions of other modern democracies. For instance, the constitution establishes separation of powers between three branches of government and a nominally independent judiciary. But in other important ways, the document exposes self-dealing practices that are entirely inconsistent with key international standards such as limited government and checks and balances. As robust comparative data on constitutions' structural provisions are not widely available at present,[6] we must look elsewhere for evidence of structural influence and potential institutional self-dealing. The strongest evidence that South Sudan's constitutional structural provisions are products of the latter phenomenon is these provisions' evolution over the four documents, most notably between the 2005 Interim and 2011 Transitional Constitution. Specifically, even though the 2005 and 2011 constitutions are in many ways highly similar, a great many of the 2011 "Technical" Committee's changes consolidated power in the central government or executive and expanded the power of the government generally. So while South Sudan's bill of rights contains strong rights protections in many fields (in some cases implausibly so), the provisions addressing the powers mitigate those protections.

For instance, as mentioned, the president's powers include the abilities to suspend much of the bill of rights and to take any measures he "deem[s] necessary" upon a declared state of emergency, which can arise from as little as economic danger to some segment of the country. (The legislature can override the president's declared state of

---

[6] But see Comparative Constitutions Project, at http://www.comparativeconstitutions project.org (providing limited cross-sectional data on structural provisions).

emergency, but given that the president can dissolve the legislature upon declaration, it may not be around to do so.) It has been argued that the ongoing security crisis contributed to the adoption of these provisions, as SPLM central leaders felt threatened by militias – many of which are led by disgruntled members of the SPLM – and believed that the most effective device to manage these threats was the flexibility of an unrestrained executive. Some members of the Legislative Assembly suggested alternative options, including provisions like those contained in South Africa's constitution, a document that features several meaningful checks on presidential power. But SPLM defenders of President Kiir responded that such provisions were unnecessary. Kiir was "a good president," they argued, and would never abuse the authority.

The revisions also erode judicial checks on the executive. As mentioned, the president arguably has the power, unburdened by legislative consent, to dismiss the (nominally independent) national justices whenever he deems them "incompetent." In other countries, including the United States, judges with life tenure are frequently labeled "incompetent," sometimes by government officials, especially when those judges nullify popular – but unconstitutional or otherwise unlawful – government actions (Vanaskie 2001: 757–758; Currie 1998: 255).

As stated, the 2011 drafters also placed all public attorneys under national control and eliminated state-level courts. In addition, the 2011 document gives the president the unilateral power to dissolve state councils, dismiss state governors, and even dissolve the national legislature, pursuant to the state-of-emergency provision. And the constitution arguably provides that existing laws, even those at odds with the constitution, will remain in force until the legislature acts to repeal them, as it states, "All current Laws of Southern Sudan shall remain in force and all current institutions shall continue to perform their functions and duties, unless new actions are taken in accordance with the provisions of this Constitution." In essence, it appears that under the current constitution, the president of South Sudan can now (lawfully) render moot many of the rest of the constitution's hard-fought, internationally approved guarantees.

How did these regressive, potentially abusive provisions survive under such international scrutiny? With the SPLM firmly in control of the central government and the presidency, but with far less secure grip on local governments, the SPLM may have seen and seized a chance for an under-the-radar power grab. This move will affect many South Sudanese, but unsurprisingly, international organizations' public statements touting the groups' work on the 2011 constitution are largely silent on the issue. The success of these domestic self-dealing phenomena can be explained by reasons mirroring those that explained the transnational rights diffusion.

Some of the factors that contribute to a transnational bill of rights also help explain why the structural provisions are less transnational and more indigenous, or more precisely, self-dealt. Namely, the confluence of international focus on human rights and Sudan's "sham" constitution appear to have enabled those leaders to self-deal a structural power play. I posit that research showing that hegemonic political parties are less likely to adopt judicial review because they "anticipate successfully advancing their interests in the post-constitutional legislature" (Ginsburg and Versteeg 2013: 16) may apply in the case of constitutional self-dealing. In a nutshell, the broad, mostly unchecked executive power that emerged in the 2011 Transitional Constitution is not an international norm, and it most certainly was not suggested or endorsed by most foreign consultants. But it proved to be easy power: despite the international magnifying glass over the process, the drafters could implement it with few political costs.

As stated, it appears that the human rights movement, including international conventions, is comparatively focused less on structural provisions than on substantive humanitarian rights. If consultants and legal instruments are not particularly committed to a standardized constitutional structure, then it is unsurprising that constitutional adopters are unlikely to incorporate this aspect of constitutionalism. Because robust democratic regimes and other institutions that disperse power are not prerequisite to complying with international human rights treaties, human rights initiatives must de-emphasize democratic governmental structural provisions in favor of pushing enumerated substantive rights. With international focus away from structural provisions, domestic drafters have a freer hand to design systems that they expect will meet local goals, whether those are the goals of the nation, those of the government, the dominant political party, or the individual drafters. In that cynical sense, drafters' political cost-benefit analysis maximizes the impact of the international human rights focus phenomenon. When self-dealing would-be leaders have agreed to strong substantive rights protections that nominally limit the power of government vis-à-vis citizenry, avoiding structures that give teeth to those rights to the detriment of government power takes on increased importance.

Moreover, it seems that the extensive 2011 structural changes reflected what Southern leaders sought all along. These leaders always preferred a strong, centralized Southern Sudanese government, but in 2005, the South was interested in maximizing Southern Sudan's autonomy, which meant *de*centralization at the Sudanese national level. To realize this goal, however, the South had to give its lower orders of government – the states and localities – those rights it was demanding from the NCP and the government of Sudan. The Interim Constitution crystallized this phenomenon, stating that South Sudan "is composed of ten states governed on the basis of decentralization." Without this decentralized structure, it may have been more difficult for the South to argue credibly for a decentralized Sudan, a prerequisite to Southern Sudan's receiving a semiautonomous government. But after the vote for South Sudan's independence, Southern elites lost their political competition, and with it the incentive to maintain decentralization. With the international community relatively more concerned with human rights and freedom than with federalism

(Feldman 2005: 867), the SPLM-dominated committee had no compunction about restructuring the document in a politically beneficial way.

Finally, a variation of Tom Ginsburg's political insurance theory may apply to self-dealing in South Sudan (Ginsburg 2004). Ginsburg has proposed that politically dominant parties will be less likely to adopt judicial (or constitutional) review because they anticipate successfully advancing their agenda through political means, and they fear that judicial review could strengthen the hand of minority opposition parties. That theory has received some additional support in recent empirical research (Ginsburg and Versteeg 2013). The same logic may apply to dominant-party drafters avoiding structural mechanisms, such as limited government and a truly independent judiciary. These systems, like de jure judicial review, can bolster the power of minority parties, level the political playing field, and impose constraints on government vis-à-vis the citizens.

In South Sudan, the SPLM's political hegemony incentivized it to eschew structural mechanisms such as effective judicial review that would constrain power or facilitate meaningful rights enforcement. Given the party's relative political security and the overwhelming popularity of SPLM member Preisdent Kiir in particular, it would make political sense to concentrate power in the central government and toward the president and away from the judiciary. Especially given that Kiir was likely to serve as president for at least the remainder of the transitional period (until July 2015), and that he enjoys the trust of his fellow SPLM members, shifting extraordinary, unchecked power to the presidency may have been the best way for the SPLM to obtain political insurance. If the SPLM and its leaders could use these constitutional measures to *lawfully* usurp power from the opposition, they had no reason to resort to extralegal measures, which, given the current international scrutiny, could unnecessarily risk domestic and international political fallout.

The Transitional Constitution has presided over a longer transition than many had expected. South Sudan minority parties were eager to get written guarantees of a firm road map, especially after the 2011 "technical review" debacle, and they got one. At a lecture in Juba in March 2011, Mr. Jok said that work on a permanent constitution would begin after South Sudan obtained formal independence in July 2011. President Kiir pledged that "all walks of life" would be included in that process (Miday 2011: 7). Indeed, the Transitional Constitution spells out in the last provision an end date for the next, longer-term version. The National Constitutional Review Commission had until January 2013 to complete its initial draft, after which a presidentially appointed national constitutional conference was scheduled to review the draft for six months. Once approved, that version is scheduled to be presented to the National Legislature no later than May 2015, and it must be approved by the end of the transitional period on July 9, 2015.

But while the Transitional Constitution outlines a timetable for the drafting of the next version, thus far, the process has lagged far behind. Although the drafting process was to begin in January 2012, the Commission was only fully constituted in late spring 2012, as struggles over its political composition had delayed the process. As of August 2012, five of its sixty members had not yet been sworn in, and the commission had not yet met (Eragu 2012).

11.5 CONCLUSION

South Sudan is a critical study in constitution-making, in part, because the conditions surrounding the Transitional Constitution's creation are not unique in the world. The degree to which transnational rights are generally effective in practice is not clear, but as stated, some have argued that transnationally developed constitutional provisions tend to be less well received than indigenous, organically generated provisions. The constitution's impact is difficult to gauge, but early signs are not promising. In addition to the human rights and corruption detailed earlier in the chapter, the country faces continuing threats from the north: while South Sudan officials were working to redraft their constitution, tensions with the Republic of Sudan continued to flare. In February 2012, ongoing disputes over oil resources let President Bashir to announce that another war with the South was imminently possible.

As the political and economic conditions evolve over the coming years, the process will reveal much about the role of external pressures, international organizations, and domestic elites in modern constitution-making. More important for the South Sudanese, it will affect whether they can realize the high hopes of the January 2011 referendum and the lofty promises set forth in their nation's governing document.

REFERENCES

Ahmed, Einas 2009. 'The Comprehensive Peace Agreement and the Dynamics of Post-Conflict Political Partnership in Sudan', *African Spectrum* 44: 133.

Ajawin, Yoanes 2005. 'Southern Civil Society Participation in the Development of the South Sudan Constitution', in Africa Peace Forum, InterAfrica Group, Saferworld (eds.), *Enhancing Sudanese Civil Society Participation in Peace-Building*. http://www.saferworld.org.uk/smartweb/resources/view-resource/186.

Antwi-Boateng, Osman and O'Mahoney, Geraldine Maria 2008. 'A Framework for the Analysis of Peace Agreements and Lessons Learned: The Case of the Sudanese Comprehensive Peace Agreement', *Policy and Policy* 36: 132.

Brady, Paul 2013. 'Social, Political and Philosophical Foundations of the Irish Constitutional Order,' in Denis Galligan and Mila Versteeg (eds.), *Social and Political Foundations of Constitutions*. Cambridge: Cambridge University Press.

Bureau of Democracy, Human Rights & Labor, U.S. Dep't of State. 2012. 'South Sudan Country Report on Human Rights Practices for 2011'.

ButleRitchie, David T. 2004. 'Critiquing Modern Constitutionalism', *Appalachian Law Journal* 3: 37.

Cope, Kevin L. 2013. 'The Intermestic Constitution: Lessons From the World's Newest Nation', *Virginia Journal of International Law* 53.

Currie, David P. 1998. 'The Constitution in Congress: The Most Endangered Branch, 1801–1805', *Wake Forest Law Review* 33: 219.

Dagne, Ted 2011. 'Sudan: The Crisis in Darfur and Status of the North-South Peace Agreement', *Congressional Research Service* Rl 33574 20.

Dann, Al-Ali 2006. 'The Internationalized Pouvoir Constituant: Constitution-Making Under External Influence in Iraq, Sudan and East Timor', *Max Planck Y.B. of UN L.* 10: 423.

Elkins, Zachary, Ginsburg, Tom, and Melton, James. 2009. *The Endurance of National Constitutions*. Cambridge: Cambridge University Press.

Eltahir, Yasir Awad Abdalla 2010. 'Empowered Deliberative Democracy (EDD): A Start from the Bottom', in Grawert, Elke (ed.), *After The Comprehensive Peace Agreement in Sudan*. Rochester, NY: James Currey.

Eragu, Veronica, Panelist, at U.S. Institute of Peace, *Constitution-Making in the Two Sudans* (March 27, 2012).

'FACTBOX: Sudan Presidential Election Results', *Sudan Tribune*, April 27, 2010, http://www.sudantribune.com/spip.php?article34901.

Feldman, Noah 2005. 'Imposed Constitutionalism', *Connecticut Law Review.* 37: 857.

Final Communique – All-Southern Sudanese Political Parties Conference, 2010, http://www.southsudannewsagency.com/news/press-releases/all-southern-sudanese-political-parties-conference – final-communique.

Galligan, Denis 2013. 'The People, the Constitution, and the Idea of Representation', in Galligan, Denis and Versteeg, Mila (eds.). *Social and Political Foundations of Constitutions*. Cambridge: Cambridge University Press.

Ginsburg, Tom 2004. *Judicial Review in New Democracies: Constitutional Courts in Asian Cases*. Cambridge: Cambridge University Press.

Ginsburg, Tom, Elkins, Zachary, and Blount, Justin 2009, 'Does the Process of Constitution-Making Matter?', *Annual Review of Law and Society* 5: 201.

Ginsburg, Tom and Versteeg, Mila 2013. 'Why do Countries Adopt Constitutional Review?', *UCLA Law Review*.

Goderis, Benedikt and Versteeg, Mila 2013. 'Transnational constitutionalism: A conceptual framework', in Galligan, Denis and Versteeg, Mila (eds.). *Social and Political Foundations of Constitutions*. Cambridge: Cambridge University Press.

Howard, A. E. Dick 1996, 'The Indeterminacy of Constitutions', *Wake Forest Law Review.* 31: 383.

Human Rights Watch, World Report 2012: South Sudan, available at http://www.hrw.org/world-report-2012/world-report-2012-south-sudan.

International Crisis Group 2011. *Politics and Transition in the New South Sudan*, Crisis Group Africa Report N°172, April 4.

Jacobson, Gary 2011. *Constitutional Identity*. Cambridge, MA: Harvard University Press.

Johnson, Douglas H. 2003, *The Root Causes of Sudan's Civil Wars*. Bloomington: Indiana University Press.

Lango, John W. and Patterson, Eric. 2010. 'South Sudan Independence: Contingency Planning about Just Armed Intervention', *International Journal of Applied Philosophy* 24: 117.

Law, David and Versteeg, Mila. 2011. 'The Evolution and Ideology of Global Constitutionalism', *California Law Review* 99: 1163.

2012. 'The Declining Influence of the United States Constitution', *New York University Law Review* 87: 762.

2013. 'Sham constitutions', *California Law Review* 101: 863–952.

Miday, Antonette 2011. 'New State, New Constitution', *United Nations Mission in Sudan Public Information Office* June: 7.

Murray, Christina and Maywald, Catherine 2006. 'Subnational Constitution-Making in Southern Sudan', *Rutgers Law Journal* 37: 1203.

Nouwen, Sarah 2007. 'Sudan's Divided (and Divisive?) Peace Agreements', *Hague Y.B. Int'l L.* 19: 113.

O'Ballance, Edgar 1977. *The Secret War In The Sudan: 1955–1972*. Hamden, CT: Archon Books.

Parkinson, Charles O.H. 2013. 'The Social and Political Foundations of the Nigerian Constitution', in Galligan, Denis and Versteeg, Mila (eds.). *Social and Political Foundations of Constitutions*. Cambridge: Cambridge University Press.

Pimental, David 2010. 'Rule of Law Reform without Cultural Imperialism: Reinforcing Customary Justice through Collateral Review in Southern Sudan' (unpublished manuscript), available at http://works.bepress.com/david_pimentel/5.

Sidahmed, Abdel Salam and Soderlund, Walter 2008. 'Sudan, 1992: Humanitarian Relief efforts Confront an Intractable Civil War', in *Humanitarian Crises and Intervention: Reassessing the Impact of Mass Media* 73 (Walter Soderlund & E. Donald Briggs eds.).

Steinitz, Maya 2009. 'Internationalized Pro Bono and A New Global Role for Lawyers in the 21st Century: Lessons from Nation-Building in Southern Sudan,' *Yale Human Rights & Development Law Journal* 12: 205.

'South Sudan backs independence – results', *BBC News*, February 7, 2011, http://www.bbc.co.uk/news/world-africa-12379431.

Sub-Saharan Africa, Public International Law and Policy Group, http://publicinternational-lawandpolicygroup.org.

'Sudan', *U.S. Department of State*, April 8, 2011, http://www.state.gov/r/pa/ei/bgn/5424.htm.

Support in Constitution-Making Processes, Max Planck Institute for Comparative Public Law and International Law, support_in_the_constitution_ma.cfm#elaboration (last updated March 2012).

U.S. Committee for Refugees, Sudan: Nearly 2 Million Dead as a Result of the World's Longest Running Civil War (2001).

USAID 2011. *Assistance to the Development of the First Ever Constitution for Southern Sudan*, USAID, formerly available at http://africastories.usaid.gov/search_details.cfm?storyID=420&countryID=25&sectorID=0&yearID=6.1.

Vanaskie, Thomas I. 2001. 'The Independence and Responsibility of the Federal Judiciary,' *Villanova Law Review* 46: 745.

Wassara, Samson 2010. 'Rebels, Militias and Governance in Sudan', in Okumo, Wafula and Ikelegbe, Augustine (eds.). *Militias, Rebels and Islamist Militants: Human Insecurity and State Crises in Africa*. Tshwane, South Africa: Institute for Security Studies.

12

New Zealand: Abandoning Westminster?

David Erdos

This chapter examines the constitution of New Zealand. It particularly analyzes the 1984–1993 period, asking whether the changes then implemented by the Fourth Labour and Fourth National Governments resulted in the forging of a new post-'Westminster' constitutional framework for the country. This decade-long period was marked by a number of institutional and legal changes including the promulgation of a new Constitution Act, bill of rights and electoral law, the enactment of new legislation on both government openness and individual privacy, and the first substantive legislation recognizing the particular rights of the indigenous Māori under the Treaty of Waitangi. It has been argued that, either individually or severally, this resulted in the establishment of a new constitutional settlement in the country. For example, Geoffrey and Matthew Palmer writing in 1997 stated that "in constitutional terms" New Zealand was a "different nation" (Palmer and Palmer 1997: vii) to when Geoffrey Palmer first penned his seminal monograph on the New Zealand constitution *Unbridled Power?* (Palmer 1979). Assessing the veracity of this claim, however, is a complex matter. In particular, any analysis must confront the fact that "constitution" is a term with multiple, albeit related, meanings. Rather than seeking to obscure this diversity, this chapter deploys it as an orientation for analysis. Thus, Section 12.1 specifically considers this term, breaking it down into a number of both formal and substantive conceptualizations. Flowing on from this, the subsequent sections systematically analyze the principal changes. It is demonstrated that, looked at generally, these changes fail to meet the various thresholds for a new constitutional settlement. Moreover, the failings of the reforms from a constitutional perspective are deeply interlinked. Underpinned by the *grundnorm* of parliamentary sovereignty, New Zealand's pragmatic and flexible 'Westminster' constitutional tradition – a tradition it shares with the United Kingdom (Scott 1962: 20) – continues to dominate. Nevertheless, the unprecedented nature of developments between 1984 and 1993 does have profound constitutional significance. Firstly, as a result of both its substantive importance and the manner in which it was carried out, the electoral shift to a system of proportional representation did constitute a fundamental constitutional change. Secondly, while less radical, the various "dividing-power" reforms of the period were at least cumulatively of constitutional significance. These frameworks will constitute critical reference points in any future attempt to engage in a full process of constitution-making in this country.

12.1 INTRODUCTION

The question of whether New Zealand acquired a new constitution between 1984 and 1993 raises two overlapping, yet distinct, conceptual questions: firstly, what do we mean by the term "constitution," and second and relatedly, what changes would be required for a country to acquire a new one? At least within the context of this chapter, all definitions of a constitution share a common core in that they refer to rules that regulate public power. Beyond this, definitions diverge significantly. Thus, Elster argues:

> If we want to distinguish the constitution from other legal texts, three criteria offer themselves. First, many countries have a set of laws collectively referred to as "the constitution." Second, some laws may be deemed "constitutional" because they regulate matters that are in some sense more fundamental than others. And third, the constitution may be distinguished from ordinary legislation by more stringent amendment procedures. (Elster 1995: 366)

To these nominal, substantive, and procedural definitions, this chapter adds a fourth, more socio-legal and historicist definition developed by Ackerman. This definition holds that, at least within democratic settings, what makes governmental rules "constitutional" is that they are the product of a moment of "higher politics," which may properly be held to represent the will of "We the People" as opposed to the outcomes of ordinary politics which may be more rooted in faction and, therefore, readily contestable (Ackerman 1989; 1991). Finally, the chapter considers a fifth "philosophical" definition that would confine the term to those rules that form a coherent logical structure and thereby genuinely "constitute" or "frame" the country's government. Thus, according to Lord Bolingbroke, "By Constitution We mean, whenever We speak with Propriety and Exactness, that Assemblage of Laws, Institutions and Customs, derived from certain fix'd Principles of Reason ... that compose the general System, according to which the Community hath agreed to be govern'd" (Quoted in King 2001: 80). As Table 12.1 further elucidates, the definition of constitution relied on critically determines what threshold must be surpassed for a new constitution to be brought into being. The first three definitions of constitution and

TABLE 12.1. *Definitions of "Constitution" and "Constitution-Making"*

	Constitution	Constitution-Making
Nominal	Those governmental rules that are included in a legal document entitled "The Constitution."	The authoritative promulgating of a new document entitled "The Constitution."
Procedural	A set of governmental rules that are specifically institutionally protected against amendment or repeal.	Promulgation of a new set of governmental rules that are specifically institutionally protected.
Substantive	Those rules that together fundamentally determine the nature of governmental power.	Rule changes that are important enough so as to fundamentally change the nature of governmental power.
Historicist	Those governmental rules that are the product of a "constitutional moment" of "We the People" "higher politics."	The enactment of new governmental rules during, and clearly as a product of, a "constitutional moment."
Philosophical	Those governmental rules that together cohere and constitute the essence of a particular pattern of governance.	The enactment of a body of rules that together bring a new coherence to governance arrangements.

their threshold should be referred to during following three sections, which outline the New Zealand case. Section 12.5 then considers the relevance of the historicist perspective while Section 12.6 also touches on relevance of the philosophical definition in coming to a conclusion on this topic.

12.2 CONSTITUTION ACT 1986

At least from a nominal perspective, the best evidence in favor of the thesis that New Zealand acquired a new constitution in the 1984–1993 period lies in the fact that in 1986 it enacted a new law entitled the Constitution Act. This Act replaced the erstwhile New Zealand Constitution Act that had been bequeathed by the UK Parliament in 1852. Moreover, the instrument covers much of the same institutional ground that is commonly found in modern constitutions. Thus:

- Part One sets out the identity and powers of the Sovereign of New Zealand, including the manner in which the latter may be exercised by her representative (ordinarily, the Governor-General).
- Part Two identifies and sets out powers of the Executive including the Executive Council, Ministers of the Crown, and both the Attorney and Solicitor-General.

- Part Three deals with the identity and powers of the legislature including the term of parliament and its summoning, proroguing, and dissolution.
- Part Four states certain matters that pertain to the judiciary in New Zealand.

One notable absence, however, is any mention of human rights or even the relationship between the New Zealand government and the people of that country. This immediately marks this Act apart from most modern constitutions. Nevertheless, even a cursory glance at an exemplar of a clearly constitutional text – the original U.S. Constitution – leads to the observation of some uncanny resemblances. This document, it should be remembered, also originally largely eschewed the question of defining individual rights vis-à-vis the state. Moreover, there is substantial positive overlap. Parts One and Two of the Constitution Act clearly relate to Article II of the U.S. Constitution, Part Three does likewise with Article I, and Part Four displays some resemblance with Article III.

Nevertheless, even putting aside both the absence of a bill of rights (which, as a result of the first ten amendments of the U.S. Constitution, were soon included in that instrument) and those parts of the text that deal with the fact that the United States is a federal as opposed to a unitary state like New Zealand, a closer comparison leads to the identification of some telling divergences. In the first place, it is important to note that the New Zealand instrument is not actually designated a "Constitution" at all; rather, it is a "Constitution Act." As with all Acts, it started life as an ordinary bill of the New Zealand parliament (then formally known as the General Assembly), achieving legal force through the operation of an ordinary legislative procedure. Its designation as a simple Act of Parliament must cast doubt on whether it can satisfy the nominal definition of a new constitution. More importantly, it correctly suggests that this instrument was not foundational. Rather it was "declaratory rather than the source of New Zealand's state instruments and authority" (Joseph 2007: 124). The Act was also "fragmentary" (Palmer 1992: 45). "Much of the detail which matters [in New Zealand constitutional law] is found elsewhere" (*ibid*). The strongly derivate nature of the Act links to its limited substantive effects. This is not to say that the Act was not designed to effect any alteration in governance arrangements. To the contrary, it has its origins in a need to respond substantively to what has been labeled a "constitutional crisis" that emerged during the handover between the National and Labour Governments in 1984. In brief, prior to the general election, the New Zealand dollar came under severe pressure. Following its election victory, Labour requested that the outgoing National Government effect an immediate 20 percent devaluation. However, Robert Muldoon, as the still duly appointed prime minister, refused to accede to this request, prompting severe and unsustainable selling of currency. The constitutional aspect of the problem emerged from the fact that, as under the Civil List Act 1979 no new Minister or member of the Executive Council could be appointed "unless the person is at the time of appointment a member of Parliament" (section 9 (1)), it was strongly arguable that Muldoon could not be removed as prime minister until the newly elected parliament was sworn in. The immediate crisis was averted by outgoing Attorney-General Jim McLay stating a new "constitutional convention" according to which an outgoing administration would be obliged to accept its successor's advice "on any matter of great constitutional, economic or other significance that cannot be delayed until the new government formally takes office" (Quoted in Joseph 2007: 127). Nevertheless, the affair had exposed major and apparently pressing uncertainties in constitutional law. Section 6 (2) resolved these by providing that:

> A person who is not a member of Parliament may be appointed and may hold office as a member of the Executive Council or as a Minister of the Crown if that person was a candidate for election at the general election of members of the House of Representatives held immediately preceding that person's appointment as a member of the Executive Council or as Minister of the Crown but shall vacate office at the expiration of the period of 40 days beginning with the date of the appointment unless, within that period, that person becomes a member of Parliament.

Another linked change was made by section 19 which provided that:

> After any general election of members of the House of Representatives, Parliament shall meet not later than 6 weeks after the day fixed for the return of the writs for that election.

Astonishingly, prior to this, it had been common to have an "inter-regnum" between parliaments of between seven and eight months (Joseph 2007: 129). Meanwhile, by repealing key UK enactments (The New Zealand Constitution Act 1852, the Statute of Westminster 1931, and the New Zealand Constitution (Amendment) Act 1947), the Act widened the legal gap between New Zealand and the erstwhile imperial authority. Notably, as a result of the repeal of the New Zealand Constitution (Amendment) Act 1947, the UK parliament lost its power to legislate for New Zealand by and with the consent of the New Zealand parliament. Nevertheless, in the main, the general effect and purpose of the Act was simply to map "the parameters of its [New Zealand's] uncodified constitution" (Joseph 2007: 125). Moreover, the Act's provisions were not legally entrenched,[1] and neither the Act itself nor any substantive changes it effected registered significantly on the New Zealand public's consciousness (Joseph 2007: 124). The Act's essentially apolitical task ensured that, in contrast to many of the changes examined later in the chapter, it benefited from cross-party support. However, it also ensured that the Act can in no sense be considered the substantive harbinger of a new constitutional settlement.

---

[1]   With one exception, the maximum three-year term of parliament (section 17 (1)), which was already entrenched under the Electoral Act in any case (discussed further later in the chapter).

12.3 ELECTORAL CHANGE

After several years of debate, in 1993 New Zealand abandoned "over eighty years' uninterrupted use of single member plurality" form of election to its parliament in order adopt a new Mixed-Member Proportional (MMP) system (Renwick 2010:194). This is a change about which none of the limitations noted regarding the Constitution Act can easily be made. Substantively, this change was a radical one in at least three ways. To begin with, from the perspective of electoral law itself, effecting an unmediated shift from a long-standing simple plurality system to full proportional representation (tempered only by a standard 5 percent threshold requirement[2]) is almost unprecedented. Thus, Renwick, states that, "[i]n no other case of post-war electoral reform has such a long-standing system been so comprehensively overturned" (*ibid*). Moreover, from a broader perspective, the electoral system that a country adopts for election to its parliament[3] has widely been acknowledged as exerting a pervasive and systemic influence on the nature of public power (and therefore on the substantive constitution as defined in section one of this chapter) (Lijphart 1999). Thus, it is clear that this reform has led to the end not only of parliaments dominated by (and in many cases solely composed of) two parties (National and Labour), but also of a long tradition of single-party government. As Levine notes:

> By 1996, prior to the first MMP election, there were already six parties (and one independent) in Parliament as internal divisions in the run-up to MMP led to the formation of new party groups. After the election there were still six Parties in Parliament – National, Labour, New Zealand First (NZF), the Alliance, ACT, and United. The 1999 election led to a seven-party Parliament, as the Green Party separated from the multi-party Alliance to compete on its own, and the 2002 results also produced a seven-party outcome (with the Progressives replacing the Alliance). (Levine 2004: 649)

Secondly, this change was the product of several years of protracted political deliberation and manoeuvring, much of it involving substantial public engagement. This process, which can be likened to Ackerman's "higher lawmaking," is fully analyzed in Section 12.5. Third and finally, the electoral law changes were facially entrenched. Specifically, according to section 268 of the Electoral Act 1993, the electoral system may only be changed either by:

- A parliamentary vote in which 75 percent of all members of the House vote in favor, or

---

[2] Or through winning of a seat reserved for the representation of certain geographical (or Māori) constituencies.

[3] Or, in cases where this parliament has more than one chamber, the lower and more powerful of these.

- A referendum of the New Zealand electorate, carried by a majority of those voting.

Notwithstanding its clearly constitutional nature, however, the change did not in itself bequeath a new constitution settlement. In the first place, turning to the issue of entrenchment, the concept behind section 268 clearly modifies New Zealand's constitutional *grundnorm* of parliamentary sovereignty. However, this modification dates back to the erstwhile section 189 of the Electoral Act 1956. Moreover, as these clauses have not themselves been entrenched, they are technically legally ineffective (Scott 1962). Additionally, the absence of any explicitly constitutional labeling casts doubt on its status at least from a nominalist perspective, while its narrow (albeit very deep) substantive nature raises further questions. Although Lijphart's analysis correctly identifies the broader indirect significance of electoral system choice for a number of other constitutional variables, these all relate to the "joint-power" dimensions of democracy or, in other words, the extent to which power within the main organs of government should be subject a "shared responsibility" (Lijphart 1999: 5). In contrast, electoral system choice has practically no effect on a whole swathe of constitutional questions that all revolve around the extent to which a polity should divide power between a range of governmental agencies. Nevertheless, this period also witnessed a number of other reforms that were aimed at this "dividing-power" dimension. The most high-profile and overarching of these was the New Zealand Bill of Rights Act 1990, to which this chapter now turns.

12.4 PRINCIPAL DIVIDING-POWER CHANGES

12.4.1 *The New Zealand Bill of Rights Act (NZBORA) 1990*

New Zealand's public debate on electoral reform originally emerged from a commitment by Labour in both its 1981 and 1984 general elections manifestos to establish a Royal Commission on this issue. Paralleling this, these manifestos also included a commitment to a bill of rights, a policy that led to a White Paper on the subject in 1985. From the perspective of New Zealand's constitutional tradition, this White Paper was extremely ambitious. In brief, it proposed a new instrument granting a range of relatively abstract civil and political rights supreme legal status. Moreover, this Bill of Rights would, similarly to the Electoral Act, be entrenched. The Officials Committee looking into drafting of the Constitution Act (analyzed earlier) even suggested that, should such a process be successful, then the provisions of the Constitution Act might also be entrenched (Quoted in Joseph 2007: 125). Notwithstanding the doubts about the legal effectiveness of such entrenchment, if these provisions had been successfully enacted, New Zealand would have taken a large step toward the written, higher law constitutions so common elsewhere in the democratic world.

However, in the light of widespread civil society and elite political opposition (Erdos 2007), in 1988 Parliament's Justice and Law Reform Committee rejected the proposals. Despite this, its Labour majority endorsed the value of an unentrenched instrument. This would for the very first time set out the core civil and political rights identified as important in the White Paper but would be explicitly designed to have only an "interpretative," as opposed to "trumping," effect on other law. The broad thrust of these proposals was accepted by the government. A new bill was drafted and referred again to the Law and Justice Committee where it received a much more positive, albeit far less high-profile, reception (Rishworth 1995: 21). After some further limiting amendments, the bill was reported back to parliament. In August 1990 it received a third reading, albeit on the basis of a strict party vote (National still being opposed).

The New Zealand Bill of Rights Act (NZBORA) is an important piece of legislation. It has had a key effect on criminal procedure and on freedom of expression. However, its wider legal impact has been limited. While this may partly be explained by a rather conservative judicial culture (Erdos 2009), these limitations clearly chime with its initial design. Painfully aware of the tension with parliamentary sovereignty, this design is at the weakest end of the "new Commonwealth" model also adopted in Canada and the United Kingdom (Gardbaum 2013; Erdos 2010). Thus, far from granting the judges a power to strike down incompatible legislation, NZBORA explicitly limits the extent to which the courts can use its provisions as an interpretative guide (NZBORA: section 4). Finally, it is in no way legally entrenched. In sum, while marking a significant reform from *within* New Zealand's constitutional setup, it in no sense brought into being a new constitutional framework for the country in a nominal, procedural, or substantive sense.

12.4.2 *Māori Treaty Rights*

Sitting alongside its general rights proposals, the 1985 White Paper also argued that the rights of the Māori people under the Treaty of Waitangi 1840 should be recognized, affirmed, and entrenched on the same basis. This Treaty had attempted to cede the governance (or *kawanatanga*) of New Zealand to the Crown while guaranteeing to Māori certain rights. There were two significantly different versions, one in English (which was, for the British, authoritative), the other in Māori (which the majority of Māori signed). While Article 3 of both versions guaranteed Māori something akin to British subjecthood, Article 2 guaranteed either, in the English, property rights or, in Māori, their *tino rangitiratanga* (perhaps best translated as "full chieftainship"). These divergences, as well as a more general tension between Māori

and Pakeha (or European) New Zealanders (which even led to war in the later nineteenth century), prompted a heated and continuing interpretative debate within
New Zealand politics (Orange 1987; Levine 2004). Within legal debate, however,
the Treaty was almost absent; indeed, in the famous case of *Wi Parata v. Bishop of
Wellington* [1877] 3 NZ Jr (NS) 72, the Court of Appeal declared the Treaty "a simple
nullity" as regards domestic law. Seen in this light, the government's proposals were
constitutionally radical. The clause would not only have placed a formidable new
interpretative power in the hands of the judiciary but could have fundamentally
shifted the nature of public power away from a unified (and ultimately majoritarian)
democracy and toward a status-based divided polity. In fact, however, this provision
failed to be included even in the watered-down NZBORA. The general problems
with Labour's rights entrenchment policy have already been noted. Some further
issues confronted the so-called Treaty clause specifically. In the first place, many
non-Māori New Zealanders expressed fear that the change would result in Māori
interests being inappropriately prioritized. More remarkably, many Māori came out
against the change. Māori criticized the fact that the clause did not make referral
to the Waitangi Tribunal (a quasi-judicial advisory commission of inquiry set up in
1975 with substantial Māori representation) compulsory, that the Bill's allowance
for "reasonable limitations" could be applied to their detriment, and that the entire
clause could be changed or repealed through an amendment process that would not
require support of at least the majority of Māoridom itself.

Despite this, the Treaty's legal standing was significantly enhanced during this
period. In sum:

- In 1985, the government empowered the Waitangi Tribunal to examine alleged
  Crown breaches of the Treaty dating back to 1840 (as opposed to 1975 as before).[4]
- In June 1986, in preparation for adoption of the Treaty clause, the Cabinet
  required that all future legislation referred to Cabinet at the policy approval
  stage should "draw attention to any implications for recognition of the Treaty of
  Waitangi" (Palmer 2008: 219). Despite the non-implementation of the clause,
  this intragovernmental provision has remained in force until today.
- From the 1986 Environment Act onward, the government began, as a matter
  of policy, to explicitly and substantively refer to the Treaty of Waitangi (or its
  principles) on the face of a range of legislation. These provisions were concentrated on environmental matters, but also encompassed areas as diverse as
  finance[5] and education.[6]

---

[4]   Treaty of Waitangi Amendment Act 1985; Treaty of Waitangi Act 1975.
[5]   Section 2, Finance Act 1995.
[6]   Section 210, Education Act 1989.

- In a related, but distinct, development, it was agreed to include a section in the State-Owned Enterprises (SOE) Act 1986 (the government's flagship corporatization legislation) stating that "Nothing in this Act shall permit the Crown to act in a manner that is inconsistent with the principles of the Treaty of Waitangi" (section 9).

In *Attorney-General v. New Zealand Maori Council* [1987] 1 NZLR 687, possibly the most momentous court decision in New Zealand history, the Court of Appeal held that the section 9 of the SOE Act could override all its other provisions. It then held that the detailed code that had been put in place to take into account Māori interests in the corporatization process was not sufficient to ensure Treaty compliance. The government was required "to devise an acceptable monitoring system to ensure that the transfer of assets would not violate Treaty principles" (Joseph 2007: 71). More generally, the court forwarded a "partnership between races"[7] understanding of the Treaty, holding, in particular, that "the relationship between the Treaty partners [i.e., the Crown and various Māori entities] creates responsibilities analogous to fiduciary duties."[8] The Treaty of Waitangi Amendment Act 1988 was the immediate legislative outcome of this litigation. This Act provided that memorials would be placed on all land or interests in land transferred to a state-owned enterprise stating that the Waitangi Tribunal could make a binding decision to return that land or interest in land to Māori ownership.[9] Given that the land in question amounted to four million hectares (Palmer 2008),[10] the implications of this Act are potentially enormous. A plethora of cases flowed from these developments, many encompassing subject matter such as radio frequencies[11] and broadcasting,[12] which were at a considerable distance from the interests traditionally conceived as falling within the Treaty. Thus, the 1987 case can be considered "a circuit-breaker for modern Treaty jurisprudence, giving birth to an entire area of legal study" (Joseph 2007: 47).

From the constitution-making perspective, however, these developments present considerable problems of interpretation. At least once the Treaty clause proposals were abandoned, none of the changes were presented within an intrinsically constitutional format. This is not only relevant from a nominalist perspective, but underlines the substantive uncertainty as to whether the political decisions from which Treaty gained its legal status are in fact constitutional in nature. In attempting to provide for a non-majoritarian mechanism that might allow Māori to both resolve

---

[7] Cooke P in *Attorney-General v. New Zealand Maori Council* at [35].
[8] Cooke P in *Attorney-General v. New Zealand Maori Council* at [37].
[9] This became section 27 of the SOE Act. The memorial (and potential for a binding order) remains live even if the land or interest in land is subsequently resold.
[10] That is, 40,000 square kilometres.
[11] *Attorney-General v. New Zealand Maori Council* [1991] 2 NZLR 129 (CA).
[12] *New Zealand Maori Council v. Attorney-General* [1992] 2 NZLR 576 (CA).

past historic complaints and current grievances, a constitutional purpose was apparent in the very early political decisions of the Fourth Labour Government. Geoffrey Palmer, who as attorney-general and deputy prime minister acted as a key architect of these initiatives, stated its logic thus:

> Some parliamentary action by way of legislation was needed to make a base. But if that legislation itself redressed the grievances it would run into the problem that the majority of the community would oppose it. If, on the other hand, legislation was used to set up processes, and procedures and the principles on which decisions should be based were stated, it may be possible to get even a majoritarian legislature to act. The initial commitment required was to a process. (Quoted in Palmer 2008: 93)[13]

On the other hand, section 9 of the SOE Act, from which the most momentous aspects of the Treaty jurisprudence arose, sprung from the much more pragmatic need to secure the smooth enactment of one of the government's flagship economic bills. As Joseph states, "these provisions were inserted by supplementary order paper when the bill was before the House to allay Maori concerns that the transfer of Crown assets would undermine the jurisdiction of the [Waitangi] tribunal" (Joseph 2007: 70). Moreover, while approximately thirty pieces of legislation now refer in some way to the Treaty (New Zealand Government Te Puni Kokhi [Ministry of Maori Affairs] 2002: 20), these provisions remain partial, fragmented, and piecemeal.[14] Moreover, even when a Treaty provision is applicable, its effects may be limited. Thus, despite the bold "partnership" rhetoric of the Courts in the 1987–1993 period, the concrete duties of the Crown may extend to little more the good-faith consultation with Māori representatives. Thus, outside the binding decision provisions of section 27 of the SOE Act,[15] such duties may be entirely compatible with Crown action that is in opposition to the opinion of both Māori and the Waitangi Tribunal.[16] Finally, from a procedural perspective, it should be noted that none of these changes were in any

---

[13] While Palmer does not explicitly state it here, it is clear from the White Paper that a similar logic underlay his proposed Treaty of Waitangi clause in the suggested bill of rights.

[14] The Treaty (and since 2004 also aboriginal customary title) can and has been given legal weight even in situations where there is no statutory provision. This weight is generally much more slender than the provisions under discussion here. In any case, this usage is outside of this chapter's focus on the extent to which political decisions in the 1984–1993 period themselves gave constitutional status to the Treaty.

[15] Despite the increasingly shrill and "over-assertive" rhetoric of the Waitangi Tribunal's fact-finding and recommendations (in one particularly blatant case the Tribunal even stated that the Taranaki land confiscations of the nineteenth century amounted to a "holocaust" [Palmer 2008: 198]), the Tribunal has made almost no use of its potentially enormous powers under this provision.

[16] Cf. *Attorney-General v. New Zealand Maori Council* [1991] 2 NZLR 129 (CA) (the *Radio Frequencies* case).

way entrenched. All this underscores the fact that the approach to the Treaty that emerged in the mid- to late 1980s remains, from a constitutional viewpoint, both uncertain and contested.

12.4.3 *Other Dividing-Power Reforms*

Before drawing certain strands together, it should briefly be mentioned that a number of other dividing-power reforms came to fruition around this time. These included the Official Information Act 1982 (a freedom of information enactment that, while strictly speaking outside the period under analysis, was, as the next section outlines, clearly linked to it), the Reserve Bank of New Zealand Act 1989 (granting the central bank a substantial measure of independence), the Privacy Act 1993 (establishing a set of privacy standards that all organizations – including government itself – were generally required to adhere to), and the Citizens Initiated Referenda Act 1993 (establishing a mechanism via which referenda had to be held, at governmental expense, on any question that was approved by no less than 10 percent of all eligible voters). At least when considered collectively, these provisions significantly strengthened the dividing-power reforms of the period. Nevertheless, all were clearly subject to significant constitutional limitations. In the first place, they were usually not framed at the time as having a clearly constitutional, as opposed to general policy, significance. Secondly, none were in any way entrenched. Third, most were subject to significant legal limitation. To take one example, the citizens' referendums were explicitly made nonbinding. This has rendered the "utility" of the polls "questionable" (Joseph 2007: 293).[17] In sum, as with the other dividing-power developments, the changes were of constitutional significance. At the same time, however, they took effect from *within* New Zealand's existing constitutional framework of parliamentary sovereignty, pragmatism, and flexibility. The next section seeks to explain both the origins and limits of the changes during this period from a historicist perspective.

12.5 POLITICAL TRIGGERS, NOT CONSTITUTIONAL MOMENTS?

According to the historicist school, for a political decision to constitute constitution-making, it is essential that it is legitimated by a process of "higher lawmaking" that ensures the decision is genuinely "by the People," as opposed to the usual case of being "by their government" (Ackerman 1989: 461). Focusing on the American case,

---

17 Four polls have been held in New Zealand since the coming into force of these provisions. All have been carried overwhelmingly. By contrast, however, the government has implemented none of them.

Bruce Ackerman, the prime exponent of this "dualist democracy" perspective, sets out the requirements of such constitutional moments in the following manner:

> Decisions by the People occur rarely, and under special constitutional conditions. Before gaining the authority to enact its proposals into the nation's *higher* law, a political movement must, first, convince an extraordinary number of its fellow citizens to take its proposed initiative with a seriousness that they do not normally accord to politics; second, allow opponents a fair opportunity to organize their own forces; third, convince a majority of Americans to support transformative initiatives as their merits are discussed, time and again, in the deliberative fora provided by the dualist constitutional order for this purpose. It is only those initiatives that survive this specially onerous higher lawmaking system that earn the special kind of legitimacy the dualist accords to decisions made by the People. (Ackerman 1989: 462)

As explored at the end of this section, in New Zealand the electoral shift to MMP was the product of a special process of "elite-mass interaction" and so can plausibly be thought to amount to a constitutional initiative in this sense. In contrast, while the other reforms considered earlier in the chapter did have clear roots in a relatively rare political trigger (labeled here "aversive" constitutionalism) that provided relevant actors with an immediate rationale for significant institutional change, this trigger fails to meet the participatory threshold criteria Ackerman sets out.

12.5.1 *"Aversive" Constitutionalism*

The rise of a political momentum behind the dividing-power reforms of the period had their roots in an "aversive" reaction against the activities and outlook of National's Robert Muldoon, prime minister between 1975 and 1984. Substantively, Muldoon's premiership was perceived as displaying a woeful disregard for traditional conventional understandings of how public power should be exercised. A large number of his actions were thought to be in violation of the rule of law. These included:

- The attempt in 1976 to suspend the government's superannuation scheme by issuing a press statement in advance of legislation.[18]
- The decision in 1982 to immediately overturn a court judgment on its water rights application relating to a dam project on the river Clyde.[19]

---

[18] In *Fitzgerald v. Muldoon* [1976] 2 NZLR 615, the High Court ruled that this action had indeed amounted to an illegal executive suspension of the law contrary to the Bill of Rights (UK) 1688 – an "imperial" statute that remained in force in New Zealand.

[19] Clutha Development (Clyde Dam) Empowering Act 1982. Geoffrey Palmer described this as "the greatest attack made on the rule of law in this country within living memory" (Speech to New Zealand Labour Party Central North Island Regional Conference, April 7–8, 1984 [Rishworth 1995: 10]).

- The enactment of special legislation to penalize striking workers at the Marsden Point Refinery Expansion Project in 1984.[20]

Muldoon also engaged in a further centralization of political power. In particular:

- He decided to combine the roles of both prime minister and minister of finance.
- He nominated sitting National Party cabinet minister, Sir Keith Holyoke, as New Zealand's governor-general, ignoring both the conventional consultation with the Official Opposition on such appointments and the traditionally non-partisan nature of this office (Palmer 1979: 21).

More generally, Muldoon's sudden and frequent implementation of various broad, and potentially draconian, initiatives was increasingly seen as an abuse of the separation of powers, especially given that these changes were made not through parliament but rather utilizing general statutes that granted the executive wide-ranging regulatory powers.[21] Wage and price freezes, professional fee freezes, and rent freezes were all implemented using such powers (Rishworth 1995: 11).

Secondly, and probably as importantly, the aggressive modus operandi of Muldoon was itself alienating. The late Labour leader and prime minister, David Lange, states that Muldoon had "an extraordinary capacity to intimidate ... [A] number of Labour members were genuinely afraid of him and he often had a free run. His stare alone could quell some of our front bench into inertia" (Lange 2005: 122). This view is echoed by New Zealand historian James Belich who argues that Muldoon generated "real fear and hatred in his opponents both within and without his own party" (Belich 2001: 396).

Muldoon's activities ignited concern within public debate about the extreme centralization of power within the New Zealand constitution. Thus, during the late 1970s and early 1980s, many important public figures indicated that that they believed that a decisive move toward greater institutional checks and balances was now necessary. Particularly important in this regard were Sir Owen Woodhouse, President of the Court of Appeal (then New Zealand's highest autochthonous court), and Kenneth Keith, Professor of Law at Victoria University of Wellington (Woodhouse 1979; Keith 1978). The new constitutionalizing *zeitgeist* even effected the thinking of a number of Muldoon's opponents within his own party. In particular, Deputy Prime Minister Jim McLay was converted to the cause of freedom of information and successfully placed the Official Information Act on the Statute Book in 1982. Muldoon, who enjoyed a very strong rivalry within McLay (Belich 2001), famously derided this law

---

[20]   Section 11, Whangerei Refinery Expansion Project Disputes Act 1984.
[21]   For example, the Economic Stabilization Act 1948, the Public Safety Conservation Act 1932, and the Primary Products Marketing Act 1953.

as "a nine day wonder" (quoted in Palmer 2004: 172). The new *zeitgeist* had a particular effect on Labour politicians. Not only did these actors find themselves at the brunt end of Muldoon's heavy-handed and authoritarian actions on a daily basis, but their openness to new restrictions on executive power increased as their period of non-incumbency lengthened. Development of new Labour policy in this area was importantly catalyzed by Geoffrey Palmer, a former law professor and committed constitutional activist. In 1979, Palmer wrote a book setting out the case for, and modalities to, check the "unbridled power" at the heart of New Zealand's constitutional setup (Palmer 1979). As Secretary of Labour's Policy Council, Palmer was able to ensure that the core of these proposals was included in Labour's program as part of a dedicated "Open Government" policy (see Palmer 1987: 281–285). The Māori dimension was not originally a strong element of this. However, the fact that Māoridom's grievances were also premised on a need to constrain or "bridle" centralized power in New Zealand, coupled with Labour's traditionally strong relationship with Māori, led to an integration of this agenda with Labour's emerging constitutional vision (Palmer 1992: 78–81). In sum, therefore, it was this political dynamic that paved the way for almost all of the dividing-power reforms of the 1980s and early 1990s.[22]

The emergence of a strong political dynamic favoring institutional change is clearly a relatively rare occurrence in any basically stable political system. It is this factor that makes much of this period so broadly fecund in a constitutional sense. However, this agenda was not pursued in the type of transparent and participatory form that would be required for it to constitute a constitutional moment of "higher lawmaking" in an Ackermanian sense. Moreover, it is clear that if a higher lawmaking framework had been adopted, then most if not all of these changes would have failed to gain the requisite popular interest or backing. The absence of wide support for Labour's bill of rights policy has already been noted. Opposition to Māori Treaty entrenchment was even more vociferous. Thus, Palmer has candidly noted, "[t]he [Labour] Government secured a reputation of doing things for Maori but not for anybody else ... a white backlash of strong proportions set in" (Palmer 1992: 91).

12.5.2 *Electoral Reform and Elite-Mass Interaction*

The beginnings of the electoral and parliamentary reform agenda also had its roots in the trigger just considered. A strengthening of parliament vis-à-vis the executive was seen as one mechanism via which the latter's "overweening powers" could be

---

[22] The main exception to this was the Citizens Initiated Referendum Act 1993. This reform was "promoted at the 1990 elections [primarily in order] to dampen demand for electoral reform" (Joseph 2007: 294). Therefore, in a sense, its roots lie in the same dynamic as the transition to MMP. Nevertheless, somewhat ironically given its substance, its implementation was devoid of the participatory elements that accompanied the MMP transition. The specific and more pragmatic origins of section 9 of the SOE Act 1986 should also be noted.

brought to heel (Jackson and McRobie 1998: 9). Additionally, the fact that National gained the most seats in both the 1978 and 1981 general elections despite the Labour gaining the most votes further galvanized a "degree of receptiveness towards the idea of electoral reform" within Labour's ranks (Renwick 2010: 196). This receptiveness led to a Royal Commission whose Report issued in 1986 backed a move to MMP secured via a public referendum.

The Royal Commission's Report came to play an important role in subsequent events. Its intellectual credibility "helped to *reassure* the public that proportional representation was indeed a viable alternative" (Jackson and McRobie 1998: 338) to the existing electoral system. In addition, "its findings provided a necessary focus" (Jackson and McRobie 1998: 123) for future political activity. Nevertheless, without a further galvanizing dynamic, these findings would have languished unimplemented. Reaction from the political class was "largely hostile" (Renwick 2010: 200), and there was anything but a mass clamour for reform (Jackson and McRobie 1998: 45). This changed, however, as the question of electoral reform came to be linked to public anger against the established Labour and National Parties. This anger emerged as a result of both parties' violation of their election promises in the core area of socioeconomic policy. In sum:

- Notwithstanding its very different ideological roots, post 1984 Labour engaged in significant market-based reforms. Moreover, despite promising a return to core Labour values during the 1987 general election, the government actually engaged in an even more free market agenda (at least up until the resignation of Finance Minister Roger Douglas in late 1988).
- Meanwhile, with regards to National, despite promising a return to a "decent society" in the 1990 general election, the new government advanced a radical program of neoliberalism. More specifically, notwithstanding its promise to abolish Labour's hated superannuation tax, the new government decided to increase this tax in the 1991 budget.

These egregious breaches of the doctrine of the electoral "mandate"[23] occurred in the context of a deep economic recession. This may have been determinative of the extent of public dissatisfaction with the political system that ensued (See Renwick 2010: 219). Meanwhile, the linkage between this and electoral reform developed both from the Royal Commission Report and from other almost happenchance factors. In particular:

- During the televised general election debate in 1987, Prime Minister David Lange unexpectedly (and seeming as a result of a "gaffe") (Jackson and

---

[23] A critical concept in New Zealand politics (Mulgan 1978) and, one might even add, New Zealand constitutional conventions.

McRobie 1998: 47) committed Labour to holding a referendum on electoral reform. Despite Palmer's best efforts, however, no such poll was conducted during Labour's second term.

• Subsequently, during the lead-up to the 1990 general election, National stated that, if elected, it would deliver this commitment to a referendum, which would be binding (Renwick 2010: 201).

At this stage, it was not expected that a referendum would produce more than moderate change that, not completely coincidentally, was actually supported by certain political figures especially within the National Party (Renwick 2010: 202). This assumption of moderateness, however, changed as a result of National's broken election promises and the ongoing economic slump. Politicians, now firmly committed to the holding of a referendum, "lost control of the issue" (Renwick 2010: 207). Thus, spurred on by the strong campaigning by the grassroots Electoral Reform Coalition, the first indicative referendum in 1992 delivered (on a 55.2 percent turnout) a resounding defeat of the existing system, with 84.7 percent backing change. Meanwhile, among the four alternatives offered, some 70.5 percent indicated a preference for MMP should reform be forthcoming (Renwick 2010). Finally, in 1993, a binding referendum was held alongside the general election of that year. Partly as a result of the rise of the pro-First Past the Post (FPTP) Campaign for Better Government (also led by a non-politician, businessman Peter Shirtcliffe), the result here was much narrower. Nevertheless, on the basis of 85.2 percent turnout, some 53.9 percent of voters supported change.[24] New Zealand's shift from FPTP to MMP was complete.

This process of "elite-mass interaction" fits Ackerman's concept of a constitutional moment much better than the "aversive" dynamic described earlier. The shift was structured around a process of popular deliberation, there was a significant amount of civil society organizing within the debate, and the final change was secured through two popular referendums, the last of which was understood by all sides to be binding. Also significantly, the existing provisions of electoral law dating back to 1956 provided an authoritative basis for deciding this through a "higher" decision-making procedure. Nevertheless, there remain at least two discrete reasons to doubt that this development can, from a historicist point of view, be thought to have bequeathed New Zealand a new "constitution." In the first place, the extent to which the "merits" of the proposed electoral law changes were "discussed, time and again" may be questioned (Ackerman 1989: 461). Thus, Levine argues that

---

[24] National's official policy had been to hold a binding referendum prior to the end of 1992 in order that the 1993 general election itself could be held on the basis of the popularly preferred system. However, apparently as a result of insurmountable practical difficulties, this tight timeframe was not achieved (Renwick 2010, 205–206).

"[t]he move to change the electoral system was fuelled more by anger than by cogent analysis of alternative electoral systems and their likely consequences" (Levine 2004: 649).[25] Similarly, Palmer describes the transition to MMP as "almost accidental" (Palmer 2007: 574). Secondly, and more importantly, while this reform may have been constitutionally transformative in an Ackermanian sense, its focus on just one, albeit very important, change was simply too narrow to bring about a new constitutional settlement for the country. Much of the core of New Zealand's constitutional approach continued unaltered. Thus, in surprisingly nonconstitutional language, Levine describes MMP as a "policy instrument," "designed with a specific purpose in mind" (Levine 2004: 649). Overall he states that "[t]he vote for MMP began a new process of institutional change, one that has diluted the purity of New Zealand's Westminster system without impairing its overall health. Some things have been changed; many have not" (*ibid*). Most especially, as previously noted in Section 12.3, the dividing-power dimension of New Zealand's constitutional setup was left unaddressed by this process.

12.6 THE CONSTITUTIONAL LIMITATIONS, AND SIGNIFICANCE, OF THE 1984–1993 PERIOD

The chapter began by laying out a number of different definitions of "constitution" together with the threshold that was required to satisfy an act of constitution-making from these various perspectives. As the preceding discussion has indicated, while clearly of constitutional importance, the changes considered earlier in the chapter failed, with the singular exception of the electoral shift to MMP, to meet these thresholds. In sum:

- Contrary, most especially, to the nominal definition, the changes not only failed to be encapsulated in a document titled "The Constitution," but were often not even couched within an explicitly constitutional language.
- With the exception of the electoral change, the reforms were adopted through administrative decisions or ordinary Acts of Parliament, which were not entrenched in any way against repeal or amendment. The requirements for the procedural definition were therefore generally not met.
- While significant from the perspective of New Zealand's existing institutional setup, none of the changes (again with the notable exception of electoral reform) were explicitly designed to constitute a radical substantive break with past practice.

---

[25] Nevertheless, it should be noted that prior to the two referendums, an extensive program of public education and deliberation was organized, in particular by the newly established Electoral Commission. See http://www.nzhistory.net.nz/politics/fpp-to-mmp (accessed November 2, 2012).

- Finally, contrary to the historicist definition, the reforms were, also with the exception of electoral change, not implemented through a deliberate and popular process of higher lawmaking.

The ability of the reforms to satisfy a philosophical definition of a constitution-making has so far not been directly addressed. This too may be questioned. At one level, it is clear that the various changes did have a philosophic coherence: all the proposals originally emerged out of a desire to constrain what had come to be seen as the "elective dictatorship" of the executive. It can further be argued that, in adopting strong electoral mechanisms for reducing this power alongside only accepting much more limited dividing power limitations, New Zealand adopted a coherent (albeit contestable) constitutional vision. Nevertheless, when looked at more deeply, tensions abound. Some, for example enacting statutory provisions that both promoted openness (Official Information Act) and secrecy (Privacy Act), are common to most contemporary industrialized democracies and largely inevitable. Others, however, are both more specific to the New Zealand situation and potentially more corrosive. Most particularly, there was a tension between the generally liberal and egalitarian philosophy of the bill of rights project conceived generally and the goal of entrenching particularized status-based rights for members of a particular racial/ethnic group (Māori) under the Treaty of Waitangi. Practically speaking, this problem of coherence was exacerbated by the fact that Māori and Pakeha are, in reality, significantly integrated through the country. These tensions have continued to develop strongly into the present. As Levine states:

> Differences of opinion about the meaning of the Treaty of Waitangi and its place in New Zealand law and governance have not been narrowing. The dispute about sovereignty – about whose country, ultimately, New Zealand is – has arrived on the nation's agenda at a time when the country's sense of itself as Western, or British, or European, has never been weaker. It also marks the end of a period of optimism about the ultimate resolution of Maori grievances over the consequences of British settlement. (Levine 2004: 651)

These differences have led, on the one hand, to the founding of a separate Māori Party in 2004 and, on the other, to a decision in 2007 by a Labour-led administration to join only three other governments internationally to vote against adoption of the UN Declaration on the Rights of Indigenous Peoples.[26] Thus, it can be argued that the half-hearted fashion in which the various dividing-power reforms were implemented related not only to an intrinsic procedural distrust of such provisions but also to a serious lack of consensus as to what they should look like substantively.

---

[26] For some analysis of why, despite the presence of numerous special Treaty provisions for Māori, the New Zealand Government voted in this way, see Palmer (2008: 217).

In sum, therefore, this period cannot be seen as one in which a new constitution was forged in New Zealand. Generally speaking, New Zealand's pragmatic and flexible constitutional habits continue to dominate. Despite this, the importance of the 1984–1993 period from a constitutional point of view should not be underestimated. The shift to MMP has clearly fundamentally transformed the system of representation, the way in which parliament functions and the relationship between parliament and the executive. Moreover, propelled by the "aversive" political dynamic outlined in Section 12.5, the sheer number of other institutional reforms was unprecedented. While these latter reforms were enacted *within* the existing constitution setup, they also broke new ground, especially as regards the role of the judiciary in protecting human rights and Māori Treaty rights. They continue to play a significant role in shaping the nature of public power to this day. Moreover, should New Zealand ever attempt to engage fully in a process of constitution-making, these new frameworks will undoubtedly be reference points. Nevertheless, because of the philosophical tensions between them, they will not constitute simple building blocks of a new constitutional order. To the contrary, resolving their contradictions and ambiguities will represent a formidable and doubtless controversial task in any attempt to create a new Constitution for the country.

REFERENCES

Ackerman, B. (1989). "Constitutional Politics/Constitutional Law." *Yale Law Journal* 99: 453–547.
(1991). *We the People Foundations*. Cambridge, MA and London: Belknap Press of Harvard University Press.
Attorney-General v. New Zealand Maori Council [1987] 1 NZLR 687.
Attorney-General v. New Zealand Maori Council [1991] 2 NZLR 129 (CA).
Belich, J. (2001). *Paradise Reforged: A History of the New Zealanders from the 1880s to the Year 2000*. Auckland: Allen Lane and Penguin Press.
Elster, J. (1995). "Forces and Mechanisms in the Constitution-Making Process." *Duke Law Journal* 45(2): 364–396.
Erdos, D. (2007). "Aversive Constitutionalim in the Westminster World: The Genesis of the New Zealand Bill of Rights Act (1990)." *International Journal of Constitutional Law* 5(2): 343–369.
(2009). "Judicial Culture and the Politicolegal Opportunity Structure: Explaining Bill of Rights Legal Impact in New Zealand." *Law and Social Inquiry* 34(1): 95–127.
(2010). *Delegating Rights Protection: The Rise of Bills of Rights in the Westminster World*. Oxford: Oxford University Press.
Fitzgerald v. Muldoon [1976] 2 NZLR 615.
Gardbaum, S. (2013). *The New Commonwealth Model of Constitutionalism*. Cambridge: Cambridge University Press.
Jackson, K. and A. McRobie (1998). *New Zealand Adopts Proportional Representation: Accident? Design? Evolution?* Aldershot: Ashgate.

Joseph, P. A. (2007). *Constitutional and Administrative Law in New Zealand*. Wellington: Brookers.

Keith, K. (1978). "A Lawyer Looks at Parliament." In *The Reform of Parliament: Papers Presented in Memory of Dr. Alan Robinson*. J. Marshall, ed. Wellington: New Zealand Institute of Public Administration.

King, A. (2001). *Does the United Kingdom Still Have a Constitution?* London: Sweet and Maxwell.

Lange, D. (2005). *My Life*. Auckland: Penguin.

Levine, S. (2004). "Parliamentary Democracy in New Zealand." *Parliamentary Affairs* 57(3): 646–665.

Lijphart, A. (1999). *Patterns of Democracy: Government Forms and Performance in Thirty-Six Countries*. New Haven, CT and London: Yale University Press.

Mulgan, R. (1978). "The Concept of Mandate in New Zealand Politics." *Political Science* 30(2): 88–96.

New Zealand Government Te Puni Kokhi (Ministry of Maori Affairs) (2002). *He Tirohanga o Kawa ki te Tiriti o Waitangi*. Wellington: Te Puni Kokiri.

New Zealand Maori Council v. Attorney-General [1992] 2 NZLR 576 (CA).

Orange, C. (1987). *The Treaty of Waitangi*. Wellington: Bridget Williams Books.

Palmer, G. (1979). *Unbridled Power?: An Interpretation of New Zealand's Constitution and Government*. Wellington and Oxford: Oxford University Press.

  (1987). *Unbridled Power: An Interpretation of New Zealand's Constitution and Government*. Auckland and Oxford: Oxford University Press.

  (1992). *New Zealand's Constitution in Crisis: Reforming our Political System*. Dunedin: John McIndoe.

  (2004). "Muldoon and the Constitution." In *Muldoon Revisited*. M. Clark, ed. Palmerston North: Dunmore Press.

Palmer, M. (2007). "New Zealand Constitutional Culture." *New Zealand Universities Law Review* 2007(22): 565–597.

  (2008). *The Treaty of Waitangi in New Zealand's Law and Constitution*. Wellington: Victoria University Press.

Renwick, A. (2010). *The Politics of Electoral Reform*. Cambridge: Cambridge University Press.

Rishworth, P (1995). "The Birth and Rebirth of the Bill of Rights." In *Rights and Freedoms: The New Zealand Bill of Rights Act 1990 and the Human Rights Act 1993*. G. Hunscroft and P. Rishworth, eds. Wellington: Brooker's.

Scott, K. J. (1962). *The New Zealand Constitution*. Oxford: Oxford University Press.

Wi Parata v. Bishop of Wellington [1877] 3 NZ Jr (NS) 72.

Woodhouse, O. (1979). *Government Under the Law*. Wellington: New Zealand Council for Civil Liberties.

13

The Juristic Republic of Iran

Binesh Hass

13.1 INTRODUCTION

Legitimacy is a notoriously elusive concept in any political setting. The concept can be legal or moral, both or neither, and the way in which we think about it is doubtless structured by the sociopolitical and historical context where it is invoked. In times of revolution, the conceptual difficulties are even greater because nothing is stable for very long and the reasons for which people take to the streets can likewise shift, hence altering the reasons why the falling regime has become at least popularly illegitimate. The Iranian revolution of 1979 is a straightforward example of legitimacy's elusiveness, and what follows here is an attempt to capture its attendant complications in the rancorous assembly debates that prefaced the ratification of the country's eventual constitution.

The case of revolutionary Iran is interesting for constitutional theory partly because the formative conversations between the then-vanguard political elites about how to develop legitimacy as the moral and political right to govern are exceptionally well documented. They left nothing to doubt in this regard – they sought to emphasise the importance of legitimacy as a moral and political concept right through their assembly debates. And the documentation, in the original Persian, drips with their exhortations that the new regime, above all else, needs to be seen in the eyes of the people as irreproachably legitimate and that the way to do this was to underscore the people's alleged endorsement of the Islamic nature of the revolution. Two thousand five hundred pages comprise the four volumes of what can be translated as the *Minutes from the Negotiations of the Assembly for the Final Examination of the Constitution of the Islamic Republic* – or, less clumsily, the *Negotiations*.[1] They

---

[1] These are the *Ṣūrat-i mashrūḥ-i muzākirāt-i Majlis-i Barʾrasī-i Nihāʾī-i Qānūn-i Asāsī-i Jumhūrī-i Islāmī-i Īrān* (*Minutes from the Negotiations of The Assembly for the Final Examination of the*

record the surprisingly candid arguments between erstwhile revolutionaries-in-arms who subsequently became political opponents and then ultimately oppressor and oppressed. The debates reflect the obvious difficulties they faced in making the principle of political rule by the guardian jurist – the Supreme Leader – somehow square with the popular nature of the revolution and its putative ideals of democratic government. In other words, how were they to legitimate the jurist's guardianship in the face of the boisterous calls from both inside and outside the Assembly for popular self-government? What emerged in Iranian constitutional theory, then, was an idea of political legitimacy that partly reflected the sociopolitical setting from which it was derived and which moreover remains an important locus of political contestation today. It would be hardly controversial, especially in light of the enduring legacy of the Green Movement, to say that political legitimacy remains a topic of robust dispute.

Against this backdrop, the task here will be to be consider the *Negotiations* as a medium for making sense of why the revolutionaries wrote the constitution in the way that they did and, moreover, why they made such fundamental changes to it upon Khomeini's death in 1989. It goes without saying that the *Negotiations*, notwithstanding their detail and expansiveness, cannot by themselves propound a complete account of these questions. But their perspective on the explosive period between August 1979 and 1981 is invaluable, especially with regard to the ways in which political legitimacy is contested today.

The argument proceeds in four steps. The task in Section 13.2 is to lay out how and why the doctrine of the jurist's guardianship came to the fore of the debate amongst the revolutionaries on what should and should not be included in the constitution. Section 13.3 begins with a reading of the tension between the right to self-determination and the jurist's doctrine, illustrating how the initial discourse witnessed a simultaneous rejection and acceptance of the democratic political and nominal form. Section 13.4 considers the Constitution's Article Five, the jurist's guardianship, and asks why it took the form that it did in 1979 in light of the arguments for and against the divinity of the jurist and the problems this would pose for the people's right to self-determination. Lastly, Section 13.5 examines the implications of the jurist's move into the public sphere as a regulative political principle – it is argued that in redrawing the relation between state and religion, the jurist comes into conflict with both and this, in turn, has been one of the defining features of contemporary Iranian political theory.

Constitution of the Islamic Republic), Tehran: Idārah-'i Kull-i Umūr-i Farhangī va Ravābiṭ-i 'Umūmī-i Majlis-i Shūrā-yi Islāmī, 1985–1989, four volumes. Also available online in PDF format at the following, accessed 10 March 2010: http://www.majlesekhobregan.ir/index.php?option=com_content&task=view&id=714&Itemid=44.The pagination of the PDFs is the same as the hard copies, and so all citations are uniform between them.

13.2 THE ROAD TO THE JURIST

Between January and June 1978, Hassan Habibi, a prominent political activist and noted liberal jurist, was instructed by Ayatollah Khomeini to draft the preliminary version of the new regime's constitution while in Paris. The drafted document would come to centre on Khomeini's then-recent assertions that the regime he wished to establish was to be a republic not unlike those found elsewhere. When asked, as he frequently was, to distinguish between an Islamic republic and other republics, he was always very conciliatory. In an interview with *Le Monde*, for example, he was asked the following:

> *Le Monde:* Your Excellency wishes to establish an Islamic republic in Iran. For the French people this is ambiguous because a republic cannot have a religious foundation. Is your republic based on socialism? Constitutionalism? Would you hold elections? Is it democratic?
>
> *Khomeini:* Our republic has the same meaning as anywhere else. We call it 'Islamic Republic' because the conditions of its emergence are embedded in Islam, but the choice belongs to the people. The meaning of the republic is the same as any other republics in the world.[2]

Some have argued that Khomeini's position before the victory of the revolution was primarily informed by shrewd political calculation (Ghamari-Tabrizi 2008: 42). Although Khomeini expounded his theory of government well before the actual revolution in 1979, its political implementation was to be an experimental exercise for everyone concerned (Khomeini 1981). Mehdi Bazargan argued the same when, after resigning from the head of the provisional government in 1979, he recalled that neither Khomeini nor the members of the Revolutionary Council had any clear idea of what institutions or regulatory bodies would be needed to implement the government's revolutionary ideals (Bazargan 1981; Ghamari-Tabrizi 2008).[3]

In assigning the task of formulating the new constitution to Habibi, Khomeini reified his rhetorical endorsement of Western understandings of republicanism. After

---

[2] Khomeini, R., *Sahifeh-ye Noor: Majmu'e-ye rahnemudha-ye Imam Khomeini* (hereafter cited as the *Pages* or Khomeini 1983), Tehran: The Organization of the Islamic Revolution's Cultural Documents, 1983, vol. 2, p. 351. Also cited in Ghamari-Tabrizi, B., *Islam and Dissent in Postrevolutionary Iran: Abdolkarim Soroush, Religious Politics, and Democratic Reform*, London: I.B. Tauris, 2008, p. 42. All twenty-one volumes of the *Pages* are available online at the following, accessed 1 April 2010: http://www.imam-khomeini.com/ShowItem.aspx?id=11749&cat=0&lang=fa

[3] The Revolutionary Council was established on 12 January 1979, shortly before the arrival of Khomeini in Tehran. It was responsible for the management of the country until the proper governmental institutions could be arranged. Initially operating in secret, its responsibilities were truly exhaustive, encompassing everything from the salaries of nurses to the nationalisation of the banks. In this respect, it acted as a parallel government to the provisional government of Bazargan (although he, too, was a member of the Council). For more on the Council, see Bakhash (1986: 64–66).

all, French republicanism, especially the Gaullist heritage of the Fifth Republic and its emphasis on the executive office, profoundly influenced Habibi's political and legal worldview. As with the 1958 Constitution of the Fifth Republic that transformed France from a parliamentary polity into a presidential one, Habibi sought to bestow wide-ranging executive powers on the president as well as establish a judicial body that reserved the right to review and reject parliamentary legislation. The president of the new regime was to wield sweeping executive powers, and the Guardian Council, a twelve-member upper house with considerable legislative and judicial powers, was to bear the right to scrutinise the religiosity and hence constitutionality of all parliamentary legislation. Khomeini's endorsement of Habibi and the other civil jurists who were drafting the constitution was, indeed, very public and, perhaps more importantly, without mention of his own theory of political governance, the guardianship of the jurist (*vilayat-i faqih*), a concept to which I shall return shortly (Schirazi 1997: 23).[4] In a meeting with the Tehran Preachers' Society on 17 June 1979, for example, Khomeini urged support for Habibi's published draft and hoped that it would be ratified without delay (Ghamari-Tabrizi 2008: 43). The doctrine of the guardianship was not passed by the Assembly of Experts until 12 September 1979,[5] and until that very day, Khomeini remained faithful to his Paris declaration from 1978 – namely, that the clergy (*ruhaniyat*) would assume no more than advisory roles in the new regime.[6] And, simpler still, as regards the guardianship of the jurist, Khomeini confessed at the time that "the realities of our society do not allow a full appreciation of the [doctrine]" (Kadivar 1998: 183). The idea that an Islamic jurist would rule the new republic, then, was initially shelved.

Six days after the publication of the preliminary draft, Khomeini appealed to the public by inviting all "groups, clergy, intellectuals, and theologians to examine this new [constitution] and write [their] opinions in existing newspapers about

---

[4] *Vilayat-i faqih* is more appropriately translated from Persian as the "guardianship of the Islamic jurist," but for brevity's sake it will be referred to in the present chapter as the guardianship of the jurist, or doctrine, or the jurist's doctrine, and so forth. In all places, I mean the same thing.

[5] The Assembly of Experts was initially called the Assembly for the Final Examination of the Constitution of the Islamic Republic of Iran and was established by a bill of the same name by the Revolutionary Council on 5 July 1979, convening for the first time on 19 August 1979. For the first four months, Ayatollah Montazeri was its speaker until Ayatollah Beheshti replaced him in November 1979. The body was later renamed the Assembly of Experts of the Leadership (*majlis-i khobregan-i rahbari*) or, more simply, the Assembly of Experts.

[6] The second and third volumes of Khomeini's *Pages* (1983) are largely concerned with his theory for an Islamic republic and the role of the clergy in its polity. As regards the advisory role of the clergy, see especially volume two, p. 250, and volume three, p. 110, as well as p. 135, which reads "I, and other clerics, will not hold a position in the future government, the duty of the clerics is to guide, I shall only take upon myself the responsibility of guiding the future government." On p. 140, he continues: "I have never said that the clerics are going to be in charge of the government; the clerics have other responsibilities."

all the things [that] might be deem[ed] useful for Islam and consistent with the Islamic Republic" (Khomeini 1983: vol. 4, 463). By positioning the constitution as an object for public epistemic contest and, prior to even that, by appointing a secular civil jurist as the chief author for the preliminary drafting of the fundamental law, Khomeini put into a motion a process that, much to the chagrin of the clerical establishment, secularised both the country's jurisprudence and constitution – a defining phenomenon of the new polity I will emphasise and describe in greater detail in the final section of this chapter.

The public responded to Khomeini's invitation in large numbers and in varying ways. Although a minority of the political parties, such as the National Front, reluctantly supported the draft formulated by the civil jurists, most political parties of the left castigated its framers for abandoning the movement's revolutionary ideals (Bakhash 1986: 71–91; Ghamari-Tabrizi 2008: 45). The draft, making no mention of the doctrine of the jurist's guardianship, enjoyed significant support from Khomeini as well as the Revolutionary Council.[7] Noticeably, however, it lacked the support of the intelligentsia. And of this last group, the most organised critique came from a group of civil jurists from the Iranian Lawyers Guild. This group demanded that the United Nations Declaration of Human Rights be incorporated into the body of the constitution and that international organisations and lawyers ought to be granted the authority to defend Iranian nationals before domestic courts. They moreover called for a curtailing of presidential powers in favour of a more politically potent parliament (Bakhash 1986: 77). And although the draft constitution was sparing in its delegation of power to the clergy, it generated a formidable negative reaction from the more secular quarters of the country's post-revolutionary mosaic. The draft intended to satisfy the political aspirations of a variegated set of interest groups, but it failed to engender enough support from any single group that could then facilitate its ratification.

The younger generation of clerical leadership, led by Akbar Hashemi Rafsanjani, were expressly satisfied with the draft of the civil jurists and were agitating for ratification at an early stage through a national referendum and not a constituent assembly. Bazargan and Abolhassan Banisadr, the regime's first president, worked against this position and advocated securing the constitution to its sociopolitical foundations by establishing a publicly elected constituent assembly that would review the jurists' draft constitution. In an oft-quoted and highly prescient moment, Rajsanjani retorted: "Who do you think will be elected to a constituent assembly? A fistful of

---

7   The draft of Habibi et al. is available online at the following, accessed 15 April 2010: http://tiny.cc/daah2, or by querying on http://fa.wikisource.org for *"qanun-i asasi"* in Arabic script. See also Abdol Karim Lahiji's commentary on penning the draft at the following, accessed 15 April 2010: http://www.radiofarda.com/content/f35_Lahiji_IV_Post_Revolutionary_Constitution/1957037.html

ignorant and fanatical fundamentalists who will do such damage that you will regret
ever having convened them" (Arjomand 1993: 90). Khomeini initially sided with
Rafsanjani for a direct and quick ratification through referendum but was, according to one source, eventually persuaded against this by Bazargan (Sanjabi 1989: 334;
Ghamari-Tabrizi 2008: 259). In the end, the task to review and approve the draft
constitution fell neither to the public via a referendum nor to an elected constituent assembly. Khomeini decided that task should be undertaken by an Assembly
of Experts that was to be carefully engineered so as to minimise what he saw as the
more aberrant elements of the immediate post-revolutionary period. He worried
that positioning the debate on the constitution so openly, either in a freely elected
constituent assembly or through a national referendum, would allow the left and
modernists to expand the popular political gains they had made in criticising the
draft constitution (e.g., the critiques that came from the Lawyers Guild). At the end
of June 1979, he galvanised the clerics who had comprised the backbone of the
Islamist camp of the revolution thus:

> This right belongs to you. Those knowledgeable about Islam may express an opin-
> ion on its law. The constitution of the Islamic Republic means the constitution of
> Islam. Do not sit back while "westoxicated" [foreignised] intellectuals, who have
> no faith in Islam, give their views and write the things they write. Pick up your pens
> and in the mosques, from the altars, in the streets and bazaars, speak of the things
> that in your view should be included in the constitution (Bakhash 1986: 78).

It was at this crucial juncture in Iran's post-revolutionary narrative that the doctrine of
the jurist's guardianship moved to the fore of the constitutional debates. The clerics
responded to Khomeini's urgings and convened the Congress of Muslim Critics of
the Constitution. Not long after its formation, it authored a resolution proposing that
"the duties of the president ought to be carried out by the ruling jurist [*faqih*]."[8]

It was the Grand Ayatollah Hussein-Ali Montazeri who spearheaded the clerical campaign to formally institutionalise the jurist's doctrine of guardianship in the
constitution. At a time when the revolution's clerical backers felt that they might
be sidelined by modernists and leftists, other grand ayatollahs also joined the growing chorus in favour of the jurist's doctrine: Golpayegani and Mar'ashi-Najafi, both
belonging to the class of traditionalist clerics which generally abstained from political engagement, argued against a constitution that would exclude the doctrine's
constitutional entrenchment (Ghamari-Tabrizi 2008: 46). Montazeri then struck
the hardest blows to the draft constitution, partly because he was the most articulate of the Assembly of Experts' interlocutors and partly because he challenged
both the traditional tripartite separation of governmental powers as well as the very

---

[8] Daily newspaper *Jomhuri-ye Islami*, 16 July 1979, cited in Kadivar (1998: 184).

idea that self-determination – understood as the people's supreme political right to elect the state's government and determine its composition and trajectory – ought to be the defining capacity of the people. Self-determination was a right that functioned centrifugally in the draft constitution, defining and limiting all its other articles. Montazeri sought to abrogate its fundamental position on the grounds that it contradicted the claim to the political and juridical primacy that was rightly inherent in the doctrine of the jurist's guardianship. The philosophical basis for this had to do with idea that subjectivity (i.e., the self) could only realise freedom by overcoming its materiality in the movement from the materiality of nature to transcendence. If freedom or the right to self-determination, then, could only be the effect of this movement toward transcendence or divinity, and if divinity is the proper interpretive remit of the *imāmat* (that is to say, the religious leadership that had dedicated itself to the pursuit of divine truths), then "self-determination" or "individual liberty" are empty concepts when divorced from the mediatory role of the religious leadership. Without divine guidance, no individual, however free to do as they wish, could shed the bondage of materiality and hence enjoy the freedom that Khomeini and Montazeri, along with Mottahari and even Shariati, had in mind. On these grounds, the jurist's doctrine is charged with concatenating, on the one hand, the aspirations of the people to be free and self-determinative and, on the other, the higher divinity that renders these aspirations a real possibility. This is why absolute political power must by necessity be vested in the jurist or, as Montazeri argued, he must have the right "to dissolve the parliament ... to declare war and peace ... to be commander in chief of the armed forces ... to nominate candidates for the presidency and approve the president after a general election" (*Jomhuri-ye Islami* 1979; Kadivar 1998: 186–187; Ghamari-Tabrizi 2008: 46). And when Montazeri was the first to advocate the soteriological qualities of juristic guardianship in a Friday sermon on 14 September 1979, the worshippers bellowed that "the jurist, by God, is the guardian of our revolution" (Ghamari-Tabrizi 2008: 46).

Although Khomeini encouraged the clerics to engage in the constitutional debates, he tactfully avoided directly sanctioning the doctrine that was proving to cause such turmoil within the ranks of the revolutionaries. When the Assembly of Experts first convened on 19 August 1979, the doctrine had already been widely touted by Montazeri and others as the foundational principle of the revolution. But when Rafsanjani inaugurated the Assembly by reading a six-point message from Khomeini on that day, he mentioned nothing of the juristic doctrine (Khomeini 1983: vol. 1, 5–6). The first point asserted the Islamic identity of the revolution and the second reaffirmed the Islamic basis of the constitution: "The constitution ought to be based on Islam. If even one article contradicts Islamic ordinances, it is a deviation from the Republic and the vote of the great majority of the people" (*ibid.*). Taken for what it means – that is, to account for its logic but not necessarily its politics – Khomeini stipulated that, if an article is un-Islamic, then it is subsequently against the wishes of the majority. To be sure, he took the figures reported in the national referendum that established the country as an Islamic republic earlier in April 1979 literally and very seriously. The referendum provided the Iranian voter with two options – abolish the monarchy and replace it with an Islamic republic, yes or no – without indicating what a third or fourth choice might look like. Doubtless, Iran in 1979 was by and large virulently anti-monarchical and the revolution was broadly popular, but neither of these meant that the people were as pro-Islamist as they were anti-monarchical. The referendum exploited the anti-monarchical sentiments of the people but denied them the opportunity to express this in the referendum except under an Islamist rubric. The wishes of "the great majority of people" were thus declared as nothing other than Islam and, by extension, all its social and political derivatives. In his third point, Khomeini reaffirmed the right of the jurists to interpret Islam and, by extension, to adjudicate the validity of the constitution in both its draft and ratified forms. This, however, was not to bar the input of legal, administrative and political experts who, he urged in the same line, ought to be consulted and have their knowledge reflected in the constitution (*ibid.*). The remaining three points had nothing at all to do with the role of the jurist, but the first three, in their omissions of direct advocacy of particular policies, went a long way to cultivate the space that was necessary for the members of the Assembly of Experts to determine the nascent contours of a distinctly Islamic form of political legitimacy.

13.3 CONTESTING THE DISCOURSE

Khomeini was well aware of the antinomy of legitimacy between the rule of the Islamic jurist and the political and moral rights related to self-determination. The religious factions of the revolution were unanimous in positioning Islam as the defining identity of the new state, but their opinions about the role of the jurist and clerics remained decidedly disparate. For Khomeini, when the national referendum of April 1979 presented the voter with two options with regard to the abolishment of the monarchy and the establishment of an Islamic republic ("yes or no"), inherent in the affirmative was a concomitant affirmation of what it meant to establish such a state, namely to be governed by the laws of Islam. And given that the jurist has privileged access to the discernment of such laws, a "yes" on the ballot was also a "yes" to the jurist's guardianship. This follows if one's view is to establish the best possible form of the state's appellation. For others, like Grand Ayatollah Shariatmadari, the referendum should have been more open-ended, and he criticised the simple "yes or no" of the ballot. In a (literally nominal) attempt to ground legitimacy in the people, a large and variegated coalition of clerical and liberal parties espoused affixing "Democratic" to the suggested "Islamic Republic" referent of the new state. Khomeini warned against suggestions of this type on two grounds. First, he followed Montazeri in arguing that the concept of democracy was already embedded in Islam and, further, that the suggested prefix implied that Islam was undemocratic and therefore necessitated an ameliorative appellation – indeed, when asked in an interview why "Democratic" was dropped from the suggested name, he lamented: "It is saddening to me when Islam is emptied of its essence, and then some believe that we need to add a prefix, such as 'democratic,' to define it. Islam encompasses everything."[9] This followed from a position more fully developed by Ayatollah Motahhari:

> The word "democratic" in the "Democratic Islamic Republic" is tautological. Moreover, soon people will gain certain freedoms and democratic rights under the Islamic Republic, and some might believe that they have attained these rights because of the democratic principle of the regime, not for its Islamic essence.... When we speak of the Islamic Republic, naturally we recognise individual rights, freedom, and democracy (*ibid.*).

The logic for this opinion can be traced further back to a polemical work by Motahhari called *The Allure of Materialism*, wherein he argued that inherent in the idea of Islam is the advocacy of plurality (Motahhari 1978: 85). This is evidenced by the wide array of opinions available in Islamic jurisprudence and, he continues, contrasted to the monolithic canon of Catholicism. And moreover, secularism's rapid growth in Europe but allegedly stymied presence in Iran could, in part, be explained by the adverse repercussions that followed from the oppressiveness of Catholic canon's singularity. In its plurality of jurisprudential opinions, Motahhari saw Islam's natural inclusion of the democratic ethos. Hence the redundancy of "Democratic Islamic Republic."

The aforementioned argument constituted the first approach to jettisoning the "Democratic" prefix. The second was linked to one of the more consistent trajectories of Khomeini's discourse, namely its anti-colonialism. He used it to admonish the "westoxicated intellectuals" that threatened the Islamic identity of the revolution, as well as to void the opinions that came from Shariatmadari and others regarding the nominal prefix. Upon arriving in Qom on 1 March 1979, for example, he warned that democracy was a Western idea, and that the new state would neither be the "Republic of Iran" nor the "Democratic Islamic Republic of Iran," but simply the "Islamic Republic of Iran, neither a word more nor less" (Khomeini 1983: vol. 5, 125). This, in part, was a trenchant opposition to any attempt that would shift the fundamental basis of political legitimacy from divinity to the people.

---

[9] Interview with Oriana Fallaci, Khomeini (1983: vol. 9, 88); Ghamari-Tabrizi (2008: 49).

The matter was finally concluded and the proposal regarding the prefix was dropped. Coupled with victory at the ballot box on referendum day (government numbers put the affirmative vote to 98.6 per cent), the clerics who were allied with Khomeini and Montazeri gained the requisite momentum to successfully demand the institutionalisation of clerical positions. These victories, however, were against a chaotic backdrop that had seen the growth of numerous and often conflicting sources of political power. These included grassroots organisations in the factories, revolutionary foundations, ethnic self-determination movements, as well as a number of state institutions that had been left behind by the ancien régime. Some historians have argued that Khomeini's seemingly contradictory positions on the state's basis of legitimacy can be explained when contextualised within the immediate post-revolutionary power struggles (Ghamari-Tabrizi 2008: 51). I think this is accurate. Why and how he abandoned his previous commitments to keep the clerics out of politics – let alone permanently institutionalising their roles in the government's operative apparatus – are questions that cannot be addressed without accounting for the turmoil of the immediate post-revolutionary context and the ensuing threat Khomeini perceived to the Islamic identity of the revolution. And ultimately, understanding the genesis of the jurist's guardianship as the fulcrum of Iranian politics, too, is bound to how one explicates Khomeini's response to, and manoeuvring of, the cuts and cleavages of, the fractured agonal context. This is the point to which I now turn.

Although the abolishment of the monarchy was relatively peaceful insofar as, for example, the country did not undergo a civil war between revolutionaries and monarchists, there was nevertheless a considerable degree of internal conflict. As previously mentioned, there were various self-determination movements from within the country's ethnic populations: beginning in March 1979, a large Kurdish uprising overtook the northern provinces of Western Azerbaijan and Kurdistan; in the same month, Iran's Arab population began to agitate for greater rights in the southern province of Khuzestan; and in the northeast, Turkomans were at loggerheads with the provisional government over land distribution and access to water. All three conflicts led to considerable bloodshed and, in the case of the Turkomans, full-scale urban warfare between the Fedayin-i Khalq and government forces. In another important theatre, trade unionists in the cities were mobilising with the help of a variegated array of socialists to demand ameliorative policies for a working class that had been mistreated under the monarchy. Perhaps above and beyond these conflicts, however, the clerics were finding it very difficult to win the discursive battles with the liberals, dissident clerics, and, more preponderantly, the socialists who were applying pressure from within the revolutionary ranks and throughout the ever-important university campuses. The clerics were, in short, losing the conversation. This is why Khomeini had to shut down the universities for three years and employ individuals like Abdolkarim Soroush, now a "doyen" of religious dialogue at several American universities, and others to purge the faculties of those whose Islamic credentials were lax. Of the dissident clerics who were at variance with the doctrine of the jurist, perhaps it was Grand Ayatollah Shariatmadari who was the most unlucky: the man who had prevented the Shah from executing Khomeini in 1963 by recognising him as a grand ayatollah was eventually "demoted" by the state and had his political party banned and many of his followers imprisoned and executed.[10] And amidst the conflict and dissension that was riddling the country, Khomeini lost faith in the capacity of Banisadr's provisional government of technocrats to protect the Islamic essence of the revolution.[11] To service this end, he found it necessary, as he would later recall in 1981, to secure the political appointments of the clergy:

> From the beginning of the revolution, my position as I conveyed it in many interviews and declarations in Najaf, Paris, and upon returning to Tehran was that the clergy [*ruhaniyat*] has a higher responsibility than those who hold executive appointments. In case the revolution should triumph, I had suggested, they would return to their cherished responsibilities. But when we entered the political arena, we realised if we asked them to return to their mosques, the Americans [i.e., the Westernised intelligentsia] and the Soviets [i.e., the socialists and Marxist] would swallow up the country. We experienced and learned that those non-clerics who assumed power, albeit many of them were devout Muslims, failed to realise our basic desire for independence.... *Therefore, since we did not find a person who could be faithful to the cause for which this nation had sacrificed its youth, we felt obliged to accept clerics in the office of the president or other governmental positions.* I reiterate that we do not intend to run the country, and on the day we realise that non-clerics are able to *manage the country according to God's desires*, the respected [then-Hojatoleslam] Khamenei [the President] shall return to his spiritual duties. We asked the clergy to attend to their spiritual and guiding roles after the revolution. But we made a mistake, and we should have the courage to admit our mistakes. We seek the realisation of Islam, not the advancement of our own words [i.e., commitments to previous statements regarding clerical forbearance from politics]. During the revolution, we thought that these educated, devout, and intellectual groups

[10] Shariatmadari's official demotion was paradoxical because the title of grand ayatollah is established through an irreversible process of recognition by other leading ayatollahs and grand ayatollahs. Note, however, that the causes of his demotion had less to do with his dissension and more with his indirect associations with a group of clerics and army officers that was plotting to assassinate Khomeini in 1982.

[11] Both the Cultural Revolution that purged the universities (1980–1982) and the demotion of Shariatmadari (1982) came after the consolidation of clerical power in 1981. This does not, however, detract from the argument presented here. What I am illustrating is that the dissent and discord were of such a degree that it made the clerical establishment uncomfortable enough that they felt it necessary to institutionalise their positions in the political apparatus of the country. The doctrine of the jurist's guardianship was, in this regard, the flagship institution.

would advance the country according to the divine will, but we were mistaken.... *If we suspect that the integrity of Islam is in jeopardy, it is our responsibility to intervene.* Let them accuse us of anything; let them promulgate [the idea] that this is the country of mullahs run by an akhundist [a pejorative term for clerics] regime. This is propaganda to force us to leave. No! We shall not leave the scene. (Khomeini 1983: vol. 16, 211–212, emphases added; Ghamari-Tabrizi 2008: 54).

The institutionalisation of clerical power throughout the political structure met with a chorus of dissent from both secular and theological quarters. The arguments centred on the doctrine of the jurist's guardianship, which had become the defining dogma of the regime during the summer of 1979. The political space to oppose the doctrine was made possible by the fact that Khomeini at that early stage was unconvinced that the nation was amenable to its implementation. He was reluctant to publicly endorse the political theory of Islamic government he had lectured on and written about since at least the Najaf lectures of January and February 1970. By not publicly speaking in its favour, Khomeini serviced the grounds for a relatively free and frank discussion of the doctrine on the floors of the Assembly of Experts. By "free and frank" I, of course, mean those discussions that occurred between the constituent members who had not been vetted and subsequently precluded from running for a seat on the Assembly by Khomeini and his ad hoc judiciary. Indeed, the composition of the Assembly had been engineered so carefully that even Tehran's constituency lines were redrawn in order to ensure the victory of certain candidates. Notwithstanding these and probably other restrictions, opposition to the jurist's doctrine within the chamber was hardly diffident.[12]

13.4 POLEMICS

Ezatollah Sahabi, a prominent civilian from the ministry of industry, was one the most vocal opponents of the doctrine of the jurist's guardianship. He argued that by "bestowing divinity upon the ruler," the doctrine amounted to idolatry in addition to undermining the democratic spirit of the constitution (Khomeini 1983: vol. 1, 88–89). Along with other more democratically minded Assembly members like Mohammad Moqadam Maraqe'i and Banisadr, he urged that the doctrine would estrange the

---

[12] As one would imagine, opposition to the doctrine of the jurist's guardianship was equally if not more intense beyond the walls of the Assembly. Because this essay is concerned with how the doctrine was forged and ratified within the purview of government, however, I cannot, for oft-repeated reasons of space, engage with the material on external opposition. One helpful source on this aspect of the debates on the constitution is the weekly journal published by the Muslim People's Republican Party, which was closely aligned with Grand Ayatollah Shariatmadari. In its final evaluation, the journal, *Khalgh-e Mosalman* (*Muslim Nation*), concluded: "The Assembly of Experts has approved the establishment of a dictatorial regime."

ruling class from the country's intellectuals as well as the international community (*ibid.*). Banisadr would argue that the right to govern belongs to the people only, and that the role of the jurist could in this respect do no more than guarantee it (Khomeini 1983: vol. 1, 520–521). Moreover, if the Assembly of Experts could not guarantee the right of self-determination for Iran's people, then it was, by extension, rendering them vulnerable to similar violations by foreign countries, mentioning by name the English, Americans, and others (*ibid.*). After all, how could a government claim to champion the rights of its people in the face of foreign aggression when it was itself violating them? The right to rule and the source of legitimacy must not be reduced to one man, Banisadr continued, however divine or whatever their claims to divinity were (i.e., the jurist or the *seyyeds*), otherwise the country would risk regressing back to the old monarchic despotism of governance by fiat (*ibid.*).[13]

The doctrine of the jurist, Article Five, was fundamentally altering the basis for legitimate government which was given to the people in Article Three.[14] Maraqe'i demanded that this shift be submitted to "a separate referendum," and that "If [the Assembly] change[d] the fundamental basis of the system's political legitimacy from popular vote to the rule of the jurist, then [it would also] need to revise all the [other] articles accordingly" (*ibid.*). In undermining the sovereignty of the people by subordinating it to political divinity, the Assembly was generating tension between religious jurisprudence (*ijtihad*) and parliamentary legislation. Whereas the former operates to further the ends of Islam, the latter labours in the interests of the state and, ideally, the people it represents. The project of the Islamic Republic was to eliminate the structural boundaries between the two by ensconcing the jurist at its apex. Khomeini denied distinguishing between the people's interests and Islam's, between state and religion, but in the act of subordinating one to the guardianship of the other he reaffirmed their distinctness – for if they really were one and the same, then there would be no need to subordinate one to the other in the form of the jurist's guardianship over the state. Banisadr and others endeavoured to inverse the relation: the jurist's guardianship, if it were to be institutionalised in the constitution, must act to ensure that the sovereignty of the people is not infringed by anyone or anything – presumably even by religious interests (Khomeini 1983: vol. 1, 520–521).

---

[13] Banisadr jokes that even in cases of those whose claims to divine descent are valid – like his own and that of Beheshti – the nation would do better to err on the side of caution and not trust even *seyyeds* with such power. Why, he asks? Because even they (alluding to Ayatollah Taleghani) admit that sometimes they are crazy, and that this would be particularly insalubrious for the country, he answers, and to which Montazeri adds: "Mr Banisadr, all jokes have serious undertones."

[14] Moqadam Maraqe'i argued that the "jurist's guardianship directly contradicts Article Three of the draft of the constitution, which assigns the ultimate legitimacy of government to the people" (Khomeini 1983: vol. 1, 375–376).

The opponents of the jurist's doctrine were significantly outnumbered. The chairman of the Assembly alternated between Montazeri to the heavier-handed Ayatollah Beheshti, who frequently rebuked Maraqe'i and others for "failing to understand the doctrine of the jurist" and for advocating a Western-inspired constitution for an incontrovertibly Islamic nation. The tired dichotomy of East and West and the essentialisation of each were met with the equally tired attempt to rehabilitate the purported ideals of one into the other by claiming that the principles of democracy, for example, could be found in Islam. Bazargan would make this argument in the opening session of the Assembly:

> All references to the principles of freedom, the right to criticism, self-determination rights, and majority rule in the proposed draft of the constitution are neither borrowed from the West nor imposed upon us by Westerners. . . . Rather, these principles derive from the Islamic doctrine of free will, the notion of promoting the good and forbidding evil, and the necessity of consultation. These principles have Quranic roots and are consistent with Divine Providence. (Ghamari-Tabrizi 2008: 58)

Grand Ayatollah Naser Makarem Shirazi, a leading seminarian from Qom, a long-time disciple and friend of Khomeini, and arguably one of the bravest men in the Assembly, supported Bazargan in this position and went much further with his dissent. He argued that Khomeini's leadership was an exception in history and that the Assembly would be foolish to attempt to institutionalise an exception given that the constitution was to be "for all times" and, perhaps more interestingly, "for all places" (Khomeini 1983: vol. 2, 1113 ff.). Along with Ahmad Nourbakhsh, Makarem Shirazi was one of the more cosmopolitan members of the Assembly who saw the need to formulate a constitution that was congruent with international law, for the Iranian revolution was considered to be an event that was inextricable from its international sociopolitical setting (Khomeini 1983: vol. 1, 363; vol. 2, 1113–1115). He continued, "ought" must imply "can," and this was a litmus test that the doctrine of the jurist's guardianship failed given the conditions of the "contemporary world" – this was the principal reason as to why the doctrine must not be accepted by the Assembly as a politically viable mechanism of government (Khomeini 1983: vol. 2, 1115). It would be incongruent with its historical, sociopolitical and international setting – it was, in short, backward. This was in addition to abrogating the sovereignty of the people in favour of a "despotic" clerical rationalisation for their own grip of power: "Do not allow our enemies to say that a bunch of mullahs sat there and wrote a constitution to justify their own rule. For God's sake do not do this" (*ibid.*). The Assembly erupted in clamorous protest and the documentation illustrates how Beheshti, the chairman at the time, struggled to maintain order and urged the members of the Assembly to allow Makarem Shirazi to continue. When one protester shouted that Makarem Shirazi's speech was poisonous to the revolution and contemptuous for those gathered in the Assembly, Beheshti came down hard: "Who gave *you* permission to speak?" Makarem Shirazi was asked to continue, and he did: embedding the doctrine of the jurist in the way that the Assembly envisioned and not as an advisory mechanism without sweeping executive powers (an interpretation that he and others had already voted for), the government was risking mass dissent:

> People might remain silent today, but as God as my witness, tomorrow they will reject [the jurist's guardian] ... [This doctrine] neither furthers the interests of Islam, nor those of the revolution. We have recognised the sovereignty and right of governance of the people in the previous article [Article Three], let us not maim this lion. (*ibid.*)

Montazeri, who would later become one of the most vociferous critics of the regime and the doctrine of the jurist's guardianship, was in the early revolutionary years a firebrand apologist for the most reactionary elements of the revolution and arguably the leading proponent of the jurist's doctrine. He attacked Makarem Shirazi in particular for likening the doctrine to despotism and for his concern for international law and the way in which the world would perceive the jurist's doctrine (*ibid.*). He would argue that the nation had chosen to become an Islamic republic and that its people were endowed with a reason of their own that need not be corroborated by Western opinion, extolling his colleagues not to "concern themselves with what goes on in the world" (*ibid.*). He not only defended the jurist's guardianship as an overarching principle of governance, but also thrice tried to further limit the executive powers of the president and superimpose the jurist over the three other branches of government (Khomeini 1983: vol. 2, 1182).[15] When all three attempts failed, Montazeri admonished his critics and attacked Mohammad Javad Hojjati-Kermani (the representative from Kerman) in particular with a series of ad hominems for his more vocal opposition. Montazeri likened him to the childish and "westoxicated intellectuals" in the media who were constantly seeking the approval of Europe and the United States (*ibid.*). Hojjati-Kermani responded to these attacks by claiming that neither he nor the grand ayatollahs and sources of emulation he had consulted both within and outside the Assembly were westoxicated or infants, and that their opposition to the doctrine was on principled grounds related to its fundamental incompatibility with the objectives of the revolution, the earlier precepts of the constitution, and the social and political bases of the popular uprising that ousted the Shah (*ibid.*).

Some commentators, including Mohsen Kadivar, argue that even before Montazeri became the primus persona non grata of the regime, he genuinely believed in the people's right to govern themselves, but that this right, for reasons related in part to

---

[15] Montazeri would also argue that the independence of the three branches of government, as a principle, was typical of the West and so those who advocated such a system were also westoxicated. Note also his interview years later with *l'Humanité*, cited later in the chapter.

the philosophical exegesis of subjectivity discussed earlier, could only be successfully exercised under the aegis of the jurist (*Jomhuri-ye Islami*, 1979; Kadivar 1998:
183; Ghamari-Tabrizi 2008: 260).[16] Kadivar, for instance, relates how his teacher was
keen to keep the revolutionary spirit alive by institutionalising its most revolutionary
political doctrine. That investing plenary power into one man remains one of the
most antiquated and hence least revolutionary forms of governance in the history of
politics was apparently lost on him. Kadivar attempts to explain this away by arguing that Montazeri read Khomeini's texts to literally mean that the jurist embodied
the "general will" of the nation. This reading of Montazeri is supported by the fact
that Khomeini, too, believed that the vote to abolish the monarchy and establish an
Islamic government was an expression of general will to establish Islamic law and
therefore abide by its supreme authority, the jurist.

Indeed, the language of "the general will of the nation" is actually used throughout the debates of the Assembly. At least one member, the conservative Hassan Ayat,
even invokes Rousseau's theory of the same name to advocate the position that the
jurist was the general will's embodiment (Khomeini 1983: vol. 2, 1093). What Ayat
implied Mohammad Yazdi made explicit: the reason as to why the jurist's doctrine
was politically legitimate was because the people had consented to relinquish a
degree of their right to self-determination to the sovereign in order to lead securer
and better moral lives (Khomeini 1983: vol. 1, 517–518). Like Locke, he argued that
man is born with the God-given gift of freedom and that the only legitimate way
to diminish this divinely ordained right is through rational consent. This is exactly
what the people of Iran had consented to in voting for an Islamic government, whose
regulative principles were Islamic law and whose ultimate juridical authority was
naturally the jurist.[17] Thus, this social contract, he continued, was no different than
what other constitutions had to say about the right to self-determination (*ibid.*).[18]

[16] The daily *Jomhuri-ye Islami*, 15 July 1979, is cited in Kadivar (whose supervisor at Qom was Montazeri);
     note especially Ghamari-Tabrizi, citing an interview Montazeri gave to Françoise Germain-Robin of
     l'Humanité in July 2001, where Montazeri admits that he was overtaken by the revolutionary fervour
     that typified the early years of the Islamic Republic. He would go on to confess that "when power
     becomes absolute and concentrated in the hands of a fallible person who is not accountable to any
     other institution – even though he may be the most pious, wisest, and the most knowledgeable – it
     would inevitably lead to the rise of despotism and authoritarianism." In this interview, Montazeri
     adumbrates, even repeats, many of the arguments that the dissidents of the Assembly had posited and
     which he led in demolishing with ad hominem attacks such as the ones landed at Hojjati-Kermani.
     The interview with *l'Humanité* is available online in French at the following, accessed 30 April 2010:
     http://www.humanite.fr/2001–07–19_International_Le-regime-a-perdu-sa-legitimite
[17] The obvious tension glossed over in Yazdi's argument is that the Shi'ite jurist is only one amongst
     many who interpret Islamic law, and that no one source of emulation ranks higher than any other in
     juridical terms. The doctrine of the jurist's guardianship eliminates the tradition of jurisprudential
     pluralism that has been with Shi'ism since its emergence.
[18] Another Assembly member, Abdolrahman Heidari, makes a bungled attempt after Yazdi to link this
     point with the French Revolution; see *ibid.*: 519.

As Ali Morad Tehrani, the representative from Khorasan, would observe, the jurist's doctrine was founded on the basis of consent and the right of self-determination, and it would only be through these that the doctrine could be legitimately exercised (*ibid.*).

Yazdi's position pivoted on consent and so contrasted with the more conservative position taken by ayatollahs Saduqi, Meshkini, and many others. In the tradition of Sheikh Fazlollah Nuri, they espoused an unstinting theocratic caliphate whose basis of legitimacy was divinity, and made no allusions to the idea that the people were related to the legitimacy of the government (*ibid.*: 77). These arguments invoked considerable ire amongst the minority, those who, like Banisadr and Makarem Shirazi, voiced premonitions of impending dictatorship. Beheshti would try to respond to these fears at one point:

> Does Article Five [the doctrine of the jurist's guardianship] negate the significance of the public ballot? Does Article Five undermine basic liberties? Does Article Five relegate all power to a particular group or social class? Does it suggest that the president and prime minister from now on ought to be turban-wearing clerics? Never. (*ibid.*: 378)

The Assembly would continue to oscillate on the issue of fundamental political and juridical legitimacy. When Article Five finally passed, it did so with a vote of fifty-three in favour, eight against, and four abstentions. The text of 1979 reads as follows:

> During the Occultation [etc.], the governance and leadership of the nation devolve upon the just and pious jurist who is acquainted with the circumstances of his age; courageous, resourceful, and possessed of administrative ability; and *recognised and accepted as leader by the majority of the people*. In the event that no jurist should be recognised by the majority, the leader, or the Leadership Council, composed of jurists possessing the aforementioned qualifications, will assume these responsibilities in accordance with Article 107.[19]

The 1979 version of Article Five hence divorced the guardian jurist, the Supreme Leader, from the clerical seminaries of central Iran and married him to his sociopolitical base in the streets of Tehran and the country's other major cities. His legitimacy became predicated on the "recognition and acceptance of the majority of the people" and his license to rule became foundationally embossed in the body of the people. In principle, Article Five extended an open invitation to the people to adjudicate the legitimacy of their government by being able to challenge or affirm

---

[19] *Constitution of the Islamic Republic of Iran*, emphasis is mine. The executive responsibilities of the jurist are laid out in Chapter VIII of the constitution, headed by Article 107, which also reaffirms that the people's consent is the basis for the jurist's power. These powers are broad and absolute.

the apex of its political structure, the guardian jurist. This, to be sure, was to prove explosive as the years went by and as the revolutionary fervour withered. In July 1989, just one month after the death of Khomeini, and presumably upon realising that the measure of dissent in the country posed a serious democratic challenge to a doctrine whose form was expressly grounded in the acceptance and recognition of the people, Article Five was rewritten. The article was no longer to make any mention of the people, let alone of acceptance and recognition.[20] This rewriting could hardly be overemphasised in any consideration of just how important the regime viewed the question of legitimacy. The clerics who did the rewriting in 1989 were intent on retaining legal legitimacy even if they knew they could no longer claim its moral or political forms.

The legacy of 1979's Article Five and the theories that upheld and challenged it continue to shape Iranian politics primarily through its invitation to the people to utilise the public sphere to adjudicate on matters of political legitimacy. The argument that is obviously not being made is that without the formal invitation of Article Five to the people to adjudicate in this way, the people would not have engaged the public sphere to do so. It would be foolish to suggest that political dissent is premised on government solicitation. What the 1979 version of Article Five did was to engender formal and legally sanctioned channels of dissent, and these were readily used by the people within the system to agitate for greater democracy. As I show in the following section, even when Article Five was rewritten to eliminate the consent basis of the jurist's legitimacy, the legacy of its initial invitation remained and, ultimately, manifested in material form in the Second of Khordad Movement. The principal challenge of this movement was, indeed, to take issue with the idea that the doctrine of the jurist's guardianship was the discursive remit of the theologians. What was once sacrosanct had been submitted to public scrutiny for "recognition and acceptance," and in the process divested of its privileged form. Thus the jurist and his divine guardianship were brought into the public sphere, and thus were sullied with the quotidian quibbles of everyday politics.

13.5 PUBLICISING THE JURIST AND THE END OF DIVINITY

Jurisprudence before 1979 was localised to the highly esoteric seminars of Qom and other centres of clerical teaching. As a rule, they were independent from the state and, perhaps more importantly, immured from public discourse and scrutiny. The

---

[20] Interestingly, in addition to striking out mentions of the people's acceptance and recognition of the jurist's legitimacy, the constitutional amendments of 1989, among other things, renamed the parliament from "The People's Parliament" (*majlis-i meli*) to "The Islamic Parliament" (*majlis-i islami*). Doubtless, this further illustrates the perceived democratic threat that was posed by Article Five's encouragement of public jurisprudential participation.

new constitution redefined the relationship between state and religion through the doctrine of the jurist's guardianship, which simultaneously invoked divinity and the people as its bases for legitimate rule. The doctrine was forged to engender a "truly Islamic" society by submitting the latter to the a priori truths of religious law that could then be implemented in public policy and enforced by the coercive organs of state. Far from becoming a point of authoritative reference, however, the jurist's claim to matters requiring political adjudication morphed – theoretically and practically – into the most contested juncture of contact between state and society.

In fighting for ownership over the meaning of Islam, the clergy discovered that the father of the revolution purveyed little assistance in his theoretical work. Khomeini was a revolutionary theologian who had threatened the existing clerical structure of his time by elevating the jurist to its apex and thereby subordinating everyone else to its adjudications, which were to be both public and political. By establishing a hierarchy that could be cited to overrule one grand ayatollah over another, he undermined the generally egalitarian and pluralist core of jurisprudence that historically typified Shi'ism. Paradoxically, however, in diminishing the pluralism that existed within the ambit of clerics, and by shifting the focal point of the jurist to matters of public governance, he exponentially increased jurisprudential pluralism by provoking public participation. This was the express concern of a group of high-ranking ayatollahs which lamented the turgid effects of public participation in jurisprudence. Khomeini expressly rejected the exclusionary and esoteric commitments of his colleagues and erstwhile equals when he argued that "there is an urgent need" for the discussions of the clerics to be freed from their seminarian confines and brought into the radio, television, and newspapers because it would be in these media where the opinions of jurists and other experts would find their broadest audience (Khomeini 1983: vol. 21, 46; Ghamari-Tabrizi 2008: 84).[21] He emphasised the desirability of publicly disseminating these opinions, especially on the "limits and boundaries of individuals and social liberties ... and most importantly, on defining and illustrating the principles of governance under the guardianship of the jurist" (*ibid.*). It almost goes without saying that Khomeini hardly envisioned a society in which secular and lay intellectuals would engage in discussion on equal terms with the clergy on matters related to jurisprudence. Of course, this was not what

---

[21] The entire passage reads as follows: "The treatises of the great jurists of Islam are filled with differences of opinion, predilections, and interpretations on military, cultural, political, economic, and spiritual issues. In the past, these disagreements stayed behind the confines of the seminary, written in Arabic in specialist books. Inevitably, people were unaware of these debates, and showed no interest in engaging with them. Today, the Islamic revolution has brought the words of the jurists *and other experts* to the radio, television, and the newspapers, for there is an urgent need for such discussion, for example, on the limits and boundaries of individual and social liberties ... and most importantly, on defining and illustrating the principles of governance under the guardianship of the jurist."

he meant by a free exchange of jurisprudential opinion. However, by making the daily affairs of the people the concern of a body of civil and criminal laws predicated upon a form of religious jurisprudence, the institutionalisation of the jurist's doctrine underwent a process of secularisation. This is because the jurist now had to compete and engage agonally with various conceptions of what constitutes the good, and had to do so with contestants who did not necessarily abide by the same rules of the game. This, of course, is a truism of at least modern politics. The conversation no longer operated within the fixed logic of the seminary, and the jurist was now theoretically susceptible to paradigm shifts of Kuhnian magnitudes. This theory has been reified by the Second of Khordad Movement which witnessed dozens of prominent lay intellectuals and clerics successfully engage the public sphere with new foundational ideas that were distinct from the canon of the jurist. In the final analysis, the jurist could not discursively compete and so availed himself of state coercion. The thugs were called out and the Movement ended in bloodshed.

The second unintended consequence of publicising the jurist's doctrine can be found in the works of Saeed Hajjarian, a celebrated public intellectual who played a formative role in the theoretical development of the Second of Khordad Movement. He argued that the jurist's doctrine transmuted Shi'ism into a state ideology by secularising the former and ostensibly sacralising the latter (Hajjarian 2001: 83). This has meant that the interests of state could now compete on equal terms with those of divinity, and this would happen in spite of protestations that either asserted the independence of each or the confluence of one into the other. This was the express concern of Grand Ayatollah Golpayegani when he wrote a premonitory letter to Khomeini in March 1981 and warned that there needed to be a firm demarcation between the interests of the state and those of religion (*ibid.* 120 ff.). Parliament, he continued, was guilty of two things: first, it was legislating on matters that were the rightful purview of the clergy, thereby violating the independence of the seminary; and second, in the name of necessity it was ratifying laws that concerned Islam but contravened the jurisprudential opinions of leading sources of religious emulation (*marja-i taqlid*). This was especially problematic because parliament could enforce its laws, whereas the grand ayatollahs could not do the same with their opinions. As mentioned earlier, since at least the Najaf lectures of 1970, Khomeini theorised against distinguishing between political and religious interests so long as the former laboured to augment the latter (Khomeini 1983: vol. 21, 46). He argued that contradictions between contemporary practical necessities and the primary demands of Islamic law need not exist under a responsible legislature. And indeed, under Islamic government, the interests of religion are subordinated to that of the legislature. In the Islamic Republic, Khomeini stipulated that in cases regarding political necessity, parliament could pass the appropriate laws with a two-thirds majority (Hajjarian 2001: 120). Many of the grand ayatollahs politely remonstrated

Khomeini's interference with the sovereignty of the clergy and for polluting Islamic jurisprudence with the legislation of a parliament whose members were not qualified to give jurisprudential opinions. This view decried public participation in what was once the exclusive juridical terrain of the clergy. Golpayegani's letter would continue in this regard:

> I believe that bestowing the authority of discerning necessity to the majority of the parliament, or any other experts in that matter, is erroneous.... In the determination of necessity and the interaction of Islamic law and state policies, the jurist should not relinquish his power in favour of any other institution (*ibid.*).

The exigencies of statehood and its supreme political office would see Khomeini develop a utilitarian ethic of governance that could potentially justify any state policy. He argued that the expediency and fortification of the Islamic Republic was "the paramount issue," that the expediency of the system the "highest importance" and that those who would neglect these principles were precipitating the "collapse of our precious Islam" (Khomeini 1983: vol. 20, 176). This was written in 1988, with the hindsight of more than eight long years at the helm of a tremendous political edifice that had demanded practical expertise and sensitivity to the social and political bases of the revolution more than religious jurisprudence for its survival. Khomeini would admit as much when he wrote that the "discernment of necessity" must be writ under the guardianship of not the jurist but the "expert" whose field the necessity at hand concerned (*ibid.*). Shortly after this letter, the Council for Discernment of Expediency was founded and its chamber has since accommodated lay jurists like Hassan Habibi and artists-turned-politicians like Mir-Hossein Mousavi. And so continues the secularisation of the jurist's guardianship and its corollary powers.[22]

13.6 CLOSING THOUGHTS

The appellations that states use to refer to their organs of power can oftentimes say a lot about the way in which they perceive their relations of power with society. How these appellatives change over time can also say as much. When the jurist's doctrine was first introduced into the discourse of the upper echelons of Iran's politics, it is highly doubtful that Khomeini meant for it to engage society dialogically.[23] Power

---

[22] In 2005, upon the "election" of Mahmoud Ahmadinejad, Grand Ayatollah Ali Seyyed Khamenei relegated more of the jurist's executive powers to the Council for the Discernment of Expediency. For a discussion, see Majd (2008: 246 ff).

[23] Khomeini ruled out the participation of the people in government in his book *Islamic Government* (1981); see, for example, section three, "The Form of Islamic Government." It does not follow that this abrogation in theory entails the same in practice, especially given Khomeini's early views on the unfeasibility of implementing the jurist's doctrine in Iran and the need to engage the people in dialogue. Cf. Khomeini (1983: vol. 1, 58).

was meant to be exerted by the jurist onto the people, and not the other way around. The jurist is the guardian of society, and under it operate the Guardian Council and the Assembly of Experts – each of which attempt the same top-down monological relationship with the people. But the exigencies of the public sphere are very different than those of the seminaries in which these theories of governance were first expounded. That the power relations between state and society are always dialogical in significant ways is an important truth of politics that Khomeini first understood when even the generally handpicked members of the Assembly of Experts began to agitate against a guardianship of a jurist who was divorced from the "acceptance and recognition" of the people. In the ensuing debates, the jurist's guardianship in the constitution was forged in a very different way than its initial conceptualisation. This chapter worked to interpret the doctrine's development into the dialogical form it eventually took in 1979 as Article Five. That this was an unintended consequence was apparent in the constitutional amendments of 1989, which attempted to eliminate the dialogue between society and the polity's apex of power, and continues to be apparent today, as the state labours to minimise public participation and abolish the most meaningful elements of dissent to the deepest cells of its prisons.

Article Five today is a neutered form of the revolutionary ideals it espoused in 1979. It was rewritten in 1989 upon Khomeini's death in order to free the guardian jurist, the Supreme Leader, of the sociopolitical pressures that were embedded in its initial formulation – the pressure, that is, to have the jurist's legitimacy welded to the acceptance and recognition of the majority. When it became clear that this sort of ideal would be unattainable, the revolutionaries became the reactionaries they were always accused to be. The current and mostly empty form, which eliminated 1979's mention of the stated pressures, reads thus:

> During the Occultation … the leadership of the Islamic community will devolve upon an appointed just and pious person, who is fully aware of the circumstances of his age, courageous, resourceful, and possessed of administrative ability, and who will assume the responsibilities of the office [of the Supreme Leader, the guardian jurist] in accordance with Article 107.[24]

---

[24] Article 107 and 109, referenced in the former, are as follows:

107: After the demise of [Khomeini], who was recognized and accepted as marji' and Leader by a decisive majority of the people, the task of appointing the Leader shall be vested in the experts elected by the people. The experts will review and consult among themselves concerning all the jurists possessing the qualifications specified in Articles 5 and 109. In the event they find one of them better versed in Islamic regulations, the subjects of the jurisprudence, or in political and social issues, or possessing general popularity or special prominence for any of the qualifications mentioned in Article 109, they shall elect him as the Leader. Otherwise, in the absence of such a superiority, they shall elect and declare one of them as the Leader. The Leader thus elected by the Assembly of Experts shall assume all the powers of the guardian jurist and all the responsibilities arising therefrom. The Leader is equal with the rest of the people of the country in the eyes of law.

But the legacy of the 1979 version, along with revolutionary dreams and aspirations of the people it inadvertently contained, remains a veritable source of theoretically sanctioned dissent both for those who operate (or operated until very recently) within foundations of the system, and, more importantly, for those who happen to be in the public sphere but operate with different social and political commitments.

REFERENCES

Arjomand, S. 1993. Shi'ite Jurisprudence and Constitution Making in Iran. In *Fundamentalisms and the State: Remaking Polities, Economies, and Militance*, edited by M.E. Marty and R.S. Appleby. Chicago: University of Chicago Press.

Bakhash, S. 1986. *The Reign of the Ayatollahs*. New York: Basic Books.

Bazargan, M. 1984. *Enqelab dar dow harekat* [*The Revolution in Two Movements*]. Tehran: Nehzat-e Azadi.

Ghamari-Tabrizi, B. 2008. *Islam and Dissent in Postrevolutionary Iran: Abdolkarim Soroush, Religious Politics, and Democratic Reform*. London: I.B. Tauris.

Hajjarian, S. 2001. *Az shahed-e qodsi ta shahed-e bazari: 'Urfi-shodan-e din dar sepehr-e siyasat* [*From the Divine to the Bazaari Witness: The Secularisation of Religion in the Sphere of Politics*]. Tehran: Tarh-e Now.

Kadivar, M. 1998. *Hokumat-i vela'i* [*Governance by Guardianship*]. Tehran: Nay.

Khomeini, R. 1981. *Islam and Revolution: Writings and Declarations of Imam Khomeini*, translated and annotated by H. Algar. Berkeley, CA: Mizan Press.

   1983. *Sahifeh-ye Noor: Majmu'e-ye rahnemudha-ye Imam Khomeini* [*Scriptures of Light: A Collection of Imam Khomeini's Counsel*]. Tehran: The Organization of the Islamic Revolution's Cultural Documents.

Majd, H. 2008. *The Ayatollah Begs to Differ: The Paradox of Modern Iran*. New York: Doubleday.

Motahhari, M. 1978. *Elal-i gerayesh be maddi-gari* [*The Allure of Materialism*]. Qom: Sadra Publishers.

Sanjabi, K. 1989. *Omid-ha va na-omidi-ha: khaterat-i siyasi* [*Hopes and Disappointments: A political memoir*]. London: The National Front.

Schirazi, A. 1997. *The Constitution of Iran: Politics and the State in the Islamic Republic*. London: I.B. Tauris.

Ṣūrat-i mashrūḥ-i muẕākirāt-i Majlis-i Bar'rasī-i Nihā'ī-i Qānūn-i Asāsī-i Jumhūrī-i Islāmī-i Īrān [*Minutes from the Negotiations of The Assembly for the Final Examination of the Constitution of the Islamic Republic*]. 1985–1989. Tehran: Idārah-'i Kull-i Umūr-i Farhangī va Ravābiṭ-i 'Umūmī-i Majlis-i Shūrā-yi Islāmī.

109: The following are the essential qualifications and conditions for the Leader: (a) scholarship, as required for performing the functions of a mufti in different fields of jurisprudence; (b) justice and piety, as required for the leadership of the Islamic Ummah; and (c) the right political and social perspicacity, prudence, courage, administrative facilities and adequate capability for leadership. In case of multiplicity of persons fulfilling the above qualifications and conditions, the person possessing the better jurisprudential and political perspicacity will be given preference.

14

Neo-Bolivarian Constitutional Design

Comparing the 1999 Venezuelan, 2008 Ecuadorian,
and 2009 Bolivian Constitutions

Phoebe King

14.1 INTRODUCTION

In his 2007 inaugural address, Ecuador's sixty-fifth president, Raphael Correa, proclaimed, "the Citizens' Revolution has just begun and no one can stop it while we have a united people decided on change" (Correa, 2007).[1] With this proclamation, President Correa identified himself as the third in a triumvirate leading what Carlos de la Torre called the "populist seduction" of Latin America (de la Torre, 2010). Correa's call for revolution echoed that of Bolivia's Evo Morales in 2006[2] and that of Venezuela's Hugo Chávez in 1999.[3]

In their respective inaugural addresses, presidents Correa, Morales, and Chávez each claimed that key to their revolution would be the promulgation of a new constitutive document for their country. In Ecuador, Rafael Correa declared, "the first axis of the Citizen's Revolution is the constitutional revolution" (Correa, 2007). In Bolivia, Evo Morales announced, "all sectors [of the population] want a Constituent Assembly committed to refoundation, and not simply constitutional reform" (Morales, 2006). In Venezuela, Chávez proclaimed that the existing constitution "must die, and with it the disastrous model that gave birth to the last forty years.... Accept it, everyone, that it is necessary that they die, because of course, it is necessary for another model to be born." (Chávez, 1999). Each president succeeded in

The author thanks Mark Harris, Melinda Koster, Sophia Kortchmar, Erica Simmons, Mila Versteeg, and Tom Ginsburg for their comments, suggestions, and encouragement.

[1]   All quotations of Correa, Chávez, and Morales are the author's translations, unless stated otherwise.
[2]   "The democratic cultural revolution, is part of the struggle of our ancestors, is the continuation of the struggle of Tupac Katari; this struggle and these results are the continuation of Che Guevara"; Morales, 2006.
[3]   "We must have revolution, even within ourselves, it is time to listen to Bolívar again and time for Venezuelans to hear me speak of Bolívar because he is the beacon"; Chávez, 1999.

promulgating a new constitution in his country: Chávez in 1999, Correa in 2008, and Morales in 2009.

Now is a critical time to take a closer look at these charters. Chávez's death has forced Venezuela's second presidential election in just seven months. It remains to be seen whether the 1999 constitution will endure as a part of Chávez's legacy or whether it will, like so many constitutions before it, be scrapped for a version that better approximates the political needs of one of his successors. Bolivia and Ecuador will hold presidential elections in 2014 and 2017, respectively. These elections will test each constitution's ability to bind and, depending on the outcome of each election, its ability to endure. This chapter provides an initial investigation into the nature of these documents. Although comparative examination of the three countries' constitutive documents reveals similarities in specific provisions, I do not perform a quantitative comparative study. Instead, I highlight broadly shared features, of which I identify three:

1) The three constitutions incorporate provisions that pointedly appeal to deep national grievances. They contain promises for a better future and enunciate the policies of the president's revolutionary ideology while patently seeking to align the population with this ideology. I adopt Jeff King's term "mission statement provisions" to describe the enunciation of these core state values (King, 2013).

2) The three constitutions are highly radical documents that pull each state further left than any constitution's recent predecessor has done. This feature offers the hint that the documents may not simply be the caudillo creations that students of Latin American constitutions have come to expect.

3) Each constitution is hybridized in that it contains principles that pull the document in different ideological directions, often irreconcilably. This hybridization fuels, to use Gary Jacobsohn's phrase, "internal disharmony" within each document, and underlines the opposing foundational principles at work in each (Jacobsohn, 2011: 130).

Mission statement provisions, radicalism, and internal disharmony have been seen in past Latin American charters. These three constitutions, however, contain unprecedented levels of aspirational and ideological content tied to specific experiences and grievances, are more radical than their recent predecessors, and encompass substantial internal disharmony. Together, these characteristics typify the three documents that Chávez, Correa, and Morales named as key to their revolutions. These constitutions, which are among the newest in Latin America, mark a trend in Latin American constitutional design. I call this trend Neo-Bolivarian constitutional design after the Venezuelan document.

14.2 CONSTITUTIONS IN THE LATIN AMERICAN CONTEXT

To study the Venezuelan, Ecuadorian, and Bolivian constitutions is to study constitutive documents in countries where respect for the rule of law has a turbulent record. Latin America has historically been a region governed by authoritarian leaders[4] who demonstrate little respect for institutional rules that impede their own objectives. Between 1930 and 1980, Latin American countries experienced 133 extra-constitutional changes in government and, collectively, Latin American countries have written more than 253 constitutional documents since their independence from Spain in the early nineteenth century (Rosenn, 1991: 57). Chávez, Correa, and Morales have themselves demonstrated authoritarian tendencies.[5]

Students of Latin American constitutions may, therefore, find textual limitations to their work. As scholar John Crabtree writes, "it is frequently the case in Latin America ... that the wording of the constitution does not reflect the way in which the state is constructed, how it actually works, how power is distributed within in it, or the way in which governance is carried out" (Crabtree and Whitehead, 2008: 163). Indeed, among certain circles constitution-writing is known as "Latin America's favorite indoor sport," and the drafting of Latin American constitutions has even been called "wiki-constitutionalism" for the ease and frequency with which they are rewritten (Rosenn, 1991: 57; Lansburg-Rodriguez, 2010).

This chapter is inspired by the scholarship of Niclas Berggren, Nils Karlson, and Joakim Nergelius and adopts the premise that constitutions matter. But as scholar Keith Rosenn cautions, "despite the long-standing belief in Latin America that constitutions and laws can perform magic if only they are drafted properly, history offers compelling evidence that democracies cannot be produced by simply adopting democratic constitutions" (Rosenn, 1991: 75). Indeed, with Latin America's history of constitutional juris-ambivalence, most Latin American constitutions seem to refute Donald Lutz's claim that "a written constitution is a bit like a self-fulfilling prophecy" (Lutz, 2000: 122). Questions abound for those interested in constitutions as documents and their potential to "contribute to coordination" (Galligan and Versteeg, 2013). The foremost of these questions is whether or not theories describing "unintended [constitutional] consequences" (Brown, 2002: 93) and the development of "rights consciousness" (Minow, 1987: 1867) can be reconciled with knowledge that constitutions are not "magic" documents that

---

[4]   This essay adopts the definition proffered by Adam Przeworski. For Przeworski, authoritarianism exists if there is "some power apparatus capable of overturning the outcomes of the institutionalized political process" (Przeworski 1988: 60).

[5]   See Levitsky and Loxton, 2012.

produce liberal constitutionalism and respect for the rule of law when written "correctly."[6]

14.3 ESTABLISHING THE CONSTITUTIONAL TREND

Before delving into an examination of the radicalism of these documents, it is helpful to specify a conception of constitutional radicalism. Although there are several classificatory systems, Roberto Gargarella's *The Legal Foundations of Inequality* provides a particularly compelling method for the classification of Latin American constitutions. In this book, Gargarella examines the archetypal models that emerged between 1810 and 1860 when the "basic features of [Latin American] constitutions were shaped" (Gargarella, 2010: 2). He identifies three models: the radical model, the conservative model, and the liberal model.

According to Gargarella, "the history of radical constitutionalism in America is the history of failure," and "in most cases, radicals did not manage to put their constitutional ideas into practice" (ibid.: 49). Latin American constitutional documents have tended to be governed by the principles of the other two remaining models: the conservative and the liberal. Radicals, who are committed to political majoritarianism and moral populism, have a "difficult relationship" with constitutions: for the radical, the promulgation of a constitution represents "a way of giving legal support to the self-governing ideal, but also a threatening risk, that of preventing the future generations' self-government" (ibid.: 3, 54). With this tense relationship in mind, it is not surprising that the radical constitutional model typically incorporates a federal or decentralized system of government, separation of state powers, and "a strong congress" to which the other two branches are "subordinatated" (ibid.: 54). These constitutions often call for redistribution of political rights so as to remedy past political inequality. Because radicals "found [economic equality] indispensable for making ... self-government possible," these constitutions similarly enshrine economic policies that ensure subsistence and egalitarian distribution of resources (ibid.: 38–39).

Instead of enshrining majoritarian exceptionalism, conservative documents divergently seek to "improve or directly replace those views" with the views of a leader who is characterized as best able to identify the path to moral perfectionism (ibid.: 93). As Gargarella explains, these documents insinuate that the "coercive powers of the state," especially when concentrated in one individual, are those best equipped to "guard the 'moral basis' of the community against those [usually foreign forces] aimed at undermining them" (ibid.: 94). Conservative constitutions characteristically concentrate authority in the hands of the president. They typically afford the executive legislative powers, the right to reelection, broad veto powers, the power to

---

[6] For an article regarding the survival extending benefits of constitution writing for autocratic coalitions in Latin America, see Albertus and Menaldo (2012).

designate and remove state officials, control over the armed forces, and sometimes even the power to dissolve congress (ibid.: 117).

By contrast, liberal constitutions, as described by Gargarella, are motivated by a conception "of the state as the main threat to individual freedoms," and these documents "use[] all their energy to reduce it to its minimal expression" (ibid.: 172). Liberal constitutions strengthen individuals' rights, diminish the powers of the executive, and promote a weak decentralized federal system of government. Unlike radical documents, liberal constitutions protect individuals from both the conservative powers of the state *and* the will of the majority. Unlike the radical impulse, which also favors a federal system, liberals protect individual property rights and prohibit the state from unnecessarily interfering in private economic activity.

This chapter examines each constitution individually and in the order in which it was promulgated. Bolivian constitutional architect José de la Fuente Jeria declared that "it is only natural" that the constitutional process forms "dynamic links with society, the economy, political parties, power groups or international politics" (de la Fuente Jeria, 2010: 8) (author's translation). In keeping with this philosophy, I begin each section with a brief topology of the political and economic climate out of which each document emerged.

14.4 VENEZUELA

14.4.1 *Setting the Stage for the 1999 Constitution*

Since Venezuela issued its first charter in 1811, the country has promulgated roughly twenty-six constitutions. This number, the greatest of any country in South America, is a testament to Venezuela's long history of authoritarian rule and the flippancy with which Venezuelan strongmen abrogated and promulgated constitutions to legitimize and satisfy their whims. The tenure of General Gómez (1908–1935) is perhaps the best example of Venezuelan juris-ambivalence. Adopting a piece of advice given to one of his predecessors – *"la Constitución sirve para todo"* ("the Constitution serves any purpose") – Gómez used constitutions to satisfy his political whims, and issued seven different constitutions between 1908 and 1935 (Kornblith, 1991: 62).

Caudillos and strongmen consistently injected themselves into Venezuelan politics until 1958, when a military-civilian coalition ousted General Marcos Pérez Jiménez and called for democratic elections later that year. In a power-sharing agreement known as the Punto Fijo Pact, Venezuela's three leading political parties, Acción Democratica (AD), Comité de Organización Politica Electoral Independiente: Partido Social Cristiano (COPEI), and Unión Republicana Democrática (URD), agreed to "avoid[] harsh inter-party antagonism during the electoral campaign, to respect[] the outcome and to form[] a government of national unity with the participation of the three parties irrespective of the election results" (Kornblith, 1991: 70–71). The election that followed the Punto Fijo Pact was, by all accounts, a democratic success and served as the foundation for a half-century of majoritarian elections. On January 28, days after the new congress took office, a bipartisan committee proposed the drafting of a new constitution for Venezuela (Kornblith, 1991: 71). On February 2, the Bicameral Commission for Constitutional Reform was born and twenty-two representatives were appointed to serve as its members. By 1961, a new constitution for Venezuela had been ratified. This 1961 document survived thirty-eight years, making it the longest-lasting constitution in Venezuelan history. Writing in 1991, scholar Miriam Kornblith attributed the document's strength and endurance to the political consensus that grounded its pragmatic fundamental principles; "the updated [1961] constitution was conceived as a long-term political project and not as another normative law" (Kornblith, 1991: 76).

Democracy began to crumble in the late 1980s when Venezuela began to experience social and economic crisis. In 1989, and in an economy already heavily recessed from declining international oil prices (McCoy, 1999: 65), President Carlos Andrés Pérez signed a Letter of Intention with the International Monetary Fund (IMF) and introduced neoliberal reforms reducing government spending, deregulating exchange rates, reducing subsidies, eliminating tariffs, and introducing a sales tax (Ciccariello-Maher, 2008). On Monday, February 27, the day before the signing, gasoline prices were up 100 percent and National Transport fares were up 30 percent (Ciccariello-Maher, 2008). Massive protest demonstrations erupted, and were violently suppressed by the government. Known as *el Caracazo*, "the massacre," the incident became a touchstone for Venezuelan disillusionment with the political, social, and economic policies of the State. By the end of that year, 44 percent of Venezuelan households were in poverty (Ciccariello-Maher, 2008). Not ten years prior, Venezuela had been among only four Latin American countries that the World Bank had designated as "upper-middle-income" economies (Corrales, 1999).

Dissatisfaction reverberated through all sectors of the population, and in 1992 a paratrooper commander called Hugo Chávez staged a coup against the Pérez government. In a massive political blunder, the Pérez government allowed Chávez to speak unedited on national television. He demanded "cost-of-living clauses for wages, tax reform facilitating a redistribution of wealth, and renegotiation of debt" (Walsh, 2009: 5). Although Hugo Chávez failed militarily, he became a household name. By 1993, Pérez was impeached on corruption charges, and succeeded by Rafael Caldera Rodríguez (Salomon, 2010).

Despite the change in government following Peréz's impeachment, Venezuelans continued to suffer economically. By 1998, the share of the population below the poverty line had risen to 68 percent, and in 1999 real wages were nearly 70 percent below that which Venezuelans had experienced two decades earlier in 1979 (Corrales, 1999). The inability of traditional party politicians to follow through on campaign promises, unshakable beliefs that corruption lay at the root of Venezuelan economic troubles, and grievances inflamed by relative deprivation opened the door to political outsiders in the 1998 elections (Corrales, 1999). Performing a tactical 180-degree turn, Chávez joined the electoral race and became a quick leader in the polls (McCoy, 1999: 66).

On December 6, 1998, Chávez was elected president of the Venezuelan Republic. For students of the country's constitutions, Chávez's first words as president were ironic: he exclaimed, "I am sure that we Venezuelans are writing pages of a new history! Today we are reviving the national spirit!" (Cristancho, 1998). Chávez was indeed sure those pages would be rewritten – just a few hours later, the new president of Venezuela called for a referendum on the convocation of an assembly to rewrite the nation's constitution. The referendum asked citizens whether or not they approved of the creation of a national constituent assembly tasked with writing a new constitution. On April 25, 1999, more than 92 percent of Venezuelans participating in the referendum answered in the affirmative (Van Cott, 2003: 54).

14.4.2 *The Document Itself*

The 1999 constitution is criticized for having been written behind closed doors by an elite group on whom the president had a tight grip. In preparation for a popular referendum on the text, Chávez distributed millions of copies of the new constitution and showcased his favorite provisions during public events (Kelly, 2000: 17). The new charter passed referendum and entered into force on December 30, 1999. Despite Chávez's claims that the 1961 constitution was "moribund," his new constitution was, as member of the constituent assembly, Roberto Pastor notes, "clearly inspired by its immediate ancestor" (Viciano Pastor and Martínez Dalmau, 2001: 206) (author's translation). Evidence of influence, and occasionally nearly identical articles, appear throughout the document. Regardless of its genetic heritage, the 1999 constitution also marks a break from the previous one, and there are numerous differences between the documents. The significance of these differences is, I argue, best understood through a lens that highlights the constitution's ideological content, radicalism, and its hybridized nature.

14.4.2.1 Ideological and Aspirational Content

"Mission statement provisions" – provisions that enunciate core state values and principles – abound in the 1999 Venezuelan constitutive document, and are a defining feature of the constitution. Mission statement provisions appear almost everywhere King tells us we might expect to find them: they are found in a section describing the "basic organizing principles of the state," in the preamble, in "ad hoc statements of principle," and in rights provisions (King, 2013). These mission statements refer to shared grievances as well as unifying political aspirations. In many instances, they appear to be deliberate bids for solidarity with the president's revolutionary ideology. Consider the preamble to the 1999 constitution:

> The people of Venezuela,
>
> invoking ... the historic example of our liberator Simon Bolívar and the heroism and sacrifice of our aboriginal ancestors ... establish a democratic participatory and self-reliant, multiethnic, multicultural society in a just, federal and decentralized State that embodies the values of freedom, independence, peace, solidarity, the common good for this and future generations.[7][8]

The preamble, then, both enunciates the embodying values of the new Bolivarian republic and invokes historical pride. As the official government "*Exposición de Motivos*" (Explanation of Motives) explains, reference to Bolívar was included because of "popular sentiment that distinguishes him as a symbol of national unity."[9] The reference was a highly intentional bid for solidarity with the new constitution.[10] The reference to the "heroism and sacrifice of our aboriginal ancestors" was likely intended to accomplish the same function among Venezuela's small but organized indigenous population. This impetus flows through the document.

The 1999 constitution was drafted after a period of severe economic hardship and political turmoil. Many of the rights provisions included in the document acknowledge this hardship and promise a better future. Acknowledgment of grievance and aspirational promises for the future are especially present in provisions governing the right to work.

The constitution not only explicitly grants all people the "right and duty to work," it also guarantees each individual the ability "to obtain ... a dignified and decent existence"[11] and "the right to a salary sufficient to enable him or her to live with dignity and cover the basic material, social, and intellectual needs for himself or herself and his or her family."[12] These elements appeal to the grievances

---

7 República Bolivariana de Venezuela, Constitución de 1999 con Reformas Hasta 2009, Preamble.

8 All quoted provisions of the Venezuelan, Ecuadorian, and Bolivian constitutions are the author's unofficial translations of their text. The author relied heavily on the unofficial English language translation of the 1999 Venezuelan Constitution made available by the venezuelanalysis.com, on the unofficial English language translation of the 2008 Ecuadorian Constitution made available by Georgetown University's Political Database of the Americas, and on Luis Valle Velascos's translation of the 2009 Bolivian Constitution see Valle Velasco, 2012.

9 Venezuela, *Gaceta Official* 5453, March 24 2000.

10 Many past Venezuelan constitutions have contained preambular references meant to spark solidarity and engender popular support. Ideological preambular content is nonetheless significant to identifying this document as an unusually ideological constitution.

11 República Bolivariana de Venezuela, Constitución de 1999 con Reformas Hasta 2009, Article 87.

12 *Ibid.*, Article 91.

that backed Chávez's rise to power, and they promise citizens that the state will safeguard against the kind of economic hardship that Venezuelans suffered under the last regime – a promise that is, of course, more aspirational than enforceable. Similar provisions include the declaration that "every person has the right to adequate, safe and comfortable, hygienic housing, with appropriate essential basic services,"[13] the constitution's guarantee that "everyone has the right, individually and collectively, to enjoy life and a safe healthful and ecologically balanced environment."[14]

Although aspirational mission provisions appear as rights throughout the document, mission statements are more recognizable in portions of the Venezuelan constitution that stipulate not rights, per se, but, as Brewer-Carías terms them, "teleological declarations of principles and intent" (Brewer-Carías, 2010: 149). Title 1, "Fundamental Principles of the State," contains many of these declarations, but these mission statements appear throughout the document. Chapter VI, "Culture and Education Rights," for example, explains that "the State recognizes as being in the public interest science, innovation and the resulting applications," and that "the State shall allocate sufficient resources and shall create a national science and technology system in accordance with the law."[15] Article 311 stipulates that "fiscal policy shall be governed and implemented based on principles of efficiency, solvency, transparency, accountability and fiscal balance." Such abundance of aspirational and "mission statement" provisions is atypical in the constitutional history of Venezuela.

14.4.2.2 Evidence of Radicalism

The political structure introduced by the 1999 constitution, the economic structure it promises, and the novel provisions regarding popular referendum all demonstrate significant radical influence.

The 1999 constitution decentralizes the government and disproportionally grants power to the legislative branch.[16] The constitution explicitly identifies the country as a "decentralized federal state,"[17] and it establishes decentralization as a "national policy" that "must add depth to democracy, bring power closer to the people, and

[13] Article 82. The aspirational nature of this article is noted by Brewer-Carías, 2010: 149.
[14] República Bolivariana de Venezuela, Constitución de 1999 con Reformas Hasta 2009, Article 127.
[15] *Ibid.*, Article 110.
[16] Decentralization, in itself, is not is not necessarily indicative of radical impulse – decentralization is also characteristic of liberal constitutions. Given Venezuela's specific history – one in which rural sectors have historically been marginalized – decentralization, because it calls for greater inclusion, access, and control over government politics, is euphemistic for the expansion of inclusive, populist, majoritarian politics typical of radical documents.
[17] República Bolivariana de Venezuela, Constitución de 1999 con reformas hasta 2009, Article 4. The 1961 constitution does not use the adjective "decentralized" to describe the state...

create optimum conditions both for the exercise of democracy and for the effective and efficient fulfillment of government commitments."[18] According to the constitution, Venezuelan federal power is divided among the national, municipal, and state authorities. Power vested at the national level is further distributed among five branches – two more than outlined by the 1961 document.

Alan Brewer-Carías, a Venezuelan constitutional scholar, strong critic of the 1999 constitution, and member of the 1998 constituent assembly, holds that the powers granted to the legislative branch in the 1999 document "absurdly distort" typical notions of separation of powers. Indeed, the constitution grants the legislative organ broad powers – the legislature may appoint and dismiss judges of the Supreme Tribunal of Justice, the Prosecutor General, the Comptroller General, the People's Defender, and Members of the National Electoral Council. In some cases, dismissal requires a simple majority vote (Brewer-Carías, 2010: 124).

As Gargarella explains, radicals are traditionally suspicious of bicameralism and upper houses of government. The upper houses "not only restrain the decision making powers of the majority, [they] also, and more importantly, guarantee a 'fixed' legislative place for the powerful 'few'" (Gargarella, 2010: 61). In a dramatic shift, the 1999 constitution collapsed Venezuela's upper house and reorganized the legislature as a unicameral legislative body.

Like its political structure, the economic structure of the 1999 Venezuelan constitution contains radical constitutional tenets. Since Venezuela's first oil well was drilled in 1912 (Wilpert, 2003), the state has promoted a "mixed economy," namely one in which, as Brewer-Carías says, "private initiative, and a free-market economic model" are combined "with the possibility of state intervention in the economy to uphold principles of social justice" (Brewer-Carías, 2010: 156–157). Given that Hugo Chávez rose to power on a platform that explicitly rejected his predecessors' neoliberal reforms, it is not surprising that Title IV of the new constitution, "Socioeconomic Order and the Function of the State in the Economy," augments radical egalitarian economic policies.

Like the 1961 document, the 1999 constitution explains that the "economic regime" is based on the principles of social justice, productivity, and solidarity and aims to ensure "human development and a dignified and useful existence for the community."[19] The 1999 constitution further obligates the state to "promote conditions for overall rural development for the purpose of generating employment and ensuring the rural population an adequate level of well-being."[20] Moreover, the constitution requires the federal government to "promote actions in the national and

---

[18] *Ibid.*, Article 158.
[19] *Ibid.*, Article 299.
[20] *Ibid.*, Article 306.

international economic context to compensate for the disadvantages inherent to agricultural activity."[21] The strength of the 1999 constitution's commitment to egalitarian social welfare is innovative and has its roots in radical constitutional theory. It should be seen as a culmination of radical impulses that were incubated in the disastrous social and political climate that provided tinder for Chávez's explosive rise to power.

The most radical innovations of the 1999 Venezuelan constitution are its provisions establishing a citizen's right to referendum. The 1999 document introduces four types of general referendum at the disposal of the citizenry: on matters of consultation, on matters of revocation, on matters concerning national sovereignty, and on matters concerning the abrogation of law.[22] For the first time in Venezuela's history, the new constitution guarantees the people a voice in the impetus of constitutional amendment and reform. The new document promises that if 15 percent of registered voters request the adoption of a constitutional amendment, the issue will be taken to popular referendum.[23] A mere 15 percent of registered voters may also initiate processes of constitutional reform. Once a draft of the reformed constitution has been approved by two-thirds of the National Assembly, it must be submitted to national referendum. A simple majority of cast votes is required for the successful passage of reform provisions.[24]

14.4.2.3 Constitutional Hybridism

Despite the constitution's highly radical character, this document contains elements of all three typologies described by Gargarella. It is a far-reaching and ambitious

---

[21] Ibid., Article 305.

[22] Article 71 introduces citizen's rights to participate in consultative referendum. This type of referendum, on issues of "matters of special national transcendence," may be called by the President of the Republic, by resolution of the National Assembly, or, importantly, by at least 10% of voters on the electoral registry. Article 72 introduces citizen's rights to call referendum on the revocation of any popularly elected public official once one-half of his or her term has been completed. According to the constitution, only 20% of the registered voters in the politician's constituency is required to initiate such a hearing. If more than 25% of registered voters participate in the subsequent referendum, and "a number of voters equal to or greater than the number of those who elected the official vote in favor of revocation," "the official's mandate shall be deemed revoked, and immediate action shall be taken to fill the permanent vacancy." Article 73 requires that "treaties, conventions or international agreements that might compromise the national sovereignty or transfer authority to supranational organs may be submitted to referendum on the initiative of the President," by two-thirds majority vote of the National Assembly or by 15% of voters registered in the civil and electoral registry. Article 74 establishes the rights to the last form of referendum – that of abrogatory referendum. This article guarantees citizens' rights to abrogate both statutes and presidential decrees when 10% of the population calls for referendum and 40% vote for abrogation. These rights to referenda strongly incorporate citizens into governmental decision making and are grounded in radical ideology.

[23] República Bolivariana de Venezuela, Constitución de 1999 con reformas hasta 2009, Article 341.

[24] Ibid., Article 342–344.

constitution that, in its hybridity, arguably communicates a lack of authenticity: a hint that, despite innovative radicalism, it is akin to a caudillo creation meant to "*sirve para todo.*"

Despite radical provisions decentralizing power, the constitution communicates a marked discomfort with decentralization.[25] Article 162 is one example of foundational ambiguity. This article stipulates that "legislative authority shall be exercised in each State by a legislative council" and that these councils hold power to legislate matters within state competence, enforce the State's Budget Law, and others "established by this Constitution or by the law." On the surface, this article upholds a commitment to decentralization. The same provision, however, stipulates that "the organization and functioning of the Legislative Councils shall be regulated by the national law."[26] The powers and independence of state legislative councils are therefore taken away in the same breath in which they are "granted." According to Brewer-Carías, the 1999 constitution also retracted several powers previously "designated as exclusive to the states" (Brewer-Carías, 2010: 97). As evidence, he points to the right to tax. States were granted the authority to tax in the 1961 constitution. The 1999 constitution reserves all rights to tax "not expressly assigned by this Constitution and the law to the States and Municipalities"[27] to the National Public Power. As the constitution does not grant states or municipalities any power over taxation, this authority was transferred back to the federal government (Brewer-Carías, 2010: 98).

Centralization of power within the federal government also suggests conservative leanings. Unlike the 1961 document, the new constitution gives the president, rather than the legislative assembly, exclusive authority over military advancements, and power, with legislative acquiescence, to both declare states of emergency and dissolve the legislative branch entirely.[28] The new constitution also increases the presidential term limit by a year,[29] allows for immediate reelection, expands executive authority to initiate legislation,[30] outlines the process for the creation of communal councils directly dependent on the president (Brewer-Carías, 2010: 22), and, after the reform procedures in 2009, removes term limits on all public officials.[31] The president is also granted the power to "designate and remove those officials whose appointment is made subject to his discretion by this Constitution or the law,"[32] "to formulate

---

[25] Tension between decentralization and centralization of power is noted and discussed by Brewer-Carías, 2010: 216–220.

[26] República Bolivariana de Venezuela, *Constitución de 1999 con reformas hasta 2009*, Article 162.

[27] *Ibid.*, 156 Section 12.

[28] *Ibid.*, Article 236. For a discussion of presidential power, see Brewer-Carías, 2010: 219.

[29] *Ibid.*, Article 230.

[30] *Ibid.*, Articles 203, 230. The previous constitution had only allowed the executive to initiate decree laws in economic and fiscal matters. See Article 190 of the 1961 Constitution.

[31] *Ibid.*, Article 160.

[32] República Bolivariana de Venezuela, *Constitución de 1999 con reformas hasta 2009*, Article 236 Section 16.

the National Development Plan, and, subject to the approval in advance from the National Assembly, direct the implementation of the same."[33] In addition, the president has the power to "determine the number, organization, and competencies of the Ministries and other organs comprising the National Public Administrative Branch, as well as the organization and functions of the Cabinet Ministers, within the principles and guidelines set forth in the pertinent organic law."[34]

Although disharmony within the document largely lies in contradictory radical and conservative impulses, the constitution insulates individual rights and liberties in a liberal fashion. The enormous increase in the number and depth of individual rights protected by the constitution is one initial indication of the document's liberal bias. Especially liberal, in the sense that it insulates groups of individuals from the will of the majority, is its novel incorporation of indigenous rights guarantees.

14.5 ECUADOR

14.5.1 *Setting the Stage for the 2008 Document*

Ecuador's constitutional history is nearly as fraught with juris-ambivalence and constitutional tinkering as Venezuela's. Democracy returned to Ecuador only in 1979 (Andolina, 2003: 726), and its current constitutive document is the country's twentieth since Ecuador's independence in 1822 (Cordeiro, 2008). Ecuador's current constitution, promulgated on September 28, 2008, was the brainchild of President Rafael Correa and emerged into an economic and political climate reminiscent of that which birthed the Venezuelan constitution.

Although neoliberal economic policies were more modestly implemented in Ecuador than in other South American countries, they nonetheless caused significant economic hardship for the poorest sectors of the country and sparked the emergence of populist indigenous movements throughout the end of the twentieth and beginning of the twenty-first centuries. In the 1996 national presidential elections, Ecuadorians decisively opted to turn from former President Sixto Duran Ballen's conservative political agenda and elected center-left and populist candidate Abadlá Bucaram (Silva, 2009: 170). Although Bucaram's constituents hoped that he would abandon his predecessor's neoliberal posture, once in power and settled with the nation's economic burdens, Bucaram quickly caved to pressures from the IMF and the World Bank. Almost immediately following Bucaram's implementation of neoliberal shock treatments, Ecuadorians saw the prices of staples skyrocket: gasoline prices increased 270 percent, public transport fares rose 60 percent, and telephone

---

[33] *Ibid.*, Article 236 Section 18.
[34] *Ibid.*, Article 236 Section 20.

and electricity bills rose 1,000 percent and 300 percent, respectively (ibid.: 171). Drawing on both the "cronyism and nepotism" of the Bucaram government and rapid increases in the cost of living, opposition parties fanned cross-class resistance to the Bucaram regime (ibid.: 171). Bucaram was forced to leave office less than six months into his first term (Andolina, 2003: 731).

In May 1997, appointed president Fabian Alarcón called for the convening of a constituent assembly, a long-sought goal of the *Confederación de Nacionalidades Indígenas del Ecuador* (CONAIE), a leading indigenous populist organization (International Crisis Group, 2007: 4). Despite high hopes, traditional parties controlled the constituent assembly. The 1998 constitution included new social rights and guarantees but its various failures, among the most important of which were its failure to establish plurinationality and the inclusion of provisions facilitating privatization, "reinforced," according to Silva, "the conviction that contentious politics was the principal, if not the only, means the popular sectors and indigenous had to defend against commodification from neoliberal reforms" (Silva, 2009: 175).

Ecuadorian politics followed a similar cyclical pattern in which politicians promised social reforms but largely abandoned those promises for neoliberal economic policies once in office.[35] The unfulfilled campaign promises of the presidents who followed Alarcón into office and the subsequent economic meltdown in the late nineties – the worst economic depression Ecuador had seen since the 1930s and one in which 68 percent of the population descended below the poverty line – enflamed tensions between government and mobilized popular sectors (Silva, 2009: 180–181).

Rafael Correa first entered the public spotlight as President Alredo Palacio's finance minister. In that position, Correa controversially refused advice from the IMF and publicly voiced opposition against free-trade agreements with the United States (Fernandez, 2009). Venezuelan newspaper *El Universo* reported that in doing so, Correa garnered "the backing of social organizations, the public sector and trade unions" (*El Universo*, 2005) (author's translation). Despite his popularity, Correa resigned after only four months in office. Although the official press release issued by President Palacio does not include an explanation for Correa's decision, *El Universo* postulated that Correa chose to resign because of President Palacio's renunciation, under World Bank pressure, of Correa's plan to issue $300 million in bonds to Venezuela in order to reduce reliance on international organizations.

The following year, Correa ran for president and carried a remarkable 56.7 percent of the vote (Silva, 2009: 191). The same day he was elected, Correa issued a

---

[35] As to why Latin American politicians so often changed their mandate once in office, see Stokes (2001).

decree calling for the convening of a constituent assembly (*El Universo*, 2007). By September 2008, the Ecuadorian people had ratified a new constitution: 63.9 percent of Ecuadorians participating in the referendum voted in favor of the new document.[36]

14.5.2 *The Document Itself*

Like the Venezuelan constitution of 1999, the 2008 Ecuadorian constitution's characteristic features are its inclusion of specific, egalitarian, value-laden missions, its radicalism, and the fact that it is governed not by one consistent ideological framework, but by an unusual and, in places, irreconcilable hybrid of the three models described by Roberto Gargarella. Unlike the Venezuelan constitution, the 2008 Ecuadorian document followed on the heels of a constitution drafted under very similar conditions of social and economic crisis. As such, its content embodies the culmination of radical and aspirational influence.

14.5.2.1 Ideological and Aspirational Content

Ecuadorians, the preamble to the 2008 constitution explains, "decide to build … [a] new form of public coexistence … to achieve the sumak kawsay," establish "a society that respects, in all its dimensions, the dignity of individuals and community groups" as well as "a democratic country." The Ecuadorian preamble appeals to Ecuadorian notions of collective history, self, and aspirations for the future state. It serves as the first indication that the 2008 document is a highly ideological, mission-driven constitution.

Rights provisions throughout the document appeal to grievances in the population and establish their recompense as a mission for the state. Chapter 2, section eight, which concerns labor and social security, is one example. This section provides that the state "shall guarantee full respect for the dignity of working persons, a decent life, fair pay and retribution, and performance of a healthy job that is freely chosen and accepted."[37] These guarantees appeal to specific and raw economic grievances felt by Ecuadorians in the late twentieth and early twenty-first centuries. Provisions granting "persons … the right to safe and healthy habitat and adequate and decent housing, regardless of their social and economic status,"[38] and the extension of social security rights to include "persons who carry out unpaid work in households, livelihood activities in the rural sector, all forms of self-employed and [those] who are

---

[36] Data from http://pdba.georgetown.edu/Elecdata/Ecuador/refconsto8.html
[37] Republic of Ecuador, Constitution of 2008, Article 33.
[38] *Ibid.*, Article 30.

unemployed"[39] similarly appeal to impoverished sectors of the state. The constitution guarantees other value-laden and aspirational rights including "[t]he right to honor and a good reputation," "[t]he right to personal and family intimacy," "the right to live in a healthy environment that is ecologically balanced, pollution-free and in harmony with nature,"[40] "and "the right to recreation and leisure, the practice of sports and free time."[41]

In addition to containing rights provisions that guarantee protection from sources of historic grievance, the constitution includes provisions that more strictly communicate policies of the state. The "Basic Principles of the State," are, for example, outlined in Title 1 of the document. These basic principles include "eliminating poverty, promoting sustainable development and the equitable redistribution of resources," and "guaranteeing its inhabitants the right to a culture of peace, to integral security and to live in a democratic society free of corruption." In reference to the role played by social movements in Ecuador's history, Article 96 establishes that "all forms of organizing society are recognized as an expression of the people's sovereignty to develop processes of self-determination and to influence public decisions and policymaking, and for social monitoring of all levels of government."

The 2008 constitution, like the 1998 constitution, enunciates both state values and policies and identifies the amelioration of economic hardship and past grievance as missions for the state. The current constitutive document, with its lengthier preamble, its delineation of fundamental principles, and sections regarding rights and guarantees, includes augmented aspirational and mission-driven content.

14.5.2.2 *Evidence of Radical Impulse*

Radical influence on the 2008 Ecuadorian constitution, like that on Venezuela's constitutive document, manifests itself in the constitution's political structure, in its economic structure, and in constitutional provisions guaranteeing rights to participation and referendum.

The political structure of the Ecuadorian constitution institutionalizes commitment to decentralization and citizen access both through emotively phrased policy provisions[42] and through substantive articles demarcating political powers. One of the latter such provisions is the constitution's addition of two new branches of government – in addition to the legislative, executive, and judiciary, the constitution

---

[39] *Ibid.*, Article 34.
[40] *Ibid.*, Article 66 Sections 18, 20, 27.
[41] *Ibid.*, Article 24.
[42] For an example of the former, see Article 95: "Citizens, individually and collectively, shall participate as leading players in decision making, planning, and management of public affairs and in the people's monitoring of State institutions and society."

creates the Electoral branch and the Transparency and Social Control branches. The mandate of the Transparency and Social Control Branch is particularly demonstrative of radical influence. This branch is tasked with the duty to "promote and encourage the exercise of the rights involving public participation," and its composition, according to the constitution, is "deconcentrated": its members are selected from "among candidates proposed by social organizations and the citizenry."[43] Although critics of the constitution are quick to claim that this change does little to dilute central power or to augment citizen participation beyond the levels established in the 1998 document, historian Agustín Grijalva of the Universidad Andia Simón Bolívar explains otherwise. He writes that while the Transparency and Social Control Branch functions very similarly to the watchdog Commission for Civic Control of Corruption (established in articles 220–221 of the 1998 constitution), the transference of authority from the Commission to a formal branch of government not only grants policies of transparency and social control equal footing with the executive, the legislative, and the judicial mandates; it also adds an additional branch whose appointees are determined by open competition to the highest tier of public authority (Grijalva, 2009). The 2008 constitution preserved the existing unicameral legislative structure.[44]

The new constitution's provisions decentralizing power to substate authorities deepen constitutional commitment to popular participation and universal access. The older document conferred few explicit powers to substate governments, instead specifying that decentralization to regional bodies be obligatory when requested and the capacity demonstrated.[45] By contrast, the new constitution automatically and explicitly grants a large number of powers to decentralized regional, provincial, municipal, and parish government bodies.[46] Moreover, the constitution requires the state to "create economic and other incentives to encourage" the creation of autonomous regions.[47] The 2008 constitution also establishes an unprecedented "empty seat policy" – one that requires the sessions of the decentralized autonomous governments not only to be public, but also to contain an "empty seat that shall be held by a representative of the citizens."[48] Manifestly, these provisions enshrine radical commitment to universal citizen access and participation in politics.

Like its political structure, the economic structure of the Ecuadorian state incorporates elements of the radical constitutional model. Although the economic structure is officially "mixed," one indication of its radical egalitarian underpinnings is

---

43 Republic of Ecuador, Constitution of 2008, Articles 204–207.
44 *Ibid.*, Article 18.
45 Article 226 of the 1998 constitution.
46 Republic of Ecuador, Constitution of 2008, Articles 262–264, 267.
47 *Ibid.*, Article 244.
48 *Ibid.*, Article 101.

that Title VI, the portion of the constitution governing economic policy, demarcates the "Development Structure" of the state, rather than the "Economic Structure" of the state. According to the constitution, this "development structure" is a "dynamic" system designed to "ensure the production and reproduction of the material and immaterial conditions that make the good life possible."[49] Interestingly, this portion of the constitution also stipulates that, "to achieve the good life, it is the duty of people and communities ... to participate in all stages and spaces of public management and national and local development planning."[50] By explaining that the economic system is designed to facilitate "the good life," and that "the good life" requires active participation in government, this economic rights section explicitly extols a key radical principle: economic subsistence is required for proper participation in government. Explicit commitment to economic egalitarianism further reveals radical ideological foundations: the constitution holds that the "general principles" of the "development structure" include the creation of an "economic system based on the egalitarian distribution of the benefits of development and the means of production,"[51] and the promotion of "balanced, equitable land use planning."[52] These economic provisions show radical influence in that they guarantee to all citizens the basic prerequisites for political engagement.

The 2008 constitution broadens and deepens participatory rights established in 1998 constitutive document. In the current document, citizens hold rights to initiate "the creation, amendment or repeal of legal regulations,"[53] to submit "constitutional amendment proposals" for the mandatory review of the legislative branch, to initiate the "recall of elected authorities,"[54] and to call referenda "on any matter" they wish.[55] [56] A mere 0.25 percent of the individuals registered to vote in the applicable jurisdiction are needed to propose or abrogate legislation. To initiate legislative review of proposals for constitutional amendment, only 8 percent of the registered population need voice their favor. To call a national referendum requires only 5 percent of the electorate.[57]

---

[49] *Ibid.*, Article 283.

[50] *Ibid.*, Article 278 Section 1.

[51] *Ibid.*, Article 276 Section 2.

[52] *Ibid.*, Article 276 Section 6.

[53] *Ibid.*, Article 103.

[54] *Ibid.*, Article 105.

[55] *Ibid.*, Article 104.

[56] The 1998 Constitution granted citizen's rights to initiate referenda on "matters of vital importance," excluding constitutional amendment (Article 105) and referenda to revoke the mandate of "mayors, governors, and other elected officials" on corruption or breach of mandate charges (Article 109); República de Ecuador, Constituciones de 1998, Articles 105, 109. In the 2009 document, referendum initiated by the citizenry is restricted from considering "tax-related matters or the country's political and administrative structure, except for what is provided for in the Constitution"; Article 104.

[57] *Ibid.*, Article 103.

Although there are numerous radical elements in the 1998 constitution, radical influence culminates in the 2008 constitution: its political structure retains the unicameral legislature and furthers decentralization, its economic provisions explicitly appeal to the necessity of economic subsistence for political participation, it qualifies rights as contingent,[58] and it deepens direct citizen participation.

14.5.2.3 Constitutional Hybridism

Although the 2008 constitution exhibits highly radical content, it also borrows from the liberal and conservative models. In direct conflict with its earlier mentioned provision subsuming individual rights to the "prevalence of public welfare," the constitution holds that "all principles and rights are unalienable, obligatory, indivisible, interdependent and of equal importance."[59] Moreover, an entire chapter of the constitution is dedicated to the demarcation of the rights of indigenous peoples. This type of protection, one that insulates minority groups from the will of the majority, is highly liberal in its impetus.

The 2008 constitution also incorporates significant elements from the conservative model. The constitution allows the executive the possibility of serving a second term in office,[60] grants him the power to decree a state of exception,[61] and grants the executive, with favorable ruling from the constitutional court,[62] the "authority to dissolve the National Assembly when, in his/her opinion, it has taken up duties that do not pertain to it under the Constitution."[63]

14.6 BOLIVIA

14.6.1 *Setting the Stage for the 2009 Document*

As in both Venezuela and in Ecuador, the path leading to the promulgation of the 2009 Bolivian constitution was one fraught with political and economic turmoil. Three major events framed the economic debate. The first occurred in 1985,

---

[58] The constitution indicates that while public policy should not infringe upon constitutional rights, prevention of this infringement should not go so far as to undermine "the prevalence of public welfare over individual well being"; Article 85 section 2.

[59] *Ibid.*, Article 11, Section 6.

[60] *Ibid.*, Article 114 – the prior constitution did not allow reelection.

[61] *Ibid.*, Article 164 – during this state of exception, the president is allowed to "suspend or limit the exercise of the right to the inviolability of domicile, inviolability of correspondence, freedom of movement, freedom to associate and assemble, and freedom of information, under terms set forth by the Constitution." See Articles 165–166.

[62] A qualifying commission selects members of the Constitutional court. Two of the members of this commission are directly appointed by the president; Article 434.

[63] *Ibid.*, Article 148.

when the International Tin Agreement collapsed (McFadden, 1986). Under the auspices of this agreement, which supported and stabilized international prices for tin, Bolivia had fostered a single-commodity economy. In the absence of an international stabilizing mechanism, tin prices plummeted and Bolivian inflation rates soared to as high as 24,000 percent (Zwass, 2002: 133). Facing enormous popular disapproval, then-president Hernán Siles Zuazo, ceded the presidency to former president, Víctor Paz Estenssoro of the populist *Movimiento Nacionalista Revolucionario* (MNR) party in 1985. Contrary to expectation, Estenssoro adopted neoliberal policies designed to rejuvenate the economy; his New Economic Policy devalued the currency, established free-floating exchange rates, and eliminated price and wage controls (Silva, 2009: 106–107). According to the Council on Hemispheric Affairs, the "result was the best and worst of free markets" (COHA, 2009). Within a year of implementation, Bolivian inflation rates dropped from 8,170 percent to 9 percent. Yet the policies were catastrophic for Bolivian workers: 20,000 miners and 35,000 factory workers lost their jobs (COHA, 2009). Workers rallied around claims that "neoliberal reforms created unemployment, hunger, and impoverishment and that they surrendered Bolivia to foreign capital" (Silva, 2009: 112)

Tensions between the government and the people of Bolivia intensified and eventually erupted in two subsequent events: the "Water War" of 2000 and the "Gas War" or "October War" of 2003. The former erupted when President Hugo Banzer privatized the Bolivian Water industry in Cochabamba, the nation's third-largest city. Banzer awarded the contract to foreign owned consortium Aguas del Tunari. Following the privatization, water prices increased up to 150 percent and coalitions formed to protest against the privatization. According to Nancy Postero, these protests, which became known as the "Water War," were a touchstone for "shared notion[s] of exploitation based on both culture and poverty" (Postero, 2006: 195). In the minds of the participants, the protests were "an all-out last-ditch stand against neoliberalism" (Silva, 2009: 127). Across Cochabamba, banners proclaimed "water is life" and protestors decried taking what they called a gift from mother earth, "the pachamama" (ibid.: 128). Among the many social organizations that joined the Cochabamban protestors in solidarity were the *cocaleros* and their organizer, Evo Morales. Although the protestors eventually convinced the government to rescind the contract it had established with Aguas del Tunari, the government refused to allow the protestors to establish a democratic water utility system owned by its users. The government argued that this kind of "social property," was not permissible under Bolivian law (Spronk and Webber, 2007: 88).

The "Gas War" occurred two years later when, in 2003, President Sánchez de Lozada, attempted a similar privatization scheme, this time with Bolivia's natural gas reserves. Around this time, and in the context of this conflict, the Movement for

Socialism (MAS) began to emerge center stage (Webber, 2006). Under Evo Morales's skilled leadership, MAS came to represent "the shared vision of Bolivia's primary social movements" (Sweeney, 2009). Sánchez de Lozada was forced to flee the country, and his successor Carlos Mesa resigned in 2005. Morales, the MAS candidate, became a quick favorite in the 2005 election. On December 18, 2005, Morales was declared the winner of the 2005 vote. He captured 54 percent of the vote, winning a margin larger than any other candidate in recent Bolivian history (Webber, 2005).

One of the first actions of the Morales presidency was to call for the convocation of a constitutional assembly and deliver on a key MAS campaign promise – the "refounding" of Bolivia and its restoration as a plurinational state free from the clutches of the international white elite. In August 2006, the constitutional assembly was inaugurated. Amidst deep contention within the constituent assembly, the draft constitution was approved in 2008 with only 164 of 255 delegates present. It was later approved by popular referendum on January 25, 2009, and came into force on February 9, 2009.[64] As Morales declared, it was the first time a Bolivian constitution was submitted to "al voto del pueblo" (the vote of the people) (Los Tiempos, 2009).[65]

14.6.2 *The Document Itself*

Like the Venezuelan Constitution of 1999 and the Ecuadorian Constitution of 2008, the Bolivian document contains mission statement provisions, strong radical elements, and is a constitutional hybrid ungoverned by any one consistent ideological impulse. The 2009 Bolivian document followed on the heels of several constitutional reforms in the early twenty-first century, is the product of culminating radicalism, and does not mark a clean break with the prior constitution in its amended form. Much like in Ecuador, the incorporation of radical principles into the 2009 Bolivian constitution is neither unexpected nor unprecedented. The 2009 constitution is, however, undeniably more radical than its predecessor.

14.6.2.1 Ideological and Aspirational Content

According to one of the architects of the 2009 constitution, this constitution is an intentionally aspirational document. José de la Fuente Jeria, a member of the constituent assembly charged with drafting the constitution, reflected afterward that one of the challenges facing the assembly was to "incorporate in the new document new state visions of the country and development that ... certainly, had little to do

---

[64] "La Contituyente de Bolivia," accessed April 25, 2011. http://www.laconstituyente.org/

[65] "Un texto para una Bolivia Plurinacional, autonómica, y de economía." *Los Tiempos*, January 21, 2009. Accessed November 1, 2011. http://www.lostiempos.com/diario/actualidad/nacional/20090121/un-texto-para-una-bolivia-plurinacional-autonomica-y-de-economia_22175_34809.html

with the reality of [Bolivia's] democratic caricature" (de la Fuente Jeria, 2010: 6–7) (author's translation). Aspirationalism is apparent throughout the text of the charter that passed referendum in January 2009. Like in the other two constitutions examined, ideological mission statements and aspirational content are apparent in the document's preamble, in its grant of specific grievance-associated rights, and in provisions that communicate broad policy aims rather than specific rights or duties.

The preamble to the 2009 Bolivian constitution is both the longest and the most ideological of the three examined in this chapter. Although the text does not reference Bolívar or a similarly revered hero, the first few lines are evocative of the country's collective past. The preamble announces that, during ancient times, "mountains arose, rivers moved and lakes were formed. Our Amazonia, our swamps, our highland and our plains and valleys were covered with greenery and flowers." In both tone and content, this document's preambular lines are more reminiscent of a national fable or myth than constitutional text. The preamble not only appeals to shared collective past, but it also consciously identifies the constitution as a document that emerged from social struggles. The Bolivian constitution calls itself a document "inspired by the struggles of the past," a product of the "water and October wars," and one through which the Bolivian people "leave the colonial, republican and neoliberal State in the past."[66] Similar to the Venezuelan and Ecuadorian constitutions, such ideological content is not confined to the preamble and, indeed, permeates the whole document. As with the Venezuelan and Ecuadorian constitutions, mission statement provisions can be found in the Bolivian constitution's rights provisions, in a portion of the constitution demarcating the basic principles of the state, and in ad hoc policy declarations throughout the constitution.

Just as in the Venezuelan and Ecuadorian constitutions, the Bolivian constitution guarantees many rights guaranteed by the Bolivian constitution that appeal to the deepest of Bolivians' recent grievances. The document, for example, guarantees "every person the right to potable water" and establishes this right "as [a] human right" never to become "the object of concession or privatization."[67] Article 373, which describes water as a "right for life," may even pay tribute to the "water is life" chants and slogans of Cochabamban protestors at the turn of the twenty-first century. Although desires for rights to collective ownership of land go far deeper into Bolivian history than the Water War of 2000, Bolivians would likely see the 2009 constitution's explicit grant of this right[68] as a direct repudiation of the prior government's infuriating claim that such ownership of land was not "legally permissible." A similar grievance-based mission statement is contained in Article 384, which provides, "the State protects the native and ancestral coca as cultural patrimony, as

[66] Republic of Bolivia, Constitución de 2009, Preamble
[67] Republic of Bolivia, Constitución de 2009, Article 20.
[68] *Ibid.*, Article 311 Section 2.6 and Article 394 Section 3.

a renewable natural resource of the biodiversity of Bolivia, and as a factor of social unity."[69] The 2009 constitution is the first specifically to enshrine the right to coca cultivation.

Not only does the Bolivian constitution contain mission statement provisions targeting specific grievances, but the document also features general declarations of aspirational policy. Provisions regarding education provide especially vivid examples of aspirational content: the constitution promises that education will be "unitary, public, universal, democratic, participative, communitarian, decolonizing," "intra-cultural, inter-cultural," and "of quality."[70]

Like the Venezuelan and Ecuadorian constitutions, the Bolivian constitution includes an entire chapter dedicated to "Principles, Values, and State Purposes." This chapter includes a list of "ethical, moral principles" that should guide the state. These principles – "*ama quhilla, ama lulla, ama suway* (do not be lazy, do not be a liar or thief), *suma qamaña* (live well), *ñandereko* (harmonious life), *teko kavi* (good life), *ivi maraei* (land without evil), and *qhapaj ñan* (noble path or noble life)"[71] –patently appeal to Bolivia's majority indigenous population. Elsewhere, the constitution also specifies that the state shall be pacifist,[72] shall "constitute a just and harmonious society, founded in decolonization,"[73] and shall "preserve … plurinational diversity as historical and human patrimony."[74] This constitution is replete with aspirational and value-laden mission statement provisions.

14.6.2.2 Evidence of Radical Influence

Bolivia's mission statement provisions are not always hollow: appeals to inclusivity, populism, and pluralism are substantiated, like in the prior two constitutions, in radical elements in this constitution's political structure, economic structure, and in provisions regarding referendum.

Although Bolivia remains a "Social Unitary State,"[75] Miguel Centellas explains that the political structure of the 2009 constitution provides "a new structure for subnational autonomies that is more comprehensive and far-reaching" than any the country has seen before (Centellas, 2010). Chapter VIII of the Constitution, which governs "Distribution of Competencies," outlines the prerogative, exclusive, con-current, and shared powers of the central state, the "autonomous departmental governments," the "autonomous municipal governments," and the "native indigenous

---

[69] *Ibid.*, Article 384.
[70] *Ibid.*, Article 78 Sections 1 and 2.
[71] *Ibid.*, Article 8.
[72] *Ibid.*, Article 10.
[73] *Ibid.*, Article 9 Section 1.
[74] *Ibid.*, Article 9 Section 3.
[75] *Ibid.*, Article 1.

communities."[76] These provisions break from Bolivia's past constitutional tradition in that they grant significant and substantive rights to autonomous substate authorities. This new constitution also adds the "autonomous governments of the territorial entities" to the list of bodies with powers to initiate legislation that the Plurinaitonal Legislative Assembly is "obligated to process."[77]

The 2009 constitution rests substantial power in the legislative organ of Bolivia's unitary government. The constitution grants the Plurinational Legislative Assembly significant authority over the Supreme Court of Justice, the Council of Ministers of Justice, the General Comptroller, the Electoral Organ, and the Public Defender. This branch of government is granted authority to determine the "composition and organization" of the Supreme Court of Justice via passage of law,[78] to designate the "General Comptroller,"[79] and to "elect six of the members"[80] and define the "jurisdiction, competency and powers" of the Plurinational Electoral Organ within the precepts of the constitution.[81] Although the legislature remains bicameral, its strength is typical of radical instruments.

Like the political structure outlined in the new constitution, the economic structure detailed in the constitution unveils a radical agenda for Bolivia. Part IV of the 2008 constitution describes the "Economic Structure and Organization of the State." According to this section, the economic organization of the state "places the highest value on human beings and assures development through the equitable redistribution of economic surplus in social policies related to health, education, culture and the re-investment in productive economic development."[82]

Tellingly, the constitution dictates that the "economic organization of Bolivia" should promote the "reduction of inequality of access to productive resources" and "the reduction of regional inequality."[83] Like its predecessors, the constitution requires the state to "recognize, respect, and protect private initiative,"[84] yet qualifies these rights: Article 56 grants that "everyone has the right to private ... property *provided that it serves a social function*" (author's emphasis).[85] Article 395 requires "fiscal lands" be granted to certain agrarian communities that do not have land or have "insufficient land," and Article 398 limits private ownership of land to

---

[76] Republic of Bolivia, Constitución de 2009, Articles 297–304.
[77] Republic of Bolivia, Constitución de 2009, Article 162, Section 5.
[78] Republic of Bolivia, Constitución de 2009, Article 181.
[79] *Ibid.*, Article 214.
[80] *Ibid.*, Article 206.
[81] *Ibid.*, Article 205.
[82] *Ibid.*, Article 306 Section 5.
[83] *Ibid.*, Article 313 Sections 3–4.
[84] *Ibid.*, Article 308.
[85] See also Articles 309, 393, and 397. Article 56 shares language with a 2002 amendment to the 1967 constitution (see Republic of Bolivia, Constitución de 1967 con reformas de 1994, texto concordado de 1995, y reformas de 2002, 2004 y 2005, Article 7 Section J).

5,000 hectares. Additionally, Articles 399 and 401 allow for the expropriation of private land where new ownership exceeds 5,000 hectares or where individuals have "failed to fulfill the social economic purpose" of land ownership.[86] The economic policy of the state is therefore not designed to uphold liberal individual rights, but rather is explicitly designed to augment social welfare, economic subsistence, and the egalitarian distribution of wealth.[87]

Like the 1999 Venezuelan and the 2008 Ecuadorian constitutions, the 2009 Bolivian constitution expands citizens' control through new provisions deepening rights to referendum. The 2009 document grants citizens the right, at the request of 15 percent of the voters "on the electoral roll of the district that elected the public servant," to initiate popular referendum on the recall of any public official.[88] It also forbids the state from signing international treaties altering borders, monetary integration, and structural economic integration without popular referenda on these issues.[89]

In addition, the 2009 constitution expands citizens' control over the constitutional reform processes. In its original form, the 1967 constitution required that constitutional reform proposals be reviewed and approved by both houses before amendment.[90] Bolivia's 2009 constitution grants the people of Bolivia power over constitutional reform. Article 411 grants citizens the right, with the signatures of 20 percent of the electorate, to initiate a binding referendum on the question of whether to convoke a constituent assembly tasked with the total reform of the constitution.[91] The constitution also grants citizens the right to initiate, with the signatures of 20 percent of the electorate, a referendum on the partial reform of the constitution. The Plurinational Legislative Assembly is required to submit any constitutional reform proposal to referendum by the people.[92]

[86] The state's power to expropriate land deemed not to be serving a social function can be traced at least as far back as the constitution of 1945.
[87] For a discussion of Bolivian efforts toward land reform, including a discussion of the 2009 constitution's role in these reforms, see Gross, 2010.
[88] Republic of Bolivia, Constitución de 2009, Article 240 Section 3.
[89] Ibid., Article 257 Section 2, 1–4.
[90] In August 2002, the Bolivian congress passed Ley 2410 de Necesidad de Reformas a la Constitución Política del Estado (Law No. 2410 on the Necessity to Reform the Constitution). This law brought sweeping constitutional reforms, including changes to the constitutional reform procedure. Two new sections were added to Article 231 – one of these sections required congress to "convoke a Constitutional Referendum whose objective is to allow the citizens [to] accept or reject the Constitutional Reform." In 2004, the Bolivian congress passed Lay 2631 de Reforma de la Constitucion (Law 2631 on the Reform of the Constitution) in violation of the requirements of the amended Article 231. Law 2631 removed the requirement for popular referendum. See Constitución de 1967, Articles 231–232. Republic of Bolivia, Constitución de 1967 con Reformas de 1994 y Texto Concordado de 1995; y Reformas de 2002, Article 231. Republic of Bolivia, Constitución de 1967 con reformas de 1994, texto concordado de 1995, y reformas de 2002, 2004 y 2005, Article 231.
[91] Republic of Bolivia, Constitución de 2009, Article 411 Section 1.
[92] Ibid., Article 411 Section 2.

The political structure, the economic structure, and the expanded rights to referendum demonstrate the institutionalization of radical constitutional ideology – each of these features brings power closer to the people.

14.6.2.3 Constitutional Hybridism

The 2009 Bolivian document, despite its highly radical provisions, is a constitutional hybrid containing elements of each of the three models.

Although less presidentialist than the Venezuelan document, the new Bolivian constitution similarly contains conservative elements suggesting that members of the MAS party, the party that launched Morales into power and had control of the constituent assembly, hoped to maintain stability both by appealing to the key demands of their constituent members and by concentrating executive power. For example, the constitution grants the executive the authority to: "propose and direct the policies of the government of the state"; "present the economic and social development plan to the Plurinational Legislative Assembly"; name "from among the candidates proposed by the Plurinational Legislative Assembly … the Controller General of the State, the President of the Bank of Bolivia, [and] the maximum authority of the Regulatory Organ of the Banks and Financial Entities."; "appoint and dismiss the General Commander of the Bolivian Police" as well as the "Commander in Chief of the Armed Forces" ; and "declare a state of exception."[93] The constitution also grants the president power to call a national referendum on the recall of any government official – a veiled but potentially significant political weapon.

Radical economic policies guaranteeing egalitarianism and redistribution of wealth are coupled with statist provisions augmenting control of the unitary government. Article 311 guarantees the state the power to "intervene in every part of the chain of productivity in the strategic sectors, seeking to guarantee its supply in or in order to preserve the quality of life of all male and female Bolivians.[94] Given Bolivia's large hydrocarbon reserves, these economic duties and imperatives could grant the national government significant economic power.

The constitution also incorporates elements of the liberal model. Central to this constitution is its promise of plurinationality – of protection for Bolivia's majority indigenous, but historically marginalized, population. The document explicitly grants indigenous peoples rights and autonomies designed to protect them from infringement from the state.[95] Lastly, this constitution, keeping with precedent,

---

[93] Republic of Bolivia, Constitución de 2009, Article 172.
[94] *Ibid.*, Article 311 Section 2.4.
[95] Republic of Bolivia, Constitución de 2009. See Article 190: "the native indigenous rural peoples will exercise their jurisdictional functions and competency through their authorities, and shall apply their own principles, cultural values, norms and procedures."

empowers a legislative branch with an upper house of government – a provision typical of liberal constitutional documents and indicative of distrust for the majority.

14.7 CONCLUSION

Speaking about the new 2009 Constitution, Bolivian Vice President Alváro Garcia Linera said, "up to now, each of our 17 or 18 constitutions has just tried to copy the latest intuitional fashion- French, US, European" (Escobar, 2010: 5). Linera suggested that the new document was different – a unique and organic product of Bolivian society. This chapter has sought to establish that the 2009 Bolivian constitution shares its most characteristic features with the 1999 Venezuelan and 2008 Ecuadorian constitutions. South America's newest constitutions thus appear to represent the newest "institutional fashion" in Latin America – one which might be called Neo-Bolivarian constitutional design. Projecting what this trend might mean for the entrenchment of constitutionalism in each country must, of course, be a very modest task. Here, I merely caution against unexamined disregard for these documents and encourage future study.

Treating these documents as crystallizations of the sociopolitical moment in which they were birthed is not heartening. Although the documents are illustrative of the specific grievances and aspirations of each polity, these constitutions reflect deep institutional uncertainty in each country – they contain manifest pulls toward radical populism, opposite liberal pressure to protect the marginalized, and strong statist provisions reminiscent of those from each country's caudillo past.

Perhaps because of this internal disharmony, David King, professor of public policy at the John F. Kennedy School of Government, asked this hypothetical question in 2005: "Does anyone, for example, think that Venezuela's 1999 Constitution will last even four years after President Chávez leaves office?" "Of course not," he answered (King, 2006: 14).

I believe this answer was preemptive. Consider, for example, Gary Jacobsohn's argument that "a constitution acquires an identity through experience" (Jacobsohn, 2011: 129).[96] According to Jacobsohn, this experience is a dynamic and dialogical process fueled by two forms of tension: internal disharmony within the document and disharmony between the constitution and the social order it governs. Jacobsohn suggests that the process according to which constitutions acquire "identity" – jurisgenerative discourse fueled by internal and external tensions – forms part of a "developmental process endemic to the phenomenon of constitutionalism" (Jacobsohn,

---

[96] Gary Jacobsohn is H. Malcolm Macdonald Professor in Constitutional and Comparative Law at the University of Texas at Austin.

2011: 130). Following from this argument, these tensions fuel grievances and political discourse, which, because couched in the terms of the document, deepen rights consciousness and so might breathe life into sentiments tied to respect for the rule of law.

These constitutions, as radical documents, explicitly name all citizens as participants and sovereign in political discourse. Furthermore, these constitutions institutionalize and officially guarantee the kinds of outlets through which citizens may themselves engage in dialogue. Each constitution promises to provide the basic levels of economic subsistence required for participation, to bring government closer to the people through decentralization, and guarantees rights to referendum. More important than the institutions they create is their message: citizens are actors and citizens' voices are empowered. Constitutional hybridism, an essential feature of these constitutions, creates what Jacobsohn calls "internal disharmony." Aspirational content, "mission statement provisions," and the temporal nature their anti-neoliberal focus pattern disharmony between the society the document promises and the society these constitutions govern. Moreover, these missions appeal deeply to the grievances of the population and so involve citizen's sentiments in a particularly potent manner.

Justification for the future study of these documents is twofold. Firstly, historic instability frames questions about whether radicalism, targeted value-laden content, and internal disharmony have the potential to foster constitutional transformation – these countries are apt crucibles in which to study the emergence of jurisgenerative dialogue, and their experience may be used to couch and strengthen the claims of existing theories. Secondly, deep ideological ties between the polity and the constitution, the empowerment of citizens in the process of rulemaking, and apparent concessions between the interests of traditional power players and those of populist social movements also signal, on very initial blush, the possibility that it may become more politically expedient for future parties to proceed with, rather than against, these constitutions. If it is possible that these constitutions will guide rulemaking in each country, they merit very close attention indeed.

REFERENCES

Albertus, Michael and Medaldo, Victor 2012. "Dictators as Founding Fathers? The Role of Constitutions under Autocracy," *Economics & Politics* **24** (3): 279–306.

Alexander, Robert J. 1982. *Bolivia: Past, Present, and Future of its Politics*. Politics in Latin America. New York: Praeger.

Andolina, Robert 2003. "The Sovereign and Its Shadow: Constituent Assembly and Indigenous Movement in Ecuador," *Journal of Latin American Studies* **35** (4): 721–750.

Berggren, Niclas, Nils Karlson, and Joakim Nergelius 2000. *Why Constitutions Matter*. Stockholm: City University Press.

Blanksten, George I. 1951. *Ecuador: Constitutions and Caudillos* 3 (1). Berkeley: University of California Press.

Brewer-Carías, Alan 2010. *Dismantling Democracy in Venezuela: The Chávez Authoritarian Experiment*. Cambridge: Cambridge University Press.

Brown, Nathan J. 2002. *Constitutions in a Nonconstitutional World: Arab Basic Laws and the Prospects for Accountable Government*. SUNY Series in Near Eastern Studies; SUNY Series in Middle Eastern Studies. Albany: State University of New York Press.

Centellas, Miguel 2010. "Bolivia's Radical Decentralization," *America's Quarterly*, Summer 2010. Accessed April 4, 2013. http://www.americasquarterly.org/node/1700 (accessed April 4, 2013).

Chávez, Hugo 1999. '*Discurso de Posesión*'. Accessed April 10, 2013. http://www.analitica.com/bitblioteca/hchavez/toma.asp

Ciccariello-Maher, George 2008. "The Fourth World War Started in Venezuela." *Hands Off Venezuela!* Accessed April 25, 2011. http://www.handsoffvenezuela.org/caracazo_anniversary_19_years.htm

Cordeiro, Jose Luis 2008. "Latin America: Constitution Crazy." *Latin Business Chronicle*. Accessed April 9, 2013. http://www.latinbusinesschronicle.com/app/article.aspx?id=2799

Corrales, Javier 1999. "Venezuela in the 1980s, the 1990s, and Beyond: Why Citizen-Detached Parties Imperil Economic Governance." *Harvard Review of Latin America*. Accessed April 4, 2013. http://www.drclas.harvard.edu/publications/revistaonline/fall-1999/venezuela-1980s-1990s-and-beyond

Correa, Rafael 2007. *Discurso de Posesión del Presidente de la República, Econ. Rafael Correa en La Mitad Del Mundo*. Accessed April 4, 2013. http://www.presidencia.gob.ec/discursos/

Van Cott, Donna Lee 2003. "Andean Indigenous Movements and Constitutional Transformation: Venezuela in Comparative Perspective," *Latin American Perspectives, Indigenous Transformational Movements in Contemporary Latin America* 30 (1): 49–69.

Council on Hemispheric Affairs (COHA) 2009. "A Brief History of Bolivia and the Rise of President Morales," *Council on Hemispheric Affairs*, January 24, 2009. Accessed April 10, 2013. http://www.coha.org/a-brief-recent-history-of-bolivia-and-the-rise-of-president-morales/

Couso, Javier. "Models of Democracy and Models of Constitutionalism: The Case of Chile's Constitutional Court: 1970–2010." Paper presented at Texas Law Review Symposium: Latin American Constitutionalism, March 4–5, Austin, Texas.

Crabtree, John and Whitehead, Laurence 2008. *Unresolved Tensions: Bolivia Past and Present*. Pitt Latin American Series. Pittsburgh, PA: University of Pittsburgh Press.

Cristancho, Maria Victoria 1998. "Hugo Chávez Barrió en Venezuela," *El Tiempo*. Accessed April 25, 2011. http://www.eltiempo.com/archivo/documento/MAM-809896

Dahl, Robert Alan 1989. *Democracy and Its Critics*. New Haven, CT: Yale University Press.

2007 "Déjà vu Venezolano," *El Universo*, October 2, 2007. Accessed June 5, 2013. http://www.eluniverso.com/2007/10/02/0001/21/7626942A6A68449C835C68EB7DEB6117.html

2007 "Ecuador: Overcoming Instability?" International Crisis Group. Latin America Report N°22. Accessed April 6, 2013. Available: http://www.crisisgroup.org/~/media/Files/latin-america/ecuador/22_ecuador__overcoming_instability.pdf

Escobar, Arturo 2010. "Latin America at a Crossroads: Alternative Modernizations, Postliberalism, or Postdevelopment?" *Cultural Studies* 24 (1): 1–24.

Fernandez, Norma 2009. "Ecuador's Correa: The Citizen's Revolution." *Global Research.* Accessed April 4, 2013.http://www.globalresearch.ca/index.php?context=va&aid=13649.

Franklin, Daniel P. and Baun, Michael J. 1995. *Political Culture and Constitutionalism: A Comparative Approach.* Comparative Politics Series. Armonk, NY: M. E. Sharpe.

Fuente Jeria, José de la. 2010. "El difícil parto de otra democracia: La Asamblea Constituyente de Bolivia." Latin American Research Review 45.S: 5–26. Project MUSE. Accessed March 15, 2011. http://muse.jhu.edu/

Galdari, Eduardo 2005. *Bolivian Leader Won't OK Cocoa Eradication.* AP Newswire. Accessed April 4, 2013. http://www.apnewsarchive.com/2005/Bolivia-Leader-Won-t-OK-Coca-Eradication/id-9ef3045770086c7bof88fdc8e935e88fd

Galligan, D. G. and Versteeg, M 2013. "Introduction" D. J. Galligan and M. Versteeg eds. *Social and Political Foundations of Constitutions.* Cambridge.

Gargarella, Roberto 2010. *The Legal Foundations of Inequality: Constitutionalism in the Americas, 1776–1860.* Cambridge and New York: Cambridge University Press.

González, Luis E. 1988. *Latin-American Institute on Comparative Constitutionalism: A Rapporteur's Report.* American Council of Learned Societies Comparative Constitutionalism Project Latin American, Regional Institute, and Centro de Informaciones y Estudios,del Uruguay.

Grijalva, Agustín 2009. "Principales Innovaciones en la Constitución de Ecuador del 2008." *Institute for Research and Debate on Governance.* Accessed April 12, 2013. http://www.institut-gouvernance.org/en/analyse/fiche-analyse-454.html

Gross, Joshua 2010. "A Covenant with Uncertainty: Considering Contemporary Constitutional Land Reform in Bolivia," *The Journal of International Policy Solutions* 12:3–15.

Harris, William 1993. *The Interpretable Constitution.* Baltimore; Johns Hopkins University Press.

Jacobsohn, Gary 2011. "The Formation of Constitutional Identities," in Tom Ginsburg and Rosalind Dixon, eds., *Elgar Handbook in Comparative Constitutional Law.* Glos: Elgar Press.

Kelly, Janet 2000. "Thoughts on the Constitution: Realignment of Ideas about the Economy and Chages in the Political System in Venezuela." *Instituto de Estudios Superiores de Administración.* Carcaras, Venezuela. Accessed April 5, 2013. https://lasa.international. pitt.edu/members/congress-papers/lasa2000/files/Kelly.PDF

King, David C. 2006. "*Constitutional Reform in Bolivia: The 2005 Presidential Election,*" ReVista: Harvard Review of Latin America (Spring): 11–15.

King, Jeff 2013. "Constitutions as Mission Statements" D. J. Galligan and M. Versteeg eds. *Social and Political Foundations of Constitutions.* Cambridge.

Kornblith, Miriam 1991. "The Politics of Constitution-Making: Constitutions and Democracy in Venezuela," *Journal of Latin American Studies* 23 (1): 61–89.

  2007, "*Democracia Directa y Revocatoria de Mandato en Venezuela,*" commissioned by International IDA as a contribution for the International Conference on Direct Democracy in Latin America. Accessed April 5, 2013. http://www.cholonautas.edu.pe/modulo/upload/democracia%20directa%20venezuela.pdf

Lansburg-Rodriguez, Daniel 2010. "Wiki-Constitutionalism: The Strange Phenomenon that's destroying Latin America." *The New Republic.* Accessed April 10, 2013. http://www.tnr. com/article/politics/75150/wiki-constitutionalism

Levitsky, Steven and Loxton, James 2012. "Populism and Competitive Authoritarianism in the Andes." Accessed April 10, 2013. http://scholar.harvard.edu/levitsky/files/levitsky-loxton-democratization-revisedversion-june2012.pdf

Lucero, José Antionio 2001. "High Anxiety in the Andes: Crisis and Contention in Ecuador," *Journal of Democracy* **12** (2): 59–73.

Lutz, Donald S. 2000. "Thinking about Constitutionalism at the Start of the Twenty-First Century," Essays in Memory of Daniels J. Elazar. *Publius* **30** (4): 115–135.

Marcano, Cristina, Alberto Barrera, and Kristina Cordero 2007. *Hugo Chávez.* 1st U.S. ed. New York: Random House.

McCoy, Jennifer L. 1999. "Chávez and the End of 'Partyarchy' in Venezuela," *Journal of Democracy* **10** (3): 64–77.

McFadden, Eric 1986. "The Collapse of Tin: Restructuring a Failed Commodity Agreement," *American Journal of International Law* **80** (4): 811–830.

Minow, Martha 1987. "Interpreting Rights: An Essay for Robert Cover," *The Yale Law Journal* **96** (8): 1860–1915.

Morales, Evo 2006. *Discurso De Evo Morales al sumir la presidencla de Bolivia.* Accessed April 6, 2013. http://www.democraciasur.com/documentos/BoliviaEvoMoralesAsuncion Pres.htm

Norton, Anne 1988. "Transubstantiation: The Dialectic of Constitutional Authority," *The University of Chicago Law Review* **55** (2): 458–472.

Postero, Nancy 2006. *Now We Are Citizens.* Stanford, CA: Stanford University Press.

Przeworski, Adam 1988. "Democracy as a Contingent outcome of Conflicts," in Jon Elster and Gudmund Hernes, eds., *Constitutionalism and Democracy*, Cambridge: Cambridge University Press.

2005 "Rafael Correa renunció al ministerio del economía," *El Universo*, August 5, 2005. Accessed April 7, 2013. http://www.eluniverso.com/2005/08/05/0001/9/A99FF2FCCCAE4D70BE0A1E92B2AC69D1.html

Rosenn, Keith 1991. "Success of Constitutionalism in the United States and Its Failure in Latin America: An Explanation by Keith Rosenn," in The *U.S. Constitution and the Constitutions of Latin America* vol. 7, ed. Kenneth W. Thompson. Lanham, MD / Charlottesville: University Press of America / White Burkett Miller Center of Public Affairs, University of Virginia.

Sajó, András 2003. *Out of and into Authoritarian Law.* The Hague and London: Kluwer Law International.

Salomon, Gisela 2010. "Carlos Andres Perez, Two-Time Venezuelan president, Dies at 88." *The Washington Post.* Accessed April 25, 2011. http://www.washingtonpost.com/wp-dyn/content/article/2010/12/27/AR2010122703506.html

Sawyer, Suzana 2004. *Crude Chronicles: Indigenous Politics, Multinational Oil, and Neoliberalism in Ecuador.* Durham, NC: Duke University Press.

Silva, Eduardo 2009. *Challenging Neoliberalism in Latin America.* Cambridge Studies in Contentious Politics. Cambridge and New York: Cambridge University Press.

Spronk, Susan and Webber, Jeffery 2007. "Accumulation by Dispossession in Bolivia: The Political Economy of Natural Resource Contention," *Latin American Perspectives* **34** (31): 31–47.

Stokes, Susan 2001. *Mandates and Democracy: Neoliberalism by Surprise in Latin America.* Cambridge and New York: Cambridge University Press.

Sweeney, Chris 2009. "From Rightist Chaos to Leftist Constitutionalism: The Institutionalization of Bolivian Populism." *Council on Hemispheric Affairs.* Accessed

April 8, 2013. http://www.coha.org/from-rightist-chaos-to-leftist-constitutionalism-the-institutionalization-of-bolivian-populism/

Torre, Carlos de la 2010. *Populist Seduction in Latin America*. 2nd ed. Athens: Ohio University Press.

Valle Velasco, Luis Francisco, ed. and trans. 2012. *Essential Laws of the Bolivian Revolution*. La Paz: CreateSpace Independent Publishing Platform.

Viciano Pastor, Roberto and Martínez Dalmau, Rubén 2001. *Cambio Político y Proceso Constituyente En Venezuela, 1998–2000*. Caracas: Vadell Hermanos.

Webber, Jeffrey 2006. "Will Evo Morales Change Bolivia?" *International Viewpoint*. Accessed April 12, 2013. http://www.internationalviewpoint.org/spip.php?article958

Wilpert, Gregory 2003. "The Economics, Culture, and Politics of Oil in Venezuela." *Venezuelanalysis: News Views and Analysis*. Accessed April 6, 2013. http://venezuelanalysis.com/analysis/74

Walsh, Frank M. 2009. "The Legal Death of the Latin American Democracy: Bolivarian Populism's Model for Centralizing Power, Eliminating Political Opposition, and Undermining the Rule of Law." Bepress.com. Accessed April 5, 2013. http://works.bepress.com/frank_walsh/

Zwass, Adam 2002. *Globalization of Unequal National Economies: Players and Controversies*. New York: M. E. Sharpe.

Constitutions:

Constitution of the Bolivian Republic of Venezuela. Accessed June 6, 2011. Available: https:/venezuelanalysis.com/constitution

República Bolivariana de Venezuela, Constitución de 1999 con reformas hasta 2009, Accessed April 5, 2013. Available: http://pdba.georgetown.edu/Constitutions/Venezuela/vigente.html

República del Bolivia, Constitución de 2009. Accessed April 5, 2013. Available: http://pdba.georgetown.edu/Constitutions/Bolivia/bolivia09.html

República del Bolivia, Constitución de 1967 con Reformas de 1994 y Texto Concordado de 1995; y Reformas de 2002. Accessed April 5, 2013. Available: http://pdba.georgetown.edu/Constitutions/Bolivia/consboliv2002.html

República del Bolivia, Constitución de 1967 con reformas de 1994, texto concordado de 1995, y reformas de 2002, 2004 y 2005. Accessed April 5, 2013. Available: http://pdba.georgetown.edu/Constitutions/Bolivia/consboliv2005.html

Republic of Ecuador, Constitution of 2008. Accessed April 5, 2013. Available: http://pdba.georgetown.edu/Constitutions/Ecuador/english08.html

República de Ecuador, Constituciones de 1998. Accessed April 5, 2013. Available: http://pdba.georgetown.edu/Constitutions/Ecuador/ecuador98.html

15

The Constitution as Agreement to Agree

The Social and Political Foundations (and Effects) of the 1971 Egyptian Constitution

Clark B. Lombardi

15.1 INTRODUCTION

From 1971 until 2011, Egypt was governed by the Permanent Constitution of 1971 (henceforth "1971 Constitution" or "Constitution"). This constitution was drafted at the instruction of a new president, Anwar al-Sadat – the heir to an authoritarian regime that had come under massive criticism from both liberals and Islamists. The new constitution seemed, at first, to be welcomed by a broad cross-section of Egyptians and it continued in force for nearly forty years.

The public's initial embrace of the new constitution seems, in retrospect, somewhat mysterious. The 1971 Constitution was a remarkably ambiguous text. Admittedly, no constitution answers clearly *all* questions about the structure of government or about the nature of the constraints that a government will recognize on its powers. Even so, the drafters of Egypt's 1971 Constitution left a number of important questions glaringly unresolved. The 1971 Constitution in its preamble and early provisions reflected considerable confusion about the nature of the state and the ideology of its governing institutions. Was the state to be Pan-Arabist or Egyptian Nationalist? Socialist or capitalist? Secular or Islamic? The Constitution also did not clarify whether its institutions would operate in an authoritarian or liberal fashion. Rights guarantees were deeply ambiguous – the scope of protection left to be established by sub-constitutional "regulation." Similarly, the Constitution made clear that state legislation should respect

The author wishes to thank Greta Austin, Nathan Brown, Simon Chesterman, Dennis Galligan, Tom Ginsburg, Andrew Harding, Ran Hirschl, David Law, Victor Ramjraj, Bruce Rutherford, Mila Versteeg, Arun Thiruvengadam, the participants in the Foundation for Law, Justice and Society December 2010 workshops on the Social and Political Foundations of Constitutions, and the participants in the National University of Singapore Faculty Research Colloquium for their comments and suggestions on drafts of this chapter. He thanks Matthew Goldman for research assistance. All remaining errors are the author's alone.

Islam, but it did not make clear exactly how much, nor did it make clear whose inter-pretation of Islam was controlling. Not only did the early provisions suggest consider-able confusion about vision and constraint, but the remarkably plastic Constitution created embryonic institutions that could operate in very different modes. Details about how institutions were to be staffed or to operate were supposed to be set out in implementing litigation. The Constitution only vaguely described judicial institu-tions that would resolve disputes about state constitutional compliance. Ultimately, someone who voted in 1971 to approve the new constitution could not be certain about what type of government would emerge.

Perhaps more surprising than Egyptians' initial support for this open-ended con-stitution was their continuing willingness to operate under it. After the ratification of the Constitution, Egypt witnessed a fairly long period of genuine contest over whether the executive-dominated government of Egypt should allow the ambi-guities in the constitution to be resolved in favor of liberalization or Islamization. Ultimately, however, the government decided it would permit neither. Operating within the letter of the open-ended constitution, Egypt's president and his allies entrenched themselves and repressed those who called for effective liberalization or Islamization. Nevertheless, a large number of liberals and Islamists continued to try and work within the terms of the increasingly unfair political and legal sys-tem. Indeed, even as popular unrest toppled the regime of President Mubarak in 2011, many of the political opponents who had suffered under Mubarak's regime questioned whether it was necessary to abolish the 1971 Constitution. After Egypt's military finally decided to abrogate and replace the Constitution, a temporary con-stitution retained significant portions of the new constitution, and, at the time of this writing, it remains possible, though not inevitable, that the next permanent consti-tution (as yet undrafted) will do so as well.

This chapter explores the social and political backgrounds to the 1971 Egyptian Constitution and to the actions of those who operated under it. It examines the reasons for the Constitution's ambiguities and then considers why the Constitution was, early on, attractive to a broad cross-section of Egyptians and, finally, how these ambiguities shaped political discourse and behavior. The contest over how to imple-ment and elaborate on the 1971 Constitution created an environment in which rival political factions could focus on a few important open questions of constitutional structure and interpretation and each could try to get these questions answered to their satisfaction. Authoritarian factions within the executive branch convinced the executive not to cede power, and to flesh out the constitution in a way that ensured his continued control over all aspects of government. In the process, however, they energized and changed their Islamist and liberal opponents. Initially struggling sep-arately against authoritarians, these mutually mistrustful opposition factions found themselves by necessity cooperating more than they had historically done. They worked together to ensure that the few institutions that could protect them retained the independence and power to do so. In the process many among them came to conclude that, when it came to concrete questions of institutional design, they agreed more than they heretofore realized. By 2011, the tentative rapprochement between Egypt's liberals and Islamists had progressed far enough to affect Egyptian politics in a dramatic way. Young liberals and Islamists engaged in joint action demanding the ouster of President Mubarak and the reform of Egypt's constitutional regime. This action was sufficiently powerful that the military felt compelled to oust President Mubarak and, shortly thereafter, to abrogate the 1971 Constitution.

The conclusion to this chapter considers the lessons we might draw from the history of Egypt's 1971 Constitution. While recent research suggests that the average constitution dies in less than twenty years (Ginsburg et al. 2007: 47; Elkins et al. 2009), the 1971 Constitution survived for almost forty. The history of the 1971 constitution thus provides evidence to support the claim, recently made by Dixon and Ginsburg (2011), that although it is often dangerous for drafters to defer a large number of important questions of constitutional design, there are some circumstances under which certain types of significant constitutional deferral can help constitutions survive. At the same time, it is important to remember that the 1971 Constitution collapsed extremely suddenly. Studying the death of this Constitution helps us understand how once-sustaining deferral policies can cease preserving and can instead make a constitution fragile. Finally, the history of this constitution also provides some provocative, if inconclusive, insight into the vexed question of whether political Islamism can under some circumstances be compatible with political liberalism.

15.2 THE SOCIAL AND POLITICAL FOUNDATIONS OF THE 1971 CONSTITUTION

The 1971 Constitution was drafted against the backdrop of almost a century of debate among Egyptian elites about executive constraint. When Egypt first entered the modern era, its government was dominated by the executive branch. Over the next century, as Egypt gained independence from the Ottoman Empire and modernized its political system, Egypt's political elites debated the degree to which the executive should be subject to any checks at all and, if so, of what these constraints should consist. While authoritarian factions tended to be dominant, they constantly struggled with rival factions that favored either (1) liberal constraints of a sort that were modeled on the constraints being imposed in Western liberal democracies or (2) "Islamic" constraints inspired by classical Islamic political structures as reimagined by modern Islamic intellectuals. The 1971 Constitution was drafted when authoritarians had weakened and their rivals were beginning to pose a significant challenge to their hegemony. Its ambiguities reflect the contemporary uncertainty about Egypt's future direction.

15.2.1 *The Emergence of Modern Egypt and Early Debates about Executive Constraint*

Egypt began the nineteenth century as a province of the Ottoman Empire. In the middle of the nineteenth century, a hereditary dynasty of autonomous governors was ruling over Egypt with the title of *khedive*. In the late nineteenth century, khedival Egypt fell under British control, the khedive thereafter being forced to coordinate all important policy decisions with a British advisor. In 1922, Egypt was given formal independence and its khedive was henceforth recognized as head of an independent nation-state. As Egypt moved toward independence, it abandoned its aspiration to operate on a traditional Ottoman model of government, one that had been stable and enjoyed considerable popular legitimacy, and struggled to find an effective, alternative model.

In the classical Ottoman model of government, the head of government and its chief executive was supposed to be constrained by respect for a particular type of Islam. In theory, the Ottoman ruler was supposed to recognize his obligation to act in consultation with a class of Islamic scholars known as the *fuqaha'*. These scholars were masters of a particular interpretation of Islamic law, an interpretation called *fiqh*. Theoretically, the sultan and his governors were supposed to rely on the *fuqaha'* as legal advisors and as judges in the courts of general jurisdiction. The ruler would then be able to assert his legitimacy partly through the fact that his advisors and judges ensured that the state acted in an Islamically moral fashion and adjudicated disputes according to law that was consistent with *fiqh*.

The central Ottoman government itself, and governors in Ottoman provinces, did not always faithfully follow in all respects the traditional model just described. Starting in the early nineteenth century, Egypt's increasingly independent khedives over time became willing to abandon it more or less completely. The roots of the divorce began in the khedive's commitment to structure his government on European models (Hunter 1984; Vatikiotis 1991: 52–64). Over the protests of the *fuqaha'*, the khedive started to expand and centralize the bureaucracy, to impose a more intrusive regulatory apparatus, and to restructure the court system. Given the unwillingness of many *fuqaha'* to train their students for the new system, the khedive was forced to supplement the *fuqaha'* serving the state with people who had not received a traditional Islamic education but had rather been trained in Western-style institutions that taught European theories of governance and law as well as the practical skills needed to administrate a European style administrative system (Marsot 1984: 66–70, Vatikiotis 1991: 58–59, 90–123).

The displacement of the *fuqaha'* by these new legal elites accelerated as the influence of the British over state policy grew during the last quarter of the nineteenth century. The process reached a tipping point when the khedive decided in 1882 to replace the Ottoman-style legal system with the one modeled on the civil law regimes of continental Europe (Brown 1997: 29–31). Thereafter, a new Egyptian national court system modeled on the French system was given jurisdiction over all disputes outside the areas of personal status and instructed to resolve disputes according to comprehensive codes promulgated by the ruler. These new codes themselves contained rules drawn from European legal systems rather than traditional Islamic legal systems. Personal status issues, such as family law and inheritance, continued to be resolved on the basis of partly codified *fiqh* in special courts staffed by members of the *fuqaha'*. Even these special Shari'a courts were abolished in the 1950s and their jurisdiction transferred to the courts of general jurisdiction staffed by lawyers rather than *fuqaha'* (Sfeir 1956).

By the early twentieth century, outside of the area of personal status law, the ruler of Egypt was no longer cooperating in a meaningful sense with the traditional Islamic scholars. This raised an important question: Should the khedive be subject to any constraints at all? While factions close to the khedive resisted any meaningful constraints on executive power, many Egyptians rejected the idea that a ruler should be unconstrained and struggled to articulate new visions of constrained Egyptian government.

Some, particularly in the judiciary and the legal profession, came to advocate a continental style of liberal government; they would argue that the government should enact a constitution that committed it to govern as efficiently as possible without violating liberal rights (Brown 1997: Rutherford 2008: 32–42; Ziadeh 1968). To ensure that it met its obligations, this faction wanted the executive to be subject to oversight by a democratically elected legislature. An independent judiciary would ensure more than the fair and equitable administration of the laws developed by the political branches. While it should show deference to the political branches, it would ultimately have the power, in extreme cases, to void government action that violated constitutionally guaranteed liberal rights.

As the liberal faction was taking shape, new Islamist political factions were also slowly coming together. In the late nineteenth and early twentieth centuries, Islamic intellectuals began to reimagine what it meant for a state to be Islamic and to build organizations calling for the Islamization of the state (Lombardi 2006: 78–100). Political Islamists tended to have a deeply ambivalent relationship with political and legal liberals. While the movements were potentially symbiotic, they had different focuses and appealed to different constituencies. Their adherents failed for decades meaningfully to explore where their commitments might overlap.

Political Islamism in modern Egypt had its roots in a movement that one might call, with caution, lay Islamism. Lay Islamists generally did not desire or acquire the classical Islamic education that would allow them to be recognized as *fuqaha'*. Questioning the value of such an education, they challenged the *fuqaha*'s claims to define Islamic law and questioned many of the traditional interpretations of Islamic law that the *fuqaha'* had developed in the past. Instead, lay Islamists used new, distinctly modern methods of interpretation to develop new bodies of Islamic law. Agreeing with the *fuqaha'* that the state must never contradict the core principles of Islamic law or the public interest, lay Islamists proposed a variety of untraditional methods of determining what the "core" principles of Islamic law were, as well as untraditional methods of determining whether the public interest was being promoted (*ibid.*).

The most powerful modern Egyptian Islamist organization was largely a product of lay Islamism. The Muslim Brotherhood was founded in 1928 by an admirer of the modernist Islamic thinker Rashid Rida (Mitchell 1993: 321). Rida had argued that no state law was legitimate if it forced people either to violate explicit scriptural rules or act against the interests of the Muslim community. Decrying the complex methods that the *fuqaha'* used to interpret text, Rida insisted that God had revealed in plain language all rules that God expected the state to obey. Any literate person who studied the Islamic scriptures could find them. Crucially, he insisted that among the rules that an informed, literate person would find was a utilitarian principle that said that, having granted reason to men, God required Muslims to promote the well-being of the Muslim community (on Rida's thought generally, see Hallaq 1997: 214–220; Kerr 1966: 187–208; Lombardi 2006: 83–90).

For Rida, the process of Islamic legal reasoning must start with an analysis of scripture, because God would never clearly command something that was unjust or harmful to humans. Whenever the law was unclear or failed to address a situation, however, the interpreter should supplement the law in whatever manner would best promote the spiritual and material welfare of the people (*ibid.*). Implicit in this message was a claim that anyone possessing piety, literacy, familiarity with scripture, an ability to understand the economic, political, and social consequences of a law, and the commitment to engage fully with the text could understand what state laws were consistent with God's command.

Teaching this theory, the Muslim Brotherhood spread quickly among the rapidly growing literate and politically disaffected middle classes, particularly in urban centers (Rutherford 2008: 78–82). The organization early on demonstrated a talent for political agitation (and at times violence) to promote the call that the state should promote Islamic piety and discourse and should recognize an obligation to respect Islamic law as soon as Islam's requirements became clear. By the late 1930s it had become Egypt's most important mass political organization.

Not all lay Islamists embraced Rida's neo-scripturalist vision of Islam. As the Brotherhood was attracting a popular following, an eminent French-trained lawyer and professor Abd al-Razaq al-Sanhuri was promoting a different method of modernist Islamic legal reasoning (Lombardi 2006: 92–99; Lombardi and Brown 2006:

411–413). Sanhuri argued that Muslims should not identify the core principles of Islamic law (which included a utilitarian principle) by rereading of scripture, but rather by rereading the *fiqh* tradition. He argued that properly trained lawyers could use inductive reasoning to find certain overarching principles implicit in the totality of the Islamic interpretive tradition. Sanhuri's method proved highly popular among legal elites.

By the middle of the twentieth century, lay Islamist thought in its various forms had begun to shape the thinking of members of the *fuqaha'*. Leading members of the *fuqaha'* were calling for a state that was Islamic in largely the sense that Rida and Sanhuri and their followers described it, that is, one whose laws and policies were consistent with a handful of rules and with general principles that included a utilitarian principle. These modernist *fuqaha'* insisted, however, that professional scholars with traditional training should play an important role in debates about those principles and their implications (Lombardi 2006: 80–83).

Lay Islamists and those *fuqaha'* influenced by them promoted a remarkably plastic vision of the state. Agreeing on the need for the state to respect Islamic law, Islamists often disagreed among themselves about whether a textual passage (or a historical pattern) was clear enough to establish binding principles. Even when they agreed on the rules and principles that a state would have to take into account, they often disagreed about how to apply a principle in the context of modern Egypt. Most obviously, they contested the nature of utility and often disagreed about whether a particular policy was likely to promote it. Islamist organizations like the Muslim Brotherhood seem implicitly to have accepted it as unavoidable that their members' understanding of Islam would evolve and their views about how modern life should be lived would change. To formulate a clear and detailed political platform would invite premature and divisive internal debates as well as possible external criticism. As a result, the Muslim Brotherhood did not commit to many specific policies (Rutherford 2008: 91–92, cf. Wickham 2002).

The vagueness of Islamist political rhetoric suggested implicitly that Islamization should have to proceed in steps. After accepting a commitment to apply Islamic law and after ensuring that all law was consistent with clear rules and principles, the state would have to promote discourse to illuminate the other rules and principles it would have to obey. The state would then have to conform its policy to the emerging understanding of Islamic principles. Ultimately, then, the central demand of Islamists up through the turn of the twenty-first century seemed to be that Egyptians and the state accept an obligation to respect Islamic principles whose ramifications for governance were still far from clear. Neither Egypt's authoritarian rulers nor their liberal opponents – each of whom had very clear ideas about how the state should be governed – were comfortable accepting this demand.

15.2.2 *The Contest between Authoritarians, Liberals, and Islamists: 1922–1971*

Constitutional struggle in Egypt during the early twentieth century can be conceptualized as a three-way struggle between dominant authoritarians and two opposition factions embracing rival visions of executive constraint. Liberals, whose strength lay primarily in the judiciary and legal profession, championed liberal constitutionalism; Islamists, who had considerable popularity among the masses, favored a somewhat nebulous set of "Islamic" constraints. The boundaries between liberals and Islamists were not entirely rigid: some conservative lawyers and judges had a foot in both camps.[1] By and large, however, the mainstreams of these factions were distinct and mutually suspicious.

The struggle between these factions heated up after the First World War, when the Ottoman Empire collapsed and Egypt could no longer be treated as an autonomous province of the empire. After Egypt was declared to be an independent state, the khedive was recognized as a sultan and later as a king. The newly promoted ruler proposed to write a constitution that would create very few checks on his power. As Islamists had not yet become a major political force, the constitution made no mention of Islamic law.[2] Liberal lawyers and judges together with wealthy landowners were, however, able to generate popular support for liberal constraints on executive power. Egypt's 1923 Constitution was ultimately modeled on the relatively liberal constitutions of Belgium and Prussia (Brown 2001: 38; Rutherford 1999: 143).[3] It required the king to cooperate with an elected parliament and it empowered the judiciary to protect an impressive list of property rights as well as political rights (Rutherford 1999:144; cf. Ziadeh 1968 and Marsot 1977.)

The 1923 Constitution was not a success. The checks it placed on the ruler were not as effective as liberals had hoped. The king and his allies were largely able to avoid parliamentary checks on his power.[4] Although judges asserted the power,

---

[1] My thanks to Nathan Brown for reminding me of the importance of this point.

[2] Article 149 made Islam the official religion of the state but did not clarify what the implications of this might be. No provision explicitly mentioned Islamic law or the obligation of the state either to respect or apply it.

[3] "Minutes of the drafting committee, later published, show its members to be very conversant in matters of constitutional law and design" (Brown 2001: 38). "While [the drafters] worked primarily from Ottoman and continental European constitutional models, they showed particular interest in writing a document that would help the country assert its independence and establish a measure of parliamentarism" (*ibid.*).

[4] Effective constitutional monarchy, Brown points out, was not an inevitable product of the language found in the European constitutions on which the Egyptian Constitution was modeled. Rather, it was the product of European interpretation of that language – and even then was only imperfectly realist. "Thus, the [Egyptian] drafting committee appropriated [from European constitutions] language that had admitted non-constitutionalist interpretations in Europe and would almost certain do so in

in theory, to conduct judicial review of legislation and executive actions, they never actually exercised these powers (Brown 2001: 41, 148; Rutherford 1999: 211). Squabbling between liberals and authoritarians prevented the government from dealing effectively with Egypt's many ills. The government's growing paralysis was exacerbated by the growing power of Islamists as a major force in Egyptian politics – a force that was not able to form meaningful alliances with the king or with the liberals in parliament.[5]

By the late 1940s, the Egyptian masses, and even some members of the elite, had grown dangerously frustrated with Egypt's parliamentary experiment. In 1952, a group of army officers including Gamal Abdel-Nasser took power in a coup. These officers quickly abrogated the 1923 Constitution, deposed and exiled the king, declared martial law, and then considered how to proceed. Over four years, a group of officers with authoritarian proclivities, led by Nasser, established their hegemony within the junta. Thereafter, they established a radically authoritarian regime with Nasser at its head.

Nasser's new regime imposed by executive decree a series of constitutions that reflected an ever-deepening commitment to authoritarian socialism as practiced in Soviet bloc states. A single political party led by the president, the Arab Socialist Union (ASU), controlled the executive and legislative functions of the state. With the support of his party, the president suppressed the advocates of both liberal and Islamic constraints. Concerned about the popular prestige of the independent and ideologically liberal judiciary, Nasser took steps to marginalize judges and cabin their power. He established laws that declared state action to be "acts of state" that individuals were unable to challenge, and he also gave himself the power to create specialized courts in which the bar and judiciary exercised little power. While doing this, Nasser attacked Islamists more directly. He had Sanhuri, then serving as a judge, physically assaulted and forced to leave public life. Although this was attributable primarily to Sanhuri's advocacy of liberal philosophy and judicial power, it nevertheless marginalized (as a political figure) an important Islamist. Nasser also

---

Egypt." As a result, "the king refused to accept the anticipated limits of a constitutional monarchy and exercised the full range of his constitutional authority directly" (Brown 2001: 41).

5   In the 1940s, the leadership of the Muslim Brotherhood considered running candidates for parliament, which would presumably have forced the Brotherhood to clarify what governmental reforms, exactly, they wanted to introduce and what policies they wanted a government to pursue. Ultimately, however, they chose not to do so, continuing to agitate for an open-ended commitment to respect an as-yet-largely-undetermined set of Islamic policies (Mitchell 1993: 248; Rutherford 1999: 105). Mitchell also points out that the Brotherhood, during Egypt's liberal experiment, considered running candidates for parliament (Mitchell 1993: 309). Given their dislike of the figures who dominated parliament, however, they initially supported the 1952 coup and joined the government (Rutherford 1999: 184–185). Frustrated by governmental dysfunction in the 1940s and 1950s, even Sanhuri wavered in his commitment to democracy, though never to liberalism (ibid. 179–181).

intimidated the *fuqaha'*, whose thinking had begun to resemble that of lay Islamists. To that end, he nationalized the school at the Mosque of al-Azhar, which trained nearly all members of the Egyptian *fuqaha'*, and he abolished the Shari'a courts where members of the *fuqaha'* had continued to resolve issues of Islamic family law and inheritance (Sfeir 1956). By far the most savage repression, however, was directed at the Muslim Brotherhood. Notwithstanding its early cooperation with the 1952 coup, the Muslim Brotherhood had become skeptical of Nasser's intentions and had dabbled in violent resistance to his regime. By the end of the 1960s, after ruthless suppression, the Muslim Brothers' leadership had all been executed or jailed, and the organization was in disarray.

Although Nasser's tactics at first seemed effective at defanging both the liberal and Islamist opposition, both groups would eventually reappear on the political screen.[6] Growing discontent at all levels of Egyptian society was fueled by economic stagnation. Egypt's shocking defeat by Israel in the 1967 war seemed to confirm in the eyes of many that Nasser's authoritarian experiment had failed. In the face of growing popular unrest both from inside and outside government, Nasser's advisors came to opposite conclusions about how to respond. One faction, apparently reflecting the views of the increasingly sick and demoralized Nasser himself, argued that the regime could not survive unless it made concessions to liberals and Islamists. In March 1968, shortly before suffering a debilitating heart attack, Nasser promulgated a series of executive orders that imposed some liberalization and promised more (Baer 1978). As a result, Islamist political prisoners were released from jail and slowly began to reorganize. Nasser's leading lieutenants, however, rejected the idea of democratizing, liberalizing, or Islamizing. They called for even more aggressive seizure of private property and redistribution and greater repression. While Nasser was incapacitated by illness, Nasser's authoritarian lieutenants began to act on their own. They repudiated the recently enacted liberalization measures and unleashed an unprecedented series of executive orders designed to bring the judiciary, still the center of liberal opposition to the regime, firmly under ASU control. Judges were for the first time, effectively, fired. Furthermore, the power of judicial review was taken out of the hands of the courts (where legal liberals might have still lurked) and placed in the hands of the new Supreme Court, which was dominated by government yes-

---

[6] By the late 1960s, his policies of providing free education through university and employing new graduates in the growing state bureaucracy had unexpected effects. For statistics on this, see Waterbury (1983). Far from being a grateful and loyal bloc, the new "state bourgeoisie" came over time to share many of the concerns of the traditional middle class – both about economic freedoms and opportunities and personal liberties. On this development, see the discussion in Baer (1978). To Nasser's distress, they resented his increasingly arbitrary exercises of power, providing a new bloc of supporters for liberals and Islamists alike. Because the Islamist opposition had lost its organizational infrastructure, Islamist opponents were less visible than liberals, but, as would become clear in the 1970s, the Islamists' influence was becoming significant below the surface.

men. As popular discontent with these developments grew, liberalizers and authoritarians continued to struggle and Islamists continued to reorganize.

In the fall of 1970, as the struggle between authoritarians, liberals, and Islamists reached fever pitch, Nasser died. His death weakened the hand of radical authoritarians in the fight to shape state policies and strengthened the hand of those who wanted to make concessions to liberals and Islamists. The balance of power became highly unstable. In this fraught environment, a new president came to power and decided to draft a new constitution.

15.2.3 *The Drafting of the 1971 Constitution*

When Nasser's vice president, Anwar al-Sadat, ascended to the presidency and leadership of the ASU, his position was extremely precarious. Deeply unpopular among the authoritarian faction of the ASU, Sadat was also concerned that the ASU was losing popular legitimacy. Even if he won control of the party, the party might lose the state to popular unrest. In this environment, Sadat felt he had no choice but to ally himself with those who, out of personal conviction, pragmatic fears of growing opposition, or some combination of the two wanted the state to make concessions to liberals and Islamists. As Rutherford puts it:

> Sadat turned to the Parliament, the judiciary and the press for support largely because these were the only institutions that were not controlled by his enemies and, once he had successfully turned to them, they became the logical foundation on which to build further support for his regime.... This process became self-reinforcing: the more liberalizing steps that he took, the more Sadat became dependent on the advocates of liberalization for support and, thus, the more pressure he faced to continue liberalizing. (Rutherford, 1999: 272)

In the spring of 1971, with great public fanfare, Sadat appointed an ideologically diverse committee to draft a new "Permanent Constitution" that would soften the authoritarian features of the existing regime and thereby would make the political modus vivendi of the country acceptable to liberal and Islamist factions.

In a 1983 speech, Ibrahim Saleh, a member of the committee that helped draft the 1971 Constitution (and a representative of the liberal faction among the elites to which Sadat was trying to appeal), recalled the environment in which the drafting was done:

> When President Sadat assumed control of the government in 1970, the Egyptian people had already been shattered by the 1967 defeat, by worsening economic conditions, and by their diminishing leadership in the Arab world. It was necessary to strengthen the people's identification with their political leadership. Establishing democracy and constitutional legitimacy would legitimize the regime and accurately express the true sentiments and aspirations of the populace. (Saleh 1983: 338)

To ensure that it was legitimate in the eyes of a broad spectrum, the regime ensured that the drafting committee (and the subcommittees that would be most closely involved in drafting the constitution) had representation from across the ideological spectrum. Leading liberal members of the legal profession, including Saleh himself, articulated some controversial proposals for liberal change. The state should embrace a liberal ideology, and parliament and the judiciary would each be given independence from the executive and enough power to ensure that a genuine liberal democracy is allowed to emerge (Saleh 1983: 338). At the same time, Islamic scholars were included to ensure that the interests of Islamists were considered and integrated into the constitution. Coptic religious leaders were also included to check whether Islamization provisions did not take a form threatening to Copts (Rutherford 1999: 275–276; Saleh 1983: 314–317, 344). At the same time, numerous authoritarians on the committee were supposed to ensure that the new constitution did not include provisions that would overly disempower the ASU.

What structure of government and what system of constraints would be acceptable to all these different factions? Authoritarians and liberals had irreconcilable visions of the state. Liberals found some of the essential features of the Nasserist structure intolerable and authoritarians found many of the liberals' most cherished ideas repugnant. Neither of these factions was willing to accept Islamists' demand that the state recognize an open-ended obligation to respect principles that Islamist thinkers were still struggling to elaborate through study of scripture, history, and utilitarian intuition. Given only two months to complete a draft and submit it for approval by the ASU (and thereafter for ratification by the public), the deeply divided group of drafters despaired in identifying mutually acceptable principles of governmental constraint and designing satisfactory governmental structures that would implement any such constraints (Rutherford 1999: 275–276). Instructed to come up with a "compromise," they found they could not, and instead simply agreed to disagree on core issues. They produced a constitution that, although long and turgid, proved on close inspection to be full of ambiguities and gaps. These were all left to be resolved at a later date by institutions that were themselves poorly described.

The text of the 1971 Constitution makes clear that its drafters systematically engaged in what Rosalind Dixon and Tom Ginsburg have called constitutional "deferral." Deferral, as these scholars describe it, is a conscious decision not to decide a controversial issue of government structure or of judicially enforceable limits on government behavior (Dixon and Ginsburg 2011). They suggest that deferral can take two forms. The first is explicitly to identify an issue and to state that it is to be resolved by legislation after the constitution is ratified. The second is a form of implicit deferral. In this case, the drafters deliberately describe a structural rule or a constitutional right in unclear language, thus requiring that the rule should be elaborated by the institution that has been entrusted with judicial interpretation (ibid.).

In an illuminating section of his 1999 dissertation, Bruce Rutherford explored the notes of the drafting committee for the 1971 Constitution (Rutherford 1999: 215–296). Although he did not analyze their work through a paradigm of deferral, his analysis suggests that the liberals and authoritarians who sat on the committee regularly engaged in both types of deferral and sometimes combined the two types by creating a vague provision that was meant to be interpreted down the line by a legal institution which had not yet been created.

The 1971 Constitution, as eventually ratified, began with a schizophrenic section outlining the principles that are to guide Egypt in the post-Nasser era. The first two recalled Nasser's Arab nationalism and socialism, which Nasser had seen as inconsistent with democracy, liberalism, or Islamism. They were then paradoxically followed by principles of democracy, rule of law, and, in an elliptical fashion, Islam. The Constitution left it to future politicians and judges to determine how such principles could be harmonized in a practical form.

The new constitution attempted to guarantee liberal democracy and governance by providing a long list of protected rights, including political, property, and social rights. The Constitution did not, however, simply declare most rights to be constitutionally protected. Rather, it instructed the legislature to define the scope of the protected rights and then to enact laws that would define the powers of the judiciary to protect them (Brown 2001: 82).[7]

Who did the Constitution's drafters expect to resolve the questions about Egypt's direction? The answer is not clear, and this is probably because the drafters and the public simply could not reach any consensus on this point.[8] The Constitution initially maintained a unicameral legislature that was effectively under the control of the executive. Thus, the parliament could emerge as a more independent institution only by dint of executive permission.[9] At the same time, under the social and political condition of 1971, it was not impossible to imagine that the parliament *would* be permitted to emerge as an independent institution. If popular demands for liberalization continued, the Constitution permitted the legislature (with the assent of the executive) to open the political space. In that case, the parliament itself would become a check on executive power and might well establish more robust judicial checks.

---

[7] Brown thus suggests that the overall effect was not to provide absolute defenses of basic rights, "but to ensure that legal and judicial processes would be faithfully followed in most cases in which rights were at issue."

[8] My analysis of the drafting process for the 1971 Constitution is heavily informed by Bruce Rutherford's PhD dissertation (Rutherford 1999), which includes an invaluable, detailed study of several volumes of the unpublished minutes of the drafting committee.

[9] As Rutherford puts it, "the framers of the Constitution went to considerable lengths to improve the procedures that govern the operation of Parliament, but they paid little attention to the electoral process that produces a weak and docile parliament … In practice, the executive branch retained decisive influence over the Parliament" (Rutherford 1999: 232).

That the drafters were deliberately creating a situation in which Egypt could evolve in either an authoritarian or liberal direction is suggested by the evolution of the Constitution's provisions dealing with the question of judicial review. Toward the end of Nasser's regime, a Supreme Court with few guarantees of independence had been created and given the exclusive right to exercise judicial review. Authoritarians wished to retain this institution, whereas the liberals wanted the Constitution to invest judicial review either in the regular judiciary, which was still controlled by liberals, or in a more independent institution. Although the minutes of the committee meetings suggest that the committee was willing to accept the position of the authoritarians, something seems to have happened when the draft was sent for review to the president (Rutherford 1999: 235–237). For reasons that have never been explained, the final draft of the Constitution turned down the drafters' offer of a constitutionally weakened court. Instead, the Constitution deferred the question of what the Court should look like to a later date. Articles 174 to 178 thus created a Constitutional Court to be staffed by judges who would serve for life, and they granted this court the power of judicial review. They also explicitly left all questions about the court's structure, its procedures, and any further jurisdiction to be resolved by "future legislation."

The constitutional drafters also deferred on the extremely controversial questions of whether to establish courts in which judges without full guarantees of independence would try political crimes (Rutherford 1999: 231–234). Article 171 of the Constitution as ratified stated that they might exist, but left all details of their staffing and procedures to be determined by future legislation. Similar ambiguities were allowed to remain with respect to the question of prosecution. Alongside the traditional office of the prosecutor, which traditionally enjoyed significant independence,[10] Article 179 of the Constitution created the possibility of a second prosecutorial office whose jurisdiction, staffing, and operating procedures were to be established by legislation down the line.[11]

Finally, the drafters of the 1971 Constitution decided not to take a position on the debate over whether the president should continue to have expansive powers to prosecute political crimes outside of the normal judicial process. They denied such power to the president in the normal course of affairs, but at the same time, Article 148 gave the president, in consultation with the legislature, considerable power to declare a state of emergency and to exercise extraordinary powers during the duration of the emergency. Such a provision deferred to the executive and legislature the question of whether and under what circumstances the president could exercise

---

[10] On the evolution of the office of the *niyaba* in Egypt, see Hill (1979). For a short comparative discussion of the offices of the *niyaba* in Egypt and other Arab countries, see Nasr, Crystal, and Brown (1994).

[11] For a discussion about the committee debates about this provision, see Rutherford (1999: 241–243).

powers beyond those granted by normal law and perhaps in contravention of the limits established by normal law.

Alongside the remarkable series of deferrals on questions of democracy and liberalism, the Constitution also deferred on the question of whether the state should respect Islam – primarily through the mechanism of leaving references to the role of Islam in the state extremely vague. Not grasping perhaps that important representatives of Islamism were found among lay Islamists, Sadat had placed on the committee two members of the Azharite *fuqaha'* but had not included any representatives of the Muslim Brotherhood, which was only beginning to regroup after the repression of the late Nasser years.[12] Even so, lay Islamism was able to make its presence felt. When the *fuqaha'* proved weak advocates for Islamism, more aggressive proposals came, ironically, from figures who were not formally representatives of Islamist factions, but whose thinking had been shaped by lay Islamist thought. One insisted that parliament be required to implement Shari'a, without explaining what that would mean. Yet another, probably inspired by recent developments in Pakistan, suggested the creation of a Council of Islamic Studies that would be specifically tasked with the job of reviewing legislation to ensure its consistency with Islamic law. Yet another member proposed that the Constitution pledge to implement a form of democracy and socialism that – in terms reminiscent of Sanhuri – would be consistent with "the historical traditions and spirit of Islam" (Rutherford 1999: 247–248).[13]

Ultimately, the Constitution only included in Article 2, a vague sentence that seemed to leave the question of the law's Islamicness in the hands of the legislature. Article 2 of the Constitution declared that "the principles of the Islamic Shari'a shall be a chief source of legislation." That Islam would play a still-to-be-determined role in the state was squarely in the constitutional text. The language, however, raised significant questions. Islam was to share space with other ideologies, and this implied that the new state might have discretion in some cases not to abide by Shari'a. What these cases were was not clear. Islamists in the 1970s eventually generated pressure to amend the Constitution in order to clarify and strengthen the position of Islam within it.

Seen as a whole, the final text of the 1971 Constitution was a symphony of strategic ambiguity. The questions of whether the state would be restrained by democratic institutions, by liberal institutions, or by a principle of respect for Islam were all left in the hands of a legislature that would operate, at first, under the control of the executive, assisted by judicial institutions that would be created and regulated by the

---

[12] For the leading members of the drafting committee, including the two "Islamic" representatives, see Rutherford (1999: 247).

[13] For a discussion of these debates, see Rutherford (1999: 247–248), citing the comments of Abdel Nasir al-'Atar, Abdel Halim Guindy, and an unnamed source as recorded in the committee minutes for the drafting committee of the 1971 Constitution.

legislature itself. Egypt's future path thus rested entirely on the opposition's ability to continue to create political pressure on the executive and to force him to allow for the free election of a representative parliament that would by law establish the makings of a liberal state.

On September 8, 1971, the ASU approved the proposed Constitution with support from both its authoritarian and liberal factions. On September 11, the new constitution was overwhelmingly approved in a national referendum (el-Shaeir 1983: 336). One has to be careful about taking the results of this poll entirely at face value; nevertheless, there seems to have been some genuine enthusiasm for the new document across a broad cross-section of Egyptians.

Why would liberal and Islamist factions support such an open-ended constitution? In light of the fact that constitutional ambiguity would be resolved, at least at the outset, by executive controlled institutions, this constitution might see to be less a compromise than a capitulation to the executive branch, which ultimately had the power to determine the direction Egypt took. From the vantage point of liberals and Islamists alike, however, it was very much an improvement. Liberals and Islamists who felt that their star was in the ascendant understood that they were being given the opportunity to keep building their popular strength and to pressure the executive to make choices that, once made, would set Egypt inexorably down a path of democratization and liberalization or Islamization.

15.2.4 *Deepening Ambiguity: Implementing Legislation and the 1980 Amendments*

As liberals and Islamists struggled to create social and political pressure in favor of liberalization and Islamization, respectively, President Sadat remained weak. Authoritarian factions continued to threaten him within the party. Sadat also needed to rebuild the economy, which required both foreign direct investment and foreign aid from the West. In this environment, liberals were able to press effectively for some of the Constitution's deferred questions to be answered in a "liberal" way. Islamists were likewise able to have the Constitution amended to strengthen the role of Islamic law in the state.

In 1972, a series of laws clarified the scope of rights that were granted in the Constitution but subject to regulation by the legislature. These outlawed a number of practices that had aroused fierce opposition in the latter years of the Nasser regime. These included torture, indefinite detention, and the stripping of former prisoners' political rights (Saleh 1983: 318–320). Even more dramatically, supplementary legislation created the possibility that the judiciary would create a real check on executive power. Laws in 1972 lifted prohibitions against citizens suing the state (*ibid.*). Then, after years of difficult negotiations and relentless pressure from liberals, the legislature promulgated the law organizing the new Supreme Constitutional Court (SCC). In 1979, in a striking triumph for liberals, parliament created the SCC in a form that gave it remarkably strong guarantees of independence. According to the law, the president's control would be exercised almost entirely through appointments (Lombardi 2008: 241–242). He had total discretion over the appointment of the Chief Justice and indirectly had the ability to exercise significant control over appointments of associate justices. Once a judge was appointed, however, the executive had almost no ability to control them. Strikingly, given this fact, the president permitted the Court to be staffed by a liberal chief and a majority of judges with liberal proclivities.[14]

Notwithstanding these developments, neither democratic nor judicial power had ever reached a point where it could fully constrain the executive on issues of importance to him, and it is not clear that Sadat wanted them to grow to that point. Shortly after taking power, he arranged for the legislature to establish a state of emergency and thereafter to renew it regularly. Notwithstanding the entrenchment of liberals within an independent judiciary, Sadat was thus able to use his extraordinary emergency powers to repress political opponents when he felt it necessary without either parliamentary or judicial oversight.

A series of constitutional amendments in 1980 made clear the undecided state of the conflict between liberals who were trying to further strengthen the still-evolving democratic and liberal institutions in Egypt and authoritarians who wished to stop the process of liberalization before it created real constraints on executive power. Some made important steps toward political liberalization. One of the 1980 amendments significantly ended the one-party political system. Sadat had already disbanded Nasser's ASU and started a new ruling party, the National Democratic Party (NDP). Alongside the NDP, opposition parties were permitted to form. At the same time, other amendments created new tools that the executive could use to entrench himself if the existing parliament and judiciary ever began to exercise independence. For example, a new upper house of the parliament was created, a third of whose staff would be presidential appointees. Ominously, presidential term limits were also eliminated.

During the 1970s, Islamists too had made significant but incomplete progress in their attempt to compel the government to respect Islamic principles. As the 1970s

---

[14] A number of scholars have recently discussed why the executive would permit the Court to be created in the form it was and to allow liberals to staff it, and have argued about whether it should be seen as something akin to an act of "hegemonic preservation" of the type described by Ran Hirschl in this volume (Hirschl 2013). Compare Moustafa (2007), Rutherford (1999), and Lombardi (2008) with Nathan J. Brown (2009: 6, n 10) (arguing that those who created the court were interested in more than creating a vehicle that would attract foreign investment). Although I myself laid out the "hegemonic preservation" argument in the article cited earlier, I find Brown's caution convincing, and this chapter implicitly reflects Brown's more qualified view.

progressed, Islamists grew in power and pushed relentlessly for the state to recognize a clear commitment to act in accordance with Islamic moral principles.[15] As the decade dragged on, Islamists benefited enormously from Sadat's periodic bouts of political liberalization. Several times during the 1970s Islamists were released from jail, allowing the Muslim Brotherhood to reorganize and rally support for a more meaningful constitutional commitment to Islam. Other, more radical and violent lay Islamist organizations appeared as well.

To deal with the growing threat, Sadat used his emergency powers to repress the most radical Islamist groups. He sometimes suppressed the more moderate Muslim Brothers as well, but generally seemed more interested in co-opting them. He thus instructed the legislature to review Egypt's laws for consistency with Islam and arranged for constitutional amendments in 1980 to include an amendment to Article 2 (Lombardi 2006: chapter 7). After the 1980 amendments, "the principles of Islamic Shari'a" ceased to be merely "a chief source" and were instead be elevated to "the chief source" of Egyptian legislation. This change of wording added significant new ambiguity to the Constitution. In Arabic, the amended Article 2 could easily be read to create a justiciable requirement that all state laws would have to be consistent with the principles of the Islamic Shari'a – and this is clearly how Islamists interpreted it.[16]

Ultimately, then, legislation during the 1970s and constitutional amendments of 1980 further deferred the ultimate questions of whether Egypt would evolve into a liberal democratic or Islamic state of some kind. As of 1980, the trajectory seemed generally to be both liberalizing and Islamizing. It remained to be seen whether this would continue. Although the parliament and judiciary had each been empowered to enforce to impose liberal and Islamic constraints, the president of the republic retained significant ability to slow down or even reverse these developments. The question of whether this would occur and, if so, the question of how liberals and Islamists would react would be resolved under a new president.

---

[15] The then-semiofficial newspaper, *al-Ahram*, reported that in public meetings held by the government to get feedback on the draft, the Constitution was criticized for making Islamic Shari'a merely "a" chief source of legislation instead of "the" chief source. A series of letters to *al-Ahram* made similar criticisms. This response was so surprising and alarming that one of Sadat's secularist (and authoritarian) legal advisers, and a member of the constitutional drafting committee, Gamal al-Otayfi, wrote a column in *al-Ahram* explaining why the Constitution did not require the state more firmly to respect Islamic legal norms. Islamists were not convinced. See Otayfi (1971), described in Rutherford (1999: 250).

[16] This was, however, not the only possible reading. There was a good argument that Article 2 should be considered non-justiciable, and Sadat probably expected the new SCC to adopt this view. Furthermore, even if the SCC were to interpret Article 2 as amended to require a form of Islamic review, Sadat probably expected it to find the vast majority of laws consistent with the principles of Shari`a. On these points, see the discussion in Lombardi (2006: chapter 8).

15.3 THE SOCIAL AND POLITICAL EFFECTS OF THE AMBIGUOUS 1971 CONSTITUTION

In October 1981, shortly after the new amendments had taken effect, a cell of radical Islamists assassinated President Sadat. Receiving conflicting advice from advisors who counseled a retreat from democratization, liberalization, and Islamization and advisors who argued for further concessions, Sadat's successor, Hosni Mubarak, vacillated. By the second half of the 1980s, Mubarak had decided to move in an authoritarian direction – albeit in a cautious way. He abandoned any further attempt to reach out to liberals and Islamists. Instead, he began to subvert institutions that had been structured in a way to enable liberal governance. The challenge of operating under a new "semi-authoritarian" system drove both liberals and Islamists into a long and painful but productive period of introspection. As a result, they, for the first time in modern Egyptian history, began to build meaningful (although still embryonic) relationships.

15.3.1 *Executive Entrenchment and the New Incentive for Liberal-Islamist Cooperation*

Mubarak's policy of political de-liberalization was gradual. Incrementally, however, the authoritarian tendencies of his regime became apparent. The new president's willingness to ignore public opinion if it suited him was on display when in 1985 his handpicked Speaker of Parliament definitively terminated Sadat's program of negotiating with Islamists to amend Egypt's laws. Thereafter, Mubarak's regime gradually closed off the political sphere to Islamists, who represented the best-organized and most important source of popular opposition to the regime. Through increasing limitations on political speech and assembly, through electoral manipulation, and occasionally through outright suppression under the emergency laws, the executive prevented Islamists and other opposition groups from achieving more than token representation in parliament. In response, opposition groups ran for leadership positions in professional syndicates. This forced Mubarak to employ a variety of legal and extralegal tools to prevent them from taking control of these institutions and establishing bases of power there.

By carrying out its repression in a manner that was incremental and could plausibly be read as respecting the letter of the law (or at least to be judicially unreviewable), the executive made it difficult for a judiciary committed to a continental European model of separation of powers to step in forcefully. By the 1990s, political scientists around the world were commenting on Mubarak's ability to work within the confines of an incomplete democratic and liberal constitutional and legal structure in order to entrench himself further. They described Egypt as the exemplar of a new type of regime, a "semi-authoritarian" regime where "despite all the formal trappings [of a liberal democracy], power remain[ed] concentrated in the hands of an unaccountable government that [could not] be removed by democratic means" (Olcott and Ottoway 1999).

Liberals and Islamist actors who were emerging as "losers" in the constitutional deal continued to counsel respect for the Constitution and attempted to operate under its terms. To be sure, acquiescence in the grossly one-sided contest between the authoritarian executive and the champions of restraint was not universal. A strain of radical Islamist thought had emerged in the 1960s, which argued that irretrievably corrupt and un-Islamic legal systems must be resisted with every tool available, including violence.[17] Some smaller opposition factions such as nationalists and Nasserists responded with vocal criticism of the authoritarian policies of the government. Notably, however, the two most important opposition factions – liberals and mainstream Islamists – chose not to call for revolutionary change. Instead, they continued grudgingly to operate under the legal limits established by the Mubarak regime. The surprising decision of Islamists and liberals to keep operating within the system was driven partly by fear. The repressive power of the state was enormous and the costs of extralegal resistance would have been very high. Furthermore, the benefits of changing the Constitution were not entirely clear for these actors.

In the 1980s, the Muslim Brotherhood's leadership was drawn from a generation that had had suffered grievously in the 1960s after the Brotherhood's resistance to Nasser had provoked violent suppression. Furthermore, because their organization had been largely destroyed during this period, the Muslim Brothers had been unable to capitalize fully when the regime had unexpectedly weakened at the end of Nasser's life. Indeed, liberals rather than Islamists had been the main beneficiaries of the government's concessions, and it had taken Islamists all of the 1970s to establish their power sufficiently to get Article 2 amended. Understandably, many leading Muslim Brothers in the 1980s were inclined to continue building a popular base for support in the future and to avoid actions that might again invite repression so severe that they would be unable to capitalize if the regime ever faltered. Not only were the costs of revolutionary activity high, but the Brotherhood was not sure that radical constitutional change was necessary for it to gain the power it craved. Even under the 1971 Constitution, winning elections might give Islamists all the power necessary to create their ideal Islamic state – particularly

---

[17] During the Nasserist period, this became an alternative vision alongside the mainstream Muslim Brotherhood, which counseled resistance within the bounds of law. Sadat's assassins had accepted this "radical Islamist" vision. The revolt provided an excuse for Mubarak to suppress a growing number of Islamists under the Emergency Law – and these included not only radical revolutionary Islamists but also ones who wanted to press the Islamist cause through constitutional means.

after Article 2 explicitly encouraged legislation to conform to an as-yet-undefined set of Islamic principles.

Similarly, liberals, and particularly liberals on the judiciary, believed that radical attempts to work outside the emerging constitutional structure were dangerous and possibly counterproductive. Like the Muslim Brotherhood, the judiciary had suffered at the end of the Nasser years and had spent the 1970s rebuilding both their independence and their popular prestige. Judges did not want to risk reliving this experience unless there was a clear benefit to be gained. Bringing down the Constitution and ushering in a popular debate over what the new constitution would say was not only a risky proposition, but it might play into the hands of Islamists. Suspicious of Islamists' commitment to liberal values, they feared that the 1971 Constitution might be replaced by a document that was even less liberal. They too, therefore, decided to focus on leveraging the powers that the 1971 Constitution left them. They would impose liberal values whenever possible, building their prestige and popular support for a judicial role in governance. This strategy would allow them to capitalize on any period of executive weakness. Moreover, it would ensure that they had the popular prestige necessary to restrain Islamists, if those Islamists were ever to replace the military as illiberal rulers of Egypt.

15.3.2 *Responses to Executive Entrenchment: The Formation of an Embryonic Liberal-Islamist Alliance*

Having opted to work within the constraints of the existing constitutional order, Islamists and liberals had incentive to work together. For Islamists to pry open the political sphere, and perhaps to avoid repression of the sort that nearly broke them during the Nasser period, they needed the support of the courts to interpret broadly the constitution's guarantees of political participation and to strike down repressive laws. Conversely, liberals, and particularly liberals in the judiciary, wanted the courts to maintain their independence and their aura of moral authority and popular respect. It would be hard to do this without Islamists' public support.

Although the interests of Islamists and liberals were symbiotic, there was still mutual mistrust. As discussed already, Islamists had long doubted liberals' willingness to qualify their expectations for a liberal state if that proved necessary to meet the demands of the Islamic tradition (which was still being interpreted). Islamists were nervous about unequivocally supporting liberal-dominated institutions that might be inclined to compel an Islamist government, if such a government were ever to take power, to respect expansive interpretations of personal freedoms. Conversely, liberals in the judiciary and liberal intellectuals were concerned by the nebulousness of Islamists' political philosophy and the lack of any public commitment on the part of leading Islamists to affirm the centrality of individual freedoms in an Islamic state. Liberals were thus wary of employing their precious prestige to empower a group that might prove less liberal than the regime. Seeking to overcome these hurdles to a valuable alliance, a few Islamists and liberals began to explore tentatively whether they might be able to imagine, within the broad framework set by the 1971 Constitution, a state structure and a set of individual rights and principles that Islamists and liberals alike could support.

On the Islamist side, this process of reaching out began in the 1980s. During that decade, a diverse group of Islamist intellectuals began to articulate far more precise visions of the Islamic state than previous Islamist thinkers. Among these new intellectuals was Yusuf al-Qaradawi, an al-Azhar-trained member of the *fuqaha'*, albeit one who had been trained after leading *fuqaha'* had adopted elements of modernist thought. There were also the likes of Kamal Abu-al Majd, Muhammad Salim al'Awwa, and Tariq al-Bishri, all of whom were lawyers – the last being a former leftist intellectual who had served as a high-ranking judge on the powerful High Administrative Court.[18] Each proposed a state constrained by both democratic checks and the protection of numerous liberal rights, not because freedom was an end in itself, but because the promotion of both personal and political freedom and the promotion of political participation were necessary for a truly Islamic state to come into being.[19] The visions of these thinkers were sufficiently consistent that Raymond Baker has argued that they represent a "New Islamist" political philosophy (Baker 2003). Their work provoked considerable discussion. Notwithstanding the gaps that remained between new Islamist thought and traditional liberal thought, the new Islamists and liberals saw eye to eye on a number of issues (Baker 2003; Brown 2001: 161–193; Rutherford 2008: 99–130). Many Egyptians began to wonder whether this thought provided a basis for cooperation between Islamists and liberals. Responding to the public's growing interest in this question, some members of the Muslim Brotherhood and a powerful group of judges each began publicly to describe in more detail the type of "Islamic" state with which they would be comfortable. In the 1990s, some leading young members of the Muslim Brotherhood began to press the older leaders publicly to clarify which, if any, of these New Islamist ideas the

---

[18] On these thinkers, see generally Baker (2003), Brown (2001: 161–193), and Rutherford (2008: 99–130).

[19] According to these thinkers, living in a state of freedom allows people to have a more varied experience of life, and this in turn leads to deeper understandings of God's will and to more productive discourse about what God wants Muslims to do. As should be clear, this type of theory had areas of overlap with liberal theory, but it was not exactly the same. Because freedom's value is dependent on the degree to which it promotes truer understandings of God's will, however, it can be constrained where it becomes unproductive. For this reason, apostasy can be banned and it is possible for a state to deny non-Muslims some of the rights that it is required to give Muslims. Similarly, although they are clear that women are *equal* to men, it remains unclear whether these thinkers believe women have the *same* rights as men. See generally Baker (2003), Brown (2001: 161–193), and Rutherford (2008: 99–130).

Brotherhood could endorse. In response, in the mid-1990s the Muslim Brotherhood issued pamphlets embracing much of the thinking of the new Islamists and clarifying that they expected women in an Islamic state not only to have full voting rights, but the right to run for any elected seat except for the "leader of the *umma*" and the right to serve as judges except in cases where it would "compromise her honor" (Rutherford 2008: 97). At roughly the same time, the Supreme Constitutional Court tentatively began to embark on the type of liberal jurisprudence that might open the state. As they began to do so, however, they also articulated a liberal vision of the Islamic state – one in which a ruler was constrained to respect Islamic values that were to be defined by judges and appeared to be largely (and perhaps entirely) consistent with liberal values.

The SCC's articulation of its vision took place in the context of Article 2 litigation. In 1985, the SCC had declared Article 2 cases to be partially justiciable, holding that Article 2 required the courts to strike down any *new* Egyptian legislation that it found to be inconsistent with the principles of Shari'a. It remained unclear for some time, however, exactly how the Court would interpret Islamic law.[20] In 1992, shortly after issuing a daring and controversial ruling stating that the Egyptian government was constitutionally obliged to respect evolving international rights norms (a ruling deeply threatening to and resented by Mubarak), the Court confirmed that the government also had to respect the principles of Islamic law and clarified that it believed that Islamic law could and should be interpreted in a manner that was consistent with international human rights norms (Lombardi 2008: 244–248). In short, the Court claimed that the principles requiring the state to respect international liberal rights norms and Shari'a mutually reinforced each other.

In its opinions, the SCC identified the principles of the Islamic Shari'a and employed them using a method of interpretation that combined elements of the methods proposed by Rashid Rida, Sanhuri, and some members of the Muslim Brotherhood (Lombardi 2006: 174–258; Lombardi and Brown 2006: 415–425).[21] More striking than this theory of interpretation – which was fully consistent with leading lay Islamist theories – were the liberal conclusions it reached. Indeed, although the SCC never said so explicitly, the pattern of decisions suggested that the Court

[20] In the late 1980s, the Supreme Constitutional Court's only Article 2 opinions came in property rights cases. The court extrapolated expansive property rights from vague provisions of the Constitution. With very little explanation, the court insisted that the law violated not only specific property rights provisions, but also violated Article 2. It did not explain its reasoning.

[21] According to this theory, Article 2 forbade the government from engaging in acts that do either of two things: (1) violate a small number of scriptural principles whose authenticity is considered by the judges to be unimpeachable and whose meaning is clear, *or* (2) impede human welfare as Islam understands it. When applying its theory, the Court identified very few indubitably "authentic" and clear scriptural principles. The constitutionality of a law thus turned, usually, on whether it promoted human welfare as the Court understands it.

believed society could not enjoy Islamic justice or welfare when its people were being denied the full panoply of liberal rights.[22] The Justices were ambiguous in their opinions about whether they thought Article 2 always required the state to respect liberal rights in the expansive way that they were understood in Western settings, or whether they accepted the possibility that such rights might be qualified.[23]

The Muslim Brotherhood pamphlets and the SCC's Article 2 cases of the early to mid-1990s can be conceptualized as opening offers in an attempt to negotiate mutually acceptable visions of the Islamic state. Increasing repression by the Mubarak regime drove the parties to continue bargaining and, arguably, to come a bit closer together.

In the late 1990s and early 2000s, the regime not only increased the suppression of the Muslim Brotherhood to a nearly intolerable degree, but, as Tamir Moustafa has described in detail, it began effectively to attack the independence of the courts. Most dramatically, the regime increased the size of the SCC and eliminated its liberal majority by filling the new places largely with non-liberals (Moustafa 2007: 178–219). In this environment, pressure to cooperate increased, and both the judiciary and Islamist political groups began subtly to indicate a willingness to clarify their positions and, it seemed, a willingness to explore further compromise on "hot button" issues.

Although the newly reformed SCC issued fewer important decisions explicitly articulating how Islamic thought and liberal thought could be integrated, other courts, which had retained more independence, began to issue opinions dealing indirectly with the question of what types of law should be deemed consistent with Islam's fundamental principles. These opinions clarified that although most Egyptian judges thought a genuinely Islamic state would be basically liberal, some thought

---

[22] To give some examples of rulings: the SCC held during this period that the state did not violate the principles of Islamic law when it guaranteed women the same rights to divorce and child custody as men – something that traditional *fiqh* had denied them and that some conservative Islamists still felt to be un-Islamic. (For discussions of these cases, see Lombardi 2006: 201–236; Arabi 2001.) The Court also held that Article 2 *did* bar the state from seizing property (or even regulating it in a way that significantly decreased its value) without adequate compensation. (For a discussion of these cases, see Lombardi 2006: 174–178, 236–240.) Islam also barred the state from prohibiting marriages between government officials in sensitive positions and foreigners. (See the description of the case and analysis in Lombardi 2006: 253–258). Strikingly, however, the SCC also held the state did not violate Islamic principles when it prohibited girls from wearing a veil in public schools (for an analysis and translation of this case, see Lombardi 2006: 240–253; Lombardi and Brown 2006: 415–434; Brown and Lombardi 2006: 437–460).

[23] The ambiguities were in full display in a case where the SCC upheld a governmental ban on parents sending their girls to public school in veils. It admitted that Islam required "modest" dress, and that this needed to be taken into account, but then it decried the psychological harm and symbolism of veiling in a way that was fully out of sync with (and insensitive to) Islamist perspectives. For a discussion of this case, see Lombardi and Brown (2006) and for a translation, see Brown and Lombardi (2006).

that a genuinely Islamic Egypt might occasionally have to apply laws that diverged in some ways from traditional Western understandings of liberalism.[24] Whether these cases were consciously designed to signal a concession and invite a closer alliance of liberal judges and Islamists is impossible to say, given the available information. These were striking decisions because they took place in an environment in which mainstream Islamists were also aggressively trying to reach out to liberals and suggesting that they too might be willing to embrace some liberal positions about which they had long been ambivalent.

Pressed by its would-be partners to clarify its position on specific key issues, between 2004 and 2007, the Muslim Brotherhood produced and explained a "draft party platform" that was supposed to describe the type of platform that they would champion were they ever to be permitted to form a political party. The platform seemed to reflect considerable debate and internal disagreement about the overlap between traditional liberals' goals and those of the Brotherhood. Read alongside explanatory comments from leading members, the platform seemed to suggest, first, that the Muslim Brotherhood was willing to try in good faith to find acceptable compromises in areas where Islamic law seemed to be in tension with liberal values, and second, that the Brotherhood was divided over how many concessions the group could make to the liberals (Brown and Hamzawy 2010: 18–23; Rutherford 2008: 163–190). It was an ambivalent message about the possibilities of a future alliance and it gave the leadership of liberal organizations, as well as many members of the public, cause for concern.

The attempt to create a viable liberal-Islamist alliance did not bear immediate fruit. Suspicions remained strong between the traditional leadership of liberal and Islamist factions. The Muslim Brotherhood's draft platform had done little to alleviate

---

[24] In 1997, the Supreme Administrative Court in Egyptian Supreme Administrative Court and Female Circumcision issued a decision in Appeal no. 5257/43 (28 Dec. 1997). Arguably Egypt's most powerful court outside the SCC, the Supreme Administrative Court here resolved an Article 2 challenge. It mostly followed the SCC's method of analysis and reached a liberal conclusion but one that demonstrated a willingness to engage more thoroughly than the SCC had traditionally done with both traditional sources and the views of contemporary Islamic thinkers outside the court (for a discussion of the case, see Bälz 1998). More striking was a 2007 case from the High Administrative Court, which stood in sharp distinction to the 1996 decision discussed earlier in which the SCC had held that the government was within its rights (and perhaps wise) to ban the veil in public high schools. The High Administrative Court held that the government had no right to ban grown women who wish to wear the veil in government-supervised universities. See Appeal 3219 of Supreme Judicial Year 48 (6 September 2007). More striking even than the result was the sympathy for the woman who had been denied the ability to wear the veil and the rejection of the government's claim (accepted by the SCC) that a ban on veiling might serve a useful government purpose. It seemed to represent a sign that the courts were willing to commit to moderating their liberalism in order to establish a form of liberalism that was legitimate in Islamic terms and that would be vigorously endorsed by the Muslim Brotherhood.

these suspicions. Furthermore, the administration was able, with typical cunning, to scuttle any budding alliance by proposing a massive set of legal and constitutional reforms that disadvantaged the Muslim Brotherhood more than its liberal would-be allies (Hamzawy 2007). Falling out over how vigorously to protest these reforms, liberals and Islamists failed to present a united front against the regime's proposals. This failure proved disastrous in the short term. The 2007 reforms changed thirty-four provisions of the Constitution, thereby modifying almost every provision of the Constitution that the courts had used to preserve openness in the political sphere.[25] A new provision introduced new and rigid succession procedures, which ensured that, on the incapacity or removal of a president, power would transfer to one of his handpicked allies – a change that would have unexpected consequences in 2011.

In the aftermath of these reforms, the Muslim Brothers and the liberal opposition watched in despair as Mubarak, who was widely thought to be grooming his son to succeed him as president, ran an election in 2010 that made no pretensions of being free or fair. It resulted in the Brotherhood, indisputably Egypt's most popular opposition bloc, losing every one of their eighty-eight seats in parliament (Saleh 2010). The political and legal spheres became so stifling that the opposition seemed, at first, to give up. The liberal opposition, which had little experience of forcible repression, was devastated by the jailing and harassment of its leaders. In January 2010, the Muslim Brotherhood elected Muhammad Badie as its new leader, a veteran of the Nasserist repression who had long been skeptical about the Brotherhood's prospects of gaining anything by its participation in a rigged political system (Brown and Hamzawy 2010: 45–46).

However, the experience of liberals and Islamists reaching out to clarify their mutual goals had had a more powerful effect than many initially realized. Some common priorities had been established and trust had been built up among a subset of the major liberal and Islamist factions. This was particularly among youth groups, whose latent power was unleashed in early 2011. In January 2011, an uprising in Tunisia against the military regime sparked massive and apparently spontaneous urban demonstrations against Mubarak's rule. The demonstrations were primarily an urban phenomenon and did not, at first, have a strong Islamist presence. Indeed, the Muslim Brotherhood initially instructed its members *not* to take part in the demonstrations. However, under severe pressure from its younger members, the leadership relented and permitted its members to join the protests. Some report that they were *instructed* to take part (see, e.g., Trager 2011: 119–120).

---

[25] For example, the constitutional provision stating that political crimes could be tried before military courts only if the legislature declared a state of emergency was changed. Among the thirty-four changes to the Constitution, it permitted the president, even in the absence of a state of emergency, to try citizens for any crime before military courts at his discretion. Another amendment limited the traditional judicial role in overseeing elections.

The presence of young Islamists alongside secular liberals was crucial to the success of the demonstrations. The ideologically diverse crowd literally risking their lives to resist an autocrat attracted domestic and international sympathy. Such sympathy was dangerous to an Egyptian military that thrived on foreign military aid from Western allies. In February 2011, the Army prepared to remove President Mubarak from office. It was clear, however, that the demonstrators would not tolerate a transfer of power to his handpicked deputies, something that the Constitution after its 2007 amendments required. Egyptians debated whether to amend the 1971 Constitution to change the succession provisions or simply to remove the president extra-constitutionally. Ultimately, circumstances required the latter.

15.4 SURPRISING SOLICITUDE FOR THE 1971 CONSTITUTION

There was, during the lead-up to Mubarak's removal, a surprising amount of support for retaining the 1971 Constitution in an amended form. By 2011, Islamists and liberals alike had for years operated under that constitution. They believed that many aspects of the Constitution were consistent with their vision for Egypt, even though some aspects clearly were not. The Muslim Brotherhood thus made clear even prior to the removal of Mubarak that it was willing to consider amending the Constitution rather than replacing it wholesale. Similarly in the days prior to Mubarak's ousting, a delegation of leading liberals proposed complex schemes that would allow Mubarak to be effectively removed and the Constitution amended quickly, schemes that would achieve the removal of both Mubarak and his cronies while allowing the Constitution to survive.[26]

Some of Mubarak's most implacable critics apparently believed that, after some significant amendments, Egypt's 1971 Constitution could serve as the constitution of a new and truly democratic Egypt.[27] Amendment ceased to be an option, however, after an inexplicable speech that Mubarak gave on February 10, 2011. On that day, President Mubarak addressed the nation on television and gave what one American political scientist later dubbed the "Worst Speech Ever" (Lynch 2011). This speech, which insulted the protestors and patronized Egyptians as a whole, so infuriated the entire Egyptian public that the military felt compelled to remove him immediately so as to avoid even more violent unrest. Because the president had been removed before constitutional amendments had been negotiated, the removal formally triggered the transition to Mubarak's deputies. To prevent such a politically explosive

---

[26] "Statement of Egyptian Activists," available at http://www.carnegieendowment.org/2011/02/03/statement-of-egyptian-activists/lwh

[27] See "Poison pill in Egypt's constitution may hobble anti-Mubarak drive," *Agence France-Presse* (February 9, 2011), available at http://www.thenational.ae/news/worldwide/middle-east/poison-pill-in-egypts-constitution-may-hobble-anti-mubarak-drive

transition from occurring, the military dissolved the 1971 Constitution and took power itself. Had Mubarak been more circumspect, the 1971 Constitution might have survived, albeit with a number of significant amendments designed to ensure more participatory government and judicial independence.

It remains possible that elements of the 1971 Constitution will be incorporated into a new constitution. As of the time of this writing, a year and a half after the ouster of Mubarak, Egypt is in a state of constitutional confusion. Its military rulers have produced a number of interim constitutional documents that place massive power in the hands of the military. Although new parliamentary elections have been held, the results of the parliamentary election were recently nullified by the courts on the ground that those elections were held according to a procedure that violated the interim constitutional documents, and the courts thereafter ordered the parliament to be disbanded. A member of the Muslim Brotherhood has been elected president, but the scope of his powers under the interim constitutional documents remains unclear. No new "permanent constitution" has yet been drafted. When a permanent new constitution is put together, its drafters will be able to draw on some lessons from the history of the 1971 Constitution. Perhaps the drafters of other constitutions around the world will be able to do so as well.

15.5 CONCLUSION

In a contribution in this volume, Russell Hardin outlines two possible ways to conceptualize constitutions: as contracts or as coordination devices (Hardin 2013). The 1971 Constitution seems to be most easily characterized as a coordination device. As initially drafted and even as amended in 1980, the 1971 Constitution was riddled with ambiguities and open questions on key terms. It resolved a small number of issues, and also identified a large number of vitally important issues that would have to be resolved in the future through mechanisms only partly set defined in the constitution. In some ways, it resembles an unenforceable "term sheet" for a complicated deal-in-the-making rather than a final "contract" enshrining any genuine agreement about the shape and form of Egyptian polity. In the decades after 1971, authoritarians within the regime were able to answer some deferred questions and to leave other ambiguities all in a manner that allowed them to entrench themselves and repress regime opponents. Nevertheless, many Egyptians who suffered under the emerging constitutional and legal regime agreed to operate under its terms. In so doing, they "acquiesced" on an ongoing basis in the emerging constitutional order – without ever really accepting that emerging order.

As a coordination device, the 1971 Constitution seems to have been an unusually successful one. Born at a time of popular unrest, elite fragmentation, and regime fragility, the Constitution coordinated political and social life in Egypt for a remarkably long time and allowed an authoritarian government to remain in power longer than it could reasonably expect to have done. In an exhaustive survey of written constitutions, Ginsburg, Elkins, and Melton found that the average constitution survives less than twenty years (Ginsburg et al. 2007: 47; Elkins et al. 2009). The 1971 Constitution thus seems to have coordinated political life two times longer than the average constitution would do. It did so notwithstanding the fact that the regime that actually controlled Egypt under the terms of this Constitution and many of its policies were often quite unpopular.

The 1971 Constitution's longevity should interest those who want to understand the impact of ambiguity and open-endedness on a constitution. Ginsburg, Elkins, and Melton suggest that longer-lived constitutions tend to share three characteristics: (1) they emerge through an open participatory process; (2) they tend to be specific; and (3) they tend to be flexible, providing "reasonable" mechanisms for amendment or binding reinterpretation (Ginsburg et al. 2007: 51; compare Elkins et al. 2009: 65–92). It is hard to know how to score the 1971 Constitution on issues (1) and (3). On issue (2), however, the 1971 Constitution is shockingly deficient, and one might have expected it to die young. In a follow-up work, however, Dixon and Ginsburg investigate further whether constitutions containing deferrals of the type that we see in the 1971 Constitution – delegation of constitutional questions to a legislature and a decision to deal with important issues in vague language – are constitutionally fragile. They argue that certain types of deferral can occasionally be useful in promoting productive ongoing negotiation of constitutional principles and thus can help a constitution survive (Dixon and Ginsburg 2011). The history of Egypt's 1971 Constitution provides evidence to support this conclusion. Furthermore, it gives us some insight into the circumstances under which it can be productive.

The ambiguities in the 1971 Constitution helped coordinate factions during the 1970s. The 1971 Constitution was drafted at a time in which political factions that had long battled each other stood in positions of relative equipoise. The constitution left unanswered a series of contested constitutional questions and set up a mechanism for resolving these questions that, although dominated by the executive, seemed potentially open to influence from important opposition factions. Every major political faction thought that under current conditions, the scheme would work to its advantage, and thus each had incentive to play by the rules set down by the constitution. Authoritarians believed they could convince the executive to direct the legislature *not* to create robust checks or engender a judiciary that would constrain them. Liberals and authoritarians, for their part, believed they could continue to generate social and political pressure that would force the executive to liberalize or Islamize. In this environment, all factions had an incentive to work within the system – leading to constitutional survival.

It is less obvious why the 1971 Constitution continued to serve as an effective coordinating mechanism from the 1990s onward. By that time, a new president, President Mubarak slowly squelched liberal and Islamist hopes for Egypt's government to evolve into one that they could celebrate. Notwithstanding some of the liberalization during the 1970s and early to mid-1980s, the Mubarak regime retained significant powers. Over time, the executive made clear that, going forward, it would not relinquish any of these powers and, indeed, would try to bolster and exploit them. It tried to ensure that the electoral system and, to some extent, the public sphere was closed to those who wanted to increase the liberal or Islamic constraints. It tried to keep judges from aggressively interpreting or enforcing the constitutional or legal nebulous guarantees of rights and respect for Islam. In this situation, ambiguity would seem to be much less attractive to liberals and Islamists. Nevertheless, until 2011, much of the opposition continued to operate under the terms of the constitution.

The continuing acquiescence to the 1971 Constitution reminds us that the attractions of constitutional resistance are always relative. If a regime has the power to suppress opposition, then those who suffer under an ambiguous constitution are likely to acquiesce in it simply because the costs of resistance are high. Similarly, if the opposition feels that it will be unable to influence the process of amending an ambiguous constitution or of drafting a new, less ambiguous one, then it will have little incentive to push for changes. Given power dynamics, the opposition is simply unlikely to benefit. Massive constitutional deferral is thus unlikely to weaken constitutions in states where political power is grossly imbalanced. Indeed, it may sustain it – for the opposition has incentive to avoid setting in motion a process that will formalize and further embed their current plight.

Although empirical work needs to be done on the question, it is possible that massive deferral may help preserve authoritarian regimes that depend on foreign aid because it can help forestall criticism from donor regimes. Governments like Mubarak's Egypt, which repress through the operation of legislated answers to deferred questions, may suffer less international pressure than explicitly authoritarian regimes whose constitutions are nakedly illiberal. When an authoritarian regime's constitution has no guarantee of free speech and international actors, other international actors are likely to criticize that government. If, instead, a constitution guarantees free speech in the abstract but allows the scope of free speech rights to be defined by law, a regime may be able to punish free speech without attracting the same degree of international or even domestic criticism. The regulations or cases that effectively gut a constitutional guarantee of free speech rights are often unnoticed or ill-understood outside the country and sometimes, even, within it.

Thus far the history of Egypt's 1971 Constitution might seem to suggest that massive constitutional deferral helps preserve authoritarian regimes. Normatively, those who favor the spread of the liberal rule of law might thus wish for less ambiguity in a constitution – even in cases where ambiguity preserves constitutional life. Yet the history of the 1971 Constitution provides some intriguing, if inconclusive, evidence that in the medium-to-long term, constitutional ambiguities can help produce something more salutary than regime survival. It can create a more productive opposition and can thereby help promote not merely regime change but a broad commitment to a shared constitutional vision.

Ambiguity that is abused by a regime may, over the long term, encourage productive discourse among ideologically divided opposition factions. Opposition factions are likely to explore shared preferences regarding certain open constitutional questions and, if they find points of agreement, to coordinate activities so as to ensure that those open questions are answered to their mutual benefit. The massive ambiguities in the 1973 Constitution combined with an executive that was exploiting those ambiguities to its own advantage seem to have promoted stalled dialogue between liberal and Islamist factions in Egypt.

Egypt's 1971 Constitution was ambiguous about the degree to which the state would respect either Islamic norms or liberal norms. As a result, the Constitution invited considerable debate about the implications both of Islamism and of liberalism in the Egyptian context. At the same time, social and political conditions created incentive for the Islamist and liberal opposition to explore whether their ideologies could be harmonized and, if so, to cooperate to push for constitutional changes that would promote common goals. Because the Constitution granted courts the power to interpret a vague Islamization provision, liberal judges had the ability to insert themselves into Islamic discussions in which they would not normally have engaged. And because it gave judges this power at a time when they were vulnerable and needed popular support, judges may have had incentive to use this power. Conversely, because the provisions requiring the state to respect Islam were placed within a constitution that simultaneously espoused some liberal principles – and because this schizophrenic constitution was to be interpreted by a largely liberal judiciary – Islamists were encouraged to consider and opine on the concessions that they believed Islamic states could (and could not) make to liberalism. Importantly, because Islamists needed judicial protection for their political and social activities, they had strong incentives to engage in good faith with liberal judges and seek compromise.

In the aftermath of Mubarak's fall, the suspension of the 1971 Constitution, and the Egyptian Army's attempt to maintain significant power in Egypt, it remains unclear what constitution will replace the 1971 Constitution. In this fraught environment, Egyptian Islamists and liberals are still exploring the possible points of agreement on questions of political philosophy and constitutional design. At the time of this writing in mid-2012, it is clear that Islamists and liberals have points both of agreement and of disagreement. It is still possible that no stable, consensus vision of the Egyptian state, and thus no broadly welcomed constitution, will emerge. Nevertheless, the dialogue that occurred in the 1990s and early 2000s over how to answer deferred constitutional questions and how to interpret ambiguous constitutional passages has surely helped make difficult current political and constitutional discussions in the fraught period after the fall of Mubarak more productive than they otherwise would be.

REFERENCES

Arabi, Ousama 2001. "The Dawning of the 3rd Millennium on Shari'a: Egypt's Law No. 1 of the Year 2000, or Women May Divorce at Will," *Arab Law Quarterly* **16** (2001): 85–104.

Baer, Gabriel 1978. *Population and Society in the Arab East*. New York: Praeger.

Baker, Raymond 2003. *Islam without Fear: Egypt and the New Islamists*. Cambridge, MA: Harvard University Press.

Bälz, Kilian 1998. "Human Rights, the Rule of Law, and the Construction of Tradition: The Egyptian Supreme Administrative Court and Female Circumcision (appeal no. 5257/43, Dec. 28, 1997)," *Egypte Monde Arabe* **34**: 141–153.

Brown, Nathan 1997. *The Rule of Law in the Arab World: Courts in Egypt and the Gulf*. Cambridge: Cambridge University Press.

2001. *Constitutions in a Nonconstitutional World: Arab Basic Laws & the Prospects for Accountable Government*. Albany: SUNY Press.

2009. "Bumpy Democratic Routes to Dictatorial Ends?" Unpublished paper, prepared for the conference "Democracy and Development in the Middle East," held in honor of John Waterbury, Princeton University, April.

Brown, Nathan and Hamzawy, Amr 2010. *Between Religion and Politics*. Washington, DC: Carnegie Endowment for International Peace.

Brown, Nathan and Lombardi, Clark 2006. "Translation: The Supreme Constitutional Court of Egypt on Islamic Law, Veiling and Civil Rights: An Annotated Translation of Supreme Constitutional Court of Egypt Case No. 8 of Judicial Year 17 (May 18, 1996)," *American University International Law Review* **21**: 437–460.

Dixon, Rosalind and Ginsburg, Tom 2011. "Deciding Not to Decide: Deferral in Constitutional Design," *International Journal of Constitutional Law* **9**: 636–672.

El-Shaeir, Mohamad Taha 1983. "Commentary" in Goldwin, Robert and Kaufmann, Art (eds.) *Constitution Makers on Constitution Making: The Experience of Eight Nations*. Washington, DC: American Enterprise Institute, 332–352.

Elkins, Zachary, Ginsburg, Tom, and Melton, James 2009. *The Endurance of National Constitutions*. Cambridge: Cambridge University Press.

Ginsburg, Tom, Elkins, Zachary, and Melton, James 2007. "The Lifespan of Written Constitutions," Unpublished Paper (December 26) available at http://www.yale.edu/macmillan/ruleoflaw/papers/Ginsburg-Lifespans-California.pdf.

Hallaq, Wael 1997. *A History of Islamic Legal Theories: An Introduction to Sunnī 'Uṣūl al Fiqh*. Cambridge: Cambridge University.

Hamzawy, Amr 2007. "Political Motivations and Implications" in Brown, Nathan, Dunn, Michele, and Hamzawy, Amr (eds.) "Egypt's Controversial Constitutional Amendments,"

Carnegie Endowment for International Peace Paper, March 23, http://www.carnegieendowment.org/files/egypt_constitution_webcommentary01.pdf

Hardin, Russell 2013. "Why a Constitution?" in Galligan, Denis and Versteeg, Mila (eds.), *Social and Political Foundations of Constitutions*. Cambridge: Cambridge University Press.

Hill, Enid 1979. *Mahkama!: Studies in the Egyptian Legal System*. London: Ithaca.

Hirschl, Ran 2013. "The Strategic Foundations of Constitutions" in Galligan, Denis and Versteeg, Mila (eds.), *Social and Political Foundations of Constitutions*. Cambridge: Cambridge University Press.

Hunter, F. Robert 1984. *Egypt under the Khedives 1805–1879: From Household Government to Modern Bureaucracy*. Pittsburgh, PA: University of Pittsburgh Press.

Kerr, Malcolm 1966. *Islamic Reform: The Political and Legal Theories of Muhammad Abduh and Rashid Rida*. Berkeley: University of California.

Lombardi, Clark 2006. *State Law as Islamic Law in Modern Egypt: The Incorporation of the Shari'a into Egyptian Constitutional Law*. Boston: Brill.

2008. "Egypt's Supreme Constitutional Court: Managing Constitutional Conflict in an Authoritarian, Aspirationally 'Islamic' State," *Journal of Comparative Law* 3: 234–253.

Lombardi, Clark and Brown, Nathan 2006. "Do Constitutions Requiring Adherence to Shari'a Threaten Human Rights?" *American University International Law Review* 21: 379–435.

Lynch, Marc 2011. "Responding to the Worst Speech Ever," *Foreign Policy*, February 10, http://lynch.foreignpolicy.com/posts/2011/02/10/responding_to_the_worst_speech_ever

Marsot, Afaf 1984. *Egypt in the Reign of Muhammad `Ali*. Cambridge: Cambridge University.

1977. *Egypt's Liberal Experiment: 1922–1936*. Berkeley: University of California Press.

Mitchell, Richard 1993. *The Society of the Muslim Brothers*. New York: Oxford University Press.

Moustafa, Tamir 2007. *The Struggle for Constitutional Power: Law, Politics and Economic Development in Egypt*. Cambridge: Cambridge University Press.

Nasr, Hesham, Crystal, Jill, and Brown, Nathan 1994. *Criminal Justice and Prosecution in the Arab World: A Study Prepared for the United Nations Development Program on Governance in the Arab World*, available at http://www.pogar.org/publications/judiciary/criminaljustice-brown-e.pdf

Olcott, Martha Brill and Ottoway, Marina 1999. "Challenge of Semi-Authoritarianism," Carnegie Paper, No. 7, Washington DC: Carnegie Endowment for International Peace, available at http://www.carnegieendowment.org/1999/10/01/challenge-of-semi-authoritarianism/cm8

al-Otayfi, Gamal 1971. "Al-Shari'a al-Islamiyya wa'l Dustur al-Daim." *Al-Ahram*, July 14.

Rutherford, Bruce 1999. *The Struggle for Constitutionalism in Egypt: Understanding the Obstacles to Democratic Transition in the Arab World*. New Haven, CT: Yale University.

2008. *Egypt after Mubarak: Liberalism, Islam and Democracy in the Arab World*. Princeton, NJ: Princeton University Press.

Saleh, Heba 2010 "Monitors Allege Fraud in Egypt Elections," *The Financial Times*, December 6, http://www.ft.com/cms/s/0/cd7d12a4-0107-11e0-8894-00144feab49a.html#axzz1WSyvUpmq

Saleh, Ibrahim 1983. "The Writing of the Egyptian Constitution" in Goldwin, Robert and Kaufmann, Art (eds.) *Constitution Makers on Constitution Making: The Experience of Eight Nations*. Washington, DC: American Enterprise Institute, 332–343.

Sfeir, George 1956. "The Abolition of Confessional Jurisidiction in Egypt: The Non-Muslim Courts," *Middle East Journal* 10: 248–256.

Trager, Eric 2011. "The Unbreakable Muslim Brotherhood," *Foreign Affairs* September–October: 119–120.

Vatikiotis, P. J. 1991. *The History of Modern Egypt*, 4th ed. Baltimore: Johns Hopkins University Press.

Waterbury, John 1983. *The Egypt of Nasser and Sadat: The Political Economy of Two Regimes* Princeton, NJ: Princeton University.

Wickham, Carrie 2002. *Mobilizing Islam: Religion, Activism and Political Change in Egypt.* New York: Columbia University Press.

Ziadeh, Farhat J. 1968. *Lawyers, the Rule of Law, and Liberalism in Modern Egypt.* Stanford, CA: Hoover Institution.

16

Explaining the Constitutionalization of Social Rights

Portuguese Hypotheses and a Cross-National Test

Pedro C. Magalhães

16.1 INTRODUCTION

On April 25, 1976, exactly two years after a military coup that put an end to decades of authoritarianism, the current Portuguese Constitution entered into force. Although it was the sixth such document adopted in the country in the modern era, it was really the first to have been adopted by a democratically elected parliament. In the final vote that took place on April 2, ten months after the inauguration of the constituent assembly and almost one year after its election by popular vote, only 16 of the 250 members voted against the text, all of them belonging to the CDS (Centro Democrático e Social), the party furthest to the ideological right in the assembly.

Among historical constitutions approved by democratically elected assemblies, this particular document was strikingly original in several respects. It established a transitory Council of the Revolution, composed of members of the military, which would enjoy not only jurisdiction over military issues and defense policy but also consultation rights in all major political decisions, and even the ability to examine the constitutionality of legislation. Furthermore, it introduced a complex system of

Research for this chapter has been conducted with the support from a grant (PTDC/CPO/71295/2006) from the Fundaçãopara a Ciência e Tecnologia (FCT, the Portuguese Science Foundation) awarded to the project "Social Rights in Portugal: Their Constitutionalization and Sociopolitical Implications," coordinated by Filipe Carreira da Silva. I am particularly grateful to Bárbara Direito for her collection of documents and analysis of the political and legal debates about social rights in Portugal. Those documents are available at: http://www.filipecarreiradasilva.net/ds_documents.html. I am also grateful to the participants at the May 2010 conference on "The Social and Political Foundations of Constitutions," organized by the Foundation for Law, Justice and Society at Oxford University, Wolfson College, for their comments and suggestions. Finally, I thank the editors of this volume for their helpful guidance and discussion of an earlier version of this chapter.

executive-legislative relations through which an elected president would coexist with a prime minister accountable before an elected parliament, a particular modality of semi-presidentialism that was further complicated not only by the role of the Council of the Revolution but also by the ability of the president to dismiss the government at will.

However, these were not the most original or, in any case, the most enduring features of the 1976 Portuguese Constitution. By 1982, the Council of the Revolution was abolished and its tasks assumed by the parliament, the government, and a newly created Constitutional Court, thus completing Portugal's transition to a fully democratic regime. Also in that first constitutional revision, the system of executive-legislative relations was reformed, shifting from a president-parliamentary to a premier-presidential modality (Shugart and Carey 1992) – that is, from a system of dual accountability of the prime minister before both parliament and president to single accountability before the former, greatly clarifying the workings of Portuguese semi-presidentialism. Thus, what ended up being the most enduring originality of the Portuguese Constitution was something else: its catalogue of social rights, arguably the most exhaustive and detailed of such catalogues in any constitution before or since. In a document that was more than 300 articles long, its section on Economic, Social, and Cultural Rights and Duties contained no less than 29 articles, including rights to work, social security, health, housing, "environment and quality of life," education, and "physical culture and sports," as well as protection for family, maternity, infancy, disability, and old age. Furthermore, the Constitution specified how the state should fulfill its obligations in several of these respects, including, for example, the creation of a unified social security system, access of all citizens to health care regardless of income by means of a universal and totally free national health service, a universal and free basic education system, and housing and rental market policies compatible with family income. Although the Constitution has already been amended on six additional occasions after 1982, this has not changed Portugal's status as one of the countries where the level of formal constitutional commitment to social rights is highest. As Fabre (2000) notes, in Europe, most countries fall in between two ends of the scale: countries like Germany or Austria, which do not recognize any social rights in the constitution; and, at the other extreme, the "very detailed" Portuguese case. Even when we expand the scope of comparison, Portugal still emerges as extreme in this respect: in a recent study ranking the level of constitutional commitment to social rights – defined as "one that grants a personal entitlement to monetary transfers (including social insurance) or transfer in kind on a universal basis" – in sixty-eight countries, Portugal is the one where such level is highest in a summary measure that includes rights to social security, education, health, housing, and workers' rights (Ben-Bassat and Dahan 2008: 107–108).

Constitutional social rights have been addressed by scholars mostly in terms of their purported consequences, both from a normative and (unfortunately much less so) an empirical point of view. It has been argued that social rights lead to an overextension of the role of the judiciary, introduce mutually conflicting claims to scarce goods, put excessive limits to democratic deliberation and popular sovereignty, delegitimize the constitution by filling it with unenforceable aspirations in lieu of actually enforceable norms, and interfere with the development of free market economies, civil societies, and property rights.[1] Conversely, it has also been argued that the basic requirements of a "decent life" entitle individuals to social rights protecting them against arbitrary deprivation, that the distinction between enforceable negative rights and unenforceable positive rights is questionable at best, and that social rights provide a needed antidote against the failure of economic and political markets to address the interests of the needy.[2] But regardless of where one stands in these controversies, it seems clear that constitutionalizing social rights has measurable and important consequences, no matter how beneficial, contradictory, or politically contentious one finds them (Elster 1994). Granted, the absence of formal social rights has not prevented the development of strong welfare states and high levels of social provision, as the Canadian, German, Austrian, or British cases show (Macklem 2006). It is also true that several studies have found no direct effects of constitutionalized social rights on either economic development or economic growth (De Vanssay and Spindler 1994; Blume and Voigt 2006), and some have even suggested that the relationship between the constitutionalization of social rights and the capability of ensuring them might be negative (Preuss 1995). However, there is also empirical evidence suggesting that greater levels of constitutional pre-commitment to social security do have measurable consequences on transfer payments as a share of GDP, while the constitutionalization of the right to health care seems to be related to positive health outcomes (Ben-Bassat and Dahan 2008). And in Portugal, for example, in academic and political debates on issues such as labor market, education, and health policies, reforms and outcomes have been almost constantly permeated by opposing views about the need to change constitutional articles such as those explicitly prohibiting dismissals with "just cause" (Article 52, 1976 Constitution), creating a "universal, general, and free of charge national health service" (Article 64), or instituting the need to establish, by stages, "free education at all levels" (Article 74.). Throughout the last thirty years, concrete government policies, such as those increasing university fees and copayments in public hospitals, or expanding the freedom of employers to dismiss employees, have been successfully challenged

---

[1] For different arguments, see Nozick (1974), Pereira-Menaut (1987), Sunstein (1993; 1996), Cross (2001), and Neier (2006). In the Portuguese context, see Lucena (1978), Otero (2001), and Alexandrino (2007).

[2] See, for example, Sager (1993; 2004), Beetham (2006), Fabre (2000), Scheppele (2002), Forbath (2001), Michelman (2007), and Tushnet (2008), among others.

in the courts, which have declared them wholly or partially unconstitutional. Constitutionalizing social rights matters.

My approach in this chapter is, however, somewhat different from that followed in most works on the subject. Instead of focusing on the consequences, real or alleged, of constitutional social rights, I focus on the causes of this kind of constitutionalization. More specifically, I take on a particular question that arises from the Portuguese case: why did the 1976 Constitution end up giving such extensive constitutional recognition to social rights? Here, I follow Whytock's (2007) injunction to "take causality seriously in comparative constitutional law" by using a two-pronged approach to the subject. On the one hand, I start by adopting a small-N approach (in fact, the smallest possible N) by presenting arguments and historically detailed evidence (as detailed as space permits in this chapter) as to why the outcome of Portugal's constitution-making ended up being such a profound commitment to enshrining social rights in a rigid constitutional text. On the other hand, I use that analysis as a hypothesis-generating tool, which will allow us to test some generalizations about the constitutionalization of social rights, this time with the help of a dataset on more than 180 countries and constitutions. In sum, the chapter tries to show that the Portuguese case was the product of a combination of circumstances and factors that, when properly specified, may help us understand cross-national differences in the widely varying extent to which constitution-makers entrench social rights. More generally, I hope to be able to use this particular question as an illustration of how different theoretical approaches to institutional design can combine – rather than collide – to account for constitutional outcomes. We start our inquiry by addressing those theoretical approaches in the following section.

16.2 INTERESTS AND IDEAS IN CONSTITUTIONAL DESIGN

In 1995, Jon Elster remarked with dismay on the almost absolute lack of studies on the constitution-making processes from a general and positive perspective (Elster 1995: 364). Almost two decades later, the diagnosis can be somewhat less pessimistic. Elster himself, in works alone or with others, provided a crucial contribution to the expansion of this literature (Elster 1991, 1994, 1996, 2000; Elster, Offe, and Preuss 1998), and a very significant body of research has emerged since then attempting to explain not only the broad outcomes of constitution-making processes, but also a variety of specific constitutional choices (for a review, see Ginsburg, Elkins, and Blount 2009). Any attempt to do justice to this entire literature here would inevitably fail, but it is probably not unfair to say that it has led us to two main conclusions.

The first is that, among all the different theoretical approaches that have been employed, the one that has presented the most readily identifiable, explicit, and testable set of assumptions is the one affiliated with "rational-choice institutionalism" (particularly its "distributional" – rather than "functional" – version; Knight 1995). From this point of view, different actors form different preferences about institutional (and in this case, constitutional) rules, based on the extent to which such rules favor or disfavor the pursuit of their interests. The institutional outcomes that result from the interaction of those societal and political actors will reflect both their differential bargaining power and the level of uncertainty about the consequences of institutional rules. Prevalent views tended to take particular formal-legal aspects of constitutions, their similarities with other texts, and the particular functions performed by such rules as sufficient evidence about how and why they had come about. However, studies inspired by "rational-choice institutionalism" on the design of rules regulating the judicial system,[3] the electoral system,[4] and executive-legislative relations[5] have successfully illuminated features of constitution-making processes and of constitution-makers' motivations that had previously remained hidden.

The second main conclusion that emerges from all this literature, however, is that an exclusive focus on the self-interested motivations of political actors, seen as single-minded power-aggrandizers, is probably insufficient to explain the outcomes of constitution-making processes. A few examples can illustrate the basic point. Jillson and Eubanks (1984), for instance, showed how proposals and choices made at the American constitutional convention seemed to take place at different levels, namely a "lower" level of self-interested considerations and a "higher" level where judgments about general principles and appropriateness seemed to prevail. Similarly, looking at the different proposals and choices made in the Eastern European constituent processes, Elster showed that, while many of them clearly flowed from a logic of "interest" – "the pursuit of individual, group or institutional advantage" (Elster 1999: 500) – there were clearly other instances where political actors seemed able, for example, to propose, on generally principled grounds, electoral rules that actually worked against their future representation in parliament. Scholars studying the development of the European Union have suggested that the positions adopted by states in several crucial moments of institutional development have flowed not only (and not always) from clearly identifiable interests but also from "polity-ideas," different "convictions about the rightfulness of governance" (Jachtenfuchs et al. 1998: 413) that were more or less consensual among political and state actors. In my own research on the constitutional design of judicial review in Southern Europe, I suggested that the realm of possibilities envisaged by the different political actors and their willingness to pursue distributional advantages through institutional choices regarding the judiciary seem to have been constrained both by historical legacies of existing legal

---

3   See, among others, Ramseyer (1994), Magalhães (1999), Ginsburg (2003), and Hirschl (2004).
4   See Boix (1999), Benoit and Schiemman (2001), and Benoit (2004), for example.
5   See Geddes (1995), Frye (1997), Negretto (1999), Voigt (1999), and Ticchi and Vindigni (2010), among others.

institutions and by consideration of a "larger game" where the costs of a complete breakdown in negotiations and future noncompliance loomed very large (Magalhães 2003; Magalhães, Guarnieri, and Kaminis 2006). In a similar vein, focusing on the Chilean and Spanish cases, Hilbink suggests that the need to "find common ground and move the transition forward" and to avoid past catastrophic experiences, as well as the main actors' shared agreements around liberal-democratic principles, led them to advance proposals and reach agreements that would have otherwise been impossible under pure "power-maximization" strategies (Hilbink 2009).

Admittedly, these and many other examples that could be provided do not necessarily make up for a particularly well-specified theory that manages to encompass the role of "ideas" (or even "ideals") in institutional change without throwing out completely the quite reasonable assumption that political elites are to a large extent rational and self-interested, or that institutional outcomes are affected by the bargaining power of the different actors.[6] They do suggest, however, in line with the abundant literature on "sociological," "constructivist," and "discursive" institutionalisms (Schneiberg and Clemens 2006; Hay 2006; Schmidt 2008), that explaining institutional (in this case, "constitutional") change requires attention to how preferences are formed and interests perceived, how particular contexts and prevailing norms shape the perceptions of what is possible and appropriate, and, more generally, to how ideas, values, and norms can work as independent variables in their own right when trying to account for institutional outcomes.

The study of constitutional social rights can be a particularly interesting application to illustrate this (admittedly very general) point. In many of the studies about institutional design cited earlier, what is being explained is a set of rules that have quite a direct and obvious impact on the distribution of power among political actors, such as those regulating electoral systems, judicial independence, judicial review, and executive-legislative relations. However, in what concerns choices regarding whether and how to introduce, protect, and implement constitutional social rights, although they also have, in a general sense, consequences on the distribution of *power* – empowering particular social groups and organizations and serving the interests of particular electoral constituencies – they are first and foremost about *policy*, particularly about what roles they impose for the state and market in the social and economic realms. Furthermore, the constitutionalization of social rights, regardless of their specific consequences in the actual delivery of social provisions, has, as Sadurski (2009) notes, a "symbolic significance": it has a "declaratory" nature, as a "statement of intentions, aspirations, and goals." Thus, unlike the cases where choices mostly have distributional consequences for the

---

[6] For broader discussions of the role of ideas in institutional and policy change, see, for example, Blyth (1997; 2003) and Campbell (1998).

power of different political and societal actors, choices concerning the constitutionalization of social rights are especially likely to be influenced by normative, ideological, and ideational factors.

The question that follows can be stated thus: what particular combination of interests and ideas may have given rise to the exhaustive protection of social rights in the 1976 Portuguese Constitution? In the following sections, we look at two different narratives than can be built around this question. The first focuses on the particular configuration of powers that prevailed while the Portuguese Constitution was drafted, the actors involved, their preferences, and how they were constrained. The second narrative focuses on cultural legacies and ideational factors. As I hope to show, both narratives constitute plausible explanations as to why the Portuguese Constitution ended up going to such extreme lengths in the constitutionalization of social rights. Then, in the last section of this chapter, I suggest that, rather than seen as contradictory or mutually exclusive, both narratives – and the theoretical approaches that inspire them – can contribute to account for the variance in the extent to which modern constitutions accommodate social and economic rights.

16.3 THE 1976 CONSTITUTION-MAKING PROCESS: CONTEXT AND CONSTRAINTS

What was the particular context in which the Portuguese constitution-making process took place? What where the major actors, their preferences, and the bargaining power they enjoyed? To answer these questions, one should probably start by focusing on the central aspect of the Portuguese regime change in 1974, specifically the fact that it was a "transition by collapse."

What collapsed was the *Estado Novo*, the conservative authoritarian regime that had ruled the country for the five preceding decades. The collapse was brought about in the April 1974 military coup led by the junior military officers that formed the Movement of the Armed Forces (MFA). A military junta was formed to oversee the transition, composed of seven of the highest-ranking officers deemed trustworthy by the MFA. Later on, the MFA ended up becoming institutionalized in a Council of the Revolution, which would assure the military tutelage of the political transition, and would even become a proper constitutional body in the 1976 Constitution, only to be disbanded in 1982. One of the crucial aspects of the MFA's program, presented to the Portuguese following the coup, had been the elimination of the previous regime's repressive apparatus, with amnesties to political prisoners, the abolition of censorship, freedom of association, and the calling of free and fair elections to a new Constituent Assembly. However, that program also collected many of the claims of the most severely persecuted "anti-fascist" movements, including "a new social policy" with the goal of "defending the working classes" and a "anti-monopolistic strategy" that would serve as the base of a "new economic policy … put in favour of the most disfavoured segments of the population," coupling legal and political change with a policy platform that, although not necessarily "revolutionary," contained a strong social and economic welfare component.

There is certainly no point in retelling here all the extremely complex events that took place between 1974 and 1976.[7] However, the main features of interest to us here can be summarized. Over the course of the following year and a half, many internal contradictions within the MFA were to unfold, first and foremost a contradiction between its more radicalized and revolutionary left-wing faction – allied with the Communist Party or other extreme left-wing parties – and its more moderate faction, which, allied with the centrist parties (most notably, the center-left Socialist Party), ultimately prevailed. However, even after the moderate military took control of the Council of the Revolution (CR) in late 1975, the entire constitution-making process still took place under the shadow of military tutelage. Two extra-parliamentary pacts were signed between the political parties and the CR concerning the content of the future constitution. The First Pact, signed just before the election of the Constituent Assembly in April 1975, was aimed not only at imposing a strong version of military tutelage over the future regime but also at consecrating in the Constitution the developments that were taking place as the revolutionary process unfolded, including nationalizations and agrarian reform, thus "committing the country in an original path towards a Portuguese socialism" (Miranda 1978: 203). The Second Pact, signed already in 1976, albeit exclusively focused on the design of future political institutions – including the constitutionalization of the CR itself – still showed that the political parties in the constituent assembly were far from being fully in command of the constitution-making process. Instead, they were constrained by the preferences of a military apparatus that, although purged of its more extreme-left elements, still retained the basic commitment to a general "democratic Socialism" platform originally expressed in the MFA's program. Thus, the first crucial point to retain from this point of view ends up being quite simple: the transition to democracy and the constitution-making process in Portugal took place under the tutelage of a nonhierarchical military that, even after the fundamental changes that occurred between 1974 and 1976, remained fundamentally leftist in its orientations and worldviews (Gómez Fortes 2009).

The second relevant point to retain about the context and constraints under which the constitution-making process unfolded is that none of the political parties that had survived the transition to the new regime (most notably, the Communist Party, founded in 1921, and the much more recent Socialist Party, founded in 1973) or formed after the military coup (the Popular Democratic Party, PPD, and the Social Democratic Center, CDS) claimed any relationship with

---

[7] For that purpose, see, for example, Maxwell (1997).

the ruling elites of the previous right-wing authoritarian regime. Instead, the 1974 coup brought about the ousting and delegitimization of the actors involved with the *Estado Novo*. Among the players in the new regime, and quite unlike what would happen in the following years in nearby Spain, no relevant segment of the civil or military elites of the old regime was represented. This was especially true, as we have seen, in the new military establishment, but it was also the case in the emerging party system. In the elections to the constituent assembly, there was a clear dominance on the part of leftist parties. The center-left Socialists won the elections, obtaining about 46 percent of seats, and the combined forces of the Socialist Party, the Communist Party, and two other smaller parties on the left represented about 61 percent of all seats. Furthermore, while the right was represented by the PPD and the CDS, their leaderships (although not necessarily all their membership bases or electoral constituencies) were formed by individuals who had early become disaffected with the previous regime following the failed liberalization efforts that had taken place in its later years (Fernandes, 2006).

A third and final major consequence of regime collapse in Portugal was acute social mobilization. In 1975 and 1976, while the constituent assembly was discussing the different drafts and proposals, the streets and the fields outside were brimming with activity. As divisions with the regime mounted and state authority floundered, a process of increasing social mobilization occurred, supported by – but in many cases escaping the control of – left-wing parties and factions of the military. Demonstrations by varied parties, movements, and informal groups took place on a daily basis, "informal" purges in the state and private sectors were conducted, and, with staggering speed, occupations of factories, vacant housing, and the lands of absentee landlords took place – occupations that were later to be legally legitimized by the provisional governments (Graham and Wheeler 1983; Bermeo 1986; Durán 2000; Palacios 2003). The constituent assembly started its work at the very height of this process and was certainly not immune to it. Although the situation would slowly normalize after the recomposition of state authority brought about by the November 1975 countercoup, leading progressively to popular demobilization, the preceding period created heightened expectations among the population about social entitlements and the redistribution of power and privilege (Fishman 2011), as well as an acute awareness of those expectations on the part of political and military elites.

The consequences of all this for the constitutionalization of social rights can be discerned if we look into some detail at the debates on the constituent assembly around "economic, social, and cultural rights," particularly those concerning the text prepared by the Third Commission, which was responsible for dealing with the initial partisan drafts pertaining to that part of the Constitution. Different parties had different preferences about the content of the Constitution in what concerned social rights, and not all parties got what they wanted. Several disagreements occurred and they all followed predictable patterns. For example, both the PPD and the CDS criticized the openly Marxist language of the proposed text and went on, in the debates around specific social rights, to criticize, for instance, the discrimination that the articles dedicated to the "right to education" seemed to introduce against private schools or the weak recognition of the role of the family in education. The CDS went as far as proposing that the notion of a separation between church and state should be qualified with a (ultimately rejected) mention of the role of the Catholic Church in education. Conversely, the Communist Party, as well as other smaller parties on the left, proposed that the Constitution should have prescribed, for example, "the confiscation of the goods and fortunes of monopolist capitalists," a much stronger role for "popular organizations" in policymaking, the nationalization of the entire chemical and pharmaceutical industry, and a fully unified (i.e., totally state-controlled) educational system, again just to give a few examples. More generally, as could be expected, both the CDS and the PPD gave systematically greater emphasis in their proposals and positions to civil and political liberties than to "second" and "third" generation rights (Miranda 1978: 316–324). In the end, an analysis of the proposals of amendment to the report of the Third Commission that were voted shows that not all parties got exactly what they wanted. Predictably, the largest party, the Socialist Party (PS), was the one that saw its amendments more frequently approved, especially in the chapter specifically dedicated to "social rights and duties." In sum, the constitution-making debates clearly revealed that parties had different preferences and that the final outcome reflected, to a large extent, the bargaining power of the Socialist Party.

On the other hand, however, the disagreements between the parties and the outcome of the votes are not the only relevant aspects of the whole process. After all, it is rather striking to note that the CDS, the party furthest to the right in the assembly, had advanced a draft that, in its preamble, discussed the role of the Revolution in "suppressing the inequalities that so deeply affected Portuguese society" and in "affirming the principles of economic and social equality in the path to a Portuguese socialism" and a "society without classes." In that same draft, it was stated that Portugal was to adopt a "social market economy" with the "socialization of the means of production," including the state's ownership of companies in the industrial and service sectors. The remaining parties to the left of the CDS tended, of course, to go much further in this respect. The constitutional prohibition of laying off workers without having proved their wrongful conduct, and most of the extensive regulation of individual and collective workers' rights, although heavily debated on the details, remained mostly unchallenged by any party in their core elements. And all major parties, in their constitutional drafts, had contemplated the creation of a national social security system, of a national health service, of a right to housing, or of a national free basic education system. In sum, then, even more striking than the disagreements between the parties and the predictably more influential role of the PS in the final outcome was the fact that those disagreements took place within a very narrow band of views about the degree to which the Constitution should contain a commitment to social and economic rights, to the point where none of the parties even contested the notion that such a commitment should exist at all.

What explains this? One possible approach is to focus on how the constraints under which the constitution-making process took place – particularly the tutelage of the transition by a left-wing military apparatus and the radicalization of mass movements – contributed to suppress dissent in this respect. We can clearly see, for example, how parties were sensitive to changes in the overarching constraints under which they operated. For example, after November 25, 1975, as the moderate military took control of the Council of the Revolution and popular demobilization ensued, the CDS felt free to display its progressively increasing alienation from the partisan coalitions that were being formed in the constituent assembly (Magalhães 2003: 89). The CDS became increasingly willing to state its divergence vis-à-vis the "paternalism" of the Constitution and the "anti-democratic binding of the Armed Forces and the Government to a restrictive political project,"[8] to the point where the party became the only one that voted against the Constitution in early April 1976. Just a few years later, as the democratically elected parliament took hold and the "civilianization" of the Portuguese political institutions progressed, rightist parties started to employ a significantly different policy discourse than the one used before. By the end of the decade, several constitutional revision projects emanating from the center-right of the party system aimed at, among other things, "amplifying the role of private initiative" (Carneiro 1979) or more explicitly undoing what was then described as the anachronistic legacy of the First Pact between the parties and the MFA. Instead, they proposed a "profound" revision that limited the role of the state in health and education. In other words, as the constraints under which parties operated eased, something closer to their "true" preferences started to emerge. In 1976, however, they were still operating under constraints that dictated a broad convergence over a strong constitutionalization of social rights.

In sum, there is one particular narrative that could be told about the constitutionalization of social rights in Portugal. It is a narrative mostly concerned with defining the main political actors, their preferences, and their bargaining power as explanations of the outcome in terms of social rights. Following a transition by collapse of a right-wing regime, no relevant legitimate political actors were around to advance a conservative economic agenda concerning the role of the state in the economy and society. The range of preferences expressed by the political actors was further constrained by the

---

[8] Statements by Member of Parliament Sá Machado, *Diário da Assembleia Constituinte*, 132, April 3, 1976.

tutelary role of a totally revamped military apparatus that, after flirting with socialist revolution, was later dominated by more moderate but nonetheless socialist views, in alliance with the largest party in parliament, the Socialist Party. The outcome of the constituent process, in what concerns the commitment with social and economic rights, reflects this configuration of powers: while staying clear of the Soviet matrix of the constitutional drafts proposed by the Communist Party and the smaller parties on the extreme left, it nonetheless lacked the "neutrality" of other Western constitutions, by clearly taking sides for "the rights and interests of workers, socialism and social liberation" (Canotilho and Moreira 1991: 29).

16.4 CIVIL LAW, SOCIAL CATHOLICISM, AND THE ZEITGEIST

It is possible, however, to construct a rather different narrative about the constitutionalization of social rights in Portugal. It is one that abstracts from the bargaining power of the different political and military elites and the constraints under which they operated and focuses instead on the factors that shaped the preferences and worldviews of those actors and facilitated consensus on social rights. There are at least three major elements in that narrative: the ideas about the role of law and the state prevalent in a civil law country like Portugal; the legacies of fundamental Catholic values, which contributed to imbue the Portuguese right with views supporting the state's commitment to social goals; and the prevalent postwar Zeitgeist regarding social rights.

16.4.1 *Civil Law*

Portugal is firmly set in the civil law tradition, the result of a historical sequence shared by many continental European nations: Roman Law, its revival in medieval and Renaissance Europe, the thrust toward the transfer of sovereignty from the "King" to the "Nation" represented in parliament, and, finally, particularly in the French tradition, the Napoleonic invasions and the spread of the *Code Napoléon*. There are several crucial differences between this legal tradition and that represented by common law. They include the distinction between the accepted sources of law (codes and statutes produced by supreme legislatures versus the judicial creation of law), how the law should be applied (conceptualism and deduction versus pragmatism and induction), penal procedure (inquisitorial versus adversarial), the role of precedent, and the organization of the judiciary and the role of the judge (hierarchical-bureaucratic versus autonomous and independent).[9]

---

[9]   See, among many, Merryman (1969),Damaška(1986), Pejovic (2001), and Glaeser and Shleifer (2002).

Civil and common law, however, denote even deeper historical distinctions between ideologies and worldviews. These two different "legal origins" also stand for different strategies of social control that flow from "different ideas about law and its purpose" (La Porta et al. 2008: 286). They tend to survive through time, constituting the kind of "normative abstractions ... that are important themselves in placing limits to action" (Buchanan 1975: 904). And there is by now a large literature suggesting how these "legal origins" have contemporary consequences for investment, growth, stock market capitalization, and other economic outcomes, through their effects on institutional choices (La Porta et al. 1999; Djankov et al. 2002; La Porta et al. 2008).

We have good reasons to believe that different legal origins may have also been consequential for the constitutionalization of social rights. Continental law systems are characterized by notions of the "state" and the "constitution" that are very different from those that prevail either in England or the United States. Common law became closely entwined with the notion of economic freedom and the preservation of liberty vis-à-vis the crown, as landowning judges developed property rights in a succession of disputes against the crown – an activity that, by the eighteenth century, had converted into a more general judicial review of executive acts against arbitrary actions by the government (Mahoney 2001). Even more fundamentally, rights, in the common law tradition, are seen as "God-given," and law as a pre-constitutional limit placed on sovereignty. As Fleiner (2005: 6) notes, the "pursuit of happiness" in common law systems tends to be seen as a purely individual goal, with the state serving only as a moderator of social groups, and law as fundamentally concerned with securing economic liberty and property rights. In contrast, the civil law tradition treats rights as given by the state, and the "pursuit of happiness" is seen not as a purely individual endeavor but as something that is tied to general will and welfare, that is, to its interpreter and promoter, the state. As a result, "constitution" also means a rather different thing in both traditions. In the common law tradition, it is an instrument to limit state power; in the civil law tradition, it is a tool to transform society (*ibid.*).

If these are the long-term ideational and normative patterns that have characterized civil law countries, then it is clear that Portugal was clearly not an exception in this regard. Looking at the history of constitutional ideas in nineteenth-century Portugal, Hespanha (2004: 525) notes that even in the period immediately following the French invasions, when political and legal liberal ideologies became most prevalent, state interventionism remained popular in Portuguese political thought, and the idea of "rule by law" was "dominated by the notion of public interest, a sort of civic pact, to which all most subordinate." Later in the nineteenth century, this gave way to an even stronger version of "statism," where the state was to "rationalize society" and to intervene for the "continuation of social harmony and the realization of the public good" (*ibid.*:526). In this light, it is unsurprising that, even under very different political and strategic constitution-making contexts, most of the pre-1976 Portuguese constitutional texts already formally prescribed a number of social tasks for the state. In the 1822 Constitution, for example, articles 231 and 240 prescribed the promotion of "public health" as one of the responsibilities of parliament and attributed a role for the government in promoting the creation of hospitals. "Public help for the needy" was introduced as a "constitutional guarantee" in the 1826, 1838, and 1911 constitutions. The creation of "sufficiently endowed" schools was prescribed in Article 237 of the 1822 Constitution, and free primary education was introduced in the 1826 Constitution, never to be abandoned in any text since.

The entrenchment of this tradition has ensured that the legal, political, and intellectual elites in civil law countries such as Portugal have tended to share a conceptualization of the role of the law that has been "more congenial to economic intervention and redistribution," elevating "collective over individual rights" (Mahoney 2001: 511). In other words, while the political and strategic context of constitution-making in 1976 was particularly favorable to a strong constitutional commitment to social rights, such a context may not have been the only explanation for the observed outcome: the entire weight of the Portuguese legal tradition was already quite supportive of a convergence among the main political actors, regardless of their ideological placement, around the constitutionalization of social rights.

16.4.2 *Social Catholicism*

A second factor that may have favored a strong commitment to social rights in the Portuguese 1976 Constitution was Catholicism, more specifically the way in which the "social doctrine of the church" ultimately contributed to produce, even within the conservative Catholicism of the *Estado Novo* and the Portuguese center-right parties following democratization, a view of "social rights" as legitimate and necessary.

Since the late nineteenth century, Roman Catholic doctrine moved from its alignment with the *ancien régime* into a more qualified and, to a large extent, entirely transformed critique of secular political and economic liberalism, first exemplified by Pope Leo XIII's *Rerum Novarum*. While maintaining a strong attack of socialism, the "social doctrine of the church" inaugurated with *Rerum Novarum* also called for the role of the state in regulating the economy, providing for the needs of the poor, and even ensuring the "right" to a living wage. Throughout the twentieth century, the Church's social doctrine has developed in the direction of appropriating "modern rights language to discuss the meaning of political and economic justice" (Calo 2009: 17). That appropriation encompassed, for example, an unequivocal adherence to the notion of "social rights," including rights to "food, clothing, shelter, rest, medical care... and social services" (*Pacem in Terris* 1963, #11), as well as to the notion of redistributive justice (*Octogesima Adveniens* 1971, #23) and, more generally, to an active role of the state in defending needs and common goods that cannot be satisfied by the market (*Mater and Magistra* 1961, #20 and *Centesimus Annus* 1991, #40).

One of the main features of Salazar's *Estado Novo* was, of course, its Catholic roots, which were mingled with conservative nationalist ideas and even, at least up until the Second World War, with Italian fascist corporatism. It has been argued that the main intellectual source of Salazar's *Estado Novo* was the Church's social doctrine, despite its "perversion" by anti-democratic or even fascistic elements (Cruz 1980). But it is probably more precise to say that Salazar's thought, although touching many themes of "social Catholicism," was indeed more closely aligned with traditionalist Catholic views. In any case, "social Catholicism" in the first decades of the twentieth century was still sufficiently vague to have served both as an ideological reference to the *Estado Novo* (and other corporatist and anti-pluralist movements elsewhere) and to the "critical" Catholic movements than would ultimately align with the opposition to the regime (Barreto 1994). In fact, the actual policies pursued by the *Estado Novo* in the first decades suggest a great weariness of having the state engaging in social policy, not to mention conceiving of the existence of anything like "social rights" (Pereira 2009). The incipient social policies were mostly directly at the urban poor, in order to prevent their radicalization (Guibentif 1985; Pimentel 2000; Cardoso and Rocha 2003), and to the protection of the nucleus of society, the "family," which would in turn be in charge of perpetuating "Christian values" and providing the only kind of protection against social risks.

Starting in the early 1960s, however, a new discourse started to impose itself within the regime, a discourse that was mostly driven by rising technocratic elites within the ministerial offices. These elites were, in fact, mostly composed of "technocatholics" (Alho 2008; Pereira 2009), who started to promote a view of state intervention highly inspired by the Catholic social doctrine as revised by Vatican II and John XXIII's papacy. In the legitimization of the regime, social protection would increasingly replace its original conservative core element – the social control and appeasement of the urban working class – with a discourse that openly used the language of "social justice" and "equity." After Marcelo Caetano replaced Salazar in 1968, these views blossomed into a full rebranding of the *Estado Novo* as a "Social State" with which Caetano sought to legitimize a regime experiencing increasing difficulties domestically and abroad (Guibentif 1997), leading to important reforms in the health system (Simões 2004), education (Teodoro 2001), and housing (Pinto 2009) policies. Such welfarist discourse and its inspiration in the Church's social doctrine became itself a weapon for the opposition. As Pinto (2009: 210) notes with regard to the issue of housing policy, "the criticism of the oppositionists was aided by the regime's failure to deliver, as it consistently fell short of its publicly stated goals." But here, as in other fields of social policy, vigorous criticism came precisely from sectors of the "progressive Catholics" that claimed the same ideological inspiration – social Catholicism – as the regime. Ultimately, many of the "technocatholics" became disaffected with Caetano's failed liberalization and would affiliate with the PS, the PPD, and the CDS after the 1974 coup.

Thus, although it is certainly accurate to talk about the Portuguese democratic transition as a "rupture" with authoritarianism, there are interesting continuities in what concerns the conception of the role of the state in society and the economy. The previous regime's collapse and delegitimization, together with constraints under which political parties operated, certainly contributed to the fact that the parties of the right "tended to define themselves much more to the left than their leadership and social bases would suggest" (Bruneau and MacLeod 1986: 87). However, the claims to a "social right" to housing, social security, or health, which became nearly unanimous after the coup, were preceded by a set of government policies that had "created a space where the use of public resources ... could be freely discussed" and made "the case for their universalisation possible" (Pinto 2009: 202–205). Catholic social doctrine seems to have played an important role both in legitimizing those government policies and in creating a line of continuity between the technocratic elites within the previous regime and the political elites in the center-left and the center-right of the new regime.

16.4.3 *Zeitgeist*

Addressing the unfolding of the "third wave of democracy" in the last decades of the twentieth century, Huntington was one of the first to call attention to the role of the *Zeitgeist* in driving the liberalization and democratization of political regimes. Facing a variety of different circumstances, different countries may be driven to respond with similar remedies, based on a set of commonly shared beliefs (Huntington 1991; see also Linz and Stepan 1996). But it is probably not a stretch to say that, to some extent, the Portuguese transition to democracy – which initiated the "third wave" – also occurred at the historical crest of another "wave," one of recognition and legitimization of social rights.

As it has been demonstrated by a large literature, the implementation of social rights through concrete policy measures and the overall configuration of welfare states is affected by many historically, politically, and socially contingent factors. The particular timing of democratization (Lenski 1966; Orloff and Skocpol 1984), the relative success of social democratic and Christian democratic parties in electoral politics (Esping-Andersen 1985; Korpi 1989; Van Kersbergen 1995), and the shape of constitutional structures and political institutions in a country (Huber et al. 1993), for example, have all contributed to produce important variations in this respect, showing that social rights are "artefacts of political struggles" and "time- and place-specific" products (Rittich 2007: 112). However, given the "symbolic" and "declaratory" nature of social rights (Sadurski 2009), the willingness of constitution-makers to include them in texts is particularly likely to have been affected by the more generic ebb and flow of ideas and beliefs in the twentieth century about citizenship rights, regardless of the way other factors dictate effectively high or low levels of social transfers and provisions.

As Marshall famously argued for the case of Britain, the expansion of rights can be thought of as a temporal sequence: first civil rights in the eighteenth century, then political rights in the late nineteenth and early twentieth century, and finally social rights after the Second World War (Marshall 1950). To a large extent, this seems to represent a broader sequence in general thinking about the relative importance and interdependence of rights both in international treaties and domestic constitutional texts. The postwar period, after all, was also the moment when "embedded liberalism" became the dominant economic system (Ruggie 1982) and Keynesianism the main "policy paradigm" in the Western world, aiming at restoring market economies while mitigating their negative social consequences. By 1948, the Universal Declaration of Human Rights (UDHR), alongside civil and political rights, included rights to social security, work, education, and adequate standard of living. It is true that the inclusion of the latter was always subject to criticism and one of the main sources of disagreements between countries, which received their full expression in the 1966 split between two separate treaties, the International Covenant on Civil and Political Rights (ICCPR) and the International Covenant on Economic, Social and Cultural Rights (ICESCR), with only the former carrying an immediate duty of implementation. However, by the 1970s, there was a general acknowledgment at the international level among large segments of the legal community about the "indivisible and interdependent" nature of civil, political, and social rights (Craven 1998: 2; Barak-Erez and Gross 2007: 5).

All this suggests that there should be a relationship between the timing of constitution-making and the extent to which social rights are formally recognized. More specifically, regardless of the specific political context of the Portuguese democratic transition, post–Second World War constitutions such as the Portuguese were always likely to have been very different from those drafted earlier. As Sadurski (2009) notes, in Scandinavia, very developed social policies coexist with a limited formal recognition of social rights in the constitutions. He attributes that to the fact that, although they have been often amended, those constitutions still bear the imprint of the time when most of them were originally drafted, that is, the nineteenth century (*ibid.*: 4). In contrast, by the mid-1960s, ideas about the centrality of social and economic rights had changed considerably: by then they were fully entrenched and normalized in the international community (Rittich 2007). This does not seem to have been lost on Portuguese constitution-makers. After all, the year 1976, when the Portuguese constitution was approved, was also the year that the ICESCR came into force. The Portuguese constitution made explicit mention of the UDHR in Article 16, prescribing it as the general text that should inspire the interpretation and integration of all legal and constitutional rules pertaining to fundamental rights. In this way, all social and economic rights contained there were implicitly included in Article 290, which established the limits for future constitutional amendments (Miranda 1993).

16.5 FROM SMALL- TO LARGE(R)-N

The previous sections provided us with two alternative narratives about the constitutionalization of social rights in Portugal. The first focuses on the concrete political context in which the constitution was approved: a regime change through collapse of right-wing authoritarianism, the ousting and delegitimization of right-wing political actors, and the dominance of the constitution-making process by left-wing military and partisan forces. From this point of view, a strong constitutional pre-commitment of the state to the protection of social rights was to be expected. The second narrative points out that such events and the balance of power they imposed occurred in a broader setting. Obviously, within the communist and part of the socialist left in Portugal, the discourse of "social rights" after the revolution flowed naturally from an ideology defending a fully socialized economy, something very different from the "personalist humanism" that flowed from the social Catholicism that dominated the views of the center-right parties and part of the Socialist Party elites. And as one would observe after the constitution entered into force, different actors shared different views about the status of social rights vis-à-vis civil and political rights, how they should be interpreted in practice, and how they conflicted or agreed with proposed social and economic policies. However, it is understandable why a generic and broad consensus about social rights could have easily emerged even if the left had not been dominant in the constitution-making process. The overall conception of the role of the law and of the state in the Portuguese (and continental) legal tradition, the values of social Catholicism that influenced important segments of both former and the new regime elites, and an international Zeitgeist favorable to social rights, all combined to form an ideological environment that was incompatible with the tenets of a "minimal state" and "economic liberalism."

Turning these two different narratives and the way they adjust to the peculiarities of the Portuguese case into general hypotheses that can be systematically tested requires a considerable amount of simplification. However, this should not deter us from attempting to move from a descriptive account of the Portuguese case to broader hypothesis testing. The latter has been attempted before, namely by Ben-Bassat and Dahan's (2008) study on the determinants and consequences of constitutional social rights. It is the only published study that, as far as I know, measures the extent to which constitutional texts are committed to the protection of social rights and tests generic hypotheses concerning the correlates of that phenomenon. The authors construct a summary index based on the extent to which "current" constitutions include strong, weak, general, or no commitments to the protection of rights to social security, education, health, housing, and workers' rights. Values theoretically range from 0 to 3, and the empirical range goes from 0 (which characterizes constitutions such as the Australian, Austrian, Canadian, Czech, German, and others) to 2.45 (precisely, the Portuguese Constitution). That score is then regressed on several variables measuring attributes of countries.

Ben-Bassat and Dahan reach several conclusions about the correlates of social rights in constitutions. First, legal origins do seem to matter. Countries sharing either French civil law or socialist law traditions display a significantly higher level of commitment to social rights in their constitutions than German, Scandinavian, and especially common law countries. Second, the share of the population with Catholic beliefs also seems to be relevant: the higher that share, the higher the level of constitutional commitment to social rights. Third, they find a relationship between democracy and a stronger generic commitment to social rights (as captured by their summary measure). At the same time, a glaring non-finding also emerges from their analysis: there is no relationship between the year when a particular constitution was promulgated and whether it entrenches social rights. They attribute this to the fact that their measurement of social rights is contemporary rather than tied to the particular version of the constitution as it was approved. Since older constitutions can be amended with different degrees of difficulty, making some (but not others) amenable to "be 'updated' to incorporate changes in preferences for social rights" (Ben-Bassat and Dahan 2008: 111), it is understandable that the effects of timing of promulgation might have been diluted.

However, their study has two major shortcomings that raise doubts about some of the main findings. The first is potential sample bias. The study collects data on sixty-nine constitutions – including sixty-five written constitutions and four other countries with a legal document whose status is higher than ordinary law – evaluated at an undisclosed moment in time, but which we assume to be around 2005–2006. The problem, of course, is that this constitutes only about a third of the entire set of constitutional orders in the world today. Criteria for case selection had almost certainly to do with data availability at the time of the writing, mainly through Internet-based sources of translated constitutional texts. The second potential problem concerns model specification. Ben-Bassat and Dahan mostly address the kind of long-standing structural factors that pertain to the second narrative discussed in the chapter thus far, that is, legal origins, age of constitution, and predominant religious beliefs. However, the political context at the time of promulgation is not an aspect of concern in their analysis. How can we replicate and extend the analysis by Ben-Bassat and Dahan while addressing some of these shortcomings? This is the issue I will address in what follows.

16.5.1 *The Dependent Variable*

We can substantially increase the number of cases under examination by resorting to the several datasets recently made available as a result of the work of the *Comparative Constitutions Project* (CCP). One of the CCP datasets, *Characteristics of National Constitutions* (Elkins, Ginsburg, and Melton 2010), includes data on 184 of the 190 constitutional systems that were in force within the 191 independent countries as of 2006. One set of characteristics measured for each constitution is precisely whether it includes social rights provisions. More specifically, it codes constitutions for whether they "provide for a right to an adequate or reasonable standard of living" (STANDLIV), "right to safe/healthy working conditions" (SAFEWORK), "right to shelter or housing" (SHELTER), "right to health care" (HEALTHR), and if the constitution stipulates "that education should be free, at least up to some level" (EDFREE). In other words, we can obtain, for no less than 184 constitutions, information comparable to that obtained by Ben-Bassat and Dahan for their 69 cases: the constitutionalization of rights to social security, education, health, housing, and workers' rights. The index in this chapter simply counts the number of affirmative answers to the questions about the presence of absence of such provisions, thus ranging from 0 to 5. For the cases also covered by Ben-Bassat and Dahan, the correlation between their index of social rights and the one resulting from the CCP dataset is quite high (.75).

Figure 16.1 shows how the 184 cases are distributed in terms of our social rights index. As we can see, about one in every four constitutions in the world includes none of these kinds of social rights provisions. However, 21 percent of them do include at least four of the social rights measured in the dataset, including fourteen cases where the index reaches its maximum value of 5. Among those cases we can find Portugal, together with Armenia, Belarus, Ecuador, Guatemala, Honduras, Mexico, Panama, Paraguay, Seychelles, Spain, Turkey, Ukraine, and Venezuela.

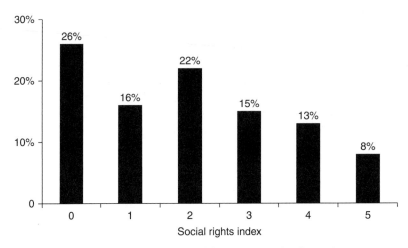

FIGURE 16.1. Distribution of the CCP social rights index.

16.5.2 *The Context of Constitution-Making*

One aspect that is missing in Ben-Bassat and Dahan's (2008) analysis is the political context of constitution-making. One might argue that variables capturing such political contexts are unlikely to have any relationship with our measure of social rights. After all, because the attributes of constitutions (in both their study and the CCP dataset) were captured by a "contemporary" measure – the extent to which constitutional texts prescribed social rights around 2006 – any variables that capture aspects of constitution-making processes that may have occurred long ago are arguably unlikely to sustain any relationships with current features of constitutions. Although such relationships may have existed with the text as it was approved, constitutions may have been amended to reflect changing ideas and political conditions.

However, another way of thinking about this is to note that looking for a relationship between contextual aspects of constitution-making and the nature of current constitutional rights only makes our hypothesis test more demanding: if any significant relationship is indeed found, one can reasonably conclude that, in spite of all changes that may have been introduced between the promulgation of a text and its current version – changes whose direction we are not able to trace on the basis of our data – current constitutional texts nevertheless still bear the marks of the context in which they were originally drafted. One should not be excessively surprised if that turns out to be the case. After all, as "historical institutionalism" has often reminded us, changing institutional rules often requires a combination of blatant inefficiency, major exogenous shocks, permissive rules for change, convergence in preferences of the relevant political actors, and low uncertainty about outcomes (Pierson 2000). Thus, fundamental institutional choices, including "constitutional" choices, may indeed persist even if economic, political, and social environments change dramatically.

In my analysis of the Portuguese case, I argued that constitutions that were approved following the collapse of previous regimes might display different features from those that were promulgated after less dramatic changes or in the absence of regime change. Unfortunately, the kind of detailed, contextual, and narrative information we presented for the Portuguese context is impossible to collect systematically for the almost 200 cases in our dataset. However, we can try to approximate this by focusing on a measurable aspect of the process that might indicate situations such as those that occurred in Portugal. One of the crucial contributions of the study of democratization in the last three decades has been the notion that there are different modes of regime transition that can be typified, and that those types of transition have enduring consequences. In some cases, regime change takes place by means of a "pact" (Linz 1981), a "transaction" (Mainwaring 1992), or, more generally, "consensually" (Share 1987), that is, with some amount of participation or consent on the part of the leaders of the previous regime. Naturally, in these cases, we should expect any new rules of the game that might be adopted to reflect to some extent a compromise between the leaders of the outgoing regime and the interests they represent and those of the opposition to the previous regime. However, in "non-consensual" regime changes, where "rupture" or "collapse" takes place – either through military coups, revolutionary change, military defeat, or simply "extrication" (as the ruling elites loses legitimacy and hand power to the opposition) – the opposite is likely to happen. The new regime "will likely eschew the support – and may actively prohibit the participation" of political forces linked to the old regime, resulting in clear discontinuities in "political institutions, political symbols, political culture, and even socioeconomic arrangements" (Share 1987: 530). The new rules of the game will be drafted without participation of the elites from the previous regime and, thus, reflect mostly the interests of the newly dominant actors.

Of particular interest to us, of course, are the situations where a new constitution is drafted following a regime change through a rupture away from markedly right-wing or left-wing political regimes. In the case of Portugal, a rupture with an authoritarian right-wing regime contributed to create an imbalance in the correlation of forces among political and societal actors that allowed left-wing forces to be dominant in the constitution-making process. Several other constitutions have been drafted in comparable contexts. A famous example is Mexico's 1917 Constitution. It was drafted following a protracted revolutionary struggle, first against the *Porfiriato* and, later, against the dictatorship of Victoriano Huerta. Venustiano Carranza, who ultimately became president and convoked the Querétaro Constitutional Convention, had envisaged a new constitution that did not differ too much from the liberal 1857 document. However, the Convention ended up being dominated by the leftist radical reformers, supported by the man who had been the military victor of the Revolution, General Álvaro Obregón (Niemeyer 1974). The issue of land reform was crucial, and one where the radicals and Obregón threw in their weight to ensure, in the famous Article 27, limits on private property and the division of large landed estates. Furthermore, Article 123 occupies a whole section "On Labor and Social Welfare," collecting the claims of the radicals concerning the rights of workers and unemployment, pension, and accident insurance. As Carozza notes, "these social and economic provisions were the first of their kind in any constitutional document, not just in Latin America but in all the world" (Carozza 2003: 304). Interestingly, in spite of the many years that have elapsed since 1917 and the sixty-five subsequent amendments, the Mexican constitution still scores among those with the highest scores in social rights constitutionalization (5, the maximum, in our measure, and 1.97 in Ben-Bassat and Dahan's index).

This suggests a more general pattern through which constitutions approved following the collapse of right-wing regimes, such as the *Porfiriato* and the short-lived Huerta dictatorship, might be more likely to reflect the dominance of political actors interested in (and capable of) entrenching social policies and positive rights in the constitution. Using *Keesing's Record of World Events*, I codified all constitutions in force (as of 2006) for which we had measures of social rights constitutionalization according to this basic criterion: whether they were approved following nonconsensual changes away from right-wing regimes (right-wing *rupture*, coded as a dummy variable with value 1 for positive occurrences and 0 for the others). This led us to include not only Portugal (1976) and Mexico (1917), but also the Philippines (1986, following the ousting of Ferdinand Marcos), Paraguay (1992, following the coup ousting the Stroessner dictatorship), Nicaragua (1987, the first constitution approved following the ousting of Somoza's dictatorship by the Sandinistas), Iran (1979, adopted following the Islamic Revolution that ousted Mohammad Reza Pahlavi), the new Italian (1947) and German (1949) constitutions, approved following defeat of fascist regimes and occupation, Japan (1946, following the defeat of the Japanese militarist regime), Guatemala (1985, following the 1983 coup against the rule of General Ríos Montt), Haiti (1987, after the ousting of Jean-Claude Duvalier), Hungary (1949, following the ousting of Ferenc Szálasi's fascist government), Korea (1948, following the end of Japanese rule), and Malawi (1994, after the deposition of Hastings Banda).

Furthermore, we can also determine the opposite situation, that is, cases of constitutions approved following nonconsensual regime changes away from left-wing regimes. We hypothesize that these are the cases where the constitutionalization of social rights is *less* likely. Many of the prominent candidates for this situation are, of course, the new constitutions approved in Eastern Europe immediately following the demise of Soviet-sponsored socialist regimes. However, many of these transitions do not qualify as a *rupture*. Regardless of the legacies of totalitarian or post-totalitarian rule and the extent to which new democratic authors might be interested in undoing them, the fact is that most of the regime transitions in these cases were, to a large extent, "consensual," in the sense that they involved the participation of parties connected to the previous regime in setting the rules of the game in the new one. That participation varied in intensity, from the case of Bulgaria (where the transition was highly controlled by the communist regime) to the case of Poland (where a contractual transition did take place, involving compromises between the Communist Party and Solidarity), but few cases qualify as a full *rupture*. Even the case of Romania, where Ceauşescu's regime was indeed toppled, is one where ex- or neo-communists quickly took control of the "revolution."

There are, however, several cases where a constitution can be said to have been approved following the collapse of a markedly left-wing regime. These include Czechoslovakia (Linz and Stepan 1996), through the "Velvet Revolution" (including the 1992 Constitution in Slovakia and the 1993 Constitution of the Czech Republic); Estonia (1992), Lithuania (1992), Armenia (1995) and Georgia (1995), following independence from the Soviet Union, and Croatia (1991), Slovenia (1991), and Bosnia-Herzegovina (1995), following the disintegration of Yugoslavia. Three additional cases were also coded as 1 in this *Left-wing rupture* variable: the Bolivian Constitution of 1967, the first approved following the overthrow in 1964 of the *Movimiento Nacionalista Revolucionario* by a military coup; Costa Rica (1949, following the 1948 civil war pitting the forces of communist-backed Rafael Calderón and the ultimately triumphant forces of José Figueres Ferrer); and Ethiopia (1994, following the collapse of the Derg regime).

The third variable we can add capturing the political context of constitution-making concerns the nature of the regime at the time of promulgation. Ben-Bassat and Dahan (2008) detect a positive relationship between contemporary measures of social rights and contemporary measures of democracy. In other words, countries that have free political competition and participation and protect the political and civic rights that accompany them are also more likely to have constitutions that accommodate social rights, a finding that is interpreted as a confirmation of the hypothesis that "democracy shapes beliefs and values" related to constitutional commitments to social rights (*ibid.*: 110). However, instead of focusing exclusively on the nature of the regime at the time the features of the constitution were measured, we can also capture regime type when the constitution was promulgated. It is not entirely clear, however, what relationship we should expect. To be sure, it has been argued that the accommodation of social claims concerning positive rights requires that "the process whereby the constitution is designed must therefore be a relatively open, democratic and transparent one" (Waylen 2006: 1217), conditions that are unlikely to be present under dictatorship. On the other hand, however, a different argument could be made: whereas the connection between the very concept of "democracy" and civil and political (negative) rights is fundamentally unquestioned, the notion that constitutions should include positive rights is much more politically and ideologically contested. Thus, to the extent that constitutions typically require supermajorities to be approved and enter into force, open political competition and participation by political actors and social interests with divergent views about the kinds of commitments the state should be tied to in terms of social policies is not a necessary congenial condition for the adoption of social rights.

We can confront these different expectations with the data by testing the relationship between social rights and regime type as of 2006 *and* at the year of promulgation. *Democracy in 2006* – that is, at the time the characteristics of each constitution were measured – is obtained from the *Democracy-Dictatorship* dataset originally presented in Alvarez et al. (1996) and updated up to 2008 by Cheibub et al. (2010). It is a dichotomous dummy variable, coded 1 if the country was a democracy at year 2006. For *Democracy at year of promulgation*, we again resort to one of the datasets made available by the CCP project, this time the replication data used for *The Endurance of National Constitutions* (Elkins et al. 2009a). One of those variables (*democ_prom*) is a binary variable coded 1 if the state was a democracy when the constitution was promulgated. However, although such cases were rare, we found that, for some country-years, coding of *democ_prom* was inconsistent with the coding assigned by the *Democracy-Dictatorship* dataset (Cheibub et al. 2010). In order to maximize comparability between measures of democracy in 2006 and at time of promulgation, in such cases, we revised *democ_prom* according to the Cheibub et al. dataset.

16.5.3 Analysis

Model 1 in Table 16.1 is a replication of Ben-Bassat and Dahan's (2008) analysis, but this time using CCP data. One of the independent variables is *Age of constitution (in years)*. We resorted to a second dataset made available by the CCP project: the *Chronology of Constitutional Events* (Elkins, Ginsburg, and Melton 2009b). For each country, we can determine the year when the constitution was promulgated, and thus create a new variable that simply represents the number of years elapsed from the year of promulgation until 2006. I also use dummy variables for legal origins. Like Ben-Bassat and Dahan, we use data from the *Lex Mundi* project

TABLE 16.1. *Explaining the constitutionalization of social rights (Poisson regression)*

	Model 1		Model 2		Model 3	
	Coef.	SE	Coef.	SE	Coef.	SE
French origin	.63**	.18	.34*	.17	.39*	.17
German origin	.37	.33	−.02	.31	.20	.22
Scandinavian origin	.35	.26	.99**	.34	.94**	.34
Socialist origin	.91***	.19	.66**	.19	–	–
Predominantly Catholic	.25	.15	−.06	.13	−.09	.13
Predominantly Muslim	.03	.18	−.20	.17	−.26	.17
Age of constitution in years	−.004	.003	–	–	–	–
Democracy by 2006	.24	.16	.26	.18	.27	.18
Log of GDP per capita	−.06	.04	−.05	.04	−.04	.04
Latin America	.29	.16	.29	.15	.23	.15
Log of age of constitution	–	–	−.13*	.06	−.14*	.06
Predominantly Protestant	–	–	−1.17***	.25	−1.18***	.26
Right-wing rupture	–	–	.46***	.10	.45***	.11
Left-wing rupture	–	–	−.01	.18	.19	.15
Democracy at promulgation	–	–	−.03	.12	−.04	.12
Constant			1.16***	.30	1.11***	.20
N	178		178		178	
Pseudo R2 (Nagelkerke):	.34		.44		.42	
Highest VIF	1.73		2.28		2.09	

*p<.05; **p<.01; ***p<.001; robust standard errors in parenthesis

(Djankov et al. 2002), which classifies countries in terms of their English, socialist, French, German, and Scandinavian legal origins, which I coded as dummy variables, using English law as the reference category. Because the *Lex Mundi* project covers just 109 countries, I completed the dataset by resorting to the CIA Factbook, which provides information on every country's legal system. For every socialist/communist or postcommunist country, we coded legal origins as "socialist."

As far as predominant religious values are concerned, we lack information about the precise shares of each country's population holding different religious beliefs. However, on the basis of the CIA Factbook (as collected by Norris 2009), I coded each country by means of dummy variables, determining whether it is predominantly Catholic or Muslim, with other religions treated as the reference category. I also control for levels of economic development, introducing the *(Log of) GDP per capita*, in U.S. dollars as of 2006 (source: World Bank);[10] finally, I add a dummy variable for *Latin America*, which Ben-Bassat and Dahan found to

[10] This causes the loss of 6 of the 184 cases for which no data on GDP per capita was available: Cuba, People's Republic of Korea, Nauru, Somalia, Taiwan, and Tuvalu. We are left with 178 observations.

be significant in their analysis. Our dependent variable is a scale of 0 to 5, representing how many social rights are enshrined in each constitutional text. In other words, we are dealing with count data, with a distribution skewed to the right, as Figure 16.1 shows. Linear regression, OLS, is therefore inappropriate. One alternative is the use of Poisson regression, which I employ here.[11]

One major positive result obtained by Ben-Bassat and Dahan is confirmed by our analysis in Model 1, this time using data on 178 countries: legal origins do seem to matter. The constitutions enacted in countries sharing either French civil law or socialist law traditions are indeed more likely to contain social rights. However, three major differences already emerge in comparison with their results. First, we find no relationship between whether a country is democratic or not and the level of social rights constitutionalization. Second, in Model 1, we find no relationship between the predominant religion in any given country and social rights. In particular, there is no evidence that predominantly Catholic countries are significantly more likely to contain social rights in their constitutions in comparison with others. Finally, there is no relationship between age of constitution in years and social rights.

Model 2 introduces new variables and two innovations in the measurement of previous variables. First, the year when a constitution was promulgated or the number of years elapsed since its promulgation is probably not the best way to capture the effects of the historical Zeitgeist in constitutional texts. While there are a few constitutions in force that have been adopted many years ago – in countries such as the United States, Norway, or the Netherlands – there are many constitutions that had been promulgated much more recently. This suggests that *Age of constitution in years* are highly skewed variables and that some transformation is desirable before we estimate its relationship with the constitutionalization of social rights. In our dataset, the number of years elapsed since promulgation ranges from zero (in three cases where the constitution was promulgated in 2006) to more than 100 years in eleven cases, and displays a skewness of 2.7 and a kurtosis of 11.2. Thus, for Model 2, we replace the Age of constitution variable by its natural log. The second change in relation to Model 2 consists in adding an additional contrast concerning religious values: instead of estimating the effects of Catholicism or Islam as predominant religions in comparison with all remaining religions, we add a third dummy variable for Protestantism. Finally, we add three already discussed variables to take into account the political context of constitution-making: *Left-wing rupture* and *Right-wing rupture*, and *Democracy at year of promulgation*.

---

[11] Running the same models as negative binomial regressions, the likelihood-ratio test of alpha (the over-dispersion parameter) was never statistically significant, suggesting that Poisson regression is an appropriate model.

Table 16.2. Predicted probabilities of social rights

Legal origins	Social rights index		Predominant religion	Social rights index	
	0–2	3–5		0–2	3–5
English law	.82	.18	Protestant	.98	.02
German law	.85	.15	Catholic	.85	.15
French law	.68	.32	Muslim	.88	.12
Socialist law	.49	.51	Others	.82	.18
Scandinavian law	.26	.74			

A look at Model 2 in Table 16.1 shows, first of all, an increase in the pseudo R-squared from .34 to .44, suggesting that Model 2 provides a better fit to the data. Some of the previous findings stand: even though, in comparison with common law countries, French civil law and socialist law countries are more likely to enact and keep in force constitutions with more social rights, there remains no evidence that predominantly Catholic countries are more likely to constitutionalize social rights. However, several new findings emerge. First, once a dummy for Protestantism is introduced, an unanticipated relationship between religious values and social rights emerges: Protestant countries are *less* likely to constitutionalize social rights than all other countries, even when legal origins are controlled for. Second, once Protestantism is controlled for, Scandinavian legal origins show a positive and significant impact on social rights, albeit one that is estimated with less precision than the impact of French or socialist legal origins. A more intuitive way to depict the findings is to compute the predicted probabilities for the counts of civil rights in the constitutions of the world contingent upon different values of the independent variables related to legal origins or predominant religions.[12] Table 16.2 displays those results, showing, by type of legal origin and by predominant religion, the added predicted probabilities of counts of 0 to 2 (low) and 3 to 5 (high) while keeping all other continuous variables constant at their mean values and the remaining dummy variables at zero. The probability that constitutions enacted in countries with French (.32), socialist (.51), and (especially) Scandinavian legal origins countries (.74) exhibit a high (3–5) index of social rights is significantly higher than what occurs in German (.15) or common law (.18) countries. Conversely, predominantly Protestant countries are extremely unlikely (.02) to have adopted constitutions with a high social rights index, in comparison with all other countries.

Another crucial finding that results from Model 2 concerns the importance of the political context under which the constitution was drafted. Our results show an asymmetry in this respect: constitutions drafted following the collapse of left-wing

---

[12]   We use the command *prvalue* in STATA, part of the *Spost* package.

regimes are no different from constitutions drafted following all other sorts of regime change or even the absence of regime change. However, in the case of ruptures against right-wing regimes, the probability of a constitution currently scoring 3 or higher in our social rights index is .38, a full twenty percentage points above the same probability for other situations. This is a sizeable effect, and it is all the more striking as it captures the relationship between the context under which a particular constitution was approved with its *current* contents, regardless of the age of that constitution and without taking into account any number of amendments that may have been introduced in the meantime. Ruptures against right-wing regimes seem to leave a powerful and resistant legacy of entrenchment of social rights. In contrast, the same occurs neither with the particular regime type under which constitutions were approved nor with current regime type: we find no evidence that democracy is related in any way to the constitutionalization of social rights.

Finally, the timing of constitutional promulgation does seem to matter. Taking into account that the age of constitution in years was log-transformed, the results of Model 2 – a negative and significant coefficient for our *Log of age of constitution* variable – suggest that there is a relationship between the age of constitutions and the extent to which they constitutionalize social rights: that relationship is nonlinear, but older constitutions are indeed much less likely to contain social rights provisions than newer ones. Here, again, the legacies of the context in which constitutions were promulgated – in this case, the historical context – are still visible today. Finally, Model 3 simply recodes our *Socialist law* dummy by replacing it with the legal system that prevailed before these countries experienced socialist regimes, leaving again common law as a reference category. While the coefficients for French and Scandinavian law change slightly (the former increasing and the latter decreasing), no major changes in our conclusions or in the strength of the variables occur.

16.6 CONCLUSION

I started by arguing that the extraordinary extent to which a full constitutionalization of social rights took place in 1976 Portugal seemed to result from a combination of several factors. Some had to do with the correlation of forces in the constitution-making process, others with prevalent ideas about the role of law and state, fostered by legal origins, religious values and doctrine, and the shifting international worldviews and policy paradigms of the twentieth century. In other words, some had to do with the particular political and historical circumstances in which the constitution was drafted, others with longer-term legacies. This line of argument, of course, can easily sound like a somewhat wishy-washy attempt to join apparently irreconcilable theoretical approaches about the causes of institutional choices, rooted, in some cases, in strict assumptions about rationality and power maximization and, in others, in slightly looser considerations about cultural and ideological understandings, moral appropriateness, "polity-ideas," and "higher-level" choices. However, I hope to have been able to at least suggest, like others have done before when addressing different objects of study, that looking at the Portuguese constitution-making process both through the lens of rational-choice institutionalism and the lens of the "ideational" factors is neither impossible nor necessarily inconsequential. In fact, as we moved from the small-N narrative, qualitative, and speculative analysis of the Portuguese case to a broad cross-national comparison, we saw that the two approaches are complementary.

On the one hand, we saw, first in Portugal and then more generally, how the collapse of right-wing regimes is likely to be followed – if it leads to the promulgation of new constitutions – by the constitutional entrenchment of policies preferred by left-wing political and societal actors, whose fulfillment addresses the claims of social interests that were marginalized under the previous regimes. At the same time, however, we also saw how the constitutionalization of social rights in 1976 was perhaps less divisive than one might have imagined. One plausible explanation for that concerns the politically constrained environment under which the constituent assembly and the parties worked in those years. However, our cross-national comparison suggested a broader explanation: in French civil law countries, in historically recent constitution-making processes, and in non-Protestant countries – such as the Portuguese case – social rights have tended to receive a stronger recognition in constitutional texts. This suggests that the political actors involved in crafting constitutional rules do so in an ideational context that, regardless of the particular circumstances of the transition, may be either adverse or congenial (as in Portugal) to the constitutionalization of social rights. In sum, this suggests a rather simple but, we hope, powerful idea: "interests" and "ideas" are not mutually exclusive lenses with which to look at institutional design.

Constitutional social rights raise other questions besides the particular ones we addressed here. What effects do they actually produce on actual welfare and its social distribution? Different studies have given us reasons to be both somewhat positive (Ben-Bassat and Dahan 2008) and rather sceptical (De Vanssay and Spindler 1994; Blume and Voigt 2006). Two things, however, seem clear after looking both at the Portuguese case and at the constitutions of the world. First, social rights do seem to matter at some level. In Portugal, different political actors had different preferences regarding their constitutionalization, differences that began to be expressed more fully, as we documented, as soon as the overarching constraints over parliamentary sovereignty and state authority that existed early in the Portuguese transition started to ease. How social rights should be interpreted in the Portuguese context has remained a heated doctrinal question among constitutional lawyers, but also, and more importantly, a relevant judicial and political issue. Throughout the last three decades, several bills and laws central to the health, labor, education, and housing policies of successive governments have been either repealed or amended as a result of Constitutional Court rulings invoking constitutional social rights. And just to give one fairly recent example, in March 2010, the Social Democratic Party, by then still in the opposition, proposed the approval of amendments that would produce a "liberal update" of the "social area" of the Constitution, presenting this into one of the party's main priorities.[13] Social rights matter. Second, the line of enquiry followed in this chapter, although focused on the causes of social rights, may also contribute to illuminating the discussion about their consequences. By calling attention to some of the potential factors behind the constitutionalization of social rights, the chapter also provides an admonition against treating those rights as exogenous variables in explanations of social and economic outcomes, because some of the factors that lead to particular constitutional commitments – legal origins and the balance of power between partisan actors, for example – may turn out to be themselves important factors behind the adoption of particular policies, their implementation, and their consequences.

Finally, by calling attention to the factors behind the emergence of certain constitutional rules, and particularly to the interplay between interests, norms, and ideas, I hope to raise new questions about the issue of institutional survival. Rational choice institutionalism has also looked at what happens after constitutional rules are chosen, suggesting that this "post-constitutional" game is fundamentally noncooperative (Riley 2001) and that the survival of rules results from their distributional consequences and the satisfaction of dominant actors with those consequences (Knight 1992). However, one potentially interesting question raised by this study concerns the remarkable resilience of the historical and political legacies of the original context under which constitutions were approved. In Portugal, social rights in the Constitution have remained mostly untouched, more than thirty years after promulgation and after no less than seven constitutional revision processes. Since then, the correlation of forces in the Portuguese party system changed dramatically: the Communist Party lost considerable force, the Socialist Party became a moderate leftist party (and, in fact, one of the most economically conservative social democratic parties in Europe), and the center-right spent considerable time in government (from 1985 to 1995 and then from 2002 to 2005). However, in Portugal, as in many constitutions all over the world, the marks of the contexts in which constitutions were once promulgated are still clearly visible today.

---

[13] Paulo Pinto Mascarenhas, "MexernaConstituiçãorapidamente e emforça", Jornal I, April 12, 2009. Available at: http://www.ionline.pt/conteudo/54873-passos-mexer-na-constituicao-rapidamente-e-emforca

Further studies could look at this surprising resilience. In Portugal, there are reasons to believe that litigation and judicial rulings, particularly from the Constitutional Court, have contributed to impose a "pragmatic" interpretation of the social rights in the Portuguese constitution. While their "minimal content" has been preserved, their application in concrete cases has been, like in other jurisdictions, characterized by standards of protection that are less strict than those applied to fundamental political and civil rights, weighing them against budgetary constraints and the (modest) capabilities of the Portuguese welfare state (Canotilho e Moreira 1991). To be sure, the imposition of this particular interpretation to the 1976 settlement can be seen as the result of the "contestation over rules" (Knight 1992) that followed, adapting those rules to the new balance of forces that developed as Portugal moved away from revolution while allowing the survival of constitutionalized social rights as slightly less "operative" and more "declaratory" than many had envisaged. At the same time, however, it is also clear that social rights – such as the right to education, health, and work – have remained powerful focal points of social and political mobilization for unions, student movements, and left-wing parties, and may even have contributed to shape public preferences and views about the role of the state in Portugal. At the very least, the resilient constitutionalization of these rights – seen as shared social aspirations and guiding principles for social policy – seems to fit rather well with the notion that Portugal's revolutionary road to democracy left an enduring legacy in both elite and popular value systems (Fishman 2011). In sum, interests and ideas may both play important and complementary roles not only in explaining the original design of institutions, but also why and how they survive and adapt through time.

REFERENCES

Alho, A.A.C. 2008. *A Fábrica Leccionada. Aventuras dos Tecnocatólicos no Ministério das Corporações*. Profedições.

Alvarez, M., Cheibub, J. A., Limongi, F. and Przeworski, A. 1996.Classifying Political Regimes.*Studies in Comparative International Development (SCID)* **31**(2): 3–36.

Barak-Erez, D. and A.M. Gross. 2007. *Exploring Social Rights: Between Theory and Practice*. Hart Publishing.

Barreto, J. 1994. Comunistas, católicos e os sindicatos sob Salazar. *Análise Social* **29**(125–126): 287–317.

Beetham, D. 2006. What Future for Economic and Social Rights? *Political Studies* **43**(1): 41–60.

Ben-Bassat, A. and M. Dahan. 2008. Social Rights in the Constitution and in Practice. *Journal of Comparative Economics* **36**(1): 103–119.

Benoit, K. 2004. Models of Electoral System Change.*Electoral Studies* **23**(3): 363–389.

Benoit, K. and J. W. Schiemann. 2001. Institutional Choice in New Democracies: Bargaining over Hungary's 1989 Electoral Law. *Journal of Theoretical Politics* **13**(2): 153–182.

Bermeo, N.G. 1986. *The Revolution within the Revolution: Workers' Control in Rural Portugal.* Princeton University Press.

Blume, L. and S. Voigt. 2006. The Economic Effects of Human Rights. *Kyklos* 60(4): 509–538.

Blyth, M. 1997. Any More Bright Ideas? The Ideational Turn of Comparative Political Economy. *Comparative Politics* 29(2): 229–250.

2004. Structures Do Not Come with an Instruction Sheet: Interests, Ideas, and Progress in Political Science. *Perspectives on Politics* 1(4): 695–706.

Boix, C. 1999. Setting the Rules of the Game: The Choice of Electoral Systems in Advanced Democracies.*American Political Science Review* 93(3): 609–624.

Buchanan, J. 1975. Comment (on Landes and Posner, 1975). *Journal of Law and Economics* 18 (3): 903–905.

Bruneau, T.C. and A. Macleod. 1986. *Politics in Contemporary Portugal: Parties and the Consolidation of Democracy.* L. Rienner Publishers.

Búrca, G., B. de Witte, and L. Ogertschnig. 2005. *Social Rights in Europe.* Oxford University Press.

Calo, Z. 2009. Catholic Social Thought, Political Liberalism, and the Idea of Human Rights. Available at SSRN: http://ssrn.com/abstract=1407072.

Campbell, J. L. 1998. Institutional Analysis and the Role of Ideas in Political Economy.*Theory and Society* 27(3): 377–409.

Canotilho, J.J.G. and V. Moreira. 1991. *Fundamentos da constituição.* Coimbra Editora.

Cardoso, J.L. and M.M. Rocha. 2003. Corporativismo e Estado-providência (1933–1962). *LerHistória* 45: 111–135.

Carneiro, F.S. 1979. *Uma constituição para os anos 80: contributopara um projecto de revisão.* Publicaç\ oes Dom Quixote.

Carozza, P.G. 2003. From Conquest to Constitutions: Retrieving a Latin American Tradition of the Idea of Human Rights. *Human Rights Quarterly* 25(2): 281–313.

Cheibub, J.A., J. Gandhi, and J.R. Vreeland. 2010. Democracy and Dictatorship Revisited. *Public Choice*: 1–35.

Craven, M.C.R. 1998.*The International Covenant on Economic, Social, and Cultural Rights.*Oxford University Press.

Cross, F.B. 2001. The Error of Positive Rights.*UCLA Law Review* 48: 857–924.

Cruz, M.B. 1980. *As origens da democracia cristã e o salazarismo.* Presença.

Damaška, M.R. 1986. *The Faces of Justice and State Authority.*Yale University Press.

De Vanssay, X., and Z.A. Spindler. 1994. Freedom and Growth: Do Constitutions Matter? *Public Choice* 78(3): 359–372.

Djankov, S., La Porta, R., Lopez-de-Silanes, F., Shleifer, A. 2002.*Courts: The Lex Mundi Project.* National Bureau of Economic Research.

Durán R. 2000.*Contención y transgresión: las movilizaciones sociales y el estado en lastransiciones Española y Portuguesa.* Centro de Estudios Políticos y Constitucionales.

Elkins, Z., T. Ginsburg, and J. Melton. 2009a. *The Endurance of National Constitutions.* Cambridge University Press.

2009b. Chronology of Constitutional Events, Version 1.0.*Comparative Constitutions Project.* Available at: http://www.comparativeconstitutionsproject.org/index.htm.

2010. Characteristics of National Constitutions, Version 1.0.*Comparative Constitutions Project.* Available at: http://www.comparativeconstitutionsproject.org/index.htm.

Elster, J. 1991. "Constitutionalism in Eastern Europe: An Introduction."*The University of Chicago Law Review* 58(2): 447–482.

1994. *The Impact of Constitutions on Economic Performance*. World Bank.

1995. Forces and Mechanisms in the Constitution-Making Process.*Duke Law Journal* **45** (2): 364–396.

1996. The Role of Institutional Interest in East European Constitution-Making. *East European Constitutional Review* **5**: 63–65.

1999. Reason, Interest and Passion in the East European Transitions.*Social Science Information* **38**(4): 499–519.

2000. Arguing and Bargaining in Two Constituent Assemblies. *University of Pennsylvania Journal of Constitutional Law* **2**(2): 345–421.

Elster, J., C. Offe, and U.K. Preuss. 1998. *Institutional Design in post-Communist Societies*. Cambridge University Press.

Esping-Andersen, G. 1985.*Politics against Markets: The Social Democratic Road to Power*. Princeton University Press.

Fabre, C. 2000. *Social Rights under the Constitution*.Oxford University Press.

Fernandes, T. 2006. *Nem ditadura, nem revolução: aAla Liberal e o Marcelismo, 1968–1974*. Dom Quixote.

Fishman, R. M. 2011. Democratic Practice After the Revolution: The Case of Portugal and Beyond. *Politics & Society* **39** (2): 233–267.

Fleiner, T. 2005. *Common Law and Continental Law: Two Legal Systems*. Working Paper, Institute of Federalism, Fribourg.

Forbath, W.E. 2000.Constitutional Welfare Rights: A History, Critique and Reconstruction. *Fordham Law Review* **69**: 1821–1891.

Frye, T. 1997. A Politics of Institutional Choice: Post-Communist Presidencies. *Comparative Political Studies* **30**(5): 523–552.

Geddes, B. 1995.A Comparative Perspective on the Leninist Legacy in Eastern Europe.*Comparative Political Studies* **28**(2): 239–274.

Ginsburg, T. 2003. *Judicial Review in New Democracies*.Cambridge University Press.

Ginsburg, T., Z. Elkins, and J. Blount. 2009. Does the Process of Constitution-Making Matter? *Annual Review of Law and Social Science* **5**(1): 201–223.

Glaeser, E. L. and A. Shleifer. 2002. Legal Origins. *Quarterly Journal of Economics* **117**(4): 1193–1229.

Graham, L.S. and D.L. Wheeler. 1983. *In Search of Modern Portugal: The Revolution and Its Consequences*. University of Wisconsin Press.

Gómez Fortes, B. 2009.*O controlo politico dos processos constituintes: os casos de Espanha e Portugal*. Imprensa de CiênciasSociais.

Guibentif, P. 1985. Génese da previdência social.Elementos sobre as origens da segurança social portuguesa e suas ligações com o corporativismo. *LerHistória* **5**: 27–58.

1997. Les transformations de l'appareil portugais de sécurité sociale. Working paper, EUI, Florence.

Hansen, F. and C.N. Silva. 2000. Transformation of the welfare states after World War 2: the cases of Portugal and Denmark. *Environment and Planning* **18**(6): 749–772.

Hay, C. 2006. Constructivist Institutionalism. In R.A.W. Rhodes, S.A. Binder, and B.A. Rockman (eds.), *The Oxford Handbook of Political Institutions*. Oxford University Press, 56–74.

Hespanha, A. M. 2004. *Guiando a mão invisível. Direitos, lei e Estado no liberalismo monárquico português*. Almedina.

Hilbink, L. 2009. The Constituted Nature of Constituents' Interests: Historical and Ideational Factors in Judicial Empowerment. *Political Research Quarterly* **62**(4): 781–797.

Hirschl, R. 2004. *Towards Juristocracy.*Harvard University Press.

Huber, E., C. Ragin, and J. D. Stephens. 1993. Social Democracy, Christian Democracy, Constitutional Structure, and the Welfare State. *American Journal of Sociology* 99(3): 711–749.

Huntington, S. P. 1991. *The Third Wave.*University of Oklahoma Press.

Jachtenfuchs, M., T. Diez, and S. Jung. 1998. Which Europe? Conflicting Models of a Legitimate European Political Order. *European Journal of International Relations* 4(4): 409–445.

Jillson, C.C., and C.L. Eubanks. 1984. The Political Structure of Constitution Making: The Federal Convention of 1787. *American Journal of Political Science* 28(3): 435–458.

Knight, J. 1992. *Institutions and Social Conflict.* Cambridge University Press.

1995. Models, Interpretations, and Theories: Constructing Explanations of Institutional Emergence and Change. In J. Knight and I. Sened (eds.), *Explaining Social Institutions.* University of Michigan Press, 95–119.

Korpi, W. 1989. Power, Politics, and State Autonomy in the Development of Social Citizenship: Social Rights during Sickness in Eighteen OECD Countries since 1930. *American Sociological Review* 54(3): 309–328.

La Porta, R., F. Lopez-de-Silanes, and A. Shleifer. 2008. The Economic Consequences of Legal Origins. *Journal of Economic Literature* 46(2): 285–332.

La Porta, R., Lopez-de Silanes, F., Shleifer, A., and Vishny, R. 1999. The Quality of Government. *Journal of Law, Economics, and Organization* 15(1): 222–279.

Lenski, G.E. 1966. *Power and Privilege: A Theory of Social Stratification.* The University of North Carolina Press.

Linz, J. 1981. Some Comparative Thoughts on the Transition to Democracy in Portugal and Spain. In J. B. Macedo and S. Serfaty (eds.),*Portugal since the Revolution: Economic and Political Perspectives.* Westview Press, 25–45.

Linz, J., and A.C. Stepan. 1996. *Problems of Democratic Transition and Consolidation.* Johns Hopkins University Press.

Macklem, P. 2006. "Social Rights in Canada."*SSRN eLibrary.* Available at: http://papers.ssrn. com/sol3/papers.cfm?abstract_id=894327.

Maddison, A. 2001. *The World Economy: A Millennial Perspective.* Organization for Economic Co-operation and Development.

Magalhães, P.C. 1999. The Politics of Judicial Reform in Eastern Europe. *Comparative Politics* 32(1): 43–62.

2003. The Limits to Judicialization: Legislative Politics and Constitutional Review in the Iberian Democracies. PhD Dissertation, Ohio State University.

Magalhães, P., C. Guarnieri, and Y. Kaminis. 2006. Democratic Consolidation, Judicial Reform, and the Judicialization of Politics in Southern Europe. In R. Gunther, P.N. Diamandouros, and D.A. Sotiropoulos (eds.), *Democracy and the State in the New Southern Europe.* Oxford University Press.

Mahoney, P.G. 2001. The Common Law and Economic Growth: Hayek Might Be Right. *The Journal of Legal Studies*30 (2): 503–525.

Mainwaring, S. 1992. Transitions to Democracy and Democratic Consolidation: Theoretical and Comparative Issues. In S. Mainwaring, G. O'Donnell, and J.S. Valenzuela (eds.),*Issues in Democratic Consolidation: The New South American Democracies in Comparative Perspective.* University of Notre Dame Press: 294–341.

Marshall, M.G, K. Jaggers, and T. R Gurr. 2005. *POLITY IV. Political Regime Characteristics and Transitions, 1800–2003.* Center for International Development and Conflict Management (CIDCM), University of Maryland, College Park.

Marshall, T.H. 1950. *Citizenship and Social Class and Other Essays.* Cambridge University Press.

Maxwell, K. 1987. *The Making of Portuguese Democracy.* Cambridge University Press.

Merryman, J. 1969. *The Civil Law Tradition.* Stanford University Press.

Miranda, J. 1978. *A constituição de 1976: formação, estrutura, princípios fundamentais.* Livraria Petrony.

1993. *Manual de DireitoConstitucional. Vol. 4: DireitosFundamentais.* Coimbra Editoral.

Neier, A. 2006. Social and Economic Rights: A Critique. *Human Rights Brief* **13**: 1–3.

Niemeyer, E.V. 1974. *Revolution at Querétaro: The Mexican Constitutional Convention of 1916–1917.* University of Texas Press.

Nozick, Robert. 1974. *Anarchy, State, and Utopia.* Basic Books.

Orloff, A. S. and T. Skocpol. 1984. Why Not Equal Protection? Explaining the Politics of Public Social Spending in Britain, 1900–1911, and the United States, 1880s–1920. *American Sociological Review* **49** (6):726–750.

Palacios, D. (2003)*O podercaiunarua: crise de estado e acções colectivas na revolução portuguesa: 1974–1975.* Imprensa de CiênciasSociais.

Pejovic, C. 2001. Civil Law and Common Law: Two Different Paths Leading to the Same Goal. *Victoria University Wellington Law Review* **32**: 817–841.

Pereira-Menaut, A.C. 1987. Against Positive Rights. *Valparaiso University Law Review* **22**: 359–383.

Pereira, V. 2009.Emigração e desenvolvimento da previdência social em Portugal. *Análise social* **44**(192): 471–510.

Pierson, P. 2000. Increasing Returns, Path Dependence, and the Study of Politics. *American Political Science Review* **94**(2): 251–267.

Pimentel, I.F. 2000. Aassistência social e familiar do Estado Novo nosanos 30 e 40. *Análise Social* **34**: 151–152.

Pinto, P.R. 2009. Housing and Citizenship: Building Social Rights in Twentieth-Century Portugal. *Contemporary European History* **18**(2): 199–215.

Preuss, U.K. 1995. Patterns of Constitutional Evolution and Change in Eastern Europe.In J.J. Hesse and N. Johnson (eds.), *Constitutional Policy and Change in Europe.* Oxford University Press.

Ramseyer, J.M. 1994. Puzzling (In)Dependence of Courts: A Comparative Approach. *The Journal of Legal Studies* **23**: 721–747.

Riley, J. 2001. Constitutional Democracy as a Two-Stage Game.In J. Ferejohn, J.N. Rakove, and J. Riley (eds.), *Constitutional Culture and Democratic Rule.* Cambridge University Press, 147–169.

Rittich, K. 2007. Social Rights and Social Policy: Transformations on the International Landscape. In D. Barak-Erez and A. M. Gross (eds.), *Exploring Social Rights: Between Theory and Practice.* Hart Publishing, 107–134.

Ruggie, J. G. 1982. International Regimes, Transactions, and Change: Embedded Liberalism in the Postwar Economic Order. *International Organization* **36**(2): 379–415.

Sadurski, W. 2009. *Constitutional Socio-Economic Rights: Lessons from Central Europe.* The Foundation for Law, Justice and Society.

Sager, L.G. 1993. Justice in Plain Clothes: Reflections on the Thinness of Constitutional Law. *Northwestern University Law Review* 88(1):410–487.

Scheppele, K.L. 2003. A Realpolitik Defense of Social Rights. *Texas Law Review* 82: 1921.

Schmidt, V.A. 2008. Discursive Institutionalism: The Explanatory Power of Ideas and Discourse. *Annual Review of Political Science* 11: 303–326.

Schneiberg, M., and E.S. Clemens. 2006. The Typical Tools for the Job: Research Strategies in Institutional Analysis. *Sociological Theory* 24(3):95–227.

Share, D. 1987. Transitions to Democracy and Transition through Transaction. *Comparative Political Studies* 19(4): 525–548.

Shugart, M.S., and J.M. Carey. 1992. *Presidents and Assemblies*. Cambridge University Press.

Simões, J. 2004. *Retrato politico da saúde. Dependência do percurso e inovação em saúde. Da ideologia ao desempenho*. Almedina.

Sunstein, C. 1993. Against Positive Rights. *East European Constitutional Review* 2: 35–37.

Teodoro, A. 2001. *A construção política da educação.Estado, mudança social e as políticas educativas sociais*. Afrontamento.

Ticchi, D. and A. Vindigni. 2010. Endogenous Constitutions. *The Economic Journal* 120(543): 1–39.

Tushnet, M.V. 2008. *Weak Courts, Strong Rights*. Princeton University Press.

Van Kersbergen, K. 1995. *Social Capitalism: A Study of Christian Democracy and the Welfare State*. London: Routledge.

Voigt, S. 1999. *Explaining Constitutional Change.*E. Elgar.

Waylen, G. 2006. Constitutional Engineering: What Opportunities for the Enhancement of Gender Rights? *Third World Quarterly* 27(7): 1209–1221.

Whytock, C.A. 2007. Taking Causality Seriously in Comparative Constitutional Law: Insights from Comparative Politics and Comparative Political Economy.*Loyola of Los Angeles Law Review* 41: 629–682.

World Bank. 1994. *Proceedings of the World Bank Annual Conference on Development Economics*. International Bank for Reconstruction and Development.

17

Popular Constitution-Making

The Case of Iceland

Anne Meuwese

Never again can the world be told by the custodians of the old that the people cannot be relied upon to write the contract between citizens and government, and write it well.

From Richard Bater, "Hope from below: composing the commons in Iceland," December 1, 2011, www.opendemocracy.net, as shared by the Icelandic Constitutional Council (Stjórnlagaráð) on Facebook.

17.1 INTRODUCTION

In at least two senses the quote opening this chapter is illustrative of the recent Icelandic experiment with popular constitution-making through a process heavily adorned with social media utensils in the wake of the banking crisis. First of all, the wording "custodians of the old" points to the anti-establishment mood that surrounds large parts of the enterprise. At the basis of the Icelandic constitution-drafting enterprise was the idea that parliaments are not best placed to revise constitutions, given that their incumbent members have vested interests in the organizational structure of the state (Gylfason 2012: 11). Second, the fact that the quote was shared on Facebook by the Constitutional Council (CC), the "constitutional assembly," whose members were originally elected but formally appointed by the Parliament after the Supreme Court invalidated the elections, is rather telling. The enthusiastic embracing of social media by the CC means engaging more actively with media in

Comments on an earlier draft of this chapter by David Law, who acted as a discussant at the workshop on The Social and Political Foundations of Constitutions organized by the editors of this volume on December 8–9, 2011, in association with the Centre for Socio-Legal Studies of the University of Oxford and the Foundation for Law, Justice and Society, and other participants at this workshop, as well as by Thorvaldur Gylfason, are gratefully acknowledged. This chapter was finalized before the Icelandic elections of April 2013 when the faith of the constitutional draft was not yet clear.

general, at the expense of a professional distance that would have been more typical of such assemblies.

The experience has the ring of a "constitutional moment" (Ackerman 1998; Choudhry and Mount 2006) of a very contemporary kind. As the editors of a recent book on financial crises and constitutions have put it, "[a] constitutional moment emerges when a catastrophe begins and societal forces for change are mobilised of such intensity that the 'inner constitution' of the economy transforms itself under their pressure" (Kjaer et al. 2011: xvi). At the same time – also very much in line with the spirit of our times – Iceland provides an example of popular involvement in constitution-making; not the first,[1] but probably one of the most clear-cut. At almost every stage of the process the public was involved and often very actively so. Not only was the public involved in "selecting those who will draft or deliberate over aspects of the [constitution]" (Ginsburg et al. 2009: 208 citing Widner 2005: 7–8), but also in the process itself through a dialogue with the Constitutional Council (CC). Icelandic voters also had the opportunity to voice their stance on the draft in a referendum that was organized in the fall of 2012.

Given this combination of a very modern crisis and a real effort at popular involvement, the Icelandic constitution-writing process could serve as a dream test case for theories about constitutions and constitution-making in particular. In fact, those directly involved in the process have shown a degree of self-consciousness regarding the unique combination of characteristics of the enterprise.[2] Recently there has been a fair bit of attention in academic literature on the idea that constitution-making processes – and especially the extent and manner of popular involvement in them – matter (Elster 1995: 364; Elster 1997). Systematic analysis is warranted because "a central dimension on which constitution-making processes differ is the degree of public participation" (Ginsburg et al. 2009: 206). This literature can be divided into a strand that takes "popular involvement" as the independent variable ("the effects of popular involvement") and a strand that is more interested in "the determinants of popular involvement," thus taking popular involvement as the dependent variable.

The range of possible effects of participation of the people in constitution-making is large. Some have emphasized the need to better understand the relationship between the constitution-making process and its outcome ("content effects") (Ginsburg et al. 2009; Voigt 2009). It is still an open question to what extent constitution-making through direct input from the people produces "better" or at least different outcomes (Ginsburg et al. 2009). Others have pointed to public

---

[1] Other cases of popular involvement in constitution-making that are often mentioned are South Africa and Uganda. For other case studies on popular involvement in constitution-making, see Moehler 2006.

[2] Interview with a member of the Constitutional Council, August 2011.

support for the constitution as well as possible improvements in understanding of democratic principles by the citizens ("attitude effects"). Intuitively, we tend to believe that public participation in the constitution-making and legitimacy and acceptance of the constitution are positively correlated, but empirical evidence to support this is lacking as yet (Klein and Sajó 2012: 424). Moehler has put forward a hypothesis in contravention of this idea, namely that citizens who participated in the process were not more likely to support the produced constitution than citizens who did not (Moehler 2006). Perhaps there are trade-offs in play, for instance processes that generate learning could be less effective in achieving consensus. As Klein and Sajó have pointed out "even where participation has created constitutional enthusiasm this may not result in lasting or widespread acceptance of the constitution, especially where high expectations of empowerment do not materialize" (Klein and Sajó 2012: 424). Regardless of empirics, could it be that more and more popular involvement is increasingly seen as a precondition for legitimate constitution-writing (Claes 2011: 107), as it is "urged by scholars, governments, and international organizations" (Ginsburg et al. 2009: 205)? A further interesting question is how the interplay of popular involvement and these various effects impacts on the durability of the constitutional contract (Voigt 2009).

The questions raised in the preceding paragraph can only be answered through a longitudinal, comparative research design and/or in-depth ethnographic case studies. The current contribution includes neither. A further limitation is the fact that at the time of writing the new Icelandic constitution has not even been ratified yet, and given the amount of contention in the parliament, it is – despite the favorable outcome of the advisory referendum – uncertain what the experiment will lead to. As a single-country study, this contribution is aimed at clarifying the nature of the enterprise from the point of view of the Icelandic experience as a potential social-scientific case study. According to current theories, the two characteristics of the Icelandic experiment – the fact that constitution-making was triggered by a crisis and high degree of popular involvement – both point to a likelihood of a drafting process and constitution "less likely to be dominated by special interests" (Ginsburg et al. 2009: 210). In the text of the constitutional draft this could materialize in a tendency to delegate powers away from the legislature. This contribution analyzes whether this prediction holds in the Icelandic case by answering the following sets of questions. The chapter assesses the nature of the Icelandic experiment and the presumptions made in that regard: what triggered constitution-writing (Section 17.2) and is it indeed a case of "constitution-writing by the people" (Section 17.3)? Subsequently, I address the question of whether there are traces of diffusion or elimination of special interests in the result (Section 17.4). The methodology employed consists of content analysis supported by informal interactions with a few people directly involved in the process. A remarkable number of insiders in the constitution-writing process have spoken out – often in English – in interviews, videos, blogs, and academic papers.[3] In the interpretation of these materials, the fact that the main sources are also subjects with an active role or at least a stake in the process – both a challenge and a blessing for an outsider analyzing the events in Iceland – has been taken into account.

17.2 BUILDING UP TO A VERY MODERN "CONSTITUTIONAL MOMENT"

Stating that the recent process of writing a new Icelandic Constitution by a directly elected Constitutional Council that made extensive use of crowdsourcing is a "test case" risks reducing it to a gimmick. And regardless of some undeniable quirky elements in Icelandic politics,[4] the financial crisis of 2008 that prompted the constitution-making process was a dead-serious affair. The events had such a profound impact on Icelandic society that political space for the rethinking of the fundamentals of the Constitution – something that had proven impossible since the formal independence from Denmark in 1944 – emerged. Paradoxically, the systemic shocks of the recent past and heavily burdened public finances brought the country – with a population of a middle-sized city[5] – closer to a "clean slate" situation than most countries ever get. If it is obvious that the basic structures of the sociopolitical system do not work anymore, constitutions no longer seem like things to be complacent about. In fact, it is well-known that social and economic crises are among the main triggers of constitution-making (Elster 1995).[6]

The following subsections describe three factors that contributed to the recent decision to resort to "constitutional re-booting" (Claes 2011: 106): (1) the fact that most provisions in the current constitution essentially date from the days that Iceland was part of the Danish kingdom; (2) the special interest-driven and clientelistic institutional behavior; and (3) the financial crisis. The question of EU accession of Iceland as an "inside-outsider" (Árnason 2006: 27) is always looming in the background but does not seem to have been a self-standing factor in the constitutional debate.[7]

---

[3] See, e.g., Gudrun Petursdottir, 'Unique Approach to Revise the Icelandic Constitution', talk at TEDxReykjavik, see http://www.youtube.com/watch?v=AiO9oNbpN14&feature=relmfu. Gudrun was chairman of the Constitutional Committee. Gylfason 2011b reports that "[m]ore than 50 interviews with CAC members and others concerned were posted on YouTube and they have ... been viewed 5,000 times."

[4] One example is the BEST party of the comedian-turned-mayor of Reykjavik, which consists of celebrities mainly and is having a lot of success with its "anti-politics" approach.

[5] Iceland's population is 318,000 – significantly less than the population of Manchester and comparable to Leicester, to use British reference points. As a reference point for American readers: Iceland has more or less the same number of inhabitants as St. Louis, Missouri.

[6] Cf the U.S. Constitution of 1787 and the French Constitution of 1791.

[7] Personal communication with a CC member.

17.2.1 *The Danish Heritage*

Iceland's development from being part of the Danish kingdom to a sovereign state that was a recognized actor on the international stage took place over the course of a century and a half (Kristinsson 2000: 142; Árnason 2006). Between the middle of the nineteenth century and the middle of the twentieth century, independence from Demark was achieved incrementally. The Icelandic Constitution of 1874 was a limited one that was based on the Danish Constitution of 1849 (Árnason 2011: 343). Iceland was granted home rule in 1904 and – on the basis of a Union Act – sovereignty within the context of a monarchical union with Denmark in 1918. The Union Act contained a "sunset" clause stipulating that either state could request a revision in twenty-five years time and that, if agreement could not be reached, the monarchical Union would cease to exist. The new Icelandic Constitution of 1920 was more or less identical to the Danish Constitution. The Second World War caused a physical loss of contact between Iceland and far-away Denmark, which accelerated the separation process that was already underway. When the time came to revise the Union Act in 1943, it was clear that expiry was the logical option.

The Icelandic Parliament, the *Alþingi*, had already decided in 1941 that the priority would lie with smoothly paving the way for the new republic and not with changing the constitutional framework (Árnason 2011: 344). So in the Constitution of 1944 the Danish king was replaced by an Icelandic president and some minor technical changes needed for ending the monarchical Union with Denmark were made. In 1944, there was general agreement that Iceland should remain a neutral state (Árnason 2011: 345), making the presence of a NATO base on the island a controversial issue later on (Kristjánsson 2003: 414–415). Independence was more a reflection of political reality than a revolution, but politicians at the time promised a wholesale revision of the 1944 constitution no later than the spring of 1945 (Gylfason 2012: 10). This revision never took place.

Several commentators claim that the strategic manoeuvring in 1943–1944 laid the basis for a tradition of constitutional "laziness" that was to characterize Icelandic constitutional law for the next sixty-five years. Of course there have been calls for constitutional change and even concrete proposals,[8] but these were hardly ever followed through, exceptions being the shift from a bicameral to a unicameral system in 1991 and the 1995 addition of a human rights catalog with the aim of complying with the international human rights treaties Iceland ratified (Kristjánsson 2003: 400). Another exception is a change in the weight of the electoral constituencies

---

[8] In 1974, a constitutional committee presided over by Gunnar Thoroddsen was established. Almost ten years later, Thoroddsen, who had become prime minister in the meantime, proposed a constitutional revision bill that was shelved for lack of political agreement. Constitutional committees were occasionally formed, last in 2003, but without generating any results. See Árnason 2011: 346.

in 1959 (Árnason 2011: 345). Yet the political reluctance to update and adapt a constitution that was in essence still the old Danish one also meant that there was a lingering discontent among Icelandic citizens. The absence of a real constitutional debate in 1944 or in the six decades thereafter fostered a growing list of constitutional problems – such as the existence of ambiguities, the vague operationalization of the separation of powers, and the unclear position of the president – waiting to be solved (Kristjánsson 2003: 399–400). Also the fact that Iceland signed the EEA Treaty without changing the Constitution, according to one author, amounted to a denial that the constitutional positions of national institutions had changed and that the constitutional framework might need updating (Kristjánsson 2003: 415).

17.2.2 Dysfunctioning Institutions

The strategic choice not to rewrite the Constitution in 1944 and the ensuing complacency regarding the text of the Constitution did not mean that the Icelandic institutions remained "Danish." Icelandic parliamentary democracy – mixed with semi-presidential elements – has been strongly flavored by the prevailing tradition of patronage, which in turn was fueled by nostalgic ideas around a "rebirth" of the medieval Saga period (Miller 1990) after the formal separation from Denmark (Kristjánsson 2003: 400, 413; Árnason 2011: 345). The regions are a strong force in the *Alþingi*, with many representatives viewing their task as "negotiating the best deal" for their constituents. An additional reason for this parliamentary culture mentioned in the literature is that the political and administrative center in Reykjavik has always been relatively weak vis-a-vis the regions because the country's own political and administrative apparatus developed so late (Kristinsson 2000: 150). This meant that the political elite has always had a strong incentive to oppose constitutional change – the self-interest of safeguarding the overrepresentation of the regions in the *Alþingi* (Gylfason 2011a). Or, as Gylfason, a professor, blogger and member of the Constitutional Council, put it: "[t]he parties behaved as pressure groups of political insiders" (Gylfason 2011a).

Another feature of Icelandic parliamentary democracy, and possibly a sign of its weakening, is the emergence of corporatism, as testified by the 1990 corporatist agreement called The National Consensus and another one in 1998, which effectively bypassed the *Alþingi* (Kristjánsson 2003: 413). Finally, commentators cite an alleged culture of secrecy and nepotism as a factor that contributed to Iceland's constitutional moment. It is difficult to substantiate this other than through anecdotes. One such anecdote includes appointments to the judiciary of friends and family of the prime minister, although one more qualified applicant for the job – compared to the prime minister's son – was awarded damages (Gylfason 2011b). The country's anger at its political leaders also found an outlet through criminal-legal means rather than the constitutional route when the former prime minister, Geir Haarde, was prosecuted and subsequently cleared of all but one minor offense – failing to keep his ministers sufficiently informed during the 2008 financial crisis.[9]

The position of the other powerful figure on the part of the executive – the president – in the existing constitution had long been taken for granted but suddenly became instrumental in fueling the debate on constitutional change, stemming from an event in 2004 when the president refused to sign a bill regarding media ownership, oddly not citing his conscience but a lack of deference on the side of the parliament to public opinion (Ólafsson 2012). On paper, the Icelandic Constitution has an elegant and democratic solution for this situation: the statute in question still enters into force but must be put to a referendum within two months. However, in practice, the government chose to withdraw the bill, confirming some experts' beliefs that Iceland has a de facto presidential system (Gylfason 2012). This state of affairs made it clear to many Icelanders that a constitution with a clear position on the matter was long overdue. What that position should be, however – an explicit move to a presidential system or a clear choice for a parliamentary one with a ceremonial president – was contentious. The issue was muddled by the president's perceived closeness to the bankers held responsible for the 2008 crash (Ólafsson 2012). Icelanders with a conservative view on the constitution now found a reason to call for constitutional change after all in the conduct of the president. As Ólafsson puts it: "Since the only way to express real effective criticism of the president was by arguing for a constitutional change that would severely restrict his field of action or even abolish the presidency, criticism of the president appeared in the guise of a criticism of the constitution" (Ólafsson 2012: 4). It is clear that against the backdrop of the financial crisis, in which the government so clearly failed to deliver on policy outcome, the *perception* of governmental misconduct in individual cases strengthens the case for constitutional reform. As one commentator put it: "It is demonstrative of the *pathos*... afflicting the Icelandic political elites that not only the people but also the *politicians* no longer trusted themselves to adequately rewrite a Constitution that would attain popular legitimacy" (Bater 2011).

17.2.3 *The Financial Crisis of 2008*

In the early years of the new millennium, the Icelandic banking system boomed. Three privatized banks developed assets valued at ten times the country's GDP. Property prices rose starkly, the stock market multiplied nine times in value, and heavy borrowing, also by individuals, became the norm. When Iceland suffered a financial meltdown in 2008, triggered by the collapse of these banks, "[t]he crash

[9]   http://topics.nytimes.com/top/news/international/countriesandterritories/iceland/index.html.

was fast, hard and painful, worsened by the collapse of the krona as the state, unable to bail out the banks, refused to pay foreign creditors."[10] The financial cost to both domestic and foreign stakeholders is estimated to equal seven to ten times Iceland's GDP and the fiscal cost was estimated at 64 percent of Icelandic GDP by the IMF.

Institutions came to a standstill. One blogger has called writing a new constitution part of the post-crisis "housecleaning,"[11] another wrote that "Iceland decided to hit the reset button on their government."[12] A wave of protests followed, often referred to as "the revolution of the pots and pans" after the household goods people used to drum on as they took to the streets. They called for constitutional reform, a demand that the discredited political class was no longer in a position to ignore. The collapse of the banking sector and the ensuing crisis were thus a way to force the country out of the constitutional lethargy that the political elite had been cherishing for so many decades.

As part of evidence taken before the Political and Constitutional Reform Committee of the House of Commons, Professor Guðmundur Hálfdánarson was questioned, as the British committee members wanted to learn from Iceland in order to shape their own thoughts on codification of the UK Constitution. He was asked – among other things – whether he thought the initiative regarding constitutional change would have happened had it not been for the crisis. He answered:

> [N]o. There have been attempts to change the constitution for over 60 years without any results. There have been amendments, but this kind of general rewriting of the constitution has not happened, simply because the political parties could never agree on how to change it. There is an idea that constitutional change has to be made more or less with true consensus rather than through debate. Parliament could not come to such an agreement. I think that we needed the crisis and the Constitutional Council to break that impasse. (House of Commons 2011)

17.3 CONSTITUTION-WRITING BY THE PEOPLE?

In constitutional revision processes we can distinguish several phases of constitution-making: the initiative to revise the constitution, the choice for the constituent assembly and its working technique, the actual drafting, and the approval (Klein and Sajó 2012: 425; see also Widner 2007). In all of these stages there can be more or less

---

[10] Ian Birrell, 'Iceland brought in from the cold thanks to party of punks and pop stars', *The Guardian*, June 18 2011.

[11] Blogpost from October 11, 2011 in reaction to Gylfason 2011a on http://www.nakedcapitalism.com/2011/10/iceland-from-crisis-to-constitution.html.

[12] Jason Hibbets, 'Crowdsourced Icelandic constitution submitted to parliament', August 3, 2011, http://opensource.com/government/11/8/crowdsourced-icelandic-constitution-submitted-parliament.

popular involvement. Also, for each stage there is a question to be asked regarding to what extent the existing procedure was followed, possibly along with improvisational elements. In the "transition model," the rules about constitutional change from the "old" constitution are respected; in the "revolutionary model," they are ignored (Rosenfeld 2010b). Unsurprisingly, the current Icelandic Constitution does not say anything about popular involvement in constitution-making, so it is clear that if the bill is adopted, this will have happened at least to some extent through improvised procedures, which have even been characterized as "trial-and-error" (Claes 2011: 105). This section discusses the aforementioned phases and addresses the nature of the procedures used.

17.3.1 *The Launch*

In the aftermath of the 2008 crisis, the coalition government of the Social Democratic Alliance and the Independence Party collapsed under public pressure despite still holding a majority in Parliament (Árnason 2011: 342). The Social Democratic Alliance went on to form a minority government with the Left-Green Party, which was supported by the Progressive Party. The social-democrat Jóhanna Sigurðardóttir, a long-serving member of Parliament and well-known supporter of a complete overhaul of the Constitution, became prime minister. After the elections in early 2009, the two parties formed a new government, again headed by Sigurðardóttir. In the spring of 2009, a bill proposing a Constitutional Assembly (CA) that would initiate the constitutional revisions the *Alþingi* had not been able to accomplish for so long was issued. Apart from the two parties in government, the Progressive Party and the small Liberal Party supported the bill, which was strongly opposed, however, by the Independence Party (Árnason 2011: 347). This opposition was enough – at that moment – to block the bill. In Iceland, the constitution can be amended by simple majority in two votes, the second of which must take place after new general elections. However, constitutional practice dictates that unanimity or at least consensus has to be sought before constitutional change is enacted – the changes in the electoral system in 1959 being the only example of the majority pushing through constitutional amendments (Árnason 2011: 347). However, in November 2009, a similar bill was sent to Parliament and this time Sigurðardóttir and other proponents decided to give the idea some time to mature in the minds of the opponents (Árnason 2011: 348). Sure enough, on June 16, 2010, the *Alþingi* adopted a slightly amended version of the Act on a Constitutional Assembly. It specified that the Constitutional Assembly should take place between February 15, 2011 and April 15, 2011 (Árnason 2011: 343, 348). Also the MPs from the Independence Party had insisted that an appointed Constitutional Committee would prepare the deliberations of the Constitutional Assembly. Interestingly enough, the list of issues on which the Constitutional Assembly was mandated to make proposals was extended in the final text of the act (see the final three bullet points). The list read as follows:

- The foundation of the Icelandic constitution and its fundamental concepts;
- The organization of the legislative and executive branches and the limits of their powers;
- The role and position of the President of the Republic;
- The independence of the judiciary and the supervision of other holders of governmental powers;
- Provisions on elections and electoral districts;
- Public participation in the democratic process, including the timing and organization of a referendum, including a referendum on a legislative bill for a constitutional act;
- Transfer of sovereign powers to international organizations and the conduct of foreign affairs; and
- Environmental matters, including the ownership and utilization of natural resources.[13]

17.3.2 Setting Up the "Constitutional Assembly"

The Constitutional Assembly as it was envisaged never came into existence. The process of setting up a constitutional assembly – which is described step by step in this subsection – did not happen without some serious obstacles, which in the eyes of some tainted the whole enterprise.

The first step was the formation of the Constitutional Committee that was to facilitate the process and – as the members were not only constitutional experts but also political party affiliates – represent the *Alþingi*. This Committee allegedly focused on "amending the constitution" rather than on "rewriting the constitution" (Olafsson 2012). In order to counterbalance the elitist nature of this body, a "National Forum" was convened by the Committee. The Forum consisted of about a thousand citizens – 0.3 percent of the entire population – drawn randomly from the national registry, although, as stipulated by the Act on a Constitutional Assembly, ensuring some degree of representation of different parts of the country and an equal division of gender (Árnason 2011: 348). Also, the sample was restricted to Icelandic residents with the right to vote for the CA. The group of about 950 citizens who turned up at the meeting on November 6, 2010 discussed – in conformity with its mandate – certain fundamental principles and focus points "as seen by the public" (Árnason

---

[13] See http://stjornlagarad.is/english/. I have used the translation from Árnason 2011, 347–348.

2011: 349). The main findings of the National Forum are available in English.[14] Two examples of constitutional ideas they asked the Constitutional Committee to pass on to the Constitutional Assembly were the principle of "one person, one vote" and the people's ownership rights to their natural resources. According to the Forum's website: "Participants at the National Forum placed strong emphasis on honesty and integrity, particularly in the public sector and among public officials. They wished to see ethics and morality become a more integral part of Icelandic society, via various channels such as introducing morality and ethics into education at an early age." The resolutions of the National Forum were explicitly taken into consideration by the later established Constitutional Council that did the actual drafting. Next to the National Forum there was also a "grassroots" movement called the National Assembly, a group of approximately 1,300 Icelanders who met regularly to debate on constitutional values.

As a next step, the Constitutional Committee organized a single-transferable-vote (STV) election in which the country would be a single electoral district on November 27, 2010. The 25 members of what was intended to be the Constitutional Assembly were elected from a pool of 522 candidates, approximately 30 percent of whom were women and 70 percent men.[15] The voting system was inspired by the Scottish system and entailed the possibility for each to list twenty-five candidates (Árnason 2011: 349). The limitations to stand for election were the same as the ones for parliamentary elections plus the requirements that candidates were not already elected members of the *Alþingi*. Furthermore, as candidates had to gather signatures to be allowed to appear on the ballot, they campaigned actively through social media and radio shows. Gylfason, a member of the Constitutional Council and an academic, reports that the election campaign for the Council was "exceptionally civilized, and quite different from parliamentary election campaigns" (Gylfason 2012: 13). This could well be partly attributable to the fact that the opposition parties – The Independence Party and the Progressive Party, who had been the main ruling parties until not long before – still opposed the enterprise and (selectively) boycotted the process (Ólafsson 2012). This meant that those who engaged in the process in the first place tended to view one another as "allies." It also implied that there was a large overlap between forces arguing in favor of revision of the constitution by popular involvement and those advocating far-reaching amendments to the constitution. Remarkable in Gylfason's account of the events is the low level of interference in the process from political parties, interest groups, or the media. The latter "did little to inform the electorate about the issues or the candidates who seemed to view one another as fellow advocates of a common cause rather

---

[14] See http://www.thjodfundur2010.is/english/.
[15] Some reports, including Árnason 2011, mention a number of 523.

than as competitors or opponents" (Gylfason 2011b). Already during the elections a large degree of overlap between the candidates' views, the recommendations of the National Forum, and public opinion appeared to exist (Gylfason 2011b). The Independence Party reportedly circulated a list with preferred candidates (not their own candidates) – an example of selective boycotting – but to little effect (Ólafsson 2012). Eighty-four thousand people voted in the elections, which amounts to 36 percent of the electorate. This was not a high turnout, but certainly not worryingly low either given the nature of the elections – it is not unthinkable that a large part of the Icelandic population could consider itself by and large satisfied with most conceivable sets of 25 people out of the 522 candidates. Among those finally elected were ten women and fifteen men.

At this point, however, the project experienced its first serious hiccup since the adoption of the Act. Three people, an unsuccessful candidate among them, filed a judicial complaint based on alleged procedural violations during the elections based on article 15 of the Act on a Constitutional Assembly (Árnason 2011: 349). In January 2011, the Supreme Court in a decision qualified as "extremely controversial" on the website of the Icelandic Constitutional Society[16] proceeded to invalidate the election results on several grounds (Árnason 2011: 350).[17] To begin with, polling booths has not been sufficiently closed and ballot papers had not been folded before being placed in ballot boxes. The more serious charges were that ballot papers had been numbered and barcoded, thus raising a question of traceability and that the counting of the votes had not taken place in public or in the presences of the candidates (Árnason 2011: 349–350). There was no suggestion in the judgment that irregularities had in fact taken place; it was rather a matter of clumsy adaptation of regular election procedures to a one-of-a-kind election. The competence of the Court to invalidate election results without proof that any serious wrongdoing occurred has been doubted by Icelandic legal experts (Axelsson 2011: 10, citing also Eiríkur Tómasson, now a Supreme Court Judge). The Court's judgment has also been criticized for being "not only poorly reasoned, but ... also materially wrong" (Axelsson 2011: 1), with some commentators positioning the Court in the camp of opponents to constitutional rewriting and viewing it as the defender of vested interests (Bater 2011; Gylfason 2012).

From the front of opponents to the constitution-writing endeavor, the court's decision was also accorded meaning beyond its strictly legal scope. According to one report, there was one charge put forward by the parties – not mentioned in

---

[16] See http://stjornarskrarfelagid.is/english/election-ruling/.

[17] Árnason refers to the original judgment in Icelandic, which can be found at: http://www.haestirettur. is/control/index?pid=1109. As is the case for many other important documents in the context of the rewriting of the Icelandic Constitution, the judgment is also available in English: http://stjornarskrar-felagid.is/wp-content/uploads/2011/07/Decision_of_the_Supreme_Court.pdf.

the judgment, however – that fourteen of the twenty-five seats in the CA were not supported by enough votes, which would mean that the CA lacked the authority to rewrite the Icelandic Constitution (Árnason 2011: 350). Although the Supreme Court did not pay any attention to this argument as such, some political actors – mainly from the Independence Party – argued that the Court's decision still had to be taken as an assertion that the CC lacked legitimacy. After the decision, the Independence Party argued that it was better to revert to "business as usual" by seeking broad support for some constitutional amendments in Parliament (Ólafsson 2012). However, after two months of deliberations, Parliament decided to forge ahead with the constitution-writing enterprise by appointing the twenty-five elected candidates to what then became the Constitutional *Council*, or *Stjórnlagaráð*.[18] The cost of organizing a new election – the first one reportedly cost more than US$1.5 million (Axelsson 2011), a considerable sum for a small country – undoubtedly played a role in this decision. One person refused the appointment and was replaced by the next person on the list of election results (Árnason 2011: 350). As part of the same parliamentary resolution, the CC was given three months, later extended to four, to produce a constitutional bill. The parliamentary resolution about the Constitutional Council confirmed the list of issues that were to be discussed (see the aforementioned bullet list) and added that the Council would be allowed to decide to discuss more topics than those listed.

To what extent was the CC representative of "the people?" Although among the elected there were quite a few members from professions that may be expected to be represented, such as law, political science, and journalism, the members' backgrounds varied. The elected were by and large already public figures to some extent, who were, however, according to one commentator, likely chosen for nonpartisan reasons (Bater 2011). To be more precise, they included "not only doctors, lawyers, priests, and professors, but also company board members, a farmer, a fighter for the rights of handicapped persons, mathematicians, media people, erstwhile members of parliament, a nurse, a philosopher, poets and artists, political scientists, a theatre director, and a union leader – a good cross section of society" (Gylfason 2011b).

17.3.3 *The Drafting by the Constitutional Council*

The CC, which was formally given an advisory role, set to work on April 6, 2011, a couple of months later than originally intended in the Act on a Constitutional Assembly, to write a new Constitution from scratch. The 700-page background report the Constitutional Committee had prepared was an important source for the CC, as were the recommendations by the National Forum. The members of the

---

[18] Resolution of March 24, 2011.

Council were expected to work full time and received the same salaries as members of Parliament. The CC was also in charge of establishing its own procedures and organizing its own governance. A chair was elected and three working groups were formed. The Council intended to open up the drafting process for members of the public and believes it succeeded in doing so, judging from the statement on its own website that "[t]he idea that the public had their saying in the revision of the constitution has … been preserved." In the remainder of this subsection, three interrelated mechanisms through which the CC has tried to make public involvement a reality – transparency, equal access, and technology – are being discussed.

First, the working method was designed to enable meaningful processing of comments from the public. The CC posted new proposals for constitutional provisions in batches on its website. Revised versions of these, in which feedback from the public and from experts had been taken into account, tended to be published two or three weeks later. Toward the end of the CC's term, the document as a whole, including proposals for changes, was debated, followed by an article-by-article vote. Gylfason reports that at the very end, each article was approved by an overwhelming majority and that the bill as a whole was passed unanimously (Gylfason 2011b). Ólafsson, however, emphasizes that the unanimity among CC members was born out of a perceived need to appear as a united front in the face of expected political resistance (Ólafsson 2012). In a move characteristic of the informality of the whole process, the members of the Council declared themselves ready to re-deliberate in case new ideas arose in the run-up to a possible referendum.[19] The phone numbers and email addresses of CC members were even made public (Bater 2011), and CC members did in fact answer letters and phone calls (Gylfason 2012). The processing of the comments as such appears to have taken care of in a rather ad hoc fashion. One news article quoted CC member Erikur Bergmann calling the ploughing through the public's comments "completely messy" while adding that "your average legislation in your average parliament in your average country [is] messy as well."[20] One downside of the emphasis on actual processing of each individual comment is that the Council could be reproached for not always having its methodology clear (Ólafsson 2012). Also, it seems that there could have been a bit more attention given to the best internal structure. According to one report, the working group format was misused at times, in the sense that CC members sometimes betrayed the consensus they were supposed to have reached in the working groups through deliberation, by strategically reopening a point in the plenary sessions (Ólafsson 2012).

[19] *See* http://stjornlagarad.is/english/.
[20] Agnes Valdimarsdottir (AFP), 'Icelanders hand in draft of world's first 'web' constitution', July 29, 2011.

Second, the CC was keen to depart "from standard operating procedure in parliamentary work" and guarantee "equal access" by "not invit[ing] representatives of interest organisations to special meetings" (Gylfason 2011b). Not only did the Council consider it "undesirable" to work with any stakeholder group on a privileged basis; it also considered any attempt to win political support for its proposals to be outside of its mandate (Ólafsson 2012). Within the CC, "consensus was quickly reached about not initiating any contact with the parliament, making it clear to parliamentarians that they would have to approach the CC in exactly the same way as other citizens, as individuals" (Ólafsson 2012). The importance of equal access in the eyes of many CC members is also apparent in the decision to hold general meetings – apart from working group meetings, which were in principle closed – in which all members of the Constitutional Council met and to which the public was invited "while there [was] enough room." A visit to the CC's premises during their last meeting in July 2011 taught, however, that the seats intended for the public were almost empty. This, however, may have had something to do with the popularity of the live streaming of the deliberations on the Internet.[21] Gylfason reports a regular audience of 150–450 viewers for the broadcasts of the open council meetings, which took place every Thursday (Gylfason 2011b).

One concrete example of how the CC focused on content and dialogue rather than on mandate and competence is its attitude toward the Constitutional Analysis Support Team (CAST), a "semi-formal collective of individuals sharing an interest in the Constitution process," (Bater 2011) which was established in January 2011 "in order to undertake analysis of the Constitution as it was drafted" (Bater 2011). CAST members contacted the CC, and as a result many members of the CC cooperated with the CAST project. As the drafting process came closer to the final text of the bill, CAST arranged a Constitution "Stress Test" – "an event open to citizens with a willingness to contribute to testing and finding gaps in the Constitution." (Bater 2011) The results of the different textual analyses applied were tweeted in realtime. The summary report of the findings uploaded to CAST's website was allegedly "informally reviewed by many on the Constitutional Council" (Bater 2011).

Third, the most celebrated aspect of the Icelandic constitution-drafting process among advocates of "open government" worldwide is its extensive use of technology. As the blogosphere already proclaimed "a possible paradigm shift in governing,"[22] the question is whether the title of "the world's first crowdsourced constitution" is justified. The Constitutional Council did make extensive use of Web 2.0 features

---

[21] Personal communication by a staff member of the CC.

[22] The same article was posted on several blogs, but the original source appears to be http://singularityhub.com/2011/08/03/25-ordinary-citizens-write-icelands-new-constitution-with-help-from-social-media/.

and social media, such as Twitter,[23] Facebook,[24] YouTube, Flickr, as well as the good old-fashioned website mentioned earlier.[25] The use of these forums certainly went further than window-dressing or marketing; they were not just used for dispersing information, but also for encouraging the public actively to put forward suggestions for the new constitution. Comments on Facebook were responded to by staff, who would, for instance, politely thank someone for the suggestion to ban private banks in the new Constitution while adding that the CC would not be that specific. It appears that a large number of suggestions from the public were related to proposals for a different economic model for the country, as well as to issues such as Web neutrality, transparency, and access to the Internet.[26] People who were worried that their last chance to contribute had passed were reassured that the CC would keep working in an open manner until the decision on the final text has been made. One glimpse of how these comments were processed by the CC members is offered by Gylfason who pointed out that "not only what was said, but also the things left unsaid" were informative because "[i]f no one objected to the provisional articles posted on the website, then perhaps we were on the right track" (Gylfason 2011b).

Of course, technology alone does not guarantee popular participation. An infamous counterexample is the assertion by a Hungarian politician who was involved in the unusually fast and closed process of constitution-making in Hungary recently that the constitution was written on his iPad (Claes 2011: 103). But even ICT structures specifically designed to facilitate popular involvement are no guarantee. Iceland has a very high per capita number of Internet users, but still the issue of unequal access to the constitutional crowdsourcing process needs to be addressed. The unconnected citizens are likely to belong to more vulnerable groups, such as the elderly population or those living in very remote areas. The CC reports that the number of comments received totalled 3,600 in addition to some 370 formal suggestions from

---

[23] *See* http://twitter.com/!/stjornlagarad.

[24] The mayor of Reykjavik, the comedian Jon Gnarr, who had unexpected success with his anti-politics "BEST Party," also has a Facebook page in English: http://www.facebook.com/diary.of.a.mayor. The mayor regularly uses this page to give the inhabitants of Reykjavik – and the entire world, for that matter – some food for thought, such as through quotes (e.g.,"'Too much capitalism does not mean too many capitalists, but too few capitalists.' –Chesterton"), open questions (e.g., "Is nonprofit the answer ?") or one-liners (e.g., "We don't need leaders. What we need is more individual responsibility" or "The governments don't rule the world, Goldman-Sachs rules the world").

[25] This phenomenon should not be confused with "wiki-constitutionalism," a term that refers to the constant rewriting of constitutions in certain countries in South America. See Claes 2011: 100, who refers to Daniel Lansberg-Rodriguez, 'Wiki-constitutionalism. The strange phenomenon that's destroying Latin America', *The New Republican*, May 25, 2010. Claes observes that the term "wiki-constitutionalism" is confusing here because it implies broad participation through an open-source infrastructure, which is in fact *not* a feature of the processes wiki-constitutionalism is referring to.

[26] Agnes Valdimarsdottir (AFP), 'Icelanders hand in draft of world's first 'web' constitution', July 29, 2011, quoting committee member Silja Omarsdottir.

citizens that the three committees of the CC discussed and answered. CC members also answered letters and phone calls, but this cannot solve the problem that those without Internet access are not able to keep up with the state of play of the drafting process. Particularly in countries where limited access to the Internet is more widespread, this should be kept in mind when experimenting with constitutional crowdsourcing, as has happened through private initiatives during some of the constitutional revision processes that resulted from the Arab Spring.[27]

A side effect of the extensive use of technology in the constitution-writing process was that anyone, and not just Icelandic citizens, could join the debate. Involvement from abroad – whether to comment on or to learn from the Icelandic experience – was actively encouraged by the CC and other directly involved parties by communicating in English. Requests from various people for translations of Facebook updates in Icelandic were readily given. The very day the text of the constitutional bill was decided on, it was available in a rudimentary English translation through the Google Translate feature embedded in the *Stjórnlagaráð* website. An appeal was issued asking Icelanders fluent in English to help improve the translation so that the rest of the world would have access to an accurate version as soon as possible.

It could be – and in the heat of the campaign surrounding the constitutional bill may well have been – argued that the fact that many comments on the CC's website came from people from all over the world undermined the people's mandate for the new Constitution. The common understanding seems to be, however, that it enriched the process, especially because the rewriting of the Constitution – and of any constitution for that matter – was always going to be in part a borrowing exercise and because most involved were acutely aware of the CC's status as global pioneer. Iceland already had a tradition of borrowing policy solutions from other countries, particularly fellow Scandinavian ones. Constitutional solutions CC members looked at came from a great number of constitutions from all over the world, including – but certainly not primarily – the Finnish, Swedish, and German constitutions.[28] The image of the constitutional borrowing process depicted in the blogosphere was perhaps a shade too rosy, as the following quote illustrates: "With each passing meeting, the CC attempted to achieve greater proximity between the written document and the sentiments of the people, whilst constantly referring also to 'state-of-the-art' constitutional practices from around the world" (Bater 2011). There are several indications, however, that councillors were inspired not only by foreign constitutions but also by insights from academic literature. At least one member of the CC apparently took into account Persson and Tabellini's finding that "corruption is more prevalent

[27] Claes 2011: 103, n. 22. She mentions http://www.reforme.ma for Morocco and http://www.wathiqah.com for Egypt; the latter was promoted by presidential candidate ElBaradei.
[28] Personal communication by a CC member.

in countries with small electoral districts and party slates than in countries with large electoral districts where voters have an opportunity to elect individual candidates" (Gylfason 2011a, referring to Persson and Tabellini 2005: chapter 7).

17.3.4 *From Bill to Enactment?*

The unanimous approval of the bill by the CC occurred after a last-ditch effort to remove contentious issues. According to Ólafsson, "[m]ost members thought that unity would under any circumstances be a major strength of the Council, making it all the more difficult for opposed political forces, the parliament or the government to dismiss or belittle its results" (Ólafsson 2012). Because the CC was focused on preventing privileged access to its drafting process, it did not cooperate with the parliament or political parties. Ólafsson adds that this is the main reason for a relatively cold reception in parliament when the constitutional bill was sent to the *Alþingi* on July 29, 2011 (Ólafsson 2012). The following has been reported on the atmosphere: "According to one CC member, when the [draft constitution] was submitted to the Speaker of the Parliament as the law required, the ceremony was short and in many ways embarrassing since no one knew exactly what was supposed to happen next" (Ólafsson 2012). A week later explanatory notes, reporting on the discussion within and outside of the Council, were also handed over. Originally it was on course to be debated in Parliament and put to the vote for ratification by October 1, 2011. However, in the course of the rewriting process, CC members developed a conviction that a referendum was the only appropriate way to seal the process. The final constitutional draft text assumes that one will be held. Gylfason reports that according to a poll held in late 2011, 75 percent of voters want a referendum on the constitutional bill (Gylfason 2012). The prime minister – a great proponent of the rewriting by popular involvement – declared that the bill must be put to a referendum that would take place at the same time as the presidential election of mid-2012 with extensive discussion in the *Alþingi* with active involvement of the – now formally dismantled – Constitutional Council beforehand.[29] The president, however, declared that the referendum must take place *before* the presidential election because the bill proposes changes to the role of the president. Neither of them got their way, as the matter of a referendum proved to be a difficult one to swallow for the *Alþingi*. The reluctance to put the constitutional bill to a popular vote is directly related to the fact that there are political forces opposing the bill, at least in part because of the inclusion of national ownership rights to natural resources

---

[29] The website now states: "The Constitutional Council has completed its task, handed the parliament (Althing) the proposal for a new constitution and closed its office. If any further information is needed please send email to: skrifstofa@stjornlagarad.is."

(Gylfason 2011b). Those who most strongly opposed the referendum were MPs from the opposition's Independence Party and the Progressive Party, who reasoned that substantial debate about the draft had not taken place and that solidarity on how to proceed was lacking.[30] The debate appears to have been characterized by celebratory declarations of the historic nature of events on the side of proponents of the draft and a dismissive tone on the part of the opponents, with one MP of the Independence Party allegedly calling the draft a "bad idea" and stating that "the whole affair had gone from one mess-up to the next."[31] In March 2012, a four-day meeting was held at the instigation of the *Alþingi* where some variations to the text of certain provisions were approved by some twenty of the CC members who were present. Only in May 2012 did the *Alþingi* pass a compromise decision with a 35–15 vote, stating that the changes to the constitution proposed by Iceland's Constitutional Council would be put to an advisory referendum. This means that the referendum took place only on October 20, 2012. The compromise lies in a slightly ambiguous formulation of the main question to be asked in the referendum: "Do you want the CC constitutional bill to be the basis of a parliamentary constitutional bill?" To the proponents of the bill it is clear that a reasonable interpretation of this means that once a majority votes "yes," the *Alþingi* may make only editorial or technical changes, if any.[32] Yet, in spite of the "yes" vote that followed, opponents may be tempted to emphasize the term "basis" in the question posed. For one might also argue that the fact that five further questions regarding specific provisions in the bill were put to voters indicates that the *Alþingi* is only consulting the people on specific issues.

The results of the referendum were affirmative across all six questions, but with varying percentages.[33]

- Do you wish the Constitution Council's proposals to form the basis of a new draft Constitution?
  Yes: 66.9% No: 33.1%
- In the new Constitution, do you want natural resources that are not privately owned to be declared national property?
  Yes: 82.9% No: 17.1%
- Would you like to see provisions in the new Constitution on an established (national) church in Iceland?
  Yes: 57.1% No: 42.9%

---

[30] *See* http://ruv.is.
[31] 'Referendum to Be Held on Icelandic Constitution', *Iceland Review Online*, May 25, 2012, http://www.icelandreview.com/icelandreview/daily_news/?cat_id=29314&ew_0_a_id=390328.
[32] Personal communication by a CC member.
[33] Ríkisútvarpið RUV (The Icelandic National Broadcasting Service), http://www.ruv.is/frett/lokatolur-i-thjodaratkvaedagreidslu.

- Would you like to see a provision in the new Constitution authorizing the election of particular individuals to the *Alþingi* more than is the case at present?

  Yes: 78.4% No: 21.6%
- Would you like to see a provision in the new Constitution giving equal weight to votes cast in all parts of the country?

  Yes: 66.5% No: 33.5%
- Would you like to see a provision in the new Constitution stating that a certain proportion of the electorate is able to demand that issues be put to a referendum?

  Yes: 73.3% No: 26.7%

Turnout was 48.7% for all 236,941 registered voters, with slightly higher percentages in the Reykjavik area. For all questions except the first one (less than 5%), blank votes amounted to more than 10% of total votes. The greatest majority in favor of the solution proposed by the CC (83%) was reported on the issue of national ownership of natural resources. The question regarding constitutional provisions on a national church – confusingly formulated given that the draft actually proposes to delegate the power to make these provisions to the legislator – collected the smallest majority: 57%. Finally it is noteworthy that on all questions the inhabitants of Reykjavik voted in favor of reform in higher number than Icelanders from outside Reykjavik. Still, for all but one question, a majority of voters from all electoral districts voted "yes." The exception was – unsurprisingly – the fifth question regarding a more proportionate distribution of voting weights across the country. This reform would likely see the populous capital be better represented in the *Alþingi*.

By April 2013, in the wake of new parliamentary elections, the bill still had not been put to a vote in the *Alþingi*. The current procedure for constitutional amendments is twofold approval by parliament, with an election between the two votes. Because the Independence Party, which has been against both the process and substance of the constitutional rewriting throughout, is expected to win the elections, the bill would not have had much chance to pass, even if it had been tabled in first reading. An added complication is that the *Alþingi* did pass an amendment of the constitutional provisions regulating constitutional changes in first reading. If this amendment is adopted in second reading, from then onward it will be possible to change the constitution in one reading, provided there is a two-thirds majority in parliament and more than 40 percent of all registered voters approve the change in a referendum. Whether the newly elected *Alþingi* will take action to pass constitutional changes, either on a small scale with regard to the amendment procedure or in a more fundamental way, on the basis of the draft prepared by the CC, remains to be seen.[34]

17.4 THE CONTENT OF THE CONSTITUTIONAL BILL

As mentioned earlier, the proposal made by the Constitutional Council did not simply amend the old constitution; it entailed a completely new text. The constitutional bill comprises 114 articles divided into 9 chapters. In much of the discourse in the run-up to the rewriting, "minimizing corruption" was an important goal. Do we see any textual result in that regard? And is there anything in the constitutional draft to suggest that a drafting body such as the CC is prone to introduce mechanisms to disperse special interests? After all, avoiding the problem of "institutional self-dealing" (Ginsburg et al. 2009) was an important motivation for organizing the constitution-writing process in the manner set out in Section 17.3. The current section briefly discusses some core elements of the draft: its preamble and structure as well as provisions regarding the presidency, the electoral system, open government, and national resource management.

17.4.1 *Preamble and Structure*

The preamble to the bill starts out as follows:

> We, the people of Iceland, wish to create a just society with equal opportunities for everyone. Our different origins enrich the whole, and together we are responsible for the heritage of the generations, the land and history, nature, language and culture.[35]
>
> In the English version there is a footnote after "everyone," clarifying that the literal translation is "where everyone has a seat at the same table." Interestingly this is exactly the principle the CC used when designing its procedures to ensure equal access for all to the deliberations (Gylfason 2012: 37)

The before-final version of the bill began with a fundamental rights section at the beginning of the text, whereas the final version simply replaces the current Article 1, which states that "Iceland is a Republic with a parliamentary government," with a slightly different but similar text, to which, according to the translator, no intended

---

[34] Bjarnason, B. 2013, 'Iceland's 'crowd-sourced' constitution is dead', March 29, 2013, http://studiotendra.com/2013/03/29/icelands-crowd-sourced-constitution-is-dead/; Gylfason, Th. 2013. 'Putsch: Iceland's crowd-sourced constitution killed by parliament', March 30, 2013 http://www.verfassungsblog.de/de/putsch-icelands-crowd-sourced-constitution-killed-by-parliament/#.UWembTPn-M8

[35] I have used the independent translation from http://stjornarskrarfelagid.is/english/constitutional-bill/.

change of meaning should be attributed. The fundamental rights section now starts from Article 6.

17.4.2 *The Presidency*

The contention surrounding the role and powers of the president has already been mentioned in Section 17.2 as a driving force in triggering plans for constitutional change. If we look at the final textual proposal, the extent to which the CC intended to shift the semi-presidential nature of the Icelandic system toward parliamentary democracy is open for debate. Although Article 1 states – as does the current Constitution – that Iceland is a parliamentary democracy, the new draft probably does not change enough to get rid of the categorization as a "semi-presidential" system (Elkins et al. 2012). The power of the president is further curtailed by making some details of the procedure after a presidential veto more explicit but remains "non-trivial" (Elkins et al. 2012). Whereas during the 2004 events regarding the media law it was unclear whether it was constitutional to withdraw the bill instead of putting it to a referendum, the *Alþingi* has now explicitly been given the competence to do so in Article 60. The president has even been given a slightly larger role in appointing high officials. This, in combination with stronger justification demands, the establishment of a civil service commission, and a role for the *Alþingi* in case of a presidential veto (Article 96), is seen by some as an attempt to curb the powers of ministers in this regard, and thus limit "appointment corruption" (Gylfason 2012: 27).

17.4.3 *The Electoral System*

One of the more radical changes in the bill concerns changes to the electoral system. Iceland has a district system that allows parties to keep "safe seats" with relatively few votes behind them in lightly populated areas. The system has caused a disproportionate representation of one-third of the Icelandic population living outside Reykjavik, which some partially blame for the events leading up to the crash (Gylfason 2012). The issue of representation of peripheral parts of the country – ironically also raised in relation to the composition of the CC itself – is not solved through a bicameral system in Iceland and the new bill does not propose to change that. It opts rather firmly for the principle of "one person one vote" as the starting point for organizing the electoral system, without completely abandoning the district system. In an attempt to keep the Icelandic tradition of voting for parties rather than individuals, the CC arrived at the following intricate provision:

> The Althing shall be composed of sixty-three Members, nationally elected by secret ballot for a term of four years. The votes of voters everywhere in the country

shall have equal weight. The country may be divided into electoral districts. They shall be eight at the most. Associations of candidates shall put forward slates, either district slates or national slates or both. Candidates may run simultaneously on a national slate and a single district slate of the same association. A voter selects individual candidates from slates in his electoral district or from nationwide slates or both. A voter is also permitted instead to mark a single district slate or a single nationwide slate, in which case the voter will be understood to have selected all the candidates on the slate equally. It is permitted to provide by law that the selection should be limited to the district slate or nationwide slate of the same association. Parliamentary seats shall be allocated to associations of candidates so that the number of Members representing each association is as close in proportion as possible to the total number of votes. The manner of allocating parliamentary seats to candidates based on their strength of vote shall be provided for by law. It is permitted to provide by law that a specified number of parliamentary seats should be tied to individual electoral districts, up to a maximum total of thirty. The number of voters on the electoral register behind each tied seat shall not be lower than the average for all sixty-three seats. The means of promoting as equal a proportion of men and women in the Althing shall be provided for in legislation on elections. Provisions of law relating to electoral district boundaries, the methods of allocating parliamentary seats and rules on candidature can be amended only by a two-thirds majority of the Althing. Amendments of this kind may not be made when there are less than six months until the next election and their entry into force shall be postponed if an election is called within six months from their confirmation.

17.4.4 *Open Government*

Perhaps unsurprisingly, open government is a big theme in the bill. One of the most extensive provisions is Article 15 on Freedom of Information, the core of which reads:

> Information and documents in the possession of the government shall be available without evasion and the law shall ensure public access to all documents collected or procured by public entities. A list of all cases and documents in public custody, their origin and content shall be available to all.

This provision certainly contains one of the more radical formulations of the right to obtain information from government worldwide ("without evasion" even translated as "without exception" in an earlier English translation). This is the case even to the extent that one wonders if the provision, if it enters into force, will not turn out to be of a symbolic nature, an inherent risk for freedom-of-information provisions. The effectuation of the right depends to a significant extent on the mechanisms and statutory provisions put in place as well as the judicial enforcement of these provisions.

17.4.5 *Natural Resource Management*

Another much discussed article is Article 34 on Natural Resources:

> Iceland's natural resources which are not in private ownership are the common
> and perpetual property of the nation. No one may acquire the natural resources or
> their attached rights for ownership or permanent use, and they may never be sold
> or mortgaged. Resources under national ownership include resources such as har-
> vestable fish stocks, other resources of the sea and sea bed within Icelandic jurisdic-
> tion and sources of water rights and power development rights, geothermal energy
> and mining rights. National ownership of resources below a certain depth from the
> surface of the earth may be provided for by law. The utilization of the resources
> shall be guided by sustainable development and the public interest. Government
> authorities, together with those who utilize the resources, are responsible for their
> protection. On the basis of law, government authorities may grant permits for the
> use or utilization of resources or other limited public goods against full consid-
> eration and for a reasonable period of time. Such permits shall be granted on a
> non-discriminatory basis and shall never entail ownership or irrevocable control of
> the resources.

This provision is especially salient in the context of the recent story that appeared
in the media about a Chinese businessman who had offered close to US$9 million
to buy 120 square miles of Icelandic territory in order to build a holiday resort but
who was turned down.[36] The innovative provision was also spurred by the alleged
attempts by some bankers and foreign companies to exploit and perhaps even
appropriate typical Icelandic energy production sources such as hot water springs
(Ólafsson 2012). This kind of provision, therefore, can be seen as a response to a very
contemporary danger. It is also a crusade against the perceived unfair – and even
corrupt – allocation of certain exploitation rights, such as fishing quotas (Gylfason
2012). Ólafsson points out that national ownership of natural resources is exactly the
kind of radical principle that is easy to adopt in an assembly such as the CC, which
is under constant – *social* not *political* pressure – to demonstrate its accountability
to the people.

17.5 CONCLUSIONS

It is clear that the Icelandic popular constitution-writing experiment has more to
offer to the world of social science than could be covered in this contribution. For
instance, it seems that Iceland could be interesting as an atypical case for those who

---

[36] *See*, e.g., Didi Kirsten Tatlow, 'Chinese Deal for Iceland Property Founders Over Distrust', September
21, 2011, http://www.nytimes.com/2011/09/22/world/asia/22iht-letter22.html?_r=1&ref=iceland.

expect forms of popular participation and oversight to be "scattered and usually rather anaemic" (Elkins et al. 2008: 206). In this contribution we have been interested in the questions of how to qualify the Icelandic constitution-writing process and whether the idea that public involvement will lead to constitutions that delegate powers away from the legislature hold in this case.

First, for qualification purposes, we may ask if this was constitution-making "by the rules" (Klein and Sajo 2012: 433)? The process can best be characterized as a compromise between "in compliance with existing amendment rules" and revolutionary. The *Alþingi* will still have to pass the constitutional bill at some point for it to become the new Icelandic Constitution, but all other elements of the process were "tailor-made." Second, and perhaps more importantly, does it qualify as "popular constitution-writing?" In this regard, too, the term "compromise" seems appropriate, here in the sense of a compromise between popular and parliamentary. The compromise consisted of letting the "popular track" exist in parallel to the "parliamentary track." This meant, among other things, that issues that should have been settled at the very beginning of the enterprise – such as whether or not to put the draft to referendum and, if so, under what conditions – were left up in the air only to threaten the success of the enterprise at the all-important final stage.

As Section 17.2 has set out, the combination of one of the early economic and financial crises in Europe, the lingering discontent with traditional clientelistic politics, and the fact that constitutional revision was long overdue forged a "constitutional moment." Against this backdrop the ensuing process can be seen as a form of "collective therapy" (Claes 2011: 106, n. 33), albeit certainly not as a straightforward one. Compared to the financial and economic crisis that is currently holding Europe in its grip, the 2008–2009 Icelandic crisis seems relatively straightforward and "clean" in the sense that the country is already making a recovery, with the economy expected to grow by 2.5 percent in 2012 and 2013 because of flourishing tourism and fishing industries.[37] Does this mean Iceland's constitutional moment has passed too? It is too early to tell what the final outcome of the process in Iceland will be. However, "the spirit of popular constitution-making seems to be out of the bottle in Iceland" (Claes 2011: 106). And even if this bill does not go through in its current form, the experience is likely to have contributed to expectations about public involvement in constitutional change in many countries around the world.

As shown in Section 17.3, one characteristic feature of the Icelandic constitutional rewriting experience was that popular involvement did not occur in one particular phase only but throughout. One reason why the online dialogue seems to have worked quite well is that the CC did not just *use* social media; it *embraced*

---

[37] 'Iceland', *New York Times*, July 9, 2012, http://topics.nytimes.com/top/news/international/countriesandterritories/iceland/index.html.

the possibilities technology offered and put an emphasis on the "social." The CC's website and social media accounts did not just disperse "official" information; they generously flagged press coverage at home and abroad – see the quotation in the beginning of this chapter.

There are a lot of indications that the drafters tried to counter the special-interest domination that had characterized Icelandic (constitutional) politics for so long, as expected. One noticeable gap is the relative marginal nature of the changes proposed regarding the powers of the president, even though this is one of the issues that accelerated the whole initiative to rewrite the Constitution. This seems a rare substantive compromise in an otherwise fairly radical proposal. The radical nature and specificity of certain provisions, such as the one regarding national ownership of national resources, paired with an overly "anti-establishment" attitude, now appears to be jeopardizing the constitutional draft's chances of success.

REFERENCES

Ackerman, B. 1998. _We the People: Transformations._ Cambridge, MA: Harvard University Press.

Ackerman, B. and Fishkin, J. S. 2002. 'Deliberation Day', _Journal of Political Philosophy_ 10: 129–152.

Árnason, A. Th. 2006. 'The European Union Seen From the Top – the View of an Insider-Outsider', in Nergelius, J. (ed.). _Nordic and Other European Constitutional Traditions._ Leiden, Boston: Martinus Nijhoff Publishers, 27–42.

2011. 'A Review of the Icelandic Constitution – Popular Sovereignty or Political Confusion', _Tijdschrift voor Constitutioneel Recht_ (July): 342–351.

Axelsson, R. 2011. 'Comments on the Decision of the Supreme Court to Invalidate the Election to the Constitutional Assembly', unpublished manuscript, available at: http://stjornarskrarfelagid.is/wp-content/uploads/2011/07/Article_by_Reynir_Axelsson.pdf.

Baldacchino, G. and Milne, D. (eds.) 2000. _Lessons from the Political Economy of Small Islands: The Resourcefulness of Jurisdiction._ London: Macmillan.

Bater, Richard 2011. 'Hope from Below: Composing the Commons in Iceland', December 1, available at http://www.opendemocracynet.org.

Choudhry, S. and Mount, B. 2006. 'Ackerman's Higher Lawmaking in Comparative Constitutional Perspective: Constitutional Moments as Constitutional Failures?', BePress Working Paper 1544.

Claes, M. 2011. 'The Changing Rules of Constitutional Change', in _De Regels en het Spel, Opstellen over Recht, Filosofie, Literatuur en Geschiedenis aangeboden aan Tom Eijsbouts._ The Hague: T.M.C. Asser Press, 97–111.

Egeberg, M. 2003. 'The Nordic Countries and the EU: How European Integration Integrates and Disintegrates States Domestically', Working Paper.

Ekholdt Christensen, J. 2011. 'The Economic Crisis in Ireland, Iceland and Latvia', _Monetary Review_ (1st Quarter – Part 1): 107–120.

Elazar, D. 1985. 'Constitution-Making: The Pre-eminently Political Act', in Banting, Keith G. and Simeon, Richard (eds.), _Redesigning the State: The Politics of Constitutional Change in Industrial Nations._ Toronto: University of Toronto Press, 47–62.

Elkins Z., Ginsburg, T., and Blount J. 2008. 'Citizen as Founder: Participation in Constitution Design', *Temple Law Review*, 2: 361–382.

Elkins Z., Ginsburg, T., and Melton J. 2012. 'A *Review of Iceland's Draft Constitution*', The Comparative Constitutions Project, unpublished manuscript, October 14.

Elster J. 1995. 'Forces and Mechanisms in the Constitution-Making Process', *Duke Law Journal* 45: 364–396.

1997. 'Ways of Constitution-Making' in Hadenius, A. (ed.), *Democracy's Victory and Crisis.*Cambridge: Cambridge University Press, 123–142.

Ginsburg, T., Elkins, Z., and Blount, J. 2009. 'Does the Process of Constitution-Making Matter?', *Annual Review of Law and Social Science* 5: 201–223.

Gylfason, Th. 2011a. 'From Crisis to Constitution', blog post on voxeu.org, October 11.

2011b. 'Crowds and Constitutions', blog post on voxeu.org, October 11.

2012. 'From Collapse to Constitution: The Case of Iceland', CESifo Working Paper No. 3770, Category 2: Public Choice, March.

Helgadóttir, R. 2011. 'Constitutional Reform in Iceland', talk given in Bergen, September 15, 2011.

House of Commons. 2011. Corrected transcript of oral evidence taken before the Political and Constitutional Reform Committee, 'Mapping the Path to Codifying – or not Codifying – the UK's Constitution', Questions to Professor Guðmundur Hálfdánarson, July 14, HC 1178-ii.

Kjaer, P.F., Febbrajo, A., and Teubner, G. 2011. *The Financial Crisis: A Constitutional Perspective: The Dark Side of Functional Differentiation.*Oxford: Hart Publishing

Klein, C. and Sajó, A. 2012. 'Constitution-Making: Process and Substance', in Rosenfeld, M. and Sajó, A. (eds.), *Oxford Handbook of Comparative Constitutional Law*. Oxford: Oxford University Press, 419–441.

Kristinsson, G. H. 2000. 'From Home Rule to Sovereignty: The Case of Iceland' in Baldacchino, G. and Milne, D. (eds.), *Lessons from the Political Economy of Small Islands: The Resourcefulness of Jurisdiction*. London: Macmillan, 141–158.

Kristjánsson, S. 2003. 'Iceland: A Parliamentary Democracy with a Semi-Presidential Constitution', inStröm, K., Müller, W.C. and Bergman, T. (eds.), *Delegation and accountability in parliamentary democracies*. Oxford: Oxford University Press, 399–417.

Lane Scheppele, K. 2004. 'Constitutional Ethnography: An Introduction', *Law and Society Review* 38: 389–406.

Miller, William Ian 1990. *Bloodtaking and Peacemaking: Feud, Law, and Society in Saga Iceland*. Chicago: University of Chicago Press.

Moehler D. 2006. *Distrusting Democrats: Outcomes of Participatory Constitution-Making*. Ann Arbor: University of Michigan Press.

Ólafsson, J. 2012. 'An Experiment in Iceland: Crowdsourcing a Constitution?', Working Paper.

Persson, T. and Tabellini, G. 2005. *The Economic Effects of Constitutions.*Cambridge, MA: MIT Press.

Rosenfeld, M. 2010a. 'Putting the People Back in the Constitution: On Arab Popular Revolt and Other Acts of Defiance', *International Journal of Constitutional Law* 8: 685–689.

2010b. *The Identity of the Constitutional Subject.*New York: Routledge.

Teubner, G. 2011. 'A Constitutional Moment? The Logics of 'Hit the Bottom' in Kjaer, P.F., Febbrajo, A., and Teubner, G. (eds.),*The Financial Crisis: A Constitutional Perspective: The Dark Side of Functional Differentiation.*Oxford: Hart Publishing, 3–42.

Voigt S. 2009. 'The Consequences of Popular Participation in Constitutional Choice – toward a Comparative Analysis' in Van Aaken, A., List, C., and Luetge, C. (eds.), *Deliberation and Decision*. Aldershot: Ashgate, 199–229.

Widner, J. 2005. *Constitution Writing and Conflict Resolution*. Helsinki: United Nations University, World Institute for Development Economics Research.

Widner J. 2007. Proceedings 'Workshop on Constitution Building Processes', Princeton University, May 17–20. Princeton, NJ: Bobst Center for Peace Justice, Princeton University Interpeace Int. IDEA.

18

Romania's Transnational Constitution

A Tradition of Elite Learning and Self-Empowerment

Cristina E. Parau

18.1 INTRODUCTION

This chapter takes as its starting point a substantial modification of the constitutional diffusion theory outlined in this section. Its theorization features actors instead of states, as the latter conception is too abstract and remote from the actual causes and motives that bring about constitutional diffusion (Hirschl 2013). By inquiring into agency, it is hoped that the black box of one East European State – Romania – may be opened up in order to find out who the actors are who actually conceived and drafted the several constitutions Romania has had since the eighteenth century, and what motivated them.

In every instance nearly all the actors proved to be elites, corroborating those who claim that "the people" are in fact little involved in constitutional conjunctures (Galligan 2013). The conceiving and drafting of constitutions has always been the domain of social elites and of "political entrepreneurs" originating within this class who chose to involve themselves in public affairs. The latter have always been a minority within a minority, an elite stratum of the social and economic elite.

This elite has consistently been oriented transnationally. In the case of Romania, transnational influences on the drafting of constitutions can be traced a surprisingly long way back in history. The Romanian state owes its very existence to the Western great powers, who created it in 1858 in the aftermath of the Crimean War. Even

I would like to thank my interviewees, each one of whom gave their precious time to answer my questions; to the British Academy, which funded the Postdoctoral Fellowship during which most of the empirical data presented here was collected; the John Fell Fund (University of Oxford), which funded part of this research; and the Law Faculty (Oxford), which contributed supplementary funding; and to the Foundation for Law, Justice and Society for the support they gave toward the final stages of this research. Thanks are due also to Dr. Manuel Gutan from the law faculty in Sibiu (Romania) for procuring hard-to-find historical documents.

before then Romanian elites encountering Western ideals had imported the corresponding institutional models back to the motherland. Romania has historically absorbed more transnational inspiration and influence than it has diffused, and in this sense has been a "dependency." It follows that transnational influence on the genesis of constitutions is not a phenomenon characteristic of globalization and the contemporary age. Transnational diffusion is likely to have been a perennial factor in the struggle for constitutionalism in the case of nations like Romania that have always aspired to development and (Western) civilization.

Historically, transnationalism is manifest in the Romanian elite's custom of sending its children to the West to be educated, and this became the main channel for ideas about how Romania should be governed. What started as a gentlemen's hobby in the eighteenth century later became the professional *métier* of one elite stratum of a burgeoning middle class. Their heirs in the present day are an elite class of legal professionals who claim expertise beyond the capacity of "ordinary politicians" to understand. They perceive themselves and are perceived by some but not all others as constituting an "enlightened minority" (Elster 1995: 383). Since 1900 at the latest, this elite has dominated both the initiation and the process of constitution-making in Romania.

A focus on such actors enables understanding in greater depth the social and political mechanisms of transnational diffusion of constitutional thought (Goderis and Versteeg 2013). Of the mechanisms theorized herein, learning is the one most consistently in evidence throughout Romania's history; the Romanians have always been keen to learn from the West. This has occurred through reception of texts as well as through "socialization" *via* education (*cf.* Wendt 1994; Risse and Sikkink 1999). Socialization entails immersion in the social milieu of the peoples and nations to be learned from. It may lead to, or may be preceded by, learning from texts, but is likely to make a "deeper" impression than reception of texts alone.

Legally trained elites have been those most keen to learn lessons from the West about constitutionalism, but they constitute only a small subset of the broader social elite class. Since the later nineteenth century, however, Romanian legal professionals have become conscious of themselves as a ruling class within the ruling class, by learning from the West – a historical development that might have remained invisible as long as learning was theorized to be a mechanism between states as unitary actors in an international system. The modernizing Romanians have merely lagged behind their modernized Western counterparts; in England, for example, the legal profession was wielding essentially political authority as early as the seventeenth century and certainly by the eighteenth century (Corfield 1995). By the time the 1923 Constitution came to be drafted, Romania's legal elites were well aware of their identity as a professional community who could claim unique expertise in drafting constitutions.

In the Romanian case, too, the "soft coercion" and "acculturation" mechanisms have been in play, but these have had more of an impact on other elites. Even the highest political leaders, if they are not legally trained, and so "initiated" into the profession, are likelier to be imitating the West because they fear the repercussions of singularity or seek strategic goals, rather than because they have learned to identify with an exclusive club of uncommon expertise.

The literature theorizes, in terms of states, that the learning state's "closeness" to the learned-from state is one precondition for transnational learning, and shared cultural heritage is one kind of closeness (Rogers 2003). This certainly is exemplified by the case of Romania; Romanians have always believed themselves heirs of the Roman Empire speaking a language akin to French and Italian. And yet, "remoteness" has also played a role, and perhaps a bigger one. Romanians believe in the West's superiority both to themselves and to the non-Western nations under whose yoke they have long chafed. Subjection to the Ottoman Empire for most of four hundred years has stirred Romanians to draw closer to the West, whom they perceive to be morally as well as materially superior. They see in Western models the legacy of those who have never been dominated and abused by conquerors. The elite yearning to learn from the West has been driven less by a realized affinity than by a feeling of alienation from one's true home imposed by alien occupiers. A feeling of this nature bids fair to motivate learning far more potently than simple proximity.

Learning by transnational diffusion does not only happen from the bottom up, in the sense that a constitutionalizing people takes the initiative to learn from those who invented constitutionalism. Romania's experience shows that top-down learning or *tutelage* may be just as operative. With tutelage the "tutor" state or elite proactively takes steps to diffuse its ideas to its "ward" – a proceeding likeliest to succeed when the ward is predisposed to receive such tutelage. Convinced of the tutor's superiority, the ward may even have invited it.

Empirical evidence confirming this has been drawn from a nation that historically has been of marginal interest to the West. Yet the following exploration of critical junctures of constitutionalism in Romanian history may yield lessons for others investigating transnational constitutionalism in Eastern Europe and in other democratizing regions. After all, it is not just Romanians who look to the West for inspiration. Yet Western transnational influences in East Europe have always been greater than elsewhere; indeed, they have been overwhelming – particularly with regard to judiciary institutions, the case to be studied in this chapter.

The major "founding" episodes in Romania's history begin in the later eighteenth century. Some of them were more fundamental than others for the changes they wrought to the polity; accordingly, they have been treated in greater depth. Such was the Convention of Paris of 1858, which created the modern Romanian state and for at least a decade thereafter served as its de facto constitution; likewise the Constitution of 1991, crafted in the aftermath of almost half a century of communism.

Key terms deployed throughout the chapter call for definition. *Transnationalism* is defined by the author as a voluntary process of transboundary interaction whereby cultural, social, intellectual, and other influences cross over from one nation to another without being screened by a higher control or authorized by hierarchical command. Having acquired theoretical status in the constitutionalist and international relations literature, the concept of *norm entrepreneur* is useful here as importing some conceptual consistency between the theorization in this chapter and broader debates over domestic change under the influence of external norms and institutions (Keck and Sikkink 1998; Checkel 2012). The definition perhaps most familiar to constitutionalists is that of American legal scholar Cass Sunstein, who defines it as a "political actor who might be able to exploit … dissatisfaction with existing norms in order to bring about large-scale social change" (Sunstein 1996: 929). Finally, *legal professional elites*: in a sense all legal professionals are elites; however, the jurists drawn from this professional class to be involved in the process of constitution-drafting and revision of judiciary institutions constitute an elite within that elite. They have had access to power resources that most political actors lack. In Romania at least since the eighteenth century, they have held commanding positions in the state and, since the advent of mass media and of transnational networks in the twentieth century, have acquired privileged access to these resources, to supranational institutions, and perhaps to international finance.

18.2 AN ARISTOCRATIC OCCUPATION? CONSTITUTION-MAKING IN THE EIGHTEENTH CENTURY

Constitution-making in the Romanian context began in the age of Enlightenment. In the eighteenth century, the Romanian-speaking peoples were still divided between Wallachia and Moldavia, two suzerain principalities of the Imperial Ottomans, who had won control of them in the fourteenth century. They are coterminous with the modern Romanian state except for the addition of Transylvania and the loss of Bessarabia (nowadays called Moldova). The Porte assigned the governing of these principalities to the *Phanariotes*, a class of Greek merchants of Byzantine descent. Originating in the Phanar, their eponymous quarter of Constantinople, they came to predominate in the upper reaches of the imperial administration. They acceded to these offices from the seventeenth century onward, having become wealthy enough to buy them from the Sultanate. Many settled there and intermarried with the *boyars*, or indigenous landed gentry.

The Phanariotes were generally corrupt and used the principalities like satrapies. But as with all classes of people, some were more virtuous than others.[1] From this intellectual as well as political elite sprang the Enlightenment *philosophes* (thus

---

[1] Indeed many noblemen supported the French Revolution. The Marquis de La Fayette, the general in charge of the French Army in the American Revolutionary War, was a real believer in the American cause, pursuing an ideal that clashed with his putative class interest (Lane 2003).

norm entrepreneurs) who ventured drafting the very first constitutions on the Romanian territories, an endeavor they treated as a genteel hobby.

Constitution-making as an elite province was thus already in evidence by the 1700s; not a surprising state of affairs given that the Rumanophone populace of the time was nearly entirely illiterate. Being cosmopolitan and Western-educated, the Phanariotes were receptive to Western ideas about the separation of powers, judicial independence, and constitutionalism in general (Berceanu et al. 1984: 171). Foreign classical texts and Enlightenment jurists known to have influenced Phanariot thinking include Hugo Grotius (1583–1645) and Samuel von Pufendorf (1632–1694) and their works on natural law, which have been found in the former principalities in German, Latin, and French translations (Georgescu 1972: 62–71; Stanomir 2004: 34).

The English Revolution (1642–1651) just might have exerted a far-flung influence on the principalities, too, possibly through intermediaries such as Voltaire, who was himself an Anglophile. In his works he was constantly praising the English system of government and laws over France's *ancien régime* (Voltaire 1734, 1738). His Anglophilia would have followed his books into the principalities, an inference corroborated by the high esteem in which English law has always been held by Romanian legal elites, who consider it just as respectable and venerable as the Roman law on which Romania later based her legal system. Montesquieu, Voltaire, and other French luminaries of the eighteenth century were known by jurists in Moldavia, either in French or through translations that were incorporated into the Romanian Orthodox Church school curriculum, or through contact with Russians also taking inspiration from the French Enlightenment (Carra 1781: 196; Mihaila 1995; see also Stanomir 2004: 35).

The domestic policy of Austrian and Holy Roman Emperor Joseph II (1741–1790) also exerted an influence (Stanomir 2005: 19). Known collectively as "Josephinism," his policies were based on principles featuring not just nationalism (*viz.* a unitary state with centralized, efficient government institutions such as a professional judiciary) but also greater freedoms, such as freedom from censorship, toleration of minorities, economic liberalism, and security for peasants (Ingrao 2000: 198–202), many of which implicate modern concepts of rights and other checks on arbitrary power. Classical Josephinian texts written by French barrister Jean Denis, Comte Lanjuinais (1753–1827) and by the Austrian jurist Joseph von Sonnenfels (1732–1817), later professor of political science at the University of Vienna, have been found on the bookshelves of aristocratic families and ecclesiastical libraries in both principalities (Georgescu 1972: 64; Stanomir 2004: 34).

Romanian historians have surmised that these Western exemplars influenced the Phanariot Constantin Mavrocordat to attempt in 1741 to draft what is considered the first constitution for the principalities. Mavrocordat's openness to Western influence is attested by features in it reflecting the ideas of Montesquieu and Voltaire and by the fact that he published his constitution in the French magazine *Mercure de France*, one of the many foreign periodicals read by the domestic aristocratic elites of the time (Georgescu 1972: 62; Stanomir 2004: 34). Mavrocordat attempted to reform Romania's entrenched feudal legacy, wherein the lord of the manor was the final arbiter in all things, by enshrining the principle of "equality before law for all regardless of the social or material status of the defendants" (Berceanu et al. 1984: 28). This included reforms to the justice system mandating inter alia that magistrates deliver justice in the presence of the parties; that adjudication is a profession to be remunerated by the state; and that courts must follow codified procedures (Berceanu et al. 1984: 168–169).

Mavrocrodat was not the only one thinking in constitutionalist terms. Alexandru Ipsilanti, another Phanariot of the latter eighteenth century, decreed the establishment of civil law courts in the principalities and the codification of much of their law,[2] based in part on his *Syntagmation Nomikon*, a codification of Byzantine customary law. Romanian scholars have found certain of its provisions comparable to the English writ of habeas corpus (Stanomir 2004). In principle it sought to "limit the arbitrary powers of the 'executive' through its censuring by an embryonic judiciary power" – a long-lasting reform incorporated into later constitutions (Stanomir 2004: 29).

These signal instances indicate that the idea of constitutionalism and its main features were being handed down to the Phanariotes as a class, probably through textual reception more than socialization *en milieu*. "Enlightened" Phanariotes even came to identify with the Romanians, supporting their national cause in the nineteenth century, as in the 1848 Revolution, which attempted to unite the principalities into one state according to Josephinist ideology.

18.3 ASPIRING TO A MODERN CONSTITUTION: KOGĂLNICEANU'S CONSTITUTIONAL PROJECT OF 1848

Elite learning through socialization as well as through reception of texts in the West gained momentum from the 1830s onward, when the sons of the boyars and the rising middle class began to flock to the West – France and Germany especially – to be educated, and the transnational diffusion that had begun a century earlier accelerated. The new, "illuminated" elite held Britain's tradition of law and its "orderly" constitutional government in high esteem, but felt more affinity with the Latin heritage shared by Romania and France; it thus received the English influence through

---

[2] Prince of Wallachia from 1775 to 1782 and again from 1796 to 1797, and Prince of Moldavia from 1786 to 1788.

the medium of French *philosophes*. Moreover, the new elite admired France "as the champion of the rights of man, and by extension of oppressed nations" (Hitchins 1996: 4). The numbers of Romanian intellectuals abroad swelled after the failure of the 1848 Revolution; many took refuge in Paris. There they befriended leading French intellectuals and, even before their own political elite had accepted the idea, interested them in promoting the cause of unification of the two principalities (Isar 1991). It was to France, and nations inspired by her, that they looked for models once they undertook to modernize the two principalities and their institutions.

The first modern, liberal Constitution belonged to Mihail Kogălniceanu (1817–1891). One of the most prominent Romanian intellectuals of the nineteenth century, and perhaps the first true transnational norm entrepreneur of Romanian origin, Kogălniceanu made his mark on history as a statesman as well as a lawyer and historian (Hitchins 1994: 23). Educated first in Lorena, France, by Abbot Lhommé, professor of rhetoric and Latin who had fled the Reign of Terror, Kogălniceanu arrived in Berlin in 1835, where he was trained by professor of law Eduard Gans Gans (1797–1839), a former pupil and ardent follower of Hegel's natural law philosophy, and by Friedrich Carl von Savigny (1779–1861), one of the nineteenth-century's most influential jurists (Kogălniceanu 1891).

Kogălniceanu's Constitutional Project (*Proiectul de Constituţie*) was focused mainly on limiting and taming state power (Kogălniceanu 1848 [1998]). Published in the midst of the 1848 Revolution (a revolution of the intellectuals), it reflected manifold transnational influences (Hitchins 1996). The 1848 French Constitution was a major source, as much as 60 percent of Kogălniceanu's text being "faithfully copied" from it (Gutan 2011: 229). The Belgian Constitution of 1831, too, was an inspiration (Gutan 2011: 228). Both derived their spirit and letter from the 1791 French Constitution, itself modeled in part on the U.S. Constitution (Gutan 2011: 239).

The French and Belgian models, particularly, informed Kogălniceanu's design of the judiciary institutions: its hierarchy was to culminate in a Court of Cassation nominated by parliament with power to revise decisions of the lower courts as well as "decide conflicts between the administrative and the judiciary authorities over their respective competences" (Art. 71); juries, an institutional innovation for the principalities, were to deliberate in trials over political, criminal, and libel cases (Art. 67); justices of the peace were to be elected by the people (Art. 68); judges were to be appointed by the executive according to a special law on the organization of the judiciary (Art. 69); the executive was not to interfere in judicial decisions (Art. 72); and judges were to be appointed for life, removable only for cause after due process in a "solemn trial by jurors" (Art. 76) (Kogălniceanu 1848 [1998]; Gutan 2011).

Kogălniceanu, however, eschewed other typical features of constitutionalism destined to become hallmarks of later Romanian constitutions, and which were to alter profoundly the power relations between judiciary and political branches.

One such feature was a strict or "hermetic" separation of powers, as evidenced by Kogălniceanu's involvement of parliament, the executive, and even the people in judicial appointments. This is not surprising, for the 1848 French Constitution embodied France's "unambiguously republican" tradition, which had been "born in violence during the great Revolution" (de Luna 1969: 332–333, 9).

The other typical features eschewed were the "rights and liberties" on which the French Constitution of 1848 had elaborated in great detail: freedom of speech and of the press, of assembly and religion, even an early socioeconomic right, the "right to work" (de Luna 1969: 314, 332). Kogălniceanu focused on a narrower range of duties and obligations addressing domestic priorities like abolishing slavery and capital and corporal punishment (Art. 94); freedom of religion (Art. 96); the right of persons of all classes to buy land (Art. 98); the right to free public education (Art. 100); and "abolition of censorship" (Art. 102).

Contemporary Romanian legal scholars have attributed these "lapses" to an alleged "lack of experience in drafting technical-juridical texts" (Gutan 2011: 243). This judgment is dubious, however, given Kogălniceanu's training under eminent German jurists. That he did not carry certain features as far as contemporary scholars would have liked might be attributable to Hegelian influence, which inspired in Kogălniceanu the conviction that a constitution ought to be "an indigenous plant, and expression of the customs and needs of the nation" (Vianu 1970: 273). Equally likely and quite possibly simultaneously, he may have been committed to republicanism as much as the French were. After all, the historical era in which Kogălniceanu lived long predated the judicial empowerment that today is assumed to be an essential feature of constitutionalism.

Having learned the precepts of constitutionalism via the socialization of his formative years in France and Germany, Kogălniceanu was well placed to attempt to draw Romania into the modern age politically. It was an attempt that nearly succeeded and one to which he would return later, after the Romanian state had been constituted by the Western powers.

18.4 TRANSNATIONAL *AB OVO*: THE 1858 CONVENTION OF PARIS CONSTITUTES THE ROMANIAN STATE

Learning is not always a bottom-up process; it may become top-down if a diffusing nation takes a receiving nation or people in hand. The founding of the Romanian State followed this pattern. Romanians accepted tutelage from the Western powers because they were struggling to fight free of the Ottoman Empire, which they perceived to be an alien occupation.

Once the Turks and Russians had suppressed the 1848 Revolution in Romanian lands, no new constitutions were attempted in either principality until 1858, when

the ending of the Crimean War posed the question of what to do with the principalities of Wallachia and Moldavia (Riker 1971). Also playing a lobbying role were
Romanian elites who by now had developed a strong sense of nationhood (Hitchins
1996). Even through the Dark Ages they had conserved some awareness of being
Roman and of once having made part of a mighty empire (Kellogg 1995). And the
two principalities' similarities in the language and culture were self-evident to all
who had traveled through them (Carra 1781). The Convention of Paris thus owed its
existence partly to the efforts of transnationally diffused Romanian elite norm entrepreneurs who had long awaited the next window of opportunity for pursuing a unification attempted in vain many a time since the 1600s (Djuvara 1989: 329–330).

To a greater extent the Convention was the initiative of the diplomats and statesmen representing the great powers – Austria, France, Great Britain, Prussia, Russia,
and the Ottoman Empire – who were pursuing self-interested ends (Riker 1971). But
these sometimes entailed broader ideological goals. Lord Palmerston, the British
prime minister (1855–1858) at the time of the Convention's negotiation, had supported the 1848 revolutions in Europe, as he believed in national self-determination
and constitutional liberties and saw England as "the champion of justice and right,
pursuing that course with moderation and prudence, not becoming the Quixote
of the world, but giving the weight of her moral sanction and support wherever
she thinks justice is, and whenever she thinks that wrong has been done" (Lord
Palmerston, quoted in Heath 1869: 39). Napoleon III too had pursued a policy of
helping Latin nations create their own states as a way of weakening France's rivals
(Focseneanu 1992: 15).

Some of these statesmen then asked the principalities to propose how they should
like to administer themselves (Hitchins 1994). Two ad hoc assemblies convoked for
this purpose, one in each principality, agreed to unification. Nevertheless, the political factions in both principalities distrusted each other so much that they called on
a foreign prince to rule over the united polity (Hitchins 1994: 14).

The resultant treaty, the Convention on the Organization of the Principalities,
adopted in Paris in August 1858, stipulated that the United Principalities of Moldavia
and Wallachia, although continuing under Ottoman suzerainty, were to "administer themselves freely and without interference by the Sublime Porte" (Art. 1) – an
autonomy which the Great Powers committed themselves to guarantee (Riker 1971:
179). This halfway arrangement between international sovereignty and the suzerain
status quo disappointed France and Britain but was the most that Austria or the
Ottomans would agree to (Riker 1971).

The Convention embodied many Western principles of governance that were
novel to Romanian lands, blazing the trail out of feudalism into modernity. Some
of these principles invoked a judiciary, such as individual liberties and equality
before law:

The Moldavians and the Wallachians shall all be equal before tax and shall have an equal chance to be admitted to public office. Their individual liberty is guaranteed. Nobody shall be retained, arrested or pursued except according to the law. Nobody shall be expropriated except according to the law and for public reasons and counter-compensation. The Moldavians and the Wallachians of any Christian denomination shall equally enjoy political rights. (Art. 46)

Other provisions of a judiciary nature or affecting the judiciary included the power of the executive to pardon criminal defendants (Art. 14); the prohibition of executive interference in the administration of justice (Art. 14); the division of sovereignty ("separation of powers") into an executive ("Hospodar"), a twin legislature (a parliament for each principality), and a judiciary; adjudication by "professional magistrates" – replacing the boyars and their private justice – appointed by the Hospodar, according to organic law that was also to abolish, step by step, the magistrates' removability without cause (Art. 7); and, above all, a High Court of Justice and Cassation common to both principalities to decide with finality cases initiated by the Hospodar or by the parliaments against ministers accused of breaches of law, especially dissipation of public income (or "corruption" as it is called today) (Art. 15, 38, 41). The High Court was an innovation reflecting Britain's interpretation of "broad administrative union" as a "tariff union and common judicial and military organization" (Riker 1971: 136).

Perhaps the most striking institutional design innovation was a sixteen-member "Central Commission" mandated to make laws of general applicability aimed at "the unification of legislation as well as the establishment, maintenance and improvement of the customs, postal and telegraphic unions, fixing the value of money, and special matters of public advantage common to both principalities" (Art. 34). The Commission was to "codify existing laws and harmonize them with the Constitutive Act [the Convention] of the new polity" and "revise organic laws as well as the Civil and Criminal and Procedural Codes to ensure that … in the future there should be only one body of law in both principalities, to be implemented only after they are passed by each of the Legislatures and sanctioned and promulgated by the Hospodar" (Art. 35). The Great Powers had been divided over the Central Commission idea (Riker 1971: 162), for it was manifestly intended to bring about the "legislative union" on which France strongly insisted – in effect, "a union in germ" (Riker 1971: 165). Its champions foresaw that the principalities would have little chance of achieving unity and international sovereignty without common legal standards.

Although later perceived by Romanian elites as a "juridical instrument of European powers" (Gutan 2011: 227), the Convention became the United Principalities' de facto constitution at least until 1866, when a de jure constitution came to be drafted for what by then had become known as Romania. Meanwhile, the Convention, forged in secret by a handful of interested parties (Riker 1971: 159), constituted an embryonic Romanian state based *ab ovo* on liberal-democratic principles.

A shrewd political move even effected a kind of proto-unification: Prince Alexandru Cuza was elected Hospodar by both principalities at once in 1859, after the Convention had been ratified. Cuza's rule enhanced the power of the prince at the expense of the legislature, yet judiciary independence and professionalism were also reinforced. Organic law included provisions to create competent jurists. Romanian law was further modernized by an influx of foreign ideas; for example, a Civil Code was enacted that essentially mirrored the Napoleonic Code of 1804. (It remained in force, with a few amendments, until 1992.) A Code of Civil Procedure that mirrors the 1819 Code of Geneva Canton was also adopted (Focseneanu 1992: 23).

This evidence may be interpreted as indicating either an informed consensus favoring judicial reforms or the initiative of few "Enlightened" elites acting against a background of general indifference. Circumstantial evidence makes the second interpretation more plausible. It is known, for example, that Cuza had a tendency of "allowing none to approach him but a handful of devoted followers," one of whom at least "was said to possess one of the best legal minds in the Principalities" (Riker 1971: 463). Kogălniceanu was one of Cuza's entourage and became his prime minister and right-hand man. He was thus in a position to spearhead many reforms foreshadowed by, but never realized in, his Constitutional Project of 1848. Historians have noticed in Kogălniceanu "that indomitable driving power which Cuza himself so sadly lacked ... he was ... a man of ideas and, what is more, a man of action" (Riker 1971: 462).

Kogălniceanu singlehandedly sired an "orgy of legislation," not hesitating to enact by dictatorial means: "Towards the end of December [1861] Kogălniceanuhad boasted that he had ready forty-five new laws, which he intended to have promulgated without consulting the legislature" (Riker 1971: 463). He made no attempt, however, to institute judicial review, resting content with an independent judiciary. Six more decades would pass before the first steps toward judicial review would be taken and the foundation laid for the "judicialization of politics" (Tate and Vallinder 1995).

18.5 THE 1866 CONSTITUTION: "PLAGIARIZING" THE BELGIAN CONSTITUTION?

Bottom-up learning may also happen in ways and under conditions not yet fully theorized. Romania's imitation of the Belgian Constitution in 1866 appears to be a case of learning from others who are "close" only in the sense of similarly situated in the international system. The Romanians saw that Belgium had thriven despite being overshadowed by Great Powers on all sides. Perceiving themselves to be in the same position internationally, they hoped to replicate the Belgian success story (Hitchins 1994).

The 1858 Convention had been inadequate as a constitution, and indeed never intended to be one; after all, it was an international treaty between the Great Powers of Europe to which Romania itself was not a party. One of the raisons d'être of the Central Commission set up by the Convention was precisely to draft a real, adequate constitution, and to act as its custodian once ratified (Riker 1971: 167). Cuza, however, ignored the Commission, disbanding it in 1861 before it could draft a replacement for the Convention (Riker 1971: 368).

In 1866, Cuza was driven into exile by partisans dissatisfied with his authoritarian rule. Soon a new constitution was drafted, which came to be known as the Constitution of Little Romania, as Romania then did not include Transylvania, still part of the Austrian Empire. It was drafted by elites "who never knew the Romanian milieu, who had been trained abroad and had a foreign political education" (Iorga 1921: 43). Experienced politicians like Kogălniceanu were "barred from the [newly elected] Constituent Assembly" that debated and agreed the new Constitution (Iorga 1921: 25). The result was essentially a foreign import, an imitation of the Belgian Constitution of 1831 – itself inspired by the French Constitutions of 1848 and 1789. It nonetheless came to be seen by later commentators as "one of the most liberal and most democratic in Europe" while also being one of the most "nationalistic" (a term of praise at the time) (Brătianu 1921: 73). As in a constitutional monarchy, it delimited the Hospodar's powers and provided a means for calling his ministers to account, reinforcing the separation of powers. It also detailed classical rights at length: equality before the law, freedom of conscience, of the press, of public meetings, of association, and prohibition on arbitrary searches and arrest (Hitchins 1994: 17).

Judiciary power and independence were reinforced too. In cases involving ministers condemned by the Court of Cassation, the Hospodar was prohibited to pardon their guilt or to commute their sentences without the consent of parliament which had impeached them in the first place (Art. 103). The establishment of law courts was to be done only by law (Art. 104). Juries were mandated at all criminal trials and at trials of offenses against the state and "press offenses" or libel (Art. 105). The Belgian Constitution's guarantee that duly appointed judges would be irremovable and otherwise occupationally secure was omitted, apparently not for lack of commitment to judicial independence but for lack of qualified judges. The framers envisaged irremovability being introduced progressively via organic legislation (Focseneanu 1992: 30).

This followed in 1890, when the Act on the Organization of the Judiciary guaranteed the irremovability of Appeal Court presidents and councillors; and in 1909, when a new Act extended irremovability to most judges, who might relinquish their posts only by resignation, retirement, infirmity, or disbarment. A judge or magistrate might not be transferred without his consent as well. Moreover, the probity of judges was impeachable only through a special disciplinary process, and their decisions might be overturned only by higher courts on appeal (Focseneanu 1992: 30–44).

These were advanced procedures for that time. Compare them with the Constitution of 1990 and the organic statute that immediately followed, which allowed judges to be moved around like pawns at the will of the party in power (*cf.* Ramseyer and Rasmusen 2001). Yet in 1909 judges could not be transferred without their own consent – a very strong provision in favor of independence and the rule of law. Despite the vicissitudes of the other government powers, commitment to the independence of the judiciary stood firm. It was a "bright spot" in Romania's history and never seriously contested until communism. What the Romanians felt the most keenly was the lack of human resources, of competent jurists who would know how to exert their independence under the new dispensation.

Amended in 1879, 1884, and 1917, the 1866 Constitution lasted until 1923, when after the tearing-apart of the Austro-Hungarian Empire, Transylvania was annexed to the United Principalities, creating the Greater Romania, which commended a new constitution.

18.6 TRANSNATIONAL LEGAL PROFESSIONALS ADOPT *MARBURY V. MADISON*: THE ROMANIAN SUPREME COURT CREATES A DE FACTO NEW CONSTITUTION

One very consequential development at the dawn of the twentieth century was the discovery by Romanian jurists of their professional identity and their elite position in the polity. Before this epoch, constitutional developments had been driven by "philosopher-kings," politicians legally trained but exhibiting no professional class-consciousness. This must have emerged in the period between 1866 and the epochal decision of the Romanian Supreme Court in 1911 to empower itself with the competence to control the constitution. Around the turn of the century, one begins to notice works published by a scholarly community that had become aware of itself as such; for example, a tome debating what was to become the 1923 Constitution. Each chapter was written by a different legal practitioner or academic, whose treatment of the topic was thoroughly professional (Stroe 1990). Nothing about constitutional law of this sort had ever been seen in Romania before, evidencing that a native professional legal community was already in being and fully aware of its power to influence the drafting of constitutions by virtue of superior expertise alone.

By 1911, Romanian legal scholarship attested to what many believe was "intellectual osmosis" from their French preceptors (Conac 2000: 16). Such a process, however, could hardly have been confined inside the borders of Romania and France.

Socio-legal research has found that a transnational legal professional community was by then ascendant and spreading across Europe. It had begun to emerge toward the end of the nineteenth century in tandem with and clustered around the first international law institutes. These had been established by certain governments collaborating with philanthropic foundations (Sacriste and Vauchez 2007: 90) to promote international law as a pathway to world peace: "The many sources ... testify to the emergence in the eighteen-seventies of an international consciousness ... the international lawyers hoped that some day this developing international spirit might bring about ... [a] warless era ..." (Abrams 1957: 380). If osmosis or filtration through a semi-permeable barrier is a reasonable figure of the nature of transnational diffusion, it renders inconceivable the notion that anything like an impermeable barrier could have isolated just France and Romania from all other transnational developments of the time.

Since its emergence, this transnational legal community has held a belief in the superiority of law and the judiciary (Abrams 1957; Cohen 2007; Sacriste and Vauchez 2007). Constantin G. Dissescu (1854–1932), a Paris-trained lawyer and professor of constitutional and administrative law at the law faculty in Bucharest, considered to be one of the leading Romanian jurists at the time, certainly shared this belief:

> In a country where parliamentary experience [and experience of a Supreme Court] is recent and where public opinion is still embryonic, judges may perform a pedagogical function and, only through the simple threat of its possible intervention, can illicit the legislator to respect the limits imposed on it by the Constitution. (Dissescu 1915, paraphrased by Conac 2000: 19)

This ideal of the judge as morally and intellectually superior to the "politician" would also feature in the discourses of the legal professional elites who drafted most of Romania's constitutional revisions following the fall of communism, as evidenced in the last empirical section of this chapter (*cf.* Sacriste and Vauchez 2007).

The 1866 Constitution had not provided the Supreme Court powers of constitutional control. Nevertheless, inspired by examples in the United States and Western Europe, the Romanian Supreme Court took upon itself such a competence, complete with power to strike down a parliamentary statute, in 1911. A dispute had arisen between a semipublic Bucharest tram company (plaintiff) and Bucharest City Hall and the Interior Ministry (defendants) (Sadurski 2008: 2). The company had been enacted by the Executive Cabinet (Council of Ministers) in 1909. In 1911, City Hall persuaded the Cabinet to annul the 1909 Act, a decision ratified by an Act of Parliament in 1911 that incidentally imposed retroactive conditions on the tram company's private shareholders over and above those embodied in the company bylaws. Parliament acted pursuant to its prerogative under the 1866 Constitution to interpret the law with finality. The company sued on behalf of the shareholders, claiming the 1911 Act to be unconstitutional. The Ilfov Tribunal nullified the Act as unenforceable on the grounds that the right to property is inviolable. The Supreme Court affirmed the nullification on appeal, refuting objections to its competence by reasoning that, as the Constitution did not expressly forbid it, judges could not be precluded from striking down even statutes, if these were found to be unconstitutional (Orescu 1929; Focseneanu 1992).

The Supreme Court's ruling did not meet with universal approval. Justice Ion Manu wrote a dissent arguing that parliament's interpretation agreed with the Constitution in force, and that, moreover, the Romanian penal code, modeled on the French, expressly denied the judiciary the asserted competence. In other words, the law struck down by the Supreme Court was constitutional because the 1866 Constitution gave parliament, and not the courts, the power to interpret the law (Conac 2000). The decision was also contested in the legal academy: law professor Gheorghe Alexianu argued that neither the Ilfov Tribunal nor the Supreme Court had a right to set themselves up as judges of the constitutionality of a law enacted with due parliamentary process (Alexianu, paraphrased in Conac 2000: 17). More recently, in an article reanalyzing the decision, Gérard Conac, a French jurist and Emeritus Professor of Law at the Sorbonne, concluded that "[t]he judge ought not to substitute himself for the legislator" and that "separation of powers does not permit a judge to rewrite, according to his own views, the law he interprets" (Conac 2000: 15).

The Court seems to have neglected to consider that its own reasoning – that anything not expressly forbidden to an arm of the state is permitted – must apply to all branches of government. On the basis of this principle the Court would have been unable to resist rival claims by the executive and legislative branches to an equal right to interpret the Constitution, as the Constitution forbade neither of them, either (indeed, it expressly empowered parliament). The Court's reasoning exposes itself to the contestation of its interpretation by the other branches, undermining the implicit assertion of finality of its own decision. Moreover, the principle of everything permitted that is not forbidden is far less dangerous when applied to upholding the rights of citizens before state power than applied to justifying acts of state, especially one of separated powers. After all, the purpose of a constitution is to limit government power not to license it open-endedly (Montesquieu 1777). The Court might have declined to enforce the statute without asserting a general power of interpretation that the sovereign had not granted them. Lastly, the civil law tradition generally allows judges no authority to "measure" acts of parliament against a constitution (Merryman and Perez-Perdomo 2007). Indeed, the Romanian Supreme Court's conduct was strikingly at odds with the civil law tradition of 1911 (Weber 2001), long before the judicialization arising in the aftermath of World War II. In 1911, only Norway and Greece had followed the United States' example. The

Conseil Constitutionnel of France, a country that has served as the model for many a Romanian constitution and judiciary institution, would not be established until 1958 (Conac 2000).

The other branches, however, appear to have been equally nescient. By submitting to judicial process, City Hall and the Ministry of the Interior implicitly ceded the competence of constitutional control and empowered the Supreme Court. The executive would have been exercising a legitimate check and balance had it refused to submit to such a process, carrying on regardless of the Supreme Court's opinion (*cf.* Parau 2012a; Waldron 2012). The U.S. Supreme Court itself has often been legitimately disobeyed and the general power to interpret the Constitution with finality alleged to have been asserted in *Marbury v. Madison* contested at least up until the Civil War and its fractious aftermath (Tushnet 1999; Whittington 2007). The Romanian Cabinet could have nullified the Supreme Court's self-empowerment by asserting for itself a countervailing competence on the basis of the Court's own reasoning.

The boldness of the Romanian judges may well have been a by-product of transnational diffusion and a trend toward judicial empowerment that had begun in the United States and was now even affecting countries as remote as Romania. The attorney for the tram company, a Romanian graduate of the law faculty in Paris, called in French experts as consultants. One was Henri Berthélemy, an administrative law specialist and a future dean of the Paris law faculty. Berthélemy's memorandum, disseminated via *Revista de Drept Public* ["Public Law Magazine"], Romania's premier publication for academics and practitioners in the field of law, justified and supported the Supreme Court (Conac 2000). Law scholars who have analyzed the decision concluded that in his reasoning Berthélemy "manifestly echoed the arguments of Judge Marshall in *Marbury v. Madison* of 1803" (Conac 2000: 13). Berthélemy could act with a free hand in Romania; in France he would have been confronted with a settled custom of deference to parliament and an express constitutional prohibition of judicial nonenforcement of parliament's statutes. Berthélemy's worldview and the Supreme Court's self-empowerment chimed with the theories of some of Romania's leading academic jurists who were predisposed to accept judicial control of the constitution (Conac 2000: 13–4). One was Dissescu, who seconded Berthélemy. He and others of his caliber known to have been following developments in the United States as well as in Norway and Greece (Conac 2000). Why their circle prevailed rather than their opponents' has never been brought to light. It is noteworthy that the practice that started in Romania was taken up by others in the region, such as neighboring Bulgaria (Sadurski 2008: 2), evidencing diffusion between countries that are geographically close (Goderis and Versteeg 2013).

Interlocking learning mechanisms seem to be in play. On the one hand, the evidence suggests bottom-up transnational diffusion wherein French law professors were learning from the U.S. Supreme Court and judicial practice. They were learning this independently of French judicial practice, which was expressly barred from following suit. On the other hand, there is also evidence to suggest tutelage: the French jurists invited in by the tram company took the case in hand. Bringing to bear their French legal training, they instructed all of the Romanian parties to the lawsuit – directly or indirectly – including the Supreme Court, in this otherwise alien precept that had originated across the Atlantic. Quite possibly their authority was what persuaded the defendant Cabinet to acquiesce in the Supreme Court's shiny new powers. And it was the cultural affinity between France and Romania that enabled diffusion (Berkowitz et al. 2000); without French norm entrepreneurs, the cultural barrier standing between Romania and the United States may have been insuperable. At the same time, the Romanian jurists were learning about themselves as an elite within the elite, uncommon "experts" who could lay claim to a normative authority superior to that of squabbling politicians.

18.7 CONSTITUTIONALIZING JUDICIAL REVIEW: THE 1923 CONSTITUTION

The self-construction of judicial review would impact the next Constitution, drafted in 1923 after the Transylvanian annexation, as well as the creation of a Constitutional Court decades later in 1990, after the fall of communism. Both constitutions were drafted by the emergent legal elite. Dissescu himself was appointed president of the 1923 Drafting Commission (Stroe 1990). He and others of like mind were keen to constitutionalize the Court's newly won powers of judicial review.

In stark contrast with the making of the 1990 Constitution, the process in 1923 was not left entirely up to legal professionals. Many drafters were experienced politicians or else academics hailing from fields as sundry as sociology and economics; however, perusal of the 1923 debates shows that few were concerned with rights or judiciary power (Stroe 1990), which only interested a handful of jurists such as Dissescu and elite judges on the Supreme Court who understood and wanted to imitate the U.S. Supreme Court. In the words of Emanoil Miclescu (1861–1946) who was to become president of Romania's Supreme Court:

> Some Congressmen and even some Presidents of the American Republic have contested the Supreme Court's right to interpret certain constitutional provisions, a right which is not in fact written in the Constitution. . . . Today this right is recognized by all, and the prestige acquired by its decisions, is due to a large extent to the superiority of judges called to serve in such high office, among whom the name of John Marshall occupies first place; his authority on constitutional matters is law. . . . So enlightened were the opinions he issued and judgments he pronounced that he has been styled the second maker of the Constitution. (Miclescu 1922: 402)

Miclescu and others like him were the ones who ensured that judicial review made it into the 1923 Constitution: "[T]he Court of Cassation in plenary session has the right to judge the constitutionality of laws and to declare inapplicable those that are contrary to the Constitution. The judgment regarding the unconstitutionality of laws is limited to the case at bar" (Art. 103). Judicial review was thus explicitly kept ex post, and could not be relied on as precedent. Sixty-seven years later, when a full-fledged Constitutional Court was established, it was invested with ex ante review as well.

The 1923 Constitution contained few provisions for the ordinary judiciary, limited to those believed to shore up judicial independence: judges shall be irremovable except under special circumstances specified by law (Art. 104); a person injured by an administrative act may petition for redress via judicial review (Art. 107). This contrasts starkly with the 2003–2004 revisions of the 1990 Constitution, which made the judiciary branch an autonomous and self-governing "state within a state."[3] The Communist Party abolished the 1923 Constitution in 1945 and with it all constitutional review and judicial independence. It was not until after 1989 that the next democratic Constitution was drafted.

18.8 JUDICIAL TRANSNATIONALISM CONSOLIDATED: THE POSTCOMMUNIST CONSTITUTIONS

The drafting of Romania's first postcommunist constitution was announced in December 1989, hours after the fall of Ceauşescu. The leaders of the Revolution (or rather coup d'état) formed a National Salvation Front (NSF) to oust the Communist Party as well as reform the state structures that were its legacy.[4] The NSF's stated raison d'être was to bring about "democracy, liberty and dignity to the Romanian people" (Consiliul Frontului Salvarii Nationale 1989). Its makeup included ex-Communist Party apparatchiks, especially those who had fallen out of grace with Ceauşescu. This compromised pedigree meant that the fledgling NSF leadership was immediately faced with the problem of legitimizing themselves domestically, but even more internationally. The president of the commission appointed to draft a new constitution has noted that they felt "under pressure from internal political forces and from European structures, that if we did not adopt a new constitution, we would not become credible with regard to our intentions of building a democratic

---

[3] Author's interview with former Romanian justice minister, Bucharest, October 10, 2009.

[4] Although initially intended to constitute an interim government until the first free elections would be organized, the NSF soon became a political party. With access to superior organization and resources, especially control over the state-owned media, and facing no significant political or societal opposition, the NSF won several elections and governed Romania for most of its transition period under various "social democrat" labels. Event today it continues to be a major political force in Romania.

polity" (Iorgovan 1998: 118). Romanians felt they "had no chance of entering the Council of Europe without a new constitution that was fundamentally different from the one created in Ceauşescu's time" (Iorgovan 1998: 118). This perception persisted throughout the drafting process and attests to the pressures to finish the process quickly, as "those foreigners who are helping us from abroad want to see something drafted" (Dan Lăzărescu quoted in Iorgovan 1998: 49). This evidence indicates that these newly empowered elites were behaving according to the logic of "acculturation" (Goodman 2004). They approached the new constitution instrumentally, with a view to being accepted by their "betters."

Immediately after Romania's first postcommunist Constituent Assembly was elected in May 1990, a twenty-six-member Constitution Drafting Committee had to be set up. It was headed by Antonie Iorgovan, a public law academic and one of Romania's few public law experts, and, though representing all political factions in the Assembly, it comprised jurists and professionals exclusively, constituting a small legal elite drawn from among the broader class of legal professionals – an elite within an elite within the elite. Eight of its members were academics, mostly from the law faculty in Bucharest and taken on as "independent experts," among the few in all of Romania who were learned in constitutional and public law.

Right from the beginning, effecting a "separation of powers" was a key preoccupation of the Committee. This had already emerged as a concern only hours after the flight of Ceauşescu, who had lorded over one of the Eastern Bloc's most brutal totalitarian regimes. Among the handful of revolutionaries who appeared on the balcony of the Central Committee building, where only hours earlier Ceauşescu had made his final speech denouncing the Revolution and accusing the revolutionaries of terrorism, was Dumitru Mazilu. A former head of the Foreign Ministry's Legal Department under Ceauşescu, Mazilu had lost that post in 1987 after drafting a report for the UN Human Rights Sub-Committee that was highly critical of Romania (Siani-Davies 2005: 110). Claiming inspiration from the Magna Carta, the Declaration of Independence, and the Declaration of the Rights of Man and of the Citizen (Mazilu 1991: 13), Mazilu outlined a blueprint for Romania that included a constitution guaranteeing a "separation of powers" between legislative, executive, and judiciary branches. Mazilu's speech was revolutionary in those circumstances, in that he put the idea of separation of powers on the public agenda at a time when people were still being shot and great uncertainty loomed as to the direction the Revolution was going in.

Mazilu's background is revealing: it typifies the kind of norm entrepreneur who has come to dominate the drafting of constitutions and other organic laws in Romania ever since the 1989 Revolution. He was an elite legal professional and a graduate (1959) of the faculty of law in Bucharest, who had been a professor of laws at the School of Officers of *Securitate* – perhaps Eastern Europe's most feared secret police – while also holding visiting professorships since the 1970s at Columbia, Harvard, and Berkeley. Mazilu was one of a very few Romanians who had had contact with international organizations: as a representative to the United Nations he had been a member of its Subcommittee for Combating Discrimination and Protecting Minorities. In such postings Mazilu had been able to move in transnational circles of like-minded professionals and to absorb norms, such as separation of powers, which had long been forgotten in Romania. In December 1989, his ideas had undergirded the FSN's first *Communiqué* to the Romanian people (Stoenescu 2006), in which they committed themselves to a separation of powers along with a reorientation of Romania's foreign affairs to integrate her into "a united Europe" (Consiliul Frontului Salvarii Nationale 1989). Both *desiderata* were to shape the process of institution building that then began, which would include designs to ensure judicial independence and judicial review.

The exigencies of politics and a diffidence about all things judiciary handicapped the politicians on the Committee, which explains their dependency on the academic members in all such matters. These technical experts saw themselves as "a small and enlightened minority" (Elster 1995: 383). Despite Romania's international isolation under Ceauşescu, the direct or indirect contact they were able to maintain with their counterparts in the West had been making them aware all along of constitutional developments, particularly in France (Wyrzikowski 2000). Already in tune with the contemporary ideology of constitutionalism, they were keen to embody in their new constitution everything they had learned, from Constitutional Courts to the "apolitical" insularization of the judiciary, and on to a laundry list of rights.

They shared a (possibly unwitting) assumption that judges and jurists like themselves were superior to elected politicians and best placed to bring Romania to the rule of law. For example, they set up information points to "assist" MPs to grasp new concepts such as separation of powers and judicial review, so as "to create in a short period the atmosphere of a scientific seminar on the Committee, not a political arena. … Our [the experts'] only chance was to ensure that on the Committee the scientific spirit predominated, not the allergy of political jockeying" (Iorgovan 1998: 46). Assiduously they broadcast contestable ideas such as that "Constitutional law, according to a widespread thesis [contained in a 1975 French treatise on constitutional law], is nothing but 'the juridical framing of political phenomena'" (Iorgovan 1998: 46). By designing the constitution after "scientific" rules of thumb centered on judicial arbitration of the political acts of all others, they hoped to save Romania from its communist legacy.

The communist regime had annihilated the rule-of-law tradition that had taken root in Romania before. For fifty years Romania had lain prostrate under Central and Eastern Europe's most arbitrary regime. Ceauşescu's sultan-like personalism (itself possibly a cultural legacy of the Ottomans) had purged any trace of even "socialist legality": in addition to the standard totalitarian fare of a monolithic Communist Party puppet-mastering all other institutions, both public and private, including all branches of government, and brutally punishing the slightest move toward individual or social independence (Almond 1992; Linz and Stepan 1996), Ceauşescu treated the state like a fiefdom: "[e]ven the top *nomenklatura* were hired, treated, mistreated, transferred, and fired as members of the household staff" (Linz and Stepan 1996: 347). The judiciary did not even pretend to impartiality or independence; prosecutors and judges were notoriously at the mercy of political commands (Demşorean et al. 2008: 95). "Telephone justice," whereby Party bosses dictated the judge's decision over the telephone (to avoid leaving a "paper trail"), was normal. Judges all had to belong to the *nomenklatura* (Party elite), and were vetted on the basis of loyalty, not competence (Gallagher 2009). This craven subjugation was crowned by the corruption that grew wild inside the "culture of secrecy and arbitrariness" that engulfed society (Demşorean et al. 2008: 95). The procuracy overawed the judiciary while remaining nothing but an ordinary tool of the Party's repressive apparatus (Macovei 1999). Magistrates' acts were minutely scrutinized by *Securitate*, Central and Eastern Europe's most dreaded secret police that was the judge behind the judge in politically consequential cases, dictating both verdict and punishment (Gallagher 2009).

Given this dismal legacy, it should surprise no one that those who had grown up and suffered under Ceauşescu and totalitarianism would hew so strictly to a constitutional scheme derived from the West, hoping that it would forever safeguard Romania from any repetition of such a trauma. Psychological triggers like these have been found to have inspired similar developments (e.g., bills of rights and self-governing judiciaries) in many countries that have suffered likewise (Guarnieri 2004; Bancaud 2006; Erdos 2010).

What moved the 1990 framers specifically to invite the Council of Europe (CoE) and its associated networks of transnational norm entrepreneurs into the drafting process was this anxiety to set things right for the future, coupled with a belief that politicians already mired in factionalism and power struggles were incapable of doing so (Iorgovan 1998: 16, 55). They believed these interveners would help shape "the Committee's strategy and thinking about the Constitution" and furnish it with superior technical knowledge. The drafting of organic laws being a scarce event in Romania's history, local expertise was in correspondingly short supply: "In 1990 people with a doctorate in constitutional or administrative law were very few and far between in the country and only 4 or 5 could claim real expertise with 'serious books behind them'" (Iorgovan 1998: 12).

Strategic motives also played a part: many hoped to "build relationships that would help bring Romania into the international community ... proving to politicians in Europe and the entire world that we were honest and we genuinely wanted to build a real Western democratic system" (Iorgovan 1998: 66, 68). In the process of "creating the new nation,"[5] the Romanians perceived themselves engaged in a "battle for the Constitution" with the outside world at a time when the NSF "lacked any external credibility" (Iorgovan 1998: 66).

Working through Romanian embassies abroad, the Committee made contact with judges and jurists on constitutional courts and in other institutions in France, Italy, Spain, and Portugal as well as with the CoE and its Venice Commission in Strasbourg, a body made of constitutional law academics that advises the CoE. The Romanian drafters were informed and edified by members of this network, such as Professor Francisco LaPorta, Spain's delegate to the Venice Commission, and Robert Badinter, President of the *Conseil Constitutionnel* and a close friend of President Mitterand (Iorgovan 1998: 114). The most influential of all proved to be Antonio La Pergola, president of Italy's *Corte costituzionale* and Italy's former justice minister as well as current president of the Venice Commission. A "self-declared friend and supporter of Romania," he would prove "very influential" in backing it for membership of the CoE (Iorgovan 1998: 66–67). The president of the Drafting Commission admitted that La Pergola made "the most important contribution in shaping our thinking" (Iorgovan 1998: 67). He inspired them to "adopt certain fundamental strategic directions," chief among which was that "everybody who breaches the Constitution must be brought before a Constitutional Court ... the only body that can guarantee individual rights"; that "Romania cannot aspire to 'full democracy' unless it has a Constitutional Court"; and that a Constitutional Court is "the key to open the door of Europe's sympathy" (Iorgovan 1998: 112).

If we accept that La Pergola had assessed the situation in Europe accurately and that his views on Constitutional Courts are representative of the transnational legal community to which he belonged,[6] then it would follow that Romania's accession to the CoE and later to the EU was conditioned upon her integration into this preexisting constitutional design consensus. At all events, these formative experiences produced a constitution reflecting the priorities of an elite minority of transnationally networked legal professionals, with other elites (to say nothing of the people) being effectively shut out – a trend that has continued ever since.

This transnational community consists of multiple overlapping networks interlocked with the supranational organs of the CoE, especially the Legal and Human Rights Directorate of its General Secretariat, its European Court of Human Rights, and its Venice Commission. Members are highly mobile between nations, levels

---

[5] Author's personal communication with a jurist member of the Constitution Drafting Committee, Bucharest, September 21, 2010.

[6] Author's interview with a senior civil servant, the Venice Commission, Strasbourg, March 13, 2010.

of governance, and fields of practice (*cf.* Cohen 2010). More than one hundred interviews conducted by this author between 2009 and 2011 with judicial reformers in Strasbourg and Brussels, as well as in Romania, Moldova, Croatia, the Czech Republic, Germany, Italy, and the United Kingdom, have revealed that these networks exist and are dependent for their leverage on the CoE. The European Commission itself is dependent on this transnational legal community, especially concerning the meaning of the 1993 Copenhagen Criteria of accession, the indeterminate terms of which need clarification and elaboration. Several interviewees have indicated to the author that, although in theory it should be the Commission's prerogative to improvise such determinations as it sees fit, it prefers as a matter of practice to rely on the preexisting work of the European Court of Human Rights and the Venice Commission. As one official put it, "Why reinvent the wheel?"

These particular empirical findings are corroborated by broad-based socio-legal and political science research, which has consistently found that the members of this transnational community, legal professionals holding high official positions in supranational institutions like the European Commission, have been pivotal in fostering European integration in the form of the CoE and the EU. The same community in the 1960s invented and imposed the doctrines of "direct effect" and "supremacy" of EU law (Stein 1981; Alter 2001; Cohen 2007; Cohen and Vauchez 2007; Alter 2009; Vauchez 2010). The networks connect legal elites not only in the old member-states but also in the postcommunist countries of Central and Eastern Europe, namely high court judges, top academics specializing in constitutional or human rights law, and legally trained policy practitioners and political dignitaries. Also in the loop are legal professionals working inside civil society organizations concerned with legal issues, such as Transparency International, the Soros Foundation, and the Helsinki Committees for Human Rights (Consultative Council of European Judges 2008).[7] At any one time, however, the community contains but a small fraction of all elected politicians (Parau 2012b).

Sharing a "common judicial identity" (Slaughter 1994: 102) and a sense of belonging to "the legal family,"[8] this transnational community has been in existence for half a century at a bare minimum, and well before the 1989 fall of communism (Abrams 1957; Sacriste and Vauchez 2007). It drove European integration from its beginnings in the late 1940s (Cohen 2007; Cohen and Vauchez 2007). It has settled on a consensus on their own superiority over politics, as illustrated by the

---

[7] Author's interview with the Political Affairs Directorate of the General Secretariat of the Council of Europe, Strasbourg, March 14, 2011.

[8] Author's interview with Head of the International Law Department, German Federal Ministry of Justice, President of the European Commission for the Efficiency of Justice, CoE and Chairman of the Committee on Legal Co-operation, CoE, Berlin, March 10, 2011.

opinion of the Romanian justice minister who led the 2003 constitutional revisions in Romania:

> All organs appointed by Parliament become *noxious* … all candidates [for membership of the Judiciary Council] go on a list, and the parties bargain between themselves … "you vote mine and I will vote yours." And this kind of bargaining governs everything. … President Iliescu understood me and agreed [that the Judiciary Council must be removed from Parliamentary control]. And this is how the idea prevailed … whereby the Judiciary Council is elected by their peers.[9]

Or, in the words of another Romanian lawyer-become-politician:

> Who should judge the judges in a democratic system? What about the college of doctors? Only they have the power to judge doctors, because only they are their equals.… The social status of judges is very special, and judges should be judged only by their peers.[10]

Socio-legal research into the thinking of this community at the beginning of the twentieth century corroborates the author's empirical findings in East Europe (*cf.* Cohen and Vauchez 2007; Vauchez 2008).

The community has a public policy agenda. This is embodied in institutional design templates, which Eastern enlargement has provided an opportunity to implement (cf. Parau 2012b; Sadurski 2012). The templates operate at multiple levels of governance: at supranational level, one template embodiment is in courts like the European Court of Human Rights and the European Court of Justice (Cohen 2007; Alter 2009); the national-level template features constitutional courts – insulated, self-governing judiciaries headed by a Judiciary Council, and, more recently, central academies monopolizing the formation of judges and prosecutors (Piana 2007; Piana 2010; Parau 2012a). Transnational norm entrepreneurs have disseminated the template not only all across Eastern Europe but also in other democratizing regions such as Latin America (Bill Chávez 2007; Garoupa and Ginsburg 2009; Piana 2010; Ingram 2011; Seibert-Fohr 2012). At all levels of governance the templates have in common that they empower the magistrature to use national constitutions and international conventions as "living documents," on the basis of which to forge (their own) norms unilaterally, that is, without democratic input beyond the text of the convention or constitution, which the judges may interpret freely and at will, beyond redress by democratic means. Although still evolving at the time that the 1990 Romanian Constitution was drafted, and not then fully formalized in official documents, the templates have been and continue to be promoted by norm

---

[9] Author's interview with Rodica Stanoiu, Romanian justice minister, Bucharest, October 10, 2009. Emphasis added.

[10] Author's interview with Augustin Bolcas, lawyer and MP, Bucharest, October 12, 2009.

entrepreneurs who sprang from the transnational legal community that became involved all over Eastern Europe in the design and drafting of postcommunist judiciary institutions.[11]

These templates are wide open to normative criticism. Firstly, they tend to discount and dismiss the alternative ancient traditions of European countries that have for centuries enjoyed popular participation, the rule of law, and protection of rights without an all-powerful judiciary. Indeed, imposing the latter might disrupt their complex but workable institutional balance, like in Britain, for example (Jennings 1971; Bogdanor no year). Secondly, they seem oblivious to the informal institutions on which formal ones depend to a large extent (*cf.* Guy 2000; Galligan 2013). Thirdly, the overriding priority given to political insulation and empowerment of the judiciary stultifies the separation of powers by elevating the judiciary to a position of effective sovereignty over the other branches of government (Parau 2012a).

The principle of separation of powers as exemplified in the U.S. Constitution purports to potentiate mutual checks and balances between government "departments" so that "no one could transcend their legal limits, without being effectually checked and restrained by the others," forestalling arbitrary government in which the people have little effective voice. This entailed a functional overlap where "no barrier" intervenes between separate departments (Madison 1788) – a too-absolute separation that, like the insulation striven for by the templates (especially where one branch asserts legal supremacy over the others), might prove to be as detrimental to individual liberty as no separation at all:

> The concentrating [of all the powers of government, legislative, executive, and judiciary] ... in the same hands, is precisely the definition of despotic government. It will be no alleviation, that these powers will be exercised by a plurality of hands, and not by a single one. One hundred and seventy-three despots would surely be as oppressive as one. (Madison 1788)

Fourthly, the templates ignore other institutions equally important to the rule of law. One institution that is crucial to any country's democratic consolidation is parliament. The records of the Constitution Drafting Committee in Romania in 1990 show no evidence that the transnational legal community took any interest in crafting any template for the design of parliaments. One reason might be that European integration has relied most of all on courts, both supranational and domestic, to implement at the domestic level the supranational bodies of law of the EU and the CoE (Alter 2001). In Romania, and apparently in the other East European countries

---

[11] Author's interviews with a senior civil servant, the Venice Commission, Strasbourg, March 13, 2010; Giacomo Oberto, Turin Court of Appeal Judge and CoE expert, Turin, October 4, 2010; Luca Perrili, Verona Court of Appeal Judge and expert for the European Commission, Verona, April 16, 2011; and senior civil servant, European and International Division, Ministry of Justice, London, April 7, 2011.

newly acceded to the EU, all priority has been given to this project by transnational elites regardless of its side effects on what perhaps ought to be a broader project of democratic consolidation. The author learned in conversations with various Commission officials that a major hurdle for accession candidates is the state of their judiciary systems (which in CEE is often poor). Member States must not lack the capacity to implement the acquis; to this end a candidate's judiciary practices must be adequate. In order to gauge this, the Commission examines the candidate's record before the European Court of Human Rights: how often has the Strasbourg Court ruled against the candidate, and why?

The Romanian Parliament was one of the few institutional designs that originated in Romania. Left to their own devices, the Romanians have had to find out by trial and error the proper structure and procedures for parliament. What emerged at first was a parliamentary design that was unique but more dysfunctional than others in the region (Popescu 2003). It had been hoped that a consensual form of decision making would be facilitated, but the striving for consensus created gridlock instead – a problem that persists twenty years later. Yet for all of its faults, the design did reflect native ideas about how such an institution should work.[12] It may be that consensualism is more of an Eastern than a Western value,[13] a consequence perhaps of the lack of social trust that pervades Eastern Europe and wreaks havoc in politics (Parau 2012b). A preoccupation with consensus has also been evidenced over the years in the composition of the Constitution Drafting Committees: their membership is always hand-picked to reflect the partisan composition of parliament.

Where the transnational templates do address the design of an institution, Romania is observed to have stuck to its precepts. Such was the genesis of her first Constitutional Court; of her first Judiciary Council governing the judiciary internally

---

[12] The reason why the Romanians have not been able to fix it is that the Romanian political class is still seeking to build consensus. Had they merely wanted to fix gridlock, they could have imitated a foreign constitution.

[13] In 1978, Aleksandr Solzhenitsyn publicly criticized the West for its majoritarian mode of decision making and in particular for its excessive legalism: "I have spent all my life under a communist regime and I will tell you that a society without any objective legal scale is a terrible one indeed. But a society with no other scale but the legal one is not quite worthy of man either. A society which is based on the letter of the law and never reaches any higher is taking very scarce advantage of the high level of human possibilities. The letter of the law is too cold and formal to have a beneficial influence on society. Whenever the tissue of life is woven of legalistic relations, there is an atmosphere of moral mediocrity, paralyzing man's noblest impulses". Solzhenitsyn believed that Russia ought not to imitate the West in this way but rather strive for consensus in the way of the Old Russia of the Middle Ages (before Ivan the Terrible), which when faced with adversity would wait for all the wise men to achieve consensus on what ought to be done" (Solzhenitsyn 1978). Another is the example of the classical Polish Constitution in force before Poland fell to the Russian Empire in the eighteenth century. This gave every single member of parliament a veto (*liberum veto*) (Rohac 2008).

on all matters from training to appointments to career paths to ethical discipline; and of a long list of rights ranging from the right to property to "socio-economic rights" such as the right to education, health, and social protection (Constitution of Romania 1991). And yet, in 1990, the Romanians did not go as far as they could have done. The Constitutional Court was empowered with both ex ante and ex post judicial review but lacked other powers such as the power to solve conflicts of a constitutional nature between all public authorities. Moreover, parliament could overturn the Court's decisions by a two-thirds majority of each chamber (a threshold so high that no override ever succeeded). The Judiciary Council, too, was to be elected by parliament (Constitution of Romania 1991).

Romania's new parliament offered no resistance to the templates of the transnational legal community, even though these abolished its participation in constitutional interpretation and judiciary governance. As for the people, their "involvement" was limited to ratifying, in a 1991 referendum, choices made by a professional elite most of whom they never elected and knew little about.

Since the fall of communism, it has become normal for Romania to rely on elite legal professionals of transnational orientation in all constitutional revisions. In 2003, for example, the same unelected professional community was called upon again. This revision, too, pursued strategic goals: timely integration into the EU and NATO. Once accession negotiations began in 2000, a vast *acquis* had to be transposed quickly, but this was impeded by the peculiarities of Romanian bicameralism noted earlier, which had made wholesale enactments practically impossible within a reasonable time frame (Commission for the Elaboration of Legislative Proposals Concerning the Amendment of the Romanian Constitution 2002).

Romanian politicians saw in the 2003 constitutional revision opportunities to network into the West and win the confidence of European elites generally by soliciting the advice of the legal elite on revising the Romanian Constitution: "If Romania wants to give a signal … that the way to Europe is understood in a serious and profound way … [she] must anchor the Constitution, her most fundamental Law, to the European dimension" (Commission for the Elaboration of Legislative Proposals Concerning the Amendment of the Romanian Constitution 2003). In practice, this meant conforming to the transnational legal community's templates, supposed to prove that Romania was making credible efforts to fulfill Western expectations, particularly concerning the super-empowerment of the judiciary (Commission for the Elaboration of Legislative Proposals Concerning the Amendment of the Romanian Constitution 2003).

By 2003, the ranks of the constitution-drafters had swollen to include a new generation of legal professionals who were at the same time holding high political office, such as the justice ministry or even the premiership, and who had been trained abroad or otherwise socialized in the transnational legal community:

We [the CoE] speak very often about "the Strasbourg promotion of political leaders", because many, many prime ministers, presidents of new democracies ... have been members of the Parliamentary Assembly of the CoE, and that creates a certain solidarity between [them]. ... Strasbourg has been important in the formation of the political elite in the new democracies of CEE ... they learn about the others by exchange of experience, they learn about standards, the values, the norms and ... how these ... are being implemented in other countries. It's comparative law in action.[14]

It should be noted that there was little disagreement between the different generations about what kind of, or how much, power courts must be given. Thus, the Constitutional Court was empowered to decide conflicts of a constitutional nature between any state authorities, including (nominally) coequal branches of government – a competence that in fact places it in the supreme position – while any right of parliament to check or balance the Court's decisions was abolished (Stanciulescu 2010; Parau 2012a). Contrast this with the thinking of prominent Romanian jurists at the dawn of the twentieth century. Emanoil Miclescu (1861–1946), president of the interbellum High Court of Cassation, held the idea of judicial control of the other branches to be "insulting": "[t]he judiciary does not have such a right over the other two powers" (Miclescu 1922: 402).

Ordinary judicial independence was interpreted as entire autonomy; thus, parliament's power to appoint the Judiciary Council was abolished in favor of "self-election" of Council members by the whole corps of magistrates. Just as in 1990, this rather extreme feature of the transnational templates was taken up because of the legal community's deep sense of mistrust in "noxious"[15] (but democratic) politics (Parau 2012b).

In all of these moves the Romanian jurists were confirmed by their highly esteemed transnational counterparts in the Venice Commission: "The Venice Commission is made up of first-rate experts ... real experts ... it is the Holy Place of European law" (Iorgovan in Commission for the Elaboration of Legislative Proposals Concerning the Amendment of the Romanian Constitution 2003). Gerard Batliner (1928–2008), former Head of Government of Liechtenstein and a member of the Venice Commission,[16] advised the Romanian drafters to take care that "political power does not control [judges'] nominations, promotions and disciplinary action" (European Commission for Democracy Through Law 2001), and that Parliament is "charged only with confirming [the] choices made by magistrates" (European Commission for Democracy Through Law 2002).

---

[14] Author's interview with Jean-Louis Laurence, Director of the Political Affairs Directorate of the CoE's General Secretariat, Strasbourg, March 14, 2011.

[15] Author's interview with Rodica Stanoiu, Romanian justice minister, Bucharest, October 10, 2009.

[16] Retrieved June 12, 2010 from http://en.wikipedia.org/wiki/Gerard_Batliner.

As in 1991, so in 2003, the Romanian people were involved only as an afterthought at the ratification stage, which hardly counts as popular input into the drafting process. Contrast this with America's 1787 Convention, where those delegates elected directly by the people participated fully in fashioning the result, without handing it off to "experts" (Madison [1893] 1840). Relentlessly touted by elites as necessary for timely accession to the EU, ratification was redirected to become a vote on European integration itself, which of course enjoyed a very high level of public support.

The latest proposals for constitutional revision in 2005 again saw the delegation to a commission of legal professionals of the high responsibility of designing amendments. They were mostly constitutional law academics of a new generation who had had no hand in the 1991 Constitution, but who *had* been educated and socialized abroad (Comisia Prezidenţiala de Analiză a Regimului Politic şi Constituţional din România 2009). The usual low priority accorded to the judiciary by elected politicians opened yet another window of opportunity for the experts to empower themselves and their legal professional community as a whole, this time by "forbidding the nomination of Constitutional Court judges from amongst experienced politicians who have served as elected representatives in the past" to make room for experts of "recognized professional reputation" like themselves (Comisia Prezidenţiala de Analiză a Regimului Politic şi Constituţional din România 2009: 64).

18.9 CONCLUSIONS

Several theoretical inferences might be drawn from the evidence given in this chapter, to be tested by future research. Socio-legal scholarship has much to gain from opening up the black box of the state to see what in particular works inside. Elite agency motivated by collective identities, social perceptions, and political strategies is what causes the transnational diffusion of constitutional ideas. Elite learning emerges as the common thread running through all the cases of constitution-making presented earlier. Among peoples who are poor in human capital, elites go out of their way to learn from those who they are convinced know better. By the time they become statesmen or professionals involved in running the government, elites often possess hard-won knowledge from abroad, which they are keen to deploy to transform the state. Elites have always been the only ones sufficiently well situated to access Western ideas either via translations of classical texts or via socialization through immersion in Western societies. The theorization of "learning" ought to distinguish between these two distinct forms of learning, and test whether they have different effects on how "deep" the learning is – in particular, how and how much motivations are affected.

In the case of Romanians and possibly other East Europeans who have long aspired to emulate the West, the trend has long been for non-state elite actors to take up the cause of constitutionalism. Legally trained professionals have been most pivotal. Even the more recent constitutional revisions undertaken since the fall of communism show that, notwithstanding the context of European integration, they have continued the tradition of their predecessors from centuries past. By contrast, the trend of other elites has been to follow the lead of legal elites, but more out of strategic motives; for example, the behavior of common politicians seems to reflect other logics of diffusion such as acculturation.

In Eastern Europe, elites are motivated to apply at home what they have learned abroad in the West. Models of governance far closer to home (e.g., the Ottomans) provoke little but aversion. The "aspiration to" a closeness not yet realized rather than "closeness" per se must be counted among the mechanisms that drive transnational diffusion of norms to the East in Europe. And the theorization of closeness ought also to be expanded to include a perception of closeness on the basis of similar status in the international system, as exemplified by the deliberate Romanian imitation of the Belgian Constitution of 1831.

Empirical research and theorization might wish to take into account top-down forms of learning, too. Tutelage entails the agency of elites, this time belonging to the disseminating people or community. The motives of tutors no less than of tutorees would bear investigation. They may be motivated by a sense of moral duty to help in the advancement of democratizing nations.

Finally, East European elites have not learned only about constitutionalism, judiciary institutions, judicial independence, and judicialization. They have also learned to think of themselves as an elite within an elite, with broader opportunities for self-empowerment. This is certainly the case with the legal professional elites. It remains to be seen whether this elite self-consciousness will have the same impact on more "backward" societies like Romania as it has had in the West. In the East, "we the people" scarcely exists as a witting concept: the Romanian people, at least, still lie deeply dormant. In a nation where all classes of people actively participate in politics on some level or another, so that the boundary between rulers and ruled is fuzzier, norm entrepreneurs may still come out of nowhere (*cf.* Fritz 2008). More original and more viable norms are likelier to emerge under such conditions than where only a specialized elite has expectations of defining or influencing the common good.

REFERENCES

Abrams, I. 1957. "The Emergence of the International Law Societies." *The Review of Politics.* **19**(3): 361–380.

Almond, M. 1992. *The Rise and Fall of Nicolae & Elena Ceausescu*. London: Chapmans.

Alter, K. J. 2001. *Establishing the Supremacy of European Law: The Making of an International Rule of Law in Europe*. Oxford: Oxford University Press.

2009. *The European Court's Political Power: Selected Essays.* Oxford: Oxford University Press.

Bancaud, A. 2006. "Normalisation d'une innovation: le Conseil supérieur de la magistrature sous la IVe Republique." *Droit et Société.* 63–64: 371–391.

Berceanu, B., Dvoracek, M., Firoiu, D., Georgescu, V., Gionea, V., et al. 1984. *Istoria Dreptului Romanesc Vol. II.* Bucuresti: Editura Academiei Republicii Socialiste Romania.

Berkowitz, D., Pistor, K., and Richard, J. -F. 2000. "Economic Development, Legality, and the Transplant Effect." Retrieved September 10, 2012, from http://deepblue.lib.umich. edu/bitstream/2027.42/39692/3/wp308.pdf.

Bill Chávez, R. 2007. "The Appointment and Removal Process for Judges in Argentina: The Role of Judicial Councils and Impeachment Juries in Promoting Judicial Independence." *Latin America Politics and Society.* 49(2): 33–58.

Bogdanor, V. no year. *The Conflict between the Government and the Judges.* Oxford: Foundation for Law, Justice and Society.

Brătianu, V. I. 1921. "Nevoile Statului Modern si Constitutia Romaniei Mari" in Stroe, A. (ed.) *Constitutia din 1923 in dezbaterile contemporanilor.* Location: Humanitas, 1990.

Carra, J. -L. 1781. *Histoire de la Moldavie et de la Valachie: Avec une dissertation sur l'état actuel de ces deux provinces.* Neuchâtel: Société Typographique.

Checkel, J. 2012. Norm Entrepreneurship: Theoretical and Methodological Challenges. *The Evolution of International Norms and 'Norm Entrepreneurship': The Council of Europe in Comparative Perspective,* January. Wolfson College, Oxford University, retrieved from http://www.sfu.ca/content/dam/sfu/internationalstudies/checkel/Oxford-NormWorkshop-Paper.0112.pdf.

Cohen, A. 2007. "Cold War Law: Legal Entrepreneurs and the Emergence of a European Legal Field (1945–1965)" in Gessner, V. and Nelken, D. (eds.) *European Ways of Law: Towards a European Sociology of Law.* London: Hart Publishing.

2010. "Legal Professionals or Political Entrepreneurs? Constitution Making as a Process of Social Construction and Political Mobilization." *International Political Sociology.* 4(2): 107–123.

Cohen, A. and Vauchez, A. 2007. "Law, Lawyers, and Transnational Politics in the Production of Europe." *Law & Social Inquiry.* 32(1): 75–199.

Comisia Prezidenţiala de Analiză a Regimului Politic şi Constituţional din România. 2009. *Raport al Comisiei Prezidenţiale de Analiză a Regimului Politic şi Constituţional din România – Pentru consolidarea statului de drept.* Bucuresti: Presedintia Romaniei.

Commission for the Elaboration of Legislative Proposals Concerning the Amendment of the Romanian Constitution 2002. The Minutes of the Meeting of the Commission Drafting the Legislative Amendments for Revising the Constitution on 18.12.2002. Bucharest: Romanian Parliament.

2003. The Minutes of the Meeting of the Commission for the Elaboration of Legislative Proposal Concerning the Amendment of the Romanian Constitution on 7 February 2003. Bucharest: Romanian Parliament.

Conac, G. 2000. "O anterioritate română: controlul constituţionalităţii legilor în românia de la începutul secolului XX până în 1938 " Retrieved March 19, 2012, from http://www.ccr. ro/events/2000/ro/Conac.pdf.

Consiliul Frontului Salvarii Nationale. 1989. "Comunicat din 22 decembrie 1989 catre tara al Consiliului Frontului Salvarii Nationale " *Monitorul Oficial 1.*

Consultative Council of European Judges. 2008. *4th meeting of the Bureau Tartu (Estonia), 17 June 2008 CCJE-BU(2008)3.* Strasbourg: Consultative Council of European Judges.

Corfield, P. J. 1995. *Power and the Professions in Britain 1700–1850*. London and New York: Routledge.

de Luna, F. A. 1969. *The French Republic under Cavaignac*. Princeton, NJ: Princeton University Press.

Demşorean, A., Pârvulescu, S. and Vetrici-Şoimu, B. 2008. "Romania: Vetoed Reform, Skewed Results" in Magen, A. A. and Morlino, L. (eds.) *International Actors, Democratization and the Rule of Law*. London: Routledge.

Djuvara, N. 1989. *Între Orient şi Occident. Tările române la inceputul epocii moderne (1800–1848)*. Bucureşti: Humanitas.

Elster, J. 1995. "Forces and Mechanisms in the Constitution-Making Process." *Duke Law Review*. **45**: 364–396.

Erdos, D. 2010. *Delegating Rights Protection – The Rise of Bills of Rights in the Westminster World*. Oxford: Oxford University Press.

European Commission for Democracy Through Law 2001. Draft Consolidated Advice on the Revision of the Romanian Constitution CDL (2002)96. Strasbourg: European Commission for Democracy Through Law.

2002. Supplementary Advice on the Revision of the Romanian Constitution CDL (2002)138. Strasbourg: European Commission for Democracy Through Law.

Focseneanu, E. 1992. *Istoria constitutionala a României [The Constitutional History of Romania]*. Bucureşti: Humanitas.

Fritz, C. G. 2008. *American Sovereigns: The People and America's Constitutional Tradition Before the Civil War*. Cambridge: Cambridge University Press.

Gallagher, T. 2009. *Romania and the European Union. How the Weak Vanquished the Strong*. Manchester: Manchester University Press.

Galligan, D. 2013. "The People, the Constitution, and the Idea of Representation" in Galligan, D. and Versteeg, M. (eds.) *Social and Political Foundations of Constitutions*. Cambridge: Cambridge University Press.

Garoupa, N. and Ginsburg, T. 2009. "Guarding the Guardians: Judicial Councils and Judicial Independence." *American Journal of Comparative Law*. **57**: 103–134.

Georgescu, V. 1972. *Ideile Politice şi Iluminismul în Principatele Române 1750–1831*. Bucureşti: Editura Academiei Republicii Socialiste România.

Goderis, B. and Versteeg, M. 2013. "Transnational Constitutions" in Galligan, D. and Versteeg, M. (eds.) *Social and Political Foundations of Constitutions*. Cambridge: Cambridge University Press.

Goodman, R. J., Derek. 2004. "How to Influence States: Socialization and International Human Rights Law." *Duke Law Journal*. **54**(621): 642–646.

Guarnieri, C. 2004. "Appointment and Career of Judges in Continental Europe: The Rise of Judicial Self-Government." *Legal Studies*. **24**(1–2): 169–187.

Gutan, M. 2011. "Constituţionalism şi import constituţional în România modernă. Proiectul de Constituţie de la 1848 al lui Mihail Kogălniceanu [Constitutionalism and Constitutional Transplant in Modern Romania. The 1848 Constitutional Project of Mihail Kogălniceanu]." *Studia Politica. Romanian Political Science Review*. **11**(2): 227–254.

Guy, P. B. 2000. *Institutional Theory in Political Science: The New Institutionalism*. London: Continuum.

Heath, E. 1869. "Realism in British Foreign Policy." *Foreign Affairs*. **48**(1): 39–50.

Hirschl, R. 2013. "The Strategic Foundations of Constitutions." in Galligan, D. and Versteeg, M. (eds.) *Social and Political Foundations of Constitutions*. Cambridge: Cambridge University Press.

Hitchins, K. 1994. *Rumania 1866–1947*. Oxford: Oxford University Press.

1996. *The Romanians 1774–1866*. Oxford: Clarendon Press Oxford.

Ingram, M. C. 2011. "Crafting Courts in New Democracies: Ideology and Judicial Council Reforms in Three Mexican States." *Comparative Politics*. 4(4): 439–458.

Ingrao, C. W. 2000. *The Habsburg Monarchy 1618–1815*. Cambridge: Cambridge University Press.

Iorga, N. 1921. "Istoricul Constitutiei Romanesti" in Stroe, A. 1990. (ed.) *Constitutia din 1923 în dezbaterea* contemporanilor. Bucureşti: Humanitas.

Iorgovan, A. 1998. *Odiseea elaborării Constituţiei*. Târgu Mures: Vatra Româneasca.

Isar, N. 1991. *Publicişti francezi şi cauza română: 1834–1859 [French publicists and the Romanian cause: 1834–1859]*. Bucureşti: Editura Academiei Române.

Jennings, I. 1971. *The British Constitution*. Cambridge: Cambridge University Press.

Keck, M. E. and Sikkink, K. 1998. *Activists beyond Borders: Advocacy Networks in International Politics*. Ithaca, NY: Cornell University Press.

Kellogg, F. 1995. *The Road to Romanian Independence*. West Lafayette, IN: Purdue University Press.

Kogălniceanu, M. 1848 [1998]. "Proiect de Constitutie pentru Moldova" in Ionescu, C. (ed.) *Dezvoltarea constituţională a României. Acte si documente 1741–1991 [The Constitutional Development of Romania. Documents 1741–1991]*. Bucureşti: Lumina Lex.

1891. "Dezrobirea ţiganilor, ştergerea privilegiilor boiereşti, emanciparea ţăranilor. Discurs rostit la 1/13 aprilie 1891 în şedinţa solemnă a Academiei Române organizată cu ocazia împlinirii a 25 de ani de la fondare." Retrieved February 22, 2012, from http://ro.wikisource.org/wiki/Dezrobirea_%C8%9Biganilor,_%C8%99tergere a_privilegiilor_boiere%C8%99ti,_emanciparea_%C8%9B%C4%83ranilor.

Linz, J. J. and Stepan, A. C. 1996. *Problems of Democratic Transition and Consolidation. Southern Europe, South America, and Post-Communist Europe*. Baltimore, London: Johns Hopkins University Press.

Macovei, M. 1999 "The Procuracy and Its Problems." *East European Constitutional Review* 8.

Madison, J. 1788. "The Federalist No. 48. These Departments Should Not Be So Far Separated as to Have No Constitutional Control Over Each Other." Retrieved October 2, 2009, from http://avalon.law.yale.edu/18th_century/fed48.asp.

[1893] 1840. *Notes on the Debates in the Federal Convention of 1787 reported by James Madison*. New York and London: W. W. Norton & Company.

Mazilu, D. 1991. *Revoluţia furată. Memoriu pentru ţara mea*. Bucureşti: Cozia Ed.-Co. Iordache & Armbruster.

Merryman, J. H. and Perez-Perdomo, R. 2007. *The Civil Law Tradition. An Introduction of the Legal Systems of Europe and Latin America*. Stanford, CA: Stanford University Press.

Miclescu, E. 1922. "Sistemul Constitutional Anglo-Saxon" in Stroe, A. (ed.). 1990. *Constitutia din 1923 in dezbaterile contemporanilor*. Bucureşti: Humanitas.

Mihaila, I. 1995. "Voltaire dans la culture roumaine." *Balkan Studies (Etudes balkaniques)*. 2: 33–40.

Montesquieu, C., de Secondat Baron de. 1777. *The Spirit of the Laws*. Crowder, Wark, and Payne.

Orescu, V. M. 1929. *Le Controle de la Constitutionnalité des Lois en Roumanie. Faculte de Droit*. PhD thesis, L'Universite de Paris.

Parau, C. E. 2012a. "The Drive for Judicial Supremacy" in Seibert-Fohr, A. (ed.) *Judicial Independence in Transition*. New York: Springer.

2012b. "Explaining Judiciary Governance in Central and Eastern Europe: External Incentives, Transnational Elites and Parliament Inaction." unpublished manuscript.

Piana, D. 2007. "Unpacking Policy Transfer, Discovering Actors: The French Model of Judicial Education between Enlargement and Judicial Cooperation in the EU." *French Politics.* 5: 33–65.

2010. *Judicial Accountabilities in New Europe.* Farnham: Ashgate.

Popescu, M. 2003. "Parliamentary and Presidential Elections in Romania, November 2000." *Electoral Studies.* 22(2): 325–395.

Ramseyer, M. J. and Rasmusen, E. B. 2001. "Why Are Japanese Judges So Conservative in Politically Charged Cases?" *The American Political Science Review.* 95(2): 331–344.

Riker, T. W. 1971. *The Making of Roumania.* New York: Arno Press & The New York Times.

Risse, T. and Sikkink, K. 1999. "The Socialization of International Human Rights Norms Into Domestic Practices: Introduction" in Risse, T., Ropp, S. C. and Kathryn, S. (eds.) *The Power of Human Rights: International Norms and Domestic Change.* Cambridge: Cambridge University Press.

Rogers, E. M. 2003. *Diffusion of Innovations.* New York; London: Free Press.

Sacriste, G. and Vauchez, A. 2007. "The Force of International Law: Lawyers' Diplomacy on the International Scene in the 1920s." *Law & Social Inquiry.* 32(1): 83–107.

Sadurski, W. 2008. *Rights before Courts. A Study of Constitutional Courts of Post-Communist States of Central and Eastern Europe.* Dordrecht, The Netherlands: Springer.

2012. *Constitutionalism and the Enlargement of Europe.* Oxford: Oxford University Press.

Seibert-Fohr, A. (ed.) 2012. *Judicial Independence in Transition.* Heidelberg: Springer.

Siani-Davies, P. 2005. *The Romanian Revolution of December 1989.* Ithaca, NY: Cornell University Press.

Slaughter, A. -M. 1994. "A Typology of Transjudicial Communities." *University of Richmond Law Review.* 29: 99–134.

Stanciulescu, A. M. 2010. "Romania: A Personalistic Approach to Accountability" in Morlino, L. and Sadurski, W. (eds.) *Democratization and the European Union.* London: Routledge.

Stanomir, I. 2004. *Nasterea Constitutiei.* Bucureşti: Nemira.

2005. *Constituţionalism şi Postcommunism. Un Commentariu al Constituţiei României.* Bucureşti: Bucureşti University Press.

Stein, E. 1981. "Lawyers, Judges and the Making of a Transnational Constitution." *American Journal of International Law.* 75(3): 1–28.

Stoenescu, A. M. 2006. *Din culisele luptei pentru putere 1989–1990.* Bucureşti: RAO.

Stroe, A. 1990. *Constitutia din 1923 în dezbaterea contemporanilor.* Bucureşti: Humanitas

Sunstein, C. R. 1996. "Social Norms and Social Roles." *Columbia Law Review.* 96(4): 903–968.

Tate, N. and Vallinder, T. (eds.) 1995. *The Global Expansion of Judicial Power.* New York: New York University Press.

Tushnet, M. 1999. *Taking the Constitution Away from Courts.* Princeton, NJ: Princeton University Press.

Vauchez, A. 2008. "The Force of a Weak Field: Law and Lawyers in the Government of the European Union (For a Renewed Research Agenda)." *International Political Sociology.* 2(2): 128–144.

2010. "The Making of the European Union's Constitutional Foundations: The Brokering Role of Legal Entrepreneurs and Networks" in Kaiser, W., Leucht, B., and Gehler, M.

(eds.) *Transnational Networks in Regional Integration: Governing Europe 1945–1983*. Basingstoke: Palgrave Macmillan.

Vianu, T. 1970. *Scriitori români*. Bucureşti: Minerva.

Voltaire. 1734. *Lettres Philosophiques*. Amsterdam: chez E. Lucas.

1738. *The elements of Sir Isaac Newton's philosophy (translated from the French. Revised and corrected by John Hanna)*. London: printed for Stephen Austen.

Waldron, J. 2012. "Separation of Powers or Division of Power?" *Oxford-Harvard Law Colloquium, Law Faculty. Oxford*.

Weber, R. 2001. "Constitutionalism as a Vehicle for Democratic Consolidation" in Zielonka, J. (ed.) *Democratic Consolidation in Eastern Europe Volume 1: Institutional Engineering*. Oxford: Oxford University Press.

Wendt, A. 1994. "Collective Identity Formation and the International State." *American Political Science Review*. 88(2): 384–396.

Whittington, K. E. 2007. *Political Foundations of Judicial Supremacy*. Princeton, NJ and London: Princeton University Press.

Wyrzikowski, M. 2000. *Constitutional Cultures*. Warsaw: Institute of Public Affairs.

19

The Social and Political Foundations of the Nigerian Constitution

Charles O. H. Parkinson

19.1 INTRODUCTION

During the late nineteenth century, Britain acquired the territories of numerous disparate indigenous peoples within what is now Nigeria, and came to administer those territories within a single colonial administration. After World War II, Britain faced insurmountable pressure to decolonize its empire. In a process lasting less than ten years, Britain devolved power to locally controlled authorities and on October 1, 1960 granted independence to Nigeria. On October 1, 1963, Nigeria cut all legal ties with Britain and became a republic. In January 1966, a military government took control and there followed a devastating civil war. Between 1979 and 1983, civil rule was restored, after which period a military government again seized power. In 1999, civil rule was restored once again.

Nigeria's constitutional development thereby exhibits many features that may be described as common to the constitutional experience of a great number of Sub-Saharan African nations – an ethnically diverse population forged into a nation by a colonial past, the grant of independence made to local leaders with little experience of democratic institutions, and repeated suspensions of civil government followed by periods of military rule.

The focus of this chapter is the social and political foundations of Nigeria's independence constitution of 1960, and its subsequent operation between 1960 and 1966. Specifically, it seeks to identify the social and political influences on the constitution-making process that led to Nigeria's independence constitution of 1960, and to identify how that process led to certain failings in that constitution.

The constitution-making process leading to the independence constitution of 1960 and its short-lived operation are important as a transformative period in Nigeria's constitutional development. But they also have broader significance for two reasons.

First, Nigeria's constitutional decolonization is representative of, and provides insights into, the constitutional decolonization of Britain's other overseas territories. Nigeria was one of the early British territories to obtain independence, and the process of constitutional decolonization adopted by the Colonial Office and the resulting independence constitution's perceived failings informed Britain's approach to its other geographically dispersed territories. Second, Nigeria's constitutional experience at the time of decolonization and immediately thereafter is similar to many other African nation's postcolonial experiences with colonial-era constitutions.

At the outset it may be stated that there are two overarching themes in this chapter. The first concerns the impact of Nigeria's colonial past and Britain's influence as the decolonizing power on the form of Nigeria's independence constitution. In short, Nigeria's postcolonial constitutional system was the direct result of the British decolonization process, which brought both short-term benefits and long-term problems. The main short-term benefit was the peaceful transfer of power to a local government, and the main long-term problem was that the constitutional model did not assist in accommodating the fundamental social and political divisions within Nigerian society. The second theme (which is related to the first) concerns constitutional protection of minorities. In particular, this involves the tension between the demands from minorities for greater autonomy and the form of government necessary for the continued unity of the nation. Thus, it incorporates questions about whether Nigeria should have adopted a unitary or federal model, the number of regions it should comprise, as well as the role of fundamental rights in protecting minorities.

19.2 NIGERIA'S COLONIAL PAST

Consideration of Nigeria's independence constitution properly begins with an understanding of Nigeria's colonial past. That is so because the independence constitution closely followed the existing colonial political structure and Britain, as the decolonizing power, prescribed the process of constitutional decolonization and, in important respects, the form of the constitution under which it would grant Nigeria independence.

19.2.1 *Nigeria's Creation and the British Colonial Administration*

Nigeria is a nation forged by colonialism. Between 1861 and 1906, Britain expanded its imperial interests in West Africa by conquering or annexing many independent kingdoms and empires, such as the Yoruba kingdom, the Benin kingdom, and the Fulani emirate, that comprise modern Nigeria (Lynn 2001; Grove 1963). Britain administered these territories using a system of indirect rule, whereby existing political institutions were retained.

The major landmarks in Nigeria's early constitutional development occurred in 1914, when Britain united its geographically proximate territories into a centralized state, and 1922, when Britain structured Nigeria into three regions – north, east, and west. Thereafter three regions lay at the heart of Nigeria's political structure during British rule.

The consequence of Nigeria's colonial origins was its heterogeneous peoples with ethnic, linguistic, cultural, and religious differences, both as a nation and within each of the three regions. A snapshot of the population of Nigeria at independence highlights these differences (Ezera 1964: 245; Coleman 1971: 384–396).[1] The Northern Region comprised approximately three-quarters of the landmass of Nigeria with the population of 16 million people, 10 million of whom were Muslim, with the majority of non-Muslims following customary beliefs and a small Christian minority. The Muslim majority was Hausa, but there was a large group of non-Hausa people in the "Middle Belt" and in Bornu. In the Eastern Region there were 7 million people, who were predominantly Christian and pagan. The dominant ethnic group was Ibo, but there were large enclaves of non-Ibo. The almost 7 million Western Nigerians were the most religiously diverse, two-fifths being Christian, two-fifths Muslim, and the remainder following customary beliefs. Five million Western Nigerians were Yoruba and the rest non-Yoruba people of Benin, Warri, and the Asaba-Ibos.

Beyond the regional differences, there was also a major division between the Northern Region on the one hand and the southern Eastern and Western Regions on the other. The north was predominantly Muslim, culturally Islamic, and had a comparatively poor education system. Politically it was still controlled by its Islamic hereditary rulers who adhered to conservative policies. The south was largely Christian and pagan and had been infused with Western ideas and mission schools. Its leaders were politically progressive and popularly elected. The basic cause of north/south tension was the north's apprehension that a southern cultural, religious, and political hegemony would be imposed on it.

Of particular significance for the purposes of this work is the fact that the divide between north and south also translated into major differences between their respective legal cultures. English law had first been introduced in Lagos in 1863, but its reception into the legal culture was still limited in the 1950s. That said, many of the leading southern politicians were trained lawyers and ardent advocates of British constitutional principles. In the south, customary courts operated alongside British common law courts. As a result, law was still viewed as a prerogative of rulership rather than an objective system designed to protect individuals (Adewoye 1988: 722). In the north there was a dual system of Sharia courts and British common law courts.

---

[1] Constitutional Developments in the Federations of Malaya and Nigeria, May 10, 1957, CO 1030/436; Nigeria, Constitutional and Political, Correspondence 1955–1958, CO 879/165.

But the Sharia courts had the support of the ruling elite, whose members were also the leaders of the Islamic faith. Consequently, British legal principles did not have primacy in northern legal culture (Campbell 1963: 1–7).

Finally, it must be recognized that Nigeria was, at least until World War II, primarily viewed both by Britain and most Nigerians as an administrative unit. That is, prior to World War II there was little sense of any Nigerian nationalism, which may be contrasted with the public displays made elsewhere in Britain's overseas empire, such as in India.

19.2.2 *The British Decolonization Model*

British rule also impacted upon the post-independence constitutional structure of Nigeria because Britain mandated certain constitutional steps leading to independence. The Colonial Office had developed, through its experience with the "old dominions," a template for preparing a colony for independence. It was an evolutionary process, granting powers incrementally to local political institutions and providing experience to local leaders with the Westminster system, but always under strict British control. Common steps included establishment of a local legislature for consultation purposes, but without lawmaking powers; an increasing franchise for the local legislature and the granting of limited lawmaking powers; a conferral of limited executive powers upon local leaders on principles of responsible government; and finally the granting of self-government over internal matters. Each step in this process often involved a constitutional conference, followed by the granting of new constitutional powers. The effect of this staged process was that the declared goal to which local leaders aspired was a constitutional system modeled on Westminster principles of both responsible government and representative government. Other models, such as the Washington presidential model, were simply not contemplated.

In the case of Nigeria, as with most of Britain's African territories, decolonization occurred on a much shorter timeframe than the British government expected. The Nigerian Constitution of 1951 took the first meaningful steps in the declared evolutionary stages of Nigeria's constitutional and political development leading to independence. At that time it was expected, at least by the British government, that Nigeria would not gain independence for some twenty years, thereby giving Britain the opportunity to take Nigeria through each stage. But this was not to be, because the so-called winds of change precipitated the sudden decolonization of Britain's overseas empire. The consequence was that the Nigerian political and constitutional system was established in less than ten years and the local politicians were given only three years of experience with self-government under the Westminster system before independence.

Within the confines of the declared evolutionary model leading up to independence, decolonization politics resulted in a complex interplay of actors seeking to determine the final form of the independence constitution, each with different, often competing, motivations. This was a dynamic repeated throughout the colonies. It is useful to touch on each key actor because it demonstrates the complex interplay within the constitution-making process: the Secretary of State for the Colonies was the key political figure, responsible to Westminster; the Colonial Office administered colonial policy across Britain's disparate territories; local British officials in the colony provided a local perspective; the Commonwealth Relations Office administered Britain's foreign policy with its former colonies; British legal and policy experts provided advice; local majority political parties and minority political parties jostled for advantage in the post-independence system; ethnic minority groups sought constitutional restrictions on power; and interest groups pressed sectional interests, such as church groups wanting constitutional protection for religious freedom, local bar associations wanting guarantees of judicial independence, and chambers of commerce wanting constitutional protection of property rights to protect foreign investment.

It is useful also to explain what may be termed the constitutional decolonization dynamic because it provides an insight into what took place at decolonization. In its simplest form, it may be described in the following terms (Parkinson 2007: 266–267).

The British government had two distinct but coterminous aims in decolonizing its overseas empire. First, it wanted the transfer of power at independence to take place without violence. The British experience in Palestine and India and the events then occurring in the Congo and Algeria highlighted the peril both short and long term of having to abandon a colony in the grip of civil conflict. Second, Britain wanted to create a viable long-term stable civil society. Both these aims required the involvement of the local political groups in the decolonization process and their consensus.

Decolonization created a dynamic within each territory with a vocal minority apprehensive about the withdrawal of British oversight. Throughout the dependencies, minority groups proposed constitutional instruments for independence that were designed to restrict the power of the majority group. Thus, common minority proposals were for devolution of power from the central government (often on a federal model), reserved seats for minority groups in the legislatures, a council of state with power to veto discriminatory legislation, and a justiciable bill of rights. The majority group, however, aspired to maximize its powers in the independence settlement. Thus the majority conceded only those instruments that least restricted its post-independence powers. That is one reason why there was frequently local consensus for bills of rights, because majority groups often did not view them as a meaningful limitation on their power.

The Colonial Office created a local political environment that fostered consensus. The Colonial Office wanted the peaceful transfer of power with a viable constitution within which all the major groups would participate. It was equally important that the majority group felt able to govern under the constitution and hence not rewrite it after independence as it was for the minority groups to feel able to oppose the government without recourse to violent dissent. To achieve this outcome the Colonial Office exerted great pressure on local groups to agree to the design of any new constitution. The incentive for majority groups (and frequently minority groups also) to agree was that the British government rarely granted a new constitution, and hence any extra powers of self-determination contained therein, without local agreement.

As will be seen for Nigeria, the absence of a single dominant majority group and instead, three competing groups, each dominant in one region, as well as numerous minorities, complicated this model. But it remains the case in Nigeria that the local groups acted in a self-interested way to protect their interests post-independence through constitutional means.

19.3 THE CONSTITUTION-MAKING PROCESS

The Nigerian independence constitution was drafted over a ten-year period, with each successive amendment moving the document closer to the declared goal of independence with a constitution modeled on that at Westminster. What follows is a narrative of that process, focusing on the key issue that arose during it, namely how best to protect the minorities so as to avoid future civil conflict while maintaining national unity.

19.3.1 *The Macpherson Constitution*

The start of the constitution-making process for the independence constitution may properly be said to begin with the Macpherson Constitution of 1951, named after Sir John Macpherson, the governor general who headed the constitutional review (Awolowo 1966: 6). Macpherson asked the people of Nigeria whether they wanted centralized or federal government; and if federal, whether it should be based on the existing three regions, or new regions on another basis, such as language. Ultimately, however, neither issue was resolved, and the status quo was maintained.

The Macpherson Constitution did, however, increase the number of elected members to the regional legislatures and confer upon them limited legislative powers. In addition, limited executive powers were granted to the regional ministries. But all these powers were made subject to the effective control of British officials (Nwabueze 1982a: 46–52).

After the Macpherson Constitution was proclaimed in 1951, the political land-scape of Nigeria settled into the form it would retain until independence. The rul-ing party in the Northern Region was the traditionalist Northern People's Congress, which took its support from the Hausa. Its political leader was Alhaji Ahmadu Bello, the Sardauna of Sokoto. The Eastern Region was controlled by the National Council of Nigeria and the Cameroons, an Ibo-dominated party, led by Dr. Nnmadi Azikiwe, a nominal Anglican. The Western Region was led by the Methodist Chief Obafemi Awolowo of the Action Group, which was the political party of the Yoruba. Each region was controlled by a political party whose support was based on tribal or linguistic affiliation. Consequently, the dominant party was different in each region and the main opposition in each region came principally from a political party in power in another region. But there were also many smaller tribal and linguistic minorities (Ezera 1964: 247). Certainly, there was no political party that could be described as a national party. As for politics, the main parties did not appear to have strong ideological differences in their policies (Robertson 1974: 187).

19.3.2 *The Lyttelton Constitution*

The Action Group from Western Nigeria wanted to accelerate Nigeria's progress to independence and so in 1953 withdrew its support for the Macpherson Constitution, resulting in a constitutional conference to review the Macpherson Constitution.

The constitutional conference, which began in London on July 30, 1953, dealt with two major issues. The first was the form of government for Nigeria. Immediately after the constitutional crisis, the Action Group and the National Council of Nigeria and the Cameroons formed a short-term alliance (Awolowo 1960: 180, 243), within which the Action Group took the lead on policy formulation (Awolowo 1960: 225). Awolowo was an ardent federalist and personally convinced the National Council of Nigeria and the Cameroons that federalism was the best model for Nigeria (Awolowo 1960: 160). The Northern People's Congress wanted a form of govern-ment more devolved than a traditional federation because it feared giving any power to the central government, but finally agreed. The British government, which had previously preferred a unitary system, accepted a federation based around the three regions because each region was large enough to be self-sufficient.

The other major issue considered at the conference was the timetable for independence. The Action Group and the National Council of Nigeria and the Cameroons proposed independence in 1956. The Northern People's Congress, however, did not support immediate independence as it feared that the Northern Region would be subsumed by the southern regions.[2] The British government also

---

[2] Constitutional Developments in the Federations of Malaya and Nigeria, May 10, 1957, CO 1030/436.

opposed independence in the short term because it believed that Nigeria was not yet ready to govern itself. The Secretary of State for the Colonies therefore announced that another constitutional conference would be held in three years at which self-government would be given to those regions wanting it and at which Nigeria's independence would again be considered.

A third issue, a bill of rights, also arose at the conference. The Action Group and the National Council of Nigeria and the Cameroons proposed a bill of rights,[3] which was closely linked to their demands for a federal system and independence (Azikiwi 1961: 6, 8). The impetus for the bill of rights came from Awolowo, a teacher and trade union leader who studied law in London before returning to Nigeria to practice law and pursue a political career. He had two discernable reasons for supporting a bill of rights. First, Awolowo had the ambition to be leader of Nigeria and he knew that to attain this position he would have to win a proportion of Northern electorates (Robertson 1974: 233). But the Northern People's Congress actively restricted other political parties campaigning in the North. Awolowo saw the bill of rights (with the rights to freedom of speech, assembly, and movement) as a legal mechanism that would allow the Action Group to campaign freely in the North (Adewoye 1988: 729, 736). Second, Awolowo believed that the only way to prevent a dictator taking over Nigeria was to create an enlightened community that respected the rule of law and that gave the people the opportunity to elect their leaders (Okunade 1988: 765; Awolowo 1960: 255, 272–273). As there was no tradition of the rule of law or parliamentary democracy in Nigeria, Awolowo thought that a bill of rights would help build this tradition.

When Awolowo raised the issue of fundamental rights at the conference in 1953,[4] the Secretary of State for the Colonies ridiculed a bill of rights out of serious consideration by saying that the Nigerians could put "God is Love" into their constitution if they so wished, but not while he was chairing the conference (Lyttelton 1962: 410–411).[5] This stance reflected the orthodox Colonial Office position on bills of rights in colonial constitutions, namely that such instruments are of little value and were unknown in British colonial constitutions.[6]

---

[3] Joint Memorandum by the Action Group and the National Council of Nigeria and the Cameroons, Fundamental Rights, August 12, 1953, CO 554/1184; Right to Freedom, Supplementary Joint Memorandum by the Action Group and the National Council of Nigeria and the Cameroons, August 13, 1953, CO 554/1184.

[4] NC (53) 13th meeting, CO 554/1184; Ian Watt, December 13, 1956, CO 554/828.

[5] J. B. Johnston, Lyttelton's Principal Private Secretary, recalled him saying: 'Why not also put in God is love?': J. B. Johnston, December 13, 1956, CO 554/828. That said, the conference later agreed to a right guaranteeing compensation for compulsorily acquired property in the Lyttelton Constitution of 1954: NC (53) 14th meeting, CO 554/1184; Nigeria (Constitution) Order in Council 1954, s 223.

[6] Brief No 14, Provisions for Safeguarding Religious Freedom and Declaration of Fundamental Rights, April 1, 1957, Briefs for the Secretary of State for the Colonies: Nigeria Constitutional Conference 1957, CO 554/1184; John Marnham, April 21, 1953, CO 1015/156.

The resulting Lyttelton Constitution, named after Oliver Lyttelton, the Secretary of State for the Colonies, came into operation in September 1954.

19.3.3 *The 1957 Constitutional Conference*

The foreshadowed next constitutional conference was set to commence on May 23, 1957 (Robertson 1974: 199–200).[7] The British government's position at the conference was the result of external factors. Ghana had applied for membership of the Commonwealth following its independence in March 1957. Acceptance was determined by a vote of the existing members of the Commonwealth, dominated by the "old Dominions." Although Ghana was admitted, South Africa was openly opposed and Australia and New Zealand privately expressed strong misgivings. With Malayan independence scheduled for later that year and its application for membership of the Commonwealth to follow, there was great concern among the "old Dominions" about the prospect of an independent Nigeria joining the Commonwealth and creating an Asian-African bloc that outnumbered them. The Colonial Committee of Cabinet therefore decided just before the start of the 1957 conference to slow Nigeria's progress toward independence. The method identified was to establish a commission to review the form of the independence constitution.[8]

The three regional political parties presented a uniform position to the conference calling for independence in 1959 (Robertson 1974: 207; Awolowo 1960: 225). The British government rejected this request and instead offered internal self-government to the regions and limited self-government to the federation. Both the Action Group and the National Council of Nigeria and the Cameroons grasped the offer and Awolowo and Azikiwe became the effective rulers of their regions in August 1957. The Northern People's Congress, however, decided to delay the grant of self-government until the next constitutional conference. The lower education levels in the North meant that the Northern civil service contained many southern Nigerians. The Northern People's Congress feared handing control of its civil service to southerners and consequently wanted time to "Northernize" its civil service (Ezera 1964: 233).

Self-government for the East and West required consideration of the form and powers of the regional governments. The regions were to have an elected lower house and house of chiefs. Independent commissions were to be established for all appointments to the judiciary and public service. The major issue was whether

---

[7] Constitutional Developments in the Federations of Malaya and Nigeria, May 10, 1957, CO 1030/436.
[8] Minutes of Colonial Committee of Cabinet, May 13 and 16, 1957, CO 957/6; Alan Lennox-Boyd to Harold Macmillan, September 5, 1958, C (58) 171, PREM 11/2436.

police should continue under federal control (still under effective British control) or be transferred to the control of the regions with self-government. The Action Group and Northern People's Congress pressed for regional control; the British government and Northern Council of Nigeria and the Cameroons supported the status quo, such that control remained with the federal government.

Limited self-government for the federation was to be effected by the direct election of the House of Representatives, the establishment of a senate, and the creation of the position of prime minister.[9] The governor general, Sir James Robertson, later appointed Abubakar Tafawa Balewa, the leader of the Northern People's Congress in the federal legislature, as prime minister (Robertson 1974: 213). Abubakar was a locally trained history teacher who had obtained his professional certificate from the Institute of Education at the University of London (Ezera 1964: 241). The leaders of the parties had remained as heads of their respective regional governments and instead sent their deputies to the federal legislature (Ezera 1964: 189).

The Secretary of State for the Colonies did not need to look hard to identify controversial issues for a commission to examine. The main question at the 1957 constitutional conference was how to deal with the ethnic minority groups.[10] By late 1955, the ethnic minority groups were pushing for new regions (Awolowo 1960: 184). They accused their respective regional governments of oppression, victimization, and tyranny and feared that the situation would only deteriorate after independence (Awolowo 1960: 196). The positions of the three governing parties on new states were fluid, but when the conference began, the Action Group supported one new state per region, the National Council of Nigeria and the Cameroons proposed seventeen new states, and the Northern People's Congress opposed any new states (Awolowo 1960: 183–85, 190). The stance of each party was based on a political calculation to maximize its own power (Robertson 1974: 188; Awolowo 1960: 198–199). From 1955 the Secretary of State for the Colonies and the British officials in Nigeria had strongly opposed the fragmentation of the regions because they thought that new states would undermine the unity of Nigeria (Robertson 1974: 180; Awolowo 1960: 207). Further, the Colonial Office felt that the current regional structure worked well and that the administrative difficulties in creating new states would outweigh the benefits to the ethnic minority groups.[11] There was also the fear that the Northern Region would withdraw from the federation if the conference proposed dividing the north.[12] In consequence, the conference agreed to create a commission of enquiry into safeguards for minority groups.[13]

---

[9] Cmd 207 of 1957 art 21.
[10] Nigeria Constitutional Conference 1957, NC (57), CAB 133/227.
[11] Constitutional Developments in the Federations of Malaya and Nigeria, May 10, 1957, CO 1030/436.
[12] Sir Ivor Jennings, May 10, 1957, Jennings Papers (University of London), B/14/5.
[13] *Report of the Nigerian Constitutional Conference* (Cmnd 207, 1957) para 24(b).

The conference also appointed two other minor commissions: a fiscal commission on the financial division between the state and federal governments (Robertson 1974: 205), and a federal boundaries delimitation commission to divide the country into single-member constituencies for the next federal election. All three commissions were expected to report to the resumed constitutional conference in late 1958.

The question of a bill of rights was again raised at the conference.[14] The Action Group had prepared a memorandum on fundamental rights that Awolowo informed the conference had been agreed by all the regional governments.[15] Significantly, the Northern People's Congress had dropped its opposition to a bill of rights and instead wanted something modeled on the bill of rights contained in the Sudan Self-Government Statute, which had been drafted to reflect that territory's predominantly Muslim population.[16] Abubakar, the deputy leader of the Northern People's Congress, later implied that this reversal was the result of a fear that without a bill of rights one sectional interest could "twist and change the shape of [Nigeria's] laws ... to deprive even a majority of their citizens of their rights" (Balewa 1964: 84).

Since the 1953 Constitutional Conference, the Colonial Office had reviewed its policy on colonial bills of rights and, in a fundamental policy shift, changed its position from total opposition to a bill of rights in any colonial constitution to limited support for a bill of rights for Nigeria's independence constitution.[17] The most important factor in the Colonial Office's change of policy was the lobbying of Christian Church organizations and the prospect that they would become a political embarrassment to the Secretary of State for the Colonies if a right to religious freedom was not included to allow their continued work in predominantly Muslim and Catholic areas of Nigeria.[18]

In response to the Action Group's memorandum, Lord Perth, minister of state and chair of the conference, at once suggested that owing to the complexity of the subject the Colonial Office lawyers should consider the proposal in depth and prepare a revised version to discuss at the resumed conference.[19]

[14] Nigeria Constitutional Conference, June 24, 1957, CO 554/1534.

[15] *Report of the Nigeria Constitutional Conference* (Cmnd 207, 1957) para 67; Action Group, Fundamental Rights Revised Memorandum, NC (57) 104, CO 554/1534.

[16] Sir James Robertson to Tom Williamson, 16 December 1955, Sir Ralph Grey to Tom Williamson, March 6, 1956, CO 554/1184.

[17] The catalyst for this review was fear about the absence of a guarantee for religious freedom in the Northern Region once self-government had been granted to that region: Sir Bryan Sharwood-Smith to Alan Lennox-Boyd, August 25, 1955, CO 554/1184.

[18] CO 554/1184.

[19] Nigeria Constitutional Conference, June 24, 1957, CO 554/1534.

19.3.4 *The Bill of Rights*

It is important to understand how the bill of rights was elevated to its status as the central constitutional protection for minorities in the Nigerian constitution.

Sir Henry Willink, a lawyer who had become Master of Magdalene College, Cambridge, after a short career as a Conservative MP, was appointed to chair the minorities commission. The records of Willink's meetings in Nigeria show that the real issue for the minority groups that he met was the creation of new states (Bello 1962: 215).[20] But given the opposition to new states from both the British government and the Northern People's Congress, they were not a politically viable option.

Willink therefore decided to propose a far-reaching bill of rights as one of the main minority protections. In fact, the record of Willink's meetings in Nigeria indicates that there was little local interest in a bill of rights as a mechanism for minority protection and a bill of rights was raised on only two occasions with the commission – both by Christian Church organizations (Bello 1962: 215).[21] Either the minority groups did not view a bill of rights as a minority protection or, as was more likely, they thought the 1957 constitutional conference had already decided the matter.

He also chose to recommend that control of the police force be vested in the federal government rather than the regional governments, which again had been agreed at the 1957 constitutional conference, and finally he proposed special minority areas in the Western Region and the Eastern Region.[22]

On Willink's return to England he met with Christopher Eastwood, the Assistant Under Secretary responsible for West Africa in the Colonial Office, and inquired about the Colonial Office's progress on drafting the bill of rights (as foreshadowed by Lord Perth at the constitutional conference), seeking a copy of it once completed.[23]

The Colonial Office was then preparing a draft bill of rights. While there can be no doubt that Willink's request for the bills of rights influenced the Colonial Office to prepare an expansive document, two other factors were also relevant. First, Malaya's experience with a bill of rights had demonstrated the difficulties of negotiating a document tailored to meet the specific requirements of a dependency. The lesson learned was that it would be easier to submit an extensive bill of rights and place the burden on the majority party to justify the reasons that a right should

---

[20] CO 957/1–40.
[21] See: CO 957/1–40; November 24, 1957, CO 957/6; January 30, 1958, CO 957/6.
[22] *Report of the Commission appointed to enquire into the fears of minorities and the means of allaying them* (Cmnd 505, 1958); *Report of the Nigerian Constitutional Conference* (Cmnd 207, 1957).
[23] Christopher Eastwood, March 13, 1958, CO 554/1534.

not be inserted, rather than the Colonial Office having to justify the inclusion of every right. Second, in the case of Ghana, the Colonial Office had reconsidered its attitude toward the value of bills of rights in reconciling minority communities with the transfer of power to a local government. The Colonial Office now saw real merit in a bill of rights because some minorities felt that a bill of rights would, at least to some extent, protect them after independence. Further, the human rights violations then being perpetrated in the newly independent Ghana gave the Colonial Office advisers reason to doubt their decision not to insert a bill of rights into Ghana's independence constitution.

Interestingly, it was not the Colonial Office legal advisers (or in fact any trained lawyer), but the West Africa Department that selected those rights to be included in the draft bill of rights.[24] The aim of the Nigeria Working Group, as the drafting party was called,[25] was to keep the number of rights to a minimum, but consistent with safeguarding minorities and stopping gross human rights abuses such as slavery and torture.[26]

The methodology of the Nigeria Working Group was to cut and paste a bill of rights from various sources. Eastwood later described the approach of the Nigeria Working Group to preparing the draft bill of rights in a minute: "[w]e have taken the European Convention (to which Nigeria adheres) as a model with bits and pieces from the Sudan, Pakistan, Malaya and elsewhere."[27] But the process was more complex. The Nigeria Working Group drew up a list of every right protected in a human rights instrument drafted by British lawyers within the previous thirty years as well as those in the Action Group Memorandum; if the Indian or Pakistan constitutions contained a right already covered, it too was noted. No other "foreign" examples were drawn upon, principally because the Colonial Office prepared constitutions in the British legal tradition of drafting in detail and so only considered useful precedents written by British-trained lawyers. British pride and a lack of knowledge about other precedents were other probable considerations: only Commonwealth and international precedents were ever used within the Colonial Office. As the European Convention on Human Rights was the most comprehensive bill of rights

---

[24] Anthony Rushford, December 4, 1957, CO 554/1534.

[25] It was led by Eastwood and included Aaron Emanuel, Ian Watt, E.C. Burr, and Maurice Smith.

[26] See CO 554/1534.

[27] Christopher Eastwood, August 27, 1958, CO 554/1535. The 1957 conference brief listed the precedents as the constitutions of Ghana, Ceylon, the Federation of Rhodesia and Nyasaland, the Sudan, Pakistan, India, and the proposed preamble in the constitution of the British Caribbean Federation, as well as the United Nations Declaration of Fundamental Rights: Brief No 14, Provisions for Safeguarding Religious Freedom and Declaration of Fundamental Human rights, April 1, 1957, Briefs for the Secretary of State: Nigeria Constitutional Conference 1957, CO 879/164. The 1958 conference brief added the constitutions of Malta, Malaya, and Kenya: Brief No 4, Fundamental Rights, Briefs for the Secretary of State: Resumed Nigeria Constitutional Conference 1958, Appendix C, CO 554/1535; CO 554/2594; CO 879/176.

then drafted with the input of British lawyers, it necessarily formed the backbone of the list,[28] being used in fourteen of the eighteen sections.[29]

The Nigeria Working Group then reviewed the list, deleting provisions that might be provocative to the North and adding others.[30] It would appear from the Colonial

---

[28] Note of Meeting of the Nigeria Working Party, April 16, 1958, CO 554/1534.

[29] The list, and origin of the provision, is as follows:

1. All persons free and equal before the law and all subject to the law, as administered by the courts of justice: Sudan Self-Government Statute, ss 5 and 8.

2. Right to life protected by law: European Declaration of Human Rights, s 2.

3. No torture or inhuman or degrading treatment: Ibid., s 3.

4. No slavery: Ibid., s 4(1).

5. No forced or compulsory labour with exceptions: Ibid., s 4(2).

6. Right to liberty save in accordance with law – habeas corpus: Ibid., s 5; Action Group Memorandum, s 3; Sudan Self-Government Statute, s 6.

7. Fair and public trial within reasonable time; presumption of innocence until proven guilty; right to legal assistance: European Declaration on Human Rights, s 6; Action Group Memorandum, s 4; Indian Constitution, s 20 (added later).

8. No one can be guilty of a criminal act constituted after the act: European Declaration on Human Rights, s 7.

9. Everyone has the right to respect for his private and family life, home and correspondence: Ibid, s 8.

10. (i) Freedom of thought, conscience and religion, including right to change religion and to manifest it or to propagate it: Ibid, s 9.

    (ii) no religion to be established: Action Group Memorandum, s 1.

    (iii) instruction in a different religion from his own not to be compulsory for any student at an educational institution: Constitution of Pakistan, s 13.

    (iv) Religious denominations or communities to have right to run their own educational institutions: Constitution of India, s 25; Constitution of Pakistan, s 18; Ghana (Constitution) Order in Council 1957, SI 1957 No 227, s 31(3).

    (v) No disabilities on account of race or religion: Ghana (Constitution) Order in Council 1957, SI 1957 No 227, s 30(2). No discrimination in eligibility for employment: Sudan Self-Government Statute, s 5(2); Rhodesia (Constitution) Order in Council, s 40.

11. Freedom of expression: European Declaration on Human Rights, s 10; Action Group Memorandum, s 7; Sudan Self-Government Statute, s 7(2). Freedom to address meetings in any part of Nigeria: Action Group Memorandum, s 7.

12. Freedom of association and peaceful assembly: European Declaration on Human Rights, s 11; Sudan Self-Government Statute, s 7(2).

13. The right to move freely throughout Nigeria: Action Group Memorandum, s 7(5); Malayan Constitution, s 9(2) (added later).

14. The right to marry! European Declaration on Human Rights, s 12.

15. Right to compensation if deprived of property: Ghana (Constitution) Order in Council 1957, SI 1957 No 227, s 34; Action Group Memorandum, s 6; Nigeria (Constitution) Order in Council 1957, s 223 (added later).

16. Independence of the judiciary.

17. Remedy before the courts for any violations of rights: European Declaration on Human Rights, s 13; Action Group Memorandum, s 8; Sudan Self-Government Statute, s 10.

18. All above rights secured without discrimination on grounds of sex, race, colour, language, religion, political or other opinion, national or social origin, association with a national minority, property, birth or other status: European Declaration on Human Rights, s 14.

[30] The final draft of the Nigeria Working Group deleted sections 1 and 10(ii)-(v), removed sections 16 and 17 to another part of the constitution, and added a prohibition on double jeopardy and a right

Office files that no thought was given to how the bill of rights would take root or how it would be enforced.

The major issue on which the Nigeria Working Group sought legal advice was the effectiveness of its proposed bill of rights in stopping human rights abuses. The test to which the legal advisers put the draft bill of rights was to assess whether it would have made unlawful that "most disreputable" Ghana Preventive Detention Bill; they concluded that the proposed bill of rights was quite sufficient.[31]

In August 1958, Willink released his report,[32] which, without acknowledgment,[33] produced a virtual digest of the draft bill of rights from the Colonial Office.[34]

19.3.5 *The 1958 Resumed Constitutional Conference*

The resumed constitutional conference began in September 1958. Once again the two main issues were new states and the timetable for independence. The British government endorsed the commission's proposals. The Northern People's Congress was relieved that the commission had not recommended new states and consequently accepted the rest of the report (Bello 1962: 216). The National Council of Nigeria and the Cameroons, which had proposed seventeen new states at the last constitutional conference, fell into line with the Northern People's Congress and so supported the commission's recommendations. But Awolowo, who had pushed so hard for new states, found the commission's findings "bad and astonishing." He continued:

> What the Commission apparently regards as its most important recommendations ... relate to fundamental human rights. What intrinsic and inseparable nexus is there between the fears of minorities and fundamental human rights? None whatsoever.... Fundamental rights are ordained not for the protection of ethnic minorities as such but for the protection of the citizens at large against executive and legislative tyranny or excess. In other words, even if Nigeria was divided into states on an ethnic basis, or even if it consisted of one homogeneous ethnic group,

---

against self-incrimination: Brief No 4, Fundamental Rights, Briefs for the Secretary of State: Resumed Nigeria Constitutional Conference 1957, CO 554/1535; see CO 554/2594 and CO 879/176.

[31] Anthony Rushford, July 28, 1958, CO 554/1534.

[32] *Report of the Commission appointed to enquire into the fears of minorities and the means of allaying them* (Cmnd 505, 1958).

[33] Christopher Eastwood, August 27, 1958, CO 554/1535; Sir John Macpherson, August 31, 1958, CO 554/1535.

[34] The main differences between the Colonial Office's and Willink's bills of rights was that Willink omitted the prohibition on double jeopardy and the right against self-incrimination and added a list of enumerated rights to bolster the religious freedom guarantee: *Report of the Commission appointed to enquire into the fears of minorities and the means of allaying them* (Cmnd 505, 1958).

it would still have been necessary to entrench fundamental human rights in our constitution.[35] (Awolowo 1960: 201–202)

Further, as Awolowo noted, fundamental rights were going to be incorporated into the new constitution anyway. At least in part, Awolowo's posturing was intended to win him the support of the minorities at the next federal election (Awolowo 1960: 198–199). The Action Group therefore rejected the commission's report and again proposed one new state per region.

Awolowo's assertion about the relationship between the protection of minorities and bills of rights would certainly have been treated with sympathy within the Colonial Office. On the first day of the resumed conference, the Secretary of State for the Colonies informed the delegates that "[p]erhaps the most important motive for incorporating clauses on fundamental rights in the Constitution was to prevent unobtrusive encroachment on individual rights."[36] Writing a few years later, de Smith, now a trusted Colonial Office constitutional adviser, agreed that "justiciable guarantees of fundamental rights do not in terms safeguard the rights of minorities; they safeguard the enumerated rights of individuals" (de Smith 1964: 179; de Smith 1961: 216). Similarly, Roberts-Wray, the legal adviser in the Colonial Office, asserted that apart from a section prohibiting racial discrimination, "their purpose has little or nothing to do with the protection of communal minorities" (Roberts-Wray 1966: 413).

That said, the British government needed agreement from the main political parties before it could proceed. Drawing on his extensive experience of chairing constitutional conferences, Lennox-Boyd took Awolowo aside and told him either to accept the commission's recommendations on new states or independence would be delayed until agreement was reached. The Action Group therefore backed down and the conference accepted the commission's proposals (Awolowo 1960: 193, 196). The conference also accepted the reports of the fiscal commission and the federal boundaries delimitation commission[37] without contention.

Having reached this agreement, the conference next considered the timetable for independence. As contemplated at the 1957 Constitutional Conference, the Northern People's Congress accepted internal self-government for the Northern Region, to begin in March 1959 (Bello 1962: 221). And the three governing political parties together requested independence for Nigeria in 1959. The British government agreed that if, after the federal election scheduled for 1959, the federal legislature asked for independence, it would grant independence in 1960.

---

[35] *Daily Service*, August 19, 1958.
[36] NC (58) 2nd meeting, CAB 133/230.
[37] *Report of the Constituency Delimitation Commission*, Lagos, 1958.

When the conference considered the bill of rights,[38] the Secretary of State for the Colonies immediately put forward Willink's proposals with some minor modifications proposed by the Colonial Office.[39] The conference then considered each clause, scrutinizing every word.[40] The resumed conference finally recommended fifteen rights, following almost exactly the Colonial Office's original draft bill of rights,[41] and agreed that the Colonial Office lawyers would draft the final legal instrument.

The conference also agreed that each regional High Court and the Federal Supreme Court would have jurisdiction to "make all such Orders as may be necessary and appropriate to secure the applicant the enjoyment of any of these rights."[42] Owing to concerns both within the Colonial Office and among the regional political leaders about the competency and independence of the judiciary (Awolowo 1960: 279; Adewoye 1988: 734), the capability of the Nigerian judicial system to deal with the bill of rights was also addressed. The result was a set of elaborate measures on judicial independence, such as appointment to the bench being vested in a Judicial Services Commission, salary guarantees for judges, and complex procedures on removal from judicial office (Elias 1967: 163–164).

The other major issue at the resumed conference was how to protect the constitution, and particularly the bill of rights, against arbitrary amendment by the federal parliament. British practice was to make parliament sovereign, but in a federal system it was usually not the case that the federal parliament could amend the constitution and hence alter the balance of power between the federation and the states. The conference therefore decided that amending the constitution would require a two-thirds majority of all members of both houses of the federal parliament as well as a majority in each regional legislature.[43]

One further point about the drafting of the bill of rights deserves attention, namely the inclusion of a derogation clause. The Commonwealth Relations Office,

---

[38] See CO 554/1535.

[39] NC (58) 2nd meeting, CAB 133/230. B.L. Barder, August 14, 1958, CO 554/1534; Aaron Emanuel to Sir Ralph Grey, August 14, 1958, CO 554/1534; Christopher Eastwood, August 27, 1958, CO 554/1535.

[40] See, e.g., NC (58) 27th and 39th meetings, CAB 133/230; 'Proposals of Committee of Regional Law Officers under Sir Kenneth Roberts-Wray's chairmanship to Consider Fundamental Rights', CO 554/1535.

[41] The conference recommended: the right to life, freedom from inhuman treatment, freedom from slavery or forced labor, the right to liberty, rights concerning criminal law, the right to private and family life, freedom of thought, conscience and religion, the right to freedom of expression, freedom of peaceful assembly and association, freedom of movement, the right to compensation for the compulsory acquisition of property, the enjoyment of fundamental rights without discrimination, and freedom from discriminatory legislation: *Report by the Resumed Nigeria Conference* (Cmnd 569, 1958) 4–7.

[42] NC (58) 2nd meeting, CO 554/1535.

[43] Note of a meeting held in Mr. Eastwood's room on Sierra Leone Constitutional Conference, October 16, 1959, CO 554/1670.

responsible for Britain's relationship with its former colonies, took the position that although the proposed bill of rights would successfully safeguard Nigerians against legislation such as that in Ghana, it would not allow preventive detention in cases of insurgency such as the Indian, Ghanaian, and Northern Ireland constitutions permitted.[44] The reaction in the Colonial Office was disbelief as to why the Commonwealth Relations Office were advocating the emasculation of the bill of rights so as to allow the Nigerian government to imprison its citizens without trial on the Indian, Ghanaian, and Northern Ireland models.[45] "All three of these countries," opined a Colonial Office mandarin, "seem to me to exemplify the very things we are trying to avoid."[46]

In the lead-up to the 1958 Resumed Conference, the Commonwealth Relations Office directly approached the Secretary of State for the Colonies and expressed its position that the draft bill of rights would prevent the federal government from locking up communists without public trial.[47] The Secretary of State for the Colonies was persuaded that the proposed restrictions on the bill of rights to times of war or to times of proclaimed public emergency were insufficient, and a slightly wider derogation clause resulted.[48] This debate well reflects the different outlooks of the respective offices: the Commonwealth Relations Office was concerned with the burgeoning communist threat, the Colonial Office with the long-term protection of civil rights.

The general tone of the resumed conference was characterized by suspicion between the Nigerian delegations. For example, on the question of whether a Muslim could elect to be tried by a non-Muslim court, as a non-Muslim could so elect, the premier of the Northern Region said that "if a Muslim were accused of an offence and wished to be tried in a non-Muslim court, it was open to him to renounce his faith."[49] But the distrust was not limited to religious divisions. In summing up the conference's consideration of fundamental rights, Mark Allen of the Commonwealth Relations Office concluded that "discussion round the table shows most of the Nigerians ... are frightened that other Nigerians will take strong action against them after independence."[50] The minutes of the Colonial Committee of Cabinet record the Secretary of State for the Colonies putting forward a very similar view.[51] "It is unlikely," Lennox-Boyd said,

[44] Mark Allen to Aaron Emanuel, September 12, 1958; Mark Allen, Nigerian constitutional discussions: Fundamental Rights, October 1, 1958, DO 35/10447.
[45] B. Barder, September 17, 1958, CO 554/1535.
[46] Aaron Emanuel to Mark Allen, September 24, 1958, DO 35/10447.
[47] Mark Allen, Nigerian constitutional discussions: Fundamental Rights, October 1, 1958, DO 35/10447.
[48] See ss 28, 29, and 65 of the Independence Constitution.
[49] NC (58) 27th meeting, CAB 133/230.
[50] Mark Allen, Nigerian constitutional discussions: Fundamental Rights, October 1, 1958, DO 35/10447.
[51] CC (58) 213 Nigeria, October 21, 1958, PREM 11/2436.

"that the conference will succeed in allaying the fears of the minority group." This is because "[t]here are still bitter and deep-rooted divisions, fears and suspicions among the different races and political groupings."

19.3.6 *Independence*

The federal election was held on December 12, 1959. The Action Group ran a professional and flamboyant campaign advised by an American public relations firm (Ezera 1964: 262). The Action Group put the bill of rights, which was proclaimed in October 1959,[52] to use in the lead-up to the election. Having attached at least one lawyer to every campaign team in the North, it would appear that the bill of rights was at least sought to be relied on (Adewoye 1988: 729–736). But Awolowo was not to achieve his ambition of becoming prime minister. The National Council of Nigeria and the Cameroons and the Northern People's Congress formed an alliance, under which Abubakar would remain prime minister and Azikiwe would be appointed governor general after independence (Robertson 1974: 235). At its first sitting, the federal parliament formally requested independence and an uncontroversial independence conference was held in May 1960 to finalize the independence constitution.

Thus, Nigeria gained independence on October 1, 1960, with a federal system comprising three regions (Northern, Eastern, and Western) and the Federal Territory of Lagos.[53]

The Independence Constitution provided for a bicameral legislature (ss 36–38), a prime minister who commanded the confidence of the lower house (s 81(2)), and a cabinet with collective responsibility to parliament (s 82); a High Court for Lagos (s 113) and Supreme Court of Nigeria (ss 104–113); a federal public service with its own Public Service Commission (ss 140–149) and an independent Judicial Services Commission (s 120); and a governor general who was a constitutional head of state (ss 33–35, 86, 87). In addition, the federal constitution divided the executive and legislative powers between the federal and regional governments. There was an Exclusive List of forty-four items on which only the federal parliament could legislate (The Schedule, Pt I); a Concurrent List of twenty-eight items on which either could legislate (The Schedule Pt II), but subject to federal laws overriding regional laws in the event of inconsistency (s 64(4)); and residual powers residing with the regions. There was also a chapter of fundamental rights with special jurisdiction conferred on the High Courts to declare any inconsistent federal or regional statute invalid, but subject to derogation during emergency (s 65). Appeals also lay to the Judicial Committee of the Privy Council (s 114).

---

[52] CO 554/1535.
[53] Nigeria (Constitution) Order in Council 1960, SI 1960 No 1652.

Each region had its own constitution providing for a bicameral legislature with a Westminster-style ministerial system and cabinet with collective responsibility; a High Court from which appeals lay in all important criminal and civil matters to the Supreme Court of Nigeria;[54] a regional public service with power for appointment and dismissal vested in an independent Public Service Commission and a separate Judicial Services Commission; and a governor whose functions were set out to accord with those of a constitutional head of state. In addition, the North's constitution provided for the Sharia court of appeal, a court of coordinate status with the regional High Courts and having exclusive and final appellate jurisdiction in civil cases based on Muslim family law.

19.4 THE INDEPENDENCE CONSTITUTION AT WORK, 1960–1966

The Independence Constitution operated from October 1, 1960 until January 15, 1966, when a military government was established following a coup (Elias 1967: 457–471; Keay 1966: 92). During this time, further constitutional changes were effected. In 1963, Nigeria became a republic, whereby the queen was replaced as sovereign with a president with powers as constitutional head of state. At the same time, appeals to the Privy Council were abolished; the Judicial Services Commission was abolished and control of judicial appointments was vested in the executive (s 38). Separately, a new region was established in the Western Region. But none of these changes reduced the underlying political rivalries or abated the widespread tensions from other minorities throughout the nation (Nwabueze 1982a: 136–138).

It is useful to state at the outset that the Independence Constitution was both a short-term success and a long-term failure. It was a short-term success because it allowed a peaceful transition of power from Britain to local government. The significance of a peaceful transfer should not be underestimated when compared to the British experience in India and Palestine or the events then occurring in the Congo and Algeria. It is not inappropriate to analyze the British decolonization process in terms of pre-commitments from each of the groups within Nigeria to the effect that they would abide by the agreed constitutional structure post-independence. But the commitment was only effective so long as all parties abided by its terms.

The Independence Constitution was a long-term failure because it was not a model under which the politically divided groups felt able to govern or be governed beyond the initial postcolonial period. Although a military government took control

---

[54] The Nigeria (Constitution) (Amendment No 3) Order in Council, 1959, s 57; Constitution of Nigeria, 1960, s 110; Constitution of Nigeria, 1963, s 117.

in 1966, the fact that the constitution was not satisfactorily addressing Nigeria's needs was clear at least from the time of the federal election held in 1964.

19.4.1 *The Failures of the Independence Constitution*

Before addressing the main objectionable features of the Independence Constitution, it is first necessary to consider briefly what took place between 1960 and 1966. In post -independence Nigeria, control of the federal government brought with it power to allocate resources and patronage of appointment. In consequence, each of the three regional political parties was vying for power within the federal government.

Following the 1959 federal election, the Northern People's Congress and the East's National Council of Nigerian Citizens (which had changed its name from the National Council of Nigeria and the Cameroons following the separation of the Cameroons) formed an alliance, and the West's Action Group assumed the role of opposition. A view formed within a faction of the Action Group that Yorubas (the dominant ethnic group of the Action Group) were losing out to Igbos (the dominant ethnic group of the National Council of Nigerian Citizens) because the National Council of Nigerian Citizens had agreed to act in concert with the Northern People's Congress. This faction of the Action Group, led by Chief Akintola, the premier of the Western Region, wanted to form an alliance with the Northern People's Congress to secure continued appointments for Yorubas in matters falling within federal patronage.

In May 1962, the Action Group split: the national executive, led by Awolowo, deposed Akintola as leader of the regional party and asked him to resign as premier of the Western Region. Awolowo thought that the Action Group could take control of the federal government at the next election, and opposed any alliance with the Northern People's Congress. Akintola asked the governor to dissolve the house for an election to test his faction's support with the electorate. The governor was given a letter signed by 66 of the 124 members of the Assembly stating that they no longer supported Akintola, and the governor appointed as premier the rival faction leader, Chief Adegbenro. When the assembly next met, the meeting descended into violence and the House was cleared by the police (Davies 1962).

Upon coming to the attention of the prime minister (who was affiliated with the Northern People's Congress), the federal government intervened to assume authority in the region with the passage by parliament of the Emergency Powers Act 1961.[55] The emergency administration put in place by the federal government then issued detention orders against the leaders of the Action Group, including Awolowo and

---

[55] This Act substantially reproduced the pre-independence Emergency Powers Orders in Council 1939 to 1959 SI 1952/2031, 1956/731, 1959/1310.

his lieutenants, relying on the derogation provision in the bill of rights during times of emergency.

There followed a series of legal challenges to the validity of the governor's actions in dismissing Akintola as premier, finally going on appeal to the Privy Council, which affirmed that the governor had acted constitutionally in dismissing the premier.[56] At the end of the emergency, however, Akintola and his faction of the Action Group regained government in the Western Region (Nwabueze 1982a: 160).

In the aftermath of the federal takeover of the Western Region, Awolowo and twenty-eight other members of his party were put on trial for treasonable felony. He was convicted on September 11, 1963 of conspiracy to overthrow the government and sentenced to ten years in prison (Ezera 1964: 174–175).

The 1964 federal election caused the next outbreak of political violence. The National Council of Nigerian Citizens fell out with the Northern People's Congress because of perceived benefits, in terms of the resources and appointments, being directed to the North at the East's expense. In consequence, the National Council of Nigerian Citizens formed an alliance with the Action Group to wrest the federal government from the control of the North. The 1964 election was abortive, but the Northern People's Congress claimed victory. The Northern People's Congress and National Council of Nigerian Citizens, after negotiations, agreed to form an alliance.

The next round of political fighting occurred in 1965, during the elections for the government of the Western Region. Akintola, having established a new party, the Nigerian National Democratic Party, fought a bitter campaign against the Action Group, in which election rigging and violence were commonplace. Akintola's victory was seen by supporters of the Action Party as a victory for the North and the culture of corruption and nepotism that had developed in Nigerian politics. The Western Region then descended into violence that only stopped after the military coup.

The leaders of the military coup justified their actions as the only way to stop the corruption, nepotism, and divisiveness of Nigeria's leaders. The federal prime

---

[56] The issue was whether section 33(1) of the Constitution of the Western Region, which reads:
"Subject to the provisions of subsections (8) and (9) of this section, the Ministers of the Government of the Region shall hold office during the Governor's pleasure:
Provided that–
(a) the Governor shall not remove the Premier from office unless it appears to him that the Premier no longer commands the support of a majority of the members of the House of Assembly."
meant that the governor could only dismiss a premier following a resolution of the House of Assembly. The majority of the federal Supreme Court held that it did; the Privy Council said that it did not because the words "it appears to him" in section 33(1) indicate that there is no restriction upon the material he may base his opinion upon: *Adegbenro v Akintola* [1963] AC 614. The Western Constitution was then amended so that the governor could only dismiss the premier if the Assembly passed a vote: Constitution of Western Nigeria (Amendment) Law No 1, 1963.

minister (Balewa), the premier of the Northern Region (the Sardauna of Sokoto), and the premier of the Western Region (Akintola) were executed in the coup. Although the military coup ended the immediate party-political rivalries, Nigeria was thrown into a protracted civil war between ethnic groups. Deep-seated ethnic divisions lay at the heart of the political turmoil that brought about the demise of the first democratic government.

There were two main features of the constitution that proved objectionable during the six years of civilian rule, each contributing negatively to the shape of the political landscape between 1960 and 1966. These were the size and composition of the regions and the emergency powers given to the federal government (Nwabueze 1982a: 147–160).

19.4.2 *Size and Composition of the Regions*

The first objectionable feature relating to the regions was their number. Three political units in a federation, in circumstances where a different political party controls each, can pose problems when alliances victimize one of the units. Between 1959 and 1964, the dominant political parties in the Northern and Eastern Regions formed an alliance that resulted, at the least, in the perception that the Western Region was being marginalized.

The second problem with the regions was their relative political importance. The consequence was that the same political parties that controlled the regions also controlled the federal government, such that the federal government lacked the political will to exercise its constitutional powers to assert itself over all the regions as a unifying power.

The third objectionable feature was that each region was structured around a major ethnic group comprising around two-thirds of the region's population, surrounded by minority ethnic groups. Structuring a region around an ethnic group with a two-thirds majority entrenched political control of that region with that ethnic group. Minorities, often with good reason, felt that they were politically disenfranchised and discriminated against. Moreover, many of the minority ethnic groups were then thought to be of sufficient size, often between 500,000 and 1.5 million, to form viable political units. The consequence was frequent communal violence, particularly in the Northern and Western Regions.

The fourth objectionable feature was that the Northern Region comprised over half the population of Nigeria and three-fourths of its landmass. The effect of having one region in the federation numerically greater than the rest of the federation enables that region in practical terms to override the will of the federal government (Wheare 1953: 50–51). This, in effect, is what occurred.

19.4.3 *Emergency Powers*

It was a major failing of the Constitution that it conferred power on the federal parliament, under section 65, to declare a state of emergency in any region without qualification. It left open the possibility that the party in control of the federal government could abuse this power.

As events transpired, accusations were made against the Northern People's Congress (which controlled the Northern Region) and the Northern Council of Nigerian Citizens (which controlled the Eastern Region) that they had together abused the emergency powers to break the Action Group's control of the Western Region in 1962. The strength of this accusation may be tested by consideration of the fact that in 1965, when civil turmoil gripped the Western Region following the election, the federal government (which was controlled by the Northern People's Congress) did not intervene to take power from its ally, Akintola.

This event was one important step in the breakdown of constitutional government. At the start of 1964, Dr. Kalu Ezera, the dean of the faculty of social studies at the University of Nigeria, noted, "under the pressure of domestic emergency, Nigerians have already become familiar with the instruments of 'constitutional dictatorial government.' This has tended to weaken their respect for constitutional limitations and has undermined the belief that observance of such limitations in the *sine qua non* of the preservation of liberty in a popular government" (Ezera 1964: 299).

19.4.4 *Political Culture*

One further problem, not caused by the structure of the constitution, was the lack of experience of the Nigerian politicians with the Westminster system of government. Responsibility for this failing falls largely on the truncated period of self-government prior to independence.

19.4.5 *The Rule of Law and Fundamental Rights*

Some comment is also warranted on the rule of law and the impact of the bill of rights on Nigerian political life. After independence, the judicial and practicing sides of the legal profession in Africa quickly lost their expatriate character (Allott 1968: 3–4). But it seems clear that the judiciary and bar retained a strong tradition of independence founded on British legal principles, as was particularly evident during the early years of military rule.

During the six-year operation of the bill of rights under civilian government, a considerable number of matters concerning those provisions were heard in either the regional High Courts or the federal Supreme Court. They concerned complex legal questions. One of the first cases to be litigated was a challenge to the result of the 1959 federal election, contested by a group of Seventh Day Adventists on the basis that the election was held on the Sabbath, which amounted to a denial of the right to vote and therefore a negation of the freedom of conscience and religion. The argument was rejected (*Dickson v. Ubani*). There was also litigation following the constitutional crisis in the Western Region and detention of the leaders of the Action Group. In one challenge to a detention order, the federal Supreme Court accepted the argument of Chief Rotimi Williams, the legal adviser to the Action Group, that a detention order could not be "reasonably justified," as s 28 of the Constitution required, to stop him attending the Court to argue his case (*Williams v. Majekodunmi*). Some other interesting examples include the determination that a fair hearing, under s 22(2), requires that an accused be allowed time to secure attendance of the counsel of his choice (*Gokpa v. Police*), and that the right to freedom of expression is not violated by the sedition laws, including an intention to bring into hatred or contempt the government of the federation (*DPP v. Obi*). It may reasonably be concluded that the fundamental rights were not mere window dressing, and were used to some effect. Certainly, the political elites litigated in reliance on them (Brett 1964: 185–194; Williams 1967). The more difficult question (and one on which insufficient research has yet been undertaken) is whether the fundamental rights had any direct grassroots effect on the people.

As noted earlier, a military government took control of Nigeria on January 15, 1966. The military rulers gave the 1963 constitution continuing effect, subject to banning all political parties[57] and suspending all executive and legislative powers conferred by the Constitution.[58] Thus the bill of rights, constitutional provisions on the judiciary, and the distribution of powers between the federal and regional military governments continued in operation (Aihe 1971). The central military government governed by instruments called decrees, and the state military governments governed by instruments called edicts.

The rule of law, at a procedural level at least, continued to operate during the early part of military rule. Although section 6 of Decree No 1 of 1966 barred the courts from questioning the validity of any decree or edict, questions concerning the meaning of decrees and edicts still came before the courts. For example, the courts considered whether a decree and edict were inconsistent, in circumstances where

---

[57] Decree (Public Order Decree No 33 of 1966; Public Order (New Political Associations Restriction) Notice, 1969, LN 1 of 1969).

[58] Decree No 1 of 1966. E.A. Keay, "Legal and Constitutional Changes in Nigeria under the Military Government" (1966) 10 Journal of African Law 92.

a decree prevailed to the extent of the inconsistency (*Adamolejun v. The Council of the University of Ibadan*).

Two cases deserve mention because they indicate that, at least within the legal community, the rule of law had established a meaningful foothold in Nigeria.

In *Chief Mojeed Agbaje v Commissioner of Police* (Aguda and Aguda 1972: 141), Agbaje challenged his detention under the Armed Forces and Police (Special Powers) Decree, No 24 of 1967, section 3(1) of which provides:

> If the Inspector-General of Police is … satisfied that any person is or recently has been concerned in acts prejudicial to public order, or in the preparation or instigation of such acts, and that by reason thereof it is necessary to exercise control over him, he may by order in writing direct that that person be detained in a civil prison or a police station.

The High Court of the Western State stated as follows:

> As it should be noted these are wide and arbitrary powers in derogation of the entrenched clauses of the constitution relating to fundamental rights.… It is clear, and I have not the slightest doubt in my mind that in that circumstance, there is upon the Inspector-General of Police the onus to establish before any court in which the exercise by him of powers conferred on him by above provision had been challenged that he has complied strictly with the enactment under which he has acted.

The Court then held the order null and void on the basis that the inspector-general had not satisfied himself as required by section 3(1). The decision was upheld on appeal in the Western State Court of Appeal.

In order to avoid further problems caused by Agbaje's case, however, the federal military government issued The Detention Orders (Bar to Certain Civil Proceedings) Decree, 1969, section 1(1) of which provides "[n]o civil proceedings shall lie or be instituted in any court for or on account of or in respect of any act, matter or thing done or purporting to be done … [in] connection with the making of an order … made under section 3 of the Armed Forces and Police (Special Powers) Decree 1967" (Aihe 1971: 222).

In *Lakanmi v Attorney General, Western State* (Aihe 1971: 223),[59] the federal Supreme Court held that The Forfeiture of Assets, etc. (Validation) Decree, 1968, was *ultra vires* the legislative power of the federal military government under s 3(1) of Decree No 1 of 1966 on the basis that the decree was an exercise of judicial power. The decision was nullified and all further court decisions invalidating any decree or edict were made invalid by the federal military government (Supremacy and Enforcement of Powers) Decree, No 28 of 1970.

---

[59] (1970) 6 NSCC 143; (1971) 1 *University of Ife Law Review* 201.

19.5 CONCLUSIONS

This chapter examined the social and political foundations of the Nigerian Independence Constitution of 1960 and its subsequent operation between 1960 and 1966. Nigeria was a nation forged by a colonial power and comprised of an ethnically diverse population. Nigeria's Independence Constitution of 1960 reflected both the British system of government and the British system of colonial governance; it represented a continuation, rather than a break, with the colonial past. The Independence Constitution was intended to achieve two overarching aims: create a central government with sufficient power to maintain national unity, and provide mechanisms for the protection of minority populations.

The Independence Constitution proved inadequate for the challenges Nigeria faced immediately post-independence. But it by no means follows that the constitutional design itself was in any relevant sense causative of Nigeria's post-independence political instability or descent into civil conflict. Many other post-colonial constitutions operating in nations with ethnically diverse populations have endured, most notably in other former British territories in the West Indies.

Of particular interest is how Nigeria's subsequent constitutions were drafted in light of the experiences of 1960–1966. Civil rule was restored in Nigeria between 1979 and 1983, after which military government resumed, and in 1999 the military transferred power back to a civilian government. In consequence, since independence, civilian government has operated under two further constitutions, the constitution of 1979 and the constitution of 1999. Both those constitutions sought to address the problems of the independence constitution.

The question of whether Nigeria should have reverted from a federal to a unitary government appears to have been seriously considered only once. Upon the military takeover in January 1966, it was proposed that the federal constitution be scrapped and a unitary system established on the basis that Nigeria's problems were caused by the federal character of the constitution. This led Awolowo, still serving his sentence for treason, to write a tract in defense of federalism from his cell in Calabar Prison, published as *Thoughts on Nigerian Constitution* (Awolowo 1966). In May 1966, the military government decreed that Nigeria's constitution be amended to a unitary system. A change in leadership of the military government ended this experiment when in August 1966 the new military leadership declared the new constitution a failure and reverted to the former constitution. Since this time it has been generally accepted that federalism is best placed to solve the political and constitutional problems arising from the heterogeneous nature of Nigerian society.

The 1979 constitution has been described as a version of the "Washington model," and implicitly a rejection of the "Westminster model." Just as the Independence Constitution was a continuation of the British colonial political model, so it has been argued that the 1979 constitution reflected a continuation of the actual form of government that developed during the fourteen years of military rule, namely an executive presidency (Read 1979: 132). For present purposes, the key features were a strong central government, under a Washington-style president and cabinet, and the division of the country into nineteen states to limit the power of the regions (Read 1979: 243; Nwabueze 1982b, 1985, 1989).

It should also be stated that the causes of the military coup in 1983 are not widely attributed to defects in the form of the constitution of 1979 (Read 1991).

In 1992, there was an abortive attempt to restore civilian government under a new constitution (Aniagolu 1993; Read 1991), but power was not transferred until 1999. Relevantly, the constitution of 1999 followed closely the constitution of 1979, including the "Washington model." It did, however, increase the number of states to thirty-six. Since 1999, Nigeria has been under civilian rule, but still struggles with political infighting caused by deep-seated ethnic division, a political culture of nepotism, systemic corruption, and conflict flowing from the political choices made in the allocation of funds derived from Nigeria's sizable natural resources.[60]

REFERENCES

Adamolejun v. The Council of the University of Ibadan. (1967) *Nigerian Bar Journal* 8: 59.

Adewoye, Omonivi 1988. 'Awolowo and the Rule of Law', in Ovelaran, Olasope et al. (eds.). *Obafemi Awolowo: The End of an Era?* Ibadan: Obafemi Awolowo University Press.

Aguda, Akinola and Aguda, Oluwadare 1972. 'Judicial Protection of Some Fundamental Rights in Nigeria and in the Sudan Before and During Military Rule', *Journal of African Law* 16: 130.

Aihe, D. O. 1971. 'Fundamental Human Rights and the Military Regime in Nigeria: What Did the Courts say?' *Journal of African Law* 15: 213.

Allott, A. N. 1968. 'Judicial Precedent in African Revisited', *Journal of African Law* 12: 3.

Aniagolu, A. N. 1993. *The Making of the 1989 Constitution of Nigeria.* Ibadan: Spectrum Books Limited.

Awolowo, Obafemi 1960. *Awo, the Autobiography of Chief Obafemi Awolowo.* Cambridge: Cambridge University Press.

    1966. *Thoughts on Nigerian Constitution.* Idaban: Obafemi University Press.

Azikiwi, Nnamdi 1961. *Respect for Human Dignity: An Inaugural Address Delivered by the Governor General of the Federation of Nigeria.* Enugu: Government Printer.

Balewa, Abubakar Tafawa 1964. *Nigeria Speaks: Speeches Made between 1957 and 1964.* Lagos: Longmans of Nigeria.

Bello, Ahmadu 1962. *My Life.* Cambridge: Cambridge University Press.

Brett, Lionel 1964. 'Digest of Decisions on the Nigerian Constitution', *Journal of African Law* 8: 185.

---

[60] A brief review of recent UN project reports demonstrates the extent of the problem; see, e.g., *Strengthening Judicial Integrity and Capacity in Nigeria.*

Campbell, Michael 1963. *Law and Practice of Local Government in Northern Nigeria*. London: Sweet and Maxwell.

Coleman, J. S. 1971. *Nigeria: Background to Nationalism*. Berkeley: University of California Press.

Davies, S. G. 1962. 'Nigeria – Some Recent Decisions on the Constitution', *International and Comparative Law Quarterly* 11: 919.

de Smith, Stanley 1961. 'Fundamental Rights in the New Commonwealth', *International and Comparative Law Quarterly* 10: 215.

1964. *The New Commonwealth and Its Constitutions*, London: Stevens and Sons.

Dickson Ojiegbe v. Marcus Ubani. (1961) 1 AII NLR 277.

DPP v. Obi. (1961) 1 AII NLR 186.

Elias, T. 1967. *Nigeria: The Development of Its Laws and Constitution*. London: Stevens and Sons.

Ezera, Kalu 1964. *Constitutional Developments in Nigeria*. Cambridge: Cambridge University Press.

Gokpa v. Police. (1961) 1 AII NLR 413.

Grove, D. L. 1963. 'The Nigerian Judiciary and Fundamental Rights', *Journal of African Law* 7: 152.

Igbuzor, Otice 2002. 'Nigeria's Experience in Managing the Challenges of Ethnic and Religious Diversity through Constitutional provisions', in *Report: The Role of State Constitutions in Protecting Minority Rights under Federalism: Dialogues in Support of a Democratic Transition in Burma*. Stockholm: Institute for Democracy and Electoral Assistance.

Keay, E. A. 1966. 'Legal and Constitutional Changes in Nigeria under the Military Government', *Journal of African Law* 10: 92.

Lynn, Martin (ed.) 2001. *Nigeria, British Documents on the End of Empire Project*. London: HMSO.

Lyttelton 1962. *The Memoirs of Lord Chandos*. London: The Bodley Head.

Nwabueze, Benjamin Obi 1982a. *A Constitutional History of Nigeria*. London: C. Hurst.

1982b. *The Presidential Constitution of Nigeria*. London: C. Hurst.

1985. *Nigeria's Presidential Constitution 1979–1983*. London: Longman.

1989. *Federalism in Nigeria under the Presidential Constitution*. London: Sweet and Maxwell.

Okunade, Bayo 1988. 'Awolowo and Human Rights in Nigeria', in Oyelaran, Olasope et al. (eds.). *Obafemi Awolowo: The End of an Era?* Ibadan: Obafemi Awolowo University Press.

Parkinson, Charles 2007. *Bills of Rights and Decolonization*. Oxford: Oxford University Press.

Read, James 1979. 'The New Constitution of Nigeria, 1979: "The Washington Model?"', *Journal of African Law* 23: 131.

Read, J. S. 1991. 'Nigeria's New Constitution for 1992: The Third Republic', *Journal of African Law* 35: 174.

Robertson, James 1974. *Transition in Africa*. London: C. Hurst & Co. Ltd

Roberts-Wray, Kenneth 1966. *Commonwealth and Colonial Law*. London: Stevens and Sons.

Rotimi Williams v. Majekodunmi. (1962) 1 AII NLR 413.

Wheare, Kenneth 1953. *Federal Government*. Oxford: Oxford University Press.

Williams, Rotimi 1967. 'Legal Development in Nigeria, 1957–67: A Practising Lawyer's View', *Journal of African Law* 11: 77.

20

The Once and Future Democracy

Argentina at the Bar of Constitutionalism

Miguel Schor

20.1 INTRODUCTION

When writing (and thinking) about constitutions, it is important to define the term because it has two different meanings that are often conflated. The large-C Constitution refers to the formal, written document. When ordinary citizens are asked what their constitution is, they typically point to the text, even though their expectations may vary considerably from its dictates (Kammen 1986). The small-c constitution, on the other hand, refers to the operating rules and practices of a polity. Social scientists, in particular, emphasize the small-c constitution because, unlike the constitutional text, it provides an empirically sound map of how power is exercised.

The distinction between the large-C and small-c constitutions is theoretically and historically important (Elkins et al. 2009; Law 2010). Theoretically, the links between the formal constitution and the operating rules of a polity are poorly understood. Constitutions are written in the hope that any gap that may exist between the constitutional text and political practices will prove untenable in the long term, but Latin America's rich historical experience with constitutions suggests otherwise. Historically, the distinction represents a paradigm shift in how constitutions are conceptualized (Sartori 1962). Prior to the American Revolution, the term "constitution" was coterminous with the small-c constitution. After the Revolution, a new term, "constitutionalism," entered into the political lexicon. "[P]roponents of written constitutions" coined the term "to identify their underlying beliefs" (Billias 2009: 7). Constitutionalism is, therefore, intimately related to the idea of a formal constitution.

Prepared for the Foundation for Law, Justice and Society and the Center for Socio-Legal Studies Conference on the Social and Political Foundations of Constitutions, Wolfson College, Oxford University, December 8–9, 2011.

Constitutionalism also provides a vantage point by which actors may critique existing power relations and introduces, as Hamilton (1787) argued in the very first of the
Federalist Papers, the issue of "whether societies of men are really capable or not of
establishing good government from reflection and choice, or whether they are forever destined to depend for their political constitutions on accident and force."

This chapter examines the historical development of Argentina's large-C and
small-c constitutions to explore the problem Hamilton posed, as well as the problem of democratic breakdown. These issues became conjoined in Argentina as
repeated bouts of oligarchical and dictatorial rule led scholars and citizens to fear
that Argentine democracy had become permanently marred by its constitutional
past. Latin America has a rich history of constitution-making and unmaking that
scholars marginalize in constructing theoretical models because it is deemed a
region where institutions go awry (Centeno and López-Alves 2001). When it comes
to the wreckage of (formal) constitutions, Argentina is exemplary. It has enjoyed one
written constitution since 1853–1860[1] while experiencing oligarchy, dictatorship, and
democracy. This chapter argues that scholars should pay greater attention to the
constitutional experience of Argentina and Latin America, for two reasons.

First, the links between the large-C and small-c constitutions are more visible in
Latin America than in the North Atlantic world. The gap between constitutional
reality and constitutional aspiration is highly visible and has existed since republics were founded throughout the region following independence in the nineteenth
century. The experience of Latin America liberates us, therefore, from the dominant theoretical models of constitutionalism drawn from the United States where
a fixation on normative theories has long undermined our understanding of how
constitutions operate. Pruning back the intellectual overhang created by this body
of normative scholarship facilitates the task of empirical inquiry.

Second, Argentina presents a richly textured comparative window that can be
used to explore the trajectory of a constitutional order over time. Latin America is
fertile soil for comparative inquiry. Commonalities in language and culture and a
high degree of "awareness of regional phenomena" (Smith 2005: 34) facilitate the
transmission of ideas throughout the region. Argentine constitutional exceptionalism, moreover, tests the dominant scholarly theories of what makes constitutional
democracy work. These theories suggest that Argentina's constitutional trajectory
should have been different from that of the other republics in Latin America. Stable
constitutional democracy, it is thought, emerges after oligarchs learn the rules of

---

[1] The Argentine constitution was promulgated in 1853, but Buenos Aires, the largest and most powerful
province, did not accede to the constitution until 1860. Hence the split date when referring to the
Argentine constitution. It was superseded in 1949 by a constitution imposed by Perón; the 1853–1860
constitution was restored in 1957. Elected presidents and military dictators oscillated uneasily in
power between 1957 and 1983. The constitution of 1853–1860 was restored in 1983 with the advent of
democracy and underwent important amendments in 1994.

political competition and before the electoral suffrage is extended to all citizens (Dahl 1971). Economic development, moreover, supposedly augurs well for democratic emergence and stability (Lipset 1959). Argentina, however, underwent numerous bouts of dictatorship in the twentieth century in spite of having experienced stable oligarchic rule and remarkable economic development in the late nineteenth century. Democracy was established in 1916 but broke down in 1930 and was not restored until 1983. While Argentina's dual and troubled experience with democracy falls well within the Latin American norm, it is exceptional when compared to the trajectory of constitutional democracy in the North Atlantic world.

The body of this chapter is divided into three parts. The first discusses Argentina's experience with oligarchy in the nineteenth century. The newly independent republics of Latin America adopted liberal constitutions but nowhere were constitutional guarantees fully implemented. Scholars debate whether these constitutions were authoritarian restorations with a republican façade or whether they were liberal projects that ran off the rails. The scholarly debate mistakenly assumes that liberalism and authoritarianism are dichotomous phenomena. Argentina's nineteenth-century constitutional order creatively fused authoritarian and liberal elements while submerging deep disharmonies as to how political order was to be maintained.

The next part examines the chaotic twentieth century when Argentina oscillated between dictatorship and limited democracy. In no period of Argentine history has its formal constitution done a poorer job of mapping political arrangements. Healthy constitutional orders are sufficiently flexible to facilitate the entry of new political forces into power. Dysfunctional constitutional orders, on the other hand, exhibit constitutional stasis. When political forces prevent the small-c constitution from evolving, as occurred in twentieth-century Argentina, political instability and dictatorship become the norm.

The final part examines Argentina's post-1983 experience with democracy. Latin America democratized during difficult economic circumstances in the 1980s. To surmount those difficulties, constitutions were amended to provide presidents throughout the region with legislative or decree powers. While these new powers may yet prove democracy's undoing, they are a functional response to the troubled circumstances that gave birth to democracy in the region. It may be that an elected leader who has the initiative in putting a political program into place and is accountable for the success or failure of those programs will do a better job of ensuring the long-term health of democracy than the classical model of separation of powers that has not served either Argentina or the region well.

20.2 OLIGARCHY

The first half of the nineteenth century following independence was politically chaotic, but order was established throughout Latin America in the second half of the nineteenth century. Constitutions and a thick web of ancillary institutions were fashioned to facilitate political stability and economic growth (Bushnell and Macauley 1994). The scholarly *problématique* of nineteenth-century Latin American constitutionalism arises from the gap that existed between republican constitutions and the political reality of oligarchic rule. One view is that constitutions in the region were liberal projects that went awry either because they were planted in an environment that was not conducive to republican government (Rosenn 1990) or because oligarchy was the "unintended outcome" of the institutional mechanisms used to fashion order (Negretto and Aguilar-Rivera 2000: 361). The opposing view is that constitutions throughout the region sought to restore the order of an idealized, Hispanic, Catholic past (Dealy 1968; Loveman 1993).

This chapter argues it is a mistake to read the nineteenth-century constitutions of the region through the lens of a reductionist dichotomy, for two reasons. First, authoritarianism and liberalism are not polar opposites but exist along a spectrum. All liberal democracies have emergency escape hatches that enable constitutional dictatorship (Agamben 2005). All successful dictatorships (i.e., those that endure), on the other hand, rely on institutions to mediate the raw exercise of power (Ginsburg and Moustafa 2008). Second, liberalism and authoritarianism were fused in the DNA of Latin American constitutionalism. The writing and adoption of constitutions require that competing political forces arrive at some agreement on language while uneasily papering over a maelstrom of disagreements. All constitutions contain profound disharmonies embedded in the understandings that shape the text (Jacobsohn 2010). Constitutionalism in Latin America was shaped by the framing generation's study of liberalism and by its perceptions of the problems of the past that it sought to transcend by founding a constitutional order. The intellectual formula that underpinned constitutionalism throughout the region was order and progress and it was reflected in liberal constitutions that borrowed freely from the United States, Spain, and Europe.

The framers of the Argentine constitution of 1853–1860 had good reasons to be preoccupied with the problem of order. The first part of the nineteenth century following independence was a tumultuous one throughout Spanish America. The wars of independence were longer and bloodier than the American Revolution, and civil wars between competing elites arrayed in liberal and conservative camps ensued following independence. The new republics of Latin America, unlike the United States, were not blessed with rivers and oceans that facilitated internal economic commerce. The republics in the region that were precocious in nation building, such as Costa Rica and Chile, were reasonably compact, and this facilitated the emergence of trust among elites. Larger nations, such as Argentina and Mexico, had a considerably more difficult time forging new nations.[2]

---

[2] Brazil is the exception but it too illustrates the role of social trust. Brazil, unlike the new republics of Spanish America, did not undergo civil war following independence. The Portuguese monarchy

Order was established not by constitutions but by *caudillos* or strongmen who "fulfilled a vital function on behalf of Republican elites as guardians of order and guarantors of the existing social structure" (Lynch 1992: 183). The most successful of these *caudillos* was undoubtedly Juan Manual de Rosas who governed Argentina from 1829 to 1852 with an iron hand and a minimum of constitutional verbiage. He also deserves to be considered one of Argentina's founding fathers as much as the principal actors who framed the Argentine constitution of 1853–1860. Rosas represents an important strand of intellectual thought that went into the matrix of the Argentine constitution. He despised constitutional liberalism because he believed it caused the anarchy that engulfed Argentina following independence. Rosas styled himself the Restorer of the Laws because he sought to recreate the order that Argentina enjoyed under Spain. To that end, the legislature of Buenos Aires provided him with the "sum [total] of public authority" (Loveman 1993: 279). He was an efficient and energetic dictator who made, interpreted, and applied the law. The means he used to govern were remarkably forward-looking since they anticipated the techniques used by some of the more brutal dictators of the twentieth century. He recruited a paramilitary organization that used violence, selective political murder, and terror to instill order. He required that all wear the color red, which was the color of his political party, and that appropriate political slogans be placed in newspapers and public documents. Peace and order bought him the support of the lower classes, who appreciated that they were no longer dragooned to fight in endless wars, and the temporary allegiance of elites whose economic interests fared better under autocracy than under chaos.

The elites abandoned Rosas, however, when an alternative appeared that provided "sounder legal foundations" for economic activities (Adelman 1999: 139). Rosas was defeated in 1852 by a coalition of forces that desired to replace dictatorship with constitutional government. The 1853–1860 constitution was both the fruit of military victory and the intellectual product of a generation of thinkers, some of whom, most notably Juan Batista Alberdi and Domingo Faustino Sarmiento, had spent considerable time in exile when Rosas was in power. The goals of the constitution were to facilitate economic development and to safeguard political order. The framers of Argentina's constitutional settlement understood that Argentina had land in abundance but needed capital and manpower (Alberdi 1852; Sarmiento 1845).

---

relied on Brazilian elites to govern. They were trained to be lawyers and bureaucrats at the University of Coimbra in Portugal. Spain, on the other hand, did not afford Spanish American elites important leadership positions. Elites in Spanish America were trained largely in local universities and opportunities for inter-provincial linkages were rare. In short, Brazil, unlike the newly independent republics of Spanish America, had available a cadre of trained elites who were "closely united" and "ideologically homogenous" and therefore were able to provide the social glue needed to keep the new republic from disintegrating (De Carvalho 1982: 390).

The new constitution provided the government with plenary power to promote economic development, foster education, and encourage immigration. It also protected primarily civil and economic rights as a means of encouraging commercial activity and the inflow of capital and labor.

Order was achieved by fashioning a constitution that fused liberalism and authoritarianism. Framers of Argentina's constitutional order, such as Alberdi, appreciated both the liberalism of the United States, which achieved political and economic success after overthrowing a colonial power, and the authoritarian stability that Spain had provided. The 1853–1860 constitution prohibited the fusion of powers enjoyed by Rosas,[3] and presidents were admonished that they could not utilize their emergency powers to execute their opponents at will. The constitution was formally modeled on the U.S. constitution, but presidents had strong emergency powers and could intervene in provincial affairs (Miller 1997; Negretto and Aguilar-Rivera 2000). Although the new constitution was not consonant with the spirit of the U.S. constitution (Adelman 2007: 110), the 1853–1860 constitution embraced liberalism as it was understood in nineteenth-century Latin America. Given the political and economic chaos that preceded the construction of the nation state, it is not surprising that liberalism in the region posited that the masses lacked the requisite republican virtues to engage in self-governance, and that order, not freedom, was the key to economic development (Hale 1968).

Argentina's 1853–1860 constitution proved surprisingly successful inasmuch as the formal institutions borrowed from the United States lacked indigenous antecedents (Miller 1997). The roots of that success are to be found in the small-c constitution, which facilitated the emergence of what social scientists call a self-enforcing bargain that provided incentives for key actors to cooperate (North and Weingast 1989). Conflict and violence, which had been endemic in the first part of the nineteenth century, were replaced by institutionalized political struggle in the second half of the nineteenth century. Elections were fraudulent and major decisions were made by means of *acuerdos* or informal agreements that protected the interests of elites (Smith 1974: 8). An independent judicial system played an important role in protecting the rights of political opponents who no longer had to fear being put to death (Chavez 2004: 28–44). The protection of economic rights and individual liberties facilitated the influx of immigrants and foreign capital (Conde 1993). Economic growth in Argentina from 1870 to 1914 was 5 percent per year; by World War I, Argentina's per capita income was on par with that of many European nations. Argentina's nineteenth-century small-c constitution, in short, lowered the stakes of

---

[3] Art. 29 provides that neither the national nor the provincial legislatures had the power to grant the president or a provincial governor "extraordinary faculties" or the "whole of the public authority." Somewhat poetically, art. 29 declares, "Acts of this character shall be utterly void" and "render their authors … liable to be tried and punished as infamous traitors to their country."

politics by establishing a "system of mutual security under which the political oppo-sition ... knew that it would suffer only limited oppression, and where the parties in power knew that even if the opposition came to power, it would not do them serious harm" (Miller 1997: 1492).

It would be a mistake, however, to present a balance sheet of Argentina's nineteenth -century small-c constitution that rests solely on why rational actors developed incentives to comply with the operational rules of the political game. Constitutional politics consists of a mixture of self-interested and ideologically motivated behavior. The ideas that animate constitutional discourse are only imperfectly expressed in the text of a constitution. Constitutions are written to paper over deep disharmo-nies between political actors with sharply differing views of the constitutional good. These ideas are revealed in the process of uncovering the identity of a constitution. A constitutional identity "represents a mix of political aspirations and commitments that are expressive of a nation's past, as well as the determination of those within the society who seek in some ways to transcend the past" (Jacobsohn 2010: 7).

Perhaps no polity that reached as successful a constitutional equilibrium as Argentina did in the nineteenth century had as deep a set of concomitant disharmo-nies. There was a deep and pathological divide between liberals who thought that order could best be created by utilizing institutional forms adopted from abroad and conservatives who sought to restore the order that had existed in colonial Spanish America. The result was that Argentina enjoyed two "competing pantheons, one liberal and [urban], the other nationalist and provincial" (Shumway 1991: 188). This divide is neatly captured by a seminal sociological analysis of Argentina written by Domingo Sarmiento (1845), a nineteenth-century president as well as a key public intellectual. He wrote that Argentina faced a stark choice between European civili-zation and native barbarism. Liberals such as Sarmiento found it far easier to write the tools Rosas used to govern out of the constitutional text, however, than they did the ideas he represented from Argentine constitutional politics.

20.3 DICTATORSHIP

The late nineteenth century became known as the process of national organization as Argentina constructed the sinews of a national government while experiencing spectacular economic growth. By the end of the nineteenth century, Argentina had become one of the ten wealthiest nations in the world (Bushnell and Macauley 1994: 289). Argentina appeared poised for a democratic takeoff at the dawn of the twentieth century. The two leading theories of democratization pointed toward a bright future for Argentina. One theory is that democracy is the fruit of political learning that occurs when elites in an oligarchy become acculturated to the rules of political competition before the franchise is extended to all the citizens (Dahl 1971;

Hartlyn and Valenzuela 1998). The other theory, known as modernization theory, contends that democracy is a by-product of sociological development and emerges once a polity reaches a reasonable level of economic development (Lipset 1959; Przeworski 1996). Neither theory proved particularly prescient as Argentina experienced six military coups from 1930 to 1976; a precipitous drop in national wealth, moreover, accompanied political instability.

A veritable cottage industry of scholarly and popular literature has sprung up to explain what went wrong. Oligarchic republics throughout twentieth-century Latin America experienced difficulties in incorporating the middle and lower classes into their political systems, but none of the reasonably well-institutionalized republics in the region experienced the chaos that Argentina did.[4] When it came to finding a constitutional culprit in the drama of democratic breakdown in twentieth-century Argentina, scholars point to presidentialism. There is no question that presidents fanned the tension between majoritarianism and constitutionalism into open conflict during the twentieth century. In two key political moments in the first half of the twentieth century, presidents mobilized broad popular support to win elections. Their opponents – fearing that their interests were being systematically undermined and that they would be unable to regain power democratically – opted to support a military coup.

The first of these moments occurred during Argentina's initial experience with democracy. Middle-class Argentineans, who had been excluded from political power during the oligarchic republic, formed the Unión Cívica Radical (UCR). Its principal reform goal was to establish electoral democracy, which was achieved in 1912. The leader of the UCR, Hipólito Yrigoyen, was elected president in 1916 and governed, with a two-year interlude, until he was deposed by a military coup in 1930. The crisis of 1930 was brought about by a "systematic attempt to destroy opposition parties on the part of the government in power" (Potter 1981: 105). The Radicals did not play by the rules of the oligarchic *ancien régime* under which important policy decisions were made by consensus (Smith 1974: 90–91). Yrigoyen exercised the power to intervene in provincial affairs to destroy the power base of the oligarchy. Consequently, elements of the oligarchy, fearing that they would be unable to regain power electorally, defected from democracy and invited a military coup.

The election of Juan Perón to the presidency in 1946 occasioned similar, albeit more profound, political and constitutional dislocations (Brennan 1998). Perón mobilized workers into Argentina's dominant political party, the Partido Justicialista

---

[4] Around 40% of the changes of government that occurred in Latin America from 1930 to 1980 were by military coup (Valenzuela 2004: 5), but these irregular accessions to power occurred primarily, with the exception of Argentina, in the poorer and more troubled nations of the region.

(PJ"). He used the wealth accumulated by agro-business to obtain the loyalty of the working class by increasing wages and benefits (Rock 1987). His extraordinary popularity afforded him the power to impose a new constitution in 1949 that strengthened the executive, empowered the government to deal with the nation's economic and social problems, and incorporated labor and social welfare rights. The 1949 constitution markedly increased executive authority by permitting reelection and strengthening presidential powers to declare a state of siege and intervene in provincial affairs.

Perón's vision for Argentina was dictatorial and corporatist. He repressed the opposition, purged the Supreme Court, and constrained freedom of the press. The state was the architect of social order. It set boundaries for interest group activity in return for which those groups obtained government benefits. His policies generated considerable opposition and antipathy and he was toppled from power in 1955 by the military in the so-called *Revolución Libertadora*.

The transition from oligarchy to democracy is an unsettling one for social and political elites whose interests are threatened by newly empowered political parties. That proved to be the case in Argentina when the UCR mobilized the middle class and when the PJ mobilized the working class. Scholars argue that presidentialism was the institutional source of political instability in twentieth-century Argentina. Certainly the excessive presidential powers exercised by Yrigoyen and Perón contributed to democratic breakdown. Other polities in the region, however, managed to tame presidentialism and incorporate the lower classes into politics without the chaos and violence that engulfed Argentina.

Overly strong presidents may explain why political competition proved so disruptive in Argentina, but a very different pattern occurred, for example, in Costa Rica where presidential power diminished over time (Lehoucq 1996). The 1871 constitution endowed the president with extraordinary powers. Consequently the incentives to gain power by whatever means necessary, including electoral fraud or revolt, were considerable. Over time and via political (and constitutional) learning, Costa Rica's elites came to realize that the abuse of presidential powers led to political violence and that "compromise offered an attractive solution to regulating access to key public offices" (Lehoucq 1996: 338). This evolutionary, and sometimes bloody, process culminated in the 1949 constitution that strengthened the legislature, created an independent branch to safeguard against electoral fraud, and abolished the military.

Perón's corporatist formula for bringing the lower and working classes into the political system did not have to lead to the violent maelstrom that engulfed Argentina in the twentieth century. The most successful (that is, long-lasting) authoritarian and corporatist regime of the twentieth century was Mexico. The Mexican constitution of 1917 provided a blueprint for the political settlement fashioned in the wake of the Mexican Revolution of 1910. The 1917 constitution, which proved highly influential throughout Latin America, "incorporated into fundamental law a broad range of social and labor rights ... designed to subordinate individual rights to collective needs" (Hartlyn and Valenzuela 1998: 15). The political order fashioned in the wake of the Mexican Revolution was remarkable in blending authoritarianism with a "pragmatic, fluid, and inclusive system" of politics (Morris 1995: 17). Elections were rigged, but there was a regular turnover in the presidency. The elasticity of the regime rested on the following features: "strong presidentialism, the prohibition on re-election, the existence of institutional vehicles that [could] incorporate the opposition, ... and ideological flexibility" (Morris 1995: 187). The regime fashioned constitutional reforms in 1995 that were designed to facilitate a democratic transition (Schor 2009: 180–183) that occurred in 2000 when the opposition gained the presidency.

In seeking an institutional account of Argentina's long-term twentieth-century democratic breakdown, scholars emphasize presidentialism while ignoring the remarkable inability of Argentina's constitution to adapt to changing circumstances. As constitutions age, they "become increasingly politically arbitrary and functionally obsolete as politics and society changes around them" (Levinson 2011: 657). To resolve this problem, polities write new constitutions, amend old ones, or undergo informal adaptations. Constitutional change is the norm in healthy polities (Elkins et al. 2009; Llewellyn 1934). Constitutional stasis, on the other hand, is an undertheorized phenomenon but one that bedeviled Argentina throughout the course of the twentieth century.

The military, not presidentialism, was the cause of constitutional stasis. The military continuously intervened in politics from 1930 to 1983, thereby preventing the political (and constitutional) learning that is a prerequisite for constitutional change. Political actors do not need to learn how to compromise if they can turn to the military when their interests are invaded. Politics from 1955 (the fall of Perón) to 1983 (the restoration of democracy) became the "impossible game" (O'Donnell 1973) and the military its umpire. The military would not allow the majority party, Perón's party, to engage in democratic politics. The second-strongest party, the Radicals, could win elections if constraints were placed on the Peronistas but could not govern. Democratic governments were unstable because they did not represent the majority and were met with considerable opposition from labor (Levitsky and Murillo 2005: 24). In short, as long as Peronist participation in politics was unacceptable to key players such as the military and their civilian allies, democratic politics was impossible.

The military in Latin America was not designed to fight foreign wars but to maintain internal order. Wars are uncommon in the region given the commonalities in language and culture, but disorder is endemic (Centeno 2002). The military took on the twin tasks of protecting the constitution from internal subversion and facilitating economic development (Loveman and Davies 1997). This quasi-constitutional role for the military was exacerbated in Argentina by a "strange" nationalist, ideological movement "pledged to violence and dictatorship" that took root in the armed forces (Rock 1993: xiii). The nationalists idealized the nineteenth-century dictator Juan Manuel de Rosas and favored an imagined *ancien régime* that lived in accordance with an unchanging social compact based on Catholic and Hispanic values. The military, in short, believing it "had the right to apply certain tests and standards to civilian governments, failing which they could be overthrown" (Rock 1993: 194–195), became the guardian of Argentina's constitutional order.

The last bout of dictatorship that occurred from 1976 to 1983 illustrates the ideology of the military at work. Compared to its sister dictatorships in the Southern Cone, the Argentine military dictatorship was remarkably lawless and violent (Pereira 2005). Brazil, Chile, and Uruguay, which also endured military dictatorships in the latter half of the twentieth century, relied to some extent on existing political institutions to govern. When the Argentine *junta* took power in 1976, on the other hand, it effectively gave itself the powers once exercised by Rosas. The military suspended the constitution, dissolved Congress, eliminated freedom of expression, and gave the president legislative powers. The Argentine military was also exceptionally violent. The regime murdered between 10,000 and 30,000 individuals in a secret campaign. It engaged in a higher level of violence than its sister dictatorships and killed significantly more people per capita.

The military ceded power in 1983 after it became thoroughly discredited following its defeat in the Malvinas/Falkland islands conflict. Argentina's half-century experience with dictatorship raises troubling questions about constitutional endurance and change. Healthy constitutional orders endure because they are flexible, inclusive, and lower the stakes of politics by specifying fundamental rules and procedures (Elkins et al. 2009). Argentina's small-c constitution exhibited none of these characteristics for half a century. Polarization, which plays a key role in democratic breakdown (Bermeo 2003), became the *leitmotif* of Argentine politics. The emergence of constitutional stasis, moreover, became common throughout the region in the twentieth century. In a perceptive essay, Anderson (1964: 4) notes that politics in the North Atlantic world leads to the rise of new groups competing for power and the elimination of old ones; politics in Latin America, on the other hand, is "something of a 'living museum', in which all the forms of political authority … continue to exist and operate … in a pageant that seems to violate all the rules of sequence and change involved in our understanding of the growth of Western civilization." In short, although formal constitutions throughout the region have proved highly malleable, stasis is a long-standing trope in the study of the region's small-c constitutions.

20.4 DEMOCRACY

Argentina began its second experience with democracy in very different circumstances than the first. The hope that Argentines had at the beginning of the twentieth century that they faced a new and brighter democratic dawn was replaced
at the end of the century by a sense that the past marred their constitutional and
democratic future. Democracy's triumph was accompanied by skepticism over
whether Argentina's citizens were capable of crafting good government. This section examines in two parts whether democracy in Argentina is developing the capacity to deal with the nation's problems or whether politics is reverting to its historical
mean. The first part examines the 1994 amendments to the 1853–1860 constitution.
These amendments were animated by a desire to augment checks and balances.
The second part examines Argentina's organic or post-1983 small-c constitution. The
scholarly consensus that excessive presidential authority mars Argentine democracy
overly idealizes separation of powers and underestimates the potential payoff to
democratic constitutional change.

20.4.1 *The 1994 Constitutional Reforms*

Argentina democratized in 1983 but did not reform its constitution until 1994. The
1994 constitutional reforms were intended to be far-reaching. In a manner reminiscent of the 1853–1860 constitution, the 1994 reforms fashioned a parchment barrier to the constitutional transgressions of the past. Section 36 provides that this
"Constitution shall rule even when its observance is interrupted by acts of force"
and that "citizens shall have the right to oppose resistance to those committing the
acts of force." The principal reforms revolved around the twin problems of reducing the formal power exercised by the president and strengthening checks and
balances. Presidential authority was potentially limited by provisions creating the
office of chief of cabinet – which was designed to be a counterweight to the executive – and provisions circumscribing the legislative or decree power of the president.
Presidential reelection was authorized but the term of office reduced from six to
four years. Amendments designed to enhance checks and balances include those
devolving power by electing – rather than appointing – the mayor of Buenos Aires,
enhancing legislative authority over Supreme Court appointments, and strengthening judicial independence by creating the council of the judicature, which would
be responsible for judicial selection and administration in the lower federal courts.

   Scholars differ in their assessment of the 1994 reforms in part because they disagree
over which phenomena matter. Constitutional reform can be analyzed by examining the following interrelated phenomena: (1) the design or formative period where
ideas are advanced that articulate aspirations for the future and grapple with the

problems of the past; (2) the bargaining process where self-interest and political calculation loom large; and (3) the aftermath of constitutional reforms where their efficacy is measured by examining the small-c constitution. Grindle (2000) emphasizes the importance of ideas and the design process and is sanguine about Argentina's 1994 reforms. Scholars who emphasize the *realpolitik* of bargaining and political outcomes (Finkel 2008; Negretto 1999), on the other hand, are more nuanced in their assessments.

The 1994 reforms were "an elite project designed out of concern for the functioning of democratic institutions in the country" (Grindle 2000: 150). Representatives of the two major parties met in secret in 1993 to hammer out the blueprint for the 1994 reforms in what became known as the *Pacto de Olivos*. Although the negotiations and subsequent pact came as a surprise to ordinary citizens, the negotiations were the fruit of a long period of discussion among legal elites and politicians. There was a considerable level of trust between the individuals who negotiated the *Pacto de Olivos*, even though they represented opposing parties, and they engaged in a wide-ranging "dialogue about institutional design that went far beyond" the immediate interests of the two parties and their respective political leaders (Grindle 2000: 174). There was agreement that the core problem was excessive presidential powers.

The 1994 reforms differ from previous constitutional reforms in Argentina because they were the result of bargaining between two democratic parties with very different interests. The secrecy in which the negotiations were conducted, however, undermined public confidence in the reforms. Many ordinary citizens were deeply skeptical of the reforms and believed they were part of a "cynical deal entered into by the two party bosses" (Grindle 2000: 149). The goal of the PJ and then President Menem was reelection. Menem lacked the requisite votes to amend the constitution and needed the support of the opposition UCR party and its leader, former president Raul Alfonsín. The UCR knew that Menem would win reelection but was committed to reducing presidential authority and strengthening the judiciary. Consequently Menem acceded to measures designed to enhance checks and balances but sought to derail the implementation of many reforms.

The key provisions designed to check presidential power concerned the judiciary for two intertwined reasons. First, the Argentine judiciary became hopelessly politicized in the twentieth century as a rotating sequence of presidents and military dictators engaged in court-packing schemes (Chavez 2004). Obviously, there was little reason to trust a Supreme Court whose members were handpicked by Argentina's rulers. Second, in a competitive electoral system, political parties are likely to favor reforms enhancing judicial power as a form of political "insurance" (Finkel 2008). Stronger courts make it more likely that the constitutional bargain will be respected because they afford the party out of power a lever with which it can challenge governmental policies. Consequently judicial reform "swept Latin America in the 1990s" as countries throughout the region democratized (Finkel 2008: 1).

The Argentine judicial reforms were well designed but poorly implemented. The difficulty in making constitutional bargains endure is that subsequent generations face very different circumstances than those that provided the framing generation an incentive to strike a bargain. Argentina's 1994 constitutional bargain over the judiciary fell apart within the space of months, however, not generations. To obtain reelection, President Menem agreed to constitutional language that strengthened judicial independence but he quickly reneged on his promises once the 1994 amendments were promulgated. Menem did not comply with his assurances that he would replace his cronies on the Supreme Court with independent justices (Finkel 2008: 53–54). The provisions needed to create a national judicial council, which was designed to enhance the independence of the lower federal courts, were not implemented until after Menem left office (Finkel 2008: 56–58). Nonetheless, the provisions requiring that justices to the Argentine Supreme Court be approved by two-thirds of the Senate and creating a judicial council "bode well" in the long term "for the development of a judiciary free from executive interference in Argentina" (Finkel 2008: 62).

The key reform designed to reduce executive power – the new office of the chief of cabinet – has not proven effective. When Raul Alfonsín was president, he created a presidential commission charged with institutional reform. The "core of the [commission's] proposal was the transformation of the presidentialist structure of government" (Negretto 1999: 210) by adopting a system akin to the semi-presidentialism of the French constitution of 1958. The chief of cabinet was designed to carve out some of the duties of administration from the president who would remain the head of state. During the negotiations that led to the *Pacto de Olivos*, however, the Peronists were insistent on retaining a strong presidentialist system because they were the majority party (Negretto 1999: 212). Consequently, the chief of cabinet became responsible to both Congress and the president. The chief of state is appointed by the president but can be removed by the president or by Congress. Given presidential authority over appointment and removal, the office of chief of cabinet has not proven much of a check on executive authority.

20.4.2 *Presidentialism*

The 1994 constitutional reforms occurred against the backdrop of a regional discussion over how best to strengthen democracy and prevent a reversal to dictatorship (Smith 2005: 137). This regional discussion mirrored a vigorous scholarly debate over the virtues and defects of presidentialism that was set off by Juan Linz's critique of presidentialism (1990). He argued that presidentialism's key features – a popular mandate for the chief executive and fixed terms – contributed to democratic break-down. The former facilitates dictatorial claims of "plebiscitary legitimacy" (Linz 1990: 53); the latter contributes to political instability because fixed terms do not track the exigencies of events. Presidential systems are prone to conflict between presidents and legislatures during crises. Constitutional impasses result either in a democratic breakdown or in an increase in presidential power to resolve the conflict (Posner and Vermeule 2010; Valenzuela 1998). Parliamentarism, on the other hand, Linz urged, is less prone to democratic breakdown because elections can be held to resolve a crisis.

In a highly influential essay, Guillermo O'Donnell (1994) built on scholarly criticisms of presidentialism to develop a model of how democracy operates in the developing world. In the developed world, representative democracy with robust mechanisms of horizontal accountability prevails. Delegative, not representative, democracy, on the other hand, prevails in the developing world. It rests "on the premise that whoever wins election to the presidency is thereby entitled to govern as he or she sees fit, constrained only by the hard fact of existing power relations and by a constitutionally limited term of office" (O'Donnell 1994: 59). The president's claim to a plebiscitary mandate is the defining feature of new and troubled democracies as presidents sweep away institutional constraints to grapple with national problems. The other key feature of presidentialism – the fixed term – has been upended by the emergence of delegative democracy, because presidents who fail to solve the nation's ills lose their mandate and are forced to leave office early (Valenzuela 2004).

Delegative democracy provides a plausible description of Argentina's small-c con-stitution. Argentine presidents have been forced to leave office early as a result of a toxic stew of economic crises and street protests.[5] Moreover, the governance style of the two most successful Argentine presidents – Carlos Saúl Menem and Néstor Carlos Kirchner – comported with the delegative democracy model. Menem pro-vides the paradigmatic example of a plebiscitary president. Menem circumvented the legislature by making extensive use of decrees and undermined the Supreme Court by packing it with his cronies (Levitsky and Murillo 2005). Kirchner also used executive decrees extensively but respected judicial independence and dealt with past human rights abuses (Levitsky and Murillo 2008).

---

[5] Raul Alfonsín, president from 1983 to 1989, left office five months early because his government was unable to deal with hyperinflation. Fernando de la Rúa was elected president in 1999 but was forced to resign two years later as the country faced a severe economic downturn. Protestors, incensed by the government's inability to deal with the economic crisis, swarmed around the three branches of govern-ment and rallied behind the slogan "Que se Vayan Todos" (let us get rid of all of them) (Levitsky and Murillo 2005). Three short-term interim presidents rotated through office before Congress selected Eduardo Alberto Duhalde as president.

This chapter argues that the delegative democracy model is flawed, however, for three reasons: (1) it fails to appreciate why presidential authority increased throughout Latin America; (2) it misconstrues how separation of powers operates in developed democracies such as the United States; and (3) it is overly pessimistic in its outlook on the democratic prospects of the region. For (1), the core argument is that democracy throughout Latin America is returning to its historical mean of excessively centralized power. The delegative democracy model emphasizes long-term factors such as political culture but downplays how institutions are shaped by the exigencies of events. The text of a formal constitution is, of course, designed to be difficult to change; the understandings and expectations that permeate the small-c constitution are sticky as well. It may be that patterns of centralization that were laid down when nations were constructed in the nineteenth century have proven enduring. The delegative democracy argument ignores, however, the circumstances that gave birth to democracy. Latin America democratized in the 1980s. This was a period of crisis, as political leaders sought to liberalize failed statist economies (Whitehead 1998). The power of successful presidents tends to grow during economic crises. Democracies in Latin America did a reasonable job of surmounting difficult economic circumstances, and consequently presidential lawmaking authority increased throughout the region (Cheibub at al. 2011).

Argentina, for example, underwent a severe bout of hyperinflation that led to Carlos Menem taking office six months early. No democracy in Latin America undertook market reforms as profound as those that Argentina did under Menem (Levitsky and Murillo 2005). Hyperinflation was followed by a severe recession that ushered in a period of rotating presidencies. These are events that would have caused the military to intervene in the past but instead led to instability in office for presidents who were unable to deal with the nation's problems and an increase in power for those presidents who successfully navigated the crisis.

For (2), the delegative democracy argument rests on an idealized and empirically infirm view of how separation of powers works. The United States provides the archetype because it is the most successful and longest-lasting presidential democracy in the world. Posner and Vermeule (2010) make a compelling argument that presidential democracy in the United States does not comport with Madison's model of checks and balances. The increasing complexity of the problems that the government faced in the twentieth century "sped" up politics. The executive, unlike the legislature or the judiciary, has the capacity to act quickly. Emergencies provided the catalyst for the delegation of ever-increasing authority to the executive branch. As the president and administrative agencies displaced the decision-making authority of the other branches, the importance of legal checks on executive power waned. The president is not, however, an elected despot because political constraints in the form of a "skeptical" and mobilized citizenry remain a potent "check" on executive authority (Posner and Vermeule 2010: 209). In short, the "clockwork mechanism" of checks and balances envisioned by Madison has been replaced by a "more organic system of power sharing and power constraint that depends on shifting political alliances, currents of public opinion, and the particular exigencies that demand government action" (Posner and Vermeule 2010: 209).

The broad sociological and historical forces that facilitated increased presidential authority in the United States were also at work in Latin America. The Great Depression was a constitutional watershed throughout the Americas. Governments grew in response to citizen demands that it play a larger role in economic affairs and provide a greater range of public goods to deal with the vicissitudes of life. Political checks on governmental authority, moreover, became more important throughout Latin America following the transition to democracy in the 1980s (Peruzzotti and Smulovitz 2006). The military dictatorship gave rise to a vigorous human rights movement in Argentina, which, in turn, facilitated a transformation in the notion of citizenship (Peruzzotti 2005: 229). The older notion that once a leader was elected, the "electorate abdicated all personal agency and subordinated itself to the leader's will until the next election" (Peruzzotti 2005: 231), was replaced by a more skeptical and demanding attitude. A rise in nongovernmental organizations focused on the problem of governmental accountability both reflects this transformation and helps fuel it (Peruzzotti and Smulovitz 2006). In short, presidents in Argentina, much like presidents in the United States, face a mobilized citizenry.

For (3), the delegative democracy argument is overly pessimistic in its assessment of the democratic prospects for the region. The argument is that excessive presidential authority bodes poorly for the long-term health of democracy. Presidents in Latin America undoubtedly exercise greater powers than they do in the United States. In the United States, congressional delegation has been the engine of expanded presidential authority. In Latin America, on the other hand, the difficult circumstances that gave birth to democracy in the 1980s also facilitated the constitutionalization of executive decree powers. Decree powers were relatively rare, however, in the nineteenth century when presidentialism hewed more closely to the American model (Cheibub et al. 2011: 3). Argentina illustrates the evolution of presidential authority. Although the 1853 constitution did not provide for presidential decrees, they were used sparingly to deal with emergencies (Larkins 1998: 425). Their use increased dramatically with democratization. The expanded use of decrees was the "culmination of an informal process of constitutional change initiated decades before via judicial interpretation" (Negretto 1999: 213). The 1994 amendments explicitly authorize and seek to circumscribe presidential decree power.[6]

---

[6] Art. 99, par. 3 constitutionalizes decrees of "necessity and urgency."

The primary argument against expanded presidential authority rests on the empirically questionable proposition that tyranny ineluctably flows from enhanced executive authority. Dictatorship was significantly more common in Latin America during the early part of the twentieth century when decree powers were relatively rare, however, than it is in the twenty-first century when executive decree powers have become the norm. The longest period of sustained democracy in Latin America is also the period of greatest executive authority. Parliamentary government – which fuses the executive and legislature – has a fine long-term track record, moreover, in sustaining democracy (Linz 1990).

There are functional and policy reasons, moreover, to be guardedly optimistic about the democratic implications of expanded presidential authority in Latin America. The growth in decree power was a response to the difficult political and economic environment that democracies in the region faced in the 1980s. These are circumstances that would have led to military dictatorship and constitutional stasis early in the twentieth century. Instead, democracies throughout the region surmounted these difficulties through constitutional change. This is an unprecedented development in Latin America.

The implications of this constitutional change, moreover, are not well understood because scholars have failed to grapple adequately with the analytical problems posed by "executive-legislative relations" (Cheibub et al. 2011: 3). It is unusual for presidents, but not prime ministers, to exercise strong legislative powers. All written constitutions empower government to solve collective action problems and limit the exercise of that power. There is a crucial difference, however, between constitutional systems that favor affording government the power to put in place a coherent program for which it will be held accountable and those that do not favor affording the government that power. This difference is imperfectly captured by the distinction between presidentialism and parliamentarism. Presidentialism historically emphasized the importance of limits, whereas parliamentarism historically emphasized the importance of power. By adopting decree powers, presidential government in Latin America has moved closer to the parliamentary model. Presidents in Latin America who are unable to solve their nation's ills, moreover, much like prime ministers, are not afforded a full term of office. Given that democracy in Latin America has long been bedeviled by the inability of government to solve deep -rooted, collective action problems, the expansion of presidential authority is more likely to facilitate the consolidation of democracy throughout the region than usher in a new era of dictatorship.

20.5 CONCLUSION

In T. H. White's *The Once and Future King*, Merlin lives backward through time and so is able to remember the future. This provides a charming literary conceit but a problematic means to understand constitutions. Yet that is how we understand old constitutional orders. The past weighs heavily in our understanding of the present. The criticisms of executive decree power rest, in part, on the historical memory of oligarchy and dictatorship. The belief that political and constitutional change is simply window dressing while the problems of the region remain unchanged is deeply entrenched (Colburn 2002). There is a trope in social science work on Latin America that the small-c constitution has been preserved in amber by inexorable political and social forces. The central *problématique* of Latin American constitutionalism, therefore, is distinguishing what is new from the residue of history.

The builders of nineteenth-century nation-states in Latin America framed constitutions with one eye toward the chaos that engulfed the region following independence and another toward the experiments in constitutional government that were occurring throughout the Atlantic world. Consequently, the 1853–1860 constitution of Argentina contained deep disharmonies between intellectual currents that favored a return to an idealized, Hispanic past and those that favored a transition to an equally idealized constitutionalist future. The blending of authoritarianism and liberalism is one of Latin America's contributions to the art of constitutionalism.

Argentina's 1853–1860 constitution proved successful in facilitating the construction of a national government that, in turn, provided the institutional stability needed to attract capital and labor. The virtuous feedback between institutional stability and economic growth was badly disrupted, however, in the twentieth century. Argentina's constitutional arrangements proved unable to accommodate new social and political actors. For fifty years, the military sought to enforce what it took to be the constitutional bargain made in 1853–1860, thereby preventing democratic constitutional change. Healthy constitutional orders exhibit constant change whereas dysfunctional ones are frozen in place by political forces that prevent compromise and thereby facilitate political polarization. Argentina's contribution to the art of constitutionalism lies in illustrating the role that constitutional stasis plays in democratic breakdown.

Argentina, as well as the other republics of Latin America, became democratic in the 1980s, which was a period of deep economic difficulty that occasioned the dismantling of statist economies. These difficulties also occasioned constitutional change and fermentation throughout the region. Polities wrote new constitutions and amended old ones to safeguard against past human rights abuses and to empower government to deal with the deep-rooted problems of the region. The decree powers now enjoyed by presidents throughout Latin America are not a return to the historical mean of dictatorship. Decree powers may yet prove unwise but they are also the fruit of democratic constitutionalism. For the first time since the breakdown of constitutional government in the twentieth century, democratic and constitutional learning has become possible. Decree powers are a unique development that blends presidentialism with parliamentarism. Accountable, elected governments now have the capacity to deal with the teeming ills of the region.

The scholarly criticism of decree authority conflates a description of a phenomenon with its cause. There is little doubt that dictators exercise too much power, but dictatorship emerges when constitutional systems become unhealthy and fail to evolve to deal with changing circumstances. Constitutional stasis, not the formal powers granted to presidents, is the cause of dictatorship. There are, no doubt, many paths to constitutional stasis but they are to be found in the small-c, not the large-C, constitution.

Presidential decree powers represent a profound constitutional transformation that will test whether "societies of men" are capable of fashioning "good government from reflection and choice" (Hamilton 1787). Historically, presidential government sought to achieve good government by fashioning formal shackles on power. Parliamentary government, on the other hand, at least in its original, Westminsterian form, empowered government to solve collective action problems and relied on constitutional politics to limit the exercise of that power. The deep lesson of this chapter is that the constitutional imagination became impoverished when the American innovation of etching limits to power on paper swept the globe. The emergence of decree powers in Latin America is a hybridization of two constitutional systems long thought to be at odds. It remains to be seen whether this hybrid will prove successful.

REFERENCES

Adelman, Jeremy 1999. *Republic of Capital: Buenos Aires and the Legal Transformation of the Atlantic World*. Stanford: Stanford University Press.
  2007. 'Between Order and Liberty: Juan Batista Alberdi and the Intellectual Origins of Argentine Constitutionalism', *Latin American Research Review* **42**: 86–110.
Agamben, Giorgio 2005. *States of Exception*. Trans. Kevin Attell. Chicago: University of Chicago Press.
Alberdi, Juan Bautista 1852. *Bases y punto de partida para la organización política de la República Argentina*.
Anderson, Charles W. 1964. *Toward a Theory of Latin American Politics*. Nashville: University of Vanderbilt Press, The Graduate Center for Latin American Studies.
Bermeo, Nancy 2003. *Ordinary People in Extraordinary Times: The Citizenry and the Breakdown of Democracy*. Princeton: Princeton University Press.
Billias, George Athan 2009. *American Constitutionalism Heard Around the World*. New York: New York University Press.
Brennan, James P. (ed.) 1998. *Peronism and Argentina*. Wilmington: Scholarly Resources.
Bushnell, David and Neill Macauley 1994. *The Emergence of Latin America in the Nineteenth Century*. New York: Oxford University Press.

Carey, John M. and Matthew S. Shugart 1998. 'Calling out the Tanks or Filling out the Forms', in John M. Carey and Matthew S. Shugart, *Executive Decree Authority*. Cambridge: Cambridge University Press.

Centeno, Miguel Angel 2002. *Blood and Debt: War and the Nation-State in Latin America*. University Park: Pennsylvania State University Press.

Centeno, Miguel and Fernando López-Alves 2001. *The Other Mirror: Grand Theory through the Lens of Latin America*. Princeton: Princeton University Press.

Chavez, Rebecca Bill 2004. *The Rule of Law in Nascent Democracies: Judicial Politics in Argentina*. Stanford: Stanford University Press.

Cheibub, José Antonio, Elkins, Zachary, and Ginsburg, Tom 2011. 'Latin American Presidentialism in Comparative and Historical Perspective', *Texas Law Review* 89: 1707–39.

Colburn, Forrest D. 2002. *Latin America at the End of Politics*. Princeton: Princeton University Press.

Conde, Roberto Cortés 1993. 'The Growth of the Argentine Economy, 1870–1914', in Bethell, Leslie (ed.), *Argentina since Independence*. Cambridge: Cambridge University Press.

Dahl, Robert A. 1971. *Polyarchy: Participation and Opposition*. New Haven: Yale University Press.

De Carvalho, José Murilo 1982. 'Political Elites and State Building: the Case of Nineteenth Century Brazil', *Comparative Study of Society and History* 24: 378–399.

Dealy, Glen 1968. 'Prolegomena on the Spanish American Political Tradition', *Hispanic American Historical Review* 48: 37–58.

Elkins, Zachary, Ginsburg, Tom, and Melton, James 2009. *The Endurance of National Constitutions*. New York: Cambridge University Press.

Finkel, Jodi S. 2008. *Judicial Reform as Political Insurance: Argentina, Peru, and Mexico in the 1990s*. Notre Dame: University of Notre Dame Press.

García Lema, Alberto Manual 1994. *La Reforma por dentro: La difícil construcción del consenso consitucional*. Buenos Aires: Planeta.

Ginsburg, Tom and Moustafa, Tamir (eds.) 2008. *Rule by Law: the Politics of Courts in Authoritarian Regimes*. New York: Cambridge University Press.

Grindle, Merilee S. 2000. *Audacious Reforms: Institutional Invention and Democracy in Latin America*. Baltimore: Johns Hopkins University Press.

Hale, Charles A. 1968. *Mexican Liberalism in the Age of Mora, 1831–1853*. New Haven, CT: Yale University Press.

Hamilton, Alexander 1787. *The Federalist No. 1*. Available at http://avalon.law.yale.edu/18th_century/fedo1.asp.

Hartlyn, Jonathan and Valenzuela, Arturo 1998. 'Democracy in Latin America since 1930', in Bethell, Leslie (ed.), *Latin American Politics and Society since 1930*. Cambridge: Cambridge University Press.

Jacobsohn, Gary Jeffrey 2010. *Constitutional Identity*. Cambridge, MA: Harvard University Press.

Kammen, Michael 1986. *A Machine That Would Go Of Itself: The Constitution in American Culture*. New York: Alfred A. Knopf.

Larkins, Christopher M. 1998. 'The Judiciary and Delegative Democracy in Argentina', *Comparative Politics* 30: 423–442.

Law, David 2010. 'Constitutions', in Cane, Peter and Kritzer, Herbert M. (eds.), *The Oxford Handbook of Empirical Legal Research*. New York: Oxford University Press.

Lehoucq, Fabrice Edouard 1996. 'The Institutional Foundations of Democratic Cooperation in Costa Rica', *Journal of Latin American Studies* 28: 329–355.

Levinson, Daryl 2011. 'Parchment and Politics: The Positive Puzzle of Constitutional Commitment', *Harvard Law Review* 124: 657–746.

Levitsky, Steven and Murillo, María Victoria 2008. 'From Kirchner to Kirchner', *Journal of Democracy* 19(2): 16–30.

  2005. 'Building Castles in the Sand', in Levitsky, Steven and Murillo, María Victoria (eds.), *The Politics of Institutional Weakness: Argentine Democracy*. University Park: Pennsylvania State University Press.

Llewellyn, Karl N. 1934. 'The Constitution as an Institution', *Columbia Law Review* 34: 1–40.

Linz, Juan J. 1990. 'The Perils of Presidentialism', *Journal of Democracy* 1: 51–69.

Linz, Juan J. and Stepan, Alfred 1996. *Problems of Democratic Transition and Consolidation: Southern Europe, South America, and Post-Communist Europe*. Baltimore: Johns Hopkins University Press.

Lipset, Seymour Martin 1959. 'Some Social Requisites of Democracy: Economic Development and Political Legitimacy', *American Political Science Review* 53: 69–105.

Loveman, Brian 1993. *The Constitution of Tyranny: Regimes of Exception in Spanish America*. Pittsburgh: University of Pittsburgh Press.

Loveman, Brian and Davies, Thomas M. Jr. 1997. *The Politics of Antipolitics: The Military in Latin America*. Wilmington: Scholarly Resources.

Lynch, John 1992. *Caudillos in Spanish America, 1800–1850*. Oxford: Clarendon Press.

Miller, Jonathan M. 1997. 'The Authority of a Foreign Talisman: A Study of U.S. Constitutional Practice as Authority in Nineteenth Century Argentina and the Argentine Elite's Leap of Faith', *American University Law Review* 46: 1483–1572.

Morris, Stephen D. 1995. *Political Reformism in Mexico: An Overview of Contemporary Mexican Politics*. Boulder: Lynne Rienner Publishers.

Negretto, Gabriel L. 1999. 'Constitution-Making and Institutional Design: The Transformations of Presidentialism in Argentina', *Archives Européennes de Sociologie* 40: 192–232.

Negretto, Gabriel L. and Aguilar-Rivera, José Antonio 2000. 'Rethinking the Legacy of the Liberal State in Latin America: The Cases of Argentina (1853–1916) and Mexico (1857–1910)', *Journal of Latin American Studies* 32: 361–397.

North, Douglas C. and Weingast, Barry R. 1989. 'Constitutions and Commitment: the Evolution of Institutions Governing Public Choice in Seventeenth Century England', *The Journal of Economic History* 49: 803–832.

O'Donnell, Guillermo 1994. 'Delegative Democracy', *Journal of Democracy* 5: 56–69.

  1973. *Modernization and Authoritarianism in South American Politics*. Berkeley: University of California Press.

Pereira, Anthony W. 2005. *Political (In)Justice: Authoritarianism and the Rule of Law in Brazil, Chile, and Argentina*. Pittsburgh: University of Pittsburgh Press.

Peruzzotti, Enrique and Catalina Smulovitz (eds.) 2006. *Enforcing the Rule of Law: Social Accountability in New Democracies*. Pittsburgh: University of Pittsburgh Press.

Peruzzotti, Enrique 2005. 'Demanding Accountable Government: Citizens, Politicians, and the Perils of Representative Government in Argentina', in Levitsky, Steven and Murillo, María Victoria (eds.), *The Politics of Institutional Weakness: Argentine Democracy*. University Park: Pennsylvania State University Press.

Posner, Eric A. and Adrian Vermeule 2010. *The Executive Unbound: After the Madisonian Republic*. New York: Oxford University Press.

Potter, Anne L. 1981. 'The Failure of Democracy in Argentina, 1916–1930: An Institutional Perspective', *Journal of Latin American Studies* **13**: 83–109.

Przeworski, Adam 1991. *Democracy and the Market: Political and Economic Reforms in Eastern Europe and Latin America*. New York: Cambridge University Press.

Przeworski, Adam and Limongi, Fernando 1997. 'Modernization: Theories and Facts', *World Politics* **49**: 155–183.

Przeworski et al. 1996. "What Makes Democracies Endure?" *Journal of Democracy* **7**.1: 39–55.

Rock, David 1987. *Argentina 1516–1987: From Spanish Colonization to Alfonsín*. Berkeley: University of California Press.

1993. *Authoritarian Argentina: the Nationalist Movement, Its History and Its Impact*. Berkeley: University of California Press.

Rosenn, Keith S. 1990. 'The Success of Constitutionalism in the United States and its Failure in Latin America: An Explanation', *Inter-American Law Review* **22**: 1–39.

Sabsay, Daniel A. and José M. Onainda 2000. *La Constitución de los Argentinos: Análisis y comentario de su texto luego de la reforma de 1994*. Buenos Aires: Errepar, S.A.

Sarmiento, Domingo F. 1845. *Facundo o Civilización y barbarie*. Reprinted in 1921, Buenos Aires: Biblioteca Argentina.

Sartori, Giovanni 1962. 'Constitutionalism: a Preliminary Discussion', *Political Science Review* **56**: 853–864.

Schor, Miguel 2009. An Essay on the Emergence of Constitutional Courts: The Cases of Mexico and Colombia', *Indiana Journal of Global Legal Studies* **16**: 173–194.

Shumway, Nicolas 1991. *The Invention of Argentina*. Berkeley: University of California Press.

Smith, Peter 1974. *Argentina and the Failure of Democracy: Conflict among Political Elites, 1904–1955*. Madison: University of Wisconsin Press.

2005. *Democracy in Latin America: Political Change in Comparative Perspective*. New York: Oxford University Press.

Valenzuela, Arturo 1998. 'The Crisis of Presidentialism in Latin America', in Mainwaring, Scott and Valenzuela, Arturo (eds.), *Politics, Society, Democracy: Latin America*. Boulder: Westview Press.

2004. 'Latin American Presidencies Interrupted', *Journal of Democracy* **15**: 5–19.

Weingast, Barry R. 1997. 'The Political Foundations of Democracy and the Rule of Law', *American Political Science Review* **91**: 245–263.

Whitehead, Laurence 1998. 'State Organization in Latin America since 1930', in Bethell, Leslie (ed.), *Latin America Economy and Society since 1930*. Cambridge: Cambridge University Press.

Constitutions and Institutional Acts

Argentine Constitution of 1853–1860.

Argentine Constitution of 1949.

Argentine Constitution of 1853/60 as amended in 1994.

Statute for the Process of National Reorganization, March 24, 1976.

Battle between Law and Society in Micronesia

Brian Z. Tamanaha

21.1 INTRODUCTION

Two often repeated notions run through law and society research: one, that law is a mirror of society, and two, that a gap exists between law and society. The first notion, in its extreme form, suggests that the relationship between law and society is so intimate that it is incorrect to interject the conjunction "and" between these terms – law is always integrated within and produced by society and society courses through every aspect of law such that they cannot be separated. The second notion, in its extreme form, suggests that law operates within but is autonomous from society – a self-defining and self-constituting complex of socially constructed legal practices, institutions, bodies of knowledge, and systems of communication and language.

Although many law and society scholars accept both propositions as virtual truisms, an evident tension, if not outright contradiction, exists between them, for they stake out antipodal positions on the law-society relationship. Contradiction is avoided by eschewing the extreme form of each. The middle ground – adopted by most scholars – relies on a positivistic understanding to identify law as the law -related activities of legal professionals and officials (picked out from society in this specific sense), while also acknowledging that law is always infused with and subject to social influences and factors. Under this common understanding, law is separable from society, contrary to the extreme mirror position, while law is also continuously subject to pervasive social influences, contrary to the extreme autonomy pole.

Even with this moderate view, however, the tension remains. How can it simultaneously be held that law is a mirror of society and that a gap exists between law and society? The short answer is that law is an *imperfect* mirror of society. Law can be mismatched with, or be out of sync with, society in various ways for various reasons.

Mismatch occurs when law lags behind rapid social change, or when law fails in an effort to produce social change. Mismatch occurs when law from one society is imposed upon or transplanted to another society. Mismatch occurs when society is comprised of different normative groups and the law reflects a selected group but not others. In these and other situations, when law is manifestly not a reflection of society, the gaps typically are seen as aberrations or defects, as temporary, as a failure or flaw, as a deviant legal condition that will or must be rectified – in the long run at least. This way of thinking about the well-known "gap problem," as it is called in the socio-legal literature, is a product of the notion that law is a mirror of society: the percept of a gap is parasitic on the mirror idea. That is, it is precisely the background belief that law reflects society that supplies the implicit assumptions that allow a mismatch or inconsistency between law and society to be seen as (merely) a "gap."

In this chapter I explore an instance of law engaging in a pitched *battle* with society. This is a fascinating story worth telling in its own right, which reveals interesting insights about law and society. Talks of "mirrors" and "gaps" are metaphors that constrain how we perceive the interaction between law and society. Sometimes these metaphors are entirely inapt. The battle I refer to emerged at the 1975 Micronesian Constitutional Convention and continues to this day.

21.2 THE BATTLE LINES AT THE CONSTITUTIONAL CONVENTION

The Convention was held under the auspices of United States, through its administration of Trust Territories of the Pacific Islands, a UN mandate created at the close of World War II to help territories previously under Japanese colonial rule achieve independence. Micronesia consists of hundreds of small islands across a vast expanse of the tropical equatorial region in the Western Pacific Ocean, stretching nearly 2,000 miles from the Philippines toward Hawaii. Beginning in the late nineteenth century, much of the region was successively ruled by foreign powers – namely, Spain, Germany, Japan, and the United States. The Convention was their long-awaited exercise of collective self-rule, the first concrete act on the road to political independence.

Delegates from several discrete island groupings within Micronesia (each with their own languages and cultures) – the Marianas, the Marshalls, Palau, Yap, Chuuk, Pohnpei, and Kosrae – were brought together on Saipan to draft a constitution that would then be submitted to the electorate for a vote. The convention was scheduled for 90 days in session, with a break in the middle to allow delegates to return home for rest and feedback from constituents. The delegates were supported by the Convention's administrative staff, fourteen interpreters to assist those with limited English (the language of the convention), and twenty-six persons in the Research and Drafting Section, which prepared committee reports, drafted constitutional provisions, and was responsible for much of the written product of the convention.[1]

The bulk of the discussion at the Convention focused on basic political and institutional design issues: the number of national legislators from each state and the voting system, a bicameral or unicameral house, parliamentary or presidential system, single or plural executive and method of selection, respective powers of the executive, legislative, and judicial branches (including allocation of jurisdiction between state and federal courts), respective powers of state and national governments, taxing power, division of revenue (mainly U.S. aid monies) among the federal government and the several states, citizenship and suffrage rights, and method of constitutional amendment. A separate contentious political conflict at the Convention revolved around the insistence of the Palau delegation on a set of nonnegotiable demands, including placement of the national capitol in Palau (Palau and the Marshalls later chose not to join the Federated States of Micronesia, preferring self-standing independence). Issues surrounding land ownership were also prominent – including an intense debate (and several votes) over the government's power to seize property through eminent domain; this was a contentious issue because Micronesian cultural systems are directly tied to the land, and because the Trust Territory Administration had taken land under circumstances the Micronesians considered unfair.[2] Another very important political debate revolved around what role – if any – traditional leaders would have in the national government. This was a crucial and delicate debate because traditional leaders were (and remain) influential in Micronesian societies, and a lack of support from traditional leaders, it was feared, might lead voters to reject the Constitution.

The battle between law and society that I refer to did not involve any of these political and institutional design issues. Rather the battle emerged in connection with two intersecting issues: the impact on custom and tradition of the Bill of Rights (and the Constitution generally), and how judges would interpret the Constitution and laws.

21.3 THE EXPLICIT PROTECTION OF CUSTOM AND TRADITION

The desire to preserve custom and tradition was a widely shared concern that had special salience in connection with civil rights and judging. While the delegates supported civil rights, they worried that these rights might operate to the detriment of custom and tradition. They have a hierarchical, communitarian-oriented society, not a Western individualist society, which several provisions of the Bill of Rights reflect. To alleviate this concern, an early draft of the Bill of Rights was amended to

[1] This background information is taken from an excellent firsthand account of the Convention by Norman Meller, *Constitutionalism in Micronesia* (Institute for Polynesian Studies, 1985).

[2] See Delegate Chief Bossy, Convention Journal, vol. 1, p. 136: "Many of my people have had the misfortune of owning beautiful parcels of land which the Trust Territory Government wanted, and the government took, through the exercise of eminent domain."

specifically include a provision "which will be equal in rank with the other Bill of Rights to protect and preserve our Micronesian customs, traditional laws and morality."[3] In support of this provision, a delegate explained that it would speed the work of the convention, "if there is a provision in there [along with the rest of the rights] it will eliminate unnecessary and lengthy debate concerning the relationship of custom and traditions to every civil right's measure that comes up for consideration on the floor of the Convention."[4] An early draft of this protective measure was:

> Protection of Micronesian Tradition. The traditions of the Micronesian people may be protected by legislation and administrative action taken pursuant thereto. If challenged as violative of any of the provisions of this Article [Bill of Rights], the essentiality of the Micronesian tradition protected may be considered as a compelling social purpose warranting such governmental action.[5]

Notwithstanding the apparent thrust of this proposal to accord protection to custom, a delegate opposed it on the astute grounds that it appears to grant courts the authority to hear challenges against custom, and the language ("may be considered" compelling) implies the power to rule against custom:

> I feel that the amendment clearly indicates, to me, that every time an alleged violation of our traditions and customs is taken to the court, the court's ruling is final and that ruling prevails. This means to me, further, Mr. President, that should a court in Micronesia rule against tradition and custom, one by one, our tradition and custom will undergo a very, very slow death. These customs and traditions which we are supposedly attempting to protect will slowly disappear from the face of Micronesia.[6]

To eliminate this concern, the final enacted version changed "may" into "shall" as follows: "If challenged as violative of Article IV [Bill of Rights], protection of Micronesian tradition shall be considered a compelling social purpose warranting such governmental action."[7]

21.4 THE JUDICIAL GUIDANCE CLAUSE

The second front in the battle was a pointed effort to restrict courts to Micronesian sources of law – to finally end the dominance of U.S. law in Micronesia after decades

---

[3] Delegate Sawaichi, Convention Journal, vol. 1, 134–135.

[4] Ibid., 135.

[5] Committee Proposal No. 4, as amended by the Committee of the Whole, Draft 1, Constitutional Journal, vol. 1, 148–149.

[6] Delegate Falcam, Constitutional Journal, vol. 1, 149.

[7] Article V, Section 2, Constitution of the Federated States of Micronesia. In earlier drafts this provision was included within the bill of rights, but it was later taken out and combined with the provision on the powers of traditional leaders to create a separate article specifically dealing with Traditional Rights.

under Trust Territory Courts (U.S. judges) applying law from the United States. As one delegate remarked, "I wish to point out that in the past the Trust Territory Courts have copied to a great extent English common law which I sometimes think is not relevant here in Micronesia."[8] A delegate proposed two separate provisions to achieve this effect. First, "the interpretation of this constitution shall not be made in the light of any other constitution known in Micronesia, immediately before the effective date of the constitution."[9] The intention behind this provision, as explained by its proponent, was "that the requestors did not want the Micronesian courts to interpret the Micronesian Constitution in the same way as interpreted by the courts of another jurisdiction whose constitution contained identical or similar language."[10]

As will be revealed in the course of this essay, this observation is of crucial significance to the battle between law and society. It evidences clear awareness on the part of the delegates that the language of constitutional provisions borrowed from the U.S. Constitution are likely to be interpreted relying on U.S. court decisions, and it manifests a strong desire to reject this practice of interpretation. A second provision was proposed as well: "[c]ommencing with the effective date of this constitution, all common law, foreign to Micronesia, shall cease to exist. All legal interpretations shall henceforth be drawn from this Constitution."[11] The explained intention behind this proposal was a desire "to build up a body of Micronesian common law, through court decisions based on Micronesian customs and traditions and the total social and physical configuration of Micronesian life."

There is no mistaking the sentiment behind these two proposals, which evince a heartfelt determination to halt the dominance of U.S. law in Micronesia. The Research and Drafting Section softened these proposals out of worry that they would hamstring courts by prohibiting them from drawing on anything not stated in the Constitution or statutes. They were rephrased from mandatory prohibitions to instead allow courts the freedom to consider other sources of interpretation and other bodies of law, while still emphasizing that appropriateness for Micronesian circumstances remains paramount.

The version that made it to the floor merged the two foregoing proposals into one: "Judicial Guidance: Decisions of Micronesian Courts shall be consistent with this Constitution, Micronesian customs and traditions, and the social and geographical configuration of Micronesia. Decisions of the Trust Territory Courts, and the common law of other nations, are not binding precedents."[12]

---

[8]   Delegate Wilinander, Constitutional Journal, Vol. 1, 420.
[9]   Appendix to Miscellaneous Communication No. 23, Constitutional Journal, vol. 1, 351.
[10] Ibid.
[11] Ibid.
[12] Committee Proposal No. 22, Constitutional Journal, vol. 1, 419

However, an amendment was proposed to delete the second sentence on the grounds that it is problematic and unnecessary. It was potentially problematic in the view of some delegates because a significant body of law had been built up in the preceding decades as well as by foreign courts, which could be useful sources of law for Micronesian courts to consider (albeit not as binding precedent). The main opposition was that the second sentence was unnecessary. As one delegate put it, "the new courts are not going to be bound as a practical consequence of having adopted the new Constitution by the previous decisions of courts. We need not say that. To say it means that we are overly worried about something we should not be concerned about."[13] He added that explicitly stating that they are not bound by the decisions of other courts – given that it is self-evidently true – "only shows our sense of insecurity."[14] Over the objection of a delegate that the second sentence serves as a useful reminder, the Convention voted to enact only the first sentence, which became the "Judicial Guidance Clause," Section 11 of Article XI on the Judiciary.

21.5 THE IMPENETRABILITY OF TECHNICAL LEGAL LANGUAGE

The third battle line was drawn around the fact that important constitutional provisions had obscure legal meanings and implications. This was not a problem with respect to the political and institutional design issues mentioned earlier, all of which were fully debated and crafted in accordance with the directions of the delegates. But several crucial provisions, including the entire Bill of Rights, were drafted by the legal staff, borrowing language from the U.S. Constitution and court decisions. The accompanying committee reports explained these provisions in a highly technical manner.

This issue came to a head when, on the sixty-fifth day of the Convention, a group of traditional leaders requested a one-week postponement on consideration of the Bill of Rights to allow them the time to absorb the dense, legalistic twenty-page Committee Report that explained the provisions. The delegate requesting the delay noted a general problem with legal terminology at the Convention:

> There are times that we may think and feel that we have understood important issues – and all of a sudden we find ourselves wondering why we voted yes or no on a particular issue. I am very much concerned that the language we are using in this Convention is a second language to all of us and is not well understood by most of us, if not at all. These are highly technical, highly abstract issues written in a language unfamiliar to most of us so I can sympathize with the efforts of the traditional chiefs in attempting to make sure that they fully appreciate and fully

---

[13] Delegate Toriblong, *Constitutional Journal*, vol. 1, 420.
[14] Ibid., 421.

understand what they are adopting and making a part of the Constitution or our new government.[15]

Two delegates separately objected that the Committee Report was filled with citations to U.S. cases and was extremely difficult to comprehend, and, furthermore, that the oral explanations provided by the legal staff who drafted the report did not help clear up matters.[16]

In response to these complaints, the director of Research and Drafting, Norman Meller, explained to the Convention floor that problems of this sort are inevitable when legal language is borrowed:

> Language which is being used in the Constitution has meaning. The exact meaning will be determined by Micronesian courts after the Constitution goes into effect. Meanwhile, to assist the Delegates to understand both its possible scope and limitations, reference has been made to the practices of other countries.... With regard to the Declaration of Rights portion of the Constitution, U.S. cases have been used as examples of interpretation. This is because the United States was a pioneer in the inclusion of a Bill of Rights in a national constitution and it is common for other countries to look to American experience. I hasten to add that this is *not* the same thing as saying the courts in those countries are, or in Micronesia, will be, bound by those American decisions.... If desired, staff will eliminate all references to judicial decisions in materials we prepare. Unfortunately, if called upon to answer questions on the possible legal meaning of phraseology, whether or not a case is referred to by name, the knowledge of how the courts have interpreted that language must be availed of by staff in responding, if their response is to be as accurate as they can make it.[17]

To appreciate the magnitude of this problem, to comprehend the extent to which the delegates were mystified by the legal terminology, it is necessary to read an excerpt of the committee report that accompanied the proposed Bill of Rights. While reading the excerpt, keep in mind that English was a second language for the delegates, most of whom had little or no legal training. The proposed Due Process and Equal Protection Clause read: "No person shall be deprived of life, liberty or property without due process of law nor be denied equal protection of the laws."[18] The report follows this proposed constitutional language with ten explanatory paragraphs. Here is one of the ten paragraphs:

> While procedural due process requires governmental decision-making to conform with the concept of what is fair and just, substantive due process, on the other hand,

---

15   Delegate Falcam, Convention Journal, vol. 1, 311.
16   See Miscellaneous Communication No. 23, Convention Journal vol. 1, 349.
17   Ibid., 350.
18   SCREP. No. 23, Committee on Civil Liberties, Bill of Rights (Committee Pro. No. 14), Constitutional Journal, vol. 2, 795.

addresses the rationality of the legislature. With substantive due process, the court basically looks at the rationale or legitimacy of the governmental interest. In subjecting a statute to the requirements of substantive due process, the court asks: (1) Does the government have power to regulate the subject matter? If the statute is not within the power of the government, the statute will be struck down. For example, inasmuch as public monies cannot be expended for other than public purposes, a fortiori, an exercise of the taxing power for merely private purposes is beyond the authority of the legislature. Loan Association v. Topeka, 20 Wall. 255 (1875); Carmichael v. Southern Coal and Coke co., 300 U.S. 644 (1937). (2) If the government has the power to regulate, the court next asks if what the statute proposes to do bears a rational relationship to the implementation of the legislative goal. Another way of asking the same question is, "Can any reasonable legislature choose this particular statute to achieve its goal?" In subjecting a statute to this second test, it must be pointed out that the statute is presumed to be valid. The challengers of the statute must bear the burden of proving that the statute is devoid of any rational basis. Additionally, with respect to economic measures, the courts do not substitute their social and economic beliefs for the judgment of legislative bodies. Munn v. Illinois, 94 U.S. 113 (1877); Ferguson v. Skrupa, 372 U.S. 727, 730 (1963). (3) Finally, where the statute involved arguably infringes upon individuals' fundamental rights, the court must ask how important is the legislative objective. In other words, where fundamental rights are involved, the court resorts to balancing the legislative goals against the fundamental rights which would arguably be infringed if the statute were to stand. The court must ask if there is a compelling governmental interest to justify holding the statute valid, even though the statute might limit fundamental rights. The burden of proving compelling governmental interest shifts to the government. The presumption is in favor of protecting fundamental rights, until the government proves a compelling justification to so curb these rights. Such presumption also protects against irrational application of valid statutes.[19]

One can admire the valiant effort of the legal staff to condense the complex constitutional doctrine of substantive due process into a single paragraph, while still recognizing that this passage, which assumes a great deal of background legal knowledge, would be impenetrable to most non-lawyers who read it (all the worse for nonnative English-speakers). To understand this passage one must know about the distinction between procedure and substance, the rational relation test, the balancing test, what burdens of proof and presumptions are, what fundamental rights are, how to measure a compelling government interest, at least. Now imagine twenty pages of this sort of text, which comprised the Committee Report on the Bill of Rights, and the dilemma confronting the delegates is apparent.

That is why the delegates protested. They were fully aware, and deeply discomfited, that they were giving their imprimatur to *constitutional* words that would be

---

[19]　Ibid. 796.

interpreted and applied – that would bind future lawmakers and citizens – in ways they could not fully grasp. The concern generated by this lack of comprehension was magnified by the fact that the Committee Report was filled with reference to U.S. cases, contrary to the expressed desire of the delegates to be freed of the dictates of U.S. law. Nonetheless, in response to their complaints, the delegates were in effect told by the legal staff: "That's how law is." Legal terminology has the capacity to carry and convey its own meaning that can be impervious to outside penetration.

What is remarkable is that the future Micronesia Supreme Court did precisely what the delegates feared and endeavored to prevent, namely, the adoption of a broad swath of U.S. law. In a cruel twist of events, the very delegates who labored mightily to sever the subservience to U.S. law were later to become the authority judges invoked when adopting U.S. law.

To provide a foretaste of the next phase of the battle, which is taken up in the following section, it is useful to note here that the preceding passage was recited in an opinion by Chief Judge Edward C. King in a case deciding whether a governmental immunity bar to a medical malpractice suit infringes upon the due process clause. The details of the case are not relevant here. What matters is how Judge King utilized the aforementioned passage. Immediately after quoting the passage from the Committee Report, he asserted, "This explanation reveals that the *framers anticipated* that, depending on the nature of the rights involved, one of two different kinds of tests would be applied to determine whether a particular governmental regulation or statute which affects life, liberty or property is consistent with the constitutional demand for 'due process of law.'"[20] Proceeding to apply the two tests (in the name of the framers), King continued in the same vein, asserting that "it appears quite likely that the *framers anticipated* that other rights, not specifically referred to in the declaration of rights, would be protected as fundamental rights under the due process clause."[21]

The *legal staff* that authored the report might have anticipated these things. In light of the concerns expressed by the delegates about the impenetrability of the legal terminology – and their complaints about this Committee Report in particular – it seems well warranted to assert that *the delegates* anticipated nothing of the sort. In a book recounting the Convention, Norman Meller highlighted this reality:

> All Convention actions occurred within a constraining paradigm of language and law which most delegates could vaguely sense, but about which I was acutely aware and could do little. Everything formally said and written was in English, the official language of the Convention, as was all personal intercommunication between delegates not hailing from the same district. Interpreters labored to bridge the gap

[20] Samuel v. Prior, 5 F.S.M. Intrm. 91,101–02 (1991).
[21] Ibid.

between the vernaculars of their principals and the complex English within which ideas frequently took shape, try as staff might to simplify the language employed. But there was a problem beyond interpretation or minimizing the use of "legalism," for all of the English terminology employed was technical in the sense that it depended upon a warp and woof of historical concept and legal experience with which few of the delegates were adequately conversant, regardless of their English -speaking abilities.

To give specificity to the words employed, and being trained in American law, the staff referred to American practice and judicial construction of meanings. As a matter of course, they shaped delegate and committee proposals, as well as the supporting rationale contained in committee reports, within the general conceptual frame of a common law jurisprudence. (Meller 1985: 196)

When discussing this problem, Meller – the head of Research and Drafting – writes as if the legal staff had no real option: "What other course could the staff have followed in an area which for over three decades had been and was yet being administered under the usages of the English language as embodied in American legal practice?" (ibid.).

The legal staff was indeed grappling with a difficult task. But other options were available at hand, as Meller acknowledges, in existing constitutional models from other Pacific Island countries like Fiji and Western Samoa (ibid.: 197). Choices were made by the legal staff, choices shaped by assumptions taken from their American legal training. Moreover, while the legal staff assumed the posture of merely formalizing into legal language the desires of the delegates, they did much more than that. In some instances they were active agents who shaped the substantive thrust of the constitutional provisions. This is evident in Section 4 of the Bill of Rights: "Equal Protection of the laws may not be denied or impaired on account of sex, race, ancestry, national origin, language, or social status." This is far more expansive than the Equal Protection Clause in the U.S. Constitution. Meller justified the additional categories as reflective of "the additional meanings accreted elsewhere over time through court interpretation" (ibid.: 245). Setting aside the question of whether this was indeed an accurate restatement of U.S. equal protection law at the time (rather than the legal staff's ideal version of equal protection law), the crucial point is that this *new* language inserted by the legal staff carried within it potentially fundamental implications for Micronesian culture and society. To state just the two most obvious areas, Micronesian cultures have radically different gender roles and relations from those in the United States, and they are hierarchical societies (including a caste system in Yap). The explicit inclusion of "sex" and "social status" potentially threatens these deep cultural values in uncertain and unknowable ways. This is why, as Meller recognized, one of the most contentious issues was "basic conflict on the floor touching the quick of Convention emotions regarding the primacy of

traditional rights over the civil liberties more recently introduced into Micronesia"
(ibid.: 198).

Thus was the battle between law and society joined. The delegates appeared to
prevail on behalf of society in this crucial engagement by including a provision
that explicitly protected custom and tradition when a clash arises with the Bill of
Rights, and by including the Judicial Guidance Clause to require judges to develop
a Micronesian body of law. Yet none of this would ensure that their wishes would be
heeded, as the delegates seemed to sense, owing to the immanent potential of legal
terminology to exert its own meanings.

21.6 "THE FRAMERS" OF THE CONSTITUTION IN COURT

The Constitution was ratified three years after the Convention in 1978 (the intervening delay was caused by U.S. objections to certain provisions in the draft), and
the new nation was called the Federated States of Micronesia. Edward King and
Richard Benson were appointed in 1980 as the first two judges on the national court,
called the F.S.M. Supreme Court, by the first president, Tosiwo Nakayama. The
Court began to function in May 1981. It was divided into trial and appellate levels;
because there were only two judges at the time, the judge who did not hear the case
at trial would preside on appeals, along with two temporarily appointed judges sitting by designation to hear the case. Benson and King were American expatriate lawyers, both of whom had spent time in the region prior to their appointment; Benson
as a judge on nearby Guam for several years, and King as an attorney for four years
in the Micronesian legal services corporation based in Saipan. The judges who King
and Benson invited to sit by designation on appellate panels ranged from local state
judges to American federal court judges. Given this arrangement, it was inevitable
that the approaches taken by Judges King and Benson would substantially shape the
jurisprudence of the new nation.

Judge King, in particular, embraced his mission to build a body of law for the
county. The focus herein will be limited to his decisions as they relate to the battle
between law and society traced out in this essay – his work at the intersection of custom and tradition, the Bill of Rights, subservience to U.S. case law, and the Judicial
Guidance Clause.

A notable aspect of Judge King's analysis was his frequent and heavy reliance on
"the framers" when justifying his decisions. In his eleven years on the court, from
1981 to 1992, King referred to "framers" in thirty-six separate opinions. This exceeds
the combined total references to "the framers" (twenty-seven in all) in opinions
written by all the other judges on the court from 1981 through 2007 (five judges have
secured permanent appointments to the Supreme Court since its inception). There
is nothing untoward in referring to the framers. One of the main tasks of the new

court was to work out the implications of the new Constitution, and one way for judges to work this out was to consider the purposes of the people who prepared it. But two oddities stand out about Judge King's analysis: his references to "the framers" hardly resemble the delegates who were actually at the convention, and time and again his invocation of the framers served as a prelude to (and justification for) the adoption of U.S. law.

One of King's very first decisions, when sitting as a trial judge in a criminal prosecution, considered the issue of whether evidence seized by police without a search warrant can be used in the criminal case against a defendant. The relevant Constitution provision reads: "The right of the people to be secure in their persons, houses, papers, and other possessions against unreasonable search, seizure, or invasion of privacy may not be violated."[22] As King notes, this clause, which is modeled on the Fourth Amendment of the U.S. Constitution, does not specify how to determine what makes a search "unreasonable," or what should happen to evidence obtained in constitutionally inappropriate searches. "We must probe further," King continued, "to determine the full *meaning of the framers* in employing this constitutional language."[23] King then pointed to the Journal of Constitutional Convention:

> The Journal in this instance though provides unmistakable direction. The Micronesian Constitutional Convention's Committee on Civil Rights proposed the Declaration of Rights in substantially the form subsequently incorporated within the Constitution. [citation omitted] The proposed language and supplemental discussions in the Committee Report reveal that in developing the Declaration of Rights for the Constitution of the Federated States of Micronesia, the Committee, and subsequently the Convention itself, were drawing almost exclusively upon constitutional principles under United States law.[24]

This would prove to be a fateful analytical move. For the next step – which comes after Judge King notes the substantial similarity between the wording of the U.S. search and seizure clause and the F.S.M. search and seizure clause – follows almost inexorably from the first:

> Thus, the Journal of the Micronesian Constitutional Convention teaches that, in interpreting the Declaration of Rights in the Constitution of the Federated States of Micronesia, *we should emphasize and carefully consider United States Supreme Court interpretations of comparable language in the Bill of Rights of the United States Constitution.* We therefore turn to these decisions for aid in determining the meaning of the word "unreasonable" and in framing principles to be employed in

[22] F.S.M. Const. art. IV Sec. 5.
[23] F.S.M. v. Tipen, 1 F.S.M. Intrm. 79,82 (Pon. 82)(emphasis added).
[24] Ibid., 82.

upholding the protection against unreasonable search proclaimed in Article IV, Section 5 of the Constitution of the Federated States of Micronesia.[25]

Judge King then launched into an exegesis of U.S. constitutional search and seizure doctrine, extensively quoting from or citing sixteen U.S. Supreme Court cases. He ended up adopting the U.S. reasonableness analysis for the F.S.M..

In the bootstrapping style characteristic of common law legal analysis, this case, *F.S.M. v. Tipen*, would later be cited (frequently by King himself) for the proposition that the similar language in the U.S. and Micronesian Bills of Rights suggest that U.S. case law should be considered. King did not mention the Judicial Guidance Clause in his decision, or the objections from delegates at the Convention about the heavy reliance on U.S. case law in the Committee Report, or their complaints that they could not apprehend the legal explanations in the report.

This was the beginning of a pattern Judge King would reiterate multiple times. An early appellate opinion issued the same year, *Alaphonso v. F.S.M.*, which considered what burden of proof is required in criminal cases, introduced a twist on this pattern involving the Judicial Guidance Clause. At the outset of the opinion, King chastised the lawyers for their omission:

> The parties here have ... merely cited legal authorities from the United States, including decisions of United States federal and state courts, without explaining why those authorities are pertinent to these issues before this Court. The Constitution instructs us that we may not merely assume away, or ignore, fundamental issues on the grounds that these basic issues have previously been decided in a particular way by other courts in other circumstances and under different governmental systems. The "judicial guidance" provision, Art. XI, Sec. 11 of the Constitution, tells us that our decisions must be "consistent" with the "Constitution, Micronesian customs and traditions, and the social and geographical configuration of Micronesia."[26]

King quoted two passages from the report attached to the Judicial Guidance Clause explaining the desire of the delegates to shape a body of law suitable to Micronesia, rather than blindly follow Trust Territory cases and U.S. law. In later cases Judge King would often cite *Alaphonso* for the proposition that the Court paid due regard for the unique circumstances of Micronesia.

In the case itself, however, after his extended homage to the Judicial Guidance Clause, Judge King immediately veered in a different direction. He noted that the due process clause in the F.S.M. Constitution says nothing about the burden of proof in criminal cases; he noted the parallel language between the due process clause

---

[25] Ibid., 83.
[26] *Alaphonso v. F.S.M.*, 1F.S.M. Interm. 209, 211 (1982).

in the U.S. Constitution and the due process clause in the F.S.M. Constitution; and he noted that in the committee report attached to the due process clause "the Committee relied principally upon decisions of the United States Supreme Court."[27] "The obvious lesson is that we are to look to the interpretative decisions of U.S. courts concerning the Due Process Clause of the Fifth Amendment of the United States Conclusion."[28] Thus, following his nod to the Judicial Guidance Clause, King arrived on familiar ground, citing ten U.S. cases, adopting the beyond a reasonable doubt standard for the F.S.M.

In the course of his analysis, Judge King made a seemingly odd remark that he treated as highly significant:

> The *framers* of this Constitution, and subsequently the *voters* in ratifying could only have been *aware of* constitutional interpretations rendered prior thereto and at the times of the Constitutional Convention, and ratification of the Constitution through plebiscite. We should therefore emphasize interpretations in effect at those times.[29]

Judge King touted, and often later repeated, this cutoff date as an essential "protection" for Micronesians – "a timing limitation, which diminishes the import of decisions made by the U.S. Supreme Court after July 12, 1978, the date of the plebiscite" (King 2002: 266). This remark is odd for several reasons. King's careful negative locution – they "could only have been aware" of a U.S. precedent in existence at the time they voted – is logically unassailable. (Of course they could not possibly know of anything that did not exist then.) But the soundness of his assertion that pre-1978 precedents carry greater import depends on the correctness of one or both of the following positive assertions: that the delegates and voters *were in fact aware of* and/ or that they *did in fact intend that greater weight be given* to U.S. precedents then in existence. Neither assertion is remotely true.

It is a pure pretense to suggest that the delegates had any *awareness* of U.S. constitutional decisions at the time. As described earlier, the delegates struggled to understand the legal explanations prepared by the legal staff for the Bill of Rights. None of the U.S. cases Judge King cited in *Alaphonso* (and in many other decisions King later wrote following this analysis) were actually mentioned in the Committee Report. Judge King's cutoff date is the mid-1978 ratification by voters, which is a travesty of fact and reason. It borders on deception to imply that the voters had any knowledge of or intention about pre-vote cases. The delegates at least had an opportunity to review the Committee Report (never mind understand it); the people, the mass of Micronesians in villages and towns (many with limited English and

---

[27] Ibid., 214–215.
[28] Ibid., 215.S
[29] Ibid., 215.

education) who voted to ratify the Constitution had no exposure to it and had no idea what it contained. Leading up to the vote there were public meetings and general education programs about the proposed Constitution, but there was no detailed legal analysis, which the people could not have grasped anyway.

As for their actual intent, the delegates repeated their fervent wish to halt the practice of blind obedience to U.S. precedent, although they permitted consideration of U.S. decisions for whatever insight they might offer to Micronesian judges. Remember, on this point, that several delegates explicitly *complained* about the presence of citations to U.S. Supreme Court cases in the committee report attached to the Bill of Rights – this prompted the Director of Research and Drafting to offer to excise the U.S. cases (although he said it would be pointless). The unmistakable intention of the delegates would have attached no significance to when the U.S. precedent was decided, whether before or after the Convention, because under all circumstances, U.S. precedents were not to be binding (which is exactly what the delegates said). All U.S. precedents would have the same weight: they were information for the Micronesian judge to consider.

The crucial distinction Judge King drew between pre- and post-ratification U.S. cases was meaningless with respect to what the delegates and voters actually knew, and was contrary to what they actually intended. It was an elaborate gesture of self-abnegation on the part of Judge King (and other judges who have repeated it) to maintain the veneer that his decisions comported with the consent of the people as embodied in their drafting and adoption of the Constitution. (This was a "gesture" rather than a genuine limitation because, notwithstanding his assertion, Judge King regularly cited post-1978 U.S. cases anyway.[30]) And he would point to this "protection" as a significant mark of the genuine independence of the Micronesian Court from obedience to U.S. law.

Alaphonso became the template for future cases. Judge King would begin with a nod to the Judicial Guidance Clause; then he would note the similarity between the U.S. and F.S.M. constitutional language, and mention that committee reports cited U.S. cases; then he would engage in extensive discussions of U.S. case law, concluding by adopting U.S. legal approaches. Following this mode of analysis, he adopted U.S. doctrines of judicial review,[31] search and seizure,[32] vagueness in criminal statutes,[33] abstention,[34] voluntariness standard in confessions,[35] and common law

---

[30] See United Church of Christ v. Hanno, 4 F.S.M. Intrm. 95 (App. 1989); F.S.M. v. Jonathan, 2 F.S.M. Intrm. 189 (Kos. 1986).

[31] Suldan v. F.S.M., 1 F.S.M. Intrm. 339 (Pon. 1983).

[32] F.S.M. v. George, 1 F.S.M. 449 (Kos. 1984).

[33] Laion v. F.S.M., 1 F.S.M. Intrm. (App. 1984)

[34] Panuelo v. Pohnpei, 2 F.S.M. Intrm. 150 (Pon. 1986).

[35] F.S.M. v. Jonathan, 2 F.S.M. Intrm. 189 (Kos. 1986)

claims,[36] among other legal doctrines.[37] On occasion King rejected prevailing U.S. law, but rarely on the grounds that it was unsuitable for Micronesian circumstances – he simply appeared to disagree.[38] In this manner, he steadily built up a body of law that closely resembled U.S. common law and individual liberties analysis.

At times, Judge King's analysis of the framers was perfunctory and conclusive. In a case in which the defendant argued that the police could not search an open field without a warrant, Judge King noted that since *Hester v. United States*, decided by the U.S. Supreme Court in 1924, the law was clear that warrantless open field searches do not violate the Fourth Amendment:

> The framers of the Federated States of Micronesia Constitution looked to United States court decisions to determine the meaning to the words they were selecting for the declaration of rights in this Constitution. SCREP No. 23, II J. of Micro. Con. Con. 973. The searches here fall within the Hester open fields doctrine. *There is no reason to doubt that the framers intended for that doctrine to apply here.*[39]

Contrary to King's assertion, it is unequivocally clear that the delegates had no intention at all about the matter. Needless to say, the *Hester* decision and the open fields doctrine were never mentioned at the convention – and the committee report (which King cites) on this particular provision of the Bill of Rights does not actually refer to any U.S. cases.

Most of the time, Judge King invoked the framers to draw a positive warrant for the incorporation of U.S. case law, but in a few instances he found no evidence of the framers' intent, which in turn allowed him to avoid U.S. precedents. In a case involving whether the enforcement of a mortgage on a ship is within the Court's admiralty jurisdiction, King was confronted with a 150-year-old U.S. Supreme Court precedent that mortgages fall outside admiralty jurisdiction. Judge King cited several criticisms by U.S. legal scholars of this early decision, he emphasized the import of the Judicial Guidance Clause, and then he raised the framers:

> Of course, if the constitutional history of the Federated States of Micronesia revealed that the *framers*, or the *electorate*, in embracing the language of the United

---

[36] Semes v. Continental Air Lines, Inc. 2 F.S.M. Intrm. 131 (Pon. 1985)

[37] An excellent survey of the Court's jurisprudence is provided in Dennis K. Yamase, "The Supreme Court of the Federated States of Micronesia: The First Twenty Five Years," available at http://www. docstoc.com/docs/49941580/the-supreme-court-of-the-federated-states-of-micronesia

[38] See Federal Business Development Bank v. SS Thorfinn, 4 F.S.M. Intrm. 367 (App. 1990) (decline to follow U.S. precedent that foreclosure on ship is not within maritime jurisdiction); Aisek v. Foreign Investment Board, 2 F.S.M. Intrm. 95 (Pon. 1985) (adopt the concrete adversary requirement of standing doctrine, but reject the nexus requirement); see Samuel v. Prior, 5 F.S.M. Intrm. 91 (Pon. 1991) (refuse to recognize medical malpractice claim, although other common law claims previously recognized.)

[39] F.S.M. v. Rosario, 3 F.S.M. Intrm. 387, 388–89 (Pon. 1988).

States Constitution, specifically intended to adopt the particular interpretation given those words by the United States courts, then we would not be free to seek an alternative meaning. However, the journals of the Micronesian Constitutional Convention reveal no such specific intent concerning the meaning of the words "admiralty or maritime."[40]

In light of his general approach, this is an astonishing passage. In none of the cases discussed earlier in which King relied on the framers' intent to adopt U.S. case analysis was there any evidence of *specific intention* in support. In all of these cases – for example, does the due process clause require the beyond the reasonable doubt standard – the Constitution and Journal were silent, indicating that no one had thought about the issue. Indeed, the strongest evidence of intention that bears on the issue was the general desire of the delegates that the future Court not slavishly follow U.S. precedent – a desire Judge King largely frustrated.

Another telling case raised the issue of the standing requirements plaintiffs must meet to bring suit. Issues about standing to sue are not addressed in the Constitution and were not raised at the Convention. Per usual, Judge King began with a reference to the import of the Judicial Guidance Clause, then made this assertion: "Many provisions of this Constitution are derived from the United States Constitution and *the framers surely intended that interpretation of the words adopted would be influenced by United States decisions* in existence when this Constitution was adopted, in October 1975, and ratified on July 12, 1978."[41] To the contrary, as argued earlier, they surely had no such intention. What makes this case revealing is that Judge King wanted to loosen the yolk of U.S. standing law, to adopt the "concrete adverseness" requirement of standing doctrine but not the "nexus" requirement. To provide himself this freedom, King noted that standing law happened to be "a particularly unsettled area of United States law when the F.S.M. Constitution was drafted and ratified."[42] Because it was unsettled, his reasoning went, the framers and voters would not have been certain about the law (in fact, they knew nothing about it either way). King then remarked that in 1978 the nexus requirement was limited to taxpayer suits. "Thus, ratification of the Constitution can not be seen as indicating an intention by the framers or the people of the Federated States of Micronesia that this additional obstacle to court access be adopted."[43]

[40] Federal Business Development Bank v. SS Thorfinn, 4 F.S.M. Intrm. 367,341 (App. 1990).
[41] Aisek v. Foreign Investment Board, 2 F.S.M. Intrm. 95,98 (Pon. 1985).
[42] Ibid., 99.
[43] Ibid., 102.

Judge King is indisputably correct that the framers and people had no intention to adopt the nexus requirement, but they just as surely had no intention to adopt any of the many doctrines taken from U.S. cases that Judge King positively declared in their name and by their authority. His analysis of the framers erects a convoluted castle of fictions, for the delegates and voters had no knowledge about any of this, and gave nary a thought to it. The flesh-and-blood delegates at the Convention were transformed in King's legal analysis into abstract entities who *must have intended* certain things – no matter how remote from their actual intentions – by virtue of the language they adopted and the committee reports they (purportedly) read and understood.

A process of abstraction is often utilized in law to re-describe social situations and events to conform to and serve legal categories and modes of analysis. This is one of the ways law manages, constrains, and channels social influences, sometimes to tame them or stave them off. This is not law acting on its own – Judge King skillfully wielded these modes of legal analysis to implant into Micronesian law legal doctrines he was familiar with and believed in. When so doing, every time Judge King referred to "the framers," he erased the actual identity of the Micronesian delegates and voters and used them to accomplish his own legal ends.

Micronesian law did not have to be built this way, and Judge King did not have to proceed in this fashion. While it makes sense that he would adopt legal tests with which he was familiar, and it is entirely appropriate that he would look to U.S. cases for guidance when faced with novel issues, he could have systematically consulted a range of legal sources, especially the constitutions and laws of other island countries of the Pacific. He could have taken up each issue on its own terms, evaluating the pros and cons, the relevant policies and principles as they bear on the government, the law, and the political, economic, geographical, and cultural conditions of Micronesia – indeed, Judge King decided a number of cases in this more open and straightforward fashion.[44] But to a significant extent, especially early in his tenure, he relied heavily on U.S. cases and engaged in standard American-style legal reasoning. And his utilization of the framers' intent was disingenuous, thereby building into the jurisprudence of the new nation a strain of fictional legal analysis that survived his departure.

When Judge King retired in 1993, he was replaced as Chief Justice by Andon Amaraich. Amaraich had enjoyed a long career in a variety of high-level government positions in Micronesia. Although he did not have a law degree, he worked as a public defender for ten years. He was also a long-time Congressman under the Trust Territory and the F.S.M., and he headed the national department of external

---

[44] See, e.g., Semes v. Continental Air Lines Inc. 2 F.S.M. Intrm. 200 (Pon. 1986).

affairs under two presidents.[45] Directly relevant to this analysis, Amaraich served on the legal staff at the 1975 Constitutional Convention, drafting a number of the constitutional provisions.

From 1992 until the end of 2007, Judge Amaraich issued seven written opinions that referred to "the framers," far fewer than Judge King did. His treatment of the framers stands in stark contrast to that of Judge King's. One striking difference is that Amaraich cites far fewer U.S. cases than King. In four of the seven cases mentioning the framers, he cited zero U.S. cases; in a fifth and sixth case, he cited one and three U.S. Supreme Court cases, respectively,[46] as informative on the issues – but without suggesting that the framers intended to endorse those precedents. In only one case in which he mentions the framers did Judge Amaraich engage in a significant discussion of U.S. cases, and that was in a case involving the power to tax. Judge Amaraich considers U.S. tax law doctrines (in a separate section labeled "United States Case Law") on their merits for how they might inform his decision, choosing to adopt certain tests for his analysis, but at no point does he link these cases back to the framers' intent.[47] Another striking difference is that when Amaraich discusses the framers' intent, it is in relation to things the framers really did debate and try to achieve, whereas Judge King's references to the framers tended to be purely abstract discussions of what they must have intended when borrowing U.S. constitutional language. Judge Amaraich also frankly acknowledged that legal questions arose that the framers simply had not foreseen, and he accepted responsibility for making the decision.[48] No abstract framers appear in the pages of Judge Amaraich's opinions.

21.7 THE EXISTENTIAL BATTLE BETWEEN SOCIETY AND LAW

While the struggle revolving around "the framers" was concealed in the dry legal analysis of judicial opinions, a remarkable clash between law and society erupted in plain view that exposed the depth of the conflict. In separate incidents on Yap several months apart in 1998, Joseph Tammed and Raphael Tamangrow sexually assaulted girls.[49] Ten days after his attack, Tammed was taken by relatives of the victim to her father's house and severely beaten, left with a bloodied face and a broken hand. Tamangrow was likewise seized, a week after his attack, by fellow villagers

---

[45] See "The Federated States of Micronesia Mourns the Loss of one of its Founding Fathers: Chief Justice Andon Amaraich," at http://www.fsmgov.org/press/pr012810.htm

[46] See Pohnpei v. KSVI, 10 F.S.M. Intrm. 53 (Pon. 2001); Pohnpei v. MV Hai Hsiang, 6 F.S.M. Intrm. 594 (Pon. 1994) (three cases).

[47] See Chuuk v. Secretary of Finance, 8 F.S.M. Intrm. 353 (Pon. 1998).

[48] F.S.M. v. Kotobuki Maru No 23, 6 F.S.M. Intrm. 65,74 (Pon. 1993).

[49] The facts of these incidents are set forth in the consolidated case, Tammed v. F.S.M., 4 F.S.M. Intrm. 266 (App. 1990).

of the victim, and severely beaten to the point of unconsciousness, thereafter hospitalized for five days (adding to his offense was the fact that his victim was of a higher caste). According to members of the community, both beatings were administered as customary punishment. Tammed and Tamangrow were later separately charged and convicted of sexual assault. At their respective sentencing hearings, they asked the presiding judge, Richard Benson, to reduce their sentences in light of the "customary beatings" they had suffered. Judge Benson refused to consider the beatings, stating:

> The judgments of this court do have an effect on the community and in future cases a group of men taking the law into their own hands can say, "It's all right. The Court lets us handle the punishment." I make that statement not denying that there is apparently, because it's been raised in two cases now, a Yapese custom along these lines.[50]

Both defendants then appealed their respective sentences, arguing that Judge Benson erroneously failed to take their customary punishments into consideration to reduce their sentence.

On Yap, custom and tradition have great importance in social and political life. The attorney general of Yap State, Cyprian Manmaw (now chief justice of the Yap State Court, who earned a law degree in the United States and served as the attorney general for twenty years), followed a policy of deference to customary actions. The Yap attorney general's office supported Tammed and Tamangrow on their appeal; stronger still, Manmaw would not have brought the original assault charges against Tammed and Tamangrow had the crime been under state jurisdiction because he considered the customary punishment to resolve the matter. Judge King ruled in favor of the defendants on appeal, finding that Judge Benson should have considered the customary punishments in mitigation of their sentence (citing a similar case from Australia). But Judge King spent the better part of the opinion sending a warning to Yap State that it would be held to account if it continued to defer to customary punishments. Here is the critical (threatening) passage:

> There is an even greater need for caution in this case because of the apparent policies of Yap state officials concerning these kinds of customary punishments, as reflected in the record and explained further in oral argument.... For example, government counsel during Mr. Tammed's sentencing hearing indicated to the trial court that if the office of the Yap attorney general makes a determination that a particular punishment has been carried out "in accordance with Yapese custom," then that office "would not file the charges" if the underlying criminal offense was a violation of state law rather than national law.... This practice of course amounts

---

[50] Ibid., 270.

to a substitution of the customary punishment in place of the judicial proceedings and punishment contemplated by the Constitution and state statutes. Under the policy of the Yap attorney general's office, beating is no longer just a customary punishment, but also serves as the entire official state trial and punishment for that specific offense. *The traditional leaders who authorized the punishment, and the village members who carried it out, may well be transformed through this ratification into government agents or officials....* By embracing the customary punishment as fulfillment of their own prosecutorial and governmental responsibilities, governmental officials may effectively make themselves participants in the punishments meted out pursuant to custom. This policy of the office of the Yap attorney general runs the risk of so identifying the Yap state government with attacks upon individuals, which state officials could not carry out directly, as to *transform those customary punishments into action of the state.*[51]

Through the legal speak, Judge King is saying that if this policy is continued, Yap State may be subject to civil lawsuits for customary punishments, and those who administer the punishment may be subject to suit as well for civil rights violations (in addition to simple battery). To make this message clear he cited the statutory provision for civil rights claims.[52]

Judge Benson and Judge King held the unshakable conviction that the state has a monopoly over law – and in particular a monopoly over the infliction of legitimate violence. This is what Judge Benson was thinking when he feared that men would "take the law into their own hands." This explains why Judge King could assert that the customary punishments might be "the entire official state trial and punishments" and those who carried out the punishments might be "government agents or officials." If one assumes that there is only one legitimate legal system, and that this system resides in the state, then it follows that any *valid* punishments are, by conceptual necessity, *actions of the state* no matter who carries them out.

The Yapese people saw law differently. They saw *two* legal systems existing side by side, with the state legal system mainly handling affairs of government and business. With respect to social affairs (including property rights, family affairs, altercations), they believed that customary ways of responding to problems had primacy. That is why Manmaw deferred to customary actions that effectively resolved matters. Owing to this primacy, if it happened that police officers were among the relatives of the victims and hence participated in the customary beatings (as apparently occurred in Tammed's punishment), they were acting as members of the

---

[51] Ibid., 282–283.
[52] Id. ft. 11. In a later article discussing the case, King acknowledged the point of this reminder; Edward C. King, Custom and Constitutionalism in the Federated States of Micronesia, 3 *Asian-Pac. Law & Policy J.* 249,278 n. 80 (2002).

community in their customary capacity (who just happened to be police officers), not as police officers.

This is an existential battle in the genuine sense that the judges found it unacceptable, a threat to the very idea of law, to be confronted with a competing legal system to which people accord primacy over state law in certain affairs. Judge King was not troubled by allowing the customary punishments to be considered in criminal sentencing because this meant that they operated by leave of and within the parameters established by state law. Judge King's overarching assumption that state law must have primacy was displayed, albeit implicitly, in an article he wrote ten years later, after his retirement from the bench:

> If the traditional leaders do believe that continuation of customary punishments is desirable, traditional leaders and government officials should explore why this is so. Is it because of a lack of confidence in the constitutional legal justice system? Is this in turn based on a perception that communities are unsafe? If so, those concerns should be discussed, and consideration should be given to the possibility of adjusting legislative authorizations, law enforcement actions, and court pretrial detention and sentencing practices to respond to these concerns.... On the other hand, is it possible that traditional punishments are being used primarily as a way for the local community or traditional leadership to assert greater control and to demand greater respect? Institutions typically seek self-strengthening devices, and there is no reason why this should be different for traditional leadership. If this is an important purpose of customary punishments, could that same benefit be obtained in some way that does not include physical violence or possible violation of constitutional standards? Could traditional leaders be involved more closely in the criminal justice process? If traditional leaders believe they are sufficiently certain as to the identity of an offender to justify a customary punishment, would they be willing simply to turn over their information to government officials if they knew that prompt action would be taken? (King 2002: 280–281)

His reflections on *Tammed* reveal that Judge King never really understood what was at stake. He could not envision the beatings as anything other than brutal acts of violence. Of course the traditional leaders were interested in maintaining their power within the customary system (much like judges within the state system), as King skeptically suggests, but events cannot be explained in those terms. Nor was the issue for the Yapese about improving the state legal system to better serve their needs as a community, as his questions assume. Rather, at issue was nothing less than the continued existence of *their own* thriving legal system, a system they identified with because it was the product of community actions in accordance with norms they all understood. Recall, if you will, the complaints of the delegates at the constitutional Convention about the foreign (U.S.) feel and impenetrability of state law. Their customary system raised no similar objections for the Yapese people precisely because it was *their* system. It is essential to recognize that Yapese society was (and remains) cohesive and well ordered in large part because its customary systems functioned fairly well. Manmaw's policy of deference to the customary system, to which Judge King objected, served to enhance the functioning of both legal systems in their own primary spheres, and helped negotiate their interaction when they intersected. A final incident helps demonstrate this point.[53]

When Manmaw resigned as attorney general to become chief justice, his long-time assistant in the office, Victor Nabeyan, was appointed to replace him. A few months after he took the position, Nabeyan, while drunk one day, committed assault and battery. This was especially embarrassing because the attorney general is the top legal official in the state. Nabeyan was immediately placed on administrative leave by the governor. The governor advised the speaker of the legislature that the incident involved family members, different villages, and possible criminal charges, writing:

> As the resolution of these concerns are a mixture of traditional and governmental responsibilities and functions – some more traditional than others, and vice-versa – the Lt. Governor and I, despite our strong desire to resolve the matter quickly, saw it fit to let those concerns we have limited authority over, and those beyond our authority (i.e., family feud, village disputes, and criminal investigation) be resolved first while waiting for input from other branches of the state government.[54]

Nabeyan made a public apology for his conduct, sending the statement to the Traditional Councils of Pilung and Tamol (the main island chiefs and the outer island chiefs, respectively), as well as to all state officials, while also tendering his resignation to the governor. Meanwhile, traditional means of reconciliation took place between the individuals and families in order to heal the rift. The Council of Pilung then called for a special meeting with the governor and legislature to express its view that Nabeyan be allowed to remain as attorney general to manage the state's legal business. "The Council's belief was that the matter was a 'non-issue' for the State because a 'weinig' at the family and village levels had been tendered and accepted and 'harmony between and among villages concerned has been restored.'"[55] The prosecutor's office (in Nabeyan's absence) decided to defer prosecution for battery because the victim refused to press charges owing to the reconciliation. The Council of Tamol sent a letter telling the governor they supported his decision to reinstate Nabeyan "as long as there should be no conflict between

[53] This incident and subsequent events are described in B. Gorong, "Victor Nabeyan Remains as Attorney General," *The Yap Networker* 8 (July 20, 2007): 4–5.

[54] Ibid., 5.

[55] Ibid.

our traditional custom and the State Government."[56] With these various positions arrived at, the governor lifted the three-week leave of absence, and Nebayan served as attorney general thereafter.

The handling of this incident is a brilliant example of the effective interweaving within Yapese society of traditional customs and processes with modern governmental processes, including state law, each with its own realm and ways, yet working in interaction to find workable resolutions. Judge King could not see the genuine importance of the customary system and how it worked. King was happy to allow the state legal system to recognize customary apologies but not customary punishment – but they were all of a piece, a total way of life that could not be pried apart while maintaining its integrity (King 2002: 268–269).

This final incident also reveals that, against the theme of this essay, law need not battle society, even when the social and legal systems are poised to clash with inconsistent norms and competing systems of power. Whether or not they battle depends to a large extent on the attitudes toward each system taken by the actors involved – especially the attitudes of state legal officials.

21.8 THE STRUGGLE BETWEEN LAW AND SOCIETY: GOING FORWARD

In 1990, after a decade of independence, a second Constitutional Convention was held, this time without the United States lurking in the background. Only three amendments were ultimately enacted, two of which were directed at the topics discussed earlier in the chapter. One amendment added a new second sentence to the Judicial Guidance Clause, which now reads (the amendment indicated in italics):

> Section 11. Court decisions shall be consistent with this Constitution, Micronesian customs and traditions, and the social and geographical configuration of Micronesia. *In rendering a decision, the court must consult and apply sources of the Federated States of Micronesia.*

This addition was an implicit rebuke of the court's jurisprudence – of Judge King in particular. The Committee Report proposing the Amendment reads:

> A review of Supreme Court decisions since the advent of constitutional government in the Federated States of Micronesia shows a pattern of reliance on precedent from the United States. Your Committee is concerned that the Supreme Court may not be giving proper attention to Section 11 of Article XI of the Constitution. Therefore, we support re-emphasizing our determination that courts shall first examine sources from the Federated States of Micronesia prior to relying upon precedent from other jurisdictions. The word "source" is used broadly to include not only court

---

[56] Ibid.

decisions, constitutional history, and other legal writings from the Federated States of Micronesia, but also the customs and traditions of our nation.[57]

As this explanation indicates, the second sentence adds nothing new; it merely emphasizes the point of the first sentence.

A second successful amendment removed legislative power over "major crimes" from the national government and gave it to the states, leaving national power only over crimes of a "national" nature. The effect of this amendment was to divest national courts of jurisdiction over these criminal cases. Under the previous system, the national government would handle all crimes subject to punishment for three or more years (later increased to five years, then ten years), including serious crimes like rape and murder (King 2002: 271). That is why the prosecutions of Tammed and Tamangrow for sexual assault were handled in the national court system. Following the amendment, state prosecutors and courts would have exclusive control over crimes of this sort.

Taking stock of developments thus far, a few conclusions can be drawn with some confidence. Judges King and Benson have departed, and Judge Amaraich recently died. There are currently two sitting national judges, Judge Martin Yinug, a Yapese with an American law degree, and Judge Dennis Yamase, an expatriate American lawyer who has lived and worked in Micronesia for decades. As would be expected after three decades of independence, a substantial body of law has developed. Judicial opinions today are filled with citations to Micronesian cases. Although U.S. cases are cited far less frequently than in the past, behind many of the Micronesian cases lie U.S. precedents, and many of the legal rules and doctrines are derived from the United States. In this respect Judge King was extremely effective and his enduring legacy will not likely be erased. Common law systems tend not to reexamine precedents. Nor is it necessarily desirable that the developed body of rules should be reexamined in a wholesale manner. Legal officials in Micronesia have become accustomed to their jurisprudence and the system operates well. Many of the technical legal doctrines the court adopted – for example, rules like abstention and standing – have no implications for Micronesian society, but are essential to every judicial system and must be worked out. The critical tone of this essay should not diminish the genuine achievement of the first generation of judges on the Micronesian Supreme Court.

The struggle between law and society played out in this essay will undoubtedly continue in ways that are impossible to anticipate. Certain constitutional provisions, especially in the Bill of Rights and certain aspects of the legal system – including its adversarial style, with winners and losers – are in tension with Micronesian norms.

---

[57] Fed. St. Micr. Const. Con., Report of the Comm. On Governmental Structure and Function, Standing Committee Rep. No. 27–90, at 2–3.

Owing to this structural feature of their society-law relationship, there is an ever-present potential for conflict.

REFERENCES

Aisek v. Foreign Investment Board, 2 F.S.M. Intrm. 95,98 (Pon. 1985).

Alaphonso v. FSM, 1FSM Interm. 209,211 (1982).

Appendix to Miscellaneous Communication No. 23, Constitutional Journal, vol. 1, 351.

Article V, Section 2, Constitution of the Federated States of Micronesia

Chuuk v. Secretary of Finance, 8 F.S.M. Intrm. 353 (Pon. 1998).

Committee Proposal No. 22, Constitutional Journal, vol. 1, 419

Committee Proposal No. 4, as amended by the Committee of the Whole, Draft 1, Constitutional Journal, vol. 1, 148–149.

Delegate Chief Bossy, Convention Journal, vol. 1, p. 136

Delegate Falcam, Constitutional Journal, vol. 1, 149.

Delegate Falcam, Convention Journal, vol. 1, 311

Delegate Sawaichi, Convention Journal vol. 1, 134–35.

Delegate Toriblong, Constitutional Journal, vol. 1, 420.

Delegate Wilinander, Constitutional Journal, Vol. 1, 420.

F.S.M. v. George, 1 F.S.M. 449 (Kos. 1984).

F.S.M. v. Jonathan, 2 F.S.M. Intrm. 189 (Kos. 1986)

F.S.M. v. Kotobuki Maru No 23, 6 F.S.M. Intrm. 65,74 (Pon. 1993).

F.S.M. v. Rosario, 3 F.S.M. Intrm. 387, 388–89 (Pon. 1988).

Fed. St. Micr. Const. Con., Report of the Comm. On Governmental Structure and Function, Standing Committee Rep. No. 27–90, at 2–3.

Federal Business Development Bank v. SS Thorfinn, 4 F.S.M. Intrm. 367,341 (App. 1990)

Federal Business Development Bank v. SS Thorfinn, 4 F.S.M. Intrm. 367 (App. 1990)(decline to follow U.S. precedent that foreclosure on ship is not within maritime jurisdiction); Aisek v. Foreign Investment Board, 2 F.S.M. Intrm. 95 (Pon. 1985)(adopt the concrete adversary requirement of standing doctrine, but reject the nexus requirement); see Samuel v. Prior, 5 F.S.M. Intrm. 91 (Pon. 1991)(refuse to recognize medical malpractice claim, although other common law claims previously recognized.)

FSM Const. art. IV Sec. 5.

FSM v. Tipen, 1 FSM Intrm. 79,82 (Pon. 82)(emphasis added).

Gorong, B. 2007. 'Victor Nabeyan Remains as Attorney General', *The Yap Networker* 8 (July 20): 4–5.

King, Edward C. 2002. 'Custom and Constitutionalism in the Federated States of Micronesia', *Asian-Pacific Law and Policy Journal* 3: 249.

Laion v. F.S.M., 1 F.S.M. Intrm. (App. 1984)

Miscellaneous Communication No. 23, Constitutional Journal, vol. 1, 351.

Meller, Norman 1985. *Constitutionalism in Micronesia*. Institute for Polynesian Studies.

Panuelo v. Pohnpei, 2 F.S.M. Intrm. 150 (Pon. 1986).

Pohnpei v. KSVI, 10 F.S.M. Intrm. 53 (Pon. 2001); Pohnpei v. MV Hai Hsiang, 6 F.S.M. Intrm. 594 (Pon. 1994)(three cases)

Samuel v. Prior, 5 FSM Intrm. 91,101–02 (1991).

SCREP No. 23, page 793

SCREP. No. 23, Committee on Civil Liberties, Bill of Rights (Committee Pro. No. 14), Constitutional Journal, vol. 2, 795.

Semes v. Continental Air Lines Inc. 2 F.S.M. Intrm. 200 (Pon. 1986)

Semes v. Continental Air Lines, Inc. 2 F.S.M. Intrm. 131 (Pon. 1985)

Suldan v. F.S.M., 1 F.S.M. Intrm. 339 (Pon. 1983).

Tammed v. F.S.M., 4 F.S.M. Intrm. 266 (App. 1990).

The Federated States of Micronesia Mourns the Loss of One of Its Founding Fathers: Chief Justice Andon Amaraich, at http://www.F.S.M.gov.org/press/pro12810.htm

United Church of Christ v. Hanno, 4 FSM Intrm. 95 (App. 1989); FSM v. Jonathan, 2 FSM Intrm. 189 (Kos. 1986).

Yamase, Dennis K. 'The Supreme Court of the Federated States of Micronesia: The First Twenty Five Years', available at http://www.docstoc.com/docs/49941580/THE-SUPREME-COURT-OF-THE-FEDERATED-STATES-OF-MICRONESIA

22

Constitutionalism of Shallow Foundations

The Case of Bulgaria

Daniel Smilov

22.1 INTRODUCTION

In this essay I set out to explore the dynamics of entrenchment of constitutionalism in Eastern Europe in the 1990s and its paradoxical weakening toward the middle of the 2000s. With the passing of time one should expect stabilisation and further institutionalisation of the political process, which has not been the case even in some of the most successful countries, such as Hungary or Poland. In many places the political process has become very volatile, and key structures of democracy such as parliaments and parties have become a target of serious distrust. Especially in the EU member states of Eastern Europe, democracy for the time being is secure, and they will not opt for an alternative model of governance. But their democracy is quite volatile, frustrated and disappointed, and their constitutionalism is under serious stress. Part of the explanation for this outcome, I argue, is the weakening of factors which helped the successful installation of constitutionalism in the 1990s. In short, these factors are three: the widespread public dissatisfaction with the stagnated communist regimes, which erupted after 1989; the desire to copy the political arrangements of the successful Western European democracies; and the desire to join the EU.

These three factors have created a consensual public environment very conducive to the transplantation of constitutionalism as an extensive package of rules and principles of political organisation. Large majorities shared the goals of breaking with the communist past and joining the club of developed democratic nations, and because constitutionalism would be instrumental in achieving these goals, it was generally successfully installed. The shallowness of its social roots was compensated for by public commitment to achieving the goal of modernisation. This instrumental attitude to constitutionalism, however, made it vulnerable in the middle of the first decade of the twenty-first century when the goal of EU membership had already been achieved, and the memories of the communist regime started to fade or blend with nostalgia and neo-nationalist and neo-populist fantasies.

The essay explores this dynamic, which is argued to be common to Eastern Europe, in the specific context of Bulgaria. Bulgaria, later than the others, created its own public consensus for breaking with the communist past and joining the clubs of liberal democracies, NATO and the EU. Therefore, constitutionalism in the country had a turbulent time in the first half of the 1990s, which made quite apparent all the difficulties of transplantation in an inhospitable social environment. Yet, the Bulgarian story was also a story of success already visible in the late 1990s, when the country was on its way to becoming a member of the EU together with the rest of Central Europe. In the Bulgarian case, parliamentarism, as a key element of constitutionalism, was decisive for the creation of a pluralistic model of political competition. Democracy needs to inspire the public imagination through the provision of meaningful political alternatives. Parliamentarism, in the Bulgarian case, was the forum where these alternatives emerged out of a society which had been forcefully homogenised for the previous forty-five years. Generally, the success of constitutionalism in Eastern Europe is co-extensive with the success of parliamentarism: therefore, I focus specifically on this issue.

By meaningful pluralism I understand political differences which are, on the one hand, sufficiently deep as to attract the attention of the public and mobilise it to participate in the political process, and on the other hand, not so grave that they threaten the fabric of the political community as a whole. In the Bulgarian case, the ethnic confrontation between the Bulgarian majority and the Turkish minority at the end of the 1980s was a political difference of the dangerous type, which constitutionalism needed to neutralise in order to be successful. Therefore, in one of the sections that follow, I analyse in more detail this part of the story of the transplantation of constitutionalism in Bulgarian soil.

The case study is revealing also of the problems constitutionalism started to experience in the 2000s. The fulfilment of the overriding goal of EU membership (which marked the successful break with the past) paradoxically exposed the shallow roots and instrumental attitude to the rule of law and separation of powers. Further, what has been seen as a meaningful political pluralism in the 1990s – the different visions of the speed and manner of joining the EU – was no longer capable of inspiring the political imagination of the people. Not surprisingly, the 'established' parties of the 1990s started to disappear, and were replaced by populist and nationalist competitors. As a result, parliamentarism and the party system came under serious stress: people were either dissatisfied with their performance or started to be attracted by political alternatives, populist and nationalist, threatening the fabric of society and undermining the very idea of governability. Bulgarian constitutionalism will probably survive this test, yet the difficulties it is going through are hopefully instructive from the point of view of the more general problem of borrowing and transplanting institutions.

22.2 EASTERN EUROPEAN CONSTITUTIONALISM AS A TRANSPLANT

Eastern European constitutionalism is a good example of a working transplant in a generally inhospitable environment (Dupre 2003). Never in their pre-1989 history have countries such as Hungary, Poland, Slovakia, Bulgaria, and Romania been known for their respect for constitutionalism and the rule of law. With the partial exception of interwar Czechoslovakia, these have been states ruled predominantly in an authoritarian and totalitarian fashion. Against such a historical background, the introduction of constitutions entrenching democracy, separation of powers and human rights can be interpreted as a significant societal achievement (Sadurski et al. 2006).

The specific meaning of constitutionalism as an ideology lies in the adherence to a foundational set of binding rules (Alexander 1998, pp. 152–193). The persistence of these rules in time creates stability and predictability, virtues commonly associated with the rule of law. Apart from that, constitutionalism (substantively understood) requires respect for the separation of powers and individual rights, which are both instruments for the limiting of government. In essence, constitutionalism rejects the concentration of all powers in a single centre of authority: it sees in such an unchecked concentration a threat to liberty. In brief, constitutionalism could be defined as the persistence over time of limitations (constraints) on government (Sajo 1999).

Despite the lack of a serious history prior to 1989, constitutionalism was successfully installed in Central Eastern Europe because of the following reasons. In the first place, the velvet revolutions were a statement of public rejection of the legitimacy of the authoritarian/totalitarian state and implicitly of concentration of powers. People no longer believed that manual governance by an authoritarian party elite, which had all levers of power in its hands, was either efficient or morally justifiable. These widespread attitudes opened the door for constitutionalism as an instrument of creating a limited form of government. The worry in Central Eastern Europe was not how to *create* political power. The communist state had put a lot of effort into making power felt, visible and recognisable in the daily lives of people, from the militia men in the streets, through the hanging pictures of dignitaries in the public areas, to the widespread (and often justified) suspicions that private lives were monitored and reported to the authorities. Thus, in 1989, the fear was not that political power was weak. On the contrary, the question was how to make it democratically accountable and constrained. Ideologically, constitutionalism gave the answers to those two questions.

In the second place, the fall of the communist regimes could be termed a 'refolution' because it was a set of peaceful reforms of revolutionary magnitude: the more common phrase 'velvet revolution' also denotes the general lack of violence in the transformation of society.[1] Eastern Europe was not setting on the course of discovering a new political model of governance. Rather, the idea was to *copy* the achievements of Western liberal democracy (Ash 1994). From the point of view of constitutionalism this was highly beneficial in at least two ways. On the one hand, constitutionalism is a significant element of an established liberal democracy, as examples from Western Europe and North America show. On the other hand, and even more importantly, Eastern Europeans believed that there is a specific 'rule book of democracy' which they simply needed to follow. The most successful countries in the region in the early 1990 – Hungary, the Czech Republic and Poland – were also the best students, those who took the rule book most seriously (Kaldor and Vejvoda 2002). The reference to a school here is not a coincidence: for the first in the class there were prizes in the forms of membership of important organisations (Council of Europe, NATO and the EU) and increased amounts of foreign investment. This type of social environment was highly conducive to constitutionalisation, understood as adherence to a set of rules. In fact, one could argue that the 'rule book' conception of politics was so dominant that it led at times to specific overkill in the other direction, namely to the generally incorrect presumption that everything in politics is a matter of following of pre-established rules.

Last but not least, right after the fall of the communist regime the countries in question aspired to become full members of the most prestigious club of states: the EU. This process, which has now (together with Croatia, which will complete the procedure in 2013) resulted in the membership of eleven countries from the region, has strengthened the 'rule book' account of politics to extraordinary proportions (Smilov 2006). The pre-accession process was structured as the internalisation by the Eastern Europeans of a huge number of EU norms – another instance of a process of learning by mastering rules. Specific sets of prizes and punishments were designed, as well as instruments for monitoring implementation which closely followed governmental progress in a number of areas stretching from the economy to law enforcement and foreign policy. This gigantic effort further strengthened the already widespread understanding that successful politics is about rule following, that the whole European project is an exercise in normative coherence.

Thus, as argued, the general success of constitutionalism in Central Eastern Europe over the last twenty years could be attributed to the pre-1989 discrediting of governance models based on concentration of power and the post-1989 popularity of a rule-based account of politics, insisting that the region needs to follow established

---

[1] See Ash 2009: 'The 1989 ideal type, by contrast, is nonviolent, anti-utopian, based not on a single class but on broad social coalitions, and characterized by the application of mass social pressure – "people power" – to bring the current powerholders to negotiate. It culminates not in terror but in compromise. If the totem of 1789-type revolution is the guillotine, that of 1989 is the round table'.

models. Both of these factors, and especially the second one, are highly contingent and time-bound. Thus, Russia since 2000 has developed its own brand of government, sovereign democracy, which is by no means following established Western models, and possibly is no democracy at all (Krastev 2006). The point is that by setting on the path of innovation and attempting to rewrite the 'rule book', Russia has suffered a considerable deterioration in terms of constitutionalism, which at present is rather nominal. Thus, it could be argued that in Eastern Europe there is a correlation between successful constitutional entrenchment and the following of Western models. Even one of the best students in the region, Hungary, became a target for criticism from a constitutional perspective when its politics started to be dominated by the more sovereign, more experimental Fidesz government of Viktor Orban.

If this argument is correct, it would follow that constitutionalism does not have very deep social roots in Eastern Europe. Under specific circumstances even very successful models can come under stress. Two types of circumstances questioning the success of the transplant should be specifically mentioned. One is the current economic crisis in the EU, which has exposed as problematic the vitality and logic of the entire European structure of governance. Since 2008, the very model which Eastern Europeans have followed has started to experience serious problems. Of course, for the Central European states which are already members of the EU, this has not had very dramatic implications yet, and they are still among the most loyal supporters of the EU project. But the 'rule book' conception of democracy and politics is surely no longer taken for granted. The fading attraction of the normative Western model is most visible in places like Russia and Turkey, however, which are now much more confident in following their own path of development, wherever it might lead them in the end. Particularly in the case of Russia, it is evident that the memory of the inefficiency of the communist regime has been to a degree superseded by the memory of the inefficiency of the separated powers in the 1990s. Together with the present European economic crisis, these memories cast a long shadow over the prospects of true constitutionalism in the country.

Secondly, the rule book conception of politics has lost some of its importance with the accession of Central European states to the EU. And indeed, as mentioned, it is paradoxical that countries in the region started to experience problems to do with both democracy and constitutionalism in the period around 2004, the date of the most massive accession of new members in the EU. Poland had a spell of populist conservative government headed by the Kaczynski brothers, Slovakia went through its own populist waves, joined by Bulgaria and Romania. Most spectacularly, Hungary, whose constitutionalism of the 1990s was an object of envy for the regional underachievers, has been since 2010 the arena of a politicised battle over the constitution, one in which rule-of-law and separation-of-power values and principles have been largely disregarded. All in all, the new democracies of the region have become more confident in attempting to rewrite the rules and to create new ones which are very often questionable (Meseznikov et al. 2008).

22.3 BULGARIA AS A SUBJECT OF TRANSPLANTATION

Bulgaria, the country in focus in this study, is a suitable, although slightly unorthodox, example of the travails of constitutionalism in the region. Compared to Poland, Hungary, Slovakia and the Czech Republic, Bulgaria was even a more unlikely place for a successful Western transplantation; while it did have a similar authoritarian and totalitarian past, it lacked the spells of dissident resistance to the communist regime or to Soviet dominance that other states have shown.[2] Further, whereas the other states were the offspring of the Hapsburg Empire and as such could boast some experience with the rule of law (albeit in a Kafkaesque form), as the offspring of the Ottoman Empire, Bulgaria was firmly based in the tradition of *kadi (qadi)* justice (Swedberg 2005). After liberation from the Ottoman Empire in 1878, Bulgaria went through a rapid process of forceful modernisation, the most oppressive period of which was the communist regime from 1944 to 1989. This regime was particularly violent in the period until the 1960s, when tens of thousands of the former bourgeois elite and the intelligentsia were killed, with even more detained in labour camps.

It is obvious that against such a historical background Bulgaria is a suitable choice for the examination of the shallowness of Western transplants such as constitutionalism. Yet, overall, the transplantation has been successful because of the two factors mentioned in the introduction: by the late 1980s, Bulgarians en masse were already convinced of the inefficiency and oppressiveness of the old regime and were enchanted by the Western models of governance. This enchantment was attributable primarily to a partial opening of the regime in the late 1970s, which made possible the consumption of Western goods. Most importantly, books, films, music and TV products became accessible to a degree, which publicly revealed the uncompetitive character of the communist economy and the parochial nature of communist culture. Bulgarians wanted to emulate the West and were prepared to follow its rule book of constitutional and democratic recipes. In the case of Bulgaria, there was an additional factor contributing to the viability of a constitutional transplant: the country was not only eager to emulate the West, but also wanted to preserve its place in the company of Poland, Hungary and Czechoslovakia, the backbone of the former Eastern bloc. So, the Bulgarian case is a complex copying exercise, whose primary source was Western Europe but whose more accessible and understandable examples came actually from Central Europe. Indeed, the Bulgarian transition started in serious only on November 10, 1989, a day after the fall of the Berlin Wall. By that

---

[2] On Bulgarian constitutionalism, see Ganev 2007; Smilov 2010b.

time, it was already clear where the whole region was headed, and the Bulgarian political elites in practice copied most of the liberalisation steps adopted elsewhere, starting from the revision of the 1971 communist constitution, and going through to the calling of Round Table Talks and the organisation of the first free election in the summer of 1990. The only original moment in all this was that the communist party successors managed to win these elections, and thus dominated the constituent assembly which was supposed to elaborate the new democratic constitution.

Based on the Bulgarian case study, I argue in this chapter that constitutionalism in Eastern Europe became an instrumental and valuable tool because it helped the countries to solve three pressing social problems which they faced at the beginning of the transition period. In the first place, the communist rule had left a 'flat' society in which many of the traditional social cleavages (such as capital/labour, city/country) had lost their significance. The main cleavage relevant for the communist regimes – the party nomenclatura versus the people – could not become the foundation of a genuine political pluralism in a democratic setting. The same held true of residual cleavages such as those based on ethnicity and religion, which – if instrumentalised – could rupture the political community. Given that political pluralism is crucial for the operation of any democratic regime, constitutionalism became instrumental in the artificial creation of *politically meaningful and manageable* cleavages, which were gradually translated in party systems and other representative structures.

Constitutionalism helped this process of artificial creation in at least two ways. On the one hand, the constitution-making process became the forum in which the fledgling democratic actors gained publicity and organisational resources. The so-called Round Table Talks, as an important preliminary to the adoption of the new constitutions, drew the dividing lines between the main players in a predictably haphazard way (Kolarova and Dimitrov 1996). Representatives of the elites found themselves in opposing camps despite previous biographical and ideological similarities. Once these initial dividing lines had been drawn, however, the pressure on the different groups to justify them marked the beginning of a plurality of political visions, programmes and ideologies more or less compatible with the general principles of liberal democracy and market economy.

On the other hand, constitutionalism introduced forms of parliamentary government in most of the successful Eastern European states (virtually all of which are now EU members). Parliamentarism in itself generates political pluralism, as a clearly defined majority and opposition are necessary for the creation of stable governments. The parliamentary game of ruling majority and opposition strengthened and amplified the emerging dividing lines in the political elite. More precisely put, some of the initial dividing lines were strengthened while others were refashioned or totally erased. In short, the parliamentary form of government put to the test the initial artificial and haphazard dividing lines, and forced political players to justify through actions their right to claim a distinctive political identity. The countries which introduced stronger parliamentary government, such as Hungary, Slovenia, the Czech Republic, and Bulgaria, were more successful in stabilising and legitimising their new party systems (Shugart 1998). These were the countries in which democratic turnover of governments progressed smoothly even in adverse economic circumstances, as the Bulgarian case study in this chapter shows. In contrast, countries which experimented with semi-presidential forms (Poland, Romania) or super-presidentialism (as in Russia and the post-Soviet space) were less successful in the creation of politically manageable pluralism expressed through democratic structures. Thus, at the beginning of the 1990s in Poland, there was massive fragmentation of political representation which led to the revision of the electoral system and the adoption of a new, more parliamentarian constitution (replacing the so-called Small Constitution). In Russia, politically viable pluralism never took hold, and the constitutional super-presidential model definitely played a role in this unfortunate development.

The second social problem which constitutionalism helped to solve was the achievement of a generally peaceful transition and cooperation from previously powerful groups (the nomenclatura and others), which meant that they should not automatically lose all their privileges. Settlements varied in the different Eastern European countries. In some places, like Bulgaria and Romania, ex-communists became primary players in democratic competition and dominated party politics in the first years after transition. (The case of Romania is especially revealing, because the accommodation of former communists there happened despite the initial violent outburst in which the former dictator and his wife lost their lives in a televised execution while street violence produced numerous other casualties as well.) Constitutionalism helped this development by granting to the ex-communist actors all constitutional protections (equality before the law, protection of political pluralism, prevention of lustration on rule of law grounds, etc.) which are afforded to political contestants in a liberal democracy. In other countries, constitutionalism and the rule of law were used to block attempts to carry out lustration or retroactive punishments for crimes perpetrated by the communist regime (Hungary and Poland). Elsewhere, political settlements were less generous to the former communists, like in Eastern Germany and the Czech Republic, which could be treated as partial exceptions to the aforementioned trend. In all of the countries, however, strong independent judiciaries were set out almost from the very beginning of the transition period with the hope of preventing attempts at political prosecution and persecution of members of the old regime (Šiklová 1996). The granting of judicial independence in fact stabilised the positions of judges and prosecutors who had made their careers under communism (Smilov 2012).

Finally, the third social problem which constitutionalism helped to solve was the problem of marginalisation or lack of political representation of certain ethnic minorities. Although it did try hard, communism could not eradicate ethnic and religious divisions in society. The great danger in Bulgaria was that after the fall of the regime in 1989, politics would become ethnically and religiously based, as in the case of former Yugoslavia. Further, parliamentarism and majority rule, without constitutional guarantees for the rights of minorities, would have endangered those minorities. Constitutionalism, therefore, was necessary to secure the loyalty of such groups to the new regime. The Bulgarian case is particularly revealing in this regard: the maltreatment of the Turkish minority by the communist regime in the 1980s required strong guarantees for their rights under the new democratic regime. This required the constitutionalisation, or at least the possibility, of the minority's right to political representation (which happened through an interpretation by the Constitutional Court despite the prohibition of ethnic parties in the text of the 1991 Constitution), and the recognition of certain language and educational rights. The argument is not that constitutional guarantees of minority rights are sufficient for keeping a polity together; the examples of Former Yugoslavia refute such a thesis. But constitutionalism is a factor in keeping diverse polities together, as the examples of Bulgaria, Slovakia and Romania well illustrate.

In what follows I trace the different stages through which transplanted constitutionalism has travelled in the Bulgarian context. Although comparative constitutional law tends to assume that each country is generally a separate 'model', this is not necessarily so. Constitutional frameworks normally allow for a variable geometry of separation of powers and different degrees of the defence of rights and other constitutional principles. By examining the different interpretations the Bulgarian constitution has undergone I hope to expose better the different social factors explaining particular institutional and practical solutions.

22.4 THE CONSTITUTIVE MOMENT: THE EMERGENCE OF PLURALISM

As argued earlier, constitutionalism proved a useful tool for the production of politically relevant pluralism in a society coming out of a totalitarian regime, which had successfully eliminated most of the traditional social cleavages. The egalitarianism of communism, despite the privileged position of the nomenclatura, was not a sham: social distinctions had been intentionally muted and erased among enormous masses of people. Thus, the need to generate politically meaningful distinctions able to capture the public imagination came to the fore immediately after the intra-party coup in November 1989. The constitution-making process, the preceding Round Table Talks and the adoption of the Constitution provided a forum for the emergence of the political majority and the opposition. These were later strengthened by the rules of parliamentarism, which the Constitution itself introduced.

The Bulgarian democratic forces emerged late in 1989 when a group of intellectuals and dissidents (mostly within the Communist Party) headed mass protests against the communist regime. The central point of these protests was constitutional change: the demands were for a new, democratic constitution and the repeal of the articles in the communist constitution, declaring the primary role of the Communist Party. University professors, young scholars and students, relatively independent professions such as lawyers, and dissidents who formed the backbone of the Union of Democratic Forces received an opportunity to organise themselves into political structures in the 1990 Round Table Talks, which legitimised them as the main representatives of the democratic opposition. The Talks finished with an agreement to call free elections for a constituent assembly, whose main task would be to adopt a new constitution. The elections were held in the middle of 1990 and were narrowly won by the former Communist Party (at that time renamed as Socialist), after bitter complaints of manipulation on behalf of the opposition.

The new Bulgarian Constitution was adopted on July 12, 1991 after heated debates in the Great National Assembly, the constituent representative organ convened to establish the legal basis of the transition to a democratic system of government. The Bulgarian Socialist Party (BSP) had an absolute majority in it and an opportunity to dominate the constitution-making process.[3] This dominance led to significant controversies within the opposition party, the Union of Democratic Forces (UDF). Being a large coalition comprised of parties practically covering the whole of the political spectrum, it suffered the consequences of the ideological ambiguity in its setup. The social democrats, the agrarians, and the liberals remained in the assembly, thus providing the two-thirds majority for the vote on the constitutional draft, while the rest of the coalition partners, the more radical anti-communists, boycotted the process by leaving the parliament. Given that the constitution was not to be ratified at a referendum, the leaving of parliament was a factor which at least theoretically was supposed to cast doubts on the legitimacy of the document and on its reliability as a foundation for the rule of law (Ackerman 1992). However (owing not least to the heavy amendment procedure), subsequent developments did not prove that to be an important shortcoming.

The processes preceding the adoption of the constitution (the Round Table Talks and the constitution-making process) helped to clarify the main dividing line between the political majority and the opposition in the new democratic regime. The UDF, which started as a haphazard *bricollage* of actors and ideas, was gradually

---

[3] For an account of the constitution-making activity of the Grand National Assembly, see *East European Constitutional Review* 1992, p. 4.

transformed into an ideologically and organisationally more coherent political actor. It became a staunchly anti-communist movement, although some of its key leaders had themselves been members of the communist party before 1989. The founding fathers who were willing to compromise with the ex-communists were gradually alienated and forced to leave the organisation in 1991. In a similar vein, the constitution-making processes allowed former communists to part with many of the most compromised members of the old regime and to start projecting a 'reformed' image to the public. Much in both camps, and especially in the democratic camp, was amorphous, however, and in need of further clarification, which happened only in the framework of the parliamentary model, which the 1991 Constitution established.

22.5 PARLIAMENTARISM AS A TOOL FOR CREATING POLITICALLY MEANINGFUL PLURALISM

In theory, parliaments represent the people and the different societal interests as they are. In some specific circumstances – as the post-1989 environment in Bulgaria – the parliament was called to perform a slightly different role: it was needed to create and augment politically relevant divisions and cleavages, which could not have, at that moment, any deep roots in society.

Owing to a complex mixture of traditionalism and political inertia, the Bulgarian founding fathers laid the grounds for a system of separation of powers with a strong emphasis on the assembly. The traditionalist logic used during the drafting process exploited some of the basic themes from the national constitutional mythology, all of which are connected to the first Bulgarian constitution adopted in Veliko Turnovo in April 1879. Despite the fact that this constitution provided for a monarchy, the one-chamber parliament, universal suffrage for men and especially the democratic way in which it was drafted and adopted gave a strong egalitarian impetus for future developments in the country.

The logic of political inertia, on the other hand, kept employing arguments developed in the framework of the communist ideology, not always as a result of intellectual or political conviction but often inadvertently, and because of a lack of familiar alternative solutions. The meeting point of these two lines of argumentation was the openly Rousseauistic logic of interpretation, which otherwise traditional constitutional provisions received in the Bulgarian basic law of 1989 (Friedrich 1951: 18–19).[4] Thus, according to art. 1.1 of the constitution, Bulgaria is a republic with a

---

[4] According to him, the term 'Rousseauistic tradition' 'is not necessarily something to be found in Rousseau himself, but something associated with his work and thought since the French Revolution: radical majoritarianism'. For Friedrich, the pathos of the constitutionalism in Europe after the World

parliamentary form of government. The meaning of this provision is to underline the outstanding role of the assembly in the political process and to suggest that it would be the main instrument for expressing the general will of the people, who are the only holder of the sovereignty in the state (art. 1.2). To ensure the most legitimate delegation of the sovereign powers from the people to the assembly, after an experiment with a mixed system, the Bulgarian electoral law settled firmly on a purely proportional model with a 4 percent rationalising threshold, and this system is still in use today (Kolarova and Dimitrov 1994).

Two of the basic elements of the constitutional fashion in Eastern Europe at the time of the drafting – the presidential institution and the constitutional court – were introduced into the text as a pure example of copying from Western and especially Central European models (Sadurski 2007; Smilov 2004). The presidency was mostly copied from the French Constitution of the Fifth Republic but with significantly reduced powers, while the court was transplanted from Italy. In both cases, the drafters clearly had in mind events in countries such as Poland and Hungary. No one doubted the need for the inclusion of such fashionable institutions, although there were some debates about and some creative adaptation of their role in the whole constitutional structure. The influence of the Rousseauistic interpretation was more evident in the design of the presidential institution: because the decision-making power was left largely to the assembly, the head of state, though directly elected for a five-year term, was deprived of substantive prerogatives and was supposed to intervene only in a situation of crisis between the other branches. Even in this intervention, his part was supposed to be almost automatic, limited to the creation of the necessary conditions for the continuation of the normal functioning of the regime. As a result, the legislative and executive functions were strictly divided between the council of ministers and the assembly, while the president was basically supposed to arbitrate, thus exercising so-called 'neutral powers' (Bliznashki 1992). The only element which principally did not fit the Rousseauistic trend was the constitutional court which limited the discretion of the assembly to the boundaries provided by the constitution, an effect amplified by the heavy amendment procedure. However, there were some elements intentionally limiting the powers of the court: for instance, only institutions (and not individuals) can petition this body, which makes it primarily an instrument of party politics. Further, the first few years of the operation of the court were marked by signs of self-restraint, which made its role less evident than the role of the powerful Hungarian constitutional court (Kolarova 1993).

War II was characterised by the very strong influence of this majoritarian tradition, albeit in varying proportions, in all countries. The collapse of communism left ideological confusion, which most 'organically' was pervaded by elements of Rousseauism. However, in the different countries, they led to different constitutional solutions.

The Rousseauistic rationale behind the constitutional framework did have one negative consequence in the first five years of the Bulgarian transition: the concentration of excessive powers in the assembly. The desire to grant to the National Assembly supremacy in the constitutional structure was so obsessive that a constitutional law professor ventured to advocate the idea that the governmental legislative initiative is incompatible with the separation-of-powers principle in a parliamentary system (Boitchev 1991). Legislation was not the only field where the assembly was supposed to be the main actor; its functions expanded to an extent untypical of most parliamentary regimes. For example, it practically attained control over the electronic media (through a standing committee) (Kolarova and Dimitrov 1993), it had a monopoly to initiate a referendum (art. 84.5), and it had and has a monopoly over the right to declare martial law (art. 84.12) (Elster 1992, p. 23). All these arrangements created the impression that the regime was supposed to operate under a majoritarian assembly rule. However, it has functioned in a much more nuanced fashion than simple majoritarianism would imply.

22.6 THE 1990S: THE IRRESISTIBLE ATTRACTIONS OF MAJORITARIANISM

The majoritarian bias in the parliamentary setup has created favourable conditions for intense political confrontation between the majority and the opposition. In the 1991 elections, the main democratic party, the Union of Democratic Forces, won a plurality of votes in parliament and together with the third party represented in it, the Movement for Rights and Freedoms (DPS), a Turkish minority party, formed a government. This was the first non-communist government in Bulgaria since 1944; BSP was sent in opposition. The cabinet was exclusively from members of the UDF and the leader of this party, Philip Dimitrov, became prime minister. It was the first government to plan serious reforms including privatisation of the state-owned assets in the economy and restitution of agricultural lands to their pre-communist owners. After a year, mostly because of the loose agreement between the coalition partners and their general lack of political experience, serious problems occurred, on sometimes inexplicable grounds, and finally the government lost a confidence vote in an unfortunate motion. After the defeat of Dimitrov, BSP and DPS formed a 'programmatic' coalition government. The programme itself was a compromise tilted in favour of the conservative BSP, whose goal was to preserve the communist legacy as far as possible. The formula of a government of 'experts' was introduced, conveying that ministers are chosen by technocratic standards, and in practice obfuscating party responsibility for their selection. After two years marked by a succession of unsuccessful votes of no confidence and half-heartedly given legislative approval, the 'expert' cabinet also resigned. The general elections in 1994 brought back to power the ex-communist BSP with an absolute majority of seats in the assembly. Its political programme was again conservative, attempting to slow down necessary reforms. For instance, the government was planning not to privatise what it called 'strategic economic interests', such as the energy sector, telecommunications and so on. It also continued to subsidise inefficient state-owned industries, which ultimately led to the financial crisis of 1996. This new situation amounted to a third constitutional scenario. The government enjoyed comfortable support in the chamber, and since J. Videnov, the leader of the BSP, became prime minister, the cabinet had a tight control over the majority. This electoral context was certainly much more favourable for the cabinet than those provided by the first two scenarios.

Thus, by the mid-1990s, the Bulgarians had started to master the rules of the parliamentary game and created a semblance of alternation in office of two political blocks – the conservative ex-communists and the reform-minded democrats. The constitutional infrastructure helped to entrench this political division. The division was beneficial for society because it helped the people to conceptualise and understand the logic of the transition. It is true that most Bulgarians were dissatisfied with the pre -1989 communist regime and wanted to follow the path of West European developed democracies, but there were huge differences of opinion on questions such as what to preserve of the communist legacy, how to achieve integration with the West, and what kind of links to preserve with Russia. The political system that had emerged by the mid-1990s offered a variety of choices which created meaningful political pluralism.

Constitutionalism was particularly instrumental in the structuring of a plurality of options. Parliamentary government in Bulgaria followed constitutional ideas for strengthening the cabinet and the executive popular in Western Europe after World War II, and illuminating most of the post-war constitutions (primarily the German Basic Law, but elements of the strategy could be found in the Italian Constitution, and the Constitutions of the Fourth and Fifth French Republics) (Dunner 1951). Sometimes these ideas are grouped together under the heading of 'rationalised parliamentarism', although there is no clear scholarly convention as to the constitutional techniques and arrangements falling into this category.[5] The paradigmatic example of such a technique is the German constructive vote of no confidence, which is designed to prevent parliamentary crises by combining the voting of a chancellor out of office with the appointment of a successor. Most of the techniques are designed to create durable and stable legislative majorities which can form and support a government, through the introduction of rules in areas which have been discretionary before that.[6]

[5] The coinage of the term is often attributed to Boris Mirkine-Guetzevitch 1931. For an introduction to 'rationalised parliamentarism' in Eastern Europe, see Tanchev 1993.
[6] Rationalisation of parliamentarism concerns many areas of constitutional law, but mostly: (1) the electoral procedures (introducing legislative thresholds for avoiding fragmentation of parliament,

'Rationalisation' offers very strong institutional incentives for the creation of stable parliamentary majorities and parties in general, even in political contexts where there are no established, socially grounded political groups and democratic traditions. In order to have control over the government, a political actor needs to rely on a strong (parliamentary) party, or a cohesive coalition of parties – an incentive which is largely absent in Eastern European (semi- or super-)presidential models. Thus, the very institutional logic of parliamentarism promoted the emergence of fairly recognisable and coherent parties even out of ideologically ambiguous groupings.[7]

On the negative side, the comfortable position of the legislative majority and the cabinet, provided by the rigid empty shell of rationalised parliamentarism, creates the feeling of institutional omnipotence in the ruling party or coalition of parties. This may gradually result in increasing alienation of the party from political reality, expressed in the political attitudes of the citizens. This was what actually happened in the case of Bulgaria: all Bulgarian governments since the mid-1990s, which relied on stable and lasting legislative majority, especially Videnov's 1994–1997 government and Kostov's 1997–2001 one, ended their mandates with very low levels of public support. In fact, none of the governments and parliamentary majorities since 1994 has managed to win two successive elections. The artificial institutional security granted to them by the constitutional setup predisposes the political parties to develop a sort of ideological arrogance. The BSP under Videnov was a good example of this tendency: the party won an absolute majority in the legislature in 1994 and embarked on overly ambitious, ideologically charged but clearly disastrous for the country economic policies. When the whole of Central Europe was privatising their public sector, the BSP triumphantly announced that they were going to preserve state ownership and monopoly in strategic sectors (telecommunications, big industry, the energy sector, etc.). As a result, later Bulgaria was forced

prohibiting dissolution of parliament and new elections in certain cases, limiting the discretion of presidents and executives to dissolve the parliament and call elections, etc.), (2) the process of formation of the cabinet (limiting presidential discretion in the appointment of prime minister, speeding up and facilitating the procedure, etc.), (3) the accountability process (limiting the possibilities of voting no confidence in the government) and (4) the legislative process (ensuring the dominance of the parliamentary majority and the cabinet in the production of legislation, and limiting the influence of the president, the opposition, or individual members of parliament).

Rationalisation of parliamentarism could be best understood against the background of the continuous crises in Germany, Italy and other continental states between the two world wars, which eventually led to the collapse of constitutionalism and the coming of fascists and Nazis to power. 'Rationalisation' has proven to be an almost unqualified success in eliminating such crises in Western Europe since World War II and in Central Europe and Bulgaria since 1990.

[7] Consolidation of democracy in Central Europe was achieved without established, programmatic parties of Western European type (see Toka 1997). One of the reasons for this, in my view, is the rationalisation of parliamentarism especially in countries like Hungary, the Czech Republic, Slovenia and Bulgaria.

to sell these assets for a fraction of their initial value. Secondly, despite the advice of experts, the socialists did not enforce budget discipline, but continued generously to subsidise losing enterprises, which eventually led to financial collapse, speeded up by the reluctance of the government to negotiate loans from the IMF and the World Bank. This was *an arrogance of experiment*. It is important to note, however, that this political experimentalism was made possible only by the borrowing of a constitutional model implying strong, party-based parliamentary government. From this perspective Bulgaria is an interesting case of a student who excelled in some of the disciplines but misbehaved and failed badly in others.

In 1997, after the BSP stepped down under popular pressure, the UDF formed a majority government under Prime Minister Ivan Kostov. This was the time when Bulgaria started to come back to the group of more successful Central European states and declared a firm commitment to joining NATO and the EU. Kostov learned from Videnov's experimentalism and established stable relationships with the international community (international lenders included), enforced budget discipline, and pursued a programme of speedy privatisation. His undoubted success, and the institutional 'empty shell' security of the constitutional rules, however, committed him and his government to another type of arrogance: call it the *arrogance of complacency*.

Especially with the change of attitude in the international community towards Bulgaria, expressed in the inclusion of the country in the second wave of EU enlargement, the lifting of the EU visa restrictions for Bulgarians, and the increased chances for NATO membership, the self-confidence of the government grew and transformed into a sort of neglect for other, no less important problems such as rising unemployment, the deterioration of the public services and the perception of corruption among the political elite. The UDF, as well as most of the political analysts, came to the belief that Kostov's government and its policies had no alternative: this was probably the culmination of the arrogance of complacency.

22.7 CONSTITUTIONALISM SINCE 2001: THE ADVENT OF NEW POPULISM

The model of majority and opposition, which was constitutionally set out at the beginning of the 1990s, imploded in 2001. As has become clear from the discussion thus far, during the first decade after the fall of the communist regime in 1989, the Bulgarian political process was dominated by two ideological party camps: Bulgarian Socialist Party (BSP), the successor of the Communist Party; and the Union of the Democratic Forces (UDF), the driving force behind most of the liberalisation processes initiated during this period. Thus, for more than ten years there was a resemblance of a generally established party system in Bulgaria structured along the left-right division known from the mature democracies.[8] In 2001, all of this dramatically changed. The return of the former tsar Simeon II from long years of exile was an event greeted by welcoming demonstrations in Sofia and the other major cities of the country. The government of Ivan Kostov (UDF) reacted rather nervously to the popular return of Simeon to the country and mobilised all of its resources with the intention of preventing him from participation in the political process. First, the Constitutional Court, in which the UDF had a clear dominance, banned Simeon II from participation in the presidential election because of residence requirements.[9] Secondly, and more controversially, a Sofia court denied registration to the National Movement Simeon II (NDSV), the organisation with which the ex-tsar was planning to take part in the parliamentary elections. The denial was grounded in procedural considerations including the lack of support shown by signatures.

All these efforts came to no avail, and NDSV won more than 40 percent of the vote and exactly half the seats in the Bulgarian National Assembly. The result would have been an absolute majority in the parliament had it not been for several small parties which used Simeon's name on their ballot without his authorisation: thus, some 3 percent of the vote was used on such parties through voter confusion. All established 'traditional' parties together – the right-wing UDF and the left-wing Socialists – won fewer votes than Simeon II's NDSV. The party system seemed to be the first victim of Simeon II's arrival, which showed that it was not well established, the parties were not truly programmatic, and the political culture of the population was susceptible to fits of opportunism and populism.

---

[8]   The BSP made extensive use of ideas such as the social state, greater intervention of the government in the economy, minimal privatisation and stronger ties with former foreign partners and Russia in particular. The UDF, on its part, stood for more radical economic reforms, including privatisation and restitution of agricultural lands and urban properties nationalised by the communist regime, full integration and membership into the Euroatlantic structures – EU, NATO, and the like. The two blocks had a different assessment of the communist past: the UDF was rejecting it as a period of oppressive totalitarianism, whereas the BSP was much more nuanced, attempting to stress the positive achievements of its predecessors in government. The role of personalities in politics was secondary: party supported candidates as a rule won against popular leaders. The most striking example of this was the win in the 1996 presidential primaries of the virtually unknown candidate of the UDF Petar Stoyanov against the former dissident and first democratically elected president of the country Zhelyu Zhelev.

[9]   The 1991 Constitution requires that candidates for presidential office spend the five years in the country before the elections. This provision was introduced in 1991 specifically against Simeon II – ironically, it came to be applied ten years later than the original plan. In this case the Constitutional Court faithfully stuck to the plain text of the basic law, although on other occasions the Court has proven that it could interpret rather creatively constitutional provisions. For instance, several years before that the Court had returned all of the real estate property of Simeon II and his family, which amounted to millions of euro.

It is justified to classify the coming of the former tsar to power as an instance of populism (Mudde 2004, 2007; Meny and Surel 2002) of a specific type for the following reasons:

- He appealed to the people as a whole, without stressing any cleavages, differences and distinctions within this whole.
- Simeon's campaign portrayed the then existing political elite as largely politically corrupt.
- Simeon was campaigning against the existing parties. For a long time after his arrival he refused to register the NDSV as a political party,[10] still nurturing the idea that he was the tsar of all Bulgarians, not a simple party leader.
- Simeon's movement was agnostic and indifferent towards political ideology. His main message was that the ideologies of the established political parties were already *passe*.
- The sole source of mobilisation of the people behind Simeon was personal – his personal charisma and historical legacy. Programme and party structure were non-existent as sources of mobilising electoral support.
- In terms of political presentation and communication Simeon relied much more heavily on appearance than on content. In terms of content he was minimalist and elusive.
- Finally, and probably most importantly, Simeon was campaigning not on a specific coherent programme, as it was already pointed out, but on people's expectations for what should be done. In short, he created the impression that, after years of austerity measures, a time of prosperity for everyone was finally on its way. The ex-tsar summed up these expectations in his promise to improve dramatically the situation in the country for 800 days.

It must be stressed, however, that once in office, the NDSV went through a speedy evolution which transformed it from a populist movement into a 'traditional' political party. First, after coming to power, the NDSV cut back on many of the fantastical promises its leader made or suggested in the pre-election period. Ultimately, the NDSV led a government whose politics were continuous with the previous government: financial discipline and strong commitment to integration in NATO and the EU. The overall result of this was positive for the country. From the point of view of the NDSV, however, the revision of the pre-electoral promises led to quite a dramatic fall in public confidence in the movement and its leader: only two months after the June 2001 election the fall of support began to be noticed. First, the

---

[10] Before the June 2001 elections Simeon indeed tried to do so, as stated earlier, in order to be able to compete for parliament. After he managed to send people to parliament, he refused to register a party.

movement failed to elect a president: the Socialists surprisingly won the 2001 presidential elections. Second, the ratings of Simeon and his party were steadily falling, reaching embarrassingly low levels for less than a year in government. In the 2005 parliamentary election, the NDSV, which had already been registered formally as a political party, came second to the Socialist Party with roughly a third of its 2001 electoral vote total.

A similar turbulence in the party system and parliamentarism happened in the 2005 general elections. A new political actor appeared claiming 8–9 percent of the voters' support. The new actor was a party, called Ataka, organised around Volen Siderov, a TV journalist radically criticising the political establishment as corrupt and dangerous from the point of view of the national interests. Ataka ultimately entered the Bulgarian parliament in 2005, surprisingly becoming the biggest opposition group in it (albeit for a short period of time, because the group disintegrated soon after); the other large parties – the BSP, the NDSV, and the Movement for Rights and Freedoms (DPS) – formed a grand ruling coalition. Ataka's assent was a small-size replica of the assent of the NDSV to power: much of the analysis of the pre-electoral strategy of the NMS is applicable to Ataka as well. The only difference was the nationalistic discourse and the language coming close to hate speech used by the new actor.

In 2007, there was another similar electoral shock for the political establishment in Bulgaria. At the May EU parliamentary elections yet another new political party, GERB, led by the popular mayor of Sofia Boyko Borissov, won most of the votes. Following a familiar pattern, this was an extra-parliamentary party, whose only resource was the personal charisma and appeal of its leader. The party was registered and set up only in 2006, reflecting the political ambitions of its leader to convert his general popularity into representation at the national level. Borissov, very much like Siderov, was a member of the second tier of the political elite. The first fact which brought Borissov to the attention of the public was that in the 1990s he was the bodyguard of the former communist leader Todor Zhivkov, while he was tried for crimes during his long stay at the helm of the totalitarian regime. Borissov's political career took off as late as the early 2000s, when he became the official bodyguard of Simeon II. This royal appointment elevated Borissov to the heights of politics, although it did not happen immediately. First, he became the head of the police under the government of the NDSV. In 2005, he ran as a candidate for parliament with the NDSV and won a seat. He declined to leave the police for the parliament, however, and stayed on under the coalition government of the BSP, NMS, and DPS. In 2006, Borissov decided to run for mayor of Sofia, the election which he won without any great difficulty. Borissov's party, GERB (abbreviation from Citizens for European Development of Bulgaria but also meaning 'heraldic sign' or 'coat of arms' in Bulgarian), became an electoral force only in 2007. In 2009, GERB won the parliamentary elections (five seats short of outright majority in parliament) and formed a minority government, which is still in power.

So, if we have to sum up, developments since 2001 have been characterised by:

- disintegration of the traditional, ideological, programmatic parties;
- loss of the mobilisation force of ideological and programmatic coherence, and party loyalty in elections;
- rising value of personal charisma, expressivist and aesthetic techniques of popular mobilisation;
- appeal to the people as a whole, and treating their acclamation and support as the ultimate legitimation in politics, sometimes trumping issues such as individual and minority rights, international conditionalities, etc;
- heavy reliance on the public media as a substitute for party structure in political mobilisation.

This brief overview of the developments in Bulgarian politics suggests that, first, the parliamentary model helped the creation of relatively structured political parties, which were sufficient for the functioning of parliamentarism. The social roots of these parties were rather shallow, however, and they generally failed to generate sustainable trust in themselves and the representative institutions of democracy more generally. This artificiality and shallowness were probably not such a grave problem for the beginning of the 1990s, and for the situation immediately after the fall of communism, when the society was held together by the consensual goals of breaking up with the past and the joining of the EU. Now, however, this is increasingly seen as a problem by the public at large, which accounts for the disillusionment with the constitutional model. This disillusionment is still rather mild and finds expression in regular populist outbursts of frustration. It needs to be taken seriously, however, because the gradual erosion of constitutionalism might spell serious problems for Bulgarian democracy in the future. Most importantly, Bulgarian parliamentarism starts to fail as a producer of meaningful political pluralism. People are either dissatisfied with the parties or mobilised by either nationalists or charismatic leaders. These developments put into question the operation of the model by either threatening to rupture the fabric of society or reducing politics to a contest between personalities on the grounds of issues such as individual morality and integrity. Such a political process is threatened by instability, poor governability of the state, and possible escalation of ethnic and religious tension. In the next section, I set out to explore what the constitutional guarantees against the instrumentalisation of ethnic and religious differences are in Bulgaria.

22.8 CONSTITUTIONALISM AS CEMENT FOR SOCIETY

In contrast to Central European countries, the start of the Bulgarian transition was marked by a particularly acute ethnic problem. During the 1980s, the communist regime in Bulgaria induced a significant ethnic conflict by forcibly changing the names of the Turks and Muslims for Bulgarian ones. In 1989, only months before its fall, the communist regime effectively expelled approximately 400,000 Turks from Bulgaria to Turkey. After the collapse of the Berlin Wall, the original names of the ethnic Turk citizens were restored, they were compensated for the expulsion, and many of them returned to the country. However, the 1991 Constitution included a provision banning the establishment of political parties on an ethnic and religious basis.[11] Thus, the Turks living in Bulgaria, and some other minorities such as the Macedonians, seemed to be prohibited from having their own parties running in democratic elections.

As discussed earlier, in the first election organised under the new constitution, the party of the Bulgarian Turks, Movement for Rights and Freedoms (DPS), came in third and formed a coalition government with the UDF. This led to an attempt by the BSP to ban the party in the Constitutional Court.[12] In the central part of the argument, the judges admitted for consideration the challenges based on the general constitutional principle of art. 11.2 – the prohibition against establishing parties on an ethnic and religious basis. In their reading of this constitutional provision, the judges interpreted the various prohibitions contained in it as a single 'militant democracy clause'[13] aiming to protect the constitutional order of the country. They argued that the ban is directed generally against parties which threaten the constitutional order (Nenovski 1997, p. 52). The judges further stressed the *open* and *voluntary* character of the DPS, demonstrated by its internal regulations, the membership of its governing bodies and parliamentary caucus, as well as by the presence (although by no means significant) of representatives of different ethnic groups among its rank-and-file members (the membership of the party was ethnically predominantly Turkish). Also, the Court examined the electoral platform of the Movement and ruled that although it had set for itself the goal of amending the Constitution, and although it had used the term 'minority' (not mentioned by the Constitution), the organisation had not violated the basic principles of the Constitution. The Constitutional Court ultimately held that the party was not ethnically exclusive and did not threaten the constitutional order and dismissed all challenges against it. The political soundness of the decision of the Court is beyond question: the judges prevented the escalation of ethnic tension in Bulgaria, in a time when the new constitutional order was far

---

[11] This seems to be a feature of Balkan constitutionalism – a similar prohibition exists in the constitution of Turkey as well. The Greek and the Macedonian constitutions also contain provisions against extremist and secessionist parties.

[12] Decision 4, 1992.

[13] 'Militant democracy clause' in German constitutional law is a doctrine which allows for the limiting of constitutional rights if their exercise threatens the free democratic order. (For instance, Art. 21(2) of the Basic Law, declaring the unconstitutionality of political parties 'seeking to impair or abolish the free democratic order or endanger the existence of the Federal Republic of Germany'.) (Kommers 1997: 217–218).

from established. Also, the judges diluted an express constitutional ban, which was embarrassing and damaging to the international reputation of the country. In fact, this decision made possible the membership of Bulgaria in the Council of Europe – the first major step of the country towards integration with the West.

Eight years after the DPS decision, the judges faced a challenge against the constitutionality of a tiny Macedonian party.[14] The challenge took place after the 1999 local elections, in which the party, OMO Ilinden-PIRIN, collected around 2,000 votes and managed to win only one mayoral place in a small village. The challengers in this case argued that the establishment and operation of OMO Ilinden violated art. 11.4 and art. 44.2 of the Constitution, as well as the constitutional principles of the preamble declaring the duty to protect the Bulgarian statehood and national unity. It was alleged that the party had a 'separatist character', and that its goals ran against the unity of the Bulgarian nation. One argument invoked by the petitioners was that the party was the successor to an independent Macedonian association, OMO Ilinden (formed in 1990), whose goal was the 'founding of a Macedonian state through the secession of the Pirin region from Bulgaria'. Surprisingly, and in contradiction to the logic of the DPS judgement, the judges developed another doctrine of unconstitutionality of parties, based on the constitutional ban of parties whose activity is 'directed against the *sovereignty, the territorial integrity of the country*, and the unity of the nation' (art. 44.2). The Constitutional Court held that OMO violated this provision in its part concerning the integrity of the country. The evidence revealing the violation, in the view of the judges, included the passing remarks of leaders of the party of Bulgarian occupation of Pirin Macedonia, publication of maps of the region with changed borders, statements suggesting that secession may be a desirable goal and a letter to an international NGO pleading for regional autonomy.

Not only did the Court hold that this evidence was sufficient to demonstrate that the activity of OMO Ilinden violated art. 44.2 of the Constitution in the part aimed to protect the *territorial integrity* of Bulgaria; the judges further argued that every separate piece of evidence constituted sufficient grounds for the establishment of such a violation. The Court expressed the view that no '*effective* impact on the protected … [territorial integrity] is necessary' for a declaration of the unconstitutionality of a certain political activity under art. 44.2. In other words, declarations, interviews, letters and statements – all of them forms of *speech* – could be interpreted as unconstitutional activity sufficient for the prohibition of a political party.[15]

The political effects of the decision were purely negative. It contributed to the cooling of the relationship between Macedonia and Bulgaria. Also, the decision of

---

[14] Decision 1, 2000.
[15] Ibid., 145.

the Court proved to be an embarrassment for Bulgaria, because the country lost a series of cases on the OMO question in the ECHR.[16] This brief case study suggests, however, that the principles of constitutionalism are much less strictly and carefully enforced when there is no perceived danger to social cohesion (Smilov et al. 2010). In the first case of DPS, the very fabric of the emerging Bulgarian political infrastructure was under threat; further, the international recognition and reputation of the new regime was on the line. In such circumstances, it is no surprise that the Bulgarian judges attempted carefully to copy and paste principles and values from established democracies (albeit originally interpreted). Eight years later, when a tiny Macedonian party lacking any political relevance was involved, and when there was no serious threat of a lasting isolation of Bulgaria by the international community, the principles and values of constitutionalism gave way to barely concealed nationalist rhetoric, dressed in legal terminology. Unfortunately, this is an indication of the shallowness of some constitutional transplants, and further supports the thesis that their vitality may depend on contingent, contextual factors. It also suggests formal constitutional guarantees have been relaxed with the development of Bulgarian constitutionalism. The previous sections made clear that the problem of rising nationalism and populism in the party system is quite serious: it is unfortunate that this problem coincides with a relative relaxation of the formal instrument specifically designed to curb nationalist outbursts.

22.9 CONCLUSION: THE CHANGING MEANING OF CONSTITUTIONALISM

I have argued that despite the lack of historical commitment to the values of constitutionalism, societies in Eastern Central Europe did embrace it rather enthusiastically because it promised solutions and delivered on a variety of pressing societal problems, the most important of which were the need to generate politically relevant pluralism, the need to avoid conflict with previously powerful groups and the need to strengthen the social cohesion of diverse society through securing the loyalty of all major ethnic and religious groups. In a sense, constitutionalism was instrumentally useful for a society which wanted to break with its authoritarian past and was highly motivated to join a club of developed liberal-democratic nations. These motivations explain the initial and surprising ease with which constitutionalism was transplanted in a generally inhospitable environment. The Bulgarian case study suggests, however, that twenty years after the fall of the communist regime, the initial motivation may be no longer so decisive. This diminishes the perceived instrumental value of

---

[16]   The most recent case, out of seven, is United Macedonian Organisation Ilinden and others v. Bulgaria (no. 2) of October 18, 2011.

constitutionalism as a remedy to three discussed constitutive problems. The fear of these problems, on its own, cannot any longer guarantee the widespread acceptance of constitutionalism as a necessary social instrument (Smilov 2010). Predictably, the last several years produced in the Bulgarian context political players and political sentiments which challenged the legitimacy of the Constitution and its adequacy for the post-transition period. In terms of political competition and pluralism, there is an avalanche of new populist players who argue that the Constitution helps the creation of a political cartel, which is not representative of the people, but serves the interests of corrupt elites. As to the independence of the judiciary, it is increasingly seen as a problem, preventing the introduction of necessary reforms and guaranteeing the elimination of corruption and efficient court management. And finally, revived nationalistic parties challenge the constitutional settlements on minority rights which were reached in the 1990s.

These developments are not specific only to Bulgaria, but concern other countries in the region as well, which led to the question, 'Is Central Europe Backsliding?' asked by the *Journal of Democracy* in 2007.[17] All in all, the Bulgarian case illustrates the need to revisit the social foundations of constitutionalism in Eastern Europe, because the factors which guaranteed the success of the 'transplant' during the last twenty years may be eroding and weakening. One should not forget that this transplant is of shallow roots, and that its current relatively healthy condition may be dependent on contextual and contingent factors. Of specific worry is the fact, that much of the success of constitutionalism in the region seems to depend on the application of an understanding of liberal democracy as based on a rule book, on a specific list of recipes borrowed and copied from elsewhere. Thus, whenever novel and unexpected circumstances which call for creative and intelligent response emerge, the copied-and-pasted normative systems not surprisingly destabilise.

REFERENCES

Ackerman, B. 1992, *The Future of the Liberal Revolution*, Yale University Press, New Heaven.

Alexander, L. (ed.) 1998, *Constitutionalism: Philosophical Foundations*, Cambridge University Press, Cambridge.

Ash, T. G. 1994, *The Uses of Adversity. Essays on the Fate of Central Europe*, Penguin Books, New York.

2009, 'Velvet Revolution: The Prospects' in *New York Review of Books*: http://www.nybooks. com/articles/archives/2009/dec/03/velvet-revolution-the-prospects/?pagination=false

Bliznashki, G. 1992, 'Funktzii na presidentskata institutsia v Bulgaria' *Pravna Misul*, No. 3, pp. 15–35.

---

[17]   http://www.journalofdemocracy.org/articles/gratis/Rupnik-18-4.pdf

Boitchev, G. 1991, 'Constitutsia na grajdanskoto obshtestvo i na pravovata durjava' *Pravna Misul*, No. 2, p. 5.

Dunner, J. 1951, 'Stabilisation of the Cabinet System in Western Europe' in *Constitutionalism and Constitutional Trends since World War II*, ed. Zurcher. New York University Press, New York.

Dupre, C. 2003, *Importing the Law in Post-Communist Transitions: The Hungarian Constitutional Court and the Right to Human Dignity*, Hart Publishing, Oxford.

Elster, J. 1992, 'On Majoritarianism and Rights' *East European Constitutional Review*, Vol. 1, No. 3, p. 19.

Friedrich, K. 1951, 'The Political Theory of the New Democratic Constitutions' in *Constitutions and Constitutional Trends since World War II*, ed. Zurcher. New York University Press, New York.

Ganev, V. I. 2007, *Preying on the State: The Transformation of Bulgaria since 1989*, Cornell University Press, Utica.

Kaldor, M. and Vejvoda, I. 2002, *Democratization in Central and Eastern Europe*, Continuum International Publishing Group, London.

Kolarova, R. 1993, 'A Self Restricting Court', *East European Constitutional Review (EECR)*, vol. 2/2, pp. 48–51.

Kolarova, R. and Dimitrov, D. 1993, 'Media Wars in Sofia', *East European Constitutional Review*, Vo. 2, No. 3, pp. 48–51.

1994, 'Electoral Law of Bulgaria' *East European Constitutional Review* Vol. 3, No. 2, pp. 50–55.

1996, 'Bulgaria,' in *The Roundtable Talks and the Breakdown of Communism*, ed. Elster, J. Chicago: University of Chicago Press.

Kommers, D. 1997, *The Jurisprudence of the Federal Republic of Germany*, 2nd edition, Duke University Press, Durham.

Krastev, I. 2006, 'Democracy's "Doubles"', *Journal of Democracy·* Volume 17, Number 2, pp. 52–62.

Meny Y. and Surel Y. (ed.) 2002, *Democracies and the Populist Challenge*, Palgrave, New York.

Meseznikov, Grigorij, Gyarfasova, Olga and Smilov, Daniel (eds.) 2008, *Populist Politics and Liberal Democracy in Central and Eastern Europe*, IVO (IPA), Bratislava. Available at: http://www.ivo.sk/5353/en/news/ivo-released-working-paper-populist-politics-and-liberal-democracy-in-central-and-eastern-europe

Mirkine-Guetzevitch, B. 1931, *Les nouvelles tendances du droit constitutionnel*, second edition, Paris: M. Giard.

Mudde, C. 2004, 'The Populist Zeitgeist', *Government and Opposition*, Blackwell Publishing, London.

2007, *Populist Radical Right Parties in Europe*, Cambridge University Press, Cambridge.

Nenovski, N. (ed.) 1997, *Jurisprudence 1991–1996*, COLPI/Open Society Publishing, Sofia.

Rohozinska, J. 2000, 'Struggling with the Past – Poland's Controversial Lustration Trials' *Central European Review*, http://www.ce-review.org/00/30/rohozinska30.html

Sadurski, W. 2007, *Rights Before Courts: A Study of Constitutional Courts in Postcommunist States of Central and Eastern Europe*, Springer, London.

Sadurski, W., Czarnota, A. and Krygier, M. (eds.) 2006, *Spreading Democracy and the Rule of Law? Implications of EU Enlargement for the Rule of Law, Democracy and Constitutionalism in Post-Communist Legal Orders*, Springer, London.

Sajo, A. 1999, *Limiting Government*, CEU Press, Budapest.

Shugart, M. 1998, 'The Inverse Relationship Between Party Strength and Executive Strength: A Theory of Politicians' Constitutional Choices', *British Journal of Political Science*, Vol. 28, no. 1, pp. 1–29.

Šiklová, J. 1996, 'Lustration or the Czech Way of Screening' *East European Constitutional Review*, Vol. 5, no. 1, pp. 57–62.

Smilov, D. 2004, 'The Character and Legitimacy of Constitutional Review: Eastern European Perspectives', *ICON (Journal of International Constitutional Law)*, Vol. 2, No. 1 pp. 177–194.

    2006, 'EU Enlargement and the Constitutional Principle of Judicial Independence' in *Spreading Democracy and the Rule of Law? Implications of EU Enlargement for the Rule of Law, Democracy and Constitutionalism in Post-Communist Legal Orders*, eds. Sadurski, W., Czarnota, A. and Krygier, M. Springer, London.

    2010a, 'Bulgaria: The Discontents and Frustrations of a Newly Consolidated Democracy' in *Democratization and the European Union. Comparing Central and Eastern European Post-Communist Countries*, eds. Morlino, L. and Sadurski, W. Routledge, London.

    2010b, 'The Rule of Law and the Rise of Populism: A Case Study of Post-Accession Bulgaria' in *Constitutional Evolution in the Central and Eastern Europe: Expansion and Integration in the EU*, eds. Topidi, K. and Morawa, A. Ashgate, Aldershot.

    2012, 'The Judiciary: The Least Dangerous Branch?' in *The Oxford Handbook in Comparative Constitutional Law*, eds. Rosenfeld, Michel and Sajo, Andras. Oxford University Press, Oxford.

Smilov, D., Grozev, Y. and Dorosiev, R. 2010, 'Protecting Individuals from Minorities and Other Vulnerable Groups in the ECtHR, Litigation and Jurisprudence: The Case of Bulgaria' *The European Court of Human Rights and the Rights of Marginalised Individuals and Minorities in National Context*, eds. Anagnostou, D. and Psychogiopoulou, E. Nijhoff Publishers, Leiden.

Swedberg, R. 2005, *The Max Weber Dictionary: Key Words and Central Concepts*, Stanford University Press, Stanford.

Tanchev, E. 1993, 'Parliamentarism Rationalised', *East European Constitutional Review*, Vol. 2, no. 1, pp. 33–34.

Toka, G. 1997, 'Political Parties in East Central Europe' in *Consolidating the Third Wave Democracies*, eds. Diamond, Larry, Plattner, Marc F., Chu, Yun-han and Tien, Hung-mao. The Johns Hopkins University Press, Baltimore and London.

23

The Shifting Foundations of the European Union Constitution

Neil Walker

23.1 METHODOLOGICAL POINTERS

If we want to say anything of interest about the social and political foundations of the European Union (EU) constitution, we must attend to the ways in which it is both distinctive from and comparable to other constitutional origins. This reflects a general imperative of comparative methodology (Glendon 1994, Dixon and Ginsberg 2011, Rosenfeld and Sajo 2012). We compare in order to find out both what is atypical and special about the particular case, and also what is more typical and general. We need, therefore, to have some prior sense of the general type in order to inform our understanding of the particular case, and, reciprocally, we should also be open to the new particular case augmenting our understanding of the general type.

This methodological starting point may seem to pose an immediate problem for our understanding of the constitutional character of the EU. In many ways, what at first glance is interesting about it concerns its emphatic distinctiveness. Famously described by Jacques Delors, while president of the European Commission, as "an unidentified political object" (Drake 2000: 5), the EU has also provoked many commentators to remark on its atypicality, its *sui generic* quality (MacCormick 2005, Verhoeven 2002). So much so, indeed, that we often seem to be straining to fit it into an analytical model based on standard constitutional characteristics. Even to start from the premise that the EU constitution bears a family resemblance to the general constitutional type – and so can stand in a relationship of reciprocal illumination with the general type – is perhaps, then, to beg the question, and to threaten to distort the inquiry from the outset.

This danger can be overstated. Provided we define what counts as constitutional in terms that are not slavishly tied to the tradition and template of statehood and so do not rule out non-state constitutionalism by conceptual fiat, much common

637

ground reveals itself between the kind of constitutional project the EU is engaged in and those familiar from state settings. The differences can be exaggerated as much as the similarities, and often have been, sometimes for the commentator's own ideological reasons.[1] Equally, many of the similarities are so obvious, so embedded and matter-of-fact that they seem unremarkable, and so fail to be remarked upon.

In particular, the origins of the EU constitution, like the origins of many "first" state constitution, are bound up with the formation of a new polity by means that, through a documentary project and process of what I term "multi-framing" (Walker 2009, Walker 2012), draw on and develop a combination of legal, political, and sociocultural resources. This is the key common ground between the EU's constitutionalizing experience and that of a state polity. As we shall see, to the extent that, alternatively, we can think of the EU, in its earlier phase of institutionalization, as having undergone a significant pre-documentary stage of polity development and informal constitutionalization, it may also be possible to locate some common ground between the EU's subsequent and explicit constitutionalizing project of recent years and that of successor state constitutions concerned with "mere" institutional reform or regime change. These different comparative points of departure, with much greater emphasis on the polity-formative analogy, focus our investigation of what is remarkably familiar and unfamiliar about the EU's early constitutional trajectory. However, the very fact that the EU constitution can be looked at from both perspectives – either as polity-formative or as building on a preexisting edifice – is noteworthy. It anticipates what will be a constant theme of this chapter, namely the deep and resilient absence of a common framework of understanding about the nature and course of supranational constitutionalism. As we shall see, the persistently unresolved quality of the European constitutional "settlement" is doubly significant for our attempts to make sense of its social and political foundations. For that unresolved quality is reflected not only in the uneven and unpredictable trajectory of emergence of supranational constitutional law and discourse considered from an external standpoint, but also in the shifting identification, interpretation, and utilization of these historical foundations by key actors internal to the debate.

Let us proceed, first, by investigating the deep structural reasons why the EU polity context has proved both an attractive and a controversial context for the emergence of constitutionalism. We will then examine in some depth certain key strands in the EU's early constitutional development that follow from these background considerations.

---

[1] As in Jack Straw's well-known suggestion, seeking as Foreign Secretary to defuse the significance of the UK New Labour government's support for the Constitutional Treaty process before a Eurosceptical national electorate, that nothing of importance should be read into the constitutional label. According to Straw, even "golf clubs all across Scotland have constitutions." See *The Guardian*, August 27 2002, http://www.guardian.co.uk/world/2002/aug/27/eu.politics

23.2 WHAT KIND OF CONSTITUTION FOR WHAT KIND OF POLITY?

So runs the title of an influential set of essays written in response to the well-reported "Humboldt speech"[2] in May 2000 of the then German foreign minister, Joschka Fischer, calling for some kind of "deliberate political act to re-establish Europe" (Joerges et al. 2000). This intervention, the first by a serving minister of a leading European state to call for a documentary constitutional process for the EU – is often viewed as a key catalyst for the Convention process of 2002–2003 under the Presidency of Giscard D'Estaing and the Draft Constitutional Treaty that followed in 2004. It is also an apt title for present purposes. On the one hand, it suggests, as noted earlier, that the EU's constitutional development, like that of a state, is indeed bound up with the development of the EU as a polity. On the other hand, the question mark implies that, unlike the state, the very nature of the polity and the nature of the constitution appropriate to that polity remain unresolved.

In crude terms, however obscure and controversial the path of constitutional development and the polity prognosis of any particular state, the state remains a settled and uncontentious general political *form* – a recognizable template that in turn shapes and stabilizes our understanding and expectation of the contribution made to that political form by its constitution. In contrast, the EU is not a settled political form. There is no genus of which it is a species, and our sense of the appropriate manner and function of the contribution made by its "constitution" – if indeed *any* such "constitutional" contribution is appropriate – to that unsettled political form is correspondingly uncertain and contentious. The nature of the EU polity and the potential contribution of any constitution to the making of that polity is both underdetermined on grounds of political epistemology – an unprecedented and uncharted political experiment, and controversial on grounds of value – a political experiment that is both fundamentally challenged by its opponents and the object of highly diverse justification by its supporters. Each feature – indeterminacy and controversy – reinforces the other in contributing to the unresolved constitutional status of the EU (Walker 2012).

Let us explore this unresolved quality and examine how it differs from the settled multi-frame form for the organization of the state polity (Walker 2009). The state constitutional multi-frame provides, first, for an exclusively and comprehensively authoritative and so "sovereign" *legal order*. It also provides for the institutional elaboration and coordination of the organs of that state polity conceived of as a self-contained *political system*. Finally, the constitution contributes to the

---

[2] In its English translation the speech was entitled "From Confederacy to Federation: Thoughts on the Finality of European Integration."

sociocultural substratum necessary for its own effective legal and political articulation; typically, this societal traction is sought through the deliberative resolution, adaptation (through amendments or later settlements), and resonant and lasting cultural expression of a political pact committing to the making and maintenance of the polity in the name of a collective agency collectively self-understood as the self-legislating citizenry of a political community.

It should be emphasized that these three framing features apply as much to a federal state polity as to a unitary state polity. The federal state, of course, will typically embrace multiple levels of legal and political architecture, and also of citizenship status. However, it is also true of the federal state, as opposed to the mere multi-state confederation, that these various frames – legal, political-institutional, and citizen identity – are each in the final analysis resolved in a singular fashion through the overarching constitutional settlement itself. The constitutional settlement, in other words, provides a final and undisputed authority for the federal state polity considered as a whole, dictating the relationship between the various levels. It remains the source of comprehensive legal authority, institutional capacity, and citizenship statuses, including, crucially, the various mechanism for resolving conflict or coordination problems between the different levels to which this plenary authority and capacity is distributed.

Whether, to what extent, and in what ways these various interlocked "constitutional" frames and processes are relevant to the EU and its "non-state" polity remains an open question. It is a question that casts a shadow over all matter relating to, and, indeed, all accounts of its constitutional origins and trajectory. The EU polity has its own legal order and a Court of Justice that asserts the primacy of that legal order within its own area of jurisdiction. In practice, however, it is a jurisdiction that is limited in scope and that overlaps, sometimes cooperatively and sometimes competitively, with state legal systems and their higher courts, which continue to defend the priority in the last analysis of national constitutional law against external challenges and to treat European law itself as a creature of international agreement (De Witte 2012: 350–357). Accordingly, the legal constitution of the EU lacks both the comprehensive remit and the monopoly of final authority associated with the legal-constitutional order of the "sovereign" state. Equally, even though the EU has developed a political system that possesses recognizable judicial, legislative, executive, and administrative organs, it remains a "mixed" (Majone 2002) and incomplete political system rather than a purely self-contained one. It is mixed in the sense that some of its key institutions, in particular its Council and European Council, are composed of officials from other (state) polities. It is incomplete owing to the fact that it depends not only on the courts but also on the political institutions of other polities – in particular national parliaments and governments – for the transposition and implementation of its norms and decisions. Again, this is an overlap that is sometimes cooperative, involving concerted action between national and supranational levels, and sometimes competitive, involving a clash of interest or priorities between these levels.

Finally, since the Treaty of Maastricht of 1992, the EU has proclaimed itself to possess its own citizenry and associated culture of political community. This is again a contentious category and one that has not (yet) been consecrated in the expressively collective self-legislative form of a self-styled written constitution. For some, supranational citizenship is understood in an open-ended and ambitious way, as a harbinger of a "thicker" sense of membership. For others, it is understood as derivative and secondary rather than an original and primary form of political identity, parasitic now and indefinitely upon the original member state citizenship without which one cannot be a supranational citizen (Shaw 2011).

Crucially, in none of these three areas – legal order, political institutionalization, and citizenship status – is there any overarching framework standing above both the EU and the member states and reconciling them as different levels of one and the same polity. In other words, while the EU shares many multi-level features in common with the federal state, the long-standing absence of any agreed higher authority to resolve the relationship between the supranational – considered as "federal level" – and the member states – considered as "provinces" – marks a key difference. It means that, in the last analysis, just as the EU is too limited in remit to be viewed either as a comprehensive and self-contained polity in its own terms, so, too, it cannot be considered as a mere constituent part of one larger settled "federal" constitutional polity alongside the member states (Maduro 2003; Walker 2003b). Its constitutional identity, such as it may be, must be forged in the indistinct and contentious terrain between these two possibilities.

A number of points follow from the underdetermined and contentious nature of the EU polity, which helps account for the pattern of emergence of its constitution. These will provide the focus of discussion in the three sections that follow. First, because the question of what, if anything, are the limits of the EU's polity ambition remains obscure and controversial, we should not be surprised by the persistence of the European debate over the role of the constitution in meeting that ambition. In particular, the adaptability to the supranational context of the canonical constitutional expression of polity ambition in the state context – namely the documentary pact viewed as the foundation and framework of a polity project unlimited in scope – has frequently been a contentious matter. The Treaty of Paris setting up the European Coal and Steel Community (ECSC) was signed in 1951 and the Treaties of Rome establishing the European Atomic Energy Community (EURATOM) and the European Economic Community (EEC) followed in 1957. But both before and after supranational Europe's early treaty troika, the question of a more ambitious constitutive document was a recurrent one, if also a recurrently problematic one.

Secondly, there is the question of uneven development. In the settled constitutional form of the state polity, the framework of exclusive comprehensive legal authority, institutional self-containment, and political-cultural self-authorization and identification tend, under the co-coordinating mechanism of the foundational documentary constitution, to become gradually embedded in a mutually supportive relationship, even if these legal, politico-institutional, and cultural components are typically not born together.[3] In the unresolved and as yet undocumented EU constitution, the different generative conditions and the unevenness of development of the three registers of constitutionalism are more pronounced.

Thirdly, the unresolved quality of the EU constitution is also associated with the move in recent years from implicit to explicit constitutionalism. In the early years, even in the context of debate over documentary origins, the "C" word remained in the background. Explicit constitutionalism, through an increasingly expressive discourse of constitutionalism and the use of the full array of the familiar symbology of constitutional origins and sustained development, has come rather late in the day. It has coincided with the rise and fall of the Constitutional Treaty of 2004, although its object of reference is by no means restricted to the canonical documentary form. This shift has significantly altered the texture of debate over constitutionalization and constitutional origins, with consequences that remain unpredictable today.

23.3 THE PERSISTENCE OF THE DOCUMENTARY FOUNDATIONS DEBATE

The high point – the point of maximum salience – of the debate over the documentary foundations of the EU has undoubtedly been reached in the years leading up to and following the Convention on the Future of Europe of 2001–2003 and the failed Constitutional Treaty. We will discuss this in Section 23.5. However, the issue of documentary foundations – of a basic text that is constitutive in form and function if not necessarily "constitutional" in self-description – has been present as a contemporary question from the beginning of the supranational project and remains with us after the failed Constitutional Treaty. As we shall see from the later discussion, the dominant early post–Constitutional Treaty narrative of constitutional origins and development is an incremental one – of a polity that has eschewed the foundational documentary form and ambition and instead seeks in its maturity its own distinctive type of constitutional accommodation. There are interesting reasons why this is the

---

[3] Possibilities range from the U.S. model in which the self-authorizing constitutional instrument predates the cultural construction of "national" community and the political architecture of the state to various European continental models where either (e.g., France) or both (e.g., Germany) "state" and "nation" predate the explicitly constitutional project (see Rosenfeld 2010: chs. 5–7).

case. However, on close inspection, the *actual* historical record of the debate over constitutional origins, as opposed to the dominant narrative reconstruction of that history, is as much one of the iteration of failed documentary constitutional initiatives as it is one of evolution and maturation.

The idea of Europe, of course, long predates the late-twentieth-century debates and struggles over its evolving political form. The concept itself dates back to the fifteenth century (Hay 1968), but it was only with the onset of the secular Enlightenment that it began to replace Christendom as the key designation of a unitary civilization. Eighteenth-century figures as diverse as Montesquieu, Voltaire, Vattel, and Burke came to understand Europe as a place of social similarity and political balance (Anderson 2009). This harmonious Enlightenment image did not survive the French Revolution. Yet the notion of Europe as a single cultural space containing many political units and ethnic groups persisted, creating and sustaining a sense of continental identity unknown in other global regions (Pagden 2002). Alongside this cultural development there have been many political projects of continental union, going back as far as the French Duc de Sully's Grand Design of 1620. Yet, as one writer puts it, this kind of project has always been "formally at odds with itself" (Anderson 2009: 477). The political recognition of Europe as a discrete object could from the outset only be of an entity whose basic structure and distinctive configuration was one of prior political division and plurality. On the one hand, this underlying structure made for a fragile and often broken interstate accommodation, hence the attraction of projects of union. On the other hand, some such projects, in their overweening ambition, were liable to destroy the very diversity that was Europe's distinctive political inheritance.

The approach to Europe's political configuration has always taken different forms, reflecting both horns of this dilemma. Some projects have been premised on consensus, but have remained largely theoretical. The more practical projects have tended to operate through conquest or imperial design. This speaks to a contrast, and to a relationship born of contrast, which also strongly marks the twentieth-century origins of the EU. In 1929, the French Prime Minister Aristide Briand, operating in the shadow of the First World War and in anticipation of the Third Reich, floated through the League of Nations the idea of a consensual federation of European states. The immediate origins of the contemporary continental polity can also be seen in large part as a response to the unilateral vision of regional domination that provoked the Second World War (Weiler 1999; Lindseth, 2010: chs. 2–3; Muller 2011: ch. 4; Anderson 2009: ch. 9).

Yet, even though joined by a shared reaction against the forced union of conquest and a commitment to peaceful collaboration, there were competing visions of the nascent postwar Europolity. This competition was framed by a basic division between an ambitious and overtly neo-federalist conception of the European Union, one premised on the equality of the member states, and a more modest, narrower conception of continental integration. The first saw the federal vision as a grand political project for a post-bellum continent dedicated to learn and perpetually apply the geopolitical lesson of uncoerced coexistence. In its ambition and in its desire to mark a new continental beginning, this approach, as for example anticipated in Altiero Spinelli's pan-European Ventotene Manifesto of 1940 (Burgess 2000; Urwin 2007), was one that strongly favored a "big bang" foundational solution.

The second and narrower conception was based on a platform of common or pooled economic affluence and other manifest common goods. To complicate matters further, the more modest approach included highly influential founding figures such as Jean Monnet and Robert Schuman[4] whose long-term vision was also a neo-federalist one based on a process of gradual accretion from a narrow basis through a series of limited actions and innovations. This was famously summed up in the pronouncement in the 1950 Schuman Declaration that "Europe should not be made all at once, or in accordance with a single plan" – a commitment that provided the platform for the ECSC Treaty of the following year. However, alongside this so-called Monnet method, on which so much of the subsequently influential neo-functionalist theorizing of EU integration is based (Hass 1958), there was another, more bounded approach to European integration. For those, such as the followers of German ordoliberalism according to whom the operation of the market should be ring-fenced from the exercise of social policy, and for many other pragmatic nationalists identifying discrete arenas of overlapping interest, the making of a common economic area was an end in itself. Europe was conceived of as a regulated supranational market-making framework, able to enhance the common pool of resources and improve the economic welfare of all member states, but in so doing to be excluded from influence over state-based market-correcting social and welfare policy (Mestmacker 1994; Chalmers 1995; Joerges 2001; Milward 2000).

As already suggested, the explicit neo-federalists and, to a lesser extent, even the federal incrementalists were likely to favor more broadly constitutive documentary foundations. Following on the original ECSC Treaty of 1951, there occurred the double failed initiative of the European Defense Community and the European Political Community in 1952–1953. Tellingly, the EPC blueprint, although not explicitly called a Big "C" Constitution, included within it a bicameral legislature charged with selecting its own executive – a centralizing template for a parliamentary executive still not fully achieved in the EU today. It also included the familiar

---

[4] Schuman was the French foreign minister from 1948 to 1953. Monnet, a career diplomat, was head of the postwar French General Planning Commission, and is widely regarded as the visionary mind behind the Schuman Plan.

state-constitutional and citizen-constitutive proposal of entrenching and enforcing individual human rights against the institutions of the supranational body itself, this being an issue treated by the EPC's ad hoc constituent Assembly's revealingly self-styled *Constitutional* Committee (De Burca 2011; Urwin 2007).

The EEC Treaty of 1957, emerging from the wake of this double failure as the leading documentary platform of early supranationalism, was more narrowly economically conceived and more modest in the substance and tone of its proposals. Yet from time to time over the following thirty years the question of a neo-federal "big-bang" came back on the political agenda. In 1984, the European Parliament, led by a federalist faction, launched a proposal for a new foundational document, styled the "1984 Draft Treaty Establishing the European Union." Preceding the reforms of the Single European Act of 1986 and the Maastricht Treaty of 1992, the proposal of the now veteran Spinelli was drafted against the background of the "Eurosclerosis" of the post–Luxembourg Compromise years of the late 1960s and 1970s. Under the terms of the Compromise, provoked by the French President de Gaulle through his "empty seat" policy at the Council in 1965, the national veto had been reasserted over majoritarian initiatives where important interests of one or more members were deemed to be at stake. The 1984 Draft Treaty was in part a reaction to the political blockage created by this reassertion of intergovernmentalism. The proposal was also inspired by a new culture of supranational political confidence after the introduction of direct elections to the European Parliament in 1979. Despite the near-unanimous support of the parliament, however, the treaty had little impact in the wider circles of the EU, and was sidelined by proposals, enshrined in the Single European Act, to facilitate the completion of the internal market. Ten years later a similar initiative launched by the Belgian MEP Fernand Hernan in the context of the ratification crisis of the Maastricht Treaty met with even less success. Self-styled as a Draft Constitution for the European Union, it failed even to win the approval of the plenary Parliament (Christiansen and Reh 2009: ch. 3).

What is striking about these failed constituent documents is that their occurrence is tied up with other Treaty-based initiatives that eschew or downplay the idea of a widely drawn constituent compact in favor of a narrower and more gradualist approach to integration in which no single documentary agreement is either intended or treated as a foundation in perpetuity. These include the Treaty of Rome itself, the Single European Act of 1986, and the linked sequence of treaty reforms at Maastricht, Amsterdam, and Nice in the last decade of the twentieth century (De Witte 2002). The relationship between the two reform modalities is both competitive and symbiotic. The foundational approach repeatedly recurs because it represents one resiliently neo-federalist polity vision, and a response to the inadequacies and blockages of other approaches. Yet it also acts as a prompt to more modest methods of reform. By the same token, the foundational approach repeatedly fails not just because of opposition to its content, but also because its very method begs the question of its "in-principle" appropriateness to this "new kind of polity." As we shall see, this dialectical pattern to some extent continues with the Constitutional Treaty of 2004, but with some important new variations.

23.4 UNEVEN DEVELOPMENT: THE EARLY SIGNIFICANCE OF LEGAL CONSTITUTIONALISM

Alongside these two documentary strategies – foundational and incremental – and their complex interaction, a non-document-centered idea of legal constitutionalism has also figured prominently both in the practice and the articulated tradition of European constitutionalism. The focus here is on the very notion of an autonomous and self-empowering legal order, one developed under the stewardship of a powerful judicial elite at the Court of Justice.

For much of the history of the EU, this story of legal constitutionalism has been a story *about* elites sponsored and discussed *by* other (and overlapping) elites, and indeed, one whose power depends at least in some measure on it remaining the preserve of elites. It is the story of a "quiet revolution" (Stein 1981; Weiler 1999: ch. 2), of a constitutionalization *sub rosa*, by stealth. It centers on the early boot-strapping endeavors of the Luxembourg court in the first half of the 1960s, on the basis of an uncertain and incomplete mandate in the Treaty of Rome, to ensure the direct effect *(van Gend en Loos, 1963)* and supremacy *(Costa v ENEL, 1964)* – and so the basic state-penetrative reach and supervening authority of European law.

All versions of this "grand narrative" (Stone Sweet 2011: 132) have in common the idea of law performing a vital and well-tailored role in the construction and sustenance of the EU polity. Earlier versions of the narrative tended to adopt a functionalist tone, concentrating on the integrative *consequences* of these framing moves, with less emphasis on their motivating causes. A recent body of anthropological research, however, has underlined just how consciously motivated and far-sightedly intended these judicial initiatives were. It has demonstrated how important and how well orchestrated the original network of elite supranational actors in and around the Court of Justice was in developing the theme of "Europeanization through case-law" (Vauchez 2010: 2; Cohen and Vauchez 2008). Not only did the key formative decisions on supremacy and direct effect take place in acknowledgment of and in response to contemporary difficulties and loss of momentum associated with political integration, culminating in De Gaulle's "empty chair" policy, but they also involved a highly self-aware and self-reinforcing mobilization of the very notion of the supranational community as a community of *law*. Rather than thinking of law-centered theories of integration as retrospective and mythologizing accounts of a founding (which they also are), therefore, we are now also better equipped to understand them as active structuring devices, as means by which a tight-knit circle of pro-integration judges, civil servants, academics, MEPs, national diplomats, and commissioners became engaged "in real time" in a "circular circulation of ideas" (Vauchez 2010: 22) that contributed in a cumulative manner to the ascendancy of legal constitutionalism.

But why would, and why did, the legal dimension prove so important in the constitutionalization of the EU? There are a number of aspects to this.

In the first place, in instrumental terms, we must appreciate the indispensability of law as the basic motor of supranationalism – the key means to the end that is European integration. Writing in the early 1980s, before the gradual development of qualified majority voting and the pronounced treaty-based expansion of legislative jurisdiction beyond the market-making core, Joseph Weiler drew attention to the "dual character of supranationalism" (Weiler 1981) as the defining dynamic of Europe's early evolution. At that stage, the developed character of legal or normative supranationalism in the area of the internal market, particularly the Court of Justice's assertive development of the formal properties of the EU as an autonomous legal system, stood in stark contrast to a modestly conceived decisional or political supranationalism. Yet the two were strategically related. The early prominence of legal supranationalism occurred not in spite of political underdevelopment but precisely *because* political supranationalism remained so modest, with the member states retaining a de jure or de facto veto power in most areas of European policy making. The weakness of political supranationalism not only motivated the development of a compensatory legal constitutionalism, as we have already noted of the early judicial boot-strapping. The persistence of the national veto in supranational forms of legislative integration also offered reassurance to those who might otherwise have been concerned that legal constitutionalism would offer too much encouragement to a federalist vision. The most basic key to the attractiveness of law as the vehicle of supranational agency, therefore, lay in the fine balance that is struck. It depended on its regulatory capacity to steer, to consolidate, and, typically through judicial recognition of the claims of private litigants, to guarantee positive-sum intergovernmental bargains across wide-ranging aspects of economic integration and some more limited aspects of market-correcting regulation, *yet* to do so without threatening key national political prerogatives. More specifically, the law's instrumental value was twofold. It provided a legible and stable method of charting and co-coordinating the supranational settlement. Additionally, in a context of market-making where the temptation for each national member of the continental trade-liberalizing cartel to engage in protectionism and other forms of discrimination while exploiting the general opening of the markets of the other national members posed a significant collective action problem, it performed a vital disciplining function. The consistent application and enforcement of the rules of the game by independent legal institutions was crucial in forestalling free-riding and rendering common commitments more credible (Shapiro 1999).

Structural factors reinforced the instrumental attractiveness of legal constitutionalism. The empowerment of the Court of Justice as the apex court responded to a conception of the supranational settlement understood, in the language of organizational economics, as an incomplete contract. Framework texts, even the relatively detailed codes of successive European Treaties, always allow a degree of open texture. In so doing they both lower the bar of prerequisite consensus and allow judicial adaptation of the text to changing conditions without new resort to the drawing board. The resulting margin of judicial maneuver is key to reconciling stability and flexibility in any constitutive context; all the more so in the EU, where the political conditions for regular textual reform, certainly over the first quarter century of the Union, were highly unfavorable. The Court of Justice, then, became a vital mechanism to avoid conflict or *impasse* associated with the divergence of national political interests. As a "trustee court" (Stone Sweet 2011) delegated significant power to bind its national principals, it was able through development of its formal legal-constitutional attributes to fortify and expand its zone of discretion and could approach the task of "completing" the supranational contract in incremental fashion. It would do so both by advancing the material agenda of integration case by case and by adjusting the balance, so sensitive in the mixed polity context, in boundary conflicts over the powers of the diversely sourced institutions (Shapiro 1999: 321–322).

The fiduciary role of a trustee court in the making and consolidation of a legal constitution, however, is not legitimated solely through considerations of system functionality. Ideological factors also matter. The tradition of legal neutrality, assiduously cultivated in the context of a Court composed of senior jurists from all member states and conducting its business in a typically laconic and scrupulously nonpartisan "legalese," has lent cumulative authority to the court's decision making (Weiler 1999: ch. 5). The fact that much of the constitutional jurisdiction of the EU and its judicial organs could be articulated in terms of (primarily economic) rights has reinforced this ideological advantage. It has meant that the Court of Justice, for all that it retained a considerable margin of discretion, could nevertheless engage in a constitutional vein in terms closely associated with its own ostensibly apolitical authority as an adjudicatory organ – in the language of individual rights and remedies so familiar from the historical lexicon of constitutional law (Stone Sweet 2011; Scharpf 2010).

If the assertion of such a robust legal persona has been the key to the capacity of the EU operating from its narrow stronghold of institutional power to exercise continental regulatory authority, its success also depends upon its resonance with many of the earlier and more narrowly economic justifications of the EU. In their different ways, two of the most influential of the early grand theories of integration – the German ordoliberal tradition (Mestmacker 1994; Chalmers 1995; Stolleis 2003) and Hans Ipsen's idea of the EU as a special purpose association for economic integration (Ipsen 1987) – encouraged a law-centered perspective. As already noted, for the ordoliberals, the Treaty of Rome supplied Europe with its own economic constitution, a supranational market-enhancing system of rights whose legitimacy *required* the absence of democratically responsive will formation and of consequential pressure toward market-interfering socioeconomic legislation at the supranational level, a matter best left instead to the member states, and even there only insofar as compatible with the bedrock economic constitution. Ordoliberal theory, then, provides a classic model of how an autonomous legal order, through generating and ring-fencing a framework of economic exchange centered on the four freedoms, provides a platform for the efficient operation of a capitalist economic logic.

Ipsen's theory, to which Giandomenico Majone's contemporary work on the idea of a European "regulatory state" (Joerges 2001; Majone 1994, 2009) is a notable successor, shares with ordoliberalism the idea that supranationalism should transcend partisan politics. Here, however, the ambit of law is extended so that the invisible hand of the market is supplemented by the expert hand of the technocrat. In Majone's elaborately developed conception – one that has continued to capture the sensibility of a significant part of the Brussels elite – these additional regulatory measures are concerned not with macro-politically sensitive questions of distribution. Rather, they attend to risk regulation in matters such as product and environmental standards where expert knowledge is deemed paramount, and where accountability, it is argued, is best served by administrative law measures aimed at transparency and enhanced participation in decision making by interested and knowledgeable parties rather than the volatile preferences of broad representative institutions.

Therefore, for all these reasons – instrumental, structural, formal, and philosophical – law, and in particular the judge-made law of the Court of Justice, has supplied a power motor of constitutionalization in the early years of European integration.

23.5 THE EMERGENCE OF EXPLICIT CONSTITUTIONALISM

The delicate balance achieved by locking the EU's collective agency within a law-centered discourse and a narrow market-based justification could not, however, hold indefinitely. The pursuit and perfection of the narrow economic objectives of the Union progressively impinged upon a wide range of social issues, making "spillover" (Lindberg 1998) into politically contentious areas of traditionally national jurisdiction inevitable. Both ordoliberal and regulatory state approaches became increasingly vulnerable to the charge of drawing artificial distinctions between technical questions of market-making and standard-setting and deeply contested questions of value preference and transnational resource and risk allocation (Follesdal and Hix 2006).

As previously intimated, such a tension was in truth present from the very birth of supranationalism. Economic policies always carried significant implications, whether supportive or restrictive, for wider political projects and ambitions at the national or supranational level. Indeed, it was a powerfully supportive nexus between the economic and political that, from the Treaty of Rome onward, permitted a considerable overlapping consensus between more or less federalist visions. The common market could be elevated to the defining supranational priority not just on wealth-maximizing grounds. Just as important was the wider political prize of lasting peace that a culture of economic cooperation and shared affluence could help secure (Weiler 1999: ch. 7). Less felicitous connections between the narrow economic and wider political poles of integration, however, became ever more evident. As the EU increasingly sought market-making or market-correcting interventions involving politically salient choices, it simultaneously reduced the capacity of states to act independently in these policy areas. The robust juridical elaboration and protection of the single market, which lay at the heart of legal constitutionalism, had flourished in a formative context where market-making measures impinged only lightly on other social policy objectives, or at least where states retained the procedural means to veto politically controversial collective commitments in pursuit of these other objectives, and so were slow to make such commitments in situations where there were obvious winners and losers. But the gradual expansion of the scope of negative integration from the narrow market-making sphere and the concomitant growth of positive integration decisively changed the dynamic of collective action. In particular, the Single European Act and the Maastricht Treaty cumulatively advanced the twin strategy of expanding the scope of supranational competence into traditional statist strongholds of monetary, social, and security policy and providing new qualified majoritarian means to facilitate the exercise of this expanded jurisdiction.

The gathering danger was that the very strength of the law in supplying "both the object and agent of integration" (Dehousse and Weiler 1990: 243) and by providing the main fruit of the "thin" constitutional settlement as well as the channel for arriving at that settlement would become a liability. On the one hand, as the *agent* of integration, the law threatened to become a medium whose prudent husbanding of the integration *acquis* would instead translate as excessive political rigidity. The danger was that the legal proofing of agreements against easy political reappraisal and the prevention of new initiatives except through still highly consensual and only moderately democratically inclusive procedures, or through the terse increments of the Court of Justice, would become more a way of avoiding the legitimate expression of political choice and contestation and less a means of protection against free-riding or against ideologically inspired skepticism toward positive-sum collective commitments. On the other hand, where the pressure toward positive integration *has* led to legal change, and as more and more controversial value choices have begun to be reflected onto the legal domain, this has also affected the ideological potency of law as the *object* of integration. As legislation begins to articulate more clearly the controversial political value choices between market liberalism and social protection, some of the detached, efficiency-maximizing veneer is stripped from legal supranationalism (Weiler 1999: ch. 2; Hix 2008 ch. 3)

The gradual fraying of the "permissive consensus" (Hooghe and Marx 2008) around the idea of legal supranationalism set the deep context within which the big "C" (Walker 2005) constitutional debate emerged. Other factors contributed, notably the wave of eastward Enlargement after the fall of the Berlin Wall. The increase in the size of the EU from fifteen members in 1997 to twenty-seven in 2007 raised acute questions about the adequacy of an institutional structure initially built for a homogenous Western European club of six states to a sprawling pan-European expanse of 500 million persons. Indeed, enlargement and its supposedly unmet and externally sourced institutional needs provided an important rhetorical framework for the EU's decade of reform. It was the thread that connected the busy sequence of Treaty reforms from Maastricht to Nice in 2000, whose unfinished business in turn led to the historic decision at the Laeken summit in December 2001 to establish a Convention on the Future of Europe (Walker 2003a; Hirschl 2005). Yet the focus on enlargement merely channeled, accelerated, and provided a kind of discursive common ground for a process of reflection and contestation over the kind of polity the EU was and could become that was *in any event unavoidable* in light of the increasing inadequacy of the received model.

The explicit big "C" constitutional moment, therefore, can be seen as a result of the increasing visibility of the hard choices facing Europe. Crucial both to its initial profile and success and to its eventual failure, the Convention process, unlike previous non-explicit documentary constitutional initiatives, succeeded in attracting the political energy and sponsorship of a number of different polity visions engaging with these hard choices. In other words, it was no longer just a federalist vehicle, and it was not seen as just a federalist vehicle.

Certainly one of the three key polity visions was a neo-federalist one, albeit less crude than some of its predecessors.[5] And if it was undoubtedly the candidate vision that remained most heavily invested in the big "C" solution, it was far from the most commonly endorsed approach feeding the Convention momentum. It sought for

[5] Jurgen Habermas is a key point of reference here. As an internationally prominent public intellectual of the democratic left, he was in the vanguard of a movement, largely outside the Convention process, which sought to reconstruct the terms and meaning of the Convention in a more explicitly federalist manner (see, e.g., Habermas 2001, 2006, 2008)

the new EU constitution, through a combination of inclusive Convention process, integrative content, and culturally unifying symbolic product, to deliver some kind of functional equivalent to the peaks of popular self-authorization, comprehensive design, and deep political identity associated, at least ideally, with the constitution of the modern state. In this way, the "asymmetry" (Scharpf 1999) of a settlement in which the EU lacked the pooled political resources to deliver legitimate and effective collective solutions to politically and intergovernmentally contentious issues of economic and social policy that increasingly fell outside the independent capability of national governments might be overcome. Importantly, for the most part, the neo-federalist approach did not envisage the EU *as* a federal state (Mancini 1998) and thus acknowledged the concerns of the state-centered constitutionalists. It did not, in other words, seek to replace the states as the single point of original collective agency, final authority, and deep political identity within the European domain. Rather, this more mature version of neo-federalism sought to develop or recognize these state-familiar constitutional assets of political community on an independent footing for the EU, and in a manner that envisaged neither superiority nor subordination to the states but engagement in a nonhierarchical relationship with them. So the EU would have a foundation and reference point of collective agency (i.e., the European "people" and the European states) that was distinctive and self-standing without being the only such distinctive and self-standing point of reference for the various constituencies (i.e., European "peoples") that made up the new collective agency (Walker 2007). It would have a sphere of authority that was final without being exclusive or exhaustive. Finally, and building on the formal supranational citizenship provisions in place since Maastricht,[6] it would also possess a form of framing or organizing political identity, complete with rights, obligations, and membership status, which was again distinctive but not unique in this function. Instead, it would operate in tandem with the other (predominantly state-centered) organizing political identities of its subjects (Weiler 1999: ch. 10).

Alongside this vision, however, were two others. A sharply opposing perspective was one of constitutional retrenchment. It was concerned to draw a line in the sand by resort to mechanisms such as a competence catalog, the entrenchment of the Charter of Rights, and the empowerment of national parliaments. Here, constitutionalism was invoked, both materially and symbolically, not as a generative measure but as a limiting device to ensure against the further evacuation of state power to the supranational level.[7]

---

[6] See Treaty on the Functioning of the European Union, Arts. 20–25.

[7] This explains, for example, the conversion of the famously Eurosceptic *Economist* magazine to the cause of a European Constitution (*The Economist*, December 15 2001). Tellingly, each of these constraining measures was itemized in the original post-Nice "leftovers" agenda, which triggered the Laeken summit and the Convention on the Future of Europe (see Walker 2005).

Finally, there was a more pragmatic and explicitly *sui generis* approach, concerned with pursuing or consolidating Europe's special way – its "*Sonderweg*" (Weiler 2001). Its defining priority was neither the revival of a neo-federal vision nor the protection of state prerogatives. Rather, it was ensuring against the kind of political blockage and institutional stasis that would prevent Europe from making the governance adjustments necessary for its distinctive "post-national" accommodations between market and state, supranational and intergovernmental, legal fixity and political openness, to be maintained and updated. In its practical attention to the demands of a novel problem-solving context and in its nonalignment with "old" state-sovereigntist coded oppositions, this view was in fact the quiet motor of much of the pro-Convention movement. Constitutionalism here assumed importance less for its special content or projection and more as a way of regaining political attention, of reenergizing and revalidating a macro-political reform process that, given the cumulative disappointments and deferrals of the Amsterdam and Nice Treaties, was falling foul of the law of diminishing returns (Weiler 2005; De Witte 2002). It is in this vision, indeed, that European constitutionalism appears more analogous to second- or successor-phase constitutional initiative at the state level, concerned not with a rupture of opening (federalist) or closure (retrenchment), but with harnessing and consolidating the political energy and legal resources necessary for continuing and evolutionary adaptation.

Given the disparity of polity visions brought to the table, it is no surprise that the big "C" constitutional initiative failed. Here we see the unresolved quality of the EU Constitution in bold and sustained relief. The very conditions of indeterminacy that encouraged the initiative also produced the open horizon of alternatives and the intensity of disputation that invited its ultimate failure. What is more, the requirement of the unanimous ratification of the then twenty-five member states to succeed meant that the process was indiscriminately vulnerable to negative assessment – to defeat on the basis of rejection of *any* of its various affirmative visions rather than endorsement of a concrete alternative. And, of course, the vision most vulnerable to defeat in state-framed constituencies was the proto-federal vision, as we saw in the defensive nationalism and Euroskepticism expressed in the key French and Dutch referenda defeats in the spring of 2005.

In the summer of 2007, the European Council bowed to what had seemed inevitable since these two negative votes and announced its decision to "abandon" the "constitutional concept" it had endorsed so optimistically only four years previously on receiving a draft of a first Constitutional Treaty for the European Union (EU) from the Convention on the Future of Europe.[8] It opted instead to return to the more familiar international law vehicle of a "Reform Treaty."[9] The move appeared

---

[8] German Presidency Conclusions: European Council, Brussels, June 21–22, 2007.

[9] Treaty of Lisbon amending the Treaty on European Union and the Treaty establishing the European Community, December 13, 2007, 2007 O.J. (C 306) 01.

to pay a political dividend. Agreement was reached as early as the Lisbon summit of December 2007 and, despite further delay occasioned by a fresh referendum defeat in Ireland, the new "post constitutional Treaty" (Somek 2007) was successfully implemented before the end of 2009 (Craig 2010). Significantly, the new measure retained most of the substantive reforms of the Constitutional Treaty, but was meticulous in its removal of the latter's high constitutional language and symbolism. It discarded not just the "constitutional" label and the ideal of a single foundational document, but also references to the European flag and motto, and even to European "laws" and "framework laws." Material reform of the institution system and the jurisdiction range of the EU eventually proved possible, therefore, absent the distracting and divisive baggage of the different polity visions that intense exposure to the traditional language and forms of explicit constitutionalism had encouraged.

It is a telling irony of the ultimately fatal difficulties encountered by the Convention project, however, that its trials coincided with the growing acceptance of some kind of constitutional status for the EU – even if understood in small "c" rather than documentary big "C" terms. Documentary constitutionalism may have suffered its most comprehensive and significant defeat, if only because it had for the first time been rendered explicit and had reached the center of the political agenda. Yet the very explicitness and heightened profile of the constitutional discourse across such wide range of polity visions had left its mark. In the years immediately following the failed big "C" initiative, the old incrementalist story of legal constitutionalism, and indeed the wider cumulative institutional settlement of the mature EU, was itself now increasingly viewed in expressly constitutional terms, even, and perhaps especially, by those who had opposed or lacked enthusiasm for the Convention initiative. Not just politicians and commentators, but both the Court of Justice and national constitutional courts[10] began to refer more often and more explicitly than ever to the EU's own distinctive non-documentary constitution (Besselink 2009; Walker 2012). Having rejected a formal constitution, then, the elites of the EU now appeared to have resolved not only that it was excessive in its ambition but also that it was redundant in principle; that the EU, rather like the *bourgeois gentilhomme* in Moliere's play, had been speaking informal "constitutional prose" all along. "Constitution," therefore, was recoded as an achievement concept rather than an aspiration concept – as a way of pointing to and reaffirming a form of political life, however thin and fragile, held in common, rather than as a conduit for various distinct and unreconciled visions of the polity. "Constitution," in other words, no longer signified what remains unresolved in the EU polity but what was already resolved. The narrative of

---

[10] See, for example, the explicit references to the supranational constitutional tradition in the German Constitutional Court's ruling on the (domestic) constitutionality of the Treaty of Lisbon; (2010) 3 CMLR 276 (see also Halberstam and Mollers 2009).

Europe's constitutional foundations moved from the future tense, where it had been conspicuously unsuccessful, to the safer terrain of the past tense.

23.6 CONCLUSION: A SHIFTING INHERITANCE

Is the story of the emergence of the EU constitution over? Is the shift in tone of the new phase of explicit constitutionalism from high to low, from formal to informal, and from conflicted to resolved a decisive one? Will the dominant narrative of constitutional origins remain past-oriented? Will its settled emphasis be on the stepwise development and gradual consolidation of a semiautonomous institutional system and a secondary culture of political belonging – a story in which no single documentary initiative is decisive and where much rests on the pioneering early work of the Court of Justice in securing an autonomous legal order? Or might the narrative of origins shift again?

We cannot be sure. The sovereign debt crisis has, since late 2009, returned many of the concerns that provoked the big "C" debate of the last decade center stage. It has placed unprecedented pressure on the capacity of the EU to balance the imperatives of general economic integration, in particular the need to stabilize the common Euro currency, against the social damage caused to those member states, most prominently Greece but increasingly also other predominantly Southern member states, with high levels of public debt or of publicly guaranteed private debt. Tied to a single continental monetary policy and both practically and legally unable to pursue growth-based fiscal policies, heavily indebted states find themselves in a bind that generates ever-higher levels of political tension between them and the economically stronger parts of the Union. On the one hand, the indebted states have required and sought increasing levels of financial aid through central institutions such as the European Central Bank and the European Financial Stability Facility. Such support inevitably involves politically difficult levels of redistribution from richer member states. On the other hand, the governments and populations of the indebted states resent the contribution of the lending policies of the banks of rich member states to their spiral of indebtedness and complain that they are allowed neither the legal nor the financial means to stimulate their domestic economies sufficiently to develop a viable medium terms strategy for overcoming debt.

In such circumstances, neo-federalist thinking inevitably reasserts itself. The Treaty on Stability, Co-ordination and Governance (TSCG) of March 2012, signed by all member states other than the United Kingdom and the Czech Republic, is one harbinger of this (Craig 2012). It approves the imposition, monitoring, and sanctioning from the European center of an unprecedentedly intrusive set of fiscal disciplines as the price of access to a more generous rescue funding under a new European Stability Mechanism. In turn, such a combination of financial solidarity and top-down regulation and enforcement inevitably fuels the case for greater democratic representation at the newly empowered center. At the same time, it stimulates a counterreaction. Some would prefer the reduction of the Eurozone to a strong core as part of a new multi-speed Europe (Piris 2011), while others view the loss of national sovereignty dramatized by the Euro crisis as fundamentally unacceptable and so advocate the retreat or even the breakup of supranational Europe.

The debate is polarized, and the future of the EU perhaps more uncertain than ever. In such circumstances, radically discontinuous change is more likely than incremental reform. Certainly on the neo-federalist side, such change may be contemplated as taking the form of a new constitutional foundation, of which the TSCG may be an early signal. For those who see the Euro crisis as an occasion for national retrenchment, too, the prudential case for constitutional guarantees at the center – previously made at the time of the Constitutional Treaty – may come to seem attractive again.

In either case, the focal point of the constitutional foundations may shift again. It may be projected back to the future, with the incrementalist narrative, centered on judge-led legal boot-strapping and serial Treaty reform, downgraded to the pre-constitutional overture to the main event. Alternatively, foundational constitutionalism may stay off the agenda. The political challenge of the crisis may be won without the EU being compelled to revisit the kind of explicit constitutional approach whose last failure is such a fresh memory. Conversely, the crisis may be lost without the EU being *able* to successfully revive explicit documentary constitutionalism. Whether or not we have reached the end of the EU's constitutional beginnings, therefore, remains a moot point, one tied up with the very conditions of survival of the world's first supranational polity.

BIBLIOGRAPHY

Anderson, P. 2009. *The New Old World*. London: Verso.
Besselink, L. 2009. "The Notion and Nature of the European Constitution after the Lisbon Treaty," in Wouters J., Verhey, L., and Kiiver P. (eds.), *European Constitutionalism Beyond Lisbon*. Antwerp: Intersentia, 261–282.
Burgess, M. 2000. *Federalism and the European Union: The Building of Europe, 1950–2000*. London: Routledge.
Chalmers, D. 1995. "The Single Market: From Prima Donna to Journeyman," in Shaw, J. and More, G. (eds.), *New Legal Dynamics of European Union*. Oxford: Oxford University Press, 55–72.
Christiansen, T. and Reh, C. 2009. *Constitutionalizing the European Union*. Basingstoke: Palgrave.
Cohen, A. and Vauchez, A. 2008. "Back to the 'Future of Europe': A Political Sociology of the EU's Constitutional Saga," EUI Working Papers. RSCAS 2008/33.

Craig, P. 2010. *The Lisbon Treaty: Law, Politics and Treaty Reform*. Oxford: Oxford University Press.

2012. "The Stability, Coordination and Governance Treaty: Principle, Politics and Pragmatism," *European Law Review* **37**: 231–248.

De Burca, G. 2011. "The Evolution of EU Human Rights Law," in Craig, P. and De Burca, G. (eds.), *The Evolution of EU Law*. Oxford: Oxford University Press (2nd ed.), 465–498.

De Witte, B. 2002. "The Closest Thing to a Constitutional Conversation in Europe: The Semi-Permanent Treaty Revision Process," in Beaumont, P., Lyons, C., and Walker, N. (eds.), *Convergence and Divergence in European Public Law*. Oxford: Hart, 39–57.

2012. "The European Union as an International Legal Experiment," in G. De Burca and J.h.H. Weiler (eds.), *The Worlds of European Constitutionalism*. Cambridge: Cambridge University Press, 19–56.

Dehousse, R. and Weiler, J. 1990. "The Legal Dimension," in Wallace W. (ed.), *The Dynamics of European Integration*. Oxford: Oxford University Press, 242–260.

Dixon, R. and Ginsberg, T. 2011. "Introduction," in Ginsberg, T. and Dixon, R. (eds.), *Comparative Constitutional Law*. Cheltenham: Edward Elgar, 1–15.

Drake, H. 2000. *Jacques Delors: Perspectives on a European Leader*. London: Routledge.

Follesdal, A. and Hix, S. 2006. "Why There Is a Democratic Deficit in the EU: A Reply to Majone and Moravcsik," *Journal of Common Market Studies* **44**: 533–562.

Glendon, M. A. 1994. *Comparative Legal Traditions (2nd ed.)*. Rochester, NY: West.

Haas, E. 1958. *The Uniting of Europe*. Stanford, CA: Stanford University Press.

Habermas, J. 2001. "Why Europe Needs a Constitution?" *New Left Review* **11** (Sep–Oct): 5–26.

2006. *The Divided West*. Cambridge: Polity.

2008. *Europe: The Faltering Project*. Cambridge: Polity.

Halberstam, D. and Mollers, C. 2009. "The German Constitutional Court Says 'Ja Zu Deutschland!'" *German Law Journal* **10**: 1241–1258.

Hay, D. 1968. *Europe: The Emergence of an Idea (2nd ed.)*. Edinburgh: Edinburgh University Press.

Hirschl, R. 2005. "Preserving Hegemony? Assessing the Political Origins of the EU Constitution," *International Journal of Constitutional Law* **3**: 269–294.

Hix, S. 2008. *What's Wrong with the European Union and How to Fix it*. Cambridge: Polity.

Hooghe, L. and Marks, G. 2008. "A Postfunctionalist Theory of European Integration: From Permissive Consensus to Constraining Dissensus," *British Journal of Political Science* **39**: 1–23.

Ipsen, H.-P. 1987. "europaische Verfassung – Nationale Verfassung" EuR 195.

Joerges, C. 2001. "'Good Governance' in the European Internal Market: An Essay in Honour of Claus-Dieter Ehlermann," *EUI Working Papers*, RSC No. 2001/29.

Joerges, C., Meny, Y., and Weiler, J. (eds.) 2000. *What Kind of Constitution for What Kind of Polity? Responses to Joschka Fischer*. Florence: Robert Schuman Centre.

Lindberg, L. 1998. "Political Integration: Definitions and Hypotheses," in Nelsen, B. and Stubb, A. (eds.), *The European Union: Readings on the Theory and Practice of European Integration*. Boulder, CO: Lynne Rienner (2nd ed.), 145–156.

Lindseth, P. 2010. *Power and Legitimacy: Reconciling Europe and the Nation-State*. Oxford: Oxford University Press.

MacCormick, N. 2005. *Who's Afraid of the European Constitution?* London: Imprint Academic.

Maduro, M. 2003. "Contrapunctual Law; Europe's Constitutional Pluralism in Action" in Walker, N. (ed.), *Sovereignty in Transition*. Oxford: Hart, 501–537.

Majone, G. 1994. "The Rise of the Regulatory State in Europe," *West European Politics* 17: 77–101.

2002. "Delegation of Regulatory Powers in a Mixed Polity," *European Law Journal* 8: 319–339.

2009. *Europe as the Would-be World Power: The EU at Fifty*. Oxford: Oxford University Press.

Mancini, F. 1998. "Europe: The Case for Statehood," *European Law Journal* 4: 29–42.

Mestmacker, E.-J. 1994. "On the Legitimacy of European Law," *RabelsZ*, 615–636.

Milward, A. 2000. *The European Rescue of the Nation-State (2nd ed.)*. London: Routledge.

Muller, J.-W. 2011. *Contesting Democracy: Political Ideas in Twentieth-Century Europe*. New Haven, CT: Yale University Press.

Pagden, A. 2002. "Europe: Conceptualizing a Continent," in Pagden, A. (ed.), *The Idea of Europe: From Antiquity to the European Union*. Cambridge: Cambridge University Press, 33–54.

Piris, J.-C. 2011. "It Is Time for the Euro Area to Develop Further Closer Cooperation among Its Members," Jena Monnet Working Paper 05/11. New York: New York University.

Rosenfeld, M. 2010. *The Identity of the Constitutional Subject: Selfhood, Citizenship, Culture and Community*. London: Routledge.

Rosenfeld, M. and Sajo, A. 2012. "Introduction," in Rosenfeld, M. and Sajo, A. (eds.), *The Oxford Handbook of Comparative Constitutional Law*. Oxford: Oxford University Press, 1–21.

Scharpf, F. 1999. *Governing in Europe: Effective and Democratic?* Oxford: Oxford University Press.

2010. "Legitimacy in the Multilevel European Polity," in Dobner, P. and Loughlin, M. (eds.), *The Twilight of Constitutionalism?* Oxford: Oxford University Press, 89–119.

Shapiro, M. 1999. "The European Court of Justice," in Craig, P. and De Burca, G. (eds.), *The Evolution of EU Law*. Oxford: Oxford University Press (1st ed.), 321–341.

Shaw, J. 2011. "Citizenship: Contrasting Dynamics at the Interface of Integration and Constitutionalism," in Craig, P. and De Burca, G. (eds.), *The Evolution of EU Law*. Oxford: Oxford University Press (2nd ed.), 575–610.

Somek, A. 2007. "Postconstitutional Treaty," *German Law Journal* 8: 1121–1132.

Stein, E. 1981. "Lawyers, Judges and the Making of a Transnational Constitution," *American Journal of International Law* 75: 1–27.

Stolleis, M. 2003. "Prologue: Reluctance to Glance in the Mirror: The Changing Face of German Jurisprudence after 1933 and Post-1945," in Joerges, C. and Ghaleigh, N. S. (eds.), *Darker Legacies of Law in Europe*. Oxford: Hart, 1–18.

Stone Sweet, A. 2011. "The European Court of Justice," in Craig, P. and De Burca, G. (eds.), *The Evolution of EU Law*. Oxford: Oxford University Press (2nd ed.), 121–153.

Urwin, D. 2007. "The European Community from 1945–85," in Cini, M (ed.), *European Union Politics*. Oxford: Oxford University Press (2nd ed.), 13–29.

Vauchez, A. 2010. "The Transnational Politics of Judicialization: *Van Gend en Loos* and the Making of EU Polity," *European Law Journal* 16: 1–28.

Verhoeven, A. 2002. *The European Union in Search of a Democratic and Constitutional Theory*. Dordrecht: Kluwer.

Walker, N. 2003a. "Constitutionalising Enlargement, Enlarging Constitutionalism," *European Law Journal* 9: 365–385.

2003b. "Late Sovereignty in the European Union," in Walker, N. (ed.), *Sovereignty in Transition*. Oxford: Hart, 3–32.

2005. "Europe's Constitutional Momentum and the Search for Polity Legitimacy," *International Journal of Constitutional Law* 3: 211–238.

2006. "Big 'C' or Small 'c'?" *European Law Journal* 12: 12–14.

2009. "Reframing EU Constitutionalism," in Dunoff, J. and Trachtman, J. (eds.), *Ruling the World: Constitutionalism, International Law and Global Governance*. Cambridge: Cambridge University Press, 149–177.

2012. "The European Union's Unresolved Constitution," in Rosenfeld, M. and Sajo, A. (eds.), *The Oxford Handbook of Comparative Constitutional Law*. Oxford: Oxford University Press, 1185–1208.

Weiler, J. 1981. "The Community System: The Dual Character of Supranationalism," *Yearbook of European Law* 267–306.

1999. *The Constitution of Europe*. Cambridge: Cambridge University Press.

2001. "Federalism without Constitutionalism: Europe's *Sonderweg*," in Howse, R. and Nicoladis, K. (eds.), *The Federal Vision: Legitimacy and Levels of Government in the US and the EU*. Oxford: Oxford University Press, 54–72.

2005. "On the Power of the Word: Europe's Constitutional Iconography," *International Journal of Constitutional Law* 3: 173–190.

Biographical index

Index